Journey to New England

"It is impossible to come away from *Journey to New England* without wanting to pack your bags and head out. . . . This book will not sit idly on my shelf. It will be beside me on my own New England travels."

—Mel Allen, Travel Editor, *Yankee Magazine*

"I enjoyed *Journey to New England*. It's a comfortable and very friendly introduction to New England's beauty and charm . . . a quiet and thorough celebration of place."

—Kaleel Sakakeeny, Executive Editor, Travel, *New England Parents' Papers* and *New England Booming* magazines

Help Us Keep This Guide Up to Date

Every effort has been made by the authors and editors to make this guide as accurate and useful as possible. However, many things can change after a guide is published—establishments close, phone numbers change, hiking trails are rerouted, facilities come under new management, etc.

We would love to hear from you concerning your experiences with this guide and how you feel it could be improved and be kept up to date. While we may not be able to respond to all comments and suggestions, we'll take them to heart and we'll also make certain to share them with the authors. Please send your comments and suggestions to the following address:

The Globe Pequot Press
Reader Response/Editorial Department
P.O. Box 480
Guilford, CT 06437

Or you may e-mail us at:

editorial@globe-pequot.com

Thanks for your input, and happy travels!

Journey to
New England

by
Patricia Harris
and
David Lyon

The
Globe
Pequot
Press

Guilford, Connecticut

Cover image by Jack McConnell/McConnell McNamara
Cover design by Nancy Freeborn
Text design by Lisa C. Ferreira
Maps by Lisa Reneson
Illustrations by Gil Fahey
Illustrations in The Midlands on pages 324 and 330 were derived from illustrations by L. Kenneth Townsend.
The concept of this book is based on *Journey to the High Southwest* by Robert L. Casey.

Library of Congress Cataloging-in-Publication Data
Harris, Patricia, 1949–
    Journey to New England / by Particia Harris and David Lyon. — 1st ed.
    p. cm.
    Includes bibliographical references and index.
    ISBN 0-7627-0330-X
    1. New England—Tours. 2. New England—Description and travel. 3. Automobile travel— New England—Guidebooks. I. Lyon, David, 1949– . II. Title.
    F2.3.H37 1999
    917.404'43—dc21
                                                               99-12674
                                                                      CIP

Printed on recycled paper
Manufactured in the United States of America
First Edition/Second Printing

In fond memory of childhood outings,
this book is dedicated to our fathers,
who always drove, and to our mothers,
who packed the tuna sandwiches.

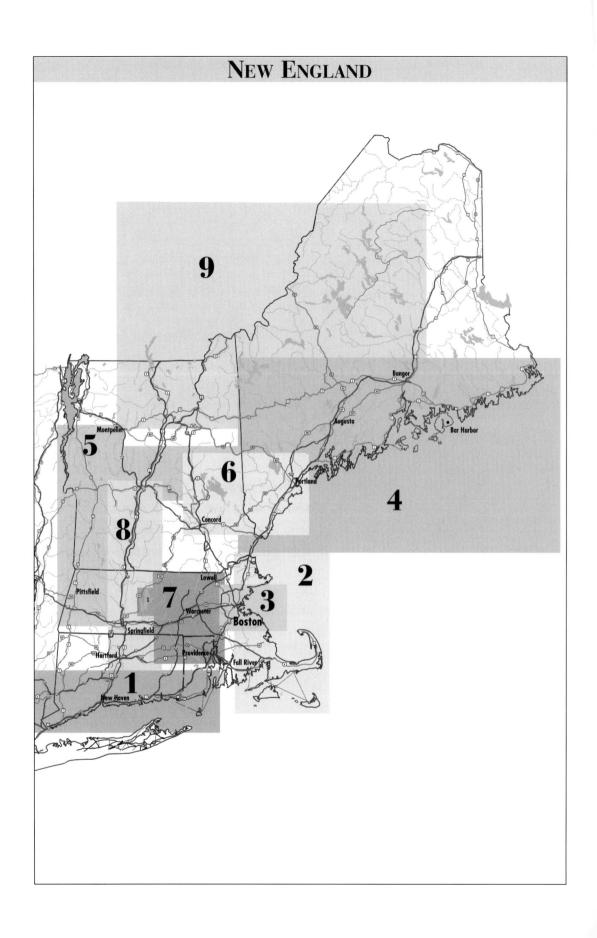

NEW ENGLAND

Contents

Experience the Wonder of Foxwoods.

 Nestled in the beautiful New England countryside, you'll find the world's favorite casino. Foxwoods Resort Casino, now even more breathtaking than ever. Inside our magnificent new Grand Pequot Tower, you'll find a world class hotel, with 800 luxurious rooms and suites. With gourmet restaurants, and more table games, slot machines and chances to win.

Our new hotel is the perfect complement to our 312-room AAA rated four diamond Great Cedar Hotel, and our quaint Two Trees Inn, with 280 charming rooms.

Foxwoods is fine dining with 24 fabulous restaurants. And room service is available 24 hours a day, for your convenience. Foxwoods is five different gaming envi-  ronments, with over 5,750 Slot Machines, Blackjack, Craps, Roulette and Baccarat, including a Smoke-Free casino.

Foxwoods is High Stakes Bingo, Keno, a Poker Room and the Ultimate Race Book.

Foxwoods is entertainment. With stars like Aretha Franklin, Engelbert Humperdinck, Paul Anka and Bill Cosby. It's two challenging golf courses. It's Championship Boxing. It's Cinetropolis, with the 1,500-seat Fox Theater. It's a Turbo Ride, Cinedrome, and our Dance Club. With its Hotels, Restaurants, Gaming and Entertainment, it's no wonder that Foxwoods has become the hottest entertainment destination in the country.

Experience the Wonder of the Connecticut Woods.
Conveniently located in Mashantucket. Exit 92 off I-95 in southeastern CT.
Call 1-800-PLAY-BIG
Visit our website at www.foxwoods.com

Mashantucket Pequot Tribal Nation

Introduction

A century ago, when large numbers of Americans began to discover the concept of travel for pleasure, *Atlantic Monthly* editor William Dean Howells wrote of what he called "the problem of summer." An Ohioan transplanted to New England, he enthusiastically explored his new corner of the country but agonized each year over the best destination. "For most people choice is a curse," Howells wrote, "and it is this curse that the summer brings upon great numbers."

Curse or not, Howells spent many summers in different areas of New England—usually with great satisfaction, occasionally with disappointment. Each year he was bedeviled by the curse of choice, fearful of making the wrong one. Our intention in this book is to still any anxiety you might have about where to go, whether you choose to travel in the summer or at any other time of year. We understand—New England offers too many choices.

New England is a region unto itself, walled off from the rest of the northeast by mountains on the west, by the deep-woods Acadian cultures of Quebec and New Brunswick along the northern rim, and by ocean to the south and east. But while New England stands apart, its solitude is filled with diversity. It is a region of metropolitan extremes (for example, the population density of Cambridge, Massachusetts, is second only to Manhattan) and virtually unpopulated wilderness. Its geography varies more than any other place in the United States, with remnants of three primordial continents and a complicated history of continental collisions and separations written in the rocks. The landscape runs the gamut from long, sandy shores to precipitous mountain ravines to vast tracts of sub-Arctic boglands. Swamp and meadow and forest and dune, boulder-strewn shore and muddy river, skyline of glass and concrete and starlight glittering on the powdery ice dust of mountain summits—it's all part of the New England experience. Even our human history is more varied, complex, and older than any other in the Americas north of the Rio Grande. One academic recently dismissed twentieth-century New England as past its prime—all "cellar holes and Robert Frost." Nothing could be further from the truth; our past is only prologue.

In putting together this book, we chose not to follow the usual arbitrary political boundaries that hash New England up into six states. Those boundaries, after all, are legacies of political disagreements that most people forgot centuries ago. Instead, we decided to divide the book the way people tour New England—which also happens to be the way that those of us who live here think about the region. If we're going to the mountains, we might be headed to Massachusetts, Vermont, New Hampshire, or Maine. State lines don't matter because we're seeking an alpine world. If we're going to the beach, it could be in any of several states. Ultimately, we carved New England into nine divisions that can stand on their own with plenty to see and do. Keeping in mind that some travelers have the time to make extended journeys, we've set up the regions to link one to another rather seamlessly.

By and large, these nine divisions might be called "geocultural." They are defined first by geography that isolates them from contiguous areas and secondarily by the local culture and mindset that further sets them apart. Most, but not all, of New England's mountainous regions are found, therefore, in the chapter called "Up Country," while the thousands of miles of New England coastline are covered in three separate chapters based on their ecological and cultural differences. The metropolitan heart of New England, Boston and its immediate environs, is delineated in its own chapter so that the attractions of the city do not overwhelm the smaller and subtler appeal of nearby small towns. Because the mightiest river valley of New England, the Connecticut, developed in splendid isolation from the rest of the area, it also receives separate treatment. The interior—neither mountain nor shore—falls into the industrious Midlands and the vacation retreats of the Lakes Region. And, finally, the rugged north country where many rivers still run wild and moose outnumber people is treated in the Great North.

As you use the book, you'll discover that we have emphasized themes in each area that we believe best represent the character of the place. The birth of American manufacturing supplies the theme, for example, of the Midlands. Other parts of New England, including all the coastal regions, also participated in the Industrial Revolution, but communities like Pawtucket, Rhode Island, and Lowell, Massachusetts, still draw their identity from that great industrial adventure. The development of the "scenery industry" lies beneath our treatment of the mountain regions in Up Country. Frankly, we often give thematic emphasis to a region based on what interests us most. We hope to provide you with a point of departure—an approach you might use to appreciate the area.

From a practical standpoint, that means that attractions and some activities central to a theme are emphasized in the narrative "Seeing" part of a chapter. (The narrative also includes other attractions and activities that are so major that you shouldn't miss them.) Still other attractions and activities—often for specialized interests—are listed in the "Staying" section of the chapter along with lodging, dining, and other practical information. Just because we have given them less emphasis doesn't mean they aren't rewarding in their own right. But ultimately, this volume is less a journey

to *the* New England than a journey to *our* New England.

So who are we to write this book? Pat is a native New Englander, raised in the Connecticut River Valley near Hartford, but transplanted to Cambridge, Massachusetts, almost thirty years ago. David moved to Penobscot Bay in Maine when he was in grade school (which means he's still considered "from away"). He also lived in coastal New Hampshire and the Pioneer Valley of Massachusetts before following Pat to Cambridge.

Our love of travel and seeing new places probably began with our own family summer vacations by car through New England. We've continued that passion as adults, earning our livings as travel writers and logging literally tens of thousands of miles throughout the region. Pat's mother continues to be amazed at our journeys because she recalls a daughter who couldn't ride for more than twenty minutes before voicing the inevitable childhood plaint: "Are we there yet?"

In these pages you will find the quintessential New England that attracts people from throughout the United States and around the world—the museums of Boston, the majestic foliage displays, the white lighthouses standing sentinel on rocky points. But we've also sought places off the beaten path that capture some essential aspect of the New England experience, whether it's the stony field where a man dropped his plow to hastily join the Revolution, a wilderness camp in the Great North where "sports" began visiting a century ago to cast flies for landlocked salmon, a small Vermont town where the library holds one of the masterpieces of American landscape painting, or a sleepy Maine village where the "fancy" house in town is adorned with a flying staircase and moldings carved with breathtaking artistry by an anonymous craftsman in 1818.

As we undertook the research for this book, we visited some places in New England for the first time, or for the first time in many years. We found ourselves embracing activities we had long ago dismissed or lost touch with, like snowshoeing and kayaking. And we discovered new and intriguing things even in areas we've visited often—the astonishing collection of Native American artifacts in Salem, Massachusetts, the rebound of once-threatened bird species all over New England, beaches and coves just around some bend where we'd never ventured before. We hope that you will experience some of the same sense of discovery—not just of what New England has to offer, but of your own interests and sense of adventure.

With all due respect, we think Howells was wearing blinders when he assumed that people would travel only in the summer. New England has several distinct seasons—winter, mud season, spring, almost summer, full-tilt summer, fall, November, and Christmas—and each season has its strengths in different areas. Some parts of New England dispense with a few of these seasons and other areas add further calendrical nuances.

Probably the biggest seasonal attraction in New England is the fall foliage. Friends from around North America argue with our contention that New England's display is the best in the world. We've discovered that arguing with them is like trying to describe the difference between scarlet and crimson to someone who has been blind from birth. Once our friends have seen New England foliage, they come around to our point of view.

Two factors account for New England foliage. While the entire region was once heavily forested with spruce and pine, most of those trees were cut in the seventeenth and eighteenth centuries for ship timbers. Then the softwood forest was leveled again in the nineteenth century to make boxes for shipping the goods produced by the Industrial Revolution. Following the normal succession of forests, deciduous trees took their place. Subsequent loggers skipped cutting the sugar maples (because their sap is so valuable) and the red maples (because their wood is useless). As a result, New England's forests consist predominantly of deciduous trees, of which nearly a third are maples.

While maple trees are found all over the globe, New England maples have evolved particularly efficient biological mechanisms for shutting down for the winter. A byproduct of this adaptation is heavy production of anthrocyanin, a pigment that gives foliage an intense red color. It's a chemical accident on a grand scale, but the red hues of the New England woods produce the world's most dramatic fall foliage. And while some of the colors in autumn leaves are simply

New London Harbor Lighthouse in summer, New London, Connecticut

masked by the chlorophyll produced during the growing season, the anthrocyanin is produced only when the night temperatures fall dramatically and the sunlight takes on that red-golden cast peculiar to this latitude. Move a New England maple to South Carolina and its fall leaves are as dull as those around it.

Foliage season varies a little every year, beginning at the highest altitudes and most northerly parts of New England in the third week of September and finishing in the cities and the south-facing islands about a month later, barring a late-season hurricane that strips the trees. No one ever successfully predicts when peak foliage will be in a given area, but it hardly matters, as the colors are as dynamic a week before and a week after.

We love the foliage season—we've had friends who walked around applauding trees—but we also find a note of melancholy in the display. It means that winter is coming. (With apologies to skiers, winter is not our favorite season.) But spring brings a rebirth of the landscape, with hints of the luscious summer to come. And from April into early July, the bloom wave sweeps over New England in a progression that reverses the foliage trend. The daffodils in full glory on Nantucket in late March may not poke out until early June in northern Maine. Rhododendrons start in May in Connecticut but their cousins, the mountain laurel, may not burst forth in the White Mountains until mid-July. Only one plant seems to synchronize throughout the region—the wild roses that dapple the beaches and cover the stream banks wherever humans and birds have managed to scatter them.

In the final analysis, each season has something to offer. Whether you come to gather rosebuds while you may, or rosehips at your leisure, when and where to go all comes down to choice—that "curse of summer" to which William Dean Howells alluded back in 1902. Some things don't change—the scope of choice—but we'd like to think that the range of New England experiences is less a burden than a blessing.

**Birch walk at Naumkeag in fall,
Stockbridge, Massachusetts**

There are a few practical things we ask you to keep in mind as you use this book.

ADMISSION COSTS AND HOURS ARE ALWAYS SUBJECT TO CHANGE.

We did our best to make sure that everything was up-to-date as the book went to press, but admission prices tend to increase slightly from year to year and opening hours change with more frequency than any printed matter can keep up with. Very local attractions, especially in small towns, keep irregular hours because they depend on volunteer staff. If Joan or Herbie gets the flu, the town history museum may not be open that Tuesday. We're not saying "don't go." On the contrary, it's almost always worth the extra effort to spend some time with people who are passionate about the subject of their attraction. You'll come away with the kind of intimate stories that even the best professional museum guide simply can't tell you.

Hours of operation (including whether an attraction is open at all) also tend to vary with the season, and the season varies with the place. For example, North Coast attractions cut back their hours or close after Labor Day. Cape Cod (except for Provincetown) locks the doors after Columbus Day and is closed tight in January when the ski slopes and Boston are in full swing. The cultural scene dies back in the cities in the summer, but it's bustling in the Berkshires.

FOOD AND LODGING LISTINGS ARE SELECTIVE AND PRICES ARE RELATIVE.

Even rural New England tends to be more expensive than many parts of the United States, but "cost" is relative. Thus, we've developed a scale for comparative pricing of lodging and restaurants. With rare exceptions, we have not listed hotels or motels that belong to national chains—mentioning them only when they depart from the national standard (usually by dint of greater local character) or offer exceptional value. Lodging is based on a double room for one night, and the scale does not include room taxes, where applicable, although it does include any meals indicated. Inexpensive covers rooms up to $75, moderate to

$140, expensive to $225, very expensive any room over $225.

Even some of the most expensive accommodations can be a bargain off season or during the so-called "shoulder seasons," either just after they open for the year or just as they prepare to close. We have tried to incorporate the full range of prices for all seasons. Many lodgings (especially hotels, motels, and campgrounds) offer discounts for active members of the United States Armed Forces and for members of AAA, AARP, and some other organizations. Be sure to ask, and while you're about it, inquire about packages, promotions, and discounts for multi-night stays.

The dining scale is based on the price of a dinner entree for one person, since this is the only section of the menu that can be readily compared across many kinds of restaurants. Inexpensive covers entrees up to $10, moderate to $17, expensive to $25, and very expensive any place where entrees average more than $25. We have not rated costs at establishments that only serve breakfast and/or lunch.

Again, we have largely omitted chain restaurants and fast food franchises. Travelers who prefer to dine at these roadside emporia hardly need our help to spy the golden arches at exit 6. Instead, we have emphasized restaurants that offer a distinctly local experience or which offer exceptional food and exceptional value. We have to be honest: There are parts of New England where we tend to picnic on what we can forage from the grocery stores. These areas contain very few restaurant listings. On the other hand, we have kept ourselves in check in the metro areas where we could easily triple or quadruple the number of restaurants we recommend, on the assumption that most travelers want to know where to eat more than they want to know where to eat the best fettuccine puttanesca on a Wednesday night.

TOLL-FREE PHONE NUMBERS ARE INCLUDED.

We included toll-free numbers whenever possible. Typically, they begin with the area codes (800) or (888) and can be dialed toll-free from within the United States.

DON'T VENTURE INTO THE WILDERNESS WITHOUT CHECKING WITH LOCAL EXPERTS.

We hope that this book will provide you with all the information you need for a journey to—and through—New England. But we caution you to expand your base of information before going into the wilderness or undertaking even "soft" adventure on your own. New England is blessed with a number of superb field guides for mountaineering, rock climbing, and even simple hiking. They can provide more information than we can possibly supply here. Moreover, most wilderness areas, including the wild rivers of the Great North, are covered in depth in several field guides to canoeing and kayaking as well as in detailed maps and field guides. We cannot emphasize how helpful these references are, and we have listed several in the bibliography in the back of this volume. Before heading into the woods, at the very least equip yourselves with a detailed U.S. Geodetic Survey map and a compass (and be sure you know how to use both). But even the best field guide cannot anticipate changes in local conditions caused by weather or other unforeseeable forces. Before heading out, check with people at the area who know exactly what you should be ready to face.

—*Patricia Harris and David Lyon*

For this guide considerable effort has been made to provide the most accurate information available at the time of publication, but readers are advised always to check ahead, since prices, seasonal openings and closings, and other travel-related factors do change over time. Neither the authors nor the publisher can be held responsible for the experiences of readers while traveling.

New England through the Years

Rather than present a long discourse on history removed from any context, we have chosen to discuss the relevant aspects of the New England past in the places where events occurred. This timeline is intended to provide a quick overview to prepare you for your journey.

—P.H. & D.L.

10,000 BC: Although most of New England was locked in ice, first inhabitants were making tools and hunting land and sea animals.

2,500 BC: Tribes of Algonquian-language group inhabit New England region.

1000 AD: Norsemen are most likely the first Europeans to explore the region.

1450–1500:   Basque fishermen exploit rich fishing grounds off New England coast.

1497–1614:   European exploration of New England.

John and Sebastian Cabot sail along the coast of Maine (1497–99).

Giovanni da Verrazzano sails from Long Island through Gulf of Maine (1524).

Bartholomew Gosnold explores coast from Narragansett Bay to Penobscot Bay (1602).

Martin Pring sails about 12 miles up the Piscataqua River (1603).

Samuel de Champlain explores and maps the coast from Cape Ann northward (1604), lands at Piscataqua Bay in New Hampshire (1605), and enters Vermont through the lake eventually named for him (1609).

Captain John Smith maps the coast from Cape Cod to Maine and establishes a fishery on Monhegan Island (1614).

Dutch navigator Adriaen Block explores Connecticut shore and attempts, unsuccessfully, to sail up the Connecticut River (1614).

1607–1639:   First European settlements in New England.

1607:   Popham Colony established near Popham Beach, Maine, but abandoned in 1608.

1620:   Pilgrims land in Plymouth, Massachusetts.

1623–24:   Saco and York settled in Maine. Dover and Strawbery Banke settled in New Hampshire.

1628:   Puritan settlement, led by John Endicott, established in Salem, Massachusetts.

1629:   Massachusetts Bay Colony chartered.

1630:   Puritans led by John Winthrop establish Boston, Massachusetts. Boston becomes the capital of the Massachusetts Bay Colony in 1632.

1635:   Puritans who consider Boston "too liberal" leave and found Windsor, Hartford, and Wethersfield along the Connecticut River in Connecticut. A fort is built at Saybrook.

1636:   Clergyman Roger Williams flees Massachusetts Bay Colony, where he is held to have "dangerous" religious views and founds Providence, Rhode Island. The first Baptist church in America is formed in Providence in 1639.

1638:   New Haven, Connecticut, founded.

1639:   Newport, Rhode Island, founded by Quakers.

1636:   Harvard University in Cambridge, Massachusetts, becomes the first English-speaking university in the New World.

1639:   Cod fishing is so critical to Massachusetts Bay Colony economy that fishermen are exempt from military duty and fishing gear is declared free from taxes for seven years.

1666:   French erect Fort St. Anne on Isle de la Motte in Lake Champlain.

1675–78:   Initial peaceful relations between Natives and European settlers erupt into warfare led by Metacom (known as King Philip), the son of Massasoit. More than fifty European settlements are raided, a dozen destroyed, and 600 settlers killed. But Colonial militia prevails, killing 3,000 Natives, driving survivors off their lands, and clearing the way for further European settlement.

1691:   A new charter incorporates Plymouth and Maine into Massachusetts.

1692:   Witchcraft trials begin in Salem, Massachusetts.

1689–1763:   New England is drawn into the struggle between Great Britain and France for control of North America, known as the French and Indian War. In 1724, Massachusetts colonists build Fort Dummer in the Connecticut River Valley near Brattleboro, Vermont, to fight French and Indians, the first permanent white settlement in Vermont. In 1759, the British drive the French from the Lake Champlain region. By the end of the conflict, New England has a generation of soldiers trained in British military tactics.

1701: Yale University is founded in Old Saybrook, Connecticut, but is moved to New Haven in 1716.

1708: Triangle trade of rum, slaves, and molasses begins in Rhode Island and quickly spreads throughout coastal Massachusetts and Connecticut.

1712: Nantucket sailor named Hussey kills first sperm whale taken by American whalers, setting Nantucket, Massachusetts whaling industry in motion.

1739: Present boundary between Maine and New Hampshire is established.

1764: Rhode Island College is founded; later moved to Providence and renamed Brown University.

1769: Dartmouth College is chartered in Hanover, New Hampshire.

1769–1776: Clashes between Colonists and the king lead the way to the American Revolution.

1769: Colonists scuttle British ship *Liberty* in Newport, Rhode Island.

1770: Five Colonists are killed by British regulars in a confrontation outside the Old State House, known as the Boston Massacre.

1772: Colonists in Providence, Rhode Island, burn the British vessel *Gaspee*. Rhode Islanders later call this incident the "Lexington of the sea."

1773: As resistance to British taxes intensifies, Colonists dump tea into Boston Harbor, an event known as the Boston Tea Party.

1774: Colonists seize military supplies from the British at Fort William and Mary in New Castle, New Hampshire. These arms are used for the Battle of Bunker Hill.

1775: Battles of Lexington and Concord and Bunker Hill mark the start of the American Revolution.

The first naval battle of the Revolution takes place in Machias, Maine, when townspeople capture British schooner *Margaretta*.

Benedict Arnold leads expedition from Augusta, Maine, up the Kennebec River and through the northern woods in an attempt to capture Quebec and bring the French and Indians into the Revolution. British defeat Arnold's troops.

Ethan Allen and the Green Mountain Boys in Vermont capture Fort Ticonderoga from the British without firing a shot. British cannon are dragged overland to Boston.

1776: With American position on Dorchester Heights fortified with British cannons captured from Ticonderoga, British evacuate Boston.

Rhode Island is first colony to declare independence. The British bombard Bristol and seize Newport. Although no other major battles are fought on New England soil, Newport remains in British control until 1779.

1777: Americans win the Battle of Bennington, which takes place in New York, 4 miles northwest of Bennington, Vermont.

1777:   Vermont separates from New Hampshire, declares itself an independent state and adopts the first state constitution to provide universal suffrage to men and to ban slavery.

1783–1807:   Massachusetts ships handle 37 percent of the country's foreign trade and comprise 88 percent of the nation's fishing fleet.

1784:   First law school in the U.S. is founded in Litchfield, Connecticut.

1785:   Elias Haskett Derby's vessel, *Grand Turk,* leaves Salem, Massachusetts, to open Canton to American trade. For next two decades, Salem leads America in international trade.

1788:   Connecticut is the fifth state to ratify the U.S. Constitution. Massachusetts is sixth state to ratify the U.S. Constitution. When New Hampshire becomes the ninth state to ratify the Constitution, the federal Union goes into effect.

1790:   Rhode Island ratifies the U.S. Constitution and becomes the thirteenth state.

1791:   Vermont becomes the fourteenth state; the University of Vermont is chartered at Burlington.

1793:   Samuel Slater launches the American textile industry by establishing mills in Pawtucket, Rhode Island. Within twenty-five years, it is estimated that Rhode Island's cotton factories employ 26,000 people and make 27,840,000 yards of cloth annually from 29,000 bales of cotton.

1796:   John Adams (born in 1735 in Quincy, Massachusetts) is elected second president of the United States.

1812–1862:   Maine leads all other states in shipbuilding. As the chief industry in about fifty coastal towns, shipbuilding supported 200,000 people.

1814:   Americans win the Battle of Plattsburg on Lake Champlain during the War of 1812.

1820:   Maine separates from Massachusetts and joins the Union as the twenty-third state.

1822:   Lowell, Massachusetts, is established as a mill town.

1824:   John Quincy Adams (born in 1767 in Quincy, Massachusetts) becomes the sixth president of the United States.

1831:   William Lloyd Garrison establishes *The Liberator* in Boston to spark the anti-slavery movement.

1836:   Ralph Waldo Emerson publishes *Nature,* which serves as manifesto of the Transcendentalist movement.

1840–1890:   Maine continues to lead country in production of three-masted square-rigged ships, but lags far behind Boston in construction of clipper ships.

1846: New Bedford becomes the largest whaling port in the world.

1850: Nathaniel Hawthorne publishes *The Scarlet Letter.*

1851: Herman Melville publishes *Moby-Dick.*

1851: Donald McKay launches the *Flying Cloud* from his East Boston shipyard, the fastest clipper ship ever under sail.

1852: Franklin Pierce (born in 1804 in Hillsboro, New Hampshire) elected fourteenth president of the United States.

1854: In record year, New England whaling industry earns $11 million.

1854: Henry David Thoreau publishes *Walden; or, Life in the Woods.*

1860s–1880s: Bangor, Maine, becomes timber capital of the world.

1863: University of Massachusetts is chartered at Amherst.

1865: Maine State College of Agriculture and Industrial Arts is founded at Orono, becomes University of Maine in 1897.

1869: First train reaches summit of Mount Washington in New Hampshire.

1869: The *Oak* sets sail from Nantucket, the last of 4,344 whaling voyages from the port.

1881: University of Connecticut is founded in Storrs.

1881: Chester A. Arthur (born in 1829 in Fairfield, Vermont) becomes the twenty-first president of the United States.

1897: First subway in the United States opens in Boston.

1910: U.S. Coast Guard Academy is relocated from Maryland to New London, Connecticut.

1914: Cape Cod Canal links Cape Cod and Buzzards Bays.

1917: U.S. Navy builds submarine base at Groton, Connecticut. *Nautilus,* the first atomic submarine, is launched here in 1954.

1917: Ripogenus Dam in northern Maine is completed and Penobscot River is tamed.

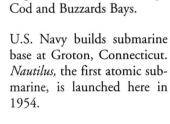

Canterbury Shaker Village in winter, Canterbury, New Hampshire

1923:   Vice President Calvin Coolidge (born in 1872 in Plymouth, Vermont, and formerly governor of Massachusetts) becomes the thirtieth president of the United States.

1923:   New Hampshire College of Agriculture and Mechanic Arts in Durham becomes the University of New Hampshire.

1947:   Maine Turnpike opens from Kittery to Portland and is extended to Augusta in 1955.

1950:   New Hampshire Turnpike is completed.

1954:   First U.S. jazz festival held in Newport, Rhode Island.

1957:   Massachusetts Turnpike opens.

1958:   Connecticut Turnpike opens.

1960:   John F. Kennedy (born in 1917 in Brookline, Massachusetts) is elected thirty-fifth president of the United States.

1969:   The Newport Bridge between Newport and Jamestown is completed.

1983:   Mashantucket Pequot tribe opens Foxwoods Casino in Ledyard, Connecticut.

1 · The South Coast

Introduction

New England's South Coast begins, at least geographically, at the New York border, but the commuter rail system has transformed the farmlands and factory towns of southwest Connecticut into a vast suburb of New York City. We don't mean this as any kind of value judgment—easy access to one of the world's most magnificent metropolises is nothing to sneeze at. But from a traveler's perspective, the chief appeal of bedroom communities is anthropological. We find ourselves sometimes charmed and often bemused by the peculiar social world of those who spend half their days in transit. If you have a similar curiosity, you can gain some considerable insight into this "Gold Coast," as some call it, from the fiction of John Cheever.

So bear with us as we whip up the coast from New York with only a few pauses until the mouth of the Housatonic River at Stratford and Milford. The stops we do make are either for nature preserves or they are historic. Among the first to take advantage of the train ride from Manhattan were the *pleine aire* painters of a century ago who found in the little coastal villages of southern Connecticut a scenic charm analogous to that sought by their French counterparts in the French countryside. About the same time, bird watchers banded together to save some of the most scenic coastal environments as natural refuges—and both resident and migrant birds have thanked them for decades by making good use of the marshes and woodlands.

With another pause in New Haven—an industrial city ennobled by the august presence of Yale University—we move swiftly again to reach the beginnings of the long sandy beaches that line the South Coast along Long Island, Block Island, and Rhode Island sounds all the way to Newport.

Some of the most idyllic of these sandy strands lie between New Haven and the mouth of the Connecticut River at Old Saybrook.

The lower reaches of the Connecticut—south of Middletown, where the river changed course some 10,000 years ago and made a dogleg along its present path—have been called by the Nature Conservancy one of forty of the "Last Great Places" in the western hemisphere. Lacking a major city at its mouth, the Connecticut broadens into a range of healthy wetlands that harbor hundreds of species of wildlife. Here too the American impressionist painters came to draw their inspiration from the netherworld where the boundaries of air, river, land, and sea seemingly disappear.

East of the Connecticut River the South Coast is no longer protected by Long Island, and the pounding seas of the Atlantic have worn down the land to bedrock. Even the names of the places let you know how the landscape changes: Rocky Neck, Bluff Point, Stonington. Here the Thames River reaches the sea and the communities again turn industrial. It seems to be a rule of thumb on the New England coast that the harder the land, the more industrial the community.

The long sandy beaches begin again just a few miles farther east at the Pawcatuck River, which forms the arbitrary border between Connecticut and Rhode Island. But here they are punctuated by equally long stretches of rocky shoals, granite outcrops, and beds of slate lifted up from ancient ocean floors by continental collisions. When the land jogs north into Narragansett Bay, our route continues east by hopscotching across Conanicut Island and over the graceful long arch of the Jamestown Bridge to reach final harbor on Aquidneck Island in many a sailor's favorite anchorage, Newport.

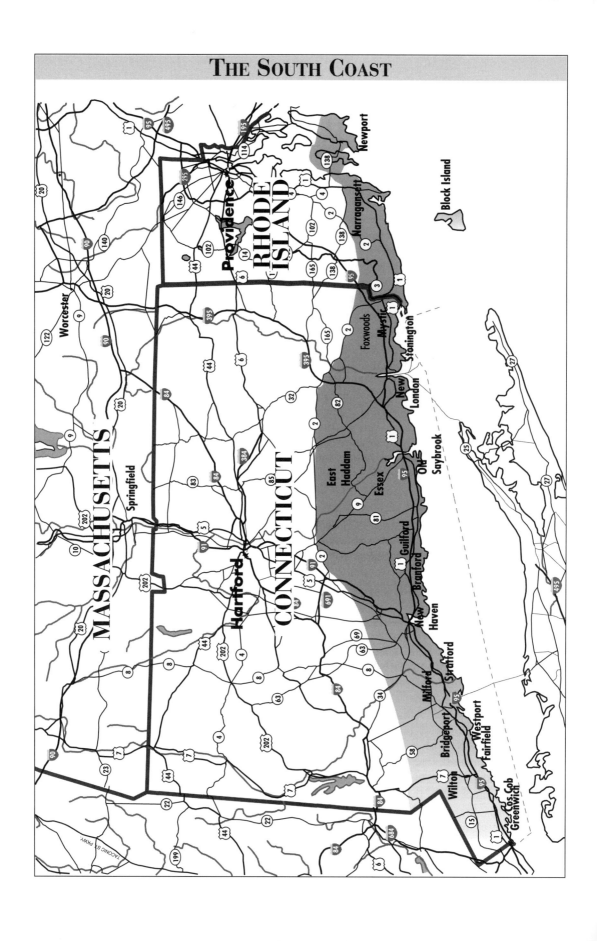

Seeing the South Coast

This journey along the South Coast moves from the painterly to the maritime, from the small harbors and broad woodlands where American impressionism began to the brawny seaports of eastern Connecticut and Rhode Island. Almost the entire stretch (minus some of the industrial patches) is picturesque and rather low-key. A century ago, American artists just back from Europe with radical ideas about light and open-air painting began riding the train from New York to the southern part of this region, where the play of light and the lay of the land created especially pleasing effects. Although the train is still a pleasant way to reach destinations along the route, you'll need an automobile to cover more ground.

The Connecticut Shore

Greenwich and Cos Cob, Connecticut

Only 13 miles from the New York border, Greenwich is one of the jewels among the coastal Connecticut towns that serve as bedroom communities for metropolitan New York. Although it was settled early—in 1640—Greenwich really began to grow when the railroad came through in 1848. Some of the smaller villages of Greenwich developed as resort communities for New Yorkers fleeing summer in the city. Hotels sprang up and wealthy New Yorkers amassed large tracts of land on which they erected palatial estates. The colonial village of Cos Cob was part of this gentrification, and in 1882 Edward and Josephine Holley purchased a roomy 1730s farmhouse (originally owned by wealthy farmer David Bush) that they converted into a boardinghouse. Among their

early boarders were New York landscape painters John Twachtman and J. Alden Weir, who would come for several weeks in the summer and happily lug their easels around quaint little Cos Cob to paint the village, the mill pond, the harbor, and anything else that struck them. It was a charming country idyll for the big-city artists, and in 1891 they set up a summer art school in the barn behind the boardinghouse, creating the first art colony of American impressionism. Over the next thirty years, the influx of painters provided a steady income to many Cos Cob families who could find a spare room to rent to the seasonal visitors.

The layout of the Bush-Holley House and its grounds gives a sense of the artistic camaraderie—of summers spent sketching and painting outdoors or on balconies overlooking the (pre-highway) Strickland Brook, eating and discussing the fine points of aesthetics in the common dining area. The best of the American impressionists to spend time here, Childe Hassam, was especially fond of posing the daughter of a local tavernkeeper around the house (Hassam had a reputation as something of a ladies' man), and some of these portraits have come back home to the house museum. Visiting artist Elmer Livingston MacRae loved more than the landscape—he married the innkeeper's daughter and lived here until his death in the 1950s. His studio is recreated in a second-floor bedroom. The **Bush-Holley House Museum** is located at 39 Strickland Road in Cos Cob. (Take exit 4 from I–95 and follow the signs.) Open Tuesday through Friday from noon to 4:00 P.M., Sunday from 1:00 to 4:00 P.M. Admission $4.00. Telephone: (203) 869–6899.

The **Bruce Museum**, the former home of textile magnate Robert Bruce, has been a forum for American impressionism since the Greenwich Society of Artists mounted its 1912 exhibition here. One small gallery holds a changing display of Connecticut landscape paintings. Among the holdings at the Bruce are some very good landscapes by Frank Dumond, Ernest Lawson, and later generations of Connecticut painters. The museum is at 1 Museum Drive and is open Tuesday through Saturday from 10:00 A.M. to 5:00 P.M. and Sunday from 1:00 to 5:00 P.M. Admission $3.50. Telephone: (203) 869–0376.

We should point out that Greenwich does have other attractions besides art. It is a great place to shop, for example. The main street of **Greenwich Avenue** is lined with excellent upscale clothing boutiques, old-fashioned downtown department stores, and a restaurant every block or so. Yes, it's suburban, consumerist, and unrelentingly upmarket. But you have to like a city with enough sense of decorum to ban skateboards, in-line skates, and bicycles from the sidewalks.

Wilton and Weir Farm, Connecticut

There are a couple of ways to move along to Weir Farm, an early center of American impressionist activity in Connecticut. One route takes about an hour and another takes as long as you care to make it. To see some additional attractions en route, continue north on I–95 to Stamford to take in the **Whitney Museum of American Art at Champion,** which makes a good break from driving or sightseeing. This small branch features changing exhibitions of American art, usually from the twentieth century, drawn from the collection of the "mother" museum in New York. Open Tuesday through Saturday 11:00 A.M. to 5:00 P.M. Free. Wheelchair accessible. 1 Champion Place, Atlantic Street and Tresser Boulevard, Stamford. Telephone: (203) 358–7630.

For the quick route, continue north on I–95 and get off the highway to pick up Route 7 in Norwalk, where the south side (South Norwalk) is the traditional oyster capital of the Northeast. The local branch of the Matabesecs (one of the lesser known Native tribes) taught the first British settlers about seeding oyster beds, and when Captain Peter Decker invented the steam-powered dredge in 1874, the industry boomed. In the late nineteenth century, Norwalk shipped three-quarters of the trans-Atlantic oyster trade as well

as supplying a large part of the domestic production. Much of this history, along with a lot of marine natural history, is recounted at the **Maritime Aquarium at Norwalk,** which is located in a restored nineteenth-century foundry overlooking Norwalk harbor. We give this institution a lot of credit for keeping a narrow focus on Long Island Sound and on the fish and marine mammals of the area, including the popular harbor seals. The aquarium also has model ships, shipbuilding demonstrations, and an IMAX theatre. Open July and August daily 10:00 A.M. to 6:00 P.M., September through June daily 10:00 A.M. to 5:00 P.M. Call for IMAX schedule. Adults $7.75 (not including IMAX). Wheelchair accessible. 10 North Water Street, Norwalk. Telephone: (203) 852–0700.

For a more scenic route to Weir Farm, follow the signs out of Greenwich to the **Merritt Parkway**, which lies about 10 miles north of town. Labeled Route 15 on many maps, this is one of the oldest parkways in America. It stretches 37.3 miles from the New York border to the Housatonic River as a four-lane road divided by a green strip and guard rail. The overpass bridges along the way are all slightly different, sporting elegant art deco designs in concrete created by architect George Dunkelberger. Stands of hemlock and red pine (the latter a product of well-intentioned but ill-conceived erosion control efforts of the 1930s), as well as beech and oak trees, line the road.

Unlike modern highways, the Merritt Parkway winds and twists gracefully through the countryside, making it a real treat to drive. It's almost a shame to leave it at exit 40 to Route 7 north. Follow Route 7 for 9 miles and turn left onto Route 102, then quickly left again up Old Branchville Road, and left yet again onto Nod Hill Road to the **Weir Farm National Historic Site.**

Painter J. Alden Weir bought the farmstead in Wilton and developed it as a painters' retreat at the turn of the century. The 153 original acres inspired hundreds of paintings and drawings by Weir and his artist friends, including Hassam, Twachtman, Albert Pinkham Ryder, and John Singer Sargent. The National Park Service acquired this site in 1990 (the only National Park in Connecticut) and it is still very much a work in progress. Although some tours include Weir's studio, none of the other buildings are open to the public, but the grounds are more than adequate compensation. Weir gradually expanded his estate to 238 acres. Over the years, he adjusted nature to suit his own sense of how it should look, adding and adapting features such as stone walls, buildings, gardens, and patches of woods. The landscapes are remarkably well-preserved and a superb walking tour of twelve spots ($2.00 for the brochure) compares the landscapes with the artists' interpretations.

Open April through November Wednesday through Saturday from 10:00 A.M. to 5:00 P.M., Sunday 1:00 to 5:00 P.M. Studio tours at 10:00 A.M. Wednesday through Saturday. Free. 735 Nod Hill Road, Wilton, Connecticut. Telephone: (203) 834–1896.

Fairfield and Bridgeport, Connecticut

The stretch of Connecticut coastline leading to New Haven harbors many half-hidden pockets of landscape that so intrigued the pleine-aire painters of a century ago. From Weir Farm return to the Merritt Parkway northbound and take exit 44 (Black Rock Turnpike, or Route 58), which goes toward Fairfield. Turn right on Congress Street, then right again on Burr Street. One mile down on the left is the **Connecticut Audubon**

Weir Farm National Historic Site, Wilton, Connecticut

Center at Fairfield and the adjacent 152-acre **Larson Sanctuary.** The sanctuary has six miles of nature trails, including a walk for the blind, handicapped, and elderly. It is open daily dawn to dusk. Admission is $2.00. The Audubon center has natural history exhibits and a shop for birdwatchers as well as a center for the rehabilitation of injured raptors. Open Tuesday through Saturday from 9:00 A.M. to 4:30 P.M. Admission free. 2325 Burr Street. Telephone: (203) 259–6305.

Continuing north from Fairfield, I–95 bypasses Bridgeport's congestion (unless you get off at exit 27 in Bridgeport for the Barnum Museum—see "Staying There"). At Milford, take exit 34 and drive south to Route 1. Turn right, go to the next stoplight and turn left onto Lansdale Avenue. At the next light, turn right onto Milford Point Road and follow the signs at the end to the parking lot for the **Connecticut Audubon Coastal Center,** where the adjacent **Milford Point Bird Sanctuary** provides some of the best year-round birding in the state. The year-round inhabitants are mostly herons and ducks. The dense thickets along the marshes are thick with orioles, warblers, flycatchers, sparrows, and finches during the May and September migrations. Long mud flats and beaches feature summer populations of several types of plovers, terns, and American oystercatchers. The sanctuary is open daily dawn to dusk, the center Tuesday to Saturday from 10:00 A.M. to 4:00 P.M., Sunday from noon to 4:00 P.M. Admission $2.00. 1 Milford Point Road, Milford. Telephone: (203) 878–7440.

Continue northward by returning to Route 1 and turning right, then taking the right fork onto Route 162 as it wanders through the marshy countryside past Woodmont and Savin Rock before rejoining I–95 north in West Haven to negotiate the trip into or through congested New Haven.

New Haven, Connecticut

There is a lot to admire about New Haven, a city laid out by Puritans in 1638 and one that suffered terribly during the American Revolution. But from our point of view, the best parts of central New Haven are associated either with pop cultural culinary history (the first hamburger and the first American pizza, or so the claims go) or Yale University, which has a pair of good art museums and an excellent theater. If you share our interests in high-brow culture or popular food, then please see "Staying There" for details. At the complex intersection of Routes 1 and 34 with interstate highways I–95 and I–91, you'll want to follow the signs carefully for Yale University.

But if the natural world along this portion of the South Coast interests you more, then continue on I–95 through New Haven and take exit 50 (Woodward Avenue). At the second stoplight, turn right onto Townsend Avenue, then right on Lighthouse Road to the eighty-four-acre **Lighthouse Point Park.** The park is open all year, but the $6.00 parking fee applies only from Memorial Day to Labor Day, when the beaches are staffed by lifeguards and the 50-cent carousel is operating. Telephone: (203) 946–8005. Near the lighthouse is a visitors center, the East Shore Ranger Station; telephone: (203) 946–8790.

This area was the mouth of the Connecticut River until about 10,000 years ago, when the river suddenly changed course. A hundred centuries of pounding by the sea have swept away the mud and revealed the peculiar combination of exposed bedrock and post-glaciation river pebbles and boulders. The lighthouse from which the park takes its name hasn't been operational since 1877, but it's kept nicely painted by the New Haven Parks Department. Boating, fishing, and picnicking are encouraged, and people do swim. The exciting time to visit Lighthouse Point Park, however, is during the three great aerial migrations that follow the original path of the Connecticut River Valley. Tens of thousands of migrating butterflies, especially monarchs, touch down at Lighthouse Point on their way to Mexico and Central America from late August into late September. They are followed by songbirds—particularly cuckoos, flycatchers, goldfinches, and robins—who fly in mostly during September. The most majestic migrants of all are the raptors, who come down low and sometimes land here during their migrations between late September and mid-November. The annual counts range between

20,000 and 30,000 hawks and owls, including the common hawks, such as the red-tailed and broadwing hawks, as well as many falcons: the still-endangered peregrines and the less threatened American kestrels and merlins.

Branford to Guilford, Connecticut

From Lighthouse Point, return to Townsend Avenue (Route 337) and turn right, following the road as it circles the peninsula through Momaugin and Route 142, which leads to Route 146 and into the beach resort community of **Branford.** Founded in 1644, the town became a vacation getaway in the early years of the twentieth century. The "five fingers"—as the protected granite coves of Short Beach, Branford Point, Indian Neck, Pine Orchard, and Stony Creek are known—became built up with both fine estates and casual beach cottages.

The Branford village of Stony Creek is the departure point for boat cruises of the **Thimble Islands.** No one seems to know for sure just how many distinct dots of land there are in this green-capped archipelago. Colonial maps called them the Hundred Islands, and locals insist there are 365—one for each day of the year. (This is a popular conceit throughout New England. Boosters of Lake Winnipesaukee in New Hampshire make the same claim, as do promoters of Maine's Calendar Islands in Casco Bay.) One thing we do know: only twenty-three are inhabited, and then mostly in the summer. (Only four islands have electricity.) Some are large enough that several cottages dot their shores; others have but a single dwelling that spreads nearly to the shore. They're named for the thimble-shaped blackberries that used to grow on them.

High Island was once the stronghold of Captain Kidd, who found its location ideal for plundering vessels passing in Long Island Sound. Legend has it that he buried his treasure on Money Island in a cave with an underground entrance, and during the 1890s there was even a hotel on the Thimbles where guests with dreams of quick riches would stay while they hunted for the pirate loot. Like all good pirate stories, the treasure has never been found—nor, for that matter, has anyone uncovered a cave with an underwater entrance. Other islands, story has it, were Indian hunting grounds. Still others hold striking Victorian mansions. From June through Columbus Day, two boats offer narrated cruises of about forty-five minutes through the Thimbles: *Sea Mist* ($7.00, 203–488–8905) and *Volsunga IV* ($7.00, 203–481–3345). Call for schedules.

The 12.3-mile stretch of **Route 146** between Branford and Guilford is designated by the state of Connecticut as a "scenic byway," and it passes through some beautifully open land of salt pond and marshes near the ocean. The countryside is flat and open here, flooding the landscape with the soft, diffuse light found only where the land and water exist in equal portions. The amazingly picturesque town of **Guilford** claims fully 500 well-preserved houses that date from 1639 (when the town was founded by Puritans coming directly from England) to 1876. The oldest house, a stone building that was restored in the 1930s, is now the **Henry Whitfield State Museum.** It's at 248 Old Whitfield Street. Open February through December 14, Wednesday through Friday from 10:00 A.M. to 4:30 P.M. Admission $3.00. Telephone: (203) 453–2457. The street continues from the gorgeous town green down to the harbor for a view of Faulkner's Island lighthouse and the Grass Island preserve.

The official scenic drive concludes where Route 146 intersects Route 1 east of Guilford, but that doesn't mean the scenery ends. Follow Route 1 north through East River to Madison, where a right turn leads to **Hammonasset Beach State Park.** Located on a 919-acre peninsula jutting into Long Island Sound, Hammonasset has a two-mile-long beach as well as Meig's Point Nature Center, which offers interpretive programs in the spring through fall. During the summer, Meig's Point itself offers some excellent fishing for bluefish, striped bass, and—on the changing tides—flounder. As Connecticut's longest public beach, Hammonasset has room for a lot of activities from swimming and saltwater fishing to scuba diving, boating, and camping. Wheelchair accessible. Parking $7.00–$12.00 for out-of-state vehicles, $5.00–$8.00 for Connecticut vehicles—but there's no charge after Labor Day until Memorial Day. Telephone: (203) 245–2785.

Route 1 continues along the coast through fine beach and marsh towns of Clinton, Grove Beach, and Westbrook. At Westbrook, the **Stuart B. Kinney National Wildlife Refuge** has 2.5 miles of trails that wind through upland forest and around the edges of a recently restored tidal salt marsh. Telephone: (860) 399–2513. Route 1 eventually converges with I–95 and Route 9 in the historic community of Old Saybrook, which happens to be both Katharine Hepburn's hometown and the headquarters of the Globe-Pequot Press.

Old Saybrook, Connecticut

This community at the mouth of the Connecticut River was among the first English colonies planted in Connecticut, when a group of Puritans led by John Winthrop, Jr. (son of the governor of Massachusetts Bay Colony) kicked out a group of Dutch traders and set down roots. Named for Lords Say and Brooke, who owned the land grant, the village became the first official seat of Yale College, when it was established here as the Collegiate School in 1701. In 1716 the trustees decided to move the college to New Haven, but when the movers came to lug off the books, the townsmen put up a fight and attacked their wagons. In the end, the books moved and Old Saybrook did not become New Haven. Instead, it grew slowly into the capital of one of the regions designated by the Nature Conservancy as the "Last Great Places"—the lower reaches of the Connecticut River.

The Connecticut River was saved from the industrial buildup that plagues other New England rivers because a large sandbar—a submerged island, really—at its mouth blocks the passage of large ships. As a result, the river-mouth towns of Old Saybrook and Old Lyme remained villages instead of becoming cities. Old Saybrook's appeal is its location in the delta country of the river mouth. Abundant marshlands have always made this area a favorite for waterfowl hunters in the fall and for birdwatchers at any season. Seaside resorts began to go up at Light House Point (now Saybrook Point) in the 1880s, and tasteful resort development continues in that part of town even today.

Fortunately, environmental laws enacted in the early 1970s helped rescue the Connecticut River from some of the worst upstream abuses of the twentieth century, including the runoff of toxic pesticides, dumping of industrial chemicals, and simple refuse disposal. A number of anadramous fish species (those that return from the sea to spawn in fresh water) have rebounded along the Connecticut and many hang around in the waters near Old Saybrook. Fish such as the primitive short-nosed sturgeon and the American shad were important food species for the Pequots who used to live on these shores, and the fish are back with a vengeance.

Up the Connecticut River

To get a little more feel for life on the Connecticut in earlier years, drive north five miles on Route 154 from Old Saybrook to **Essex** and follow Main Street to the waterfront and the **Connecticut River Museum.** Sitting right at the dock that was a port of call for the New York-Hartford steamboat service in the nineteenth century, the museum is situated in a warehouse built in 1878. Not only does the museum relate the story of shipbuilding in the area, it also boasts a substantial collection of boats that were built and used on the Connecticut River. Model ships and marine paintings are also exhibited, including one canvas depicting the burning of the Essex merchant fleet by the British Navy during the War of 1812. One of the most interesting displays is a replica of the *Turtle,* built in 1775 and said to be America's first submarine. Open Tuesday through Sunday 10:00 A.M. to 5:00 P.M. Adults $4.00. Wheelchair accessible. Steamboat Dock. 67 Main Street. Telephone: (860) 767–8269. The dock is also a pretty nice place to loll around and watch the river flow, feed the mendicant gulls, or drop a line to fish for bass and catfish.

Three miles west of Essex is the tony community of **Ivoryton,** which earned its name as the center of the ivory-fabricating trade (piano keys and the like), but is now a quiet and pricey residential community. Route 154 continues up the western bank of the Connecticut, passing through Deep River and leading up to the junction with Route 148. This road goes east less than a mile before it hits the river, where the venerable

Chester-Hadlyme ferry (since 1769) crosses the river regularly from 7:00 A.M. to 6:45 P.M. during warm weather. When the ferry isn't operating, a sign is posted at the Routes 154–148 crossroads instructing would-be riders to drive north to the bridge at Tylerville. Car and driver $2.25, additional passengers 75 cents.

Gillette Castle State Park sits on the opposite shore. The eccentric twenty-four-room castle was designed by actor William Gillette, who became famous for his portrayal of Sherlock Holmes. The 184-acre hillside park has a grand view of the Connecticut River and makes a pleasant area for hiking or picnicking. Horse-drawn carriage rides are also available. Open Memorial Day to Columbus Day daily 10:00 A.M. to 5:00 P.M. Weekends until mid-December 10:00 A.M. to 4:00 P.M. Admission to Castle: $4.00. Park admission free. 67 River Road. Telephone: (860) 526–2336.

(To continue north up the Connecticut River, see the "Connecticut River Valley" chapter.)

Old Lyme, Connecticut

The easiest way to cross the Connecticut to resume touring the saltwater coast is to return to Old Saybrook and drive on I–95 north to exit 70 for Old Lyme, Old Saybrook's companion village at the river mouth and another of the leading art colonies for American impressionism.

Prominent landscape painter Henry Ward Ranger discovered Old Lyme in the summer of 1899 and deemed it perfect for American artists returning from Europe with fresh ideas about rendering light and painting in the open air. Just as today, great saltwater marshes lay on the south side of town, while rolling open meadows and deep woods of cedar and oak bordered the north. The village featured handsome Georgian and Federal architecture, and farms divided by long stone walls lined the outlying winding roads. Moonlight and sunlight seemed to shimmer over the varied landscape throughout the year. To Ranger's eye, Old Lyme was a model of the picturesque.

He returned to New York that winter of 1899–1900 to recruit fellow artists to join him in Old Lyme. The landscape, he claimed, was "waiting to be painted." Many who flocked to Old

Gillette Castle, East Haddam, Connecticut

Lyme from 1899 into the 1930s based themselves in the home of Miss Florence Griswold, who became sort of the Gertrude Stein of American impressionism. The Griswold House, with its high-columned portico, was both the spiritual and physical center of the Old Lyme art colony. Built in 1817, the Georgian mansion was purchased by Captain Robert Griswold in 1841. It was Florence Griswold's home from her birth in 1850 until her death in 1937, when the mansion was converted into the **Florence Griswold Museum.**

When Griswold found herself in reduced circumstances in the late 1890s, she began taking in boarders and soon became the landlady of choice for the exuberant painters who summered in Old Lyme. Some of the work left by the artists can be found on the doors and on the mahogany panels set into the walls. A committee of artists chose who would paint a panel—and who would not. Being chosen to paint one was considered a great

honor, a mark of status in the Old Lyme art circle.

As more artists came to stay over the years, new panels were mounted in the dining room, which today chronicles changing styles in American painting early in this century. Among the most striking panels are those painted by Willard Metcalf and Childe Hassam, who seemed to show up at every place along the Connecticut coast where the light suited his taste. Hassam employed bright and broken colors to render the shifting and elusive character of light and his technique came to define the style for the Old Lyme art colony. The Florence Griswold Museum is open December to May Wednesday through Sunday from 1:00 to 5:00 P.M.; June to November Tuesday through Saturday from 10:00 A.M. to 5:00 P.M. and Sunday from 1:00 to 5:00 P.M. Admission $4.00. 96 Lyme Street. Telephone: (860) 434–5542.

Landscapes weren't the only subjects to inspire Old Lyme's painters. Florence Griswold's house and the First Congregational Church of Old Lyme, situated one mile apart from each other on Lyme Street, are among the most frequently painted structures in American art. The church burned down in 1907, but thanks partly to proceeds from that summer's art exhibition, a duplicate was erected on the site. The distance between the church and the Griswold Museum encompasses almost the entire Old Lyme Historic District. Old Lyme lacks a well-defined village center, but antiques shops and art galleries line Lyme Street near the town hall.

New London, Connecticut

Although most travelers arrive in New London (or pass through it) on I–95, the more interesting coastal Route 156 from Old Lyme wends through Niantic and Waterford on the way to the congested industrial and naval centers New London and Groton. **Rocky Neck State Park** in Niantic features a half-mile-long crescent beach outfitted with a boardwalk and bathhouses. The parking charge, levied only from Memorial Day to Labor Day, is $8.00–$12.00 for out-of-state cars, $5.00–$9.00 for Connecticut vehicles. Route 156, Niantic. Telephone: (860) 739–5471.

New London is the home of the Coast Guard Academy and Groton the home of Electric Boat, builder of nuclear-powered submarines, including the USS *Nautilus* (see "Staying There"). Although the cities stand across from each other on the Thames River (pronounced *Thaymz,* as it was in Old London when New London was settled in 1656), the river is sufficiently industrialized at this point that it forms less of an attraction than the modest **Lyman Allyn Art Museum.** Amid its eclectic collections donated by many private collectors, the Allyn devotes an entire gallery specifically to Connecticut impressionist painters. To reach the museum continue following Route 156 until it joins Route 1. In town, turn north on Route 32 and watch for the signs. Open Labor Day to June Tuesday to Sunday from 1:00 to 5:00 P.M., July to Labor Day Tuesday through Saturday from 10:00 A.M. to 5:00 P.M. and Sunday from 1:00 to 5:00 P.M. Admission is $3.00. 625 Williams Street. Telephone: (860) 443–2545.

Route 1 rejoins I–95 in New London to cross the Thames on the Gold Star Bridge. At exit 88 the state should erect a sign that says "Last Chance for Indian Gambling." Instead, it simply points to Route 117 north to Route 214, which in turn funnels into the Mashantucket Pequot Reservation and the Foxwoods Casino. (See "Staying There.") Otherwise, exit 90 leads to Mystic, home of one of the top educational tourism attractions in New England, Mystic Seaport.

Mystic, Connecticut

In 1929, right before the Depression, three Mystic residents formed a Marine Historical Association to try to preserve the fast-disappearing artifacts of America's maritime past. Their foresight has grown into **Mystic Seaport,** a maritime museum with the largest collection of boats and maritime photography in the world.

The town of Mystic was an appropriate choice for Mystic Seaport. With a sheltered harbor on the tidal outlet of the Mystic River, the village has long been the home of mariners and fishermen. The British Navy damned Mystic during the Revolution as a "cursed little hornets nest," and the town became a major shipbuilding center during the 1849 gold rush. The modified clipper *Andrew Jackson,* which had both ample cargo space and a fast hull design, was built here in

1860. It ultimately broke the record (by nine hours) set by Boston's *Flying Cloud* by rounding the Horn to California in eighty-nine days and four hours.

Mystic Seaport is designed to show the life of a nineteenth-century seafaring community and served as a location for Steven Spielberg's historical drama *Amistad.* Several buildings along the unpaved streets and around the town green sit in their original locations, while others have been brought to the Museum from elsewhere in New England. The bank, drugstore, grocery and hardware store, chapel, and schoolhouse typify domestic life in any nineteenth-century New England village. But few villages can boast a shipping office, mast hoop shop, nautical instrument store, or ship's chandlery.

Mystic Seaport would be reasonably impressive if it stopped there, but the museum village recognizes that visitors are most interested in maritime life. The museum's 480-plus vessels represent the largest collection of ships and boats in the world. And you can board and tour the three largest vessels, although the full-rigged *Joseph Conrad,* built in 1882, is used principally as a dormitory for Mystic Seaport's educational programs.

The most interesting of the larger vessels is the *Charles W. Morgan,* the last wooden whaleship in the country. (If you're planning to continue on to the Mid Coast to visit the famous whaling ports of Nantucket and New Bedford—see "Seeing the Mid Coast"—pay special attention to this vessel.) It was built for Quaker whaling merchant Charles W. Morgan and launched from New Bedford in 1841. Records show that in 1846, the *Morgan* was one of a fleet that numbered 736 vessels. Now it is the sole survivor. In eighty years as an active whaling ship, the 133-foot *Morgan* made thirty-seven voyages ranging from nine months to five years. She cruised back and forth across the Pacific, Indian, and South Atlantic Oceans, surviving storms, ice and—according to Mystic Seaport curators—even a cannibal attack in the South Pacific. More than 1,000 whalers served aboard the *Morgan* and they brought home 54,483 barrels of oil and 152,934 pounds of whalebone.

It's fascinating to go below decks and forward of the mast (hence the term "before the mast") to see the cramped quarters where the crew of twenty-two to twenty-five sailors lived for months at sea. Whaleships differed from other large vessels of similar type in that they carried a fleet of six-man whale boats along their rails, which seamen entered to chase, harpoon, and kill a whale before towing the beast back to the whaleship. Aft of the foremast was the "tryworks," a furnace of brick, iron, and wood where cast iron pots were used to render the oil from whale blubber. The oil was stored in casks in the lower hold. The *Morgan* was built as a full-rigged ship with square sails on three masts, but she is displayed as a bark, which she's been since the square sails were removed from her mizzenmast in 1867.

The ***L.A. Dunton*** is a 1921 fishing schooner and the last example of the round-bow fishing vessel common in New England fishing ports in the first quarter of the twentieth century when diesel-powered vessels were beginning to displace sail craft in the fishing trade. On board, staff split and salt cod, and the aroma permeates the vessel as far as the close quarters below decks. Among the other vessels afloat at Mystic Seaport's docks are the Noank smack *Emma C. Berry,* the Friendship sloop *Estella A.,* the oyster sloop *Nellie,* the sandbagger sloop *Annie,* the pinky schooner *Regina M,* the tugboat *Kingston II,* and the 1926 fishing dragger *Florence.*

The North Boat Shed displays a selection of beautifully restored small craft, including boats small and manageable enough to imagine owning. The Mystic River harbor, protected from the Atlantic by Mason Island, was a prime area for the use of catboats as small fishing and recreational craft. With a shallow draft and broad beam, the catboat hull looks rather like a large bathtub with a centerboard. The mast, placed far to the bow, holds a single large sail on a boom, making the catboat a swift little craft that's steady enough to haul lobster traps over its side.

With the beautiful harborside location, it's almost impossible not to want to get out on the water—and there are a number of options at Mystic Seaport. The ***S.S. Sabino,*** a coal-fired wooden passenger steamer, offers half-hour river tours from mid-May through mid-October. Adults $8.50. In the Boathouse, visitors can

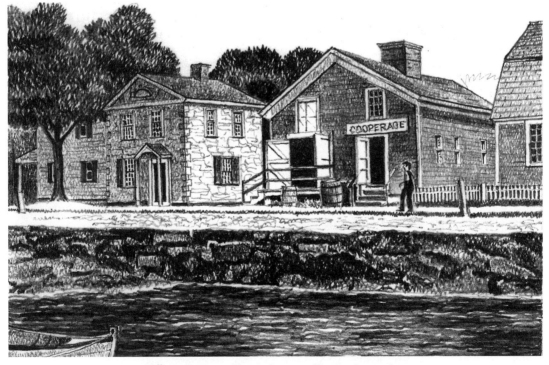

Village Street at Mystic Seaport, Mystic, Connecticut

**Charles W. Morgan at Mystic Seaport,
Mystic, Connecticut**

arrange half-hour cruises aboard a 20-foot Crosby catboat for $4.00 per person, or rent rowboats ($10.50 per hour) or sailboats ($14.00 per hour).

Mystic Seaport is more than a collection of old buildings and vessels. The skilled craftsmen of the Preservation Shipyard restore and preserve wooden vessels. A visitors' gallery overlooks the work area. In March 1998 the shipyard laid the keel for a recreation of the schooner *Amistad,* which was seized off the coast of Cuba in 1839 by fifty-three Africans who had been illegally enslaved. Few sites have Mystic Seaport's capability to undertake such a project, but the location seems doubly appropriate since the *Amistad* was brought into nearby New London after being seized by a U.S. revenue cutter off the coast of Long Island.

Throughout the year, Mystic Seaport hosts a variety of special events ranging from a Sea Music Festival in June to an Antique and Classic Boat Festival in July or Lantern Light Tours in December. Mystic Seaport is open April through Columbus Day daily from 9:00 A.M. to 5:00 P.M. and daily from 10:00 A.M. to 4:00 P.M. the rest of the year. Adults $16. One mile south of I–95, exit 90. 75 Greenmanville Avenue (Route 27). Telephone: (860) 572–5315 or (888) 9–SEAPORT.

It's a short stroll from the Seaport to the downtown area of boutiques, ice cream parlors, and restaurants, including the original **Mystic Pizza,** inspiration for the movie (see "Staying There").

Leaving the Seaport by the gift shop, turn

right and then take the first right down a short residential street to the harbor. Turn left and walk along the harbor. While downtown Mystic is a pleasant enough place for shopping, it is best known for the **bascule drawbridge** that crosses the harbor. Built in 1922 (making it the oldest drawbridge of its kind in the United States), its unusual and rare engineering features counter-weights on top of the bridge.

Stonington Borough, Connecticut

The "borough" takes in both the small port of Stonington, which has Connecticut's largest commercial fishing fleet, and agricultural inland North Stonington. Although Stonington Borough sits cheek by jowl with bustling Mystic and within a crapshoot of Foxwoods, it's a surprisingly quiet and unpresumptuous place. From Route 1 take the turnoff on Route 1A to Stonington Harbor. If a parking space appears, ditch the car for a while. Water Street is better walked than driven to appreciate the architectural details of the buildings, some of which date as far back as 1760. The majority of the structures, however, are Greek Revival in style, dating them in the second quarter of the nineteenth century. At the end of the street is the small and sandy **duBois Beach,** which is patrolled by a lifeguard during the summer and offers a very good view across Long Island Sound toward Montauk on the far eastern tip of Long Island. Also at the end of the street is the **Old Lighthouse Museum** in an 1823 structure that was the first government-operated lighthouse in Connecticut. Open May through October Tuesday through Sunday 10:00 A.M. to 4:00 P.M. Open until 5:00 P.M. in July and August. Adults $4.00. 7 Water Street, Stonington. Telephone: (860) 535–1440.

The agricultural side of Stonington is exemplifed by **Stonington Vineyards.** It is 2.5 miles from town—a verdant, wooded drive through horse country that is spectacular in the fall. The winery usually offers tours at 2:00 P.M., but the tasting room is open daily 11:00 A.M. to 5:00 P.M. 523 Taugwonk Road, North Stonington. Telephone: (860) 535–1222.

The Rhode Island Shore

Block Island Sound, Rhode Island

Route 1 continues north to cross the Pawcatuck River that forms the formal border between Connecticut and Rhode Island, and marks the beginning of a new geological region of New England. Technically, it's the outwash plain south of the terminal glacial moraine. In plain speech, it's the low country of marshes and sandy beaches between the ocean and the short hills a few miles inland. Those hills mark the southern limits of the ice sheet during the last glaciation, and they are composed of rubble picked up by the glacier in its advance, then dumped as the ice melted. All of this outwash plain is fairly new land, built up in the last 15,000 years by silts washed down the inland hills and sand thrown up by the ocean. The oceanside edge of this plain is therefore in constant flux, and one of the features at this particular point in history is that many barrier beaches have completely enclosed their lagoons and created vast ponds separated from the ocean by a thin strip of beach.

A perfect example of this phenomenon is **Misquamicut State Beach**, a spectacular sandy

Old Lighthouse Museum, Stonington, Connecticut

strand that divides Winnipaug Pond from the ocean. This beach attracts swimmers and sunbathers from great distances, and the parking lots often fill up early on the weekends. After crossing into Rhode Island from Connecticut, turn right onto Route 1A toward Avondale and follow the signs to Misquamicut. Parking: Rhode Island residents $4.00 weekdays, $8.00 weekends; out-of-state cars $8.00 weekdays, $10.00 weekends. The beach road continues through the nether world of half land and half water to Weekapaug, where it rejoins Route 1A and then merges into Route 1 to become the "Ocean Scenic Highway." Almost any right-hand turn off Route 1 leads directly to a barrier beach.

The **Ninigret National Wildlife Refuge** in Charlestown protects the northern shore of the largest of the captured coastal ponds, Ninigret Pond, along with its associated swamps, wetlands, grasslands, and uplands. Once the site of a naval air station, Ninigret has both dirt and asphalt trails through its 407 acres. More than 300 bird species have been recorded here, but the greatest concentration is found in late summer and early fall during the migration of egrets, herons, ducks, and geese. Gulls and terns are found throughout the year. Songbirds and their raptor predators also flock here in great numbers during the May and September migrations. Telephone: (401) 364–9124.

The **Ninigret Conservation Area,** which lies across the pond, contains an extraordinary two-mile-long barrier beach that can be reached from the west side by East Beach Road from Route 1. Like most terrific beaches, its parking lot fills early in the day. Charlestown Beach Road, which is a right turn off Route 1 after passing through the village of Charlestown, provides limited access to the eastern end of the strand along the scenic **Charlestown Breachway**. Beach parking costs Rhode Island residents $4.00 weekdays, $8.00 weekends; nonresidents $8.00 weekdays, $10.00 weekends.

Route 1 veers inland as the coastline makes a ninety-degree jog where Block Island Sound turns the corner into Narragansett Bay. About 17 miles after rejoining Route 1 from Trustom Pond, go south on Route 108 to **Galilee** and **Point Judith** on the Harbor of Refuge. There is truly something Biblical about the little fishing port of

Galilee (its sister village across the harbor is Jerusalem)—hard-working seiners and netters pulling fish from the inshore waters. It's a great place to get out of the car and simply walk around, and—no real surprise—it has some very good if very casual seafood restaurants. Although many other ports offer some **ferry service to Block Island,** only the ferry at Galilee operates year-round. Sailing time is seventy minutes and cars are carried (usually with an advance reservation). Departures range from ten per day in the height of the summer to two per day in the winter (no service between Christmas and New Year's Day). Adults $8.00 one-way, $13.50 same day round trip, $16.30 any day round trip. Bicycles $2.30 each way. Cars $52.60 round trip. State Pier off Point Judith Road. Telephone: (401) 783–4613.

Block Island, Rhode Island

Situated a dozen miles east of Long Island and a dozen miles south of the Rhode Island mainland, Block Island is far enough out to sea to enjoy some isolation and close enough to the human crush to become inundated in the summer. Shaped more or less like a pear with a big bite out of the middle, the island has surprisingly diverse topography. High bluffs and low marshes, windswept dunes and rocky outcrops, a huge salt-water pond and more than 300 small bodies of fresh water—all these features combine to make Block Island a topographical precis of the entire South Coast.

Although car service is available on the ferry, most travelers bring bicycles with them or rent bikes on the island. It's best to arrive early, as bicycles are in strong demand. (Mopeds are also available, but moped riders are pariahs on Block Island.) Nothing is very far away on this island of three miles by seven miles, and there are only a few roads, so it is hard to get lost. Bike rental shop staff can advise on the relative difficulty of various routes.

The ferry docks at the island's only village, **Old Harbor,** which could have been lifted from a Victorian tintype. (Local ordinances ensure it stays that way.) The waterfront inns and shops were built to capitalize on the pleasures of the shore. Large windows flood the rooms in light;

high ceilings guarantee good air circulation; and beautiful, arcade-like porches invite guests to settle into wicker chairs and observe the passing scene.

A few hundred yards from the village center is the beginning of a three-mile stretch of sandy beach—**Crescent, Scotch, and Mansion beaches**—that is great for swimming and sunbathing in the warm weather, even better for strolling during the less crowded fall and winter, and superb for surf fishing when the bluefish and striped bass are running.

A good tour of the southern end of the island starts on Spring Street, which goes south out of town past green meadows, moors, and marshy ponds. The Gothic Revival **Southeast Light** will appear on the horizon, and the road changes name somewhere along the way to Southeast Light Road. A small, free exhibit is open at the base of the 1874 lighthouse, one of the oldest on the East Coast, but there's a $5.00 fee to climb the stairs. Presumably this charge helps defray some of the expense of moving the lighthouse 150 feet back from the eroding cliffs in 1993. The light is visible for 30 miles out to sea, warning ships off the Block Island shoals that have claimed more than 1,000 vessels over the years. Open daily July through Labor Day, weekends through Columbus Day. Adults $5.00. Telephone: (401) 466–5009. A few hundred yards down the road, the **Edward S. Payne Overlook** gives a striking view of the cliffs. Known as the Mohegan Bluffs—based on the story that the resident island tribe of Manisseans drove a raiding party of forty Mohegans over the cliff in 1590—these clay banks reach as high as 200 feet in some places.

The road turns back from the cliffs inland, with the right fork returning to Old Harbor. The left fork, Cooneymus Road, leads to **Rodman's Hollow,** a glacier-scoured ravine with footpaths that wind through bayberry brush and swampland, around ponds and across meadows and marshland teeming with birds. Birders actually complain about the abundance of feathered creatures, especially during the fall migration, when thousands of warblers (mostly yellow-rumped warblers) throng the bayberry bushes.

The island's interior consists of knolls and meadows, peaceful farms delineated by stone walls, and five wildlife refuges. The gentle slope of the inland roads make easy pedaling past a broad meadow covered with wildflowers or a moor glistening with one of the island's small ponds. In the middle of the island is Great Salt Pond, actually a substantial lake that nearly bisects the island. The boat marina at New Harbor on the pond is a time-honored spot for watching the sun go down. The northern tip of the island, **Sandy Point National Wildlife Sanctuary**, is an excellent spot to watch migrating butterflies in the fall, mostly monarchs. **North Light House** functions as an interpretive center. Open daily 10:00 A.M. to 4:00 P.M. Telephone: (401) 466–3200.

Narragansett, Rhode Island

Back on the mainland in Galilee, Sand Hill Cove Road leads east to Point Judith Road, which goes a mile south to **Point Judith Light.** Built to replace the original 1806 wooden lighthouse that blew down in the Great Gale of 1815, the light marks the entrance to Narragansett Bay. The last German U-boat sunk in World War II was two miles offshore from the light. This picturesque spot attracts photographers like milkweed draws butterflies, but the lighthouse itself and the Coast Guard Station are not open. Grounds open daily 9:00 A.M. to 4:00 P.M. 1460 Ocean Road. Telephone: (401) 789–0444.

The road north to the town center of Narragansett, Ocean Road (which becomes Ocean Boulevard), passes by some stupendous bathing beaches, not the least of which is **Scarborough State Beach,** perhaps the favorite beach for youthful flirting. Narragansett center is dominated by the "Towers," the cylindrical structures on each side of Ocean Boulevard spanned by matching stone construction. This is all that remains of the old Narragansett Casino, designed by the architectural firm of McKim, Mead and White—*the* prestigious architects to the moneyed classes at the end of the nineteenth century. The towers and span form an effective ceremonial gateway to the town, especially coming from the south. The east tower (on the ocean side) contains the Narragansett Tourism Office.

We were always puzzled to hear people talk about the Narragansett "pier," as there is no structure jutting out into the water from the beach. In fact, it's a local colloquialism for the seawall and

Narragansett Casino, "The Towers," Narragansett, Rhode Island

sidewalk along the water—an area always vibrant with activity in the summer. The "pier" stops at Town Beach, which is a conventional swimming beach until there's an ocean storm. Then the beach receives big, rolling waves at a sixty-degree angle—the best surf in Rhode Island, we've been told.

Continue north from Narragansett on Route 1A (Boston Neck Road) for 8 miles to the junction with Route 138. Head east on Route 138 over the Jamestown Bridge to Jamestown (a great place to live, harder to visit) to the two-mile-long Newport Bridge.

Newport, Rhode Island

Coming into Newport from the west is every bit as dramatic and exciting as everyone claims. The Newport Bridge seems to hover in the sky, a long and graceful arc that looks down on the genteel sprawl of Newport, queen city of the southern end of Aquidneck Island on the east side of Narragansett Bay. Best of all, this rainbow of steel and concrete deposits you practically into the heart of the city.

Most people associate Newport with yachting and with the barons of commerce who built the elaborate summer "cottages" in the Gilded Age. But the city has a distinguished Colonial pedigree and much more modest roots. Newport was founded in the spring of 1639 by religious dissenters from Boston who purchased Aquidneck from the Narragansetts. The English first settled near what is now the junction of West Broadway and Marlborough Street. The **Gateway Information Center** at 23 America's Cup Avenue—one of the best visitors centers we've seen—is nearby, and has excellent free maps. It also sells admission tickets for the mansions.

About a block north of Gateway Center is the area called **The Point.** This is the neighborhood where colonial merchants had their homes and many authentically restored eighteenth-century buildings remain private residences. In fact, Newport claims to have more original Colonial houses still occupied than any other community in the United States. The **1748 Hunter House** at 54 Washington Street, which is open to visitors, is often cited as one of the best examples of residential Colonial architecture in the country. Saving it was the impetus for forming the Preservation Society of Newport County in 1945. The interior features Goddard-Townsend furniture, among the finest furniture makers in early America. Open May through September daily 10:00 A.M. to 5:00 P.M., April and October Saturday and Sunday 10:00 A.M. to 5:00 P.M. Adults $6.50. Telephone: (401) 847–1000.

Another important Colonial era building is the **Colony House,** also called the Old State House, which sits in Washington Square beneath high shade trees about a block from the visitors center. When Newport was the capital of Rhode Island, the Colony House was the capitol building. Rhode Island renounced its ties with England here on May 4, 1776, becoming the first colony to declare independence.

Rhode Islanders have always prided themselves on being free thinkers. The state's founders were thrown out of the Massachusetts Bay Colony for their unorthodox religious beliefs and Newport prospered in part by serving as a haven for religious minorities, including large numbers of Quakers unwelcome in the rest of New England. The first group of six Friends arrived in 1657, the first apostles of Quakerism in the New World, and when the movement's founder, George Fox, saw fit to visit New England in 1671, he came straightaway to Newport. The Friends won many powerful converts, and for two centuries Quakers dominated both commerce and government in the city.

Newport was also one of the few American cities to welcome the Jews with open arms, the first fifteen families arriving from Holland in 1658 and forming the congregation Jeshuat Israel. They were joined by another contingent of Jewish refugees from Curaçao in 1694 and many Portuguese Jews fleeing the earthquakes in 1755. The mid-eighteenth century also saw many other Jewish refugees arriving in Newport as they fled the last throes of the Spanish Inquisition. Among them was Jacob Rodrigues Rivera, who is credited with introducing the spermaceti industry to the American colonies, and Aaron Lopez, his son-in-law and business partner. As the numbers of the congregation swelled, they could no longer worship in private houses and in 1763 built the **Touro Synagogue** at 72 Touro Street. Just a short walk uphill from the Colony House, it is the oldest synagogue in the United States and the only one that survives from the colonial era. Designed by noted Colonial architect Peter Harrison, it is considered one of the finest examples of eighteenth-century Georgian architecture in the country. Open July 4 weekend through Labor Day Sunday through Friday 10:00 A.M. to 5:00 P.M. Call for hours during the rest of the year. Telephone: (401) 847–4794.

Indeed, in 1729 the great scholar and theologian George Berkeley, Dean of Derry, wrote to a friend in Dublin of Newport's religious diversity and tolerance. "Here are four sorts of Anabaptists, besides Presbyterians, Quakers, Independents and many of no profession at all. Notwithstanding so many differences here are fewer quarrels about religion than elsewhere, the people living peaceable with their neighbors of whatever persuasion."

Perhaps good times had to do with all that mutual tolerance. Newport's first street, **Thames Street,** was laid out to run exactly one mile along the harbor. The street is lined with wharves—a reminder that while Newport began as a farming community, it made its fortune on shipbuilding and ocean trade. By 1675, the area farms, which have the best soil in the state, were sending their goods to middle Atlantic and Southern colonies, the West Indies, and Europe. Despite liberal religious influences, Rhode Island led the colonies in slave trading and Newport was the chief Rhode Island slave center, with up to sixty vessels engaged in slaving at any one time. Nor were the Newport merchants averse to putting guns aboard their ships and turning privateer—one of the port's leading occupations during both King George's War and the French and Indian War. By the time the shots rang out to signal the American Revolution, Newport enjoyed a prosperity that rivaled Boston and New York.

Today, Thames Street and the wharves no longer deal in cotton, sugar, slaves, or booty—monetary inflation after the Revolution and the trade embargo of the War of 1812 all but killed the city's commerce and drove out half its population. But Newport rose to a new glory in the 1830s, when the wealthy from the southern states and Cuba began to spend their summers relieved by cool harbor breezes. Although the Southern clientele fell off after the Civil War, Newport became one of the key summer watering holes for America's wealthy in the last third of the nineteenth century. So these days Thames Street and the wharves that line its length have been redeveloped as a tourist destination, with shops, restaurants, and boutiques jammed into virtually every structure along the one-mile stretch.

Even if you ignore the shops and eateries, there is plenty to see on the water. Newport variously calls itself the "Yachting Capital of the Northeast" or sometimes the "Yachting Capital of the World." The great steam and sailing yachts of the nineteenth century found Newport a commodious destination and the America's Cup lodged here from 1930 through 1983. In fact, the New York Yacht Club, which launched the America's Cup competition, has a substantial presence still in Newport. On any particular day, the harbor is filled with classic wooden sailing vessels as well as the sharp-bowed, high-powered behemoth yachts much favored by oil barons, software tycoons, and Third World despots. For those whose personal fortunes do not run to eight figures, several places along the wharves offer motor or sail cruises (see "Staying There").

As gentrified as the wharf district has become, there is one anomalous reminder that it was not always such a playground: the **Seamen's Church Institute.** Newport has many famous sights, but we consider the Institute one of the few essentials. Since 1919 it has been a haven for seafarers, pro-

viding spiritual comfort in the Chapel of the Sea (which is lined with truly wonderful murals of maritime Biblical scenes), and also meeting more practical mental and physical needs for food in St. Elmo's Galley (see "Staying There"). Sailors can also enjoy the reading materials from the library (where there's always a good used-book sale) as well as the very pragmatic showers and washing machines. The **Rhode Island Fisherman & Whale Museum** is located on the second floor. It's open daily except Wednesday. Adults. $2. The library, chapel, restaurant, and restrooms are open daily. 18 Market Square. Telephone: (401) 847–4260.

If you're in search for a souvenir of bygone Newport—or just an inveterate patron of antiques and collectibles dealers, as we are—you'll want to move uphill a bit from the harbor. **Spring Street** runs parallel to Thames Street and **Franklin Street** runs perpendicular between the two. Between them, they constitute the city's primary antiques district. Interestingly, many of the Spring Street houses are modest affairs that date from the eighteenth century, making an interesting contrast with the fine furniture, export porcelain, and other goods that reflect the more opulent side of Newport's past.

Newport started becoming fashionable in the 1830s, when summer visitors faced with a hotel shortage erected modest cottages intended to last but a single season. The scale and permanence of those first cottages soon began to escalate, leading ultimately to the "cottages" for which Newport became famous—the mansions built by wealthy Northern families after the Civil War along **Bellevue Avenue** and other strategic and scenic points on the rocky promontory on the southern tip of Newport.

Before the mansions begin on Bellevue, the **International Tennis Hall of Fame** sets the style for the avenue. Known as "Newport's Sporting Mansion," it is housed in the Newport Casino, built as a social and sporting club for the summer residents—a place where the Vanderbilts and the Astors and their ilk played tennis. The first National Championship tennis matches were held here in September 1881 and the Hall of Fame continues to host some of the world's best tennis players. "Newport Tennis Week" in July features men's and women's professional events as well as enshrinement ceremonies. From May through October the **Casino Lawn Tennis Club** has daily court rentals for those who want to experience playing on its thirteen grass courts. The museum itself has fifteen galleries tracing the history and current events of the sport and makes use of interactive technology to bring the sport to life. Adults $8.00. The museum is open daily 9:30 A.M. to 5:00 P.M. 194 Bellevue Avenue. Telephone: (401) 849–3390 for Hall of Fame, (401) 846–0642 for Tennis Club.

While some summer residents stayed for the long season of four months, the fashionable season in Newport was from about the middle of July until the first of September, and the true social butterflies only stuck around in late June and July—in August one moved to Saratoga for the races, in September and October to the Berkshires for fall foliage. At its most extreme, the disparity of social status between the summer people and the townspeople was appalling, with the summer folk referring to the locals as "our footstools" and going to great lengths to keep them away from Bellevue Avenue or the private beaches and yacht marinas. The social season was known for elaborate balls and dinners—even lavish picnics. The competition between hostesses to outdo each other reached its apogee during the "gilded years" of 1890–1914, when a single ball could cost more than $100,000 and, in one infamous instance, a dinner party of considerable expense was given for one-hundred dogs and their masters. A newspaper reporter snuck in and outrage over the extravagance was expressed on several editorial pages up and down the Eastern seaboard.

The unchallenged leader was Mrs. William Astor, the grande dame of New York and Newport society whose annual ball was the greatest social event of the season. Her New York ballroom held 400 people and invitations even to her Newport party were limited to that number. Legend has it that she said there were only 400 people worth knowing. It gives us a twinge of pleasure to imagine what she would think of the crowds of hoipolloi who traipse through her mansion today.

The **Astor's Beechwood,** a forty-room mansion at 580 Bellevue Avenue, is one of eight homes the couple owned. Costumed actors portray Mrs. Astor's family, wealthy friends, and servants in a forty-five-minute guided tour—a lively *Upstairs Downstairs* alternative to a standard tour. You can also rent Beechwood for $4,400 a night during peak season. Adults $8.75. Open June through October daily 10:00 A.M. to 5:00 P.M. Call for hours during the rest of the year, as well as for special Christmas events. Telephone: (401) 846–3772.

We can also only imagine what Mrs. Astor would think if she knew that the most popular mansion is not Beechwood, but **The Breakers,** the spectacular mansion completed in 1895 for Cornelius Vanderbilt in an attempt to outdo Marble House, the home of his brother, William K. Vanderbilt. More than 2,000 laborers and craftsmen spent in excess of two years to complete the Italianate structure built of Indiana limestone. Its seventy rooms include a two-story dining room that is larger than some Newport ballrooms, twenty-three bathrooms and thirty-three servants' rooms. (It took thirty-three servants, thirteen grooms, and twelve gardeners to maintain the property and see to the needs of the family.) The Breakers covers an acre of the estate on the southern end of Ochre Point Avenue, with ocean views from the back of the house. This extraordinary exercise in conspicuous consumption was modeled after sixteenth-century northern Italian palaces. A number of the rooms were built in France, disassembled, and shipped to Newport for reassembly. Much of the furnishings came from European estates whose owners were no longer as flush as the Vanderbilts. Adults $10. Open mid-March through October daily 10:00 A.M. to 5:00 P.M. Open until 6:00 P.M. on Saturdays in July and August. Telephone: (401) 847–1000.

Because The Breakers is so popular, the wait to tour it can be very long, and those with little patience might prefer another mansion. They all look pretty spectacular compared to how most of us live, so it's unlikely that any will disappoint. If you really get into the lifestyles of the rich and famous, there is a discount if you visit two or more of the mansions owned by the Preservation Society of Newport County, which includes The Breakers, Marble House, Rosecliff, and several others.

Marble House on Bellevue Avenue adjacent

to the Astor's Beechwood was built by William K. Vanderbilt as a thirty-ninth birthday gift for his wife Alva. The fifty-two-room mansion is named for its primary building material—the façade alone consists of 100,000 cubic feet of white marble, and several more tons of yellow and pink marble were used in the interior. Yet all that stone is upstaged by the ballroom, which is gilded from floor to ceiling, with golden chandeliers to reflect the glitter. Three years after receiving this lavish gift, Alva divorced her husband. When she remarried divorce lawyer Oliver H. P. Belmont the next year, he gave her the fifty-two-room mansion **Belcourt** (657 Bellevue Avenue) as a wedding gift.

Rosecliff, also on Bellevue Avenue, might look a little familiar. This 1902 mansion was designed by Stanford White after the Grand Trianon at Versailles. It was the home of Jay Gatsby (as played by Robert Redford) in the film version of F. Scott Fitzgerald's novel *The Great Gatsby* and also appeared in the Arnold Schwarzenegger movie, *True Lies.* It has Newport's largest ballroom (80 by 40 feet) and a memorable red-carpeted, heart-shaped staircase rising from the vestibule. Adults $8.00. Open mid-March through October daily from 10:00 A.M. to 5:00 P.M. Call for hours during the rest of the year and for a schedule of Christmas events. Telephone: (401) 847–1000.

One of the things we like best about Newport is that anyone can enjoy the same view as those who lived in the "cottages." **The Cliff Walk,** a 3.6-mile path along and above Newport's rocky shoreline, stretches from Easton's Beach (the public beach where the servants swam) to Bailey's Beach (the private beach where the elite disported in bathing uniforms, monocles, and hats). The beginning of the walk is paved, but later it becomes more rocky, so sturdy shoes are a necessity. One side of the path offers incredible ocean vistas, while the other looks on the mansions and their manicured lawns. The walk, however, predates the mansions. Fishermen began tramping along the cliffs around 1640 and Newporters have used the trail ever since. In the early 1900s, one writer described it as "the most beautiful walk in the country."

Although the summer people thought little of

The Breakers, Newport, Rhode Island

the townies, they permitted the city to reserve the great sandy strand of **Easton's Beach** on the northern end of the Cliff Walk for public use. Because the beach is fairly exposed, waves here can become quite large. The beach has showers, lockers, bathhouses, a snack bar, and a carousel.

Newport's other famous scenic route is the approximately 10-mile **Ocean Drive**, around the southwestern peninsula of Aquidneck Island. It's a chance to ogle estates and enjoy great ocean views from a bicycle, although the shoulders of the road are narrow and traffic is predictably heavy. Ocean Drive begins almost where the Cliff Walk ends. The far end of Bellevue Avenue (going away from town) swings around to the right, returning to town as Spring Street (the right fork), or veering to the left as Ocean Avenue. All the way out on the tip of the peninsula, **Brenton Point Park** is a good place to take a breather and enjoy the easy access to the rocky shore. Shortly after Ocean Avenue turns into Ridge Road, there's another good stop at Castle Hill Coast Guard Station where a path leads to **Castle Hill Light.**

One of the more notable mansions along the route is **Hammersmith Farm,** established in 1640 and the only remaining working farm in the city of Newport. It is decidedly the province of a "gentleman farmer." Pastures and cows contrast with the gardens designed by Frederick Law Olmsted. Hammersmith is perhaps better known as the childhood home of Jacqueline Bouvier, the daughter of Mrs. Hugh Auchincloss. The twenty-eight-room shingle-style mansion was built in

1887 by John W. Auchincloss and four generations of the family have spent their summers here. When Jacqueline married John F. Kennedy in Newport in 1953, their wedding reception was at Hammersmith Farm. The Kennedys visited often, hence the farm is sometimes referred to as a "summer White House." The lawns lead down to the bay, where the Presidential yacht *Honey Fitz* used to berth. Adults $8.50 Open April through early November daily 10:00 A.M. to 5:00 P.M. Telephone: (401) 846–7346.

Near Hammersmith Farm is the entrance to **Fort Adams State Park,** born of Newport's long association with the U.S. Navy. The city was the site of the Naval Academy during the Civil War. The Naval Training Station and the Naval War College, the highest educational institution in the U.S. Navy, were established here in the 1880s. In the early 1900s, Narragansett Bay was the principal anchorage for the Atlantic Fleet, which was protected by Fort Adams, one of the largest bastioned forts in the nation. Fortifications can still be seen in the park, but the grounds have long since dropped their military significance in favor of recreational facilities: a roped-off swimming area, a picnic area, and a fishing pier.

Occupying a spectacular waterfront location within Fort Adams State Park is the **Museum of Yachting,** a window for most of us into the history and traditions of this sport. One exhibit explores the style of yachting in the late 1800s when the Vanderbilts, Morgans, and Astors vied to have the best yachts as well as the most elaborate mansions. By contrast, the Small Craft Gallery collects and displays a variety of classic wooden sail and power boats. The feature exhibit, the Great J-Boats, includes photos, artifacts, models, and chronicles describing the America's Cup races and their contenders in Newport during the 1930s. The Small Boat Basin displays boats dating from 1917 to the 1930s restored by the museum's School for Yacht Restoration. Adults $3.00. Open mid-May through October daily 10:00 A.M. to 5:00 P.M. Telephone: (401) 847–1018.

Soon after the park, Ocean Drive concludes at the Ida Lewis Yacht Club—named for the lighthouse, which is in turn named for the female keeper who took over the job from her father. Wellington Avenue leads back to Thames Street, and the electric buzz of Newport.

Hammersmith Farm, Newport, Rhode Island

 # Staying There

For information about Coastal Fairfield County from Greenwich to Stratford, contact Coastal Fairfield County County Convention and Visitor Bureau, MerrittView, 383 Main Avenue, Norwalk, CT 06851. Telephone: (203) 899–2799 or (800) 866–7925.

The Connecticut Shore

Greenwich, Connecticut

LODGING

The Stanton House Inn. 76 Maple Avenue. In 1900 architect Stanford White—a good friend of many of the American impressionists—oversaw the enlargement of the Stanton House. The twenty-four rooms, most with private baths and some with fireplaces, have unusual but cozy layouts, while the public areas embody a classic formality. Telephone: (203) 869–2110. Moderate with breakfast.

FOOD

Elm Street Oyster House. 11 West Elm Street. Telephone: (203) 629–5795. Right off the main street, this smartly decorated restaurant offers a number of daily fish specials as well as reliable pan-fried oysters and mini-crab cakes. Lunch and dinner. Moderate to expensive.

Stamford, Connecticut

SHOPPING

United House Wrecking Company. 535 Hope Street. Telephone: (203) 348–5371. Make sure you have plenty of room in your car if you plan to stop at this specialist in architectural salvage, collected in an area of really good pickings.

Norwalk, Connecticut

LODGING

Silvermine Tavern. 194 Perry Avenue. This 1785 country inn, overlooking a waterfall on the bucolic Silvermine River, has ten guest rooms. The Sunday brunch is a local tradition for multigenerational gatherings. Telephone: (203) 847–4558. Moderate with breakfast.

FOOD

Amberjacks Coastal Grill. 99 Washington Street. Telephone: (203) 853–4332. The marine paintings and boat-prow bar leave no question that this restaurant specializes in seafood, prepared with a bit of invention and panache. Lunch and dinner. Moderate to expensive.

OTHER ATTRACTIONS

WPA Murals. More than thirty murals in City Hall depict local scenes and constitute one of the largest collections in the country of work funded by the federal art project of the Works Progress Administration. Open Monday through Friday from 8:30 A.M. to 5:00 P.M. Free. Wheelchair accessible. 125 East Avenue. Telephone: (203) 866–0202.

FAIRS, FESTIVALS, AND EVENTS

Norwalk Oyster Festival. This three-day event in early September celebrates Long Island Sound's seafaring past with entertainment, tall ships, and oyster shucking and slurping contests. Telephone: (203) 838–9444.

Fairfield, Connecticut

FOOD

Rawley's Drive-In. 1886 Post Road (Route 1). Telephone: (203) 259–9023. This local institution serves up more than 350 hot dogs every day to regular folks and to celebrity aficionados such as Martha Stewart, Paul Newman, Mike Wallace, and David Letterman. Owner Chico Beilik is their idea of a celebrity. His most popular dogs with "the works"—mustard, relish, sauerkraut, cheese, and bacon. Lunch.

Bridgeport, Connecticut

OTHER ATTRACTIONS

The Barnum Museum. Known for his flamboyant entrepreneurship (a trait more bluntly called hucksterism), P.T. Barnum was once also mayor of Bridgeport. Hence the town established a museum in his honor in an elaborate 1893 Gothic structure. In addition to a range of offbeat memorabilia, the museum has a 1,000-square-foot scale model miniature three-ring circus. Open Tuesday through Sunday 10:00 A.M. to 4:40 P.M., Sunday noon to 4:30 P.M. Also open July and August Monday 11:00 A.M. to 4:30 P.M. Adults $5.00. Wheelchair accessible. 820 Main Street. Telephone: (203) 331–9881.

New Haven, Connecticut

For information about the Greater New Haven area contact the Greater New Haven Convention & Visitors Bureau, One Long Wharf Drive, Suite 7, New Haven, CT 06511. Telephone: (203) 777–8550 or (800) 332–STAY.

FOOD

Frank Pepe's Pizzeria Napoletana. 157 Wooster Street. Telephone: (203) 865–5762. This spot in New Haven's Italian neighborhood claims to have created the first pizzas in the United States in 1925. The coal-fired oven is still in use. Lunch on weekends and dinner. Inexpensive.

Louis' Lunch. 261–263 Crown Street. Telephone: (203) 562–5507. Legend has it that the first hamburger sandwiches were created in this little red-brick restaurant in 1900. They are still prepared by members of the same family—on the same grills. But, be advised, Louis' burgers come with tomato and onion, but no catsup. Lunch and dinner. Inexpensive.

OTHER ATTRACTIONS

Long Wharf Theatre. This well-respected regional theater presents both classics and new works and offers free backstage tours. Call for hours. 222 Sargent Drive. Telephone: (203) 787–4282.

Yale University. The college, which was established in nearby Old Saybrook in 1702 and moved to New Haven in 1718, is a major presence in the city and provides many of the cultural attractions of interest to travelers. The **Visitor Information Center** at 149 Elm Street can provide maps and offers free guided walking tours Monday through Friday 10:30 A.M. and 2:00 P.M., Saturday and Sunday 1:30 P.M. Telephone: (203) 432–2300. The leafy old campus surrounded by Victorian and Federal buildings is what most people think of when they imagine an Ivy League institution. The **Yale University Art Gallery** has an excellent collection that ranges across continents and centuries, but which is especially strong in American realist painting of the late nineteenth and early twentieth centuries and French impressionism. Travelers exploring the sites of Connecticut impressionist painting along the coast may find the comparisons interesting. Open September through July Tuesday through Saturday 10:00 A.M. to 5:00 P.M., Sunday 1:00 to 6:00 P.M. Donation requested. Wheelchair accessible. 1111 Chapel Street. Telephone: (203) 432–0600. The **Yale Center for British Art** surveys the development of British art, life, and thought from the time of Queen Elizabeth I to the modern era, with special emphasis on the eighteenth and first part of the nineteenth centuries. The J.M.W. Turner paintings were important influences on the American impressionists who painted along this coastline. The center just underwent major structural renovations, reopening in early 1999. Open September through July Tuesday through Saturday 10:00 A.M. to 5:00 P.M., Sunday 1:00 to 5:00 P.M. Donation requested. Wheelchair accessible. 1080 Chapel Street. Telephone: (203) 432–2800. **Yale Repertory Theatre** is the laboratory for the talented faculty and students of Yale's theater program. You never know what up-and-coming talent you might discover. Corner of Chapel and York Streets. Telephone: (203) 432–1234.

FAIRS, FESTIVALS, AND EVENTS

International Festival of Arts and Ideas. This five-day event in late June has a packed calendar of music, dance, theater, film, visual arts exhibits, and literature and draws performers and cultural activists from around the world. Telephone: (888) ART–IDEA.

Branford, Connecticut

FOOD

Le Petit Café. 225 Montowese Street. Telephone: (203) 483–9791. One of the best bargains along the coast is the four-course, prix-fixe dinner for less than $25. As the name suggests, the dominant cuisine is French and the dominant style is bistro, but a new chef/owner occasionally interjects some surprising touches from his native China. Dinner Wednesday through Sunday. Moderate.

Lenny's Indian Head Inn. Route 146. Telephone: (203) 488–1500. Located in the Branford "finger" of Indian Head, Lenny's is a rare find along the coast—the kind of seafood place that the locals would like to keep to themselves if they could. Alas, passing yachtsmen have whispered its name all along the Intracoastal Waterway, so it can get fairly crowded. There's not the slightest hint of "nouvelle" anything—just stupendous steamed clams, immense boiled lobsters, succulent broiled scrod, sweet fried oysters, and some good chowders and bisques. With wooden booths, pitchers of beer, and a swell salt marsh location, you could hardly ask for more. Unlike many seafood houses, Lenny's is open daily all year for lunch and dinner. Moderate.

Guilford, Connecticut

FOOD

Cilantro. 85 Whitfield Street. Telephone: (203) 458–2555. This bakery, deli, and specialty foods store has good choices of sandwiches and snacks to eat in or take out. Breakfast and lunch.

FAIRS, FESTIVALS, AND EVENTS

Guilford Handcraft Exposition. The gracious town green is the site for a three-day handcraft exposition in mid-July that has been held for more than forty years. Telephone: (203) 453–9677.

Madison, Connecticut

LODGING

Madison Beach Hotel. 94 West Wharf Road. All but three of the thirty-five guest rooms in this restored 1800 Victorian hotel have water views and everyone can take advantage of the private beach at the end of a road in a quiet neighborhood. Wheelchair accessible. Telephone: (203) 245–1404. Moderate to expensive with breakfast.

Tidewater Inn B&B. 949 Boston Post Road. At the east end of town, this Victorian inn sits up on a knoll not far from Hammonasset Beach. Departing from casual beach decor, the inn is furnished with antiques and has an English garden. Some of the nine guest rooms have canopy beds or fireplaces. Telephone: (203) 245–8457. Moderate to expensive with breakfast.

Westbrook, Connecticut

LODGING

Captain Stannard House. 138 South Main Street. This circa 1850 sea captain's home has six guest rooms set back just far enough from Route 1 to get a little peace and quiet. Telephone: (860) 399–4634. Moderate with breakfast.

FOOD

Lenny & Joe's Fish Tale. 86 Boston Post Road. Telephone: (860) 669–0767. Although it doesn't sit directly on the waterfront, Lenny & Joe's is one of the most popular clam shacks on the Connecticut coast. Regulars stick with fried whole-belly clams and cole slaw, with maybe a cup of chowder to start and an order of onion rings on the side. Lunch and dinner. Inexpensive to moderate.

SHOPPING

Westbrook Factory Stores. Flat Rock Place. Telephone: (860) 399–8656. This mall outlet north of town has more than sixty of the usual factory outlet mall establishments.

Old Saybrook, Connecticut

LODGING

Saybrook Point Inn & Spa. 2 Bridge Street. This classy waterfront inn right at the mouth of the Connecticut River offers sixty-two spacious, well-appointed rooms, most with unbeatable views of Long Island Sound. Photos throughout show the property's evolution from a 1950s motel—a peculiar bit of self-congratulatory decor—to its present-day refined English-style demeanor. Wheelchair accessible. Telephone: 860–395–2000. Expensive to very expensive.

FOOD

Aleia's. 1687 Boston Post Road. Telephone: (860) 399-5050. This popular restaurant recently moved to larger quarters. Service can often be slow, but locals wait patiently for the deft handling of seafood and the great desserts. Dinner. Moderate to expensive.

Cafe Routier. 1080 Boston Post Road. Telephone: (860) 388–6270. Locals sometimes refer to this stylish restaurant as the "Truck Stop Cafe" because of its location next to a gas station on the busy Boston Post Road, but nothing could be farther from the truth in this classic French bistro. Travelers can only wish that all truck stops were this good. Dinner. Moderate.

SHOPPING

Antiques. More than 200 antiques dealers are clustered within a two-mile driving area along Route 154.

Essex, Connecticut

FOOD

Griswold Inn. Main Street. The Griswold Inn may actually define "local institution." The main building dates to 1776 and all the public rooms are filled with mementos and the sort of character that it takes decades to accrete. The food might also define straightforward Yankee cooking, but there is no more authentic or interesting place in which to eat such things as turkey with stuffing. It's essential to reserve for the Sunday Hunt Breakfast, which is a traditional English buffet. Telephone: (860) 767–1776. Lunch, dinner, and Sunday Hunt Breakfast. Expensive.

ACTIVITIES

Essex Steam Train & Riverboat Ride. Steamboats began regular service on this stretch of the Connecticut in 1823, and while the boat involved in this attraction isn't anywhere near that old, it does give a sense of a slower, more orderly time. This old-fashioned sightseeing combo includes a ride on a restored 1920s steam train up the Connecticut River Valley to Deep River to board a multi-deck steamboat for a river cruise past the Goodspeed Opera House, Gillette Castle, and Haddam's unique swing bridge. Operates May through December. Train and boat $15 adults. Train only $10 adults. Railroad Avenue. Telephone: (860) 767–0103.

Ivoryton, Connecticut

LODGING

Copper Beech Inn. 46 Main Street. Four rooms in the main 1890 home have the most period feel, while nine rooms in the carriage house have whirlpool tubs and televisions. Smoke free. Telephone: (860) 767–0330. Expensive with breakfast.

FOOD

Copper Beech Inn. 46 Main Street. Telephone: (860) 767–0330. The inn's "nouvelle" French restaurant is one of the most popular in an area of high eating standards. Dinner. Closed some Mondays and Tuesdays during the winter. Expensive to very expensive.

OTHER ATTRACTIONS

Ivoryton Playhouse. This mainstay of the summer stock circuit runs to Broadway revivals and is heavy on light comedies and mysteries. Children's theater is performed during the winter months and the Playhouse is a venue for concerts. Wheelchair accessible. 103 Main Street. Telephone: (860) 767-7318.

East Haddam, Connecticut

FOOD

Blue Oar. 16 Snyder Road, Haddam. Telephone: (860) 345–2994. Casual as they come, the Blue Oar can be found at Midway Marina off River Road. You can sit at colorful picnic tables to enjoy the view of the Connecticut River and dine on fairly ambitious fish shack fare, such as mussel bisque or barbecued shrimp. Or you can simply settle for an excellent, if less imaginative hamburger. Lunch and dinner. Inexpensive to moderate.

The Gelston House. 8 Main Street, East Haddam. Telephone: (860) 873–1411. A convenient spot for dining if you're heading to a production at the adjacent Goodspeed Opera House, the Gelston House has undergone a recent makeover of the decor while adhering to its classic continental menu. Lunch and dinner Wednesday through Saturday, Sunday brunch. Expensive.

OTHER ATTRACTIONS

Goodspeed Opera House. The imposing white Victorian opera house overlooking the Connecticut River is a stunning setting for musical productions that run from April through December. Wheelchair accessible. Route 82. Telephone: (860) 873–8668.

Old Lyme, Connecticut

For information about coastal Connecticut from the mouth of the Connecticut River to the Rhode Island border, contact Southeastern Connecticut Tourism District, P.O. Box 89, 470 Bank Street, New London, CT 06320. Telephone: (860) 444–2206 or (800) 863–6569.

LODGING

Bee & Thistle Inn. 100 Lyme Street. The Bee & Thistle has an essential place in Old Lyme society as the standard-bearer of old-time grace and charm. The heart of the inn is a restored 1756 private home with a riverside location. Eleven bedrooms, some of which share baths, are scattered through the property. Telephone: (860) 434–1667

or (800) 622–4946. Moderate to expensive with breakfast.

Old Lyme Inn. 85 Lyme Street. Built a century after the Bee & Thistle, the Old Lyme Inn has thirteen rooms with private baths and the antique decor you'd expect in a Victorian mansion. Wheelchair accessible. Telephone: (860) 434–2600 or (800) 434–5352. Moderate to expensive with breakfast.

FOOD

Old Lyme Inn. 85 Lyme Street. Telephone: (860) 434–2600. Offering a choice between the Victorian bar with a light dinner menu and more formal Victorian dining rooms with a full menu of New American cuisine, the Old Lyme Inn is a bit of time trip to an age of grace. Wheelchair accessible. Dinner. Expensive.

New London, Connecticut

OTHER ATTRACTIONS

U.S. Coast Guard Academy and Museum. The attractive campus overlooks the Thames River.

Goodspeed Opera House, East Haddam, Connecticut

When it's in port, the barkentine *Eagle,* the only square-rigged tall ship on active duty in the U.S. government, is open for tours. It serves as a training vessel for cadets. Otherwise, the museum has a variety of exhibits that trace the history of the Coast Guard. Wheelchair accessible. Open Monday through Friday 9:00 A.M. to 4:30 P.M. (Tuesday until 8:00 P.M.), Saturday 10:00 A.M. to 5:00 P.M., Sunday noon to 5:00 P.M. Free. 15 Mohegan Avenue. Telephone: (860) 444–8270.

FAIRS, FESTIVALS, AND EVENTS

Mashantucket Pequot Thames River Fireworks. Three barges are placed in the river between Groton and New London for what is billed as one of the largest fireworks displays in the country. Held in early July. Telephone: (860) 599–2214.

Groton, Connecticut

OTHER ATTRACTIONS

Historic Ship Nautilus/*Submarine Force Museum.* Exhibits trace the history of the United States Navy's submarine service, but the real attraction is the opportunity to board the *Nautilus,* the world's first nuclear-powered vessel and the first submarine to actually journey 20,000 leagues under the sea. Open mid-May through October Wednesday through Monday 9:00 A.M. to 5:00 P.M., Tuesday 1:00 to 5:00 P.M. November through mid-May closed Tuesday. Closed first full week of May and last full week of October. Free. Naval Submarine Base (exit 86 off I–95). Telephone: (860) 694–3174.

FAIRS, FESTIVALS, AND EVENTS

SUBFEST. The Naval Submarine Base is the site of a four-day festival in early July with a boat show, carnival, and fireworks. Telephone: (860) 694–3238.

Ledyard, Connecticut

OTHER ATTRACTIONS

Foxwoods Resort Casino. The Mashantucket band of the Pequot Nation opened Connecticut's first casino in decades in 1992, and it has grown into the highest-grossing gaming complex in the world. To help smooth the way with the state (which had opposed the facility), the Pequots offered 25 percent of the slot machine earnings to the state government on the proviso that Connecticut ban all nontribal casinos. (The Mohegans cut the same deal in 1996, and between them they swell state coffers by nearly a quarter *billion* dollars each year.) The proximity to both New York and Boston has been a huge boon to the once-impoverished tribe, as the casino earns more than $1 billion a year. As a result, the Mashantucket Pequots have become some of the largest charitable donors in Connecticut, seeking to put some of that gambling money to work for good causes.

We admire the Pequot investment in their community, but casino complexes don't excite us. The casino is huge—larger than many in Atlantic City or Las Vegas—and the entire resort complex is so vast and complicated that it's connected by a bus system. The Pequot Towers and Foxwoods Resort hotels are swank, convention-style facilities with prices to match, mostly in the expensive level. The Two Trees Inn is comparatively small (280 rooms), expensive to very expensive. Information or reservation telephone: (800) FOXWOOD.

As you'd expect of such a successful gaming facility (5,000-plus slot machines, hundreds of gaming tables), top-name entertainment is featured in the show rooms and there's a place to get a drink or a bite to eat every time you turn around. In truth, the casino complex has almost nothing to do with the history or character of New England, but it is certainly a fascinating sociological phenomenon. Foxwoods is open continuously, and directions are posted at every intersection for miles around to make sure that you find your way. Bus information telephone: (888) BUS–2–FOX.

Mashantucket Pequot Museum & Research Center. This tribal museum opened in August 1998 to relate the story of the Pequot Nation from the point of view of the surviving members. In many respects, the most impressive part of the complex located near the casino is the research center, which opened with 35,000 titles of assorted film clips, videos, tribal family photos, books, historical papers, memorabilia, scrap-books, newspapers, and almost any other tangible resource to try to reconstruct tribal history and genealogy. The center aims to expand the collection to 150,000 titles, and has the financial backing to do it. Meanwhile, most people come to shuffle through the slick and contemporary exhibits that range from general New England Algonquian anthropology to specifics of tribal Pequot life. Europeans did not recognize the Pequots as a viable tribe for more than 300 years, and many members of the tribe assimilated into the general culture. As a result, many exhibits in diorama form are reconstructions from Colonial sources, mostly early seventeenth-century English diarists who didn't particularly approve of what they saw. Still, it's a more impressive presentation of pre-contact Native life than any other in New England, rivaled only by the recreated Wampanoag village at Plimoth Plantation (see "Seeing the Mid Coast"). Open daily 10:00 A.M. to 7:00 P.M. Admission $10. Telephone: (800) 411–9671.

Montville (Uncasville), Connecticut

OTHER ATTRACTIONS

Mohegan Sun. They don't talk about it much anymore, but the Mohegan tribe helped the English nearly exterminate the neighboring Pequots back in 1637, thereby winning recognition as a nation from the Connecticut colony in 1638. They were less fortunate in future wars against native peoples, but—James Fenimore Cooper to the contrary—the Mohegans didn't entirely disappear after King Philip's War and the French and Indian War. They persisted here in the marshy woods of east-central Connecticut in Montville, next to Uncasville, finally gaining recognition as a tribe from the federal government in March 1994 after a sixteen-year petition process. Thanks to the Indian Gaming Act that permits casinos on tribal lands, they now have the second largest gaming operation in the Northeast—a large Vegas-style casino in what seems like the middle of nowhere. The casino complex is reached from Foxwoods by driving five miles north on Route 117, then two miles west on Route 2A. The exterior design is very stylized—sort of Hiawatha-goes-to-Vegas—and the access roads are *very* well-marked.

The Pequots had a six-year headstart at Foxwoods, but the bus tours keep rolling into Mohegan Sun and chain-smoking seniors keep feeding the 3,000 slot machines around the clock. There are also 180 gaming tables. Mind you, as casinos go, this one is rather pleasant and low-key, with a lounge area in the center where once-famous acts play for free and a concert facility where still-famous acts play for pay. A food court with inexpensive meals supplements the more expensive restaurants on site. You have to be twenty-one to get in and it's open around the clock. Shuttle buses service some of the more farflung parking lots. 67 Sandy Desert Road. Telephone: (888) 226–7711.

Mystic, Connecticut

LODGING

Inn at Mystic. Junction Routes 1 and 27. Situated on a hill a short drive from downtown Mystic, this property has outstanding views of Mystic Harbor and Long Island Sound. Accommodation choices include a motor inn or an early twentieth-century mansion. Telephone: (203) 536–9604. Moderate to very expensive.

Steamboat Inn. 73 Steamboat Wharf. The ten rooms of the inn sit on a pier jutting out into the harbor in downtown Mystic. Appropriately enough, the rooms are named for famous Mystic ships from the schooner days. Nine rooms have water views and six have fireplaces. Telephone: (860) 536–8300. Moderate to very expensive with breakfast.

The Whaler's Inn. 20 East Main Street. Also located in a convenient downtown location, the rooms are spread over a couple of properties and offer a variety of accommodations. Telephone: (860) 536–1506 or (800) 243–2588. Moderate to expensive.

CAMPGROUNDS AND RV PARKS

Seaport Campground. Route 184. Conveniently located to take advantage of the local attractions, the facility has 130 sites and tenting facilities and offers trolley service. Telephone: (860) 536–4044.

FOOD

Flood Tide Restaurant. Junction Routes 1 and 27. Telephone: (860) 536–8140. The restaurant at the Inn at Mystic is a local favorite for special occasions. Breakfast, lunch, dinner, and Sunday buffet. Expensive to very expensive.

Mystic Pizza. 56 Main Street. Telephone: (860) 536–3700. Inspiration for the 1988 movie of the same name. Yes, there is a "secret recipe" sauce. Those who don't want to try "a slice of heaven" can order sandwiches, chicken, and Italian dinners. Lunch and dinner. Inexpensive to moderate.

S & P Oyster Company. 1 Holmes Street. Telephone: (860) 536–2674. The white clapboard restaurant overlooks the Mystic River and the drawbridge and emphasizes New England seafood, including clams, lobsters, and steamers. Lunch and dinner. Moderate.

Sea Swirl Seafood Restaurant and Ice Cream. Junction Routes 1 and 27. Telephone: (860) 536–3452. This drive-in is always getting one kind of award or another for its fried whole-belly clams, but also offers other seafood and burgers. A few picnic tables overlook the flood tide. Lunch and dinner. Inexpensive to moderate.

Mystic Pizza, Mystic, Connecticut

OTHER ATTRACTIONS

The Mystic Aquarium. A nice complement to the Mystic Seaport's focus on maritime activity, the aquarium's exhibits feature more than 6,000 creatures: exotic fish, jellyfish, dolphins, penguins, and sea lions among them. Open September through June daily 9:00 A.M. to 5:00 P.M., July and August daily 9:00 A.M. to 6:00 P.M. Adults $13. Exit 90 off I–95. Telephone: (860) 572–5955.

ACTIVITIES

Schooner Sails. The 81-foot *Argia*, a replica of a nineteenth-century gaff-rigged schooner, offers a variety of excursions, including a half-day sail. Adults $30. Steamboat Wharf. Telephone: (860) 536–0416.

FAIRS, FESTIVALS, AND EVENTS

Mystic Outdoor Art Festival. More than 250 artists and 60 craftspeople exhibit their work in this juried exhibition the second weekend of August. Telephone: (860) 572–9578.

SHOPPING

Olde Mystick Village. Junction of Route 27 and I–95. Telephone: (860) 536–4941. More than sixty specialty shops are clustered in an early-American-style village that is also the site of a number of special events.

Stonington Borough, Connecticut

FAIRS, FESTIVALS, AND EVENTS

Blessing of the Fleet. Two-day event in late July includes a lobster bake, Fisherman's Mass, and parade. Telephone: (860) 535–3930.

North Stonington Agricultural Fair. This classic country fair gets a jump on the season with four days of craft and livestock exhibitions and a carnival in mid-July. (860) 599–8498.

The Rhode Island Shore

Watch Hill, Rhode Island

For information about "South County" Rhode Island—the southern strip of the state from the Connecticut border to Narragansett—contact South County Tourism Council, 4808 Tower Hill Road, Wakefield, RI 02879. Telephone: (401) 789–4422 or (800) 548–4662.

Located south of the town of Westerly in the same direction as Misquamicut, the resort village of **Watch Hill** occupies the tip of the west-jutting little peninsula. This gorgeous point became a seaside summer retreat in the late 1860s, and the gingerbread architecture shows it. (Even the most staid Victorians got a little giddy when ornamenting their summer houses.) A one-way road circles the end of the peninsula, with the yacht marina on the north side and the small town and beach on the south. (You can also see Watch Hill Light not far away.) One of the enduring features of the village, at least in the summer, is the **Flying Horse Carousel**. Only children are allowed to ride on this 1883 carousel, in all likelihood the last of its kind in the country. The twenty horses, each hand-carved from a single piece of wood, are suspended from a center frame rather than attached to the floor—enabling them to fly out when in motion. Open mid-June to Labor Day 1:00 to 9:00 P.M. Bay Street, Watch Hill. Telephone: (401) 789–4422.

LODGING

Watch Hill Inn. 38 Bay Street. The big white inn sits just high enough off the street for good views of the harbor and beautiful sunsets. The sixteen guest rooms are in a comfortable "New England" style. Telephone: (401) 348–8912 or (800) 356–9314. Moderate to expensive with breakfast. Mid-week and weekend specials available.

FOOD

Olympia Tea Room. 74 Bay Street. Telephone: (401) 348–8211. A few tables are placed on the sidewalk in nice weather, but we much prefer to eat our BLTs and grilled cheese and tuna sandwiches while seated in a wooden booth in the dining room with its black-and-white checkerboard floor and Pepto-Bismol pink walls. The Tea Room has been serving beachgoers since 1916. Breakfast, lunch, and dinner. Inexpensive to moderate.

Charlestown, Rhode Island

CAMPGROUNDS AND RV PARKS

Burlingame State Park. U.S. 1. Located on the shore of Watchaug Pond in a 2,100-acre park, this facility accommodates 730 trailers. The park has hiking trails, boating and fishing, and is close to ocean beaches. The park lies on the north side of Route 1, across from the Ninigret National Wildlife Refuge. Telephone: (401) 322–7994 or (401) 322–7337.

Charlestown Breachway. Off Charlestown Breach Road. This sandy ocean beach is popular for fishing and has sites for seventy-five trailers. Telephone: (401) 364–7000 (summer) or (401) 322–8910 year-round.

Port of Galilee, Rhode Island

ACTIVITIES

Southland *Sightseeing Cruises.* The two-deck paddlewheel riverboat offers a narrated cruise that lasts almost two hours and takes in Point Judith, Galilee, Block Island, and the wildlife of the area. Wheelchair accessible. Adults $6.00. State Pier, next to Block Island Ferry landing. Call for schedule. Telephone: (401) 783–2954.

Block Island, Rhode Island

For general information about Block Island, contact the Block Island Tourism Council, P.O. Box 356, Block Island, RI. Telephone: (401) 466–5200 or (800) 383–2474.

LODGING

For such a tiny place, Block Island has an amazing amount of lodging—more than sixty hotels, inns, cottages, and B&Bs—at sometimes breathtaking prices. Most hotels charge $200 per night and up during the summer, and many close altogether in the off-season. The grand old Victorian hotels lining Water Street depend, to a great extent, on travelers arriving without reservations; even so, they'll be booked up on summer weekends. New lodgings open and old ones change hands with some frequency, so ask the Tourism Council office for help.

Water Street. Water Street. More casual and less well-appointed than its haute neighbors, this Victorian-era hostelry is also a little less expensive. Even the smallest rooms are of reasonable size. Telephone: (401) 466–2605 or (800) 825–6254. Moderate to expensive with breakfast.

1661 Inn & Guest House. 1 Spring Street. Part of the Hotel Manisses complex, the inn is a little more low-key and a little less pricey. It has the advantages of being removed from the harbor hubbub and remaining open all year. Bluefish breakfast comes with the room. Telephone: (401) 466–2421 or (401) 466–2063. Moderate to expensive with breakfast.

FOOD

Ballard's. Old Harbor. Telephone: (401) 466–2231. It's almost a requirement of visiting Block Island that you have at least one meal at Ballard's, a cavernous restaurant bedecked with nautical regalia. Of course, if the weather smiles on you, there's always the cement terrace overlooking the beach. The menu is as enormous as the dining room, so stick to the fresh fish. Lunch and dinner. Moderate.

Mohegan Café. Water Street. Telephone: (401) 466–5911. Located on the ground floor of the Water Street Hotel, it's a friendly spot with a casual bar menu and good fried food. Lunch and dinner. Moderate.

ACTIVITIES

Transportation Rental. **Aldo's Bikes and Mopeds.** Weldon's Way. Telephone: (401) 466–5018. **Island Moped.** Chapel Street. Telephone: (401) 466–2700.

Narragansett, Rhode Island

LODGING

The Atlantic House. 85 Ocean Road. Only a grassy front lawn and Ocean Road separate this three-story gray clapboard hotel from the ocean. Be sure to specify if you hope for an oceanview room, though specific room assignments are not guaranteed at time of booking. Telephone: (401) 783–6400. Moderate to expensive.

CAMPGROUNDS AND RV PARKS

Fishermen's Memorial State Park. 1011 Point Judith Road (Route 108). On the road to Point Judith, this park has sites for 35 tents and 147 trailers. The location is very convenient to the beaches and Block Island ferry. Telephone: (401) 789–8374.

FOOD

Coast Guard House. 40 Ocean Road. Telephone: (401) 789–0700. It's impossible to miss the big stone former Coast Guard House built in 1888 by McKim, Mead and White. Its dining room has a panoramic view of the ocean and diners can keep their eye on the surfers at Narragansett Town Beach. Lunch and dinner. Moderate to expensive.

Newport, Rhode Island

For information, contact the Newport County Convention & Visitors Bureau, 23 America's Cup Avenue, Newport, RI 02840. Telephone: (401) 845–9123 or (800) 976–5122.

LODGING

Bannister's Wharf Guest Rooms. A number of guest rooms occupy the upper floors above shops and restaurants of the Colonial era wharf. Ask for rooms one, two, three, or four—they look out on the harbor and share two small decks. Telephone: (401) 846–4500. Moderate to expensive.

Cliff Walk Manor. 117 Memorial Boulevard. Less than a mile from town center, this inn overlooks Easton's Beach and sits at the start of the Cliff Walk. The 1855 mansion contains twenty-two guest rooms (fifteen with ocean view) decorated with Victorian antiques. It's a good choice if you want to be near the beach, but a bit above and removed from it all. Telephone: (401) 847–1300. Moderate to very expensive.

Harborside Inn. Christie's Landing. This modern property sits right on the harbor and offers both rooms and suites with all the usual services of a full hotel. All the suites have harbor views, but you pay a premium for location and roominess. Telephone: (401) 846–6600 or (800) 427–9444. Expensive to very expensive with breakfast.

Hotel Viking. One Bellevue Avenue. Although it's hard to imagine that there was ever a shortage of guest rooms in Newport's grand mansions, this 1926 hotel was built to accommodate the guests of the mansion owners. Opt for rooms in the original building; they're smaller than the ones in the newer structures but have more period character. The Rooftop Bar has great harbor views. Telephone: (401) 847–3300 or (800) 556–7126. Inexpensive to expensive.

The Inn at Newport Beach. Memorial Boulevard. For those who want to be right in the middle of the action, this fifty-room inn is located right across the street from Easton's Beach and in the heart of the funky little beach community. Telephone: (401) 846–0310 or (800) 786–0310. Inexpensive to expensive.

The Jailhouse Inn. 13 Marlborough Street. In a clever adaptive reuse, a 1772 jailhouse has been converted to a stylish lodging with twenty-two guest rooms. Located directly across the street from the White Horse Tavern, it's a good base for walking around the city. Telephone: (401) 847–4638 or (800) 427–9444. Moderate to expensive with breakfast.

Newport Gateway Hotel. Corner of Route 138 and Route 114. This forty-six-room motel on the edge of town is a good budget choice, though it will be necessary to drive and park your car closer to the attractions. Telephone: (401) 847–2735 or (800) 427–9444. Moderate.

Pilgrim House. 123 Spring Street. Only three streets from the harbor, the Victorian style Pilgrim House has ten guest rooms and a rooftop deck

overlooking the harbor and the sunsets on Jamestown and Narragansett Bay. Telephone: (401) 846–0040 or (800) 525–8373. Moderate to expensive with breakfast.

Rose Island Lighthouse. Rose Island, Newport Harbor. The 1870 lighthouse was declared surplus in 1984 and restored by a local foundation. After the museum closes for the day, the two cozy keeper's bedrooms on the first floor are available for adventurous overnight guests. (No running water.) The upstairs apartment is available by the week for people willing to also do some chores, like raising the flag, recording weather data, doing some maintenance or cleaning. Both nightly and weekly rentals are available throughout the year. Additional $10 round-trip charge per person for transportation. Telephone: (401) 847–4242. Moderate to expensive, depending on season.

Savana's Inn. 41 Pelham Street. Opened in early 1998, the innkeepers have done one of the most stylish remakes of a historic home (circa 1865) that we have seen in a long while. The four elegant guest rooms have amenities (robes, phone with voicemail, TV/VCR, air conditioning) that are often only found in larger properties. Telephone: (401) 847–3801 or (888) 880–3764. expensive to very expensive with breakfast.

FOOD

Elizabeth's Cafe. 404 Thames Street. Telephone: 846–6862. The eclectic mix of tables and chairs creates a relaxed atmosphere in the big dining room that is matched by the presentation of the food on big platters for two—bouillabaisse, lobster paella, or shrimp *e piselli*, for example. Dinner. Moderate. BYOB.

Flo's Clam Shack. Wave Avenue. Telephone: (401) 847–8141. The seaside clam shack is a staple of summer on the shore and Flo's, across the street from Easton's Beach, is a classic of the genre. Lunch and dinner. Inexpensive.

La Petite Auberge. 19 Charles Street. Telephone: (401) 849–6669. The small green clapboard colonial home was built before 1714 and since 1976 has housed a tavern and dining room serving classic French cuisine prepared by Lyon native Roger

Putier. Dinner. Moderate (tavern) to expensive (dining room).

The Mooring. Sayer's Wharf. Telephone: (401) 846–2260. This restaurant in the former summer headquarters of the New York Yacht Club knows how to handle fresh fish (frozen is banned from the kitchen) and serves a multiple award-winning clam chowder. There's a great harbor view and you can complete the fantasy by pretending one of those yachts is yours. Lunch and dinner. Moderate to expensive.

Rhumb Line. 62 Bridge Street. Telephone: (401) 849–6950. This seafood restaurant in the Point neighborhood is a local favorite. Lunch and dinner. Moderate.

White Horse Tavern. Marlborough Street. Telephone: (401) 849–3600. This tavern was established in 1687 and shows its antiquity with big fireplaces and beamed ceilings. The dining (on traditional American and continental cuisine) receives a more contemporary touch with reliance on native seafood and excellent local produce. Lunch and dinner. Expensive.

OTHER ATTRACTIONS

Museum of Newport History. By using photographs, artifacts, and decorative arts to focus on the people of Newport—past and present—this museum provides a lively overview of the city's history. Adults $5.00. Open Monday and Wednesday through Saturday from 10:00 A.M. to 5:00 P.M., Sunday 1:00 to 5:00 P.M. Brick Market. Telephone: (401) 841–8770.

Naval War College Museum. The Naval War College is the oldest naval war college in the world and the highest educational institution in the U.S. Navy. To complement its teaching mission, the museum explores the history of naval warfare, as well as the history of the U.S. Navy in Narragansett Bay. Free. Open Monday through Friday 10:00 A.M. to 4:00 P.M. year-round and June through September Saturday and Sunday noon to 4:00 P.M. Wheelchair accessible. On Coasters Harbor Island. Telephone: (401) 841–4052.

Newport Art Museum and Art Association. Permanent and temporary exhibitions of Newport and New England artists are housed in an 1864 grand mansion and a 1919 Beaux Arts building. Adults $4.00. Open Memorial Day to Labor Day Monday, Tuesday, and Thursday through Saturday 10:00 A.M. to 5:00 P.M., Sunday noon to 5:00 P.M. The museum closes at 4:00 P.M. the remainder of the year. Wheelchair accessible. 76 Bellevue Avenue. Telephone: (401) 848–8200.

Redwood Library and Athenaeum. Built in 1748, the Redwood Library is the oldest existing library building in the country. It might look familiar because when Thomas Jefferson was secretary of state under George Washington, he visited and was quite taken with the portico and Doric columns that architect Peter Harrison had adapted from the Italian Renaissance master Andrea Palladio. Jefferson liked the style so much that he decreed it a model for public buildings and used it to design his own estate, Monticello. The private library was founded by Abraham Redwood, a wealthy Quaker and slave owner, and other affluent men in 1747. Among those who have used it over the years are painter Gilbert Stuart (several of his portraits are on display), William and Henry James, and Edith Wharton. Open Monday through Saturday 9:30 A.M. to 5:30 P.M. 50 Bellevue Avenue. Telephone: (401) 847–0292.

Rose Island Lighthouse. The 1870 lighthouse was declared surplus in 1984 and restored by a local foundation. Visitors can enjoy the same panoramic views as the resident keepers used to and explore other natural and historic aspects of the island, including the remains of early coastal fortifications. $1.00 landing fee. (See below for ferry transportation.) Telephone: (401) 847–4242.

ACTIVITIES

Harbor Cruises. Several operators offer tours of Newport Harbor and Narragansett Bay aboard motorized excursion boats, including the M/V *Amazing Grace* that docks at Sayer's Wharf ($7.50 adults, telephone: 401–847–9109) and the *Spirit of Newport* that docks at Newport Harbor Hotel

& Marina ($7.50 adults, telephone: 401–849–3575). *Rum Runner II,* a restored Elco Motoryacht built in 1929 and pressed into service as a bootlegger during Prohibition, docks at Bannister Wharf (adults $15.00, telephone: 401–847–0299).

Jamestown & Newport Ferry. This ferry between the two towns makes a number of stops along the harbor, including Fort Adams and Rose Island, making it convenient and scenic for sightseeing. Adults $7.00 one way. Bowen's Landing. Telephone: (401) 423–9900.

Newport Equestrian Academy. Located in Middletown, a short distance from downtown Newport, the academy offers horseback rides along the beach. Adults $55 to $65. 287 Third Beach Road. Telephone: (401) 847–7022.

Sail Cruises. For those who prefer to traverse the harbor and bay under sail, there are also a variety of options for morning, afternoon, and sunset cruises. The 72-foot schooner *Madeleine* docks at Bannister's Wharf ($20–$25 adults, telephone: 401–847–0298), while the 78-foot Schooner *Adirondack* docks at the Newport Yachting Center ($17–$25 adults, telephone: 401–846–1600). The smaller *Sightsailer* holds twelve to fourteen passengers and docks at Bowen's Wharf ($17.50–$25 adults, telephone: 401–849–3333).

TOURS

Guided Walking Tours. One-hour tours focus on architecture, history, and preservation efforts. Adults $7.00. Depart from the Visitors Center. Telephone: (401) 846–5391.

Viking Tours. If your time is short, Viking Tours offers a number of tours that will give you a quick overview of Newport—from guided bus tours to a combination of bus tour and harbor cruise. Some tours include admission to a mansion and other attractions. Adults $8.00 to $28.00. 23 America's Cup Avenue. Telephone: (401) 847–6921.

FAIRS, FESTIVALS, AND EVENTS

Annual Regatta. Sponsored by the New York Yacht Club. Held in mid-June annually since 1855. Telephone: (401) 845–9633.

Ben & Jerry's Newport Folk Festival. Newport began hosting a folk festival in 1959 and the current incarnation of this event is held for two days in early August at Fort Adams State Park. Telephone: (401) 847–3700.

Black Ships Festival. This event honors Newport native Matthew C. Perry, USN, who negotiated the first treaty between the United States and Japan that ended two centuries of Japanese isolationism. The three-day event in mid-July celebrates Japanese art and culture with a variety of events including sumo wrestling and judo, *ikebana,* origami, a tea ceremony, and a festival of drums. Telephone: (401) 846–2720.

Christmas in Newport. The town is decorated with white candles and holly during the month of December when a blizzard of holiday events occurs, including concerts, recitals, pageants, and the annual reading of "A Visit from St. Nicholas" (aka "The Night Before Christmas") written by Newport summer resident Clement C. Moore. Telephone: (401) 849–6454.

Classic Yacht Regatta. About one hundred vintage yachts of 32 feet or more participate in a Labor Day weekend event featuring a race, nautical bazaar, and parade through Newport Harbor. Sponsored by the Museum of Yachting. Telephone: (401) 847–1018.

Redwood Library and Athenaeum, Newport, Rhode Island

JVC Jazz Festival. Continuing a tradition that dates back to the early 1950s, two days of jazz performances take place in mid-August at Fort Adams State Park. Telephone: (401) 847–3700.

Newport International Polo Series. Olympic caliber polo matches are held every Saturday throughout the summer at Glen Farms in nearby Portsmouth. Telephone: (401) 846–0200.

Newport Music Festival. More than fifty-five concerts of chamber music and other special events are performed in Newport's cottages throughout the month of July. Telephone: (401) 846–1133.

SHOPPING

Buddy's Tattoo Shop. 4 Marlborough Street. Telephone: (401) 846–3520. Newport is a sailor's town and is known around the globe for its tattoo artists. Buddy's has been "keeping America beautiful since 1948" with classic designs that predate the current trends. Not ready for the tattoo needles? Get the T-shirt.

Custom Canvas of Newport. One Bowen's Landing. Telephone: (401) 847–4977. This shop makes custom marine canvas and also crafts tote bags and luggage from sail material. Just the place to have a custom jib made—and get matching luggage as well.

Thames Glass. 8 Bowen's Wharf, telephone: (401) 842–0579 and 688 Thames Street, telephone: (401) 846–0576. Local glass artist Matthew Buechner has two showrooms, but you can only see artisans at work at the Thames Street location. Both shops sell seconds at reduced prices.

Third & Elm Press. 29 Elm Street. Telephone: (401) 846–0228. This establishment in the Point neighborhood creates original woodblock prints, note paper, and Christmas cards using handset type and two wonderful period hand presses—an 1830 Acorn hand press and an 1897 Golding platen press—that replace the impersonality of quick printing with the character imparted by hand craftsmen.

2·The Mid Coast

Introduction

When Bartholomew Gosnold reported back to England on his 1602 voyage exploring the area in this chapter, he told tales of seas so full of codfish that a man could almost walk on their backs from one point of land to another without getting his feet wet. He exaggerated, but not by much. Gosnold was so excited by the commercial prospects that he named the most prominent land feature of the area "Cape Cod," and though the schools of cod are much depleted, the name has stuck for nearly four centuries.

Gosnold was a dreamer, but even his most audacious imaginings could hardly match the hopes of the English settlers who followed only a few years later to carve out a godly life in the wilderness of a New World. The Mid Coast is truly the heart of maritime New England, both in its geography and in its history. The Pilgrims who settled Plymouth and the Puritans who set up shop in Salem defined this region as a promised land, however stony its soils and hard its winters. Their descendants—and the tens of thousands of other refugees who sought a fresh start here—proved to be an adventurous and imaginative lot. They capitalized on the fisheries that Gosnold had foreseen and they turned the haphazard and primitive whale hunt into a well-oiled international commerce. Dissatisfied with the vessel designs they had brought from Europe, they created entirely new classes of sailing ships that ranged from the sturdy two-masted schooners mounted with fishing dories to the tubby whaleboats that cruised the South Pacific to the racehorses of the waves, the billowing clipper ships. In many cases, they made their dreams come true.

But those early settlers could never have dreamed of the recreational uses their land would provide centuries later. The idea of "play" might never have occurred to them. That men and women would strip off most of their clothing to deliberately expose their bodies to the sun's rays as they lay indolently on the sandy beaches would have been unthinkable. The concept of "pleasure" boats would have been anathema. And we wonder if, in a passing sinful moment, any of them took a simple joy in the diffuse light that buoys the spirit.

The Mid Coast—the stretch from Buzzards Bay around Cape Cod to Cape Ann—is a fascinating interstice between land and sea, and in many spots it can be difficult to distinguish one from the other. What would the fishing village of Gloucester be without the ledges and banks off its shores where the first harvests of the sea were found? Would Nantucket have developed whaling into an industry had it not been a dot of land thirty miles out to sea? And the outer face of Cape Cod changes all the time. A point of latitude and longitude might be solid land one year, then open water the next—all depending on the vagaries of winter storms.

This encircling crust of the eastern coast of the middle of New England is just that—a ring of land only recently (in geological time) associated with its surroundings. This area took the brunt of continental collisions, so the bedrock is a mixture of uplifted sea floor, deposits left behind from other continents, and granite formed underground when the earth's mantle was ruptured in these massive hits. The Mid Coast also represents the extreme advance of the ice sheets and the top layers of its land consist of the detritus scraped off the rest of New England. Finally, the drifting sands that swirl around these coastal features are literally flowing slowly over the ocean floor, washing up in one place, then washing away. We think of geological processes as being finished eons ago, but the Mid Coast is still changing almost before

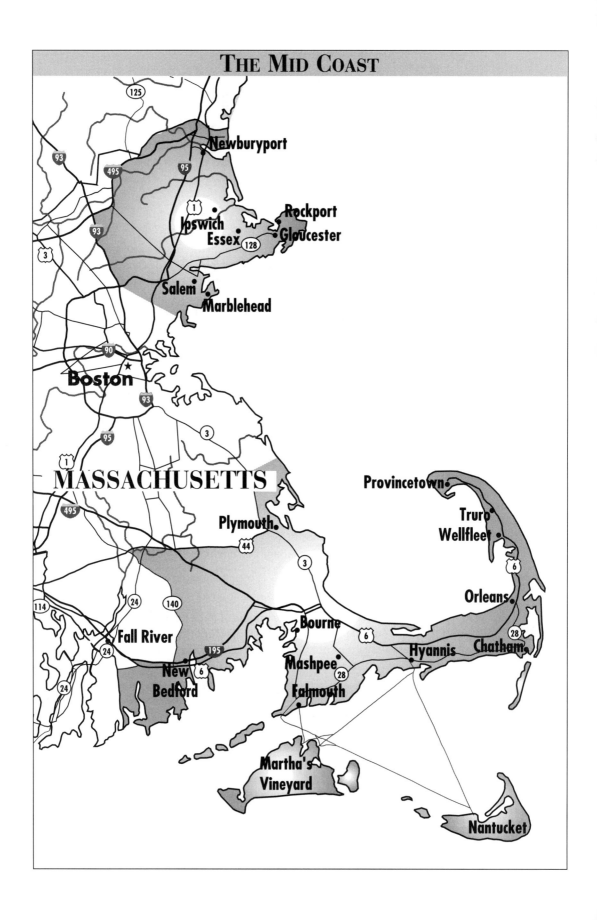

our eyes. Five thousand years ago it extended miles out to sea to what are now the nutrient-rich offshore banks. Over the next millenium, many of the coastal communities will have to migrate inland or they will disappear beneath the waves like fabled Atlantis.

By necessity, we have relegated Boston and its harbor to a separate chapter for fear that the urban attractions of the city would overwhelm the small-town and natural attractions of the rest of the Mid Coast. For that reason, the south-to-north organization of this chapter hits a hiatus after Plymouth, picking up again in Marblehead before rounding Cape Ann to conclude on the barrier beaches of Plum Island at the mouth of the Merrimack River.

History:

In Search of the Mighty Whale

Travelers in Massachusetts usually notice the state's environmental license plate, which displays the motto, "Preserve the Trust," and pictures the flukes of the northern right whale. One of the most critically endangered of all the great whales (some estimates place their population at 300 and falling), the right whale makes the nutrient-rich banks off Cape Cod and Massachusetts Bay one of its favorite roadside rest stops in the annual migration from the high Arctic to the Caribbean. The lure of these feeding grounds to the great whales made the Mid Coast a natural place for the whaling industry to develop. In these days, when "Save the Whales" has become an environmental cliché on the level of "Have a Nice Day," we forget that whaling was once an economic necessity comparable to drilling for petroleum.

Human beings began hunting whales off New England thousands of years ago, as archaeological excavations from Maine to New York have shown. The Algonquian peoples employed a straightforward technique. They would paddle out in large canoes, fill the whale full of spears and arrows attached to floats, and chase the animal until it died of exhaustion. Like the bison

hunted by tribes on the western plains, the whale served as a critical source of meat, hide, and bone during the most difficult months of the year. The European settlers soon discovered another use for the whales—light. The oil rendered from whale blubber is one of the purest, brightest burning of all animal oils, and once the Industrial Revolution began, it also proved to be the best lubricating oil available to keep machinery working smoothly.

Whales yielded other commercial products as well. The large and aggressive sperm whale, the only toothed whale commercially hunted, yielded the waxy substance known as ambergris. Sperm whales feed primarily on squid, including the rare and elusive giant squid. Scientists believe that ambergris helps the whales to safely expel razor-sharp, indigestible squid beaks from their stomachs by forming a protective coating around the beaks. A complex substance of many volatile oily compounds, ambergris was highly prized as a carrying agent for scent in the perfume industry. Baleen and whalebone from the baleen whales were also pressed into service, as the springy baleen (actually composed of keratin, the same structural substance as hair and fingernails) was a key structural component in making corsets. As a booklet on Massachusetts whaling published at the turn of the century dryly observed, "Many a whaleman has lost his life in the endeavor to improve the female figure."

Whales were once so plentiful that the log of the first *Mayflower* voyage indicates whales playing around the ship when it was anchored inside Cape Cod. Colonial records show that "drift," or dead whales washed ashore, were so common that their distribution was regulated. The Colonial government received a third of the proceeds, the town a third, and the person who found the whale a third. In 1663, the Massachusetts Bay Colony voted that a portion of every drift whale should be given to the church. But counting on whales to beach themselves meant trusting to providence, so the settlers took matters in their own hands and began to actively hunt the great beasts of the sea. In 1664 it was reported to England that "the new Plymouth colony made great profit by whale killing." The first communities whose economies were based on whaling were Southampton (Long Island), Martha's Vineyard, and Nantucket, all of which got into the trade in the third quarter of the seventeenth century.

Although early whaling in New England focused on right and humpback whales that swam close to shore, Nantucket whalers were soon circling the globe is search of the deep-water sperm whale. The oil rendered from the head matter of a sperm whale was much purer and hence more valuable than that rendered from whale blubber. Sperm whales were found in the warm waters off the coasts of Chile, Peru, Japan, New Zealand, Madagascar, California, and Brazil; in the Caribbean, China, and Red Seas; in the Indian Ocean and Persian Gulf; off the Azores, Java, Galapagos, Society, Sandwich, Fiji, and Samoan Islands, and off Cape Verde. And Nantucket (and, later, New Bedford) whalers sought them wherever they swam. The most prized baleen whale was quickly named the "right whale" because it was the "right" one to catch. The baleen strips in the mouth of a right whale number 500 to 600 and weigh about a ton. Right whales were found in the high latitudes of the Arctic Ocean, in Baffin Bay, in the Ochotsk Sea, near Tristan d'Acunha and the Desolation Islands, and in the Japan Sea. Again, American whalers sought them in all their grounds. Once ships began to sail long distances to hunt whales, they were outfitted with "tryworks"—a hoist to raise the whale above the water for easier butchering and huge pots for rendering oil from the blubber to store below decks in five-foot-high casks.

The forecastle of the whale ship, where the crew of thirty to forty lived and slept for as long as four years, was called "the Black Hole of Calcutta," and with good reason. This tiny triangular area within the curve of the bow was reached by a small hatchway and the tiered bunks were each about the size of a coffin. There was a small table in the center and seamen's chests lashed to the floor. One J. Ross Browne wrote in 1846 of his single trip as a whaler, "It would be difficult to give any idea of our forecastle. In wet weather, when most of the hands were below, cursing, smoking, singing, and spinning yarns, it was a perfect

Humpback Whale breaching

Bedlam. . . . It would seem like exaggeration to say, that I have seen in Kentucky pigsties not half so filthy, and in every respect preferable to this miserable hole: such, however, is the fact."

The officers and mates lived in steerage, where the three mates had small private staterooms and the captain had a large cabin on the starboard side. Many a whaling captain took his wife and children along. The quarters may have been better than the crew's, but everyone aboard subsisted largely on a diet of salt beef or salt pork three times a day, along with hardtack (a cracker-like bread so inedible that it didn't spoil) and coffee sweetened with molasses.

Each whale ship carried from four to seven whaleboats, which were typically 28 feet long and pointed at both ends so they could go forward and backwards with equal ease and speed. The hull was flat-bottomed, allowing for quick maneuvers to dodge any sudden movement by a whale. Shipboard life consisted of weeks, even months of tedium punctuated by brief periods of excitement. When a whale was spotted, the whaleboats were lowered and crews rowed toward the mighty beast. (Herman Melville claimed in *Moby-Dick* that the crew rowed to the refrain of "A Dead Whale or a Stove Boat.") Standing in the bow of the boat, the harpooner tried to strike the whale, tying the harpoon line to the boat as a drag to tire the whale. Eventually, if they were successful, the whalers could get close enough to the whale to spear it to death. Sometimes the whale won—smashing the boat with a fluke, or in the case of sperm whales, even crushing the boat with a bite. Enraged sperm whales—which have the largest heads of all whales and can grow longer than 60 feet and weigh more than fifty tons—were known to attack the whaleship itself. The great white whale of Melville's tale was, in fact, a sperm whale.

In the parlance of the whaling trade, the "blubber hunters" came home either "clean" or "greasy," i.e., empty or full of whale oil. In theory each man aboard shared in the proceeds, but after four years at sea buying necessities from the ship's store on credit, many an individual whaler ended up in the red. Partly for this reason, ships rarely returned to port carrying the same crew that had left. Whalers often jumped ship along the way and signed up with another in need of crew. It was a lucrative trade for the ship owners, nonetheless. In 1854, the record year, the New England whaling industry earned about $11 million.

The discovery of petroleum in Pennsylvania at the end of the 1850s abruptly trimmed the sails of the whaling industry, and when spring steel was invented in the 1880s, obviating the need for whalebone, it sounded the industry's death knell. Although a few whaleships continued to operate, hunting the small bowhead whale in the Arctic for specialty markets, New England's whaling industry collapsed. The last surviving New England whaling ship is the *Charles W. Morgan,* now permanently berthed at Mystic Seaport (see "South Coast" chapter). Built in New Bedford for $48,849.85, on her maiden voyage in 1841 she sailed around Cape Horn and into the Pacific. When she returned to New Bedford three years and four months later, she carried 2,400 barrels of whale oil and 10,000 pounds of whalebone, valued at $56,000. In her first 30 years at sea, only once did she bring back a cargo worth less than her original cost. The *Morgan* spent eighty years at sea on thirty-seven voyages before she was tied up for good in 1921.

Seeing the Mid Coast

Southeastern Massachusetts

New Bedford, Massachusetts

"Call me Ishmael"—the opening lines of *Moby-Dick* still resonate in New Bedford, a city of brick and granite that flows down a long hill to the waterfront. On a drizzly November day, when the brine fog grips the waterfront, the decades seem to roll away. Looking down at the harbor from town, we almost expect to see three barren masts laden with lines poke through the fog, the typical rigging of a wooden whaleship.

There hasn't been a whaleship moored here for generations, not since the *Charles W. Morgan* was towed to Mystic, Connecticut. And it's been many more years since an active whaler shipped from New Bedford. Yet those days cling to the town like a salt fog, never quite washed away by the brightest sunshine. Salem and Boston, Newbury and Portsmouth, Portland and Searsport—they all have their fine histories as ports of trade, where shipwrights conjured fine, fast vessels into wood on water and their handsome captains set billows of sail for the farthest shores and most exotic lands. But New Bedford is America's archetypal hunting port. Located where the Acushnet River spills south into Buzzards Bay, its exceptionally deep channel accommodates the largest ships and rarely freezes, even in the harshest winter weather. When sandy shoals gagged the mouth of Nantucket's harbor, New Bedford took over the islanders' trade. Ever larger whaleships, suited for voyages literally to the ends of the earth, could return from three or more years at sea and make port in New Bedford, even in the brutal weather of mid-February.

Originally a small farming village—the out-wash plain on which New Bedford sits is some of New England's most productive soil—New Bedford was settled by Quakers from Rhode Island and Cape Cod. Around 1760, they began to see the possibilities of the deep harbor and by 1765 Joseph Russell, whom some credit as the real founder of the city, began to send whaling ships out. During the "golden age" of whaling—1825 to 1860—New Bedford emerged as the leading whaling port in the world, even as others gave up the pursuit. In 1845 the New Bedford fleet recorded 158,000 barrels of sperm oil, 272,000 barrels of whale oil, and 3 million pounds of whalebone. Its ships carried no less than 10,000 seamen. New Bedford had turned whaling from a fishing enterprise into an industry, and as the money flowed into the community, finer and finer houses were built higher and higher on the hill above the harbor. It was said in the mid-nineteenth century, when New Bedford's fleet constituted a third of the world's whaling vessels, that the city's men fell into three categories: those away on a voyage, those returning, and those getting ready for the next trip.

Urban renewal nearly destroyed the physical reminders of New Bedford's whaling past, but a determined group of citizens stopped the wrecker's ball, salvaging many of the old buildings and wharves while they raised money to renovate and reuse them. Their efforts paid off in 1996, when a thirteen-block waterfront historic district became **New Bedford Whaling National Historical Park.** Institutions and museums stand cheek by jowl with historic buildings owned by private individuals and groups who operate shops, galleries, restaurants, coffeehouses, and bars—all within this easy-to-walk downtown area.

The imposing **New Bedford Whaling Museum** should be any visitor's first stop—a true "don't miss" attraction. The museum claims to be the largest devoted to the history of American whaling. We're less impressed by the size and quantity of artifacts than by the museum's ability to give us a sense of the life of an ordinary seaman who shipped aboard one of the 329 whaling ships that sailed from New Bedford in the mid-nineteenth century.

As the exhibits show, a young man shipping out an a whaling vessel had to cram everything he would need for the next three or four years into a chest about 18 by 18 by 46 inches. Apart from the profits—which were slim for ordinary seamen—whaling was a grim business that involved almost unbearable months of tedium followed by brief and terrifying encounters that meant certain death—usually, but not always for the whale. The twenty-two-minute segment from the 1922 film, *Down to the Sea in Ships,* gives a feel for the rugged life as the silent black-and-white footage shows a crew harpooning, capturing, and butchering a whale.

The museum's Bourne building holds a half-size replica of the *Lagoda,* one of New Bedford's last whaling barks. (To see the last existing whaling ship from New Bedford, the *Charles W. Morgan,* visit Mystic Seaport in Mystic, Connecticut. See "South Coast.") The full-size examples of the small boats that were lowered over the side of the ship make the task of whaling seem even more immediate. From these open boats, little bigger than fishing dories, men harpooned and rode the whale to its death on a "Nantucket sleigh ride." It's not exactly the vessel we'd choose to battle the largest animal on earth.

All things considered, we probably wouldn't have minded waiting for months before encountering the next whale; but time lay heavy on the hands of these sailors. During the long months at sea, they created a strikingly domestic body of art with knife and awl on bone, tooth, and ivory. These scrimshaw carvings were intended as gifts for loved ones back home and the Whaling Museum has an encyclopedic collection. We are enchanted with the entire case of pie crimpers—exquisitely carved fluted wheels turning smoothly in imaginatively carved ivory handles. Last time we visited the museum, our guide told us that a young man bringing such a loving gift to his mother or wife could expect a welcome-home pie—a fine treat after months of hardtack and salt beef.

The New Bedford Whaling Museum is open daily 9:00 A.M. to 5:00 P.M., also Thursday until 8:00 P.M. from Memorial Day to Labor Day. Adults $4.50. 18 Johnny Cake Hill. Telephone: (508) 997–0046.

The **Seamen's Bethel,** across the street from the museum, opened in 1832 and continues to serve mariners as a non-denominational Christian house of worship. Described in *Moby-Dick,* it has become best known for its bowsprit pulpit, which was installed in 1959 to match Melville's imaginary description. While visitors are always welcome, this church is dedicated to ministering to the spiritual needs of sailors, not acting as a tourist attraction. Its walls are lined with somber marble memorials to sailors lost at sea. Next door, at 15 Johnny Cake Hill, the **Mariners' Home** provides lodging to visiting sailors.

A block away, on the corner of William and North Second Streets, the **U.S. Custom House,** regally formal with its Greek columns and portico, is one of the few New England custom houses that has not become a museum. Built in 1836, it is the oldest continuously operated custom house in the country.

The historic hillside district is linked to New Bedford's working waterfront by a walkway above the highway. With a well-protected deepwater harbor, New Bedford continues to make a living from the sea. The vast whaling fleets are long

Seamen's Bethel, New Bedford, Massachusetts

gone, and even the huge fishing fleets of the 1970s have dwindled, but New Bedford remains America's leading Atlantic Ocean fishing port based on the value of the catch. In addition to cod and haddock, long the mainstays of New England fisheries, the boats also land more scallops than any other port in the country.

If it's not at sea, the **schooner** *Ernestina,* an 1894 Gloucester fishing schooner later used to carry immigrants from the Cape Verde islands to New Bedford, will be docked among the fishing boats at Fisherman's Pier. Now a training vessel offering education programs for schools and other organizations, the *Ernestina* led the Parade of Tall Ships into New York harbor at the Statue of Liberty centennial because she is the only one of the 250 ships from around the world that had brought immigrants to the United States. The **Lightship New Bedford,** a rare piece of maritime history, is docked at State Pier. Lightships served as beacons where building a lighthouse was either impossible or impractical. This one served in the Atlantic waters of the East Coast until it was decommissioned in 1971. State Pier also operates as a cargo terminal for foreign and domestic goods. Nearby, the **M/V** *Schomanchi,* which provides service to Martha's Vineyard (see Staying There) docks at Steamship Pier. The next, shorter, pier is Coal Pocket Pier, once a receiving point for casks of whale oil, now a berth for fishing and lobster boats.

The harbor, source of New Bedford's wealth, is visible from County Road, a rather steep walk from the harbor straight uphill to the crest. The wealthiest whaling merchants built their grand homes up here with enough land to support gardens that they filled with plants from around the world. The spectacular Greek Revival **Rotch-Jones-Duff House and Garden Museum** is one of the best examples of the lifestyle. It was owned by two successful whaling merchants and then by a New Bedford businessman before becoming a museum. One of the best preserved houses in New Bedford, it also has one of the best examples of the nineteenth-century whale merchants' gardens of which Herman Melville wrote: "The town itself is perhaps the dearest place to live in. . . . All these brave houses and flowery gardens came from the Atlantic, Pacific, and Indian oceans. One and all, they were harpooned and dragged up hither from the bottom of the sea." Open daily 10:00 A.M. to 4:00 P.M. Adults $4.00. 396 County Street. Telephone: (508) 997–1401.

The Massachusetts Archipelago

New Bedford's harbor—indeed, all of Buzzards Bay—is shielded from the brunt of the Atlantic Ocean by the small chain of the Elizabeth Islands trailing off from the southwestern edge of Cape Cod. The westernmost island, Cuttyhunk, has developed a substantial summer community served by a ferry from New Bedford, but the others are sparsely inhabited, again only by summer residents who arrive by private boat. At various times they have served as a base for pirates (Captain Kidd once operated from Naushon Island), French privateers, and, briefly in the early twentieth century, a leper colony.

The Elizabeths represent the southwestern edge of a larger archipelago forming a semicircle south of Cape Cod with Nantucket Sound in the center. These islands, which include the large and solid landforms of Martha's Vineyard and Nantucket as well as the shifting sands of Monomoy Island, represent the southeastern march of the great Laurentian glacier. Each of the islands—and the thousands of pieces of land just barely submerged below the sea's surface—is a dump of glacial rubble composed of soils and stones of New England and southern Canada, pushed ahead of the great ice sheet and deposited when the climate warmed and the ice retreated. No simple land map gives a clear picture of the extent of this glacial moraine, but coastal charts of the entire area show the hidden shoals very clearly. These are treacherous waters, indeed, for sailors who are unfamiliar with them, and the island communities have long histories of lifesaving stations and salvage operations.

Martha's Vineyard, Massachusetts

This hundred-square-mile island just seven miles off the coast of Cape Cod was settled by the

English in the 1640s, but carbon-dating shows signs of continuous human inhabitation dating back to nearly 4,300 years before present. Bartholomew Gosnold explored the island in 1602 for England and named it for his daughter and for the profusion of wild grapes he found growing here. A Massachusetts Bay Colony man, Thomas Mayhew, purchased Martha's Vineyard and the Elizabeth Islands from the British crown in 1641 for the grand sum of forty pounds, and the following year encouraged settlement at Great Harbor, now the community of Edgartown.

The settlers and those Wampanoags who survived the scourge of European diseases got along rather well on Martha's Vineyard, with both groups following essentially the same activities— farming, fishing, and capturing whales that had become beached on the offshore shoals. The Wampanoags who kept their distance lived principally at Gay Head, as far away as possible from Edgartown, while those who embraced the Puritan piety, the so-called "Praying Indians," founded their own community of Manitouwattootan (Christiantown) near what is now called North Tisbury. Although most Martha's Vineyard harbors are small and shallow, Vineyarders joined their brethren from Nantucket and New Bedford in the early whaling trade, sailing large vessels from the Grand Banks off Newfoundland to the West Indies in search of whales. Whaling began to diminish on the Vineyard with the Revolution, ending entirely by the Civil War.

Most travelers arrive on the north face of Martha's Vineyard by ferry (from Woods Hole, New Bedford, or Montauk on Long Island) at the village of **Vineyard Haven,** part of the town of Tisbury. Once a whaling community, Vineyard Haven's Main Street was destroyed by fire on August 11, 1883, leaving only traces of the village's history. Owen Park, a grassy expanse from Main Street to the harbor, is named for one of the first whaling captains, and William Street is lined with several fine Greek Revival sea captains' houses untouched by the fire. (Turn onto Church Street from Main Street, then onto William Street.)

Vineyard Haven today is a service community— a place where the masses of visitors eat, drink, and shop as they get off the ferry. As such, it resembles many beach towns in New England with a slightly different historical overlay. If a single motif dominates the village, it's the visage of the **Black Dog,** which once signaled the symbolic creature of darkness in Robert Louis Stevenson's *Treasure Island* but now denotes the charming waterfront tavern by that name and its profligate spawn. The ubiquity of the Labrador retriever's profile has also led to the occasional takeoff, e.g., the Bad Dog T-shirt, which shows the canine squatting in a decidedly antisocial fashion.

Oak Bluffs is the next community on the perimeter of the island if you're circumnavigating it clockwise. Before the road enters town, watch for a detour on the left that goes to **East Chop Light,** mounted on a headland in a residential neighborhood and overlooking the lagoon that separates Vineyard Haven from Oak Bluffs. The lighthouse is open on Sunday evenings for sunset viewing. $2.00. Telephone: (508) 627–4441.

When unprepared visitors descend the long hill into Oak Bluffs, the gingerbread architecture of the town sometimes makes them feel suddenly immersed in a fairy tale by the brothers Grimm. Perhaps even more surprising, this aberrant architectural style was not constructed for wealthy vacationers but for participants in Christian revival meetings. Although the first white settlers of Martha's Vineyard were Puritans and Quakers, by the late eighteenth century the island was in the throes of evangelical Methodism. The idea of revivalist "camp meetings" introduced in Kentucky in the early nineteenth century spread to New England, arriving at last in August 1827 on Martha's Vineyard when "Reformation John" Adams held forth at West Chop, near Vineyard Haven. One of Adams's staunchest followers, Jeremiah Pease, led a group from the Edgartown Methodist Church in acquiring a large sheep pasture in Oak Bluffs where the **Martha's Vineyard Camp Meeting Association** now stands. In 1859, they erected the first wooden building, which now serves as the association headquarters, and in 1879 constructed the Tabernacle, essentially a giant wooden tent that seats more than 3,000 worshippers in the center of the property.

For many years the participants slept in tents, with some building wooden platforms to get the tents off the ground. Between 1862 and 1880, members of the association erected small cottages in the Carpenter Gothic style. They are of balloon frame construction, with high peaked roofs that make them look rather like small chapels—an effect heightened by the use of stained glass in many of the windows. Today the thirty-four-acre site has more than 300 permanent cottages, each vying with the next for a more unusual color scheme to accentuate its architectural details. Over the years, the original cottages have been expanded, usually in the back, to add private kitchens and bathrooms.

The summer camp meetings continue on the MVCMA grounds, although most of the cottage dwellers come for the entire summer, more for vacation than for religious reasons. It is a pleasant community to walk around, and people are surprisingly patient with picture-takers. The **Cottage Museum**, located at the corner of Highland Avenue and Trinity Park, is staffed by volunteers who clearly enjoy relating camp association lore and explaining artifacts of the community. Open June 15 to October 15, Monday to Saturday 10:00 A.M. to 4:00 P.M. Adults $1.00. Telephone: (508) 693–0525.

About the same time that the cottages began sprouting like so many baroque mushrooms on the Camp Meeting Association grounds, the adjacent town emerged as a summer resort community, thanks to the construction of some large, boxy hotels near the beach and harbor. People from the mainland began to build summer homes here, and a number of large, mansard-roofed Victorian homes are found throughout the town. Perhaps the most attractive concentration of these structures surrounds Ocean Park, the huge green separating the downtown from the waterfront. Oak Bluffs also gained a reputation as America's premier integrated summer community. The town has had a substantial year-round African American population since before the Revolution, and developed rather naturally as a vacation destination for African Americans from metropolitan New York as early as the 1850s.

The small downtown section of Oak Bluffs is full of gift shops and places to get a quick bite to eat. Built in 1876, the venerable **Flying Horses Carousel** on Oak Bluffs Avenue is yet another contender for the title of America's oldest carousel. Rides are $1.00. Open daily in the summer 10:00 A.M. to 10:00 P.M. Call for off-season

hours. Telephone: (508) 693–9481.

Joseph Sylvia State Beach in Oak Bluffs stretches for two miles along Beach Road heading toward Edgartown and even has a few parking areas for non-residents as well as residents. With a large salt pond (Sengekontacket Pond) on one side and the long sands of Vineyard Sound beaches on the other, Sylvia Beach is flat and open, making it a fabulous spot to watch the sun go down over the pond and watch the full moon rise over the ocean.

The alternate route to Edgartown along County Road to the Edgartown-Vineyard Haven Road passes the **Felix Neck Wildlife Sanctuary,** which occupies a 300-acre peninsula jutting into Sengekontacket Pond. Named for Felix Kuttashamaquat, a Wampanoag sheep farmer who grazed his flocks here, the peninsula became a Massachusetts Audubon Society refuge in 1969. Several color-coded trails lead through a variety of habitats, where it's possible to encounter the ospreys who nest here as well as twenty-three varieties of waterfowl, turtles, frogs, deer, and several varieties of harmless snakes. Open daily sunrise to 7:00 P.M. $1.00. Telephone: (508) 627–4850.

The first settlement on Martha's Vineyard, **Edgartown,** grew rich on whaling and remains the island's seat of power, wealth, and influence. Most of the homes along Water Street were built for whaling captains in the first quarter of the nineteenth century, giving the whole town a solid Greek Revival appearance that is only enhanced by zoning ordinances and the pressure of local custom. Houses throughout the village—whether Capes or later Greek Revival—are typically painted bright white and faced with black shutters. Sidewalks are made of brick and yards surrounded by white picket fences. Many of the houses have a railed walkway on the roof between the two chimneys. These structures are often called widow's walks, and many a tour guide has painted the image of a poor captain's wife watching for her husband's return from the rooftop aerie. Actually, these platforms offered swift access to the chimneys from attic doors so the inhabitants could extinguish chimney fires without having to clamber over slippery pitched roofs in the middle of a winter night.

A good orientation to historical Edgartown is

the combined tour of the **Vincent House,** the **Dr. Daniel Fisher House,** and the **Old Whaling Church** operated by the Martha's Vineyard Preservation Trust. The tour begins at the Vincent House, the Vineyard's oldest standing residence, which was built in 1672. It is one of the earliest surviving examples of the "full Cape" house, a one-story cottage with a center chimney and two windows on each side of the central entrance. Framed in post-and-beam with native pine and oak, its exterior walls were filled with a mixture of clay and straw—so-called "wattle and daub," a holdover from English building practices.

The **Fisher House,** built in 1840, was Edgartown's style-setting Federal period home. Fisher was a very successful whaling entrepreneur and in the year he built this showpiece house owned the town wharf, a whale oil refinery, and a spermaceti candle factory. At the time, he had a national monopoly on the sale of whale oil to America's lighthouses and earned an annual income in excess of $250,000. Perhaps to keep an eye on that money, Fisher was also the first president of the Martha's Vineyard National Bank. He spared no expense in building this mansion, floating materials over from the mainland as needed and sending as far away as Italy for the marbles that encase his fireplaces. The property is now used principally as a reception facility, and the grand staircase provides a classically dramatic entrance for the bride.

The **Old Whaling Church,** now used mainly as a performance center, is a far more austere piece of architecture despite its leviathan bulk. The small congregation (fewer than fifty members) of the Edgartown United Methodist Church also worship in the minimally heated building except in the dead of winter. This 1843 church is a marvel of simple meetinghouse design, the final work of Frederic Baylies, an Edgartown architect. It echoes the capacious proportion and simple dignity of the hull of a whaling ship—not a huge surprise in a town made rich in the whale trade. The immense, hand-hewn 50-foot beams were felled in Maine and brought down to the town by schooner. One of the treasures of this church is the 1869 Simmons-Fisher tracker organ, which is still used at church services and special organ concerts.

Tours of the three properties are given several times daily in the summer and during the spring and fall Monday through Saturday at 11:00 A.M. and 1:00 P.M. Adults $6.00. 99 Main Street. Telephone: (508) 627–8619.

Walking around compact Edgartown is a pleasure, and certainly easier than driving its narrow streets. Cross Main Street from the Old Whaling Church and walk down School Street, passing a number of striking private residences from the 1760s to the 1840s. The Vineyard Museum stands at the corner of Cooke Street (see "Staying There"). One block closer to the harbor at the corner of Cooke and South Summer Streets is the Federated Church, the first of Baylies's designs (1828). Inside is a whale-oil lamp chandelier and an 1895 Hook and Hastings organ. Back toward Main Street along South Summer are the offices of the *Vineyard Gazette* in a 1760 house, noted on some maps as the Benjamin Smith House. Go down Davis Lane toward the harbor and on South Water Street you will encounter one of those wonderful botanical rarities found in

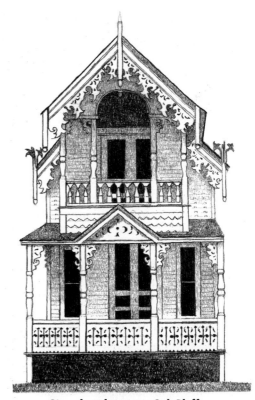

Gingerbread cottage, Oak Bluffs, Martha's Vineyard

some old seaports—the **Pagoda Tree.** It was brought from China as a potted seedling in the mid-nineteenth century by Captain Thomas Milton, predating by several decades the importation of other such trees by botanists of the Arnold Arboretum in Boston.

Water Street may be the most interesting part of Edgartown. South Water leads past many old captains' homes, now fabulously expensive private residences. We don't know how jasmine was introduced to Edgartown—possibly as an intentional planting in recent years, possibly by accident aboard the whaleships—but during the late summer it covers every horizontal surface from fences to evergreen boughs along South Water Street, spreading its heady scent everywhere. North on Water Street leads past the town wharf, more captains' homes, and, finally, picturesque Edgartown Light.

Just off North Water Street at Dock Street is the **ferry to Chappaquiddick Island,** a delightfully rustic place made infamous by the drowning death of Mary Jo Kopechne in Edward Kennedy's automobile. The ferry operates June through October 15 daily from 7:00 A.M. to midnight, October 15 through May 30 from 7:00 A.M. to 7:30 P.M. with additional runs between 9:00 and 10:00 P.M. and 11:00 to 11:15 P.M. All prices are round-trip: $5.00 for car and driver, $1.00 per additional passenger, $3.00 for bicycle and rider, $4.00 for motorcycle or moped and rider.

Chappaquiddick is actually a large island with a long barrier peninsula known as Cape Pogue sweeping around its outer edge. Less populated than the rest of the Vineyard, it's a great place for bicycle riding and nature watching. The beaches at **Cape Pogue Wildlife Refuge in Wasque Reservation** are truly stunning—two long miles of tan sand protecting an inland sandy marsh. Piping plovers nest on the beach here, and rather than bar people during the nesting season, the guardians of the beach put up wire cages to protect the nests. Seabirds abound. Tiny sanderlings skitter across the wash eating nearly microscopic mollusks thrown up on the beach by the waves. Immense black-backed gulls circle, cormorants dive for fish, and the ubiquitous wood ducks and mallards paddle around the marsh. This area is operated by the Trustees of Reservations, which charges admission from June 1 to September 30:

$3.00 per person and $3.00 per vehicle. Telephone: (508) 693–7662.

Edgartown also has another stunning bathing beach, known variously as **Katama Beach** or **South Beach.** Located about five miles from town via South Water Street, the beach has a few parking spaces, but during the summer a shuttle bus services it from Edgartown. Three incredible miles of tan sand stretch along the ocean. One side is a still pond protected by sandy islands— the best place to swim. The other end of the beach has excellent surf but swimmers need to beware of dangerous rip tides. (A rip tide is a current running perpendicular to the shore that carries the water deposited by waves back out to sea. While rip tides are usually visible as a rift in the waves, they can whisk even the strongest swimmer out into roiling deep water.)

From Katama Beach the road continues westward across the island, following the northern edges of the "great ponds," which form an open lacework along the southern perimeter of Martha's Vineyard. Following this route is a trip "up island," a term that dates from the Vineyard's nautical days: Heading west took you to a higher latitude, which mariners called "up."

The road to West Tisbury follows the terminal edge of the glacial moraine—a geologist's term for the southernmost edge of debris ploughed up in the glaciation of New England some 12,000 years ago. The road actually runs along the ridge at the end of the dirt dump, passing along the southern boundary of the 4,000-acre **Martha's Vineyard State Forest.** Most of the island was deforested by early European settlers, but this preserve in the middle of the island was set aside around the turn of the century. Crisscrossed by bicycle trails, it also contains the island airport.

Across the street from West Tisbury's fire station is the Joshua Slocum House, built by that nineteenth-century adventurer after he made his solo circumnavigation of the globe from Gloucester. The left wing of this privately owned home is modeled after Robert Louis Stevenson's house in Samoa and was visited in the 1970s by the Queen and Crown Princess of Samoa. At the first intersection, follow signs to the left toward West Tisbury Center, Chilmark, and Gay Head— all of them tiny communities. This is wooded countryside, dramatically more rural than the bustling villages of down island. At Beetlebung Corner, marked by the Chilmark Library, the road divides. Going straight leads to the fishing village of **Menemsha,** where it's worth timing an arrival to enjoy a meal of fish fresh from one of the boats. (See "Staying There.") We cringe at using the word "picturesque," but Menemsha fits the bill. Because it is so isolated from the rest of the island, the village maintains an old-fashioned equilibrium that has vanished elsewhere.

It's necessary to return to Beetlebung Corner to take the other road to Aquinnah and Gay Head. Watch carefully for a left-hand turn to **Moshup Trail,** which follows the shoreline down to Gay Head. Historically the home of the Wampanoag Aquinnah people, this 3,400-acre peninsula at the southwestern end of the island supported them for about 4,000 years before the Europeans arrived. The name "Aquinnah" means "Land Under the Hill" in Algonquian, a reference to the multi-colored cliffs of Gay Head that are sacred to the tribe. Legend has it that the people were brought here by Moshup, a giant who was so large and powerful that he caught whales with his bare hands and roasted them over bonfires of entire trees that he ripped from the ground. Legends say that Moshup created Vineyard Sound by dragging his big toe behind him on the way from the mainland and created Nantucket by knocking the ashes from his pipe. The tribe celebrates a Legends of Moshup pageant each year at the end of July and beginning of August.

Public parking near Moshup Beach and the Gay Head cliffs is expensive—$5.00 per hour to a maximum of $15.00 per day—and the vast majority of visitors arrive by tour bus rather than automobile. Because the buses only make a brief stop, we suggest gritting your teeth and paying up so you can explore at your leisure. It's one of the few sources of income for the Aquinnah tribe.

The **Gay Head cliffs** are a geological marvel. Violently uplifted ocean floor, they display the stratigraphy of 100 million years in layers of sands, gravels, and clay. The land, which rose and sank over the eons, was at one time covered with forest, then laid bare, then forested again. The fossils revealed by erosion of the cliffs include mammoth ancient sharks that once swam here, clams and crabs from ancient seas, and lignite coal from the giant ferns of the Cretaceous period. Fossils of camels and wild horses have been exposed here as well as fossils of long-extinct species of whales. No wonder the Aquinnah hold the cliffs sacred! They contain the history of the earth in a single formation. Direct access to the cliffs is now limited to tribal members and scientists with special tribal permission.

Just offshore from the cliffs is a very dangerous reef of glacial rocks that sailors call Devil's Ridge. In 1799 one of the first revolving lights in the country was erected atop the cliffs to warn of the peril, although the present red brick lighthouse dates from much more recent times. The worst wreck of the area occurred in January 1884, when the steamship *City of Columbus* grounded on the Devil's Bridge and lost all 121 passengers and crew.

Gay Head Light is open for touring from mid-June through September on Friday through Sunday evenings from an hour before sunset to an hour after. Views from the top include Vineyard Sound, the Elizabeth Islands, and—on a clear day—Block Island and Buzzards Bay. The sunset view from the cliffs is also very striking. Adults $2.00. Telephone: (508) 627–4441.

Gay Head cliffs, Martha's Vineyard

To return to the ferry at Vineyard Haven, double back to West Tisbury Center and follow Old County Road, which merges into State Road, which becomes Main Street.

Nantucket Island, Massachusetts

The Wampanoags called this spit of land thirty miles off the shore of Cape Cod Nanticut, or "far-away island," and the English, who began arriving in significant numbers in 1661, followed suit but Anglicized the name to Nantucket. These early settlers were Quakers, fleeing persecution by the Puritans of Amesbury and Salisbury, and "Far Away Island" offered them the sanctuary to practice their quiet faith in peace.

Nantucket's isolation still appeals, although the inception of a high-speed ferry from Hyannis and commuter flights every few minutes (at least during the summer) have made it far less remote than in Colonial days. The whaling industry that built Nantucket vanished long ago, but the wealth engendered by that trade persists in the old houses, the stone jetties and warehouses, the spires of its churches, the cobbles of its streets, and the solid look of Nantucket village, clinging to the hillside harbor with the tenacity of a barnacle colony. It is a small island—14 miles long and an average of 3.5 miles wide—covered in virtually every inhabitable spot with a domicile. Although some Nantucketers still go to sea, they stay closer to home, reaping the easy harvest of inshore fisheries among the reefs and shallows that surround the island. The island's chief stock in trade these days is refuge from a busy world. Nantucket is a place where wealthy metropolitans come to sit on their porches and contemplate the abiding rhythms of a life offshore.

Although there are two other notable villages on the island, most visitors by ferry arrive at Nantucket Town. And because space for automobiles is severely limited on the one car-ferry that serves the island, most arrive without a vehicle. This is hardly a problem. Nantucket parking is so scarce that a car becomes a liability, and every place on the island is easily accessed by public transportation, bicycle, or (if you're willing to endure the glint-eyed stares of the residents)

moped. (See "Staying There.") In fact, Nantucket Town has so much to explore that many travelers never venture farther than their legs will carry them.

The main part of town surrounding the harbor has much of the look that caused sailors of yore to refer to it as "the little gray lady in the sea." When the first Quaker settlers arrived, they found the island extensively covered with white cedars, which can be easily split into shingles. A simple and practical people, they covered their houses with cedar shingles, which resist rot and weather to a lovely, silvery gray color. The look became so established that subsequent settlers followed suit, and now unpainted cedar shingles are virtually required on all domiciles. Property owners within the historic district cannot alter the exteriors of their buildings. Houses that are destroyed by fire or natural disaster must be rebuilt along strict lines, generally following the original construction. Local ordinance requires new houses (still being built outside of town) to be faced with cedar clapboards or cedar shingles.

As far as we know, no local ordinance requires owners to post the construction dates of their buildings, but most do. We've observed that when we walk around a residential neighborhood, we see many small homes dating from the early 1700s, several more from the early 1800s and suddenly one house—looking every bit as old as the others—constructed in the 1980s. Over time this strict preservationism may come to seem precious. We can envision an era of buildings constructed in the twenty-first century to look like they date from the eighteenth. But barring some catastrophe that scours the town clean of human construction, the presence of these shipwright-built houses lends Nantucket an undeniable charm.

Several relics of Nantucket's treasured past are secured by the **Nantucket Historical Association (NHA),** which provides a $10 visitor pass to a dozen properties. (Individual admissions range from $2.00 to $5.00.) Telephone: (508) 228–1894. While it takes a hardcore history buff to traipse through all the historic structures, no one should visit Nantucket without an eye-opening stop at the **Whaling Museum** on the corner of Broad and South Beach Streets. It's hard to miss, as Steamboat Wharf (where the ferries land) lies directly at the foot of Broad Street.

The large brick structure occupied by the Whaling Museum was built in 1847 as a whale oil refinery and candle factory. As befits the island that launched American whaling and came to briefly dominate the industry worldwide, this museum holds one of the largest collections of whaling artifacts anywhere. It is one thing to read of Nantucket's whaling hegemony, and quite another to appreciate it in the presence of these objects.

In a way, Nantucketers were fated to become whale hunters, as farms played out on the sparse land within two generations of settlement. But Nantucket is unusual among New England islands because it is situated among extensive shoals and banks, traditionally productive areas of the sea where small fish school and larger fish come to eat them. Rich in plankton as well as animal life, these shoals were key feeding grounds for marine mammals as well. The original Wampanoag inhabitants of Nantucket took advantage of this situation, slaughtering beached whales and hunting whales as they grazed near shore, and the English settlers followed suit. Obed Macy's *History of Nantucket* offers (in hindsight) this version of a Nantucket epiphany: "In the year 1690 some persons were on a high hill observing the whales spouting and sporting with each other, when one observed: 'there'—pointing to the sea—'is a green pasture where our children's grandchildren will go for bread.'"

Baleen whales were so plentiful in Nantucket waters that the early whale hunters rarely ventured far from shore. Lookouts were posted on the south shore, with each patrolling a set territory, and when he spotted a whale, six-man crews set out in cedar-plank boats to harpoon the leviathan and ride him to exhaustion—the so-called "Nantucket sleigh ride." Old records speak of the men carrying cobblestones aboard the boat to throw at the whale to judge if they were close enough to harpoon it. The exhausted creature was speared to death and eventually rowed back to shore, where it would be beached and stripped of its meat and blubber. The hunters then rendered the blubber in large iron pots at the beach to separate the oil. There is something primitive and almost intimate about this kind of hunting—a seaborne version of large game hunting as prac-

ticed for millennia. It differs little from the European cave dwellers who surrounded and speared mastodons or the Plains dwellers who hunted the American bison. Indeed, the English settlers learned the trade from the Wampanoags.

When a Nantucket sailor named Hussey had his boat blown out to sea in 1712, he encountered and killed the first sperm whale known to be taken by American hunters. So superior was the lamp oil rendered from its blubber—and from the waxy head matter—that the more adventurous whalers took quickly to "whaling in the deep," with six sloops from Nantucket sailing as far as Newfoundland in 1715 to hunt sperm whales. By the American Revolution, Nantucketers had ceased inshore whaling and begun to hunt farther and farther afield in ever larger vessels that would stay out as long as four or five years.

Nantucket whalers were the first to build what were, in effect, factory ships—broadbeamed vessels with tryworks on board to render the oil and store it in casks for the voyage home. This development, which began around 1730, was no doubt a great relief to those who stayed ashore. Nantucket thoroughly dominated the whaling business during the first half of the eighteenth century. In 1730, the little island had more whaleships afloat than the rest of the American colonies put together and on the eve of the Revolution, in 1768, the town was home port to 125 whaling vessels. With no other way to earn a living, Nantucket continued whaling during the Revolution with disastrous results: Most of its vessels were captured, lost, or shipwrecked. More than 1,200 men aboard were either killed or taken prisoner. Yet after the war, Nantucket rebuilt its fleet and continued to hunt whales. Indeed, many a Nantucket fortune was made delivering whale oil to Great Britain during the Embargo of 1807 and even through the War of 1812.

Nantucket whalers were the first to sail the Pacific (1791) and the first to reach the coast of Japan (1820). They were the first whalers to land in Hawaii (in 1819), first to report sighting Antarctica (1821), and the first to ply the Arctic Ocean (also 1821). Like their trading cousins farther north in Salem, Nantucket ships became known in every harbor of the world. It has been said that more than thirty islands and reefs in the Pacific are named after Nantucket whaling captains and merchants. As the industry grew, so did the size of ships, a development that ultimately let New Bedford surpass Nantucket as America's leading whaling port. By 1820, profitable ships had ballooned to 300 tons, but a bar at the mouth of Nantucket Harbor made it impossible for vessels of that size to pass.

Nantucket continued to whale but the business shifted quickly from hunting whales to processing whale oil and spermaceti. In 1843, Nantucket had eighty-eight whaling ships, its record number of ships in the nineteenth century. Three years later, in the 1846 apex of American whaling, Nantucket had only sixteen, while New Bedford had sixty-nine. Racked by a great fire that destroyed the wharves and warehouses in 1846, Nantucket did not rebuild its fleet, although its dominance of the spermaceti candle industry lasted another two decades until kerosene became widely available. American whaling continued elsewhere until World War I, but when Nantucket sent out the bark *Oak* in 1869, it was the last of 4,344 whaling voyages from the port.

The Whaling Museum's collections give a genuine poignancy to this era, evoking both the adventure of the whaling trade and many of its grim realities. In addition to whale-hunting gear and whale-oil processing equipment, the museum holds a remarkable collection of artifacts that whalers brought back from islands of the South Seas. One new room is devoted principally to displaying the museum's striking scrimshaw collection, including the ever-popular pie crimpers, that could be carved from a single sperm whale tooth. Not all of the whalebone relics are so decorative. On Nantucket, whalebone was often easier to come by and usually less expensive than wood, so practical islanders used the material for everything from peg legs to hammer handles. Before leaving the museum, it's worth a stop at the shop to peruse the excellent selection of books on Nantucket history and whaling. Serious scholars of Nantucket and whaling history in particular and New England history in general might wish to spend some time at the NHA's research center on 15 Broad Street, where a nonmember's usage fee of $5.00 is charged.

The Whaling Museum of the Nantucket Historical Association is open from Memorial Day weekend through Columbus Day daily from 10:00 A.M. to 5:00 P.M., through the remainder of October daily from 11:00 A.M. to 3:00 P.M., and from November to Memorial Day weekend on Saturday and Sunday from 11:00 A.M. to 3:00 P.M. $5.00. Corner of Broad and South Beach Streets. Telephone: (508) 228–1894.

Except for the Peter Foulger Museum, directly adjacent to the Whaling Museum, the majority of NHA properties keep a more limited season (basically Memorial Day through Columbus Day) and are open only from 11:00 A.M. to 3:00 P.M. Before planning a visit, it's best to call the NHA at (508) 228–1894 to check.

Walking the route of the NHA properties can be a good way to see old Nantucket. The association's walking tour brochure suggests the entire collection can be seen in less than three and one-half hours, which is probably true unless you actually want to go inside them. Two of the closer properties, however, provide a feel for old Nantucket in a little more than an hour of careful observation.

From the Whaling Museum, Federal Street leads to the heart of the old town at Main Street, still paved with the rough cobbles laid down in 1837 to keep whale oil wagons from bogging down in the mud. Most of lower Main Street dates from the mid-nineteenth century, as the "Great Fire of 1846" ravaged the entire waterfront before firefighters halted the blaze at the Pacific Bank. The glorious large houses of Upper Main Street, however, represent the height of Nantucket's wealth. These Federal manors and Greek Revival domestic temples were mostly built between 1760 and 1830, usually for Quaker whale industry merchants.

It appears that wealth often brought about a change of church for many of these families, as the Unitarians gained a lot of ground as Nantucket flourished. The last Quaker meetinghouse, where the Society of Friends still holds services all year on Sundays at 10:00 A.M., is owned by the NHA, which operates the adjacent building on Fair Street as a museum. About 100 feet off Main Street, the **Friends Meeting House** was built as a Quaker school in 1838 and converted to a place of worship in 1864. The NHA acquired the building in 1894 as its initial restoration project. It is open for general tours June through September from 10:00 A.M. to 5:00 P.M. $2.00.

Farther up Main Street is one of the most resplendent examples of Nantucket's Greek Revival mansions, the **Hadwen House,** built in 1845 by William Hadwen, co-owner of the candleworks where the Whaling Museum is now located. Both the interior rooms and the gardens are maintained to reflect the lifestyle and taste of Hadwen and his family. Nominally a Quaker, Hadwen clearly left his ascetic roots behind as his business flourished. The Hadwen House is open June through September daily 10:00 A.M. to 5:00 P.M. Adults $5.00. 96 Main Street (corner of Pleasant Street).

Puritans followed the Quakers to Nantucket, with the result that the white-spired **First Congregational Church** sits downtown amid the gray-shingled houses. The site on Centre Street gives an idea how the congregation grew. The first Puritan church, long gone, was a Wampanoag meetinghouse mission from the 1690s staffed by "Praying Indian" pastors who had learned the faith on Martha's Vineyard. The building that serves the current congregation as its winter church (it has heat) is the North Vestry, first built in 1725 and moved to its present location. Renovated and decorated over the years, it still preserves the austere piety of an early meetinghouse. The congregation makes no claims for it being the oldest American church in continuous use as a house of worship, but it has to rank among the most venerable.

The huge church that dwarfs the cozy vestry is the "Summer Church," which was built to accommodate the swelling ranks of Congregationalists during Nantucket's economic heyday. Built in 1834, it was further enlarged in 1850. Yet most of the members in that era were women, as the men were always at sea. As the church historians note, at one point in the early nineteenth century the congregation of about 250 counted only three men among them. Church services are held here each Sunday at 10:00 A.M. with an additional 8:00 A.M. service in July and August.

Part of the original plan of the church was to provide a high **tower beneath the steeple** that could serve as "an observation tower for the convenience of the community," and that tower is open to visitors from mid-June to mid-October Monday through Saturday 10:00 A.M. to 4:00 P.M. and during July and August it is also open Wednesday evenings 6:00 to 8:00 P.M. Some ninety-two steps ascend the heights to the windowed observation room that provides a 120-foot-high lookout over all of Nantucket harbor and much of the rest of the island. The church asks a donation of $2.00. 62 Centre Street.

The long-ago chandleries and marine outfitters of Nantucket's downtown and wharf areas have given way to a plethora of pricey clothing stores, souvenir shops, restaurants, and bars of the sort one finds in similar resorts, although a few are unique to the island. We leave you to your own devices, conscience, and pocketbook to determine how much time to spend in this district—an experience that can be replicated in most upscale parts of the Mid Coast.

If the bustle of town becomes too much, Nantucket also offers some beautiful natural scenes, including several excellent swimming beaches for which there is no admission charge. **Jetties Beach,** a 20-minute walk from town out South Beach Street (also serviced by a shuttle bus from mid-June through mid-September), has everything one could ask from a recreational beach, including lifeguards, changing rooms, restrooms, take-out food service, and concessions that rent windsurfers, sailboats, and kayaks. Similar services are available at **Surfside** on the south side of the island. It is a three-mile bicycle ride from town and is also served from mid-June through mid-September by a shuttle bus. Less a swimming area than Jetties (the waves are high and strong, making for good surfing but difficult swimming), the broad beach at Surfside is favored by kite-flyers, picnickers, volleyball players, and surfcasters. (Nantucket is one of the best places in New England to surfcast for bluefish.)

One of the nicest ways to escape the hubbub of Nantucket Town's tourist scene is to make the 10-mile ride to 'Sconset on the **Polpis Bike Path,** which was completed in the fall of 1998. Technically, 'Sconset is the village of Siasconset on the far eastern tip of the island, but the longer version of the name only appears on formal maps. The bike path follows Polpis Road along the northern perimeter of the island from Nantucket

Town to Polpis Harbor, where it turns southeast toward 'Sconset. Passing through conservation lands, the path skirts the edges of Nantucket's moors.

A good stop along the way is the **Nantucket Life-Saving Museum**, 2.7 miles from the traffic rotary east of Nantucket Town. Although Nantucket's story as a whaling center is well-known, its role in saving lives at sea is often forgotten. South and east of the island the shifting sands of the shoals have made these waters the "graveyard of the Atlantic." Dangerous as the waters are, until the Cape Cod Canal opened in 1914, virtually all ship traffic between Boston and New York, as well as many ships going to and from Europe, had to pass through these treacherous waters. Literally hundreds of vessels grounded on the shoals, and Nantucketers were among the most valiant members of the U.S. Life-Saving Service. This museum recounts some of the drama of tragic disasters and daring rescues. Among the artifacts are items recovered from the Italian ocean liner *Andrea Doria,* which sank after colliding with the Swedish liner *Stockholm* off Nantucket in July 1956. Open mid-June to Columbus Day daily 9:30 A.M. to 4:00 P.M. $3.00. 158 Polpis Road. Telephone: (508) 228–1885.

It's worth detouring about a quarter-mile up Wauwinet Road to visit a new nature interpretation trail at **Squam Swamp.** This project of the Nantucket Conservation Foundation highlights the geological and natural history features of the island interior in a compact one-mile walk with nineteen interpretive stations. Waterproof shoes are useful, as parts of the path can be damp, but most of the route is well out of the water, and the vegetation varies widely depending on the saturation of the soils. Fiddlehead and cinnamon ferns unfold in the swampy lowlands, shadbush and arrowwood in the uplands. Four species of oaks are found on this tiny nature trail, but the most common tree is the tupelo, or black gum. In whaling days, this was known as the "beetlebung tree," because its hard wood was made into mallets (called beetles) to pound wooden stoppers (called bungs) in whale oil casks. The two most common low-lying plants here are sassafras (its roots provide the natural flavor for root beer) and poison ivy, which turns a brilliant scarlet in the fall. The trail is kept free of poison ivy—a good

reason not to stray.

The Polpis bike path also skirts the edge of a cranberry bog and the private Sankaty Golf Course before entering 'Sconset. On an island where land is at an extreme premium, golfing is a luxury on a par with the most conspicuous of consumption. Nonetheless, it is striking to see duffers lugging their clubs across the green almost in the shadow of **Sankaty Head Lighthouse,** which has warned ships off Nantucket's shoals since 1861. Beach erosion on this side of the island is so severe that much of the bluff on which the lighthouse stands has been eaten away.

The bike path concludes in the privileged village of **'Sconset**—where a tiny cottage can easily sell for seven figures. The community began, as all communities on Nantucket did, as a fishing village until it was discovered by the New York theatrical crowd at the end of the nineteenth century. By the turn of the century, 'Sconset was pronounced *the* place to spend the summer among a certain well-heeled Gotham crowd. Wealth here assumes the mantle of simplicity and modesty, which gives 'Sconset a distinct visual charm only enhanced by the climbing roses trellised on many of the slanting roofs of former fishermen's cottages. The houses in the upper village are secure for the time being, but be sure to have a look around below the bluff at Codfish Park and along the fast-eroding shore. Many of these ancient fishing cottages purchased by millionaires as fashionable retreats are on the verge of being reclaimed by the sea.

Riders sufficiently tuckered out by pedaling to 'Sconset will be delighted to discover that the island buses will transport two bicycles per trip back to Nantucket Town at no additional charge.

Personal Narrative: Kayaking from Wauwinet to Coskata Pond

Nantucket wash-ashore Peter Aiken has been living on the island for twenty-five years, which doesn't quite make him a Nantucketer but at least qualifies him as a "reformed tourist," as author Robert Benchley once called long-term residents who weren't born on-island. Peter is an avid sea kayaker and has been after us for years to join him on a Nantucket paddle. We are visiting Nantucket's Wauwinet Inn resort at the end of October, so David assents.

We are all enjoying a stay at the Wauwinet, an exquisite resort at the site of the Nantucket Harbor "haul-over" about nine miles from Nantucket Town on the northeast end of the island. The "haul-over" was the spot where fishermen traditionally hauled their boats across the dunes to save several miles of sailing around the long barrier beaches of Great Point and Coatue Point. In the mid-nineteenth century, the Wauwinet House opened as a restaurant serving shore dinners to patrons who arrived by boat; at the time there was no road between Nantucket Town and Wauwinet. Later the restaurant added rooms and into the mid-twentieth century the site developed as a full-fledged resort. The current incarnation of the Wauwinet is a 1988 multi-million dollar makeover that combines every imaginable creature comfort with a low-key style just right for Nantucket.

The Wauwinet has placed its small boats (a cat boat, sculls, row boats) in storage for the winter, so David and Peter put Peter's two sea kayaks in the water early in the morning, lace up and snap their skirts on to stay dry, and begin the paddle across Nantucket Harbor to Coskata Pond.

The harbor is very shallow—five to seven feet deep in most places—and the water is surprisingly warm for the end of October. With no wind in the early morning, we have no waves to contend with. We are in a hurry to get over to Coskata Pond, a little more than a mile away across open water, to maximize our time exploring the marsh system, but we stop halfway to marvel at two flocks of birds sitting on the water. We are not surprised by the eider ducks, which are among the most common birds on Nantucket in the winter, but not more than thirty feet away is a gathering of at least twenty, perhaps thirty loons. As we come up on the birds we think they are some kind of geese, because they are so big and have molted to their slate-colored winter plumage. But as soon as we startle one and it takes off with that unmistakable maniacal hooting laugh, we know exactly what they are. Neither of us realized that loons congregated, but you see a lot of things in a kayak when you sit low in the water and melt into the scene.

Since the tide is running high we're able to negotiate the tidal mouth of Coskata Pond with nearly a foot of water, picking our way around large rocks into the salt pond. Once inside, we are in an autumnal paradise of flat water and rich bird life, as many waterfowl have already settled into their winter grounds on Nantucket. We paddle through the narrows beside glades and sandy shores where we see nearly a dozen endangered American oystercatchers probing for food. As we paddle closer one looks up and lets out a loud "KLEEP!" to warn us off. Three snipes seem to be standing in the water, but we realize they are actually on a barely submerged sand bar, so we paddle around it, passing between a cluster of black ducks and another group of common mergansers, all of them diving in the shallows. We see an opening in the weeds, where two blue herons are repeatedly rising up, flapping and landing in the tall grasses about fifty yards away. As we follow the opening we are in a narrow channel that cuts into the glade. The banks are half roots and half ridged mussels, and the water is so shallow that Peter reaches down and plucks up a six-inch quahog from the bottom.

We follow the channel into the weeds until the sandy bottom seizes our kayaks and we have to climb out onto a sand bar to turn them around. The herons pay us no heed—they are still looking for fish in the tiny streams. Inland, toward the dunes that separate the pond from the pounding Atlantic surf, a northern harrier skims along the scrubby brush, listening intently for prey. Winter is coming, but life is teeming in this Nantucket salt pond and its surrounding marsh.

Cape Cod, Massachusetts

The scenic way to approach Cape Cod from New Bedford is along Route 6, which is called the "Cranberry Highway." Cranberry bogs are found all over southeastern Massachusetts and on Cape Cod and the islands, but they are so nondescript except at blossom and harvest times that most people never notice them. Not until the berries begin to ripen in September and October do the farmers flood the bogs for the harvest. In the old days, pickers walked through the bogs swinging cranberry rakes—trays with long tines on them—to pull the berries from the low-lying bushes. Most farmers now harvest using the wet method. They fill the bogs with a foot or so of water, drive through with machines that beat the berries from the bushes, and then corral the red sea of floating berries. A few still dry harvest, using a machine that shakes the vines and catches the dry berries. After passing the bounce test (overripe or spoiled fruit won't bounce over a four-inch wall on an incline), the dry-picked berries are sold as whole cranberries. The wet-harvested berries all end up in jellies, preserves, and juice products.

Cape Cod's boundaries have shrunk over time—Plymouth on the Cape Cod Bay side and Wareham on the Buzzards Bay side were once considered to belong to Cape Cod. Despite the continuing presence of a Cape Cod League base-ball team in Wareham, they're both officially "off Cape." That locution, so common to native Cape Codders, is the same phrasing islanders use to denote any place not on the island ("off island"), and is apropos because the Cape Cod Canal, dug in 1914, made the Cape into an island. The canal also radically altered shipping routes, saving vessels bound between Boston and New York from having to run the dangerous shoals around Nantucket.

Two bridges cross the Cape Cod Canal, one in Bourne on Route 28 and the other in the village of Sagamore on Route 6. Coming from New Bedford, the Bourne Bridge is the most reasonable route. The Cape's fifteen towns contain within their borders dozens of villages and communities. In towns like Falmouth, the subdivisions are relatively seamless (with the exception of the vil-lage of Woods Hole). In others, such as Barnstable, they are radically distinct. Bucolic West Barnstable, for example, shares little in common with busy Hyannis except a municipal government. This "one town with many villages" lay-out, a legacy of sixteenth-century land grants, proves confusing to most visitors, although the 200,000 or so residents of Cape Cod seem entirely unruffled. For the sake of convenience, this chapter copes with those divisions the same way as road maps and signs, as if, say, Yarmouth Port and South Yarmouth were entirely separate entities and as if West Harwichport and Harwich Port were one.

Cape Cod is shaped like a strongman's flexed arm, with the section nearest the Canal serving as the upper arm, Chatham the bent elbow, and the Outer Cape the forearm. Provincetown termi-nates the land as a clenched fist. The chief build-ing block of this unique body of land is, like the islands, terminal glacial moraine—the debris deposited when the glacial ice sheet retreated. But the stones of New England have been augmented over the centuries by sand drift on the ocean side, creating a shifting barrier shore. It is in perpetual motion, but changes in the land forms are only visible over time or following major ocean storms.

Cape Cod occupies a special place in the American imagination—a mythic spot where Patti Page's silky voice forever extols summer indolence on "Old Cape Cod" and the distant fig-ure of John Kennedy stalks an endless beach lost in his thoughts. In truth, we think there are at least three Cape Cods—the windswept dunes and relentless surf of the Outer Cape, the honky-tonk bustle of the Cape's southern edge on Nantucket Sound, and the quiet Cape Cod of former farm-ing communities and bayside ports nearly lost in the backwash of history. We've organized this tour of the Cape for a taste of all of these variations on a geographic theme by circling the mainland on Route 28.

Bourne, Cape Cod

Bourne is a transition zone between Cape Cod and mainland southeastern Massachusetts, a com-munity defined to a great extent by the Cape Cod Canal and the bridges that cross it. The Wampanoags of this region used the present-day route of the Canal as a waterway between Cape Cod Bay and Buzzards Bay by portaging their canoes between Scusset Creek and Manomet River, but ships cannot be picked up and carried like canoes, and European settlers in southeastern Massachusetts dreamed of digging an eight-mile canal to speed transport between the bays. Myles Standish, the military leader of the Plymouth settlers, first proposed the canal, and as early as 1697, the Massachusetts General Court ordered a feasibility report. George Washington even considered putting his engineers to work on such a project to provide more mobility for America's fledgling Navy. But despite many false starts, canal construction did not begin until 1909 and wasn't completed until July 29, 1914.

The paved service roads along both sides of the canal are good places to bicycle or hike for excellent close-up views of vessels of all sizes from large cruise ships and tankers to graceful sailboats, runabouts, and hard-working tugs. **The U.S. Army Corps of Engineers information center** on the Bourne Scenic Highway on the north side of the canal in Bournedale conducts walks and bicycle trips. With tidal currents that run four to seven knots, the Cape Cod Canal is also a famous fishing ground, although fishing is banned at some points along the shore so that it will not interfere with shipping. Several diving, sport fishing, sightseeing, and overnight charter boats operate from the **Bourne Marina** in the village of Bourne on the east end of the canal. Telephone: (508) 759–2512. Near the marina is the Emmons Road entrance to well-sheltered **Monument Beach,** which features showers, restrooms, and a snackbar.

Falmouth, Cape Cod

Route 28 crosses the Bourne Bridge and continues southward, skirting the western edge of Cape Cod along Buzzards Bay until it makes a 90-degree turn directly through Falmouth Center, the largest of the town's eight villages. While other parts of Cape Cod might wow with their dramatic landscapes and exposure to the elements, Falmouth is the quintessential town of the Upper Cape, with the personality of an engaging conversationalist who finds new ways to charm at every turn. Its short

Bourne Bridge over Cape Cod Canal

sandy beaches, protected harbors, and a postcard town green give Falmouth an enduring appeal.

The first stop in Falmouth should be the visitors center of the **Falmouth Chamber of Commerce** at 20 Academy Lane, just east of the town green in the center of the village. Telephone: (508) 548–8500 or (800) 526–8532. In addition to publishing an excellent guide to the town and assisting with lodging reservations, the Chamber also provides copies of "A Walk Through Falmouth History," an invaluable pamphlet that hits the local historic highlights.

Settled around 1660 by Quakers, Falmouth developed principally as a farming community. Once the Puritans saw how fertile the land was, they soon outnumbered the Quakers and the triangular town green is dominated today by the white **First Congregational Church** with a Paul Revere bell inscribed with the popular Puritan saying, "The living to the church I call: Unto the grave I summon all." In a pattern classic in English New England, as Falmouth grew wealthier, the Episcopal Church came to dominate, and the neo-Gothic **St. Barnabas Church** opposes the Congregationalist across the green. The rolling green lawns of St. Barnabas host the annual Strawberry Festival in late June in a town renowned for its berries.

Main Street is sweet and brief—really just a cluster of shops. At its east end is Shore Street, which, true to its name, leads down past pleasant little houses set back on shady lots to the open light and long vistas of **Surf Beach.** On a clear day the island of Martha's Vineyard is visible offshore. The sand here is soft and white (a glass factory once stood at the foot of Shore Street), and the strand is long enough to make for an invigorating walk in any season. During the summer, Surf Beach is also a popular bathing spot. Amazingly, the waters of Vineyard Sound typically run about ten degrees warmer than those on the other side of the Cape in Cape Cod Bay.

Falmouth has five other public beaches: Menauhaut in East Falmouth; Falmouth Heights and Trunk River beaches in Falmouth village; and Old Silver Beach in North Falmouth. Bath houses and concession stands are available at the Surf and Old Silver beaches. Old Silver Beach on Quaker Road in North Falmouth off Route 28 faces west across Buzzards Bay, and is one of the few spots in New England with an unobscured view of sunset over the water where the "green flash" (a sudden glint of green light just as the sun goes down) has been reported. Parking at Old Silver Beach, however, is the most expensive of all Falmouth beaches, running $12 per day. For beach parking permits, contact the Town Beach Committee. Telephone: (508) 548–8623.

The historic walking tour begins at the **Old Burying Ground** on Mill Road, southwest of the town green, where the oldest grave dates from 1705. Many of the older stones are engraved with the years, months, and days of the person's life— for these hardy settlers, every day counted. Because Falmouth lies on Vineyard Sound, where the tides and currents wash all sorts of flotsam and jetsam ashore and seasonal tidal rips periodically scour the beaches, the burial ground contains both gravestones without graves (for sailors lost at sea) and graves without stones (for bodies washed ashore). The tour continues toward the town green, wending past a virtual gallery of early American domestic architecture, including the **home at 16 West Main Street where Katharine Lee Bates,** author of "America the Beautiful," was born.

The most memorable line from that anthem provides the name for the best of Falmouth's bicycle paths, the rails-to-trails conversion called the **Shining Sea Bike Path** (as in "from sea to shining sea"). Beginning just outside the gate of the Old Burying Ground, the route covers a nearly flat three and one-half miles along beaches, marshes, and woodlands from Falmouth Center to the village of Woods Hole. Some of the in-town B&Bs provide loaner bicycles to guests. The closest place to rent a bicycle is **Corner Cycle** at the corner of Palmer Avenue and North Main

Street. Telephone: (508) 540–4195. Like the rest of Falmouth, the bike path's charms are subtle, but an observant person will discover a great deal. Trunk River Beach has both good ocean views and a nice swimming strand, and nearby is a marshy inlet where mute swans and a wide variety of songbirds congregate. A wide detour off the path connects to Nobska Road and ultimately, on a tall headland, to historic **Nobska Light,** built in 1828. The lighthouse is automated now but still has the poignant charm of an outpost on a bluff. Ships can see the light from seventeen miles out to sea, and the seaward view is comparable. The best photograph of the lighthouse can be taken from above the light, looking down toward the sea.

The Shining Sea Bike Path concludes in the nautically minded village of **Woods Hole,** the embarkation point for ferries to Martha's Vineyard and Nantucket. Unless you are visiting in the middle of the winter, it is almost impossible to find parking in Woods Hole, which is why a free shuttle service runs from parking lots in Falmouth Center. Originally a fishing port (although Penzance Point was the site of the Pacific Guano Co., which produced fertilizer from bird droppings), Woods Hole has grown into an interesting amalgam of marine research center, fishing village, and tourist trap.

A certain academic atmosphere pervades the village, thanks to researchers from the Marine Biological Laboratory and the Woods Hole Oceanographic Institute. The **WHOI Exhibit Center** maintains quaint if low-key historical exhibits. The short films (including an underwater tour of the wreck of the *Titanic*, which WHOI researchers found and explored) are fascinating. The center is open April through October Tuesday to Saturday 10:00 A.M. to 4:30 P.M., Sunday noon to 4:30 P.M. $1.00. 15 Market Street. Telephone: (508) 457–2000, extension 2252 or 2663.

The **National Marine Fisheries Service Aquarium** deals with the more down-to-earth side of Cape Cod waters—keeping the local fisheries alive and well. There's little glitz or glamour about this venerable facility (the oldest public aquarium in the country), but the admission is free and it's a good place to see—and even handle—the commercially important local fish. Open mid-June to mid-September daily 10:00 A.M. to 4:00 P.M., closed on weekends the rest of the year. On Albatross Street at the west end of Water Street. Telephone: (508) 548–7684.

Leaving Falmouth Center eastward on Main Street, Route 28 passes through several villages of Falmouth, including the summer-home areas of Teaticket and Menauhunt before turning inland a bit en route to Mashpee.

Mashpee, Cape Cod

Set aside in 1660 as a reservation for Wampanoags displaced from other towns in eastern Massachusetts, Mashpee's lands consist of territory that the colonists deemed too marshy, too scrubby, and too isolated. Now Mashpee has the last laugh because it is one of the least developed towns on Cape Cod and hence one of the most desirable for the construction of new summer homes. Real estate development, however, has not yet overwhelmed Mashpee, for much of its territory is watershed protected by zoning and environmental regulations.

Ten miles from Falmouth Route 28 comes to the Mashpee traffic rotary at the town commons. The northernmost of the five roads converging here is Great Neck Road North, which leads about a mile to town hall at the junction with Route 130. Immediately on the left on Route 130 is the **Mashpee Wampanoag Indian Museum.** Open all year Monday through Friday from 10:00 A.M. to 2:00 P.M., the modest structure shows off traditional Wampanoag baskets, tools, and personal articles in one room, while the exhibit in the second room chronicles Wampanoag influences on Colonial culture. Donation. Telephone: (508) 477–1536.

To see another significant Wampanoag site and continue touring Cape Cod, return toward the rotary but turn left almost immediately onto Meetinghouse Road. This road cuts through the heart of the original reservation along the headwater streams of the Mashpee River, famous for its spring run of shad. (A good place to enjoy shad roe is The Flume—see "Staying There.") Where the road rejoins Route 28 is the current site of the **Indian Meeting House,** which was built in 1684 on the shores of Santuit Pond and moved to its pre-sent location in the nineteenth century. The Mashpee Wampanoags still use the old church for worship, community meetings, and social activities. Tours can be arranged through the Indian Museum from June through August on Wednesdays between 10:00 A.M. and 4:00 P.M. and on Fridays between 10:00 A.M. and 3:00 P.M. Practically adjacent to the church is the **Old Indian Burial Ground,** where most of the graves date from the late eighteenth century and headstones are carved with traditional symbols and scenes.

Great Neck Road South from the rotary leads five miles south to the most popular resort portion of Mashpee, Pomponesset Beach. The 2,000-unit resort development of **New Seabury,** which occupies the west end of this summer community, features two championship eighteen-hole golf courses. The semi-private country club has reciprocal privileges with many other clubs and is also open to guests at the resort. Telephone: (508) 477–9110.

Hyannis, Cape Cod

As Route 28 continues east, virtually every right-hand turn winds its way down to a beach or cove surrounded by summer homes. The little communities along this stretch—Cotuit, Osterville, Wianno, and Centerville—are a respite of the "old Cape Cod" before all serenity is shattered by Hyannis. If Cape Cod were a small Caribbean country, Hyannis would be its capital. It is the nerve center, containing the main airport for the Cape, the regional government offices, and the lion's share of the stores. The summer population of Cape Cod easily surpasses a half million, and it seems like many of those people converge on Hyannis simultaneously to shop, to hop a plane to New York, or catch one of the ferries to the islands. Yes, the Kennedy family still has its compound at Hyannisport, on the west side of town, but they make a point of avoiding the town as much as possible to dodge gawkers and well-wishers. Moreover, the only way to get even a glimpse of the compound is to take a harbor cruise. For the most part, we simply advise getting through Hyannis as best you can—or cutting up Yarmouth Road north to the Cape Cod Bay side to visit the tranquil historic ports along Route 6A.

Nantucket Sound Communities

There is no nice way to say this but Route 28 east of Hyannis is one of the most dreadfully overdeveloped portions of Cape Cod. In the summer it is locked for eight hours a day in stall-and-crawl traffic and the roadside motels and attractions begin to develop the awful sameness of highway strip culture that has afflicted parts of Florida and the New Jersey shore. And yet . . . . Any right-hand turn off Route 28 toward Nantucket Sound makes it immediately clear why too many people come here for the summer. There is a distinctly dreamy quality about the beaches and marshlands, the picturesque tidal streams and rivers of this glacial outwash plain. (Route 28 more or less follows the glacial ridgeline.) Protected from the force of the Atlantic by Nantucket Island and the great barrier islands of Monomoy, these silted lowlands consist of verdant countryside leading to sandy beaches on the sea. Literally hundreds of motels line Route 28 through this stretch, and the competition is all to the benefit of travelers, as prices are among the lowest on the Cape and even the older properties are constantly refurbished.

The largest river on Cape Cod divides South Yarmouth from West Dennis at the village of **Bass River** 11 miles east of Hyannis. Legendary for its striper fishing, the Bass River also has a substantial marina where many captains offer both sightseeing and fishing excursions. South Shore Road on the Yarmouth side leads down to the swimming beach at **Parker's River** as well as to the **Bass River Beach** at the river's mouth. Both charge $9.00 per day to park. Bass River Beach features an excellent fishing pier with ramped access for wheelchairs. (Wheelchair accessibility is also unusually good at lodgings in this area— another fruit of market competition.) One mile east of the village on the West Dennis side, a right hand turn down School Street to Lower County Road allows you to follow the coastline through residential properties at a pleasant remove from the tackier aspects of Route 28. One of the best swimming and sunning beaches of this part of the Mid Cape is **West Dennis Beach,** which has lifeguards, food stands, and changing rooms. The east end of the beach is reserved for Dennis residents, but the west end is usually less crowded, if a longer walk from the parking lot. Daily parking fee is $10.

Lower County Road cruises for five miles along Nantucket Sound past private homes and resorts before rejoining Route 28 in the surprisingly pleasant village of **Harwich Port.** The Harwiches (inland Harwich and West Harwich and seaside Harwich Port and South Harwich) have learned from their crowded brethren to the west and have restricted development with minimum lot sizes and various ordinances governing signage. The town has also instituted a summer bus service (75 cents) that stops near motel groups and ferries visitors to the beaches and village centers. Consequently, travelers can book a room at one of the nicer properties (usually with good beach access in its own right) and enjoy the other beaches while squeezing in a little shopping—all without taking the car out of the parking lot.

Route 28 continues its eastward march to the center of Chatham, where it turns northwest and then north before terminating at Route 6.

Chatham, Cape Cod

Long ago a poetic wag dubbed Chatham "the first stop of the East Wind" because nothing but ocean lies between this town at Cape Cod's elbow and Portugal's west coast. In truth, the wind has less to do with Chatham's nature than the water. The boundaries of the town shift with every storm surge, creating a swirling shore whose beauty is underscored by impermanence. In contrast, Chatham's human landscape stands steadfast, re-enacting summer exactly the same way every year. The little town uphill from restless dunes and sandbars clings as tenaciously to its roots as the damask roses that border every street and lane.

Continuity counts for a lot in Chatham. Settled in 1656 by a handful of Pilgrim farmers and incorporated in 1712, Chatham is old, even by Cape Cod standards. With a year-round population of about 6,800, Chatham could be just another sleepy shore village if it were not for those shifting sands that provide a challenge to sailors, a living for shell fishermen, and a tableau for sunbathers.

Chatham's coastline is a labyrinth of barrier beaches and islands. Tiny **South Beach** near **Coast Guard Light** broadened into a long, sandy crescent in the late 1980s when hurricane-driven sands filled the strait between the mainland and the Nauset Beach peninsula just across Chatham Harbor. Even though the beach is vast, the parking lot is not, so it's best to simply walk down Main Street from town—less than ten minutes in a lazy saunter. From the center of town it's even closer to **Oyster Pond Beach,** a favorite for families with children because it lies on a well-protected inlet off Stage Harbor Road. (From the village center it's easier to walk down Queen Anne Road.) Earlier this century Oyster Pond really was a freshwater pond, but the sea breached the sands and now the waters rise and fall with the tides.

The best place to combine swimming with long walks on the dunes is **Harding Beach,** a mile-long peninsula of sand dotted at its tip by a decommissioned lighthouse. About a mile west of town on Route 28, turn down Barn Hill Road, which branches quickly to the right to Harding Beach Road. Daily parking fee is $10. The broad strand faces tame Nantucket Sound, and a nature trail, maintained more by occasional use than active care, crosses the dunes. Better yet is the walk at the ocean's edge, where sandpipers plumb the flats, sanderlings skitter at the water's edge, and fishermen cast for bass and bluefish.

Technically within the town limits of Chatham, **Monomoy Island** trails off the elbow of Cape Cod in the same way (and for the same reasons) that the Elizabeth Islands trail across Buzzards Bay. Until the early twentieth century, Monomoy was a barrier beach peninsula much favored as a base for commercial fishermen who reaped the bounty of the shallows between Monomoy and Nantucket. It separated as an island soon after World War I; in 1978, winter storms completed the process of breaking it up into North and South Monomoy Islands. The fishing shacks are almost all gone from Monomoy and the entire barrier island complex has been transformed into **Monomoy National Wildlife Refuge,** classified as a national wilderness, the strongest class of federal environmental protection. The reason for this designation is that Monomoy is one of the most vital and fragile refuges for migratory birds on the Atlantic flyway. Legendary among birders, Godwit Bar on the west side of North Monomoy has been known to simultaneously host all four known species of godwits as well as thousands of sandpipers, plovers, oystercatchers, and other

shore birds. Larger South Monomoy, which contains the remains of the now-silted-in fishing harbor as well as a substantial growth of poison ivy, is shorter and scrubbier—prime land for songbirds, rabbits, and several species of small hawks.

It can be relatively simple to get to North Monomoy—captains at Fisherman's Pier in Chatham routinely take visitors on the twenty-minute trip. Cost varies with the season and your bargaining skills. Plan on spending at least $20 per person. South Monomoy is harder and more expensive to reach. Even on the leeward beaches, landing always depends on wind and wave conditions. Trips can be arranged through the **Massachusetts Audubon Society** (telephone: 508–349–2615) and the **Cape Cod Museum of Natural History** (telephone: 508–896–3867).

From the likeliest beachhead on South Monomoy, a ten-minute walk along sandy dunes bordered by thigh-high grasses leads to an 1823 lighthouse decommissioned a century later. Nearby is silted-in Powder Hole harbor, which deepwater fishermen used as a summer base. Ninety percent of its buildings were constructed from shipwreck flotsam. Only one shack remains at the lost village, destined for dismantling when its owner dies. Outside Powder Hole, harbor seals often bask on the broad, gravelly beach.

For general information on Monomoy, contact the Monomoy National Wildlife Refuge, Wiki Way, Chatham, Massachusetts 02633. Telephone: (508) 945–0594.

Part of what we like about Chatham is that its lure extends beyond natural beauty. The town center is a cohesive and pleasant community more concentrated than any other on the Cape. Photographers and artists feast on Chatham's visual complexity. It's not surprising that Chatham's busy little Main Street has several photographic and art galleries mixed in with the more typical souvenir shops and frozen yogurt stands.

The paintings that reveal the soul of Chatham are portraits of townspeople rendered in Alice Stallknect's expressionist murals, painted 1932–1945 and preserved in a barn at the **Old Atwood House Museum.** They caused an initial stir because they showed townspeople surrounding a clean-shaven Christ depicted as a modern Cape Cod fisherman. More intriguing are her character studies of Chatham residents at a church supper. "She was a visionary—we didn't appreciate her at the time," a volunteer guide told us on a recent visit. She then proceeded to point out her own grandmother, parents, brother, and cousin among the faces in Stallknecht's paintings. The museum, which also contains a trove of local history objects, is open from mid-June through September Tuesday through Friday 1:00 to 4:00 P.M. Adults $4.00. 347 Stage Harbor Road. Telephone: (508) 947–2493.

Church suppers still figure in Chatham social life, especially on Friday evenings in the summer, when the Episcopalians offer chowder and the Methodists counter with lobster rolls in the hours leading up to Chatham's **Band Nights** in July and August. This weekly institution is a throwback to the era when every New England town had a band and bandstand. The Chatham Band has been performing since the late 1940s, and probably so have some band members in their bright red uniforms. As many as 6,000 people swarm to Kate Gould Park for the concert, so it's wise to lay out a blanket around 2:00 P.M. to secure a close-up seat for the 8:00 P.M. performance and swing by **Chatham Candies** on Main Street for a bag of chocolate-covered cranberries, a local delicacy.

Orleans, Cape Cod

Orleans has the dubious distinction of serving as the community where all roads on Cape Cod come together, or at least all the major roads. Route 6, a dull but fairly fast road through the middle of the Cape is joined here by Route 6A (which traverses the Cape Cod Bay shore) and Route 28 for the final push up the forearm of the Cape to land's end in Provincetown.

Orleans has two beaches that represent the best that Cape Cod offers. The town's single-day parking pass ($12) is valid at both. **Skaket Beach** off Route 6A is a warm-water beach on Cape Cod Bay with tides that reach nine-foot extremities, sometimes exposing as much as a mile of flats. Amenities include restrooms, lifeguards, and snack bar. Telephone: (508) 255–0572. At the end of Nauset Road off Route 6 in East Orleans is one of the East Coast's great beaches: the huge expanse of dunes called **Nauset Beach,** with parking, restrooms, showers, lifeguards, and snack

bars. The parking lot will hold a thousand vehicles, and it is usually full by 9:00 A.M. from mid-June through August. Nauset Beach stretches more or less 10 miles (winter storms trim and augment the barrier beach, depending on the year), and the high surf attracts the dudes with their own boards to the sections reserved for surfing. Boogie boards (which skim across the wash) are found everywhere else. Telephone: (508) 240–3780. Scuba, sailboarding, and surfing gear can be rented at **Pump House Surf Co.** at 9 Route 6A just south of the rotary. Telephone: (508) 240–2226.

Nauset Beach actually belongs to the Cape Cod National Seashore but recreation is managed by the town of Orleans. The protected marshlands and estuaries behind Nauset Beach are known as **Nauset Marsh,** more than thirty square miles of estuarine habitat best explored by canoe or kayak. **Goose Hummock Shop** is the nearest outfitter, and rents both kinds of vessels for about $30 per half day (including life preservers and paddles). The shop is at 15 Route 6A, just south of the rotary where all the roads converge. Telephone: (508) 255–0455. One of the nicest marked trails in the Nauset Marsh is actually reached a few miles up Route 6 in Eastham, the **Fort Hill Road Nature Trail,** part of the Cape Cod National Seashore. Amazingly, parking is free behind the nineteenth-century ship captain's manse, the Edward Penniman House, which is open for touring afternoons in the summer. The trail passes through marshlands favored by great blue herons and common terns for fishing and by peregrine falcons for hunting. Open meadows along the trail, full of milkweed plants, attract some of the largest concentrations of butterflies on the Cape.

Cape Cod National Seashore

About two-thirds of the land area of the Outer Cape now falls within the boundaries of the Cape Cod National Seashore. Established in 1961 along a 40-mile stretch between Chatham and Provincetown, the National Seashore protects the fragile environments of the forearm and fist of the Cape. Within its boundaries are almost 45,000 acres of fragile dunes, rolling beaches, fertile

Architectural Styles

Cape Cod

**Jethro Coffin House,
Nantucket, Massachusetts**

Georgian

**Hunter House,
Newport, Rhode Island**

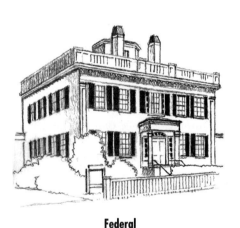

Federal

**Dr. Daniel Fisher House,
Edgartown, Martha's Vineyard**

Italianate

**Whaler's Inn,
Mystic, Connecticut**

marshes, woodlands and deserts, cranberry bogs and cedar forest. Virtually the entire eastern side of the Outer Cape is National Seashore land under the administration of the National Park Service. Admission is free.

The **Salt Pond Visitor Center** in Eastham is a great place to start exploring the National Seashore. Exhibits explain how the land was formed and the huge parking lot can serve as an access point for two of the outstanding outer strands, **Coast Guard Beach** and **Nauset Light Beach.** (Each has a closer beach parking lot with a fee. A one-day permit good at all National Seashore beaches is $7.00; a season-long permit is

$20.00.) Coast Guard Beach has excellent surfing, while Nauset Light Beach has both good surfing and good surf-casting. Lifeguards are posted on these beaches, as well as four others in the National Seashore, from late June through Labor Day, but only strong swimmers should brave the often wild waves. The center is open daily from mid-March through December during daylight hours. Route 6, Eastham. Telephone: (508) 255-3421.

The **Marconi Station Site,** the Wellfleet spot where Guglielmo Marconi sent his first transatlantic radio signal from the United States in 1901, is the administrative headquarters of the National

Seashore. The area includes both the good swimming area at **Marconi Beach** as well as a fascinating nature walk along the **Atlantic White Cedar Swamp Trail,** where a boardwalk makes it possible to penetrate the swamp without mucking through it. Birders find this trail particularly fascinating: the last of the Cape's vesper sparrows breed here, as do two species of small owls.

Almost across Route 6 from the entrance to the Marconi Station Site is the **Wellfleet Bay Wildlife Sanctuary,** where the Massachusetts Audubon Society maintains its regional headquarters in one of the few wild areas not within the National Seashore boundaries. The preserve contains almost every habitat found on Cape Cod—from deciduous forest to long tidal flats—and more than 260 species of birds have been recorded visiting this critical stop on the migrational flyway. More than 60 species nest here. Six trails, which wind through several distinct habitats in the thousand-acre refuge, are open daily 8:00 A.M. to dusk. $3.00. The visitors center is open Tuesday to Sunday 8:30 A.M. to 5:00 P.M. 291 State Highway Route 6, South Wellfleet. Telephone: (508) 349–2615.

Farther out on Route 6, **Head of the Meadow Beach** lies between Highland Light and **Pilgrim Heights,** a region of raised bluffs with astonishing overviews of the Provincetown and Truro dunelands and a favorite spot for watching migrating birds, butterflies, and dragonflies.

The **Provincelands Area** contains some of the most dramatic scenery of the entire National Seashore. Accessed from Route 6 in Provincetown, it covers almost the entire fist of Cape Cod. The **Provincelands Visitor Center,** which has free parking, sits in the least attractive part of the district—a rocky inland moor—but the outlook tower gives a splendid view of the surrounding territory. Open late May through Labor Day daily during daylight hours. Route 6, Provincetown. Telephone: (508) 487–1256. The access road to the visitors center passes through one of the last standing beech forests on Cape Cod—the original habitat that greeted the Pilgrims when they first spied land here.

Race Point Beach in the Provincelands Area has some of the most spectacular dunes on the Cape and the swimming/bathing beach is among the most beautiful. A telescope or binoculars can

come in handy here to watch the offshore activity where the water suddenly changes color from light blue to deep blue. That change demarks the sudden dropoff of the land shelf to deep water. Such junctures typically teem with aquatic life, and Race Point is no exception. Nutrient upwelling encourages the prolific growth of microorganisms, and every step on the marine food chain comes here to feed, including finback and humpback whales. Both are easy to identify—finbacks rarely show their heads, but their bodies look like a cross between a mythical sea serpent and a shark bigger than any Peter Benchley nightmare. Humpbacks frequently surface and blow from their twin holes, then dive with a splashing flip of their flukes. Seabirds also flock in this transition zone, sometimes numbering in the thousands.

Cape Cod once had thirteen stations of the U.S. Lifesaving Service along its ocean shores, but the only original station left standing is the **Old Harbor Lifesaving Museum** at Race Point. On Thursday afternoons during July and August, National Park Service rangers provide demonstrations of surf boat rescues. One other beach of note in the Provincelands is **Herring Cove Beach,** which not only has the calmest waters for swimming of all the National Seashore beaches, but also has the added benefit of facing west into the sunset over Cape Cod Bay.

Wellfleet and Truro, Cape Cod

Once great whaling and shellfishing centers, these two towns have evolved a hibernational pattern over the last century—that is, they virtually go to sleep on the Tuesday after Columbus Day and don't fully reawaken until Memorial Day. Even during the summer, both function, to a great extent, as bedroom communities for the more lively Provincetown. While many of the summer homes in Wellfleet and Truro belong to wealthy industrialists from New York and Boston, an even greater number of rather more modest swellings are occupied by painters, sculptors, and writers. Wellfleet's refreshingly old-fashioned village center rivals Provincetown for art galleries, and the simple, country feel of the place is a welcome antidote to P'town's frenetic partying. Both communities have ceded control of much of their land to the National Seashore. Each has its specialty for anglers—mackerel in Wellfleet harbor, huge bluefish on the flats of Truro.

Provincetown, Cape Cod

Both a fishing village and America's first gay and lesbian summer resort, P'town inhabits the come-hither finger at the end of Cape Cod's muscular arm. The broad arc of the summer sun, which rises over the harbor and sets over the dunes, creates a magical light that has drawn painters and photographers for well over a century. Just looking around in Provincetown makes the artist's job seem deceptively easy: an impressionist flourish of hollyhocks against weathered cedar shingles, achingly empty shorescapes where the sky goes on forever, a cubist jumble of fishing trawlers at the piers, and the whalelike humps of the looming dunes that so haunted Edward Hopper.

There are two sides to Provincetown—the natural setting, almost all of which lies in the Cape Cod National Seashore, and the rollicking human carnival of the town itself. Visitors to P'town move back and forth between the two, which is especially easy on rented bicycles. Pedal out to Herring Cove Beach and you find a strand that curves almost to the horizon, with plenty of room for families with small children, surfcasters angling for stripers, and romantic pairs strolling the coarse sands. It is a beach where sea-etched glass washes up next to the dessicated egg cases of whelks.

On a bicycle it's easy to pedal a few miles to the dunelands of Race Point, which resemble a moonscape punctuated by razor-edged clumps of beach grass. The seaward face of the foredunes is tracked with rivulets, where sand flows like slow water. But the asphalt path lets cyclists pass without doing harm. Inland, the bicycle trail cruises downhill past beach plum and bayberry, winding through beech forest, and climbing again to rejoin Race Point Road to town. These wild dunes are also the favorite spot for dune buggy tours that point out some of the historical aspects of these wild, desert lands. Several dune shacks still survive out here, grandfathered in from the days before the National Seashore was established. They will be toppled when their current owners die. We favor the environmentally sensitive trips operated

since 1946 by **Art's Dune Tours.** Telephone: (508) 487–1950.

Although the fishermen are up early—P'town still harbors a substantial fleet of trawlers—the rest of the village tends to stay up late and get up at midmorning. By noon, the scene is getting into full swing—the handsome boys in their muscle shirts, the young parents with tykes in tow, white-haired tourists from the mainland, and the swarming majority who fit no stereotype at all. The West End (west of Town Pier on Commercial Street) becomes a free-floating carnival of colorful types and dogged souvenir shoppers in the afternoons. The quieter East End of Commercial Street is where the artists hold forth.

In 1899, Charles Hawthorne put Provincetown on American impressionism's dance card by founding the **Cape Cod School of Art,** which still enrolls students enamored of the Cape light. Almost lost in the trees, the barnlike structure of the school stands at the head of Pearl Street. The view through a half-open door reveals shelf upon shelf of pottery and glassware—still life props. The schedule is unpredictable, but on many warm days, instructors give outdoor landscape painting demonstrations, completing an entire canvas in an afternoon.

Back on Commercial Street, the roster of the **Provincetown Art Association** reads like a roll call of American painting in the twentieth century: Marsden Hartley, Milton Avery, Edward Hopper, Robert Motherwell. . . . The gallery is open in May and from Labor Day through October Friday to Sunday noon to 5:00 P.M., June through Labor Day daily noon to 5:00 P.M. and again 8:00 P.M. to 10:00 P.M., and November through April on Saturday and Sunday noon to 4:00 P.M. Adults $3.00. 460 Commercial Street. Telephone: (508) 487–1750. The tradition carries on in the little galleries all along Commercial Street—landscapes, seascapes, then a sudden interjection of pure, glorious abstraction.

Provincetown also has an historic side that predates its incarnations as gay and lesbian resort, art colony, or Portuguese fishing town. In fact, the **Pilgrim Monument** towers over all. The 255-foot tower is the tallest granite structure in the United States. From its summit, the views are breathtaking—the entire interior sweep of Cape Cod's arm, with Plymouth at the other end, and, on a very clear day, Boston with the White Mountains behind it. The monument marks the Pilgrims' first landfall in the New World in 1620. They anchored in what is now Provincetown harbor, raided some Nauset tribes' grain stores in nearby Wellfleet, and moved on to settle Plymouth. But while they were in Provincetown, they drew up that document that would be the first building block of American self-governance, the Mayflower Compact.

Exhibits in the museum around the base of the monument chronicle P'town history with a dizzying assortment of relics that range from a tiny room re-creating a whaling captain's quarters aboard ship to group photographs of the town's early art colony, and even a stuffed polar bear from an Arctic expedition. Open mid-March through November daily from 9:00 A.M. to 5:00 P.M. Adults $5.00. Bradford Street. Telephone: (508) 487–1310.

Along the King's Highway, Cape Cod

Route 6A, which runs along the north shore of the shoulder and upper arm of Cape Cod, is also known as the King's Highway, though no one seems sure *which* king ordered it built. The towns along this stretch were all settled by the middle of the seventeenth century and each of them participated in the great mercantile shipping adventures of the eighteenth and nineteenth centuries. As a result, they all feature a number of stately Federal and Greek Revival homes and the shady serenity of communities enjoying a reflective old age. While many of these towns also have villages on the touristy south shore, their north shore villages have largely dodged the modern developments of auto touring culture. In place of fast food joints and shopping emporia are several score of B&Bs and possibly even a greater number of antiques shops. Contemporary craftsmen also find the King's Highway towns amenable places to practice their trades; watch for roadside signs pointing to studio shops a mile or more away in the woods.

As you return from the Outer Cape, Route 6A begins at the Orleans traffic rotary. Before reaching the town of Brewster, the highway passes through **Nickerson State Park**, one of the largest parks in Massachusetts. In addition to the most

extensive public camping on the Cape, Nickerson is laced with trails for bicycles, horseback riding, and hiking. The park is dotted with big and small glacial kettle ponds well equipped for fishing and motorboating. 3488 Main Street, Brewster. Telephone: (508) 896–3491. Directly across the highway from the main park entrance is the access road to **Linnell Landing Beach,** a gentle swimming beach with long tides that expose extensive flats. It is also one of the few beaches with boardwalks and ramps for excellent wheelchair access.

In Brewster's downtown, the **General Store** (which dates from the 1850s) is one of the nicer old-fashioned stores to explore—as well as the landmark everyone uses to give directions. It's located at the junction of Routes 6A and 124. Breakwater Road, across Route 6A, leads down to **Brewster Flats,** one of the best clamming areas on the Cape. At low tide the flats are exposed for nearly a mile into Cape Cod Bay.

Like most institutions of its type, the **Cape Cod Museum of Natural History** orients its exhibits toward schoolchildren, with an emphasis on hands-on activities. The eighty-two-acre grounds offer three well-marked, self-guided nature trails. One is a quarter-mile trail over wetlands, another leads over a marsh to a beech forest; the longest goes over salt marsh to a beach. Open Monday through Saturday 9:30 A.M. to 4:30 P.M., Sunday 12:30 to 4:30 P.M. Adults $5.00. Route 6A, Brewster. Telephone: (508) 896–3867.

Six miles farther west in **Dennis** is an unusual artistic complex on the grounds of the **Cape Museum of Fine Arts,** which emphasizes Cape Cod artists of a representational bent. Open Tuesday through Saturday 10:00 A.M. to 5:00 P.M., Sunday 1:00 to 5:00 P.M. Adults $2.00. Main Street, Route 6A. Telephone: (508) 385–4477. Some of the best art is not in the museum but in the tiny **Cape Playhouse,** an 1838 meetinghouse moved here in 1927 and decorated with murals by Rockwell Kent. Bette Davis started out as an usher at this summer theater in her first season, and was a featured actress by the second, making her debut opposite young Henry Fonda. Main Street, Route 6A. Telephone: (508) 385–3911.

Several superb nature trails cross the marshy lands between the highway and Cape Cod Bay in Yarmouth and Yarmouth Port. The **Callery-**

Darling Trail is an excellent walking area adjacent to a salt marsh and includes a boardwalk for wheelchair access to see the great blue herons, northern harriers, quail, pheasant, foxes, rabbits, and deer. The trail stretches from Homers Dock Road in Yarmouth Port to the salt marshes west of Centre Street, nearly two and one-half miles of trail concluding at the **Gray's Beach** boardwalk.

Nature runs a quiet riot on Cape Cod, so it's easy to overlook the exquisite gardens that some horticulturalists have managed to create. Several of the finest are found on the seventy-six-acre grounds of **Heritage Plantation of Sandwich.** Known specifically for its rhododendrons, which bloom from late May into the middle of June, Heritage Plantation also has striking bulb gardens and dazzling landscaping. Moreover, the gardens are only the secondary attraction. The complex is a collection of museums: Some buildings are filled with Indian artifacts, others with Colonial domestic goods, still another with early Colonial weapons. The replica Shaker round barn is filled with one of the region's finest collections of antique and vintage automobiles. One of the most charming exhibits is a 1912 carousel of carved circus animals, which whirls around to the strains of a vintage calliope. Open mid-May through October daily 10:00 A.M. to 5:00 P.M. Adults $10. Grove and Pine Streets. Telephone: (508) 888–3300.

On the way back to the mainland, it's worth swinging through the town of **Sandwich** proper, which has enough trappings of its early days to qualify as truly quaint. How else can you describe a village where people stop to fill bottles at the spring next to a 1640 grist mill that's still grinding away? Ducks, geese, and swans in the mill pond help complete the illusion.

The **Sandwich Glass Museum**'s orientation video provides a capsule history of the town as well as the story of Deming Jarves's entrepreneurial daring in establishing the glass factory here and making a one-time luxury product available to the masses. Surprisingly, Jarves found the local sand useless in making glass and had to import sand from the Berkshires. But having a harbor handy for shipping, a hardwood forest to fuel the furnaces, and all the salt hay anyone could ask for as packing material, Sandwich Glass flourished from 1828 to 1888. Several rooms in the museum also detail Sandwich's history as a trading town on the high seas, and the gift shop sells the work of local glass artisans as well as replicas of the highly collectible Sandwich pressed glass. Open April through October daily 9:00 A.M. to 5:00 P.M.; November, December, February, and March Wednesday through Sunday 9:30 A.M. to 4:00 P.M. Adults $5.00. 129 Main Street. Telephone: (508) 888–0251.

Plymouth, Massachusetts

After crossing the Sagamore Bridge, most travelers heading north toward Boston take Route 3, a limited-access highway that offers excellent views of asphalt and trees. By getting off at Exit 2 in Cedarville it is possible to follow the more scenic coastline along the high bluffs at Manomet on Route 3A. **White Horse Beach** in Manomet, about six miles south of Plymouth center, is named for a local legend, which claims that in 1778 a young woman rode a white horse into the ocean and drowned because her physician father disapproved of her sailor lover. New England, of course, is full of such tales of thwarted love, and more local attention is concentrated on the giant granite boulder about a half-mile offshore, called White Horse Rock. When someone painted a swastika on the rock during World War II, local teenagers painted over it with an American flag, establishing what has become an annual flag-painting tradition.

About three miles farther north on Route 3A is **Plymouth Beach,** a three-mile stretch of sandy shores with views of Saquish Neck to the northwest and Manomet Bluffs to the southeast. While the beach is popular with sunbathers and swimmers, it is equally popular with several species of shorebirds. Four species of terns nest here, thousands of waterfowl congregate along the beach in the summer, and tens of thousands use it as a rest stop in the spring and fall migrations. Parking fee June through September is $5.00 weekdays, $8.00 weekends.

Practically across the road from Plymouth Beach is the entrance for **Plimoth Plantation,** where signs say "Welcome to the seventeenth century." Walking from the parking lot through the orientation center and crafts exhibits and then along a woodsy path eases the time change a little.

Inside the stockade, the year is 1627, just seven years after the "Plimoth" colony was founded. Every staff member plays the role of an actual member of the community—going about daily tasks typical of that day and season. We can't overemphasize how firmly the Plimoth Plantation "colonists" stay in character. They know nothing of post-1627 life and respond with confusion and blank stares if visitors talk about current sports stars, fashion, or political scandals. But each person has an interesting story of how he or she came to be part of this colony—and of the various interests and intrigues of small town life. They are likely to start explaining the intricacy of land ownership issues or the payment of debts—just like immigrants in any time and place fretting over when they will own their homes and how they will repay the loans that made their passage possible in the first place.

This modest site at the ocean's edge strikes home what a remarkable thing the Pilgrims did—carving out a home in the wilderness literally a world away from their old lives. Hobbamock, a member of the Pokanoket band of the Wampanoag nation, lived adjacent to the English colonists with his family and he acted as interpreter and advisor to the colonists until his death in the early 1640s. Hobbamock's homesite is also recreated at Plimoth Plantation, and it's interesting to see the contrast between the wattle and daub homes of the colonists and the thatched homes of the Pokanokets. Hobbamock's garden looks precisely as our third-grade teachers told us

Plimoth Plantation, Plymouth, Massachusetts

it would: mounds of corn interplanted with beans and squash. The interpreters at this site (most of them of Wampanoag descent) speak from a twentieth-century perspective about local native culture and the long history of interaction with Europeans.

Plimoth Plantation is open late March until late November daily 9:00 A.M. to 5:00 P.M. and sponsors a variety of special events throughout the year. Adult admission to the Plantation and *Mayflower II* is $18.50, or $15 for the Plantation alone or $5.50 for *Mayflower II*. Plimoth Plantation is about 2.5 miles south of the town of Plymouth on Route 3A. Telephone: (508) 746–1622.

The Plymouth area is one of the most satisfying places in New England to explore the progression of local history because you can go directly from the 1627 village to the modern town of Plymouth to see how it evolved from the Pilgrims' bold undertaking. Plymouth boosters like to call it "America's hometown," and even today one resident in ten is descended from the *Mayflower* Pilgrims, a proud local badge of honor.

In many respects Plymouth seems like a conventional small town, with its stores, town offices, schools, restaurants, and people simply going about the daily business of the late twentieth century. And since Plymouth is a harbor town, it also has a small local fishing fleet and a marina of pleasure boats. But survivals of the past are embedded throughout the community. The most famous landmark of all is **Plymouth Rock,** a nondescript boulder inscribed with the date 1620 that is ensconced beneath a grandiose Greek Revival portico at Plymouth's waterfront. One of the country's foremost historic icons, the rock languished unheralded for the first century. Finally, in 1741, a 95-year-old man identified the stone as the place where the first Pilgrims landed. He had picked up the story from his father, who arrived in the colony in 1623 and learned the tale from one of the original colonists. In the fiery days leading up to the Revolution, patriots in Plymouth hooked a yoke of oxen to the rock to move it to Town Square as a symbol of independence. Unfortunately, their efforts split the stone in half. One piece was left in place and the rest was stored at various locations around the city until the two halves were reunited—you can see the patch—in 1880. The portico dwarfs the rock, which many visitors frankly find something of a letdown. Think of it as the patriots did—a symbol.

Within sight of Plymouth Rock is the anchorage for *Mayflower II,* Plimoth Plantation's reproduction of the startlingly small vessel that carried 102 Pilgrims, their livestock, and the ship's crew to the New World. The vessel was built in England in 1955–56 and was undergoing extensive refitting and repairs in 1998 and 1999. She is not an exact replica of the original ship, but rather a reproduction of a typical bark of the *Mayflower's* type, built using seventeenth-century methods, tools, and materials. We think that the master of the original *Mayflower,* Christopher Jones, is a genuine unsung hero of American history. When the Pilgrims ran out of their stores of beer—an essential part of their diet—Jones handed over some of the crew's supply.

Personal Narrative:
Plymouth at Thanksgiving

We have taken to spending Thanksgiving in Plymouth almost every year since 1992. Fifteen generations since the Mayflower landed, the town rightly feels it owns the holiday, and we agree. Legend says William Bradford, John Alden, Myles Standish, and all the other fifty-one survivors of that first winter broke bread here with Massasoit and his fellow Wampanoags. The story is a pretty embroidery that is poorly supported by the historical record. We try to keep in mind that Thanksgiving didn't become a national holiday until the 1860s and that the Pilgrims didn't become Thanksgiving icons until some years later. But myth overpowers mere facts—if the Pilgrims have been blown out of historical proportion, it's because their story carries some powerful lessons about community and courage.

Plymouth not only claims Thanksgiving, but it invites the rest of the world to the celebration. As we all stand around waiting for activities to begin, one Pennsylvania woman tells us, "I took this bus tour so I wouldn't have to cook dinner for fourteen and clean up afterwards." But escaping from the kitchen isn't the only reason to visit Plymouth on Thanksgiving Day. The community celebration brims with local pride. The hospitality can be a bit overwhelming (especially at your ninth cup of hot cider and napkin of warm cookies), but this hoopla actually surpasses the hype. Moreover, many of the historic buildings that close after Columbus Day (some after Labor Day) open up to mark Plymouth's most important occasion.

We arrive around 8:00 A.M., coming in on Route 44 (exit 6 from Route 3) from Boston. We're early, but we want to get a space in the parking lot between South Park Avenue and Memorial Drive just above Water Street. We head first across the lot to the Plymouth Information Center on Water Street for a map and schedule of the day's events. It is a short walk to Plymouth Rock, down in a hole beneath the grand portico. For some reason we do not quite fathom, people pitch coins at the Rock, as if it were a wishing well. We see one young girl close her eyes and fold her hands in prayer. We suspect the Pilgrims would have liked that.

The real activities of the day begin at 10:00 A.M. with Pilgrim Progress, a traditional reenactment of the first Pilgrim Thanksgiving that was established in 1921 by the Tercentenary Committee. This ceremony, in full Pilgrim garb, depicts the Pilgrims marching to church as described in 1627 by the French visitor, Isaac de Rasieres, except that the list of the March is based on the fifty-one Pilgrim passengers (out of 102) who survived the first hard winter. Pilgrim Progress is also reenacted on Fridays at 6:00 P.M. during August for the benefit of tourists, but the Thanksgiving enactment is more of a town celebration that visitors are permitted to observe. Townspeople in seventeenth-century dress gather, young and old, outside the Mayflower Society House on North Street and march down to Water Street opposite Plymouth Rock for a few prayers and hymns. With many of us onlookers following on the sidelines, they march up Leyden Street past the First Parish Church, a Unitarian-Universalist building on the site of the original Pilgrim house of worship, and the Church of the Pilgrimage, which is the Congregational Church.

The procession winds behind the churches to the ancient Burial Hill at the site of the first fort, built in 1621 under the guidance of Myles Standish. This lofty perch overlooks both the old and new buildings of the town and out to the harbor. Because it is late November, the ground is ankle-deep in fallen leaves. Old gravestones sprout all around us, but those we look at seem to date from the nineteenth century.

The Reverend Gary Marks, senior pastor of The Church of the Pilgrimage, is playing the role of William Brewster. Since none of Brewster's writings have survived, Marks has created a short sermon/prayer of Thanksgiving in what he thinks would have been the Pilgrim leader's style. He has been delivering it since at least 1989, when he gave it during a Thanksgiving day blizzard. It is a moving ceremony, as hundreds of onlookers huddle in the cold around the reenactors.

"And we think we have some hardships," says one middle-aged woman. "It's amazing what people could endure," replies her friend.

When the service concludes, the Pilgrims return to the Mayflower Society House where they pile into their station wagons and minivans, still in costume. The tour groups have all gone back to their seats to be bused to restaurants for turkey with all the trimmings, but we hang on to talk a little with the reenactors, all of whom are Mayflower descendants. One father explains, "I did it when I was a kid." Now he brings his three young children with him. A teenage girl tells us, "I've done this since I was little. My mom is one of the organizers." She is happy to pose with her mother—the two of them glowing with pleasure. Another family explains, "We're not from Plymouth, we're from Gloucester," but admit the father hails from Plymouth and still has family here. This is their second year. "It was scary the first year," one of the daughters says.

Thanksgiving Service at the First Parish Church begins at 10:45 A.M. One parishioner rushing off to take her seat tells us that the only way for a non-parishioner to get in is to join the line at 9:30, which means missing all the other activities. "It's the one day of the year when the pews are packed," she says with a twinkle.

Across Leyden Street, the Church of the Pilgrimage is holding an open house with coffee and a table laden with cookies, carrot cake, muffins, coffee, cider, and other goodies until noon, so we stop by to pay our respects. One church member, Mellicent Drake, has created two volumes that trace the lineage of current parishioners back to the Pilgrims.

"Not many churches can trace their members back more than 300 years," she observes. She's not certain, but hazards a guess that about 50 of the 500 church members are Mayflower descendants. It is difficult to count because so many Mayflower descendants have intermarried. She is convinced that many more people simply aren't aware of their distinguished ancestry, although we find such ignorance hard to fathom in a town where Pilgrim heritage is almost a fetish. Mellicent agrees, but points out that she traced her husband's lineage back to sixteen of the original Pilgrims. "And he didn't even know," she says.

Mellicent explains that The Church of the Pilgrimage is the "successor congregation" to the original house of worship. The Pilgrims lost 51 to 50 in a vote over whether or not to embrace Unitarianism when it came to a vote in 1801. The Unitarians won and kept the right to call themselves the First Church. The losers formed their own congregation, which became the Church of the Pilgrimage and now belongs to the United Church of Christ (Congregational). "They kept the charter," says Mellicent, "but we kept the faith."

Many of the historic houses in Plymouth close after Columbus Day, or only open for very limited hours on weekends, but on Thanksgiving, they're all in operation. We are fond of the **Howland House,** the 1666 home of Jabez Howland, whose parents, John and Elizabeth Tilley Howland, were both Mayflower Pilgrims. When the elder Howlands' farm burned in 1670, they moved in with Jabez and his family. As a result, this two-and-one-half story structure with hip roof and central chimney is billed as "the last house left in Plymouth whose walls have heard the voices of the Mayflower Pilgrims." The interpretation gives a very good feel for what it might have been like to live in this rural but relatively prosperous community toward the end of the seventeenth century. Open June to Columbus Day, varying hours. Adults $3.00. 33 Sandwich Street. Telephone: (508) 746–9590.

Our other historic house stop is **1677 Harlow Old Fort House,** with its wide floorboards, low ceilings, slanting floors, and balky iron latch on the front door. When the original fort on Burial Hill was torn down, the Harlow family had salvage rights and used the timbers to build this house. In the modern gift shop and workshop behind the Old Fort House, a hot Ocean Spray cranberry holiday drink and baked goods are given out to all visitors. "It wouldn't be Thanksgiving without coming here," one Plymouth woman comments.

In the main building, costumed interpreters are demonstrating open hearth cooking. Despite the snacks, we're beginning to feel hungry. A delicious looking cornbread in a big round iron skillet is coming off the fireplace after cooking for forty-five minutes, which one woman remarks is not much longer than it would take in a modern oven—except that she has to keep piling coals under it to keep the temperature high enough. The demonstrators are also preparing Jerusalem artichokes, which grow wild in the area and "were about as close as the Pilgrims had to potatoes," one cook says. They are also boiling cranberries, but admit that the Pilgrims probably gathered much tinier wild berries. Children in Pilgrim dress are using a forked stick to turn a pork roast on a jack spit. The cooks tell us that they usually eat the results at the end of the day, although one quips "sometimes we're not sure if we'll eat it." One year a turkey seemed like "salmonella for sure," she says. "But usually it's good." Open July and August daily 10:00 A.M. to 4:00 P.M. Adults $3.00. 119 Sandwich Street. Telephone: (508) 746–0012.

We also make our annual visit to **Pilgrim Hall Museum,** which calls itself "America's Museum of Pilgrim Possessions." Pilgrim Hall is one of New England's older local history museums—it was built in 1824 and enlarged over the years in the imperial version of Greek Revival. The handsome, if incongruous, Doric

Mayflower II, Plymouth, Massachusetts

portico is the work of the most prestigious architectural firm of the late nineteenth century, McKim, Mead & White. We think of Pilgrim Hall as the family attic for Plymouth. Among its venerable objects are the cradle in which Peregrine White (the first English child born in Plymouth) slept and the Bible of Governor William Bradford, printed in Geneva in 1592. Many of the Pilgrim artifacts are extremely modest items salvaged from what were probably garbage dumps—a tankard, a razor, some broken pottery—but they remind us with a certain poignancy the Pilgrims were ordinary, vulnerable humans clinging to a stony life at the edge of the wilderness. Open daily 9:30 A.M. to 4:30 P.M. Adults $5.00. 75 Court Street. Telephone: (508) 746–1620.

This tour of the Mid Coast bypasses the principally residential towns of Boston's South Shore, all of which boast rich histories but are oriented primarily to the needs and interests of residents. And while Greater Boston clearly belongs geographically with the Mid Coast, it is so large and dense that it resides in a separate chapter. So, after a geographic hiatus of more than fifty miles, this tour resumes on Boston's North Shore. The most direct route to the first stop, Marblehead, is to follow Route 1A north from Logan International Airport in East Boston, taking the right-hand fork in Swampscott onto Route 129 toward Marblehead.

The North Shore of Massachusetts

Marblehead, Massachusetts

Marblehead's self-bestowed title as the "Yachting Capital of America" contrasts mightily with the community's origins. It was settled in 1629 as a plantation of Salem by fishermen who hailed from Cornwall and the Channel Islands. Knobs, shelves, and even cliffs of granite protrude through the soil, even in the village center, as Marblehead's geology closely resembles the hard rock of neighboring Cape Ann. The Old Town still preserves narrow, winding streets of the seventeenth and eighteenth centuries that are fun to follow down to the harbor, where everything in Marblehead leads. The harbor is broad and deep, nestled between the granite ledges of the mainland and the solid granite mass of Marblehead Neck (which is largely a wildlife sanctuary today). Deep anchorages and a rocky bottom make Marblehead ideal for small boats, and local wealth sees to it that these boats are pleasure yachts rather than fishing trawlers. Marblehead has done a good job of preserving its pre-Colonial character, with several structures serving as museums. Since Boston is so close and Salem even closer, Marblehead's shops have evolved as selective boutiques.

Visitors usually start at **Abbot Hall** on Washington Street, where the massive original of the widely reproduced painting, ***The Spirit of '76,*** hangs in the Reading Room. General John Devereux bought the painting from the artist Archibald M. Willard after it had been displayed at the Centennial in Philadelphia in 1876. Devereux's son served as the model for the young boy with the drums and, although he then lived in Cleveland, Devereux donated it to his native town of Marblehead. Willard knew a marketable idea when he saw it, and painted many copies of the same patriotic image. Marblehead, however, has the original, and even if it is not a great work of art, the image has become a revered icon of popular culture. The same room houses some additional local history paintings that are far more crudely executed, yet capture more of the spirit of Marblehead. We're especially fond of a work by folk artist John O. J. Frost that depicts the Massachusetts Indians selling title to Marblehead to the English settlers—more than thirty years after they had settled.

Born in 1852, Marblehead native Frost went to sea aboard a fishing schooner as a young man and also worked as a carpenter, shoemaker, and restaurateur. In 1922, when he was 70 years old, Frost began to paint and carve. He had no formal training and did not consider himself an artist, but he wanted to record Marblehead history and folk traditions and proceeded to do so until his death in 1928. In only six years, he produced 130 paintings of scenes from Marblehead's past, scenes from his early years at sea, and forty carvings of ships, buildings, birds, and fish.

Frost's work was not much appreciated during his lifetime, but art historians now regard him as a naive artist with a lot of talent and feel for his subject. The **Marblehead Historical Society** has a treasure trove of Frost's work, donated by his son, and recently installed in a gallery on the second floor. The naive scenes of the town and the harbor have a beguiling charm, while also relaying a great deal of schematic information about how the community functioned in different eras. But we'd argue that Frost saved his real passion for painting the hard life of fishermen. You can almost feel the halibut fisherman's sore hands as he pulls on his dory. Other works show the town covered with flats to dry codfish and an attempted rescue of a fisherman ("William Chambers lost overboard"). Frost's masterpiece is a large painting of a gale in 1846 that is legendary among fishing communities on the North Shore. As Frost records in his uncertain script, "11 vessels lost, 65 men—43 widows—155 fatherless children. And the Sea Gave Up the Dead wich [sic] were in it." Open Monday through Saturday 10:00 A.M. to 4:00 P.M. Adults $2.00. The Historical Society is at 170 Washington Street. Telephone: (781) 631–1768.

Not everyone in Marblehead was involved in the hard life of fishing. Even before the American Revolution, the town also had a merchant class of traders. The Marblehead Historical Society also maintains the **home of Colonel Jeremiah Lee,** a leader of Marblehead commerce, one of the wealthiest men in the Colonies, and an active patriot. His Georgian mansion was built in 1768, but he died in 1775. Mrs. Lee remained in the house until 1789, the year in which she held a reception for President George Washington. After her death, the home served as a bank for more than a century until the historical society bought it in 1909. It is filled with period furniture and portraits of early residents. The sixteen-foot-wide entrance hall and drawing room feature English wallpaper handpainted with tempera to depict classical ruins and attest to Lee's wealth and his willingness to spend to make a good impression. Open mid-May to mid-October Monday through Saturday 10:00 A.M. to 4:00 P.M. and Sunday 1:00 to 4:00 P.M. Adults $4.00. 161 Washington Street. Telephone: (781) 631–1069.

Much as we enjoy guided tours of historic houses, we always wish we could wander around on our own—which is exactly what you can do at the **King Hooper Mansion.** Built in 1745 and purchased by the Marblehead Art Association in the 1930s, the mansion's large rooms with high ceilings make it a surprisingly good spot to hang works by the members of the association. Once the home of many sea captains, Marblehead is now rife with artists. Admission to the mansion is free. It is located less than a block from the Lee Mansion at 8 Hooper Street. Telephone: (781) 631–2608.

From the winding streets of Old Town, you can walk along the harbor on Front Street to **Fort Sewall Park.** The simple earth embankment fort here at the mouth of the harbor was built in 1742 to protect the town and harbor from the French. During the Revolution, it protected Marblehead from the British. The town was always a thorn in the British side: When the governor closed the port of Boston in 1774, Marblehead simply extended shipping privileges to Boston merchants. It's worth the short walk to appreciate its strategic location as well as the striking views of the harbor. The point on which the fort sits is a popular place to view sailing regattas.

Marblehead remained small and decorous because the next town over, Salem, quickly overwhelmed it as a mercantile center. Route 114 connects the two communities.

Salem, Massachusetts

Even in the part of New England where Euro-American settlement began, Salem has forgotten more history than other towns can remember. Although it is defined in the popular imagination by the witchcraft trials of the 1690s, Salem's real story has always been its role on the sea rather than its shameful period of religious hysteria. Founded in 1626 as a Puritan farming community, Salem (a shortened form of "Jerusalem") soon followed the familiar path of eking its living from fishing. By the end of the seventeenth century, the town had switched to coastal trade, and before the eighteenth century was out, Salem's East India men were carrying the new American flag into the farthest ports of the world. Although Salem's "fat, ugly little ships" (as they were described, even at the time) lacked the clean lines and billowing grace of the clippers that followed them by a half century, the stolid barks plodded around the globe to bring home pepper from Sumatra, cottons from India, and tea from China. So ubiquitous were Salem's ships that some traders thought the town was a sovereign nation: the "Venice of the New World."

We confess that the tales of farflung trade and adventure fascinate us. Matched only by the Penobscot Marine Museum in Searsport, Maine (see "North Coast"), the **Salem National Historic Site** does a superb job of capturing the excitement of sailing out into the unknown to bring back the riches of distant ports. And while Searsport's glories are represented only by the mansions that outlived their sea captain owners, Salem has preserved much of the infrastructure of its trading heyday. As one National Park Service ranger told us, "If it were economical, we have everything here to start it all up again tomorrow." He was exaggerating a bit, of course, but the wharves and custom house and even some of the warehouses remain. If you squint enough to make the trappings of modernity fade, you can almost hear the stevedores cursing as they roll barrels of cargo down the planks. The facilities and related sites of Salem's trading days are so extensive that the park rangers lead a variety of different tours. Adults $3.00. Check at the Orientation Center at 193 Derby Street. Open daily 9:00 A.M. to 5:00 P.M. Telephone: (978) 740–1660.

Derby Street itself is the nerve center of the historic maritime trade. From the intersection of Orange and Derby Streets, the turf and dirt of **Derby Wharf** juts several hundred feet into Salem harbor. Two hundred years ago, this wharf was covered with warehouses and lined with broad-beamed ships engaged in trade "to the farthest point of the rich East." To evoke that long-ago time, the National Park Service commissioned a full-size replica of the 1797 **East Indiaman merchant ship *Friendship,*** which was completed in 1998 and is now berthed at Derby Wharf. Built by Scarano Boat Building Inc. of the Port of Albany, New York, she is the largest wooden, Coast-Guard-certified sailing vessel to be built in this region in the twentieth century. *Friendship* is 104 feet on deck, with an overall sparred length of 171 feet. Many of the original ship's logs, three paintings, and a model built by the ship's carpenter still exist and are on display at the Peabody Essex Museum. The original 342-ton *Friendship* made sixteen voyages around the world before she was captured by the British in the War of 1812. No one knows her fate—refitted and renamed as a war ship or simply gutted and sunk.

The street and the wharf are named for the man who started it all—Salem Yankee Elias Hasket Derby. Britain banned American vessels from British ports (including the key ports of the Caribbean) after the Revolution, so Derby cast further afield. In 1785, his *Grand Turk* cleared Salem harbor to sail around the Cape of Good Hope to Canton, becoming one of the first American ships to enter a Chinese port. Soon Derby (who never went to sea himself), the Crowninshields, and Salem's other shipping families dominated the East India trade routes. At his death in 1799, Derby had become America's first millionaire and Salem was the richest town per capita in the United States.

Some of the Park Service tours enter **Derby's house,** which sits across the street from his wharf. Built in 1762, it is the oldest brick domicile still standing in Salem. It was a wedding gift and shows the merchant and his family on the way up. The kitchen is filled with brass from Holland, iron from Russia, Cantonese china, Madeira wine, and exotic fruits and spices. The eighteenth-century garden behind the house includes exotic plants that Derby instructed his captains to bring back from every voyage.

Other Park Service tours take in the **Custom House**—that reminder of the Federal government that sits in every port. In the late eighteenth century, Salem supplied one dollar of every eight that the government collected. Dating from 1819, the magisterial building topped with the federal eagle commands the harbor. Its most famous employee, Nathaniel Hawthorne, didn't occupy his first-floor office until 1846 to 1849, when he was "surveyor of the port" and Salem shipping was already in eclipse, overshadowed by the larger and faster ships that put in at Boston's deeper harbor.

When the good times rolled, Salem's sailors and traders could not have imagined that their rule of the sea would be so brief. Nonetheless, they created a series of institutions to preserve their legacy. If there's one club we wish we could have belonged to, it is the East India Marine Society, which limited membership to those who had sailed around Cape Horn or the Cape of Good Hope. We can only imagine the stories, when members sat around a fire and swapped tales. Members were requested to bring home curiosities from foreign lands, and those curios formed the basis for the collections of the **Peabody Museum,** founded in 1799 and the oldest continuously operating museum in the United States. The Peabody's giant building on Essex Street houses the most comprehensive collection of Asian export art in the world, as well as the leading collection of marine art in the United States. Altogether, the collection has more than 100,000 objects from Japan, China, Korea, India, Africa, and the Pacific islands.

In 1992, the Peabody Museum merged with the Essex Institute, just a block down the street, to form the **Peabody Essex Museum.** The **Essex Institute** counters the Peabody's global view with a domestic vision of life in Essex county. Its walls are lined with portraits of Salem's prominent citizens and its galleries brim with Salem's fine cabinetry of the seventeenth and eighteenth centuries. Three buildings in the garden behind the main museum trace Salem history—a 1684 medieval-style house, the 1727 Crowninshield-Bentley House, and the 1804–05 Gardner-Pingree

House, a brick mansion built for a rich merchant. This Federal masterpiece is considered one of the best works by Salem's master architect Samuel McIntire. Among them, the three homes sketch Salem's rising fortunes through the portraiture of architecture: a dark medieval cottage, a rationalist Georgian home for the king of the black pepper trade, and a smugly splendid declaration of Federal-era wealth.

The Peabody Essex Museum is located in East India Square, with the Plummer Hall (the Essex Institute collections) at 132 Essex Street and East India Hall (the Peabody collections) at 162 Essex Street, the corner of Liberty Street. Open Memorial Day through October Monday through Saturday 10:00 A.M. to 5:00 P.M., Sunday noon to 5:00 P.M.; November 1 to Memorial Day closed Monday. Adults $8.50. Wheelchair accessible. Telephone: (978) 745–9500.

Architecture buffs will want to stroll the length of **Chestnut Street,** a one-way street often cited as America's most beautiful. It is lined with elegant Federal mansions either designed by or inspired by Samuel McIntire and built in the early nineteenth century by prosperous merchants and sea captains. The street begins three blocks west of Old Town Hall.

Not far from the Peabody Essex Museum is the nine-acre **Salem Common,** which rivals any in New England with its central bandstand, nineteenth-century cast-iron fence, and surrounding trees. Early spring—before the trees fully leaf out and obscure the view—is the best time to get a good look at the beautiful houses that surround the common. The houses at 74, 82, and 92 Washington Street East are all associated with McIntire.

It is also an easy stroll to the **House of Seven Gables,** which has beautiful gardens facing the sea. The building inspired Nathaniel Hawthorne's second novel. (Hawthorne turned to writing full-time when he lost his job at the Customs House with a change in political administrations. His first novel, *The Scarlet Letter,* was an immediate commercial and literary success.) Originally constructed in 1688, the House of Seven Gables was added onto several times. It was owned by Hawthorne's second cousin Susannah Ingersoll, and Hawthorne visited often, drawn by the

house's deep sense of history. Also on the grounds is the modest house where Hawthorne was born and lived until his father died when Nathaniel was just four years old. The House of Seven Gables is located at 54 Turner Street. Open July through October daily 9:30 A.M. to 6:00 P.M., November through June daily 10:00 A.M. to 4:30 P.M. Adults $6.00. Combination tickets available with Salem 1630: Pioneer Village (see "Staying There"). Wheelchair accessible. Telephone: (978) 744–0991.

Hawthorne brooded over Salem's witch trial history, in which an ancestor, Judge John Hathorne, was an enthusiastic participant. He even theorized that as Hathorne's descendant, he was heir to the guilt for a sin against God and against humanity. During the 1692 witch hysteria that swept the town, more than 150 townspeople were imprisoned and twenty were executed. Salem continues to have an ambivalent attitude toward this dark blot on its history. Much of the town's promotional material focuses on more positive things like the Far East trade, yet a certain quotient of the town embraces the witch association with a full-month of events in October (see "Staying There"). In recent years, the Halloween imagery has been transfigured through New Age cant to produce a year-round industry devoted to the practice and commerce of Wicca, which purports to be a rebirth of pre-Christian European paganism. Unfortunately, it's hard to separate the palm readers and crystal gazers from the sincere practitioners of environmentally based spiritualism.

We think the best public acknowledgement and atonement for this brief period of Salem's history is the **Salem Witch Trial Memorial,** which was erected in 1992 on the occasion of the 300th anniversary. The memorial is on New Liberty Street next to the old cemetery. It's simple, tasteful, and reflective. Several other attractions are related to the Witch Trials. (See "Staying There.")

From downtown Salem, the easiest way to continue exploring the Mid Coast communities of Boston's North Shore is to cross the bridge into Beverly on Route 1A and watch carefully for signs pointing to the right for Route 127, also known as the Old Salem Trail. Most of the heavy traffic is on the swifter, inland Route 128, leaving this modest roadway relatively uncongested as it cuts through beautiful countryside with farms and fields on one side and oceanfront homes on the other. Take advantage of small roads on the seaward side—many lead to scenes made famous in the paintings of Gloucester's premier marine painter, Fitz Hugh Lane. Route 127 goes through the one-time agricultural villages of Pride's Crossing and Beverly Farms (now on Boston's commuter rail) as well as the wealthy village of Manchester-by-the-Sea. Watch for signs a few miles north for the turnout to sweet little Magnolia, an erstwhile summer village now occupied all year. The Magnolia turnout rejoins Route 127 just outside Gloucester harbor.

Gloucester, Massachusetts

Gloucester and neighboring Rockport occupy the entire peninsula of Cape Ann, a geological district distinct in New England as the oldest granite formation (c. one billion years) not ground up, folded, or metamorphosed into some other formation. Cape Ann is just about solid granite from the bluffs overlooking the Annisquam River to the quarries of Halibut State Park. Fractured when the collision of continents lifted it from beneath the sediments, Cape Ann has been scoured clean of all but its hardest rock by millennia of erosion.

The larger of the two communities, Gloucester, has the distinction of being both America's oldest fishing port and the site of America's oldest continuously operating art colony. In 1623, Plymouth fishermen set up a temporary camp where they could quickly reach the rich fishing grounds of Stellwagen Bank and where they had good exposures to dry their fish on flats. The site of that Pilgrim settlement is now **Stage Fort Park,** where the Visitors Welcoming Center is located today. With broad playing fields, seaside walking trails, and a two good swimming beaches, the park is also a great place for a picnic.

Later that same year, the Pilgrim fishermen got competition, as Puritan immigrants from Dorchester and Gloucester, England, set up a permanent settlement. The banks at the mouth of Massachusetts Bay must have seemed inexhaustible, and Gloucester jutted out toward them like a granite jaw. Moreover, its protected harbor

let fishermen haul their catch and beat it back to shore before they were caught in a storm. This fishing prowess led Gloucestermen to refine their boats as well, launching the world's first two-masted schooner in 1713 and a large version of the same vessel a few decades later. The superior speed and seaworthiness of these boats was a direct response to the declining hauls from Stellwagen Bank—at the helm of a schooner, a Gloucester fishing crew could easily reach the Grand Banks off Nova Scotia and Newfoundland and bring home a catch fresh enough to sell.

Gloucester led North America as the most productive fishing port in the nineteenth century, and fishing continued as the main source of employment throughout much of the twentieth century. You are reminded of the central place of fishing in the lives and psyche of the community as you continue into town from Stage Fort Park on Stacy Boulevard, following the edge of the harbor. The **"Man at the Wheel"** statue of a fisherman was erected by the citizens of Gloucester in 1923, the town's 300th anniversary. It was created by Leonard Craske in his studio on the pier on Rocky Neck. On the occasion of its 375th anniversary in 1998, Gloucester tallied up the records and found that about 10,000 Gloucester fishermen have been lost since the first camps were set up—an average of one man every thirteen days for 375 years. The worst year was 1879, when 249 Gloucester fishermen were lost at sea.

To appreciate the interplay of the arts and the fishing industry, continue into town on Stacy Boulevard, which becomes Rogers Street and park at the lot near **Fitz Hugh Lane Park.** Gloucester native Lane's granite house sits up on a granite outcrop with a commanding view of the working harbor front and the town, but is not open for visitors. The first floor contains the offices of Gloucester Adventure, a non-profit organization that is restoring the dory fishing schooner *Adventure,* which was built in 1926 in Essex and landed nearly $4 million in cod and halibut. When her fishing career ended in the early 1950s, she was the last American dory fishing trawler in the Atlantic. Hours for tours of the National Historical Landmark vessel *Adventure,* which berths at Harbor Loop at the Gloucester Marine Railways, are somewhat irregular due to the restoration work. Telephone: (978) 281–8079.

A **statue of Lane** sits beside the house, showing the master painter engaged in one of his favorite activities: watching boats in the harbor. Lane was a master of light and delighted in the finest details of sailing vessels, carefully delineating each line of a complicated rigging (his father was a sail maker). He especially liked to paint sunset scenes of the harbor from the top floor studio in his home—which is all the more amazing considering that he was left crippled, probably by polio, as a child and had to crawl up the steps to the third-floor studio.

An extraordinary collection of Lane's work is displayed at the **Cape Ann Historical Museum,** reached by following the red line in the road (Gloucester's version of Boston's Freedom Trail). The museum has the world's largest collection of paintings by Lane, one of the founding fathers of nineteenth-century "luminist" painting and one of the greatest marine painters who ever lived. Lane's paintings are on view in spacious galleries, interspersed with beautiful furniture. The galleries also hold works by some of the other artists who were drawn to Gloucester over the years, including Winslow Homer, Maurice Prendergast, and Milton Avery. Nor does the museum neglect other aspects of Gloucester's livelihood and heritage. Photographs and artifacts chart the changes in the fishing industry and one exhibition delineates the important granite quarrying industry that flourished in the late nineteenth and early twentieth centuries.

The **Rocky Neck Art Colony,** designated the oldest working artists' colony in America by the Smithsonian Institution, sits directly across from the main wharves on a knob of land that juts out into the middle of Gloucester harbor, providing the artists with nearly 360 degrees of sky and water. The **Harbor Water Shuttle,** which leaves from Harbor Loop at the foot of the Fitz Hugh Lane House, is a good way to get there without having to worry about the difficulties of driving the narrow streets and the even greater difficulty of finding parking. It runs from 11:00 A.M. to 5:00 P.M. in season. Adults $2.00. Rocky Neck can be fun to explore on foot, as it retains a funky, improvisational quality. The studios are hardly the "shacks" that some of the local tourist hype sug-

gests, but painters are frequently out on their decks or in their yards or standing beside the road with palette and brush in hand, canvas on the easel before them. They might also be holding down a table at any of several cafes or restaurants in the area.

If Gloucester did not already have enough distinctions, it also calls itself the "whale watching capital of the east coast" because it is so close to the major feeding grounds of Jefferys Ledge and Stellwagen Bank National Marine Sanctuary, an undersea plateau about 15 miles southeast of Cape Ann. If you are planning to take a whale watch cruise on the New England coast, Gloucester is one of the best places to take it. Most of the whales sighted in this area are baleen whales—fifty-foot humpback whales, seventy-foot finback whales (the second largest whale on earth), smaller minke whales, pilot whales, sei whales, white-sided dolphins, and—on occasion—the endangered northern right whale. (See "Staying There.")

Rockport, Massachusetts

Rockport occupies Cape Ann's northern tip. Lacking as good a harbor as Gloucester, it was a

"Man at the Wheel" statue, Gloucester, Massachusetts

THEY THAT GO DOWN TO THE SEA IN SHIPS
1623 ~ 1923

low-key fishing village until artists discovered it shortly after the Civil War. Even today, you'll see a few inshore fishing boats in the harbor, but you're more likely to see artists and photographers standing on the end of Tuna Wharf to make an image of **"Motif No. 1,"** perhaps the most popular sight on Cape Ann. Since no one could anticipate that the dusky red story-and-a-half fish shack at the end of Bradley Wharf was going to become an icon, no one bothered to note when it was built—theories now suggest the 1840s, 1860s, or 1884. What is known is that the original was destroyed in the Blizzard of 1978 and was rebuilt in the traditional board-and-batten style and dedicated on November 26, 1978. At that time, the *New York Times* observed that Motif No. 1 had been painted at least 10,000 times, with various versions displayed in Disney World,

"Motif #1," Rockport, Massachusetts

Disneyland, and in eastern Europe, South America, and Australia.

You'll probably see more than a few images of it yourself as you explore the art galleries along Beach and Main Streets near the harbor. A good place to begin looking is at the **Rockport Art Association,** which was founded in 1921 as an artists cooperative and continues to admit members based on a juried evaluation of their work. The Association is housed in an old tavern and barn dating back to the mid-1700s—making for interesting spaces in which to view members' work. On Tuesday and Thursday evenings from June through early September, artists give demonstrations of various techniques. Admission to the demonstrations is $4.00; otherwise the galleries are free. Open Monday through Saturday 10:00 A.M. to 5:00 P.M., Sunday noon to 5:00 P.M. The Rockport Art Association is located at 12 Main Street. Telephone: (978) 546–6604.

The densest concentration of galleries, boutiques, eateries, and souvenir shops is found on **Bearskin Neck,** a rocky peninsula that forms the north side of Rockport harbor. Its name derives from a bear stranded there by the tide and captured in the early days of Rockport settlement. In the ensuing years, the tidal strait has been filled, giving the village a fully protected harbor.

As you leave Rockport on Route 127, you get a good sense of the granite foundation of Cape Ann and of the region's once active quarry industry by following the road north to **Halibut Point State Park,** a fifty-four-acre park at the northernmost tip of the peninsula. The reservation has broad picnic areas as well as several walking trails through woodlands and along the ocean. The most interesting self-guided trail explores the area around a quarry that last saw active excavation in 1929. The view over the water-filled quarry to Ipswich Bay is stunning and perfectly situated for magnificent sunsets, if the season is right. (Because the park closes at 8:00 P.M. and cars in the lot after that time may be towed, sunset viewing is impractical during June, July, and most of August.) But if you're in the area at the right time and love sunsets, it's worth the trip out to the park. Cape Ann's geography makes it one of the few places in the world where you can watch the sun rise and set over the ocean. Go to **Good Harbor Beach** on the east side of Gloucester for sunrise and to **Plum Cove Beach** in the Lanesville section of Gloucester for sunset.

After circling Cape Ann on Route 127, follow Route 128 south for two exits to Route 133, which will lead you west to the river village of Essex.

Essex, Massachusetts

Essex is one of the prettiest spots around, stretching out along a sinuous tidal river lined with high marsh grasses. As if that weren't enough reason to visit, the town also claims to have more antiques shops within a square mile than anywhere else in New England. We haven't tested this hypothesis, but we do know that the seven-tenths of a mile stretch of Main Street is lined with old homes that now house antiques shops, making it easy to leave your car and stroll the length.

Essex also has a three-century tradition of shipbuilding and the **Essex Shipbuilding Museum** recalls the days when fifteen shipyards produced more than fifty vessels a year and Essex was one of the continent's major builders of fishing schooners. The museum has dioramas, full-scale construction displays, hands-on shipbuilding exhibits, photographs, antique tools, and twenty models. Its prize exhibit is the dry-docked hull of the 1927 schooner, *Evelina M. Goulart,* one of only five surviving Essex-built fishing schooners. Part of the museum is a working riverfront shipyard. As we write, the museum staff is working on a reproduction of a Chebacco boat, a type of craft built and used in these waters in the late 1700s and early 1800s. Open during the summer Monday through Friday 10:00 A.M. to 5:00 P.M., Sunday 1:00 to 5:00 P.M. Call for off-season hours. Adults $5.00. The museum is spread between two sites within walking distance of each other at 28 and 66 Main Street. Telephone: (978) 768–7541.

Essex River Basin Adventures, also located on the museum property, offers guided kayak tours for novice and experienced paddlers through the marshes, estuaries, and saltwater creeks around Essex. Choices include three-hour, day-long, sunset, and moonlight trips. Prices begin at $35. Reservations necessary. Telephone: (978) 768–3722 or (800) KAYAK04.

The marine estuary ecology is so striking in

Marshes, Essex, Massachusetts

Essex that it's worth getting out on the water. If kayaking is not your pleasure, the **Essex River Queen** offers scenic cruises for a close look at salt marshes, islands, barrier beaches, sand dunes, Crane Beach, Hog Island, and site of the movie *The Crucible.* Mosquitoes and flies thrive in marshes, but when the insect population gets to be too prolific, the boat is covered with protective screens. Cruises depart from the Essex Marina from April through October. Adults $15. Telephone: (978) 768–6981.

Continue following Route 133 north toward Ipswich, watching on the right for Northgate Road, which connects to Argilla Road. A right turn here delivers you to the naturalist's crown jewel in Ipswich.

Ipswich, Massachusetts

The Trustees of Reservations owns and manages much of the five miles of beaches and acres of dunes and marshes for which Ipswich is justly famous—all part of the turn-of-the-century, 2,000-acre estate of Chicago industrialist Richard T. Crane. **Crane's 59-room mansion** sits atop a hill and overlooks a spruce-lined *grand allée* with a sweeping view down to the sea. The house is open for guided tours from late May through early October on Wednesday and Thursday 10:00 A.M. to 4:00 P.M. Adults $7.00. Some of the rooms were shipped piece-by-piece from England, and the bathrooms have luxurious Italian marble and

sterling silver fixtures manufactured by the Crane Company. But one of the best ways to enjoy the site, known as **Castle Hill,** is to picnic on the lawn and enjoy a concert performed on the back patio. You get your chance on Thursday evenings from early July to late August. For concert evenings, parking on the grounds is $8.00; otherwise $5.00. 290 Argilla Road. Telephone: (978) 356–4351.

From Memorial Day to Columbus Day, tours are also available to the 680-acre **Crane Wildlife Refuge,** which includes Hog and Long Islands. The *Osprey* crosses the Castle Neck River, and, once ashore, visitors tour the islands from a tractor-drawn wagon. More than 180 species of birds—from herons to hawks, warblers to waterfowl—have been spotted here, and otter, mink, and deer live on both islands. Striped bass, flounder, and mackerel feed in the surrounding waters. The tour also passes the exterior of the 250-year-old Choate family homestead as well as the "Proctor" house built for the recent filming of *The Crucible.* The tour goes up to the 177-foot peak in the middle of Hog Island for panoramic views of Castle Neck and Ipswich Bay, the Isles of Shoals in New Hampshire and (when the weather is very clear) Mount Agamenticus in Wells, Maine. Adults $12. Telephone: (978) 356–4351.

But probably what most people enjoy of the Crane Estate is **Crane Beach**—four miles of sandy white barrier beach famous both for delightful swimming and spectacular viewing of shore birds. Parking $9.00 weekdays, $15.00 weekends and holidays.

North of Ipswich center the road splits between Route 133 and Route 1A. Route 133 connects to I–95 north, where two exits later you can enter Newburyport via historic Route 113. Route 1A meanders through the villages of Rowley, Newbury Old Town, and Newbury before entering Newburyport from the opposite direction on High Street.

Newburyport, Massachusetts

We recommend following I–95 to Route 113 because this end of High Street presents a march of big, blocky white **mansions of the ship own-**

ers who made and lost fortunes in the maritime trade—one of the most distinguished survivals of Federal architecture in the nation. These square three-storied buildings with hip roofs, often crowned by cupolas, are marvels of the carpenter's trade. The severity of their lines is relieved by cornices, doorways, and window treatments executed by men who had learned their craft as shipwrights in Newburyport's famous yards.

Newburyport lies at the mouth of the Merrimack River at the throat of a harbor well sheltered at its mouth by barrier beaches. Between 1681 and 1741, Newburyport shipyards launched 107 ships, most of them built with tall timbers floated down on the Merrimack from central New Hampshire. Like so many other New England ports, Newburyport was shut down during the Revolution. During the opening years of the nineteenth century the shipowners and sea captains turned to privateering, but then sat at anchor again from the Embargo of 1807 through the War of 1812. But Newburyport enjoyed another brief period of glory in the clipper ship era. After apprenticing in New York, Nova Scotia ship designer Donald McKay came to Newburyport and built three clipper ships that established his reputation and reinvigorated the town's trade with the Far East.

In contrast to white clapboard High Street, the **downtown area,** along the harbor with all the shops and boutiques so pleasing to visitors, is constructed almost entirely of red brick. An 1811 fire destroyed most of downtown Newburyport, allowing the town to be rebuilt using the bricks that had served as ballast in ships returning from Asia light of cargo. The 1835 Custom House, by contrast, was built in granite from Cape Ann. Vessels from all over the world registered their cargoes here—wine from Madeira, gunpowder from Saint Petersburg, molasses and sugar from Guadeloupe, silk from Bilbao, Spain. The Custom House is now the **Custom House Maritime Museum** full of artifacts from Newburyport's glory years at sea. Open Monday to Saturday 10:00 A.M. to 4:00 P.M. (closed November through May on Wednesday afternoons) and Sunday 1:00 to 4:00 P.M. Adults $5.00. 25 Water Street. Telephone: (978) 462–8681.

Personal Narrative:
Bird Watching at Plum Island

The long barrier island called Plum Island stretches southward from the mouth of the Merrimack River in Newburyport through parts of Rowley and Ipswich. Except for Town Beach at the northeast tip, almost the entire island is devoted to the **Parker River National Wildlife Refuge,** which has been called one of the top ten birdwatching sanctuaries in the United States. It's not surprising that its 4,662 acres of sand beach and dunes, bogs, tidal marshes, and small freshwater ponds and springs support more than 800 species of birds, plants, and animals.

We've been wanting to try our hand at birdwatching and we figure that in such a rich spot we can't fail to have some luck. To improve our chances, we decide to visit in the spring—when the birds are plentiful during their spring migration, but mosquitoes and other insects are not as pesky as they will become during warmer months. Besides, it's a great excuse to get out and enjoy the marshes as the yellow grasses are beginning to green up, the bayberry shrubs are leafing out, and the fresh spring winds are blowing in from offshore.

The refuge is just a short distance from the

Blue heron

Historic Newburyport District. Coming from Boston we follow High Street and turn left onto Rolfe's Lane, where signs direct us out the Plum Island Turnpike (which should be called the "Plum Island Secondary Road"). The Refuge is open daily from sunrise to sunset, parking is $5.00 per car, $2.00 for bikes or persons on foot. Telephone: (978) 465–5753.

We stop first at the Information Center to pick up a map of the reservation and a bird checklist from a weatherproof box. We are in luck, because the visitors center is staffed by two volunteers. One tells us that about seventy species nest in or near the refuge, and 302 different species are seen each year. (True exotics or, in birders' terms, "accidentals" add another thirty-nine to the list of birds sighted here since 1975.)

Before heading into the refuge, we walk to the crest of the dunes for a view of the beach, which is a favored nesting area for the piping plover, a bird remarkable more for its rarity than for its appearance. Without a bird identification guide and good binoculars, we think it would be almost impossible to tell the pipers from the black-bellied and semipalmated plovers that share their habitat.

The piping plovers also share their nesting habitat with the least tern and since both birds are on the federal list of endangered species, all six and one-half miles of beach in the refuge are closed beginning April 1. (Parts of the beach not used by the nesting birds begin to open in July and usually all the beach areas are open by late August.)

We're happy to give the terns and plovers their privacy. There are plenty of other chances to see even more impressive birds in the refuge and lots of other interesting habitats to explore. We leave the parking lot at the information center and drive down to Parking Lot 4 at the **Hellcat Swamp Trail.** With such a name, we don't know what to expect, but the trail turns out to be an extraordinary boardwalk through wooded wetlands at the edge of a tidal marsh. This is prime territory for spotting the migrating warblers and vireos, so we walk slowly and

quietly looking for the red-eyed vireo, the yellow warbler, the common yellowthroat, and the American redstart—all of which nest here. The season is early for nesters, but we do see some warblers that we have trouble identifying.

The area is also popular with blackpoll warblers and black-and-white warblers. The warblers live up to their names as the males stake out territory with the ornithological equivalent of chest-thumping. When we hear birdsong, we look up about two-thirds of the way up the tree canopy—until we spot the singer. Then we search lower in the canopy for the female—she looks the same, but with the contrast and color turned down.

On our way back to the parking lot, we turn right to reach the dike separating marshes from open water. The marsh grasses are a bright, almost iridescent green, but we hardly notice them as we stop and quietly observe a group of herons and egrets, some of the reservation's most striking birds. These long-legged hunters stand and wait, stand and wait—and then lunge for fish, frogs, newts, or salamanders. During the morning hours, this is a popular area for great blue herons, green herons, and snowy egrets (in descending order of size). An observation tower rises at one end of the dike, and when we climb up to the top level, we can see the full extent of the marshes, and catch views of northern harriers cruising just above the grasses like low-flying carpet bombers. Soaring in the distance over the ocean is an osprey.

Although the reservation road soon becomes a rutted path, we continue to Lot 6 to get a look at one of the broad barrier beaches that sometimes remains open during plover nesting season. (Officially, it's always closed from April into July, but when we ask back at the visitors center, the volunteers explain that beaches without nesting plovers are sometimes opened provisionally.) Looking down from the crest of the dunes we see plovers and sanderlings skittering along the wet sand. Overhead, gulls and terns soar on the thermals and cormorants plunge into the sea.

Staying There

Southeastern Massachusetts

New Bedford, Massachusetts

For information contact New Bedford Office of Tourism, Wharfinger Building, Pier #3, New Bedford, MA 02740. Telephone: (508) 979–1745.

FOOD

Antonio's. 267 Coggeshall Street. Telephone: (508) 990–3636. Outside the historic district tourist area, this neighborhood restaurant is a good place to sample Portuguese specialties. Lunch and dinner. Moderate to expensive.

Candleworks Restaurant. 72 North Water Street. Telephone: (508) 997–1294. The thick stone walls and big wooden beams in the ceiling hint at the history of this building, which was built in 1810 as a factory for the production of spermaceti candles from whale oil. One of New Bedford's "fancy" restaurants, it features a traditional New England menu with some New American fillips. Indoor tables are set with comfortable wing chairs, and there's an airy enclosed porch and cafe tables outside for nice weather. Lunch and dinner. Moderate.

Freestone's. 41 William Street. Telephone: (508) 993–7477. Located in a striking brownstone bank building from the late nineteenth century, Freestone's was a pioneer in the redevelopment of New Bedford's historic district. The menu features grill specialties, seafood, and a good range of choices for vegetarians. Lunch and dinner. Moderate.

ACTIVITIES

Cruises to Cuttyhunk Island. Only about an hour from New Bedford, the island was once the home of whaling fleet pilots. Now it's known for its beaches, birds and wildlife, and striped bass fishing in Vineyard Sound. Cruises aboard the M/V *Alert* allow several hours for exploring the island. Fisherman's Wharf, Pier 3. Adults $16 roundtrip. Telephone: (508) 992–1432.

Ferry to Martha's Vineyard. The Cape Islands Express Line ferry *Schamonchi* takes passengers and bicycles from New Bedford harbor through the Elizabeth Islands and Woods Hole Passage to Vineyard Haven Harbor in an hour and a half. Round trip adults $17. Bicycles one-way $2.50. Telephone: (508) 997–1688.

TOURS

National Park. Volunteers guide daily tours of New Bedford Whaling National Historic Park. Call for schedule. Visitor Center is at 33 William Street. Telephone: (508) 991–6200.

FAIRS, FESTIVALS, AND EVENTS

Feast of St. John Clamboil. Madeira Field, the Portuguese Feast Grounds in New Bedford's North End, is the location for this late June event that features an old-fashioned New England clamboil and live music. Telephone: (508) 992–6911.

Feast of the Blessed Sacrament. This four-day festival in late July calls itself the "largest ethnic festival in New England" and features amusement rides, entertainment, and ethnic food vendors to celebrate the heritage and culture of Portuguese residents from the island of Madeira. Telephone: (508) 992–6911.

Seamen's Bethel. Special events during the year include a Herman Melville Memorial Service in early September, a Harvest of the Sea Fisherman's Thanksgiving Service in mid-November, and a Christmas Candlelight Service in mid-December. Telephone: (508) 992–3295.

The Massachusetts Archipelago

Martha's Vineyard

For information contact Martha's Vineyard Chamber of Commerce, Beach Road, P.O. Box 1698, Vineyard Haven, MA 02568. Telephone: (508) 693–0085.

GETTING TO MARTHA'S VINEYARD

Martha's Vineyard & Nantucket Steamship Authority makes auto and passenger crossings between Woods Hole and Vineyard Haven all year and between Woods Hole and Oak Bluffs in the summer. Summer service is also operated between Oak Bluffs and Nantucket. Telephone: (508) 477–8600. Other ferry lines offer summer passenger service between Oak Bluffs and Falmouth (telephone: 508–548–4800); Hyannis and Vineyard Haven (telephone: 508–778 –2600); and between New Bedford and Vineyard Haven (telephone: 508–997–1688).

GETTING AROUND

If you don't bring your own vehicle, you'll probably want to use public transportation to shuttle among the villages of Edgartown, Oak Bluffs, and Vineyard Haven, the so-called "down island" towns. The **Yellow Line Public Bus Service** runs every half hour during peak season in July and August and less frequently from the end of May through Columbus Day. Each fare is $1.50 and tickets can be purchased at the terminals at Church Street in Edgartown and the Steamship Authority in Vineyard Haven. Additional service to other parts of the island is less frequent. Call Island Transport for details. Telephone: (508) 693–1589.

TOURS

Martha's Vineyard Bus Tour. Island Transport also operates this narrated drive of two and one-half hours around the perimeter of the island in a pink and aqua school bus. The tour includes a half-hour stop at the Gay Head cliffs. Tours depart from the Steamship Authority Terminal in Vineyard Haven as each ferry arrives. $12.50. Telephone: (508) 693–1589.

Cinnamon Traveler Vineyard Tours. Offering two three-hour van tours targeted for travelers of color, Cinnamon Tours picks up passengers at inns, hotels, and guest houses, makes frequent photo stops, and provides a written tour narrative. The Easy Living Tour concentrates on lighthouses, gardens, local farms, and beautiful local landscapes, including the Gay Head cliffs (which they call by their Wampanoag name, Aquinnah). The All Island Cultural Tour hits all six towns on the Vineyard with special attention to points significant in African American history. It also includes a cultural presentation from the education department of the Wampanoag tribe. Adults $40. Telephone: (508) 696–9665.

ACTIVITIES

Martha's Vineyard Chamber Music Society concert series. The society sponsors ten concerts at varying locations across the island during the summer. Call for program information and locations. Telephone: (508) 696–8055.

FAIRS, FESTIVALS, AND EVENTS

Striped Bass and Bluefish Derby. This annual fishing competition, which takes place mid-September to mid-October, has been held since 1946. Telephone: (508) 693–0728.

Edgartown, Martha's Vineyard

LODGING

Colonial Inn. 38 North Water Street. Nicely central to the Edgartown waterfront, the Colonial Inn is done in Cape contemporary style. There is a wheelchair lift to the accessible rooms on the second floor; otherwise guests must use the stairs to reach the guest rooms, which are on the second, third, and fourth levels. A nice if small porch on the fourth floor front overlooks the harbor. Telephone: (508) 627–4711. Moderate to expensive with breakfast.

Edgartown Inn. 56 North Water Street. Built as a home for Captain Thomas Worth in 1798, it became a hostelry in the early nineteenth century. Nathaniel Hawthorne is said to have worked on *Twice Told Tales* here in 1822–23. The rooms at the inn all have private baths, while some in the Garden House and the Barn have shared baths. It's comfortable, homey, a little less glamorous than the competition, and a lot less expensive. Telephone: (508) 627–4794. Moderate to expensive with breakfast.

Harbor View Hotel. 131 North Water Street. At the end of the street near Lighthouse Beach, the Harbor View overlooks Edgartown Lighthouse and Chappaquiddick Island. Although the property has been an inn since 1891, the contemporary reconstruction feels more like a century later—which is not all bad. The hotel has 124 rooms and suites, and verandas with rocking chairs. Telephone: (508) 627–7000 or (800) 225–6005. Expensive to very expensive.

Point Way Inn. Main Street and Pease's Point Way. New owners in 1998 have transformed the Greek Revival inn with a beachy, sunny makeover that banishes the Puritan sea captains to the waterfront and lets a little bright light shine in. The landscaped garden area has a fresh and contemporary feel. Many of the fifteen rooms have fireplaces and all have private baths. Telephone: (508) 627–8633. Moderate to expensive.

Tuscany Inn. 22 North Water Street. With just eight rooms in this beautifully rescued Italianate Victorian home (and a delectable small restaurant downstairs), book ahead. Forget Yankee austerity—the place is awash with the earthy colors and warmth of Mediterranean Europe. Innkeeper Laura Sbrana also runs Tuscan cooking classes during the off-season. Telephone: (508) 627–5999. Moderate to very expensive with breakfast.

Food

Daggett House. 59 North Water Street. Telephone: (508) 627–4600. The contemporary American bistro style—grilled pork chop in a plum tomato marinade served with an apple-

orange-cranberry chutney, for example, or grilled mahi-mahi with a pineapple salsa—fits surprisingly well with the venerable pub dining room on the lower level of the circa-1730 building. (It's part of a three-building lodging complex.) Also known for its hearty breakfasts. Breakfast, lunch, and dinner. Expensive.

Edgartown Inn. 56 North Water Street. Telephone: (508) 627–4794. Big breakfasts are quite the thing in Edgartown, and Edgartown Inn claims to make the best on the island. It's certainly one of the heartiest: cakes and breads, pancakes and waffles, eggs with bacon. It's the only meal the inn serves, but they do a great job of it. Breakfast.

Seafood Shanty. 31 Dock Street. Telephone: (508) 627–8622. With a fine view right on one of the Edgartown harbor marinas, Seafood Shanty specializes in local lobster, scrod, clams, and mussels at dinner, offering burgers and sandwiches as well at lunch. Obviously not all 200 seats look out on the water, but the spacious room is comfortable whatever the view. Lunch and dinner. Expensive.

Tuscany Inn. 22 North Water Street. Telephone: (508) 627–5999. With an elegant Florentine menu that emphasizes both the Vineyard's local seafood as well as lamb dishes, this is a place worth spending the money on. With only five tables, you have to reserve well ahead, but the meal justifies the advance planning. Dinner. Very expensive.

Other Attractions

Vineyard Museum. Operated by the Martha's Vineyard Historical Society, this community museum is a complex of houses in central Edgartown. The Vineyard Museum building is the Thomas Cooke House, built in 1765. Its dozen rooms are filled with antique furniture, scrimshaw, ship models, whaling gear, and farm implements. Outside stands an immense fresnel lens that was removed from Gay Head Light in 1952 after nearly a century of service. Also on the grounds is the Carriage Shed, which shelters an antique fire engine, a whaleboat, a fishing boat, and an old peddler's wagon. The Captain Francis Pease House contains three galleries dedicated to Vineyard art and Wampanoag artifacts. Open mid-June to mid-October Tuesday to Saturday 10:00 A.M. to 5:00 P.M., mid-October to mid-June Wednesday to Friday 1:00 to 4:00 P.M. and Saturday 10:00 A.M. to 4:00 P.M. Adults $5.00. Corner of School and Cooke Streets. Telephone: (508) 627–4441.

ACTIVITIES

Bicycle Rental. Several outfits rent bicycles, but the best established is **Wheel Happy, Inc.,** which supplies mountain bikes and hybrids for $18 per day or $75 per week. Delivery and pickup at your lodging can be arranged at no charge for most of the island, or an additional $5.00 for Chilmark and $10.00 extra for Gay Head. Wheel Happy also rents helmets ($1.00 a day if you rent the bike from them, $3.00 otherwise). The same operator also sets up bicycle tours for groups, with a guide and box lunches for participants. 8 South Water Street. Telephone: (508) 627–5928.

Live Music. The **Hot Tin Roof**—a smokefree night club—is the island's chief venue for live music, including national acts and rising stars. At the Martha's Vineyard Airport. Telephone: (508) 693–1137.

TOURS

Walking Tours. Offered as an adjunct of the Martha's Vineyard Preservation Trust, these tours alternate between an emphasis on the whaling era and an emphasis on a potpourri of tales about "ghosts, gossip and downright scandal." Given during high season Monday to Saturday at 3:00 P.M., spring and fall Monday, Wednesday, and Friday at 3:00 P.M. The $8 fee includes admission to the Vincent House Museum. Telephone: (508) 627–8219.

FAIRS, FESTIVALS, AND EVENTS

Edgartown Regatta. Four-day event in mid-July hosted by the Edgartown Yacht Club brings many a pretty boat to town. Telephone: (508) 627–4361.

SHOPPING

The Golden Basket. Dock and Kelly Streets. Telephone: (508) 627–4459, or (800) 822–3266. Edgartown is full of jewelry and crafts stores with goods on the high end of the spectrum. The Nantucket original of this small chain claims to have originated the design of miniature Nantucket Lightship baskets in gold.

Oak Bluffs, Martha's Vineyard

LODGING

Oak House. Seaview Avenue at Pequot Avenue. Exemplifying the early homes of seaside rusticators from Boston, this house was built in 1872 from plans by a Boston architect known for his work on the mansions of Newport, Rhode Island. Over the years it sprouted balconies and porches and received upgrades of oak paneling and ceilings, marble sinks, and stained-glass windows before becoming an inn. With ten rooms varying from rather small to two-room suites, the inn is literally across the street from a long sandy beach. Telephone: (508) 693–4187. Moderate to expensive.

Wesley Hotel. 70 Lake Avenue. This voluminous Victorian hotel overlooking the harbor has a newer Wesley Arms annex in the same style but with larger rooms (and slightly higher prices). One of the reasons the original hotel is such a good deal is that the rooms lack heat and air conditioning, although each has a private bath. The Wesley Annex rooms have it all. Telephone: (508) 693–6611. Moderate to expensive.

CAMPGROUNDS AND RV PARKS

Webb's Camping Area. Barnes Road. About three miles from Steamship Authority Terminals in either Vineyard Haven or Oak Bluffs, this property offers a choice of fully wooded sites or sites with view of Lagoon Pond. Telephone: (508) 693–0233.

FOOD

Nancy's. Oak Bluffs Harbor. Telephone: (508) 693–0006. With picnic tables overlooking the harbor and a license to sell beer for consumption on the premises, Nancy's does a superlative job with fish-shack standards like fish and chips, lobster rolls, and stuffed quahogs. Lunch and dinner. Inexpensive to moderate.

Sweet Life Café. Upper Circuit Avenue. Telephone: (508) 696–0200. Small and away from the central bustle, Sweet Life offers a rather simple New American menu where everything is roasted—"fire-roasted" chicken, pan-roasted salmon, roast lamb tenderloin . . . . With a good wine list that mixes Californian, French, and Italian vintages in a range of prices, Sweet Life is something of a relief after the beach resort fried food of downtown Oak Bluffs. Dinner. Moderate.

TOURS

Walking Tours. Historical tour of the village includes the Cottage City Museum and the Flying Horses Carousel and is strong on juicy tidbits of past gossip. Offered at 3:00 P.M. Tuesday, Thursday, and Saturday. Begins at the Cottage City Museum, Trinity Park. Adults $8.00. Telephone: (508) 627–8619.

FAIRS, FESTIVALS, AND EVENTS

Band Concerts. During July and August, Sunday evening concerts alternate between Owen Park in Vineyard Haven and Ocean Park in Oak Bluffs. Telephone: (508) 693–0085.

Community Sing. The Tabernacle at the Methodist Campground is the site of community sings on Wednesday evenings in July and August. Telephone: (508) 693–0525.

Illumination Night. As many as 20,000 people turn out for this spectacle, usually held the second or third Wednesday in August. When the tradition began in the 1860s, Oriental lanterns were used. Although all the lights today are electric, the illumination of Campground's gingerbread cottages seems no less magical. We've been told by a fifth generation Camp Community member that Illumination Night is "an absolute fairyland." Telephone: (508) 693–0525.

Vineyard Haven, Martha's Vineyard

LODGING

Captain Dexter House. 92 Main Street. The rooms are a little on the small side in this Greek Revival captain's house from the 1840s, but the furnishings are period and each room has a private bath. Several have canopy beds and a few have working fireplaces. Telephone: (508) 693–6564. Moderate to expensive with breakfast.

Lothrup Merry House. Owen Park. This charming cedar-shingled home with just seven guest rooms (some with fireplaces) has a long rolling lawn down to a short stretch of private beach next to a public beach. Some rooms share baths. A canoe and sunfish are available for guest use. Telephone: (508) 693–1646. Moderate to expensive with breakfast.

Ocean Side Inn. 103 Main Street. With a range of room types, including one specifically for wheelchair users, Ocean Street Inn has delightfully landscaped grounds and is less than 100 yards from a small town beach. Telephone: (508) 693–1296. Moderate to expensive with breakfast.

CAMPGROUNDS AND RV PARKS

Martha's Vineyard Family Campground. Edgartown Road. Spacious wooded sites (with separate area for tents) are located about three miles from the Steamship Authority Terminal. Telephone: (508) 693–3772.

FOOD

Note that Vineyard Haven is a dry town—i.e., alcohol sales are prohibited. Some restaurants allow you to bring your own wine; check first.

Black Dog Tavern. Beach Street Extension. Telephone: (508) 693–9223. Locals opened the Black Dog here on the waterfront in the winter of 1971, and a lot of clever marketing has carried its name far beyond the original modest aspirations to be a good waterfront pub and restaurant. The original tavern remains true to the dream, and though we're sick to death of Black Dog T-shirts, notecards, and souvenirs of every sort, the original tavern is worth a stop. Breakfast, lunch, and dinner. Expensive.

Stripers. 52 Beach Road. Telephone: (508) 693–8383. From the road you'd guess that Stripers was just another grilled fish place with a great outdoor deck that probably serves lots of fruity drinks. Wrong. The kitchen here aims for some serious treatments of local (and not so local) fish—dishes like a tamarind-glazed salmon with Israeli couscous, or seaweed-crusted pan-seared tuna with a puree of wasabi and peas. Not everything is fish—duck and lamb are usually on the menu too. Dinner. Expensive.

ACTIVITIES

Live Music. Singer-songwriters from the island and beyond hold forth at the **Wintertide Coffeehouse.** Rated in the top ten coffeehouses nationwide by *Billboard,* Wintertide programs folk, rock, and jazz. Five Corners. Telephone: (508) 693–8830.

Martha's Bike Rentals. Located conveniently near the Steamship Authority wharf, Martha's rents eighteen-speed hybrids for $18 per day, three-speeds for $12. 4 Lagoon Pond Road. Telephone: (508) 693–6593.

Vineyard Playhouse. Resident theater company performs year-round and offers, during the summer, BYOB cabarets late at night on weekends (after the main performance). 24 Church Street. Telephone: (508) 693–6450.

FAIRS, FESTIVALS, AND EVENTS

Band Concerts. During July and August, concerts alternate between Owen Park in Vineyard Haven and Ocean Park in Oak Bluffs. Telephone: (508) 693–0085.

SHOPPING

Shaw Cramer Gallery. 76 Main Street. Telephone: (508) 696–7323. Very high quality art in craft media, with an emphasis on ceramics.

Travis Tuck Weathervanes. 71 Main Street (rear entrance from alley). Telephone: (508) 693–3914. This master craftsman designs and builds custom weathervanes for clients ranging from movie mogul Steven Spielberg (a Velociraptor) to Kentucky horse breeding farms (jockeys on thoroughbreds). Stop by to get a list of Tuck weathervanes you can see around the island. Custom work begins at $8,000.

Menemsha, Martha's Vineyard

LODGING

Beach Plum Inn. Beach Plum Road. Set on a country road within walking distance of Menemsha Harbor and Menemsha Beach, this is a genuinely delightful retreat with hosts who understand hospitality. Only three of the rooms are in the main inn, which was a Cape house before it came down with a serious case of sprawl. Two more are in the wing to the house, and six more are in single or double cottages. If this looks like a spread from a bridal magazine, it should. It's been featured several times in such publications. Telephone: (508) 645–9454. Expensive to very expensive.

FOOD

Larsen's Fish Market. Menemsha Harbor. Telephone: (508) 645–2680. Menemsha is the only real fishing village on Martha's Vineyard, and Larsen's is the place to go for the fresh catch. Open daily 9:00 A.M. to 7:00 P.M., they'll also cook lobster, steamers, and mussels to order and serve crab cakes and fish chowder to boot. For swift dining, Larsen's also prepares a raw bar to order of oysters, littleneck and cherrystone clams. Inexpensive to moderate.

ACTIVITIES

Fishing Charters. Menemsha is a working fisherman's harbor, but it's also a fine spot to charter a boat for sport fishing for striped bass and bluefish. In fact, some captains will guarantee a catch or refund the fee. Two good bets are **Flashy Lady Charters** (telephone: 508–645–2462) and **North Shore Charters, Menemsha** (telephone: 508–645–2993).

Gay Head (Aquinnah), Martha's Vineyard

FAIRS, FESTIVALS, AND EVENTS

Legends of Moshup. Several times during the summer, the Wampanoag Tribe of Gay Head presents this pageant recounting the history of the people's arrival from the mainland thousands of years ago. Call for schedule. Telephone: (508) 645-9265.

Chilmark, Martha's Vineyard

SHOPPING

Chilmark Flea Market. Telephone: (508) 645-3100. Popular flea market is held Wednesday and Saturday from July through early September at the Chilmark Community Church.

West Tisbury, Martha's Vineyard

LODGING

Lambert's Cove Country Inn. Lambert's Cove Road. Set truly in the country amid apple orchards and rambling fields—yet close to a fine beach—this is a rural retreat with too much elegance to be rustic. Half the rooms are in a 1790 farmhouse greatly enlarged in the 1920s. The remainder are in the converted barn and carriage house. Many have their own decks, one its own greenhouse sitting room. Telephone: (508) 693-2298. Moderate to expensive, with breakfast.

Nantucket Island

For advance information, contact the Nantucket Chamber of Commerce, 48 Main Street, Nantucket, MA 02554-3595. Telephone: (508) 228-1700.

GETTING TO NANTUCKET

Most travelers to Nantucket take a ferry from Hyannis or, in the summer, from Wood's Hole via Martha's Vineyard. The auto and passenger ferries are operated by the **Martha's Vineyard &**

Nantucket Steamship Authority. Telephone: (508) 477-8600. **Hy-Line Cruises** operates high-speed ferry service on a catamaran and regular boat service (passengers only) from Hyannis. Telephone: (508) 778-2600 or for high-speed ferry reservations only, (800) 492-8082.

GETTING AROUND

The Nantucket Regional Transit Authority operates a bus shuttle service with several loops covering Nantucket Town and providing service to the villages of Miacomet, Madaket and Siasconset. One-way fares are 50 cents on the shorter loops, $1.00 on the longer ones. Exact fare is required. Shuttle passes are available for three days ($10), seven days ($15) or one month ($30) and may be purchased at the Visitors Services office at 25 Federal Street, Monday to Friday from 9:00 A.M. to 2:00 P.M. Season passes for town ($40) or island-wide ($65) may be purchased at the NRTA office at 22 Federal Street. Beach service is also operated from town to Jetties Beach (50 cents) and Surfside Beach ($1.00) from mid-June through mid-September daily from 10:00 A.M. to 6:00 P.M. Telephone: (508) 228-7025.

LODGING

Four Chimneys Inn. 38 Orange Street, Nantucket Town. The three grand size "master bedrooms" on the third floor have small sitting areas and the "Gardner" has a coveted private porch with harbor view. Smaller third-floor rooms have more casual country cottage decor. Telephone: (508) 228-1912. Expensive to very expensive with breakfast.

Jared Coffin House. 29 Broad Street, Nantucket Town. When it was built in 1845 for a successful shipowner, the handsome brick home on the corner of Broad and Centre Streets was the first three-story mansion on the island. It remains a social center of island life, a popular site for weddings and receptions, and a convenient base for exploring the town. Sixty guest rooms spread throughout six buildings are all comfortably furnished with period reproductions and antiques. As is expected in older buildings, the rooms vary in size, so guests should specify their needs when booking. Telephone: (508) 228-2400 or (800)

Jared Coffin House, Nantucket Island

248–2405. Moderate to expensive with breakfast. Package rates available.

Roberts House Inn. 11 India Street, Nantucket Town. The innkeepers are very friendly and the atmosphere is very relaxed at this centrally located inn. Rooms range from a king suite on the first floor to cozy rooms under the eaves on the third floor—reached by somewhat narrow and steep stairs. Telephone: (508) 228–9009 or (800) 558–0074. Moderate to expensive with breakfast.

Ship's Inn. 13 Fair Street, Nantucket Town. The ten beautifully furnished guest rooms in this 1831 whaling captain's home are larger than often found in buildings of similar vintage. You feel like you're visiting country relatives and they gave you the master bedroom. Telephone: (508) 228–0040. Moderate to expensive with breakfast.

The Wauwinet. 120 Wauwinet Road. This is as upscale as Nantucket gets, yet the pampering is all subtle, never ostentatious. Sure, the Wauwinet was once a fishermen's shore dinner spot and then a jazz-age dinner and dancing dive. Now it's the embodiment of environmentally sensitive relaxation in one of the least spoiled stretches of the island. The inn provides van and boat shuttle service to and from town as well as boat shuttles to otherwise inaccessible beaches in the wildlife preserve. Telephone: (508) 228–0145 or (800) 426–8718. Expensive to very expensive with breakfast.

CAMPGROUNDS AND RV PARKS

Camping is prohibited on Nantucket. Local ordinances provide for a fine of up to $200 for anyone pitching a tent for the purpose of sleeping or for sleeping in the open or in a vehicle.

FOOD

Café at Le Languedoc. 24 Broad Street. Telephone: (508) 228–2552. Blue-and-white checked tablecloths and big windows brighten the basement level cafe of one of Nantucket's serious French restaurants, making it a good place to try French bistro food in a relaxed atmosphere. Lunch and dinner. Moderate.

Kendrick's at the Quaker House. 5 Chestnut Street at Centre. Telephone: (508) 228–9156. Candlelight, big windows, and simple furnishings create an attractive dining room to enjoy the chef-owner's New American cuisine with Asian influences. Breakfast and dinner. Expensive to very expensive.

Jared's. 29 Broad Street. Telephone: (508) 228–2400. The elegant dining room in the Jared Coffin House is one of the island's special occasion restaurants—known equally for its candlelit dinners and bountiful breakfasts. The Wednesday and Sunday seafood buffets ($26.95) feature an extensive raw bar and cooked specialties, including Nantucket scallops. Breakfast year-round and dinner early May to mid-October. Expensive to very expensive.

Ships Inn Restaurant. 13 Fair Street. Telephone: (508) 228–0040. Before opening his own restaurant, chef/owner Mark Gottwald trained at La Varenne in Paris and cooked at Le Cirque in New York and Spago in Los Angeles. He's brought his creative flair and all that classical technique to bear on local ingredients. Islanders look forward to the new lobster dish he creates each year and his seasonal variations on classic crab cakes. Dinner. Expensive to very expensive.

Soda Fountains. Old fashioned soda fountains are getting scarce, so we were delighted to find not one—but two—cheek by jowl on Main Street. Both serve up breakfast baked goods and a variety of sandwiches and the countermen have mastered the dying art of making an ice cream soda. **Congdon's Pharmacy Fountain** is at 47 Main Street. Telephone: (508) 228–4549. **Nantucket Pharmacy Fountain** is at 45 Main Street. Telephone: (508) 228–0180.

Straight Wharf Fish Store. Straight Wharf, Harbor Square. Telephone: (508) 228–1095. In addition to superlative fresh fish and a few gourmet items (bluefish pâté, marinades), this market also provides items to go 11:00 A.M. to 7:00 P.M., including lobster rolls, raw bar (clams, scallops, oysters), swordfish or tuna steak sandwiches, crab cakes and seafood gumbo, and lobsters cooked to order. Inexpensive.

Straight Wharf Restaurant. Straight Wharf, Harbor Square. Telephone: (508) 228–4499. One year-round Islander explained to us that there are very few restaurants right at the water because it tends to get too cold. Straight Wharf Restaurant is an exception to the rule, with a dining room and outdoor patio taking full advantage of the harbor view. The kitchen knows how to handle fresh seafood perfectly—and all those same skills go into the less expensive dishes at the attached bar/cafe (without the view). Dinner. Moderate to expensive.

Toppers. At the Wauwinet, 120 Wauwinet Road. Telephone: (508) 228–0145. The Wauwinet is the top resort on the island, and Toppers prepares the food to match—except that you don't have to be a guest to eat here. You just need a reservation, preferably months in advance. Diners staying in town can take the Wauwinet's boat, with cocktails en route and the chance of a glorious sunset on the return trip. The dining is purely New American, with ever-changing variations on the great seafood available fresh on the island with little touches not usually found on Nantucket (caviar garnishes, for example). Lunch is an interesting array of tapas-sized dishes. Dinner is full-fledged a la carte dining. Breakfast, lunch, and dinner. Very expensive.

OTHER ATTRACTIONS

Maria Mitchell Association. On clear nights when the sky is full of stars, we understand why the highly talented Nantucket native Maria Mitchell became an astronomer. From her base on Nantucket, Mitchell discovered a comet with her telescope and became the first woman elected to the American Academy of Arts and Sciences and the first woman Professor of Astronomy. The Association preserves her memory with a variety of lectures and nature programs and several buildings, including Mitchell's birthplace, a library, and two observatories (one of which is open for public viewing). Call for hours and schedule of programs. 2 Vestal Street. Telephone: (508) 228–9198.

Old Mill. Built in 1746, the Old Mill is the last example of several mills that once stood on the "hills" on the west side of Nantucket Town. You can go inside to watch the hand-carved wooden gears use windpower to grind dried corn into cornmeal. Daily, weather permitting, June to September 10:00 A.M. to 5:00 P.M. Adults $3.00. Top of West York Street. Telephone: (508) 228–1894.

Oldest House. Furnished with period domestic artifacts, the "Oldest House" was built in 1686 as a wedding present for Jethro and Mary Gardner Coffin from their feuding fathers. It's a classic center-chimney saltbox, finished (of course) in cedar shingles. Guided tours tell the whole story behind the family feud and deal with the structural details of seventeenth-century domestic architecture. Open June to September daily 10:00 A.M. to 5:00 P.M. Adults $5.00. Sunset Hill Lane. Telephone: (508) 228–1894.

ACTIVITIES

Bicycle and moped rentals. If you want to leave Nantucket Town and see the rest of the island, it's best to have your own two wheels. Two agencies on Steamboat Wharf dominate the trade: **Nantucket Bike Shop** (508–228–1999) and the venerable **Young's Bicycle Shop** (508–228–1151). Another good spot on the way to Jetties Beach is **Cook's Cycles** (6 Beach Street, 508–228–0800). Bicycle rentals are typically

$16–$20 per day. Mopeds rent for $40 per day for single-rider vehicles, $60 per day for dual rider models. Be aware that mopeds and scooters require a driver's license and you must follow all motor vehicle rules, which can be tricky given that they're rather underpowered. Also be aware that locals frown on mopeds and scooters.

Christina. This classic wooden catboat from 1926 offers one and one-half hour sails. Adults $15–$20. Slip 19 Straight Wharf. Telephone: (508) 325–4000.

TOURS

Great Point Natural History Tours. The Trustees of Reservations oversee Coskata-Coatue Wildlife Refuge and remote barrier beach complex at the northeast tip of the island. Tours are conducted in nine-passenger vehicles with four-wheel drive and balloon tires. The trips include a visit to the Great Point Lighthouse at the farthest point of the refuge. When the previous version of this light washed away in a storm, the Coast Guard considered replacing it with a plain tower. Nantucketers dug into arcane regulations and forced a replica replacement. The view from the light is astounding and takes in the fierce rips a mile or so offshore, where many a boat has been literally torn apart by colliding currents. Adults $30. Reservations essential. Telephone: (508) 228–6799. Tours leave from the Wauwinet Inn, 120 Wauwinet Road, nine miles from town center.

Van Tours. One and one-half hour tours of the highlights of the town and natural features of the island provide a good overview of Nantucket's charms. Adventure Tours (adults $10; telephone: 508–228–1686) and Ara's Tours (adults $10; telephone: 508–228–1951) pick up at all in-town lodgings.

Walking Tours. One and one-half hour walking tours of the town of Nantucket are a good way to soak up history and local color. Several options are available. Historical Walking Tours of Nantucket depart from the Peter Foulger Museum on Broad Street (adults $10, telephone: 508–228–3592). Tours led by twelfth-generation Nantucketer and island-historian Dirk Gardiner Roggeveen gather

in front of the Athenaeum at the corner of India and Federal Streets (adults $10; telephone: 508–221–0075).

FAIRS, FESTIVALS, AND EVENTS

Daffodil Festival. More than three million daffodils provide the backdrop for a celebration of spring with an antique and classic car parade, tailgate picnic, birdwatching, and other activities in late April. Telephone: (508) 228–1700.

Nantucket Film Festival. This young but well-received festival in mid-June focuses on the craft of screenwriting. Telephone: (212) 642–6339.

Nantucket Harvest. Scheduled to coincide with the mid-October cranberry harvest, this festival features a range of events including an Inn Tour, Chef's Food Festival, and Harvest Marketplace. Telephone: (508) 228–1700.

SHOPPING

Golden Basket. 44 Main Street. Telephone: (508) 228–4344. This shop is one of the more credible claimants to having originated the design of miniature Nantucket Lightship baskets in gold. The Golden Basket produces exquisite models of several traditional Nantucket and Cape Cod basket styles, including some with scrimshaw medallions on the top. They must have started a trend, as variations on the Nantucket Lightship basket as jewelry appear in a range of prices throughout Nantucket.

Lightship Baskets. Nantucket is most readily associated with one item—the woven Nantucket Lightship Basket. The earliest baskets were made during the 1820s though the craft didn't become firmly established until lightships were set up offshore to guide ships and the crews would pass their time weaving. In the late 1940s, Jose Formoso Reyes popularized the basket as a purse with a lid, and Islanders carry their well-patinaed baskets as a mark of pride. Actually, as one husband confided to us, they are a bit of conspicuous consumption: Someone offered his wife $4,000 for her 30-year-old basket. Woven on a mold, with a wooden bottom, the baskets are often custom-made for buyers. We've been told

Nantucket Lightship Baskets, Nantucket Island

that the baskets are so important to the local economy that the Chamber of Commerce banned the importation of imitations. In any event, the Nantucket Lightship Basket Makers & Merchants Association offers an informative pamphlet for anyone seriously contemplating the investment (expect to pay $700 or more, often much more). Write to them at 2 Greglen Avenue, Suite 61, Nantucket, MA 02554. Several places to see a selection of baskets and perhaps see weavers in action are **The Lightship Shop** (20 Miacomet Avenue; telephone: 508–228–4164), **Nantucket Basket Works** (14 Dave Street; telephone: 508–228–2518), and **Forager House Collection** (20 Centre Street; telephone: 508–228–5977).

Sailor's Valentine Gallery. Lower Main Street. Telephone: (508) 228–2011. This gallery in a wharf warehouse has intriguing exhibitions of contemporary art. It draws its name from the permanent collection of "sailor's valentines," the shell-encrusted pictures that whalers brought home to their loved ones.

Cape Cod, Massachusetts

For information about Cape Cod, contact Cape Cod Chamber of Commerce and Visitor Bureau, P.O. Box 790, Hyannis, MA 02601. Telephone: (508) 362–3225 or (888) 33– CAPECOD.

CAPE COD-WIDE ATTRACTIONS

Cape Cod Baseball League. The venerable league has launched many collegiate players on professional careers. The *Cape Cod Times* sports section lists games played in the towns of Falmouth, Bourne, Cotuit, Hyannis, Brewster, Dennis-Yarmouth, Orleans, Chatham, and Wareham. Although some Cape League players eventually end up with major league teams, fans are less interested in the chance to see future celebrities than the opportunity to enjoy pure baseball as it was played in the days before megalomaniac owners, greedy free agents, and artificial grass. The fences are long and admission is free. As the twilight creeps in over the outfield, there's something perfect about it all: This is old Cape Cod, where the boys of summer play the American game.

Rail Trail. A bicycle trail follows the route of an abandoned railroad right-of-way for about 25 miles through Dennis, Harwich, Brewster, Orleans, and Eastham, where it connects with the 7 miles of trails in the Cape Cod National Seashore. Maps are available at all bike shops and most tourism information booths. Telephone: (508) 986–3491.

CAPE COD-WIDE EVENTS

Cape Maritime Week. A week-long festival in May includes tours of lighthouses and sailing ships, theatrical events, and lectures. Telephone: (508) 362–3828.

Heritage Week. This week-long festival in June celebrates Cape Cod history with museum and historic house tours and handcraft demonstrations. Telephone: (508) 362–3828.

Walking Weekend. Fall foliage is usually at its peak during this two-day event which features thirty to forty guided natural and historic walks in all fifteen Cape Cod towns. Telephone: (508) 362–3828.

Bourne, Cape Cod

OTHER ATTRACTIONS

Aptucxet Trading Post Museum. The museum is a modern replica of the original trading post constructed on this site in 1627. Exhibits feature Dutch, Pilgrim, and Wampanoag artifacts. Also on the grounds is President Grover Cleveland's private railroad station, an old windmill, a salt works, and an herb garden. Open for guided tours July and August Monday through Saturday 10:00 A.M. to 5:00 P.M., Sunday 2:00 to 5:00 P.M.; May, June, September and first half of October closed Monday. Adults $2.50. 24 Aptucxet Road. Telephone: (508) 759–9487.

FAIRS, FESTIVALS, AND EVENTS

Bourne Scallop Fest. Held for three days in mid-September, this event features scallop and chicken dinners, crafts, and entertainment. Wheelchair accessible. Telephone: (508) 759–6000.

Cape Cod Canal Region Striped Bass Fishing Tournament. The Cape Cod Canal region is considered by many to be one of the best saltwater fishing areas in the world. This nine-day event begins in mid-May and offers prizes up to $1,000. Registration required. Telephone: (508) 759–6000.

Falmouth, Cape Cod

LODGING

Gladstone Inn. 219 Grand Avenue South, Falmouth Heights. Eight of the fifteen rooms in this homey bed-and-breakfast have private baths. It's a good base for taking advantage of Falmouth Heights beach—which is right across the street. Telephone: (508) 548–9851. Inexpensive with breakfast.

Palmer House Inn. 81 Palmer Avenue, Falmouth. This Victorian inn in the village center has comfortable guest rooms in the main building and a separate private suite with Jacuzzi that is one of our top choices for romantic getaways. Telephone: (508) 548–1230 or (800) 472–2632. Moderate to expensive with breakfast.

Shoreway Acres. Shore Street, Falmouth. Located in the village of Falmouth, Shoreway Acres is one of the nicest of the Cape's hybrid properties—not an inn, not a hotel, and certainly more than a motel. Options include gracious if quirky rooms in three former sea captains' homes or spacious

motel accommodations in two modern buildings. It's a five-minute stroll to town in one direction or to the beach in the other. Telephone: (508) 540–3000 or (800) 352–7100. Moderate.

FOOD

Coonamesset Inn. 311 Gifford Street. Telephone: (508) 548–2300. The kitchen prepares a New American menu, while the walls of the dining room are lined with artwork by local primitive painter Ralph Cahoon. Lunch and dinner. Moderate to expensive.

Regatta of Falmouth-by-the-Sea. 217 Clinton Avenue. Telephone: (508) 548–5400. The modest exterior of this building right at the head of the harbor gives no hint of the chic dining room inside—or of the imaginative menu. Be sure to order the lobster corn chowder. Dinner. Moderate to expensive.

FAIRS, FESTIVALS, AND EVENTS

Barnstable County Fair. This week-long event in late July is a reminder of Cape Cod's agricultural roots. Wheelchair accessible. Telephone: (508) 563–3200.

Mashpee, Cape Cod

FOOD

The Flume. Route 130. Telephone: (508) 477–1456. This restaurant run by Earl Mills is a Wampanoag tribal institution. Many of the dishes are traditional, but seem anything but exotic—the Pilgrims and Puritans knew good food when they ate it and many Algonquian dishes long ago entered the general New England culinary repertoire. Menu choices might include local quahog chowder, fried smelts, codfish cakes, or other outstanding seafood preparations. Lunch and dinner. Inexpensive to expensive.

Cotuit, Massachusetts

FOOD

Regatta of Cotuit. Route 28. Telephone: (508) 428–5715. If Regatta of Falmouth-by-the-Sea has closed for the season, you can get the same excellent food and service at this sister restaurant in a historic setting. Dinner. Moderate to expensive.

OTHER ATTRACTIONS

Cahoon Museum of American Art. Ralph Cahoon painted mermaids and sailors and fanciful scenes of Cape life and life at sea in a deliberately primitive style. He was amazingly prolific, and while his work was well-received during his lifetime (he made a fine living), even he couldn't have imagined the five- and six-figure prices some of the canvases now command. This little museum that he endowed has many pieces of his work as well as painting and sculpture in a similar naïve vein by other folk artists. Open Tuesday through Saturday 10:00 A.M. to 4:00 P.M. Donation requested. Routes 28 and 130. Telephone: (508) 428–7581.

Hyannis, Cape Cod

TRANSPORTATION

The sole year-round auto and passenger ferry from the Ocean Street Dock in Hyannis to Nantucket is operated by the **Martha's Vineyard & Nantucket Steamship Authority.** Telephone: (508) 477–8600. **Hy-Line Cruises** operates high-speed passenger ferries April through October to Martha's Vineyard and Nantucket from Ocean Street Dock. Telephone: (508) 778–2600.

LODGING

DeCota Family Inn. Route 132. This twenty-four-room, family-run motel sits smack in the middle of Cape Cod, one mile from exit 6 off Route 6. With a nice lakefront beach with canoes and paddleboats, it's a good choice for families. Telephone: (508) 362–3957. Moderate.

Hyannis Travel Inn. 18 North Street. Tucked away on a private court between the Hyannis traffic circle and Main Street, this surprisingly spacious two-story motel has eighty-three rooms, two swimming pools, and a sauna. It's a convenient walk downtown and a good strategic base (a block off Route 28) for driving elsewhere. Telephone: (508) 775–8200 or (800) 352–7190. Moderate.

Palmer House Inn, Falmouth, Massachusetts

OTHER ATTRACTIONS

Cape Cod Melody Tent. Ever wonder what happened to Tom Jones? Engelbert Humperdinck? The Melody Tent claims to be the top tourist attraction on Cape Cod, and people swarm in to see Las Vegas acts perform. West Main Street at West End rotary. Telephone: (508) 775–0889.

John F. Kennedy Hyannis Museum. The photo and audio exhibits in this modest museum open a window on JFK's days on Cape Cod. Despite the glamour of the Kennedy compound and the presidential yacht, we find the photos remarkably humanizing—a family like any other savoring their time together. Open mid-April to mid-October Monday through Saturday 10:00 A.M. to 4:00 P.M., Sunday 1:00 to 4:00 P.M. Call for off-season hours. Adults $3.00. 397 Main Street. Telephone: (508) 790–3077.

ACTIVITIES

Hyannisport Harbor Cruises. Leisurely one-hour narrated cruise of Hyannis harbor circles past some of the harbor islands en route to the historic Kennedy family compound. Two replicas of Maine coastal steamers, the *Prudence* and the *Patience,* operate mid-April to late October. Hy-Line also runs food and music theme cruises aboard the same vessels. Ocean Street Dock. Harbor cruises adults $10. Telephone: (508) 778–2600.

West Yarmouth/South Yarmouth, Cape Cod

LODGING

Beach House at Bass River. 73 South Shore Drive, South Yarmouth. This tasteful cluster of four buildings on a private Nantucket Sound beach is the embodiment of serenity. Most of the twenty-six units have private balcony or patio and refrigerator. Telephone: (508) 394–6501 or (800) 345–6065. Moderate to expensive with breakfast.

Tidewater Motor Lodge. 135 Main Street (Route 28), West Yarmouth. The Tidewater is one of the most accessible lodgings on Cape Cod. Many rooms are equipped for wheelchair users and the entire pool complex (pool, whirlpool, and sauna within a giant greenhouse) is well-ramped. Assisted listening devices are also available for television sets. You get the feeling that the proprietors of this 100-room complex genuinely care about the comfort of their guests. Telephone: (508) 775–6322 or (800) 338–6322. Moderate.

Dennisport, Cape Cod

CAMPGROUNDS AND RV PARKS

Campers Haven. 184 Old Wharf Road. There are 265 sites at this spot, as well as a private beach on Nantucket Sound. Telephone: (508) 398–2811.

FOOD

Kream 'N' Kone. Route 28 and Sea Street. No phone. Great fried seafood has been served up here since 1933. Take a cue from the locals and top it off with an ice cream cone. Lunch and dinner. Inexpensive.

The Harwiches, Cape Cod

TRANSPORTATION

Nantucket passenger ferry operates daily from the Harwich Port town dock, summers only. Telephone: (508) 432–8999.

LODGING

Beach House Inn. 4 Braddock Lane, Harwich Port. This movie-set beach house looks like it lifted off the pages of *Architectural Digest*. There's a large private beach on Nantucket Sound and a grand sitting room with beach and ocean views. Telephone: (508) 432–4444 or (800) 870–0405. Expensive with breakfast.

Commodore Inn. 30 Earle Road, West Harwich. Although technically a motel, the Commodore feels more like an inn. All the rooms sit around nicely landscaped central grounds with a playground and heated pool. Several rooms have Jacuzzi tub and gas fireplace. While it's not quite on the beach, surf and sand are only about 75 yards away. Telephone: (508) 432–1180 or (800) 368–1180. Wheelchair accessible. Moderate to expensive.

Sandpiper Beach Inn. 16 Bank Street, Harwich Port. Twenty rooms and suites in new and renovated shingled beach houses/motel units have a comfortable "beach-bum" atmosphere, but with plenty of creature comforts. The property has its own private beach on Nantucket Sound. Telephone: (508) 432–0485 or (800) 433–2234. Moderate to expensive with breakfast.

West Harwich Motor Lodge. 161 Main Street (Route 28), West Harwich. The rooms are spare in this well-kept older building, but you can't beat the location facing west at the mouth of the tidal Herring River. Sunsets over the marshy inlet are spectacular and in the late summer, the waters roil with schools of striped bass. The motel is a stop on Harwich's summer beach trolley. Telephone: (508) 432–2100. Inexpensive to moderate.

FAIRS, FESTIVALS, AND EVENTS

Harwich Cranberry Festival. The harvest ritual of corralling bright red berries floating on deep blue water is a sight not to be missed. This ten-day event beginning in early September celebrates the harvest with a range of events that includes a classic car show, parade, fireworks, and carnival. Telephone: (508) 430–2811.

Chatham, Cape Cod

LODGING

Chatham Bars Inn. Shore Road. One of the few

remaining old-time Cape Cod seaside resorts, the Chatham Bars has expanded its lodgings with many newer buildings to complement the old inn with its baron-sized public lobby. The resort boasts every conceivable amenity, from tennis courts to golf club privileges to a sandy beach. Telephone: (508) 945–0096 or (800) 527–4884. Expensive to very expensive.

Chatham Wayside Inn. 512 Main Street. Restored rooms from the 1860 inn and a tasteful 1995 addition fit neatly into the central village next to the bandstand. Wheelchair accessible. Telephone: (508) 945–5550 or (800) 391–5734. Moderate to very expensive.

Port Fortune Inn. 201 Main St. Just-renovated romantic colonial B&B has fourteen rooms in two buildings a short walk from South Beach. Telephone: (508) 945–0792 or (800) 850–0792. Moderate to expensive with breakfast.

FOOD

Chatham Bars Inn. Shore Road. Telephone: (508) 945–0096. The grand dining room of the Chatham Bars is one of the Cape's true gourmet dining destinations for updated (i.e., lighter than traditional) continental fare. Breakfast, lunch, dinner, Sunday brunch. Expensive.

Impudent Oyster. 15 Chatham Bars Avenue. Telephone: 508–945–3545. Every beach town needs a salty restaurant that serves cold draft beer and knows how to cook fresh fish. This is Chatham's. Lunch and dinner. Moderate.

Sea in the Rough. Route 28. Telephone: (508) 945–1700. Chatham's shellfish may be the best in New England and this no-frills place a short distance outside of town may be one of the best places to try clams and scallops from the Chatham flats along with lobster, cod, flounder, and bluefish from the waters. Lunch and dinner. Inexpensive to moderate.

Cape Cod National Seashore, Massachusetts

For general park information, send a self-addressed, stamped envelope to Superintendent, Cape Cod National Seashore, South Wellfleet, MA 02663. Telephone: (508) 349–3785.

Wellfleet, Cape Cod

OTHER ATTRACTIONS

Wellfleet Drive-In and Flea Market. We want to invent a new category called "Local Treasures" for this winning combination. This 1957 drive-in is not only one of the last of a dying breed, but also hosts Cape Cod's largest flea market on weekends and Monday holidays from mid-April through September and also on Wednesday and Thursday in July and August. Route 6A. Telephone: (508) 349–2520.

Wellfleet Harbor Actors Theater. The theater building may look like an old motel, but this feisty company presents some of the most provocative contemporary work on the Cape. Kendrick Avenue, Wellfleet Harbor. Telephone: (508) 349–6835.

Truro, Cape Cod

LODGING

Days' Cottages. Route 6A, North Truro. You can't miss the twenty-three white cabins all lined up in a row with Route 6A on one side and the ocean on the other. The 1930s-era cabins all have two bedrooms, living room, kitchen, and dining area and are in great demand for week-long stays. A true Cape classic. $400 to $600 per week. Telephone: (508) 487–1062.

Provincetown, Cape Cod

LODGING

Beaconlight Guesthouse. 12 Winthrop Street. Inviting common rooms, open-hearth fireplace, and grand piano lend an English country house air to this fifteen-room inn—one of the friendliest we have encountered for couples of all gender combinations. Telephone: (508) 487–9603 or (800) 696–9603. Moderate to expensive with breakfast.

Dyer's Beach House. 173 Commercial Street. Five basic motel rooms on pilings over the harbor have one of the most dramatic locations in town. Telephone: (508) 487–2061. Moderate.

Watermark Inn. 603 Commercial Street. Right on the water and away from the hubbub, this architect-designed contemporary property has two decks and a private beach. Eight of the ten suites have water views and all have kitchenettes. Telephone: (508) 487–0165 or (800) 734–0165. Moderate to expensive.

FOOD

Dancing Lobster Café/Trattoria. 463 Commercial Street. Telephone: (508) 487–0900. Chef-owner Pepe Berg, scion of a famous P'town restaurant family, has masterfully reinvented both fish shack and trattoria. He started on the town pier, but demand required moving to this more spacious location. Even so, there are lines out the door almost every night. Large windows on P'town's harbor provide a fabulous view—boats in the water, moon above the bay. Dinner. Expensive to very expensive.

Martin House. 157 Commercial Street. Telephone: (508) 487–1327. A 1750 house with multiple fireplaces and cozy rooms is the setting for quiet New American dinners that seem both years and miles from the busy scene on Commercial Street. Dinner. Expensive to very expensive.

The Moors. Bradford Street Extension. Telephone: (508) 487–0840. Provincetown's fishing heritage is hard to ignore when you're dining on Portuguese variations of local seafood amid the shipwreck and whaling decor. Dinner. Moderate.

Vintage American quilt squares

OTHER ATTRACTIONS

Provincetown Rep. The latest in a long line seeking to revive the theater tradition in Provincetown, this ambitious professional company has some serious supporters, including Julie Harris and Jason Robards. Its summer season consists of new plays, along with an occasional classic by Eugene O'Neill, a founder of the legendary Provincetown Players. The company is raising funds to build a new theater space. Telephone: (508) 487–0600.

FAIRS, FESTIVALS, AND EVENTS

Arts Festival. Gallery events, demonstrations, and studio tours in late September highlight the town's role as a leading art colony. Telephone: (508) 487–3424.

Lighting of the Pilgrim Monument. The 255-foot Pilgrim Monument is strung with more than 5,000 lights to celebrate the holiday season and serve as a reminder that the Pilgrims landed first in Provincetown before heading across the bay to Plymouth. The lighting ceremony is held in late November and the lights remain lit until at least January 1. Telephone: (508) 487–1310.

Portuguese Festival. This five-day event in late June celebrates the town's Portuguese heritage with art and cultural exhibits, theatrical presentations, a food bazaar, and the Blessing of the Fleet. Telephone: (508) 487–2576.

Brewster, Cape Cod

LODGING

Ocean Edge Resort and Golf Club. 2907 Main Street. It's hard to miss the massive stone hotel with ninety rooms, but the property also has condo units available for short-term stays. Some overlook the resort's beach on Cape Cod Bay, while others are clustered around one of Cape Cod's best golf courses. Telephone: (508) 896–9000 or (800) 343–6074. Moderate to expensive.

CAMPGROUNDS AND RV PARKS

Nickerson State Park. 3488 Main Street (Route 6A). One of the most popular sites on Cape Cod includes about 420 campsites on 2,000 acres. Telephone: (508) 896–3491, reservations: (508) 896–4615.

FOOD

Chillingsworth. 2449 Main Street. Telephone: (508) 896–3640. Auguste Escoffier would likely approve of the classic French dining with all the attendant formalities. Chillingsworth is where folks at this end of the Cape head to celebrate a major development deal, a silver or golden wedding anniversary, even a mere engagement. The decor is high antique, and while they don't enforce it rigorously, there is a strongly suggested dress code. Reservations are absolutely essential. All meals are prix fixe. Lunch and dinner. Very expensive.

Dennis, Cape Cod

OTHER ATTRACTIONS

Scargo Hill Observatory. Built in 1902, this rude stone tower surveys the entire Pilgrim domain from Plymouth at one end of the great, long, arching curve of the Cape to Provincetown's Pilgrim Monument at the other. Free. Scargo Hill Road, off Route 6A.

SHOPPING

Antiques Center of Cape Cod. 243 Route 6A. Telephone: (508) 385–6400. Cape Cod has few groups of dealers in antiques and collectibles—this is the largest. Small items occupy glass-fronted cases on the first floor. Look upstairs for furniture and larger items.

Yarmouthport, Cape Cod

LODGING

The Wedgewood Inn. 83 Main Street. Located on the National Register of Historic Places, this elegant 1812 property has nine guest rooms, some with fireplaces, screened porches, or decks. Telephone: (508) 362–5157. Moderate to expensive with breakfast.

FOOD

Hallet's. 139 Main Street (Route 6A). Telephone: (508) 362–3138. This 1889 drugstore's classic marble soda fountain dispenses ice cream sodas, sandwiches, and other treats.

Barnstable/West Barnstable, Cape Cod

FOOD

Mill Way Fish & Lobster. 276 Mill Way (off Route 6A). Telephone: (508) 362–2760. One owner at this casual fresh fish market and take-out shop trained at a top culinary school, which is why you might find seafood sausage or shrimp and eggplant Parmesan available along with steamed lobster, stuffed quahogs, and fresh cherrystones.

OTHER ATTRACTIONS

Sandy Neck Beach. This eight-mile-long barrier beach extends across Barnstable Harbor from the west. The peninsula is a 100-acre habitat for a number of wildlife species. Access road is off Route 6A just over the town line in Sandwich.

Sandwich, Cape Cod

LODGING

Wingscorton Farm Inn. 11 Wing Boulevard, East Sandwich. The thirteen-acre farm has been in continuous cultivation since the eighteenth century and guests can check out the livestock—chickens, goats, sheep, pigs, even a llama. Rooms are in a 1758 farmhouse, complete with "keeping room" and enormous hearth. Telephone: (508) 888–0534. Moderate to expensive with breakfast.

CAMPGROUNDS AND RV PARKS

Peters Pond Park. 185 Cotuit Road. This 452-site facility is located on a spring-fed lake with good swimming, fishing, and boating. Telephone: (508) 477–1775.

OTHER ATTRACTIONS

Thornton Burgess Museum. The children's author made his home here in Sandwich, and this delightful little museum has a collection of his writings as well as original illustrations of his animal characters by Harrison Cady. Many of the exhibits deal with Burgess's lifelong fascination with natural history that led him to anthropomorphize everything from Mother West Wind to Chatterer the Red Squirrel. After touring, wander along by Shawme Pond, where some real-life versions of his creatures might put in an appearance. Open Monday to Saturday and holidays 10:00 A.M. to 4:00 P.M., Sunday 1:00 to 4:00 P.M. Donation requested. 4 Water Street. Telephone: (508) 888–6870.

FAIRS, FESTIVALS, AND EVENTS

Band Concerts. The all-volunteer band performs every Thursday evening from late June through late October at the bandstand behind the Henry T. Wing School. Telephone: (508) 888–5281.

Dexter Rhododendron Festival. Peak bloom for the thousands of rhododendrons at Heritage Plantation is from the last week in May until mid-June. Wheelchair accessible. Telephone: (508) 888–3300.

Plymouth, Massachusetts

For information about the Massachusetts South Shore, including Plymouth, contact Plymouth County Convention and Visitors Bureau, P.O. Box 1620, Pembroke, MA 02359. Telephone: (781) 826–3136 or (800) 231–1620.

For information about the town of Plymouth contact Destination Plymouth, 225 Water Street, Suite 202, Plymouth, MA 02360. Telephone: (508) 747–7525 or (800) USA–1620.

LODGING

Cold Spring Motel. 188 Court Street. We're particularly fond of motels from the early days of auto travel—and this nicely landscaped property a short drive from Plymouth center fits the bill. Originally opened in 1949, the property has expanded over the years and now offers thirty-one guest rooms. Telephone: (508) 746–2222 or (800) 678–8667. Moderate.

Pilgrim Sands Motel. 150 Warren Avenue, Route 3A. This two-story motel sits on its own private beach right next to Plymouth Beach and just down the road from the entrance to Plimoth Plantation. Although it is a short drive into the town of Plymouth, this is a good spot for those who like to mix history with sunbathing. Telephone: (508) 747–0900 or (800) 729–7263. Inexpensive to moderate.

Plymouth Bay Bed & Breakfast Manor. 259 Court Street. A short drive from Plymouth Center, this 1903 shingle-style home has three very comfortable and rather elegant guest rooms—all furnished with antiques and all with windows on Plymouth Bay. Telephone: (508) 830–0426. Moderate with breakfast.

CAMPGROUNDS AND RV PARKS

Pinewood Lodge Campground. 190 Pinewood Road. Tenters and RVs are both welcome at the 250 sites within 150 acres of white pine forest. The grounds include a fifty-acre freshwater lake for swimming, fishing, and boating. Telephone: (508) 746–3548.

FOOD

Cafe Nanina. Brewer's Plymouth Marina, 14 Union Street. Telephone: (508) 747–4503. Situated in a small pleasure boat marina about a five-minute walk from *Mayflower II,* Cafe Nanina has an outdoor cafe for a casual lunch. The elegant upstairs dining room features a wall of windows on the harbor and Italian-inspired treatments of fresh fish, chicken, and meats. Lunch and dinner. Moderate to expensive.

Seafood "in the rough." The town wharf is a good spot for casual dining at any of three spots that emphasize fresh fish and give you a view of the activity in the harbor while you eat. **Lobster Hut** has an outdoor deck right at the water. Telephone: (508) 746–2270. **Souza's Seafood** was founded to serve fishermen on the wharf and has been in operation for three generations. Telephone: (508) 746–5354. **Wood's** features a seafood market as well as restaurant. Telephone: (508) 746–0261. All open for lunch and dinner. All inexpensive to moderate.

Water Street Cafe. 25 Water Street. Telephone: (508) 746–2050. This very friendly spot serves hearty breakfasts (until noon) and a good selection of sandwiches and soups—and they'll pack up anything on the menu so you can take it to the beach. Breakfast and lunch.

Other Attractions

Cranberry World. The cranberry is the chief fruit crop of Massachusetts—with the bogs of southeastern Massachusetts producing nearly half the 400-million-pound national crop each year. This exhibition, sponsored by Ocean Spray, depicts the history of the fruit and of the people who cultivate it. It's quick and interesting to tour—with samples of cranberry products available at the end. Open May through November daily 9:30 A.M. to 5:00 P.M. Free. 225 Water Street. Telephone: (508) 747–2350.

Activities

Amphibious Tours. Plymouth has not been left behind in the craze for touring aboard amphibious vehicles. In fact, there are two choices. **Water Wheels** offers a ninety-minute tour of which thirty minutes are in the water. Adults $12.50. Telephone: (508) 746–7779. **Splashdown**'s sixty-minute tours are split evenly between land and sea. Adults $13. Telephone: (508) 747–7658.

Cape Cod Cruises. The Pilgrims landed first in Provincetown and later sailed the *Mayflower* across the bay to found their colony in Plymouth. Today a ferry makes the same crossing in about an hour and a half—and gives passengers about five hours on shore before the return trip. Daily mid-June through August; call for off-season schedule. Adults $24. State Pier. Telephone: (508) 747–2400 or (800) 242–2469.

Lobster Tales. Designed to give passengers a hint of the life of a fisherman, this one-hour tour includes hauling lobster traps in Plymouth harbor. Even if the traps come up empty, a touch tank on board gives a chance to handle the creepy-looking crustaceans. Adults $10. Town Wharf. Telephone: (508) 746–5342.

Tours

Colonial Lantern Tour. Each participant carries a pierced-tin lantern on tours of Plymouth at night departing at 7:30 P.M. and 9:00 P.M. The later—and darker—tour emphasizes the ghosts in Plymouth's closet. Adults $8.00. 98 Water Street. Telephone: (508) 747–4161.

Plymouth Rock Trolley. The narrated tour allows all-day reboarding. Operates daily from Memorial Day weekend through October and weekends in May and November. Includes connections to Plimoth Plantation during the summer. Adults $8.00. Telephone: (508) 747–3419.

Fairs, Festivals, and Events

Summer Evenings on Town Square. Free Tuesday evening programs from late June through late August include musical performances and lectures. Most evenings also feature open house tours of the historic buildings of Town Square: the 1749 wooden courthouse, the First Parish Church, and the Church of the Pilgrimage. Telephone: (508) 747–7525.

Shopping

The Sampler. 84 Court Street. Telephone: (508) 746–7077. We've never before encountered such a broad selection of sampler kits ranging from reproductions of historic work to modern designs inspired by the sampler tradition.

The North Shore of Massachusetts

For information about the area north of Boston, contact North of Boston Convention and Visitors Bureau, 17 Peabody Square, Peabody, MA 01960. Telephone: (978) 977–7760 or (800) 742–5306.

For information about Essex, Gloucester, Manchester-by-the-Sea, and Rockport, contact the Cape Ann Chamber of Commerce, 33 Commercial Street, Gloucester, MA 01930. Telephone: (978) 283–1601 or (800) 321–0133.

Marblehead, Massachusetts

LODGING

Marblehead Inn. 264 Pleasant Street. On the main drag between Marblehead and Salem (Route 114), this Victorian inn has ten two-room suites with full kitchenettes, making it a good option for both business people and families. Telephone: (781) 639–9999 or (800) 399–5843. Moderate with breakfast.

Oceanwatch. 8 Fort Seawall Lane. This Victorian-era home with three guest bedrooms shares a superb view of Marblehead harbor with its neighbor, Fort Sewall. Guests have their own deck to savor the view and are within easy walking distance of the historic downtown shopping and dining district. Telephone: (781) 639–8660. Moderate to expensive with breakfast.

FOOD

King's Rook. 12 State Street. Telephone: (781) 631–9838. This cafe and wine bar in a 1747 building is a local favorite for light lunches or romantic dinners. Lunch and dinner. Moderate.

Truffles. 114 Washington Street. Telephone: (781) 639–1104. This casual cafe and deli is a good place to pick up sandwiches for the beach or more elegant ready-to-cook dinner entrees if your lodging has kitchen facilities.

FAIRS, FESTIVALS, AND EVENTS

Marblehead Race Week. Sailboat regatta fills Marblehead harbor for competitions in different classes during third week of July. Telephone: (781) 631–2868

Salem, Massachusetts

LODGING

The Hawthorne Hotel. On the Common. Built in 1925, this red brick member of Historic Hotels of America is well-situated for touring, and recently completed makeovers of its eighty-nine guest rooms. Telephone: (978) 744–4080 or (800) 729–7829. Moderate to expensive.

Inn at Seven Winter Street. 7 Winter Street.

Several of the guest rooms have fireplaces or decks in this 1870s Empire-style B&B decorated with period furnishings. At least one room has a decidedly modern whirlpool tub. Telephone: (978) 745–9520. Moderate to expensive with breakfast.

Stepping Stone Inn. 19 Washington Square North. This 1846 home on Salem Common, furnished with period pieces and reproductions, offers good value for the price as well as an extremely convenient location. Telephone: (978) 741–8900. Moderate with breakfast.

FOOD

Derby Fish & Lobster. 215 Derby Street. Telephone: (978) 745–2064. The fresh fish at this casual spot is equally good if you order at the counter or choose table service. Next door you can buy fresh fillets and shellfish by the pound. Lunch and dinner. Inexpensive to moderate.

Grapevine Restaurant. 26 Congress Street. Telephone: (978) 745–9335. This stylish trattoria specializes in seafood specialties and has a broad wine list. Dinner. Moderate to expensive.

Museum Café. East India Square. Telephone: (978) 745–1876, extension 3118, or (978) 740–4551. Elegant white-linen dining room with art on the walls or an outdoor patio for nice weather make a good choice for a meal even if you are not visiting the museum. Lunch and Sunday brunch.

Red Raven's Havana. 90 Washington Street. Telephone: (978) 740–3888. Colorful and somewhat campy decor is the backdrop for large plates of food with strong flavors and straightforward preparations. Dinner and Sunday brunch. Moderate to expensive.

OTHER ATTRACTIONS

Salem 1630: Pioneer Village. With its rich maritime history and witchcraft associations, Salem's early settlement as a hardscrabble fishing village is often overlooked. This re-creation of a seventeenth-century fishing village (one of the oldest living history museums in the country, dating from 1930) keeps the early days alive. Visitors can opt for guided or self-guided tours of the site, with its thatched roof cottages, wigwams, period gardens, and costumed interpreters. Open May through December Monday to Saturday 10:00 A.M. to 5:00 P.M., Sunday noon to 5:00 P.M. Adults $6.00. Combination tickets with House of Seven Gables available (see "Seeing the Mid Coast"). Forest River Park. Telephone: (978) 745–7283.

Salem Witch Museum. Occupying the former Second Church of Salem, this attraction features an emotionally charged voice-over narrative intoning the tragic events of 1692 as illustrative dioramas are suddenly lit in the otherwise dark space. The Halloween hokiness rather effectively conveys the details of the witch hysteria. Open July and August daily 10:00 A.M. to 7:00 P.M., September through June daily 10:00 A.M. to 5:00 P.M. Adults $4.50. Washington Square. Telephone: (978) 744–1692.

Witch Dungeon Museum. A theatrical presentation drawn from transcripts of the trial of Sarah Good precedes a tour of a re-created dungeon. Open April through November daily 10:00 A.M. to 5:00 P.M. Adults $5.00. 16 Lynde Street. Telephone: (978) 741–3570.

Witch House. The dark, gabled building was the home of Judge Jonathan Corwin, who presided over many of the pretrial hearings of accused witches and was a member of the court that condemned twenty people to death. This home, which he purchased in 1675, is the only structure still standing in Salem with direct ties to the witch trials. To their credit, guides put the trials into context of the architecture, furnishings, and lifestyle of the time. Open July through Labor Day daily 10:00 A.M. to 6:00 P.M., Labor Day through November and March through June daily 10:00 A.M. to 4:30 P.M. 310 Essex Street. Telephone: (978) 744–0180.

TOURS

Haunted Footsteps Ghost Tour. Candlelight strolls make much of the "supernatural" side of Salem history. Late May through October nightly. Adults $6.00. 15 Derby Square. Telephone: (978) 745–0666.

Shaker ladder-back chair

Salem Trolley Corp. You can opt for a one-hour tour of the city's highlights or board and reboard all day. Purchase tickets on board or at the Trolley Depot. April through October daily. Adults $9. 191 Essex Street. Telephone: (978) 745–3003.

FAIRS, FESTIVALS, AND EVENTS

Haunted Happenings. Salem celebrates Halloween throughout the month of October with candlelight tours, haunted houses, psychic fairs, and other events. Telephone: (800) 777–6848.

Salem Heritage Days. This week-long celebration in August takes a more encompassing look at Salem's past and features concerts, a grand parade, a chowderfest, and other events. Telephone: (978) 745–9595, extension 206.

SHOPPING

Pickering Wharf. This waterfront development houses a range of boutiques, antiques shops, and restaurants.

Gloucester, Massachusetts

FOOD

McT's Lobster House and Tavern. 25 Rogers

Street. Telephone: (978) 282–0950. McT's may not look very promising from the street, but it has a large waterfront dock with a good view of the working waterfront. Proximity to the fish docks also guarantees good fresh fish. Lunch and dinner. Moderate.

OTHER ATTRACTIONS

Beauport (Sleeper-McCann House). There are many chances in New England to visit homes that exemplify architectural styles, such as Federal or Georgian, Italianate or Victorian. But Beauport is in a league of its own. The Society for the Preservation of New England Antiquities, which manages the property, describes it as a "fantasy house." Architect Henry Davis Sleeper decorated the mansion's forty rooms with his collection of American and European art and antiques, selecting a theme from literature or history for each. Visitors can tour twenty-six of those rooms. Open mid-May through mid-October Monday through Friday from 10:00 A.M. to 4:00 P.M. Also open mid-September through mid-October Saturday and Sunday from 1:00 to 4:00 P.M. Adults $6.00. 75 Eastern Point Boulevard. Telephone: (978) 283–0800.

Gloucester Stage Company. Headed by playwright Israel Horovitz, this company performs at the Gorton's Theater (a space donated by the fish–processing giant) and presents an ambitious summer season of premieres and contemporary plays, and works by Horovitz himself, sometimes focusing on the changing dynamics of the city of Gloucester. 267 East Main Street. Telephone: (978) 281–4099.

Hammond Castle Museum. Inspired by his journeys throughout Europe, inventor John Hays Hammond, Jr. built a medieval-style castle on the coast of the Atlantic to house his collection of early Roman, medieval, and Renaissance artifacts. Equally impressive is the view of the entrance to Gloucester Harbor and the rocky coastline. Open June through October daily from 10:00 A.M. to 5:00 P.M. Museum sometimes closes early to accommodate weekend weddings. Call for off-season hours. Adults $6.00. 80 Hesperus Avenue. Telephone: (978) 283–7673.

ACTIVITIES

Schooner Sails. Launched in June, 1997, the 65-foot schooner *Thomas E. Lannon* was the first schooner in fifty years to come out of Essex. From May through October, she sails from Gloucester daily except Tuesday, when she sails from Salem. Adults $25. Seven Seas Wharf at the Gloucester House Restaurant, Rogers Street. Telephone: (978) 281–6634.

Tiny Tug Tours. The shallow-draft, 23-foot tugboat *Time Being* is able to go where larger boats cannot, making it possible to travel the Annisquam River and salt marshes, as well Gloucester Harbor. The small boat carries only six passengers at a time—a real switch from the crowds on most boat trips. Adults $12. Harbor Loop. Telephone: (978) 638–6371.

Whale Watch Cruises. With its proximity to the whale feeding grounds, Gloucester is one of the best places on the Mid Coast to take a whale watch cruise. The following operators all have naturalists on board and in some cases, even gather research data during the cruises. The **Yankee Fleet Whale Watch** is located at 75 Essex Street; telephone: (978) 283–0313 or (800) 942–5464. **Seven Seas Whale Watch** departs from Seven Seas Wharf off Rogers Street; telephone: (978) 283–1776 or (800) 238–1776. The wharf sits in the middle of the fishing fleet and packs and sells live lobsters to go. **Cape Ann Whale Watch** sails from Rose's Wharf, and is the closest to Route 128; telephone: (978) 283–5110 or (800) 877–5110. **Captain Bill's Whale Watch** is based on Harbor Loop off Rogers Street; telephone: (978) 283–6995 or (800) 33–WHALE. Whale watch cruises are about $25 per adult. Captain Bill's and the Yankee Fleet also offer deep-sea fishing cruises for about the same price.

FAIRS, FESTIVALS, AND EVENTS

Saint Peter's Festa. This four-day religious festival in late June honors the patron saint of fishermen. Religious processions, an outdoor mass, and the Blessing of the Fishing Fleet are interspersed with music, nightly dances, a parade, food, and sporting events, including the wildly popular greasy pole walk. Telephone: (978) 283–1601.

Schooner Festival. The annual festival usually draws about a dozen schooners to compete for the Esperanto Cup. The three-day, early September event also features a parade of sail, deck tours, a Boatlight Parade, and a fish fry. Telephone: (978) 283–1601.

Rockport, Massachusetts

LODGING

Addison Choate Inn. 49 Broadway. On a side street within easy walking distance of the harbor and shops, this Greek Revival house was an early entry into the B&B business and has been in operation for more than thirty years. The inn has five rooms and a suite and a separate stable house has two suites with kitchenettes. There's also a swimming pool. Telephone: (978) 546–7543 or (800) 245–7543. Moderate with breakfast.

Bearskin Neck Motor Lodge. 74 South Road. This eight-room motel occupies a prime spot. Walk out the front door to the shops and restaurants of Bearskin Neck, or hang out on the back deck for an unobstructed view of the ocean. Telephone: (978) 546–6677. Inexpensive to moderate.

Inn on Cove Hill. 37 Mount Pleasant Street. The 1791 building was financed by pirates' gold found nearby at Gully Point. Despite this outlaw association, the inn is a fine example of quality eighteenth-century workmanship and furnishings in the eleven guest rooms and public spaces enhance the architecture. The location is convenient for walking to Bearskin Neck or to the beach. Telephone: (978) 546–2701. Inexpensive to moderate with breakfast.

FOOD

In 1856, more than 200 hatchet-wielding women destroyed every container of alcohol in Rockport and the town remains "dry" to this day. Many restaurants allow patrons to bring their own, but check first.

Flav's. 15 Mount Pleasant Street. Telephone: (978) 546–7647. Steven Spielberg and Tom Selleck ate breakfast at this unassuming local eatery during filming of the movie, *The Love Letter*. It's also a good place to grab a fish sandwich or a fried clam or scallop plate. Breakfast and lunch.

Harbor Grille. 8 Old Harbor Road. Telephone: (978) 546–3030. This little red-shingled building sits down a side street on Bearskin Neck right at the edge of the water. There are tables inside, but unless a cold wind is blowing, we think it's better to hold down a picnic table on the seawall to consume a bucket of peel-and-eat shrimp followed by seafood stew or a lobster roll served on a baguette. Lunch and dinner. Moderate.

Lobster Pool. 329 Granite Street (Route 127). Telephone: (978) 546–7808. If you visit Halibut Point late in the day, you can time your stop at this casual spot so that you can sit out back and watch the sun set over Folly Cove. Lunch and dinner. Inexpensive to moderate.

Essex, Massachusetts

LODGING

Essex River House Motel. 132 Main Street. Sitting right on the Essex River amid the marshes, this one-story motel seems nearly invisible from the road. The sixteen rooms have simple and uncluttered decor. Step out the door and you're right at the marsh. Room 15 has a terrific view of the marsh and the river. Telephone: (978) 768–6800. Inexpensive to moderate.

FOOD

Woodman's of Essex. Main Street. Telephone: (978) 768–6451. The tidal flats of Essex are famous for clams and the Woodman family claims that Lawrence "Chubby" Woodman invented the fried clam here more than eighty years ago. We can only guess how many have been served since then in this "eat-in-the-rough" restaurant, famous throughout the Northeast. Lunch and dinner. Inexpensive to moderate.

FAIRS, FESTIVALS, AND EVENTS

Essex Clamfest. This one-day event in mid-

September includes arts and crafts and entertainment along with a chowder-tasting competition. Telephone: (978) 283–1601.

Newburyport, Massachusetts

LODGING

Clark Currier Inn. 45 Green Street. Shipbuilder Thomas March Clark built this home in 1803 in the three-story "square house" style of the time. Each of the four guest rooms is decorated with antiques and retains period architectural detail. Telephone: (978) 465–8363. Moderate to expensive with breakfast.

The Windsor House. 38 Federal Street. This eighteenth-century brick Federal mansion has four guest rooms, each with a private bath. Innkeeper John Harris hails from Great Britain and his wife is a true Anglophile. This translates into traditional English breakfasts and afternoon tea. One room is decorated as a tribute to the late Princess Diana. Telephone: (978) 462–3778 or (888) TRELAWNY. Moderate with breakfast.

FOOD

Glenn's Restaurant. 44 Merrimac Street. Telephone: (978) 465–3811. This contemporary bistro favors fish on a New American menu that changes with striking frequency. The bar scene is also lively. Dinner. Moderate to expensive.

Ten Center Street. 10 Center Street. Telephone: (978) 462–6652. The first floor pub in this 1790 home-turned-restaurant is a local favorite for its cozy atmosphere and pub menu. The upstairs dining room is dressed in formal linens and the menu is more continental. Lunch, dinner, Sunday brunch. Moderate.

3·The Hub

Introduction

As Greater Boston residents, we're apt to find ourselves grumbling as we rush to a concert or lecture (or to the grocery store) and find the sidewalk blocked by a gaggle of visitors poring over a map or pointing and staring at some landmark we take for granted. Then we bring ourselves up short. We may consider Boston (actually, Cambridge, just across the river) our home turf, but in many ways the Hub is every American's hometown, and we have no business getting impatient with folks who have come to have a look around.

Boston's history belongs to America. A persistent strain of the American character began here in 1630, when Governor John Winthrop led a bunch of Puritan reformers dedicated to the virtues of intellectual achievement, hard work, thrift, sobriety, and moral conduct to this unpromising peninsula on Massachusetts Bay. Self-righteous and self-determined, they founded Boston as a "City upon a Hill" to stand as an example to the world. And while those first Puritans were hardly democrats, their reformist ideas held the seeds of democracy. Although only property-owning church members could vote, by 1634 they established a representative elected body to assume day-to-day running of community business.

By 1644, this arrangement evolved into an elected bicameral colonial legislature—a model of American governance grounded in the rejection of the divine right of kings in favor of an individual's understanding of Holy Writ. And to make sure that their successors understood the Bible, they quickly established universal and free education. Already civilized when most of America was wilderness, Boston was first to bridle under the British yoke and supplied a nascent America with the political and intellectual underpinnings for independence. The broad strokes with which merchant John Hancock signed the Declaration of Independence were a statement of determination—"big enough so King George can read it," he said. As a new nation went forward, two of its first four presidents hailed from Greater Boston. The country's literature and its early commerce began here, and even today, when the money managers of Boston speak, the world turns an attentive ear. None of that history would matter except that Boston holds onto its past with a firm Yankee grip. No other city has so many sites directly related to the American Revolution.

Yes, we grumble about sidewalk blockers and landmark gawkers, but (truth be told) we get a kick out of people from all over the globe coming to appreciate our adopted city. Once in a while we'll hang out at Faneuil Hall Marketplace—a place frequented more by visitors than by locals—just to see how many languages we can recognize. When the chemistry is right, we're treated to a vision of Boston through fresh eyes. It reminds us not to take Boston for granted, for it is a city unique among American places.

For starters, more than three and a half centuries of history are embedded in the city. As Benjamin Thompson, one of Greater Boston's most influential twentieth-century architects, once remarked, "The fact that Boston's past touches us daily is the most modern thing about the city." Yet Boston isn't constantly gazing in a rearview mirror. Around the winding streets that Paul Revere and Sam Adams walked stands a vibrant city with arts, architecture, and culture to rival any metropolis in the modern world.

All that energy and experience, however, is stacked on a small footprint. The Shawmut peninsula settled in 1630 covered about 880 acres. With centuries of filling and refashioning and annexing, Boston still only encompasses 1,900 acres—not much bigger than Denver's new

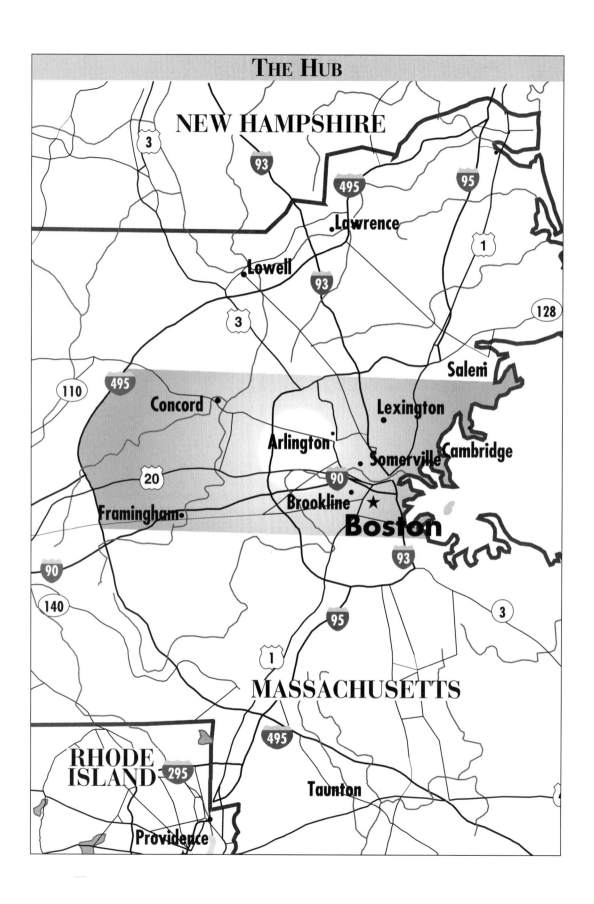

airport. In practice, that means that Boston is the "walking city" that it claims to be. There is no better way to savor the interwoven layers of history and modern life than to stroll the city's streets, and—yes—to stop suddenly on its sidewalks to consult the map and marvel over the landmarks.

History:
Making a Nation

Many New England sites played a role on the road to the American Revolution and the struggle that transformed British colonies into a nation. Vermonters Ethan Allen and his Green Mountain Boys captured Fort Ticonderoga without firing a shot on May 10, 1775. (Allen's co-commander, General Benedict Arnold, captured Crown Point, New York, the next day, thereby seizing control of Lake Champlain.) Machias, Maine, can claim the first naval battle of the war, when the townspeople captured an armed British schooner on June 12, 1775. Rhode Island took the lead in political defiance as the first colony to renounce allegiance to King George on May 4, 1776.

But we can say without local chauvinism that Boston—and its suburbs of Lexington and Concord—were the vanguard of insurrection. Even today, Boston takes much of its identity from that tumultuous period. In a 1770 letter, General Thomas Gage, commander of British forces in North America, complained "America is a mere bully, from one end to the other, and the Bostonians by far the greatest bully." Bostonians consider that high praise and wear it as a badge of honor—to rank first on the British enemies list.

When the British finally forced the French off the North American continent in 1763, Parliament began to squeeze the colonies to replenish coffers emptied by nearly a century of warfare—the conflicts we call the French and Indian War. The British tightened restrictions on where and under what terms the Colonies could trade, levied new taxes on trade goods, and put local government on a short leash. Boston was exactly the wrong

place for these strong-arm tactics. Besides a tradition of robust local rule and a trade-based economy, Boston also had a generation of soldiers and officers battle-hardened from fighting the French.

Boston quickly emerged as the most vocal opponent to the new British regulations. Protests broke out at the site of Colonial government headquarters in the Old State House, at Boston Town Meeting in Faneuil Hall, and at the hall that held the largest crowds, Old South Meeting House. An eloquent and politically savvy leadership arose to defy Britain: John Hancock, the city's richest merchant; Samuel Adams, a brilliant political organizer; Dr. Joseph Warren, one of Boston's leading physicians and political philosophers; and the indefatigable Paul Revere.

The quarrel with the mother country soon turned violent when in March 1770, a small squad of British soldiers fired on a hostile crowd in front of the Old State House and killed five Bostonians in what the rebels soon called the Boston Massacre. On December 16, 1773, rebels dumped a load of British tea in the harbor to protest a new tea tax. Britain summarily closed the port of Boston to trade and placed the entire Massachusetts colony under the military rule of General Thomas Gage. In response, the clandestine rebels came out in the open, established an illegal Provincial Congress and organized the minutemen, a select group of the Colonial militia who could be ready to fight at a minute's notice.

Public tumult grew with angry meetings characterized by heady rhetoric. The die was cast, and war came quickly. After sunset on April 18, 1775, boats began ferrying British soldiers across the Charles River to Cambridge to begin a march to Lexington to seize a cache of rebel weapons and to arrest Samuel Adams and John Hancock. In many towns throughout New England, bands of revolutionaries had organized leadership groups called "committees of safety." When Dr. Joseph Warren, head of Boston's committee, learned of the troop movements, he dispatched Paul Revere and William Dawes to warn Hancock and Adams. Young sexton Robert Newman crept to the steeple of

Old North Church to signal the Redcoats' route—"one if by land, two if by sea," as Longfellow later chronicled in "The Midnight Ride of Paul Revere."

When about 700 British soldiers marched into Lexington near dawn they were met by seventy-seven minutemen. Facing overwhelming odds, colonial Captain John Parker told his men, "Stand your ground. Don't fire unless fired upon, but if they mean to have a war, let it begin here." It did.

In the brief exchange of fire, eight Americans were killed and the Redcoats marched on to Concord to search for weapons. During the search, 400 Colonial militiamen attacked a British unit of ninety soldiers at Concord Bridge, routing them in a brief skirmish—the encounter that Ralph Waldo Emerson immortalized as "the shot heard 'round the world." A running battle back to Boston claimed the lives of seventy-three British soldiers and left 200 wounded.

There was no turning back. Within days, 16,000 armed New England Colonists descended on Boston and penned in the British on Boston's peninsula. The British sent reinforcements under General William Howe and the Continental Congress sent General George Washington to take command of the Continental Army.

On the afternoon of June 17, 1775, before Washington could arrive, Howe's forces tried to break out of Boston by attacking Patriot forces on Breed's Hill (often mistaken for Bunker Hill on Colonial-era maps). Holding fire until they could "see the whites of their eyes," the Americans mowed down the Redcoats. A second assault also failed. But a third assault with fresh troops overtook the Americans, who had spent nearly all their ammunition in the first two encounters. While the British took the hill, it was a Pyrrhic victory. British casualties were high and the troops withdrew. The Americans took heart at having met the British regulars successfully in a pitched battle.

The siege of Boston dragged on through the winter—until Washington implemented a plan to drive the British from Boston without a bloody battle. Using British cannons captured by the Green Mountain Boys at Fort Ticonderoga and laboriously hauled overland to Cambridge, he fortified Dorchester Heights on the South Boston peninsula. When dawn broke on March 5, 1776, General Howe discovered that his mighty fleet of troop- and warships was literally under the gun. He accepted Washington's offer of a peaceful retreat and on March 17 the Redcoats set sail for Halifax. The date is still celebrated as a state holiday, Evacuation Day. The battlefronts of the Revolution soon shifted south, but losing Boston was the first major setback to Britain's efforts to subjugate its rebellious colonies and the Americans' first major victory in the struggle for independence.

Seeing the Hub

Boston, Massachusetts

Travelers with only a short time to enjoy the city before taking off on the byways of New England would do well to follow the Freedom Trail. This 2.5-mile path marked by a red line connects sixteen sites linked to the American Revolution and the early history of America. First established in 1951 and significantly improved with new signage and interpreters within the last years, the **Freedom Trail** also passes through some of Boston's most interesting neighborhoods and commercial districts. Maps for self-guided tours are available at the **Boston Visitors Center** on **Boston Common,** which is the beginning point of the Freedom Trail.

Established in 1634, the Common served as a militia drill field and common pasture for two centuries. Bordered by Tremont, Boylston, Charles, and Beacon Streets, the Common's very centrality has made it the stage where many of the city's dramas have been played out. This is where Puritans hanged Quakers for heresy, where a century apart William Lloyd Garrison and the Rev. Martin Luther King, Jr. spoke for racial equality, where Pope John Paul celebrated Mass, where Boston soldiers massed to march off to the Civil War, and where antiwar protestors gathered in small groups during World Wars I and II and in the tens of thousands during the Vietnam War. We've rarely crossed the Common without encountering at least one person with a placard declaiming some political point of view.

The deep history of the Common alone hints at the tales each of Boston's historic spots can tell. The best way to get a handle on Boston for a short visit is to tag along on a free ninety-minute tour with a guide from the National Park Service for an overview and then return to spots of particular interest. (See "Staying There.") We take one of these tours every few years and find they both jog our memories and teach us something new every time. But if you can spare a few more days, Boston can be toured in four historic overlays that expand well beyond the brief era of the Revolution to embrace a dynamic, modern city with a pachydermic memory for its salad days and a sweet sense of where it is headed.

North End and Charlestown

Charlestown, which lies on its own peninsula between the Charles and Mystic Rivers, was first established in 1629 and a year later briefly housed the Puritans who would settle Boston. The original settlement of ten families constructed their houses in what is now City Square at the base of Town Hill in 1629, and a year later erected a fort near the top of the hill. The approximate dimensions of the fortress are now delineated by stone fences that set off **John Harvard Mall,** named for the minister and benefactor of Harvard College who lived nearby. A bronze plaque proclaims "this low mound of earth the memorial of a mighty nation," while another notes that "the first public worship of God" by the Puritans led by John Winthrop took place here "under a great oak."

Recent excavations for Boston's massive highway and tunnel project uncovered what archaeologists believe are the remains of the Great House built by John Winthrop in 1630 before he moved across the river to the Shawmut Peninsula. Other than the odd cellar hole, seventeenth century Charlestown has vanished and the neighborhood is less associated with its founders than with its defenders during the Revolutionary War. The looming **Bunker Hill Monument**—the tallest monolith erected in America until it was surpassed by the Washington Monument in 1885—ensures the memory of Charlestown's rebel grit, memorializing the Revolutionary War battle of June 17, 1775. Although the Americans lost this first pitched battle of the war, they prevented the British from breaking the siege of Boston and their valor inspired all of New England to arms. A statue of Colonel William Prescott, leader of the "farmer soldiers," stands by the steps leading up to the monument and a plaque marks the demise of Dr. Joseph Warren (head of Boston's "Committee of Safety"), who insisted on fighting as a private in the militia and was fatally wounded in the fracas.

Two hundred ninety-four steps lead to the top of the Bunker Hill Monument and the climb—there is no elevator—is rewarded with an extraordinary panorama of red-brick Charlestown immediately below, the skyline of Boston, and the harbor spread out to the horizon. One of the grandest sights is the USS *Constitution* floating in the harbor at the Charlestown Navy Yard. The monument is open daily 9:00 A.M. to 5:00 P.M. (until 4:30 for climbing to the top). Free. Telephone: (617) 242–5641.

The **Charlestown Navy Yard,** which sits at the spot where British troops landed for the Battle

of Bunker Hill, was established by President John Adams in 1800 and remained in active service until 1974, when it became part of Boston National Historical Park. Alexander Parris, architect of Quincy Market, also designed the yard. The complex represents one of the country's earliest examples of purpose-built architecture. A perfect example of this approach to design is the long, narrow **Rope Walk** building where most of the U.S. Navy's cordage was produced for nearly a century. Another good example is **Drydock #1,** which was the second drydock on America's Atlantic coast when it was built in 1802. A drydock is a basin large enough to hold a ship. One end is opened to the ocean and a ship scheduled for repair is floated in. Then the drydock is sealed and drained while the ship is braced in place. When the hull is repaired, the drydock is refilled and the ship floats again. The Navy Yard is open daily 9:00 A.M. to 5:00 P.M. with ranger-led tours mid-June through Labor Day at 11:00 A.M. Free. Telephone: (617) 242–5601.

The first ship in Drydock #1 was the **USS *Constitution,*** built in Edmund Hartt's North End shipyard in 1797 and now the oldest commissioned ship afloat. The *Constitution* earned the nickname "Old Ironsides" during the War of 1812 when she defeated the British ship *Guerriere* and, as the legend goes, a sailor noticing cannonballs bouncing off her oak planks called out, "Huzza! Her sides are made of iron." After extensive refitting, the *Constitution* carried her own canvas into the wind for her bicentennial. Navy personnel conduct free tours daily 9:30 A.M. to 3:50 P.M. Telephone: (617) 242–5670.

Walking from Charlestown to Boston's **North End** across the 1899 bridge provides a more immediate view of the mouth of the Charles River and the inner reaches of Boston Harbor. Although Winthrop's band had to make the passage by rowboat, the stroll emphasizes just how easy it was for the settlers to pull up their tender roots and occupy the Shawmut peninsula. Although the first settlement was on the more sheltered South Cove (in what is now Chinatown), the new Bostonians spread into the North End by the spring of 1631, making this the oldest continuously occupied neighborhood within the original confines of Boston.

USS *Constitution*
Boston, Massachusetts

The North End has been accepting immigrants ever since. In 1800, most North End residents were of English or African descent, but when the Great Famine hit Ireland in the 1840s, the neighborhood soon absorbed the brunt of the Irish immigration. The Africans moved to Beacon Hill, and most of the Irish moved on to Dorchester and then the South Shore. Russian and Polish Jews fleeing the pogroms of their homelands replaced the earlier immigrants, and at the end of the nineteenth century political and economic turmoil in Sicily and southern Italy sent tens of thousands to Boston. Other groups moved on but the Italians have remained, making the North End their own for the last three-quarters of a century.

Despite recent gentrification, southern Italian tradition is strong on the mile-long main drag of **Hanover Street.** The street is dotted with the densest concentration of trattorias and cafes in the neighborhood and the music of the mother tongue is found on every street corner. Unless a visitor comes in the height of tourist season (when the North Enders go on vacation to escape the crowds), it will seem as if everyone in this neighborhood of 15,000 seems to know each other. In many ways, the North End is a small town within the geopolitical limits of metropolitan Boston.

Most history books emphasize public buildings and squares, but we feel the real story of Boston lies in her citizens' private lives. Purely by coincidence, Paul Revere's house is the oldest residence still standing in Boston. When the 35-year-old silversmith bought the structure in 1770, it was already a century old. Over a thirty-year period, Revere sired sixteen children by two wives and the **Paul Revere House** provides detailed, even gossipy interpretation of the domestic life of the Reveres. Some Revere family possessions remain on display—an armchair, a chest of drawers, one of Revere's early silver pitchers. Paul often ducked out of the house under cover of darkness for clandestine meetings of the Sons of Liberty at one of several nearby pubs, and this is where his journey began when he slipped down to Hancock's wharf and rowed across the Charles River to Charlestown to mount his horse for their midnight ride into history. Open April 15 through October 31 daily 9:30 A.M. to 5:15 P.M.,

November through April 14 daily 9:30 A.M. to 4:15 P.M. Adults $2.50. 19 North Square. Telephone: (617) 523–2338.

Thanks to Henry Wadsworth Longfellow's poem ("Listen my children and you shall hear..."), we expect that every American knows that Revere looked to the towering spire of Boston's oldest church—the 1723 Christ Church, Episcopal, better known as **Old North Church**—to know what message to deliver. On the night of April 18, 1775, sexton Robert Newman hung lanterns in the belfry to signal British troop movements. The church remains an active parish, and the interior of the building is classic, lovely, and restrained—a model of box pews, brass chandeliers, and airy light. A small gift shop next door

Old North Church, Boston

has a more imaginative than usual collection of Boston souvenirs. The church is open daily 9:00 A.M. to 5:00 P.M. Suggested donation $2.00. 193 Salem Street. Telephone: (617) 523–6676.

Behind Old North is the uphill entrance to Paul Revere Mall (which the Italians of the neighborhood simply call "the Prado"). Across the mall at 401 Hanover Street stands **St. Stephen's Church.** Originally built as a Congregational church, it is the last meetinghouse designed by Charles Bulfinch still standing in Boston. Saved by the Catholic Archdiocese when Hanover Street was widened, St. Stephen's was the parish church of Rose Kennedy, matriarch of the Kennedy clan. Here she was christened and here her funeral Mass was said.

Uphill from the churches, on the corner of Hull and Snowhill Streets, the famous and the obscure lie side by side in **Copp's Hill Burial Ground,** Boston's second oldest cemetery. One modest crypt holds the remains of preacher-politicians Cotton and Increase Mather. A broken column marks the grave of Prince Hall, leader of Boston's African American community after the Revolution. Patriot Daniel Mather's tombstone—chipped by musketballs fired by British soldiers during target practice—notes that he lies ten feet down, presumably safe from further musket fire. Boston is a terrific town for cemetery buffs, but this is one of our favorite burying grounds because its high vantage makes it lighter and airier than most. (The Puritans often held hangings here because crowds could watch from the base of the hill and from boats in the harbor.)

Faneuil Hall Marketplace and Downtown

We've been told that Faneuil Hall Marketplace ranks as one the most popular tourist destinations in America, and the bustle of the crowds and the energy of the street performers seem to confirm that claim. But the market isn't just another mercantile sideshow. There's ample historical precedent for browsing these shops: The handsome granite buildings that anchor the market have been in place since the 1820s. When the admittedly rundown area was redeveloped in the mid-1970s, the project pioneered the concept of reusing historic buildings as festival marketplaces—an idea replicated in New York, Baltimore, New Orleans, and Miami by the same developers.

Many of the shops and restaurants are housed in the 535-foot granite **Quincy Market** building, constructed in 1827 as part of an overhaul of Boston's sanitary infrastructure. Until this produce, meat, and fish market for the entire city was built, most food was sold door to door by peddlers with pushcarts. Centralization permitted garbage control and a high standard of sanitation. And because the market stood right on the docks in those days, fresh food could be brought in by boat. Not long after Quincy Market was built, **Durgin-Park Restaurant** (see "Staying There") went into business in the adjacent **North Market** building to serve the butchers and bakers and stall tenders and stevedores. Its clientele is rather more diverse today, but we suspect there have been very few changes in the menu.

But the entire complex takes its name from Boston's still-operative 1742 temple of free speech, **Faneuil Hall,** often called "the Cradle of Liberty." Opened in 1742 as a food market and auditorium, it became a focal point of revolutionary rhetoric. Samuel Adams took the floor in 1772 to protest excesses of the British crown and established a tradition of outspokenness that continues to this day. In the first decade of the nineteenth century, the original building was renovated and enlarged under the direction of architect Charles Bulfinch, who added a larger and acoustically resonant meeting hall to the second floor. From this stage, William Lloyd Garrison, publisher of the abolitionist weekly, *The Liberator,* railed against slavery. Susan B. Anthony electrified the New England Woman Suffrage Association with her demands that women have the right to vote, and a young World War II veteran named John Fitzgerald Kennedy launched his first campaign for Congress—a campaign successful, in part, because he won the overwhelming majority of votes by women. Public discourse still rings in this venerable auditorium, where many speeches, lectures, political debates, and even poetry readings are held. Any citizen of Boston can petition to use the hall, provided that no admission is charged and the general public is admitted. Open daily 9:00 A.M. to 5:00 P.M. Free. No phone.

Historic buildings still play a vital role in the life of modern Boston, lending the substance of history to the concerns of the moment. But these historic monuments were not always so well regarded, and several nearly vanished in the make-way-for-the-new ebullience of the late nineteenth century.

The **Old State House,** Boston's oldest public building, was built in 1713 but had so deteriorated by 1880 that many citizens argued that it should be demolished to clear a prime piece of real estate. The city of Chicago even offered to purchase the building and move it to the shores of Lake Michigan, a prospect so alarming that the Bostonian Society preserved the building as a museum of Boston and Revolutionary War history. The structure itself figures prominently in that history: The 1770 Boston Massacre occurred out front and on July 18, 1776, the Declaration of Independence was read from the balcony. Open daily 9:00 A.M. to 5:00 P.M. Adults $3.00. 206 Washington Street. Telephone: (617) 720–3290.

Old South Meeting House, the second building of Boston's second oldest church, also came close to demolition when its congregation moved to fashionable Copley Square in 1876. A group of concerned citizens, including Ralph Waldo Emerson and Julia Ward Howe (grande dame of Boston society and author of the "Battle Hymn of the Republic"), raised the money to save Old South and turn it into a museum to recount its own rich history. One congregant at the 1729 structure was Phillis Wheatley, who came to Boston as a slave, won her freedom, and became the first African American poet in the colonies. The building's historical apogee was the December 16, 1773, meeting at which Samuel Adams gave the secret signal to commence the Boston Tea Party. The British Army got even by using Old South as a riding school in 1775 and 1776; it took nearly five years to repair the building once the cavalry departed. Open April through October daily 9:30 A.M. to 5:00 P.M., November through March daily 10:00 A.M. to 4:00 P.M. Adults $3. 310 Washington Street. Telephone: (617) 482–6439.

Many of those who made Colonial or Revolutionary history were laid to rest in this neighborhood and we rarely pass by without seeing someone carefully searching out their graves. **King's Chapel Burying Ground,** on the corner of Tremont and School Streets, is Boston's first cemetery. It holds the graves of Governors John Winthrop and John Endicott, William Dawes (the often-overlooked rider who spread the alarm with Paul Revere on April 18, 1775), Mary Chilton (the first Pilgrim to touch Plimoth Rock), and Elizabeth Pain (said to be Nathaniel Hawthorne's inspiration for Hester Prynne of *The Scarlet Letter*).

The **Granary Burying Ground** on Tremont Street dates from 1660. Samuel Adams, John Hancock, and the victims of the Boston Massacre are buried here. So is Paul Revere, whose very full life was also so long that when he died in 1818, his casket barely squeaked into one of the last remaining gravesites. As they lowered him down, King's Chapel tolled his loss with a bell he had cast just two years earlier.

Beacon Hill

Bounded by Boston Common on the sunny side, Charles Street at its base, and Cambridge Street on its north flank, Beacon Hill is the hump that rises in the heart of downtown Boston. Even without the sixty feet trimmed off the top in the 1790s, Beacon Hill remains the loftiest natural perch in the city, and its crowning glory is the gold-domed **Massachusetts State House.** Drivers might be interested to know that the gold dome is the Mile Zero marker for Massachusetts mapmakers—all distances are measured to this point. Boston Mayor Samuel Adams and Grand Master of the Masonic Order Paul Revere laid the cornerstone for the State House, and when the classical building designed by Charles Bulfinch was completed in 1798, it proclaimed the grandeur of self-government. The structure has been enlarged over the years, but the stateliness of the original red brick core has not been diminished by later yellow-brick wings and other architectural indignities visited on the complex. In fact, Bulfinch's design seemed so in tune with the country's democratic ideals that it served as a model for modifications to the U.S. Capitol building in

State House, Boston

Washington and influenced about half the state capitols in the country. Free tours offered Monday through Friday. Call for hours. Telephone: (617) 727–3676.

Many statues dot the lawn of the State House, including likenesses of Daniel Webster, educator Horace Mann, John F. Kennedy, and religious martyrs Anne Hutchinson and Mary Dyer. But the most moving public sculpture is directly across Beacon Street on the edge of Boston Common. The cast-bronze **Shaw Memorial,** sculpted in low relief by Augustus Saint-Gaudens (see "Connecticut River Valley"), honors the African American Civil War soldiers of the 54th Regiment, led by abolitionist Robert Gould Shaw. Half the members of that first black Union regiment, along with their white commander, Shaw, died at Fort Wagner in the harbor of Charleston, South Carolina, and their valor was depicted in the film *Glory.*

If the State House was the symbol of the grandeur of self-government, the early nineteenth-century development of the leafy south slope of Beacon Hill into an exclusive residential neighborhood reflected Boston's commercial muscle in the nation's youth. The land was purchased from portrait painter John Singleton Copley (who, as a Tory sympathizer, had taken refuge in England) in the 1790s by the Mount Vernon

Proprietors, a real estate syndicate of lawyers and politicians. They trimmed and smoothed the summits of three adjacent hills and used the dirt to fill in swampland at the base of the high ground, thereby creating even more real estate. America's first professional architect, Charles Bulfinch, did some of his most inspired work along Mount Vernon, Chestnut, and Beacon Streets, creating domestic masterpieces for himself and for Boston's richest merchants. Ultimately, he set the tone for Beacon Hill's streets, both with individual mansions on large lots and, once construction money began to dry up in the economic turndown of 1807, with handsome rows of brick townhouses.

The "best" families of Boston have lived here ever since. Henry James once called the stretch of Mount Vernon Street between the Massachusetts State House and Louisburg Square "the most civilized street in America." **Louisburg Square** itself, which runs between Mount Vernon and Pinckney Streets is considered by many to be the most prestigious address in the city. This private square of Greek Revival townhouses has been home to such local luminaries as Louisa May Alcott and William Dean Howells. The square is long on decorum and short on flash, as proper as an old-fashioned waistcoat. Among the current residents are Senator John Forbes Kerry and his wife, Teresa Heinz, as well as Robin Cook, author of various blockbuster novels.

Thanks to the generosity of Beacon Hill resident (and resident character) Rose Standish Nichols, "people from around the world without a letter of introduction" are able to "see the inside of a fine house"—notably her own family home, built in 1804 from a Bulfinch design. The Nichols family acquired the house when Rose was thirteen and she spent her life there as a Beacon Hill paradigm. Possessing a little family money, she invented a genteel career as a landscape designer, became a prominent political and social activist, and created her own version of an artist's salon. The home is furnished with family heirlooms and more quirky objects Rose acquired on her travels. The **Nichols House Museum,** created in her 1960 will, lends color to this admittedly formal neighborhood with personal details of a life on "The Hill." Open May through October Tuesday through Saturday noon to 5:00 P.M.,

November, December, and February through April Monday, Wednesday and Saturday noon to 5:00 P.M. Adults $5.00. 55 Mount Vernon Street. Telephone: (617) 227–6993.

So much of Rose Nichols' personality survives in her house museum that it often makes us speculate about other Beacon Hill residents we pass as we make our way along the frost-heaved brick sidewalks. (The Hill's residents went ballistic when one Boston mayor tried to pave these walks more than half a century ago, and brick they remain to this day.) The caricature of the Beacon Hill residents was laid out more than a century ago by Oliver Wendell Holmes (himself a Beacon Hill resident) when he defined the Boston Brahmin as a member of that "harmless, inoffensive, untitled aristocracy" with their "houses by Bulfinch, their monopoly on Beacon Street, their ancestral portraits and Chinese porcelains, humanitarianism, Unitarian faith in the march of the mind, Yankee shrewdness, and New England exclusiveness."

But in a city as vibrant as Boston, no neighborhood is monolithic, and Beacon Hill has been surprisingly diverse over the years. The largest free African American community in pre-Civil War America also lived here. The **Black Heritage Trail,** a walking tour designed by the National Park Service, links several highlights of the community, which later shifted to Roxbury and the South End. Pinckney Street, which runs parallel to Mount Vernon, divided the Caucasian south slope and the African north slope. Number 86 Pinckney was once the **home of John J. Smith,** who crossed the color bar by renting the house from an abolitionist. At the end of Pinckney Street, a left turn leads onto Joy Street and Smith Court, the center of the community when Beacon Hill's north slope was African American. The waterfront slave market in Boston opened in 1638, but by the time Massachusetts became one of the first states to outlaw slavery in 1783, the city had a large population of free blacks. They constructed the **African Meeting House** on Smith Court in 1806 to rival white churches and to serve as a social, economic, and religious center. The first black school in Boston (later absorbed into the Abiel Smith School next door) was established in its basement, and the Anti-Slavery Society was founded in the schoolroom. The

meetinghouse and the surrounding neighborhood also figured in the Underground Railroad. The warren of alleys and mews (a typical entry is visible at the end of Smith Court) was ideal for evading slave catchers, and no slave catcher was ever successful on Beacon Hill. The African Meeting House is open Monday through Friday 10:00 A.M. to 4:00 P.M. Donation requested. 46 Joy Street. Telephone: (617) 739–1200.

Charles Street lies at the foot of Beacon Hill toward the Charles River. It serves as the neighborhood's mercantile center—where the ladies purchase their lamb chops at Julia Child's butcher, Savenor's, and great-grandchildren of Boston Brahmins purchase their after-dinner madeira. This gracious street of shops and restaurants deems itself the first antiquing district in America. We wouldn't swear to that, but about two dozen shops proffer goods that range from exquisite and pricey Asian art objects and fine tableware to Victorian jewelry and nineteenth-century lithographs. Local lore suggests that many dealers began by helping scions of famous Beacon Hill families transform their heirlooms (of which they had many) into dollars (of which they had fewer).

Victorian Back Bay and the Fenway

Beacon Hill was Boston's first best address, but by the time the Civil War concluded, the fashionable folk were building townhouses on the "New Land" (as Beacon Hill snobs derided it) of Back Bay. The gateway between the two neighborhoods is the **Public Garden** (*never* plural). Established as a botanical preserve and dedicated in 1859 as the nation's first public botanical garden, its twenty-four acres are filled with flower beds, grand specimen trees, and public sculpture. But the three most popular features are not botanical at all. The bridge over the lagoon was designed in the late nineteenth century by William Preston to parody the mighty suspension bridges so in vogue in the rest of the country. Many a couple has courted on its short span, lending the nickname as the **"Bridge of Sighs."** At one time it was in the running as the smallest suspension bridge in the world, but it was long ago propped up from beneath and the cables are merely decorative. While spooners may favor the bridge, children are far more enamored of the **bronze ducklings** near the Beacon Street-Charles Street corner of the Garden. Inspired by Robert McCloskey's children's classic *Make Way for Ducklings,* their backs and heads are polished to a bright sheen by thousands of youngsters who pose atop them as parents take snapshots. But perhaps the most beloved feature in the Public Garden is the small fleet of **swan boats.** Fifteen-minute cruises aboard these elaborate foot-pedaled boats inspired by sets from Wagner's opera *Lohengrin* have been a Boston tradition since the Paget family introduced them in 1877.

Back Bay was once literally a marshy tidal bay near the mouth of the Charles River, and filling it up to create 450 acres of "new land" was the most ambitious public works project in America when it began in 1859. Using gravel brought by steam locomotive from West Needham, workers filled, on average, two house lots per day for thirteen years, with work continuing at a slower pace into the early twentieth century. The work proceeded from east to west, and as soon as a block was filled, new houses went up. The result is a decade-by-decade march of Victorian architectural styles in this lovely neighborhood where the tangled web of old Boston streets unfurls into broad boulevards.

Commonwealth Avenue affords the clearest picture of Boston's Victorian self-assurance. Modeled on Baron Haussmann's Parisian boulevards, Commonwealth Avenue is 240 feet wide with an elegant green mall punctuated by statues and trees running up the middle. It is a stroller's street and the place where some neighborhood residents settle down on a bench with the Sunday newspaper while others walk their dogs. Most buildings are residential, though several private clubs and non-profit offices also lurk behind the domestic facades. Between the world wars it became fashionable to plant the tiny dooryards with spring bulbs and magnolia trees, which put on a gaudy show each spring.

By contrast, **Newbury Street** has grown from a residential enclave to become a stage set of sorts—the street to see and be seen amid the most expensive and au courant boutiques, chic art galleries, trendy restaurants, and outdoor cafes. We have a friend who dismisses the upscale posturings

Swan boats, Boston

of Newbury Street as "rue de pretense," yet we find ourselves drawn back time and again by a really good exhibition at the Society of Arts & Crafts (175 Newbury Street; telephone: 617–266–1810), by the bistro offerings of some of the less self-conscious restaurants, or the younger, funkier scene of Newbury's last block before reaching Massachusetts Avenue.

Yet if Newbury sacrifices culture in favor of couture, the antidote is only a block away. **Copley Square** is Boston's symbolic center of art, religion, and culture. Its spiritual and architectural center is **Trinity Church,** which defines the Clarendon Street side of the Square. A perennial on the American Institute of Architects' poll of the ten best buildings in the country, the 1877 French Romanesque style church was designed by H.H. Richardson, who appealed to such artists as John LaFarge to create an inspirational interior for preachers and congregation alike. The full effect for all the senses can be enjoyed during the free half-hour organ concert every Friday from mid-September through June at 12:15 P.M. So that it will stand firmly on the soft fill of Back Bay, the monumental church rests on 2,000 piles sunk through the mud to solid ground and topped with granite pyramids. The hefty stone church literally floats on this platform, yet it seems almost ethereal as it is reflected in the mirror-like glass facade of the adjacent 790-foot **John Hancock Tower.** Completed in 1975, the Hancock's skyscraping temple to commerce will likely remain Boston's tallest building, thanks to new and tougher zoning regulations. The sixtieth floor observatory provides a sweeping view of the city. (See "Staying There.") The tower is visible from great distances—we know one immigrant who speaks no English but successfully navigates around the city by using the Hancock as a landmark. But as the viewer gets closer, the mirrored façade of the building almost disappears into reflections of the Victorian and twentieth-century buildings that surround it.

Across the plaza, Charles McKim's 1895 **Boston Public Library** is the home of the first major free municipal library in the United States. It's often called the "people's palace" and with good reason. McKim modeled it on a Renaissance palazzo, with grand marble staircase, bronze doors designed by Daniel Chester French (see "Up Country"), and murals, including those by Edward Abbey depicting the "Quest for the Holy Grail" and those by John Singer Sargent of "Judaism and Christianity." When the library outgrew its quarters, a simple and dignified addition was added in 1971. Art and architecture tours are offered Monday at 2:30 P.M., Tuesday and Thursday at 6:00 P.M., Friday and Saturday at 11:00 A.M. Free. Tours gather at the Dartmouth Street entrance on Copley Square. Telephone: (617) 536–5400, ext. 216.

First-time Boston visitors are often surprised to learn that Copley Square did not settle into its present tidy and inviting form until the mid-1990s, when the current paving and walkways were laid. Indeed, in the 1860s it was a gaping wasteland where the non-parallel street grids of the South End and Back Bay met at the erstwhile site of a railroad roundhouse. A vast temporary structure, the Peace Jubilee Coliseum, was thrown up on the site but when its second extravaganza flopped in 1872 (despite the presence of Johann Strauss conducting his own compositions), the structure came down to be replaced by the Museum of Fine Arts. The museum was super-

Trinity Church, Boston

ceded, in turn, by the **Copley Plaza Hotel,** a stately Edwardian structure that has the most ornate lobby in the city and serves as the site of many social occasions.

By the turn of the century the **Museum of Fine Art**'s swelling collections had outgrown the Victorian Gothic monstrosity built to house them in 1876, and the MFA relocated about a mile farther from the downtown core in another swampy area just beginning to be reclaimed. For those willing to spend the time (and even stop to sniff the Rose Garden), the best way to get to the MFA is to walk through the Back Bay Fens, part of the Emerald Necklace of parkland designed by Frederick Law Olmsted to stretch through the city

With more than one million objects, the MFA is one of the largest art museums in the world. The permanent collection is primarily displayed in the granite Classical Revival main building that opened in 1909, while the West Wing, added in 1981, hosts temporary exhibits, including some "blockbusters," and a cafe, restaurant, and extensive gift shop. Boston history buffs will find more than sixty portraits by John Singleton Copley, perhaps America's most gifted eighteenth-century painter. Among those who took time from their rebellious activities to pose for this Tory portraitist were John Hancock, Paul Revere, and Samuel Adams. The museum also owns two cases of silver by Paul Revere, including the "Liberty Bowl," a 1768 commission by the Sons of Liberty to honor Massachusetts legislators for taking a stand against the Townshend acts, which imposed new taxes and trade restrictions. (The protests succeeded and the acts were withdrawn.)

But the MFA's holdings are hardly parochial. The Asiatic art collection ranks among the largest under one roof in the world. The extensive holdings of Egyptian funerary arts (which kids happily call "The Mummies") have just been reinstalled in magnificent new galleries. The collection of Old Kingdom and Nubian art and artifacts is second only to the Cairo Museum. The MFA has the largest collection of paintings by Jean-François Millet in the world and a group of Monet paintings surpassed only in Paris. Boston merchants and bankers prospered at the end of the nineteenth century, and their largesse allowed the MFA to acquire some of the best art of the time, compiling one of the world's great collections of impressionism and post-impressionism. Controversial when they were first acquired, these paintings now occupy the museum's most popular galleries. Open Monday and Tuesday 10:00 A.M. to 4:45 P.M., Wednesday 10:00 A.M. to 9:45 P.M. Thursday and Friday 10:00 A.M. to 9:45 P.M. (West Wing only after 5:00 P.M.), Saturday and Sunday 10:00 A.M. to 5:45 P.M. Adults $10. 465 Huntington Avenue. Telephone: (617) 267–9300.

Yet the first painting by Henri Matisse to enter an American collection was purchased not by the MFA but by Isabella Stewart Gardner, a free-thinking New Yorker who married into Boston society and often scandalized her peers by exceeding the narrow limits of behavior for a proper Bostonian. Gardner used her considerable fortune to assemble an impressive art collection and construct a Venetian-style palazzo in the Fenway to display it. Covering the walls with paintings from the Italian Renaissance and by French, German, and Dutch masters, Gardner opened "Fenway Court" (as she called it) on New Year's night 1903 and lived on the fourth floor until her death in 1924. The following year, under the terms of her will, it became a full-fledged

The Museum of Fine Arts, Boston

museum. Gardner's broad interests also encompassed gardening and music, and, besides its fine art collection, the **Isabella Stewart Gardner Museum** is known for its glass-covered, flower-filled courtyard (a winter haven for locals) and for its concert series offered on Sunday at 1:30 from September through April.

In all, Gardner collected about 2,500 objects spanning thirty centuries and stipulated in her will that they must be displayed just as she arranged them. The visual richness of the rooms is broken here and there by some blank spaces—the result of the March 18, 1990, theft of thirteen works conservatively valued at $200 million. While rumors of their whereabouts surface every few years, so far these objects from the world's largest art theft to date are still missing. The absence of a few works is no reason, however, to overlook a delightful museum both strongly possessed of the personality of its founder and delightfully receptive to contemporary art in one of its newer galleries. Open Tuesday through Sunday from 11:00 A.M. to 5:00 P.M. Adults $10. 280 The Fenway. Telephone: (617) 566–1401.

Cambridge, Massachusetts

Mention Cambridge and most travelers—and even many locals—think of **Harvard Square.** Although we dwell in working-class Cambridge, well outside the groves of academe and the 02138 zip code (often called the most opinionated address in America), we have to concede that the identification makes sense. Harvard Square was where Cambridge was born, where the city awoke to its intellectual identity, and where most of its attractions and amenities are found.

There's something mythical about the center of Harvard Square, which isn't square at all. It is an oblique triangle whose point is blunted by an outsize sculpture called *Omphalos,* named for the navel of the universe at Delphi. (This should hint how we Cantabrigians view our place in the world.) Out of Town News, the city's leading dealer in national and international newspapers and magazines, squats in the middle of the triangle and the broad end is occupied by an information booth and the gaping mouth of the Underworld. Give Charon your coin (well, your token) and you can cross the river to the Other Side, i.e., Boston on the subway system's Red Line. This island in a sea of traffic, which carries the address of Zero Harvard Square, is truly the heart of Cambridge. The high brick walls of Harvard University stand to its east and northeast, the shops, bookstores, and cafes of commercial Harvard Square lie to the south and west, and the oldest part of the city is due north.

Historic Cambridge

The pattern of streets in Harvard Square has barely changed since shortly after Cambridge was settled in 1631 by a handful of Puritan settlers who originally called their home "Newtowne." But little remains of pre-Revolutionary Cambridge except **Cambridge Common,** which was set aside in 1631 and served originally as a pasture and later as a military drill ground. A marker beneath a scion of the Washington Elm recalls what was perhaps the Common's greatest moment—when George Washington took command of the Continental Army on July 3, 1775. Or at least that's one version of the story. In true Cambridge fashion, some academics insist that Washington assumed command on July 2 and merely reviewed the troops on July 3, but their quibbles in no way diminish Cambridge's connection with Washington, who spent nearly a year in town during the siege of Boston.

In fact, Washington worshipped at the mod-est, gray-shingled **Christ Church** at the Harvard Square end of the Common. The church was designed for Anglican Cambridge Tories in 1761, but they had little time to enjoy its bright and simple interior before fleeing the city in 1774 as the Revolution approached. The church served briefly as a barracks for Colonial troops, who melted its organ pipes for bullets. It was restored and reopened for services on New Year's Eve 1775, with George and Martha Washington in the congregation.

Drawn by the amenities of life in a college town, some of the Massachusetts Bay Colony's wealthiest merchants chose to live in Cambridge and seven of their homes still stand along the stretch of Brattle Street called "Tory Row." It begins just a block behind Christ Church (convenient strolling distance to worship services) and extends roughly a mile out of Harvard Square. Surrounded by long, green lawns and Georgian gardens, these blocky mansions sit in removed majesty as models of proportion and order. After the Revolution, the homes were seized by the Massachusetts government and auctioned off to patriots.

The best-known among them is the yellow manse at 105 Brattle Street. George Washington definitely slept here, as he made it his quarters during the siege of Boston. Henry Wadsworth Longfellow became a lodger in 1837 and received the home as a wedding gift when he married Frances Appleton, daughter of a well-to-do Beacon Hill family. His descendants ultimately turned over the **Longfellow House** to the National Park Service. Guided tours of the house open a window on comfortable middle-class life in the late nineteenth century and often digress into Professor Longfellow's place in the literary scene. (He retired from teaching when *The Song of Hiawatha* became a best-seller, but his peers always called him Professor because he kept up his scholarship, ultimately producing one of the finest English translations of Dante's *Divine Comedy.*) We are not great fans of Longfellow's own singsong verse, but we still get a kick out of visiting the study described in "The Children's Hour," and empathize with the tragedy of Fanny's death. She was sealing locks of hair from the couple's six children into envelopes when the hot wax set her clothing on fire. Longfellow sought in vain

Longfellow House, Cambridge, Massachusetts

to smother the flames, but she perished and he was left with lifelong scars that he covered by growing a beard. As this volume went to press, the Longfellow House was closed for much needed repairs and restoration, with an anticipated reopening in the fall of 1999. Call for hours and price. 105 Brattle Street. Telephone: (617) 876–4491.

Academic Cambridge

Harvard University owns more than 360 acres of land and 400 buildings throughout Cambridge—those in residential areas are often marked with a discreet Lucite plaque at the entryway. But the inner sanctum is **Harvard Yard,** cloistered behind high brick walls punctuated by nine major and several minor gates. Anyone can go through Harvard (the Square's oldest joke) to experience the leafy arcadia of academia. The **Harvard Information Center** provides maps for self-guided walking tours, but far more instructive, we think, is a guided tour by a student. Each class brings a fresh perspective on Harvard's history and architecture, as well as more mundane insights into life at the world's most prestigious university (as its alumni like to claim). Free tours are offered September through May Monday through Friday at 10:00 A.M. and 2 P.M. and Saturday at 2:00 P.M. and June through August

Monday through Saturday at 10:00 A.M., 11:15 A.M., 2:00 and 3:15 P.M., Sunday 1:30 and 3:00 P.M. Harvard Information Center is in Holyoke Center at 1350 Massachusetts Avenue. Telephone: (617) 495–1573.

The Massachusetts Bay Colony established the college in 1636 "to advance Learning and perpetuate it to Posterity: dreading to leave an illiterate Ministry to the Churches, when our present Ministers shall lie in the Dust," according to a seventeenth-century account. Two years later, young cleric John Harvard died in Charlestown and left half his money and all of his books to the college—an act of generosity that prompted the Great and General Court to rename the college in his memory. Today such a gift might possibly merit a named reading room in one of the libraries.

John Harvard was later celebrated with a statue that has a place of honor in Harvard Yard and serves as the most popular "photo op" on campus. Any student or alumni can recite the particulars of the **"statue of three lies,"** which is inscribed "John Harvard, Founder, 1638." Not only is Harvard's role exaggerated and the date incorrect, but it's not even the man's likeness, since no one even knew what he looked like by the time the statue was sculpted in the late nineteenth century.

Fictional or not, John Harvard's image still exerts a powerful force, or it would be lost in what architect James Stirling once described as "Harvard's architectural zoo"—an assemblage of buildings from almost every major architect from Charles Bulfinch to Le Corbusier to Stirling himself. Most notable in Harvard Yard are **Massachusetts Hall,** the oldest surviving Harvard building, which was constructed in 1720 and housed Colonial soldiers during the siege of Boston; **Hollis Hall,** a 1763 dormitory where Ralph Waldo Emerson and Henry David Thoreau lived as students; and handsomely classical **University Hall,** designed by Charles Bulfinch and completed in 1816. The zoo's "white elephant" could be said to be **Widener Library,** the third largest library in the United States and the largest university library in the world, with more than 4.5 million books on more than five miles of shelves. The building is named for Harry Elkins Widener of the class of 1907. When he went down on the *Titanic* in 1912, his mother donated his books to Harvard, and threw in a library to house them. Harvard Yard is the archetype of the perfect college campus, and it is a genuine pleasure to stroll its tree-lined paths around the grassy quadrangles. Outside the walls the world is in tumult; inside lies reflective serenity.

The College's two art museums sit across from each other right outside the eastern gates of Harvard Yard that open onto Quincy Street. The **Fogg Art Museum** was built in 1927 around a central courtyard adapted from a sixteenth-century Italian church. Two levels of galleries surround the courtyard and the collections on their walls manage to cover the sweep of the last millennium of Western art without being too exhausting. The museum has superb holdings of Gothic religious art, Renaissance paintings, Old Master prints and drawings, and French art from Ingres to the impressionists. Because the Fogg is a teaching museum, exhibitions are always intriguing and signage tends to be exhaustively informative. **Werner Otto Hall** was grafted onto the rear of the Fogg in 1991 to house the Germanic art of the Busch-Reisinger Museum. The collection is very deep in German Expressionism and serves as the depository of the personal papers and drawings of seminal Bauhaus figures Walter Gropius and Lyonel Feininger.

Across the street, the **Arthur M. Sackler Museum,** designed by James Stirling and opened in 1985, holds Harvard's Ancient, Asian, Islamic, and later Indian art. Stirling departed from mere functionalism and made the interior a work of art as well, with a long narrow staircase rising to the galleries. As a counterpoint to the starkness of the architecture and the antiquity of the holdings, a contemporary installation designed by Sol Lewitt and executed by a group of Harvard students was created for the entrance.

Harvard University's art museums are open Monday through Saturday from 10:00 A.M. to 5:00 P.M., Sunday 1:00 to 5:00 P.M. Adults $5.00 for entry to all three. The Fogg Art Museum is located at 32 Quincy Street. The Sackler Museum is located at 485 Broadway. Telephone: (617) 495-9400.

Commercial Harvard Square

High culture, pop culture, and counterculture all converge on Harvard Square. Its too-narrow sidewalks bustle with a symbiotic swirl of scholarship and street savvy, Gen-X and geriatric, affluent and indigent. The street front, mostly red-brick buildings from the late nineteenth and early twentieth centuries, displays almost a small-town countenance zealously guarded by the local preservation society. Yet few small towns bustle with such a concentration of cafes and restaurants, emporia of music and books, and shops that cater to every whim of a youth culture with substantial disposable income.

Harvard Square reaches its fullest expression on a Saturday afternoon. A crowd gathers outside Au Bon Pain cafe to watch hopefuls challenge the Chessmaster. (Where but in Harvard Square could anyone make a living by hustling chess?) High school kids in funereal clothing and enough rings and studs to set off a metal detector a block away hang out in the "pit" near the subway station. Political activists of a motley range of fringe organizations collect signatures on their latest petitions. Street-corner entrepreneurs energetically hawk *Spare Change,* the newspaper written and produced by the homeless from offices in one of the Square's church basements.

Not everyone is milling around. The throngs on the sidewalks pack into the bookstores to browse. While the number of booksellers ebbs and flows, Harvard Square's distinction as one of the world's greatest concentrations of bookstores seems secure. (See "Staying There.") Shoppers check out the latest CD releases in Tower Records (95 Mount Auburn Street; telephone: 617–876–3377) and HMV (1 Brattle Square; telephone: 617–868–9696), or hold down a cafe table as they wait for afternoon to stretch into evening and for the street performers to appear like some rare, night-blooming flower. Not that singers, magicians, and acrobats are all that rare in Harvard Square, which is known among buskers around the globe as one of the premier stages in America. Long before they cut their first albums or got their first break with the circus, many a performer learned to please an audience on the sidewalks of Brattle Street and Massachusetts Avenue, known universally as "Mass Ave."

Lexington and Concord, Massachusetts

Located only a few miles west of Cambridge along Route 2, Lexington and Concord were the "suburbs" of Boston where the Revolution finally caught fire. (See "Personal Narrative: Patriots Day in Lexington and Concord.") Today they function principally as bedroom communities for Boston and for the technology companies situated on the highways that ring Boston. Most travelers visit them for their sites associated with the Revolution, but a few also stop in Concord to pay their respects to the first flowering of American literature.

Although Concord's town center can be reached on commuter rail, most visitors arrive by automobile, taking the Concord exit from Route 2. One block east of the center on Heywood Street is a **Visitor Information booth,** open weekends in April and November and daily May through October. A map of all the historic sites in town is sold at the booth.

During the middle third of the nineteenth century, Concord was America's equivalent of Periclean Athens—home to a sudden and unexpected outburst of intellectual and artistic creativity. In many ways, the men and women responsible were ordinary citizens of this small town, yet their writings created a uniquely American literature that continues to resonate. They took seriously the observation made by one of their own, Henry David Thoreau: "A written word is the choicest of relics. It is at once something more intimate with us and more universal than any other work of art. It is the work of art nearest to life itself."

Ralph Waldo Emerson was the star around which Concord's other literary planets orbited, and the **Emerson House,** a solid white Federal house with black shutters and a large American flag out front, makes a fitting introduction to the lives of the authors. Emerson lived here during the most productive part of his life, from 1835 until he died in 1882. Operated by his descen-

dants, the house is kept much as it was in Emerson's day, right down to many of his books, personal effects, and furniture. (His study room is across the street at the Concord Museum. See "Staying There.") Among the regular visitors to the "Sage of Concord" were the utopian dreamer A. Bronson Alcott and his talented and dramatic daughter Louisa May; Nathaniel Hawthorne, who lived off and on in Concord; and Emerson's best friend and protégé, Henry David Thoreau. During his years in "exile" at Walden, Thoreau came to dinner every Sunday. Open mid-April through October, Thursday through Saturday 10:00 A.M. to 4:30 P.M., Sunday and holidays 2:00 to 4:30 P.M. Adults $4.50. 28 Cambridge Turnpike. Telephone: (978) 369–2236.

The compulsive storyteller Louisa May Alcott stands in counterpoint to Emerson's genial abstraction. The Alcotts moved a lot, since Bronson Alcott frequently squandered their money on high-minded schemes. But the family's tale is well told at **Orchard House,** which is described in *Little Women* with throat-catching fondness. It's more modest than Emerson's abode, and nearly a century and a half later the sagging floors and roofline speak of the family's diminished economic circumstances. Behind Orchard House stands a simple shack that aspired to be something more: Bronson Alcott's Concord School of Philosophy. Open April through October, Monday through Saturday 10:00 A.M. to 4:30 P.M., Sunday 1:00 to 4:30 P.M. Adults $5.50. 399 Lexington Road. Telephone: (978) 369–4118.

Many of the seminal figures in the movement that critic Van Wyck Brooks termed the "New England Renaissance" repose at **Sleepy Hollow Cemetery,** which is northeast of Concord Center on Bedford Street (Route 62). To find "Author's Ridge," enter at Pritchard Gate (second entrance on the left) and follow the signs to a small parking area. Up on the ridge to the right are the graves of Ralph Waldo Emerson (marked with a rugged boulder), Henry David Thoreau (a minuscule marble tablet simply inscribed "Henry"), Nathaniel Hawthorne (two stones, at head and foot), and Louisa May Alcott. Their family members lie all around them, reminders that they were not just names from American literature but persons securely attached to a broader social world. Admirers tend to leave small offerings—clusters of smooth pebbles on Emerson's stone, a hemlock cone as an oblation to Thoreau, tattered American flags at Louisa May Alcott's grave in memory of her service as a Civil War nurse. On the ridge road coming to the parking lot is the grave of Daniel Chester French (see "Up Country"), the sculptor best known for the seated Lincoln in the Lincoln Memorial. His grave is usually scattered with pennies.

Little physical evidence survives of the Concord author whose intellectual legacy remains most timely. Thoreau prided himself on his lack of property, so he is best remembered not by his gravestone, but by his beloved **Walden Pond,** located about 2 miles south of town on Walden Street (Route 126). In 1845, Thoreau went to live on Emerson's woodlot next to the Pond. He stayed for two years, keeping a journal of his thoughts and his encounters with Nature and society—a journal he tinkered with for seven more years before *Walden* was published in 1854. Walden Pond is managed by the state ($2.00 parking fee), which limits the number of visitors at any time to 1,000. It's a popular place for swimming, boating, and fishing. A model of Thoreau's cabin stands at one end of the parking lot, and rangers will provide directions for a hike to the site of the original structure, visible largely by the crumbled hearth that marks the foundation of Thoreau's chimney. The author planted more than 400 white pines on the ridge uphill from his cabin site; many were toppled in the hurricane of 1938 and their stumps are still visible.

Thoreau left Walden voluntarily because, he wrote, he had other lives to lead. His parting words were practically a précis of that strain of Yankee thought that marries abstraction and pragmatism: "I learned this, at least, by my experiment; that if one advances confidently in the directions of his dreams, and endeavors to live the life which he has imagined, he will meet with a success unexpected in common hours. . . . If you have built castles in the air, your work need not be lost; that's where they should be. Now put the foundations under them."

Personal Narrative:
Patriots Day in Lexington and Concord

Like most people who live in Greater Boston, we often drive our visitors west to the towns of Lexington and Concord. As every school child knows, these sleepy towns once rang with the musket fire of confrontations between Colonial minutemen and British regulars that marked the first volleys of the American Revolution. We find that these places, so familiar from many visits, come alive when we see them through the eyes of a friend who has only read of them in history books.

A couple of years ago, we decide that, as self-respecting Bostonians, we should witness the reenactments of the Battles of Lexington and Concord at least once. It's the least we can do, given that the state of Massachusetts claims its very own holiday—Patriots Day—in honor of the Bay Colony's role in setting the wheels of revolution in motion. These events are usually held on April 19, sometimes over the weekend closest to April 19. All the details are outlined in the *Boston Globe Calendar* section on the Thursday leading up to the big day.

Experiencing the battle requires some modern-day sacrifice, as the initial skirmish at Lexington took place at 5:30 A.M. on April 19, 1775, and the town adheres to historical accuracy. In fact, local enthusiasm is so great that when we arrive around 5:00 A.M. (well before dawn), the crowd around **Lexington Green** is already four to five deep. (Later we learn from a friend who grew up in Lexington that it's quite acceptable to show up at the last second with a stepladder and set it up at the back of the crowd.)

The call to alarm begins at 5:30 when church bells peal, a Paul Revere reenactor arrives on horseback and the militiamen come running out of the yellow clapboard **Buckman Tavern** that still sits opposite the common at 1 Bedford Street. Columns of Redcoats march up Main Street and confront the seventy-seven militiamen gathered on the common. The standoff is

tense. A reenactor portraying militia commander Captain John Parker repeats the historic
command to his men: "Stand your ground.
Don't fire unless fired upon, but if they mean to
have a war, let it begin here." History does not
record who fired the first shot, but soon we hear
gun fire and the air is full of smoke. When the
smoke clears, eight patriots lay dead (well, they
lie still and *look* dead) and the rest pursue the
British toward Concord. Given the historical
impact of this event, we are shocked by its
brevity. But even though we know it is only a
reenactment, the removal of the dead seems
poignant.

As the crowds disperse—many to pancake
breakfasts held in the white-spired churches
around the green—we take time to stroll
around the common, where the grass is just
turning green and the buds on the trees are
swelling. The Minute Man Statue, erected in
1900, holds a commanding position. It is said
to represent Captain Parker. The Old
Revolutionary Monument was built in 1799 by
those who actually still remembered the event it
honors. Seven of the eight casualties of the battle are buried here. Then we walk over to look
at the outside of the Hancock-Clarke House at
36 Hancock Street. John Hancock and Samuel
Adams were staying in this 1698 house, now a
museum, on the night of April 18 when Paul
Revere and William Dawes rode out to warn
them of the approaching columns of British soldiers.

It is too early to visit any of the town's other
attractions related to the Revolution, though we
know from experience that they do a good job
of bringing the history to life for those unable
to attend the reenactments. The **Lexington
Historical Society** conducts tours of the
Buckman Tavern and Hancock-Clarke House
from April through October, Monday through
Saturday from 10:00 A.M. to 5:00 P.M., Sunday
from 1:00 to 5:00 P.M. Adults $4.00 per site.
Telephone: (781) 862–1703.

Instead, we follow the path of the British
soldiers, going west on Massachusetts Avenue
(Route 2A) to the **Minuteman National
Historic Park's North Bridge Visitor Center.**

The park preserves the scene of the fighting at
the "rude bridge" that was immortalized by
Ralph Waldo Emerson in his poem, "Concord
Hymn." As everyone in Lexington tells us,
Emerson took a little literary license when he
proclaimed the fighting in Concord to be "the
shot heard 'round the world," since the
Lexington skirmish took place hours earlier.

But it is true that while the Colonials at
Lexington had been in a state of disarray, those
who faced the British at North Bridge did so
with stern military discipline. Their sense of
serious purpose is captured in the Minute Man
Statue by Daniel Chester French. As we watch
the reenactment, a few Redcoats advance part-
way across the bridge, fire, and retreat. They
repeat the action again. Then the minutemen
come marching across to fife and drum and fire
a volley. Their marksmanship exacts the first
British fatalities of the day, and a plaque on the
opposite side of the bridge from the Minute
Man Statue commemorates the British soldiers
who died far from home during the
Revolutionary War.

The North Bridge Visitor Center of Minute
Man National Historic Park is open daily from
9:00 A.M. to 5:30 P.M. Free. 174 Liberty Street.
Telephone: (978) 369–6993.

The path of the British retreat from North
Bridge is called Battle Road and we follow the
running troops to watch further reenactments–and we're reminded of kids playing war
games, with one chasing another and shouting
"Bang! Bang!" The road, we know, proceeds to
Meriam's Corner in Concord, through
Lincoln, to Fiske Hill in Lexington and then
onward to Boston. We're not game to follow
the entire distance, so we conclude with a visit
to the **Battle Road Visitor Center.** The center interprets the first four miles of Battle
Road with a diorama that traces the path of
the British retreat. Wall plaques tell more
about the details of the fights that day and the
long-simmering tensions that precipitated
them. Open mid-April through October daily
from 9:00 A.M. to 5:00 P.M. Free. Off Route
2A, one-half mile west of I–95. Telephone:
(781) 862–7753.

Staying There

Boston, Massachusetts

For advance information, contact the Greater Boston Convention & Visitors Bureau, 2 Copley Place, Suite 105, Boston, MA 02116–6501. Telephone: (617) 536–4100 or (888) 733–2678.

LODGING

Boston hotel occupancy has been approaching 90 percent for the last few years, making the city's rooms among the tightest in the nation. In practice, this means hotel rooms are often expensive, especially on weeknights when they are in demand for business travelers. Be sure to inquire about weekend rates and other packages, which are available at almost all hotels and can offer substantial savings over the rack rates indicated below.

Boston Harbor Hotel. 70 Rowes Wharf. If you want to make the most of Boston's revitalized waterfront, this is the perfect location right on the harbor, with docking for ferries and harbor cruise ships. Telephone: (617) 439–7000 or (800) 752–7077. Expensive to very expensive.

Copley Square Hotel. 47 Huntington Avenue. A lower-priced alternative in Copley Square, this hotel features cheerful rooms, often with peculiar floor plans, that are very popular with European guests. At this writing, it is the only older Copley Square property that has not undergone extensive renovations, which helps explain the competitive rates. Telephone: (617) 536–9000 or (800) 225–7062. Moderate to expensive.

Eliot & Pickett Houses. 6 Mount Vernon Place. Twenty guest rooms are divided between two brick townhouses steps from the State House in this charming B&B operated by the Unitarian Universalist Association but open to all. We once treated ourselves to a night, reasoning that it's the closest we'll ever get to the pinnacle of Beacon Hill. Telephone: (617) 248–8707. Moderate to expensive with breakfast.

Fairmont Copley Plaza Hotel. 138 St. James Avenue. This newly-restored Edwardian-era hotel is one of the landmarks of Copley Square and a social center for the city. Richard Burton is said to have carried Elizabeth Taylor over the threshold when the couple stayed in the Presidential Suite. Telephone: (617) 267–5300 or (800) 527–4727. Expensive to very expensive.

Four Seasons Hotel. 200 Boylston Street. This chic and cosmopolitan hotel overlooking the Public Garden balances business services with creature comforts. As the priciest hotel in town, it's very popular with rock stars and celebrity athletes. Telephone: (617) 338–4400 or (800) 332–3442. Very expensive.

Harborside Inn. 185 State Street. A former spice warehouse dating from 1858 has been converted into a fifty-four-room boutique hotel in the Financial District. It features exposed brick and granite walls and Victorian furnishings. Telephone: (617) 723–7500. Moderate to expensive.

Boston Harbor Hotel, Rowes Wharf, Boston

Newbury Guest House. 261 Newbury Street. Surrounded by cafes on Back Bay's toniest street, the comfortable rooms spread among several townhouses are one of the best deals in the city. Telephone: (617) 437–7666 or (800) 437–7668. Moderate to expensive with breakfast.

Omni Parker House. 60 School Street. Located near the Boston Common and the start of the Freedom Trail, the Parker House is the oldest continuously operating hotel in America. Though some guest rooms are fairly small, all have recently been renovated. The historic lobby is worth a visit even if you're staying elsewhere. Telephone: (617) 227–8600 or (800) THEOMNI. Expensive to very expensive.

The Ritz-Carlton, Boston. 15 Arlington Street. Anchoring one end of the Public Garden, the Ritz epitomizes proper Boston manners and elegance. It's the last Boston hotel with elevator operators who wear white gloves. Telephone: (617) 536–5700 or (800) 241–3333. Very expensive.

FOOD

Artu. 6 Prince Street; telephone: (617) 742–4336; and 89 Charles Street; telephone: (617) 227–9023. These small spots in the North End and Beacon Hill feature great roasted vegetables and offer sandwiches or full meals of roast leg of lamb or chicken. Lunch and dinner. Inexpensive to moderate.

Barking Crab. 88 Sleeper Street. Telephone: (617) 426–2722. The closest thing to a true fish shack in Greater Boston, this casual spot on Fort Point Channel has a great view across the harbor to the skyscrapers of the Financial District. Lunch and dinner. Moderate.

Daily Catch. 261 Northern Avenue; telephone: (617) 338–3093; and 323 Hanover Street; telephone: (617) 523–8567. Boston's fishing heritage and large Italian population merge in these restaurants that feature fish, especially squid, in various preparations that emphasize garlic. Lunch and dinner. Moderate.

Durgin-Park. 340 Faneuil Hall Marketplace. Telephone: (617) 227–2038. A survivor from the days before the Marketplace became a tourist destination, Durgin-Park serves big plates of traditional New England fare at family-style tables. Lunch and dinner. Inexpensive to moderate.

Figs. 42 Charles Street; telephone: (617) 742–3447; and 67 Main Street, Charlestown; telephone: (617) 242–2229. The casual kitchens of celebrity chef Todd English feature the best grilled pizza in town and boldly flavored pastas and meats from a wood-burning oven. Lunch and dinner. Moderate.

Hamersley's Bistro. 553 Tremont Street. Telephone: (617) 423–2700. This oversized bistro in the South End is a must for great French provincial fare with the occasional all-American twist. The lemon roast chicken is world class. Dinner, Saturday and Sunday brunch. Expensive to very expensive.

Ida's. 3 Mechanic Street. Telephone: (617) 523–0015. We enjoy the North End's explosion of trendy trattorias as much as the next person, but when we yearn for good old-fashioned Italian cooking in a friendly and unpretentious atmosphere, this is where we head. Dinner. Inexpensive to moderate.

L'Espalier. 30 Gloucester Street. Telephone: (617) 262–3023. If you're planning to splurge on a *big* night out, this elegant Back Bay townhouse with superb fixed-price French menu and impeccable service is the place to do it. Dinner. Very expensive.

Legal Sea Foods. Park Plaza Hotel, 35 Columbus Avenue; telephone: (617) 426–4444; Copley Place Mall, 100 Huntington Avenue; telephone: (617) 266–7775; Statler Office Building, 27 Columbus Avenue; telephone: (617) 426–5566; and Prudential Center, 800 Boylston Street; telephone: (617) 266–6800. This Boston mini-chain is as popular with locals as with visitors for its simple preparations of fresh-from-the-dock fish. For stronger spicing and more unusual preparations, the 35 Columbus Avenue location (**Legal C-Bar**) serves fish Caribbean style. Lunch and dinner. Moderate to expensive.

Maurizio's. 364 Hanover Street. Telephone: (617) 367–1123. Maurizio Lodo's delightful Sardinian fish dishes and great pastas make his small restaurant our favorite North End trattoria. Unlike most of the competition, Maurizio's takes reservations—a great way to avoid the long lines and long waits that often dog diners in the North End. Dinner. Moderate to expensive.

Oak Room. Fairmont Copley Plaza Hotel, 138 St. James Street. Telephone: (617) 267–5300. Boston has embraced the steakhouse craze sweeping the country, but the Oak Room, an Edwardian masterpiece of carved plaster, dark woodwork, and deep red draperies, adds a touch of local flair. Dinner. Expensive to very expensive.

Parish Cafe and Bar. 361 Boylston Street. Telephone: (617) 247–4777. A good spot for people watching, the intriguing sandwiches were designed by local celebrity chefs. Lunch and dinner. Inexpensive to moderate.

Pizzeria Regina. 11½ Thatcher Street. Telephone: (617) 227–0765. This North End institution is a little off the beaten path, but it's worth searching out for delicious pizza and a great neighborhood atmosphere. Although it once spawned a chain, only this original location was—and still is—the real thing. Lunch and dinner. Inexpensive to moderate.

Warren Tavern. 2 Pleasant Street, Charlestown. Telephone: (617) 241–8142. Dating from about 1780, the Warren is one of the oldest restaurants in the city. Renovations to the old building have been gentle; fortunately, the menu is truly up to the moment, if Yankee-inspired. Lunch and dinner. Moderate to expensive.

Les Zygomates. 129 South Street. Telephone: (617) 542–5108. Situated in the up-and-coming arts district near South Station, Les Zygomates serves true French bistro fare and has an impressive list of wines by the glass or bottle. Fixed-price lunch and dinner menus are a great bargain. Lunch and dinner. Moderate to expensive.

OTHER ATTRACTIONS

Boston Ballet. Artistic director Anna-Marie Holmes trained in the classical Russian style at the famed Maryinsky Theater in St. Petersburg, Russia, and oversees a full schedule of classics, new works, and the inevitable Christmas-time

Nutcracker. The company usually performs at the Wang Center for the Performing Arts. 270 Tremont Street. Telephone: (617) 695–6950.

Boston Center for the Arts. Much of the most exciting work in visual and performing arts being created in the city is presented at this landmark facility, which serves to anchor a bustling social, dining, and gallery scene in the bohemian South End. 539 Tremont Street. Telephone: (617) 426–5000.

Boston Symphony Orchestra. The BSO celebrated a quarter of a century under the baton of Seiji Ozawa in 1998. While the orchestra travels throughout the world, there's nothing like hearing it at home in the acoustical masterpiece known as Symphony Hall. 301 Massachusetts Avenue. Telephone: (617) 266–2378.

Christian Science Complex. The fourteen-acre site in the Back Bay is the world headquarters of The First Church of Christ, Scientist, founded by Mary Baker Eddy in 1879. A long reflecting pool brings order to the complex of buildings and makes a lovely setting for walking and lingering. The Mother Church houses one of the world's largest organs with 13,595 pipes covering nine octaves. Tours are offered Monday through Saturday from 10:00 A.M. to 4:00 P.M., Sunday 11:15 A.M. to 2:00 P.M. Free. 175 Huntington Avenue. Telephone for visitor information: (617) 450–3793. The Christian Science Publishing Building contains the unique Mapparium, a 30-foot stained glass globe, with a glass bridge cutting through the center. Political boundaries and worldwide activities of Christian Science are fixed at the time that the globe was created between 1932 and 1934. The building is expected to reopen for tours when renovations are completed in late 1999.

Franklin Park Zoo. New leadership and exhibitions have rescued the zoo from a lackluster past and turned it into one of the most exciting in the country. Exhibits include an African Tropical Forest, Australian Outback, and the newly opened Butterfly Landing with more than 1,000 butterflies in an enclosure with flowering plants and classical music. Open April through September, Monday through Friday 10:00 A.M. to

5:00 P.M., Saturday and Sunday 10:00 A.M. to 6:00 P.M., October through March daily 10:00 A.M. to 4:00 P.M. Adults $6.00. Telephone: (617) 442–2002.

Fenway Park. Few Bostonians can even remember the last time the Red Sox won the World Series so far this century, but as a consolation the city has the most picturesque ball park in the country—complete with real green grass and the Green Monster. Yawkey Way. Telephone: (617) 236–6666 for schedule; (617) 267–8661 for ticket office.

FleetCenter. The Boston Bruins NHL hockey team and the Boston Celtics NBA basketball team both call this new North Station arena home. It may lack the character of the old Boston Garden that once stood next door, but the FleetCenter has a lot more seats. Causeway Street. Telephone: (617) 624–1000.

Gibson House Museum. The furnishings in this 1859–60 Italian Renaissance-style townhouse have been maintained as they were during the lifetime of the first owner Catherine Hammond Gibson, and give a good picture of life during the early years of the Back Bay. Open Wednesday through Sunday for tours at 1:00, 2:00 and 3:00 P.M. Adults $5.00. 137 Beacon Street. Telephone: (617) 267–6338.

Huntington Theatre Company. This stalwart of the regional theater movement is known for ambitious productions of classics and new works, including the plays of African American playwright August Wilson. Boston University Theatre, 264 Huntington Avenue. Telephone: (617) 266–0800.

Museum of Science. Located atop the original Charles River Dam (a newer facility now controls the river from a spot farther downstream), the Museum of Science is a perfect place for kids—both the real juniors, for whom most of the exhibits were designed, and older visitors still capable of experiencing the "gee-whiz" awe of everyday science. The museum offers free stargazing at the Gilliland Observatory on Friday evenings. Open Saturday through Thursday 9:00 A.M. to 5:00 P.M., Friday 9:00 A.M. to 9:00 P.M.

Adults $9.00. Separate admission for Omni Theater. Science Park. Telephone: (617) 723–2500.

Museum Wharf. Former wool buildings on Fort Point Channel have been recycled into two of Boston's most unusual museums. The **Children's Museum** has four floors of exhibitions that prove that learning can be fun. Open Saturday through Thursday 10:00 A.M. to 5:00 P.M., Friday 10:00 A.M. to 9:00 P.M. September through June closed Monday. Adults $7.00. Telephone: (617) 426–8855. With virtual reality exhibitions, software demonstrations, and a "Walk Through Computer," it's hard to tell if adults or kids are more intrigued (and competent at operating the exhibits) at the adjacent **Computer Museum,** which both recalls Boston's pioneering days in the cyber revolution and keeps adults and children alike updated on developments since. Open Tuesday through Sunday 10:00 A.M. to 5:00 P.M. Adults $7.00. Telephone: (617) 423–6758.

New England Aquarium. With a recent expansion, the Aquarium remains a centerpiece of Boston's revitalized waterfront and in the forefront of marine ecological research. The most popular exhibits are the seals and sea otters and the endlessly amusing penguins. The giant sea tank, a column that rises through the middle of the original complex with thousands of free-swimming fish and giant turtles, is downright mesmerizing. Open July through Labor Day Monday, Tuesday, and Friday 9:00 A.M. to 6:00 P.M., Wednesday and Thursday 9:00 A.M. to 8:00 P.M., Saturday and Sunday 9:00 A.M. to 7:00 P.M. Open Labor Day through June Monday through Friday 9:00 A.M. to 5:00 P.M., Saturday and Sunday 9:00 A.M. to 6:00 P.M. Adults $11. Central Wharf. Telephone: (617) 973–5200.

New Museum at John F. Kennedy Library. The soaring white concrete and glass structure matches the drama of the site on a precipice above the Atlantic Ocean. Chronological exhibitions about Kennedy's life and political career gain immediacy through extensive use of film, newsreel, and television clips. Additional exhibits are devoted to Robert F. Kennedy and one small room holds Ernest Hemingway memorabilia. Open daily

9:00 A.M. to 5:00 P.M. Adults $8.00. Columbia Point. Telephone: (617) 929–4523.

Observatories. Two of Boston's modern office towers provide good vantage points to understand the layout of Boston. The Prudential Tower was Back Bay's first real skyscraper and the fiftieth-floor **Skywalk** has a 360-degree view and good signage to explain what you're seeing down below. Open daily 10:00 A.M. to 10:00 P.M. Adults $4.00. 800 Boylston Street. Telephone: (617) 536–1775. The **John Hancock Observatory** is located on the sixtieth floor of Boston's tallest building and includes narration by historian Walter Muir Whitehill, a student of Boston's landscape and maybe the only Bostonian to ever have a complete lay of the land. Open Monday through Saturday 9:00 A.M. to 10:00 P.M., Sunday 10:00 A.M. to 10:00 P.M. The Observatory closes at 5:00 P.M. on Sunday during the winter. Adults $5.00. John Hancock Tower. Telephone: (617) 572–6429.

Harrison Gray Otis House. This first home of one of the wealthy developers of Beacon Hill was designed by Charles Bulfinch and its opulent furnishings and rich colors depict the lifestyles of the rich and famous of the early years of the new republic. It now serves as the headquarters of the Society for the Preservation of New England Antiquities. Guides offer tours of the house and also a limited schedule of tours of Beacon Hill. The house is open Wednesday through Sunday 11:00 A.M. to 5:00 P.M. Adults $4.00. Beacon Hill tours are offered May through October on Saturday at 11:00 A.M. and 3:00 P.M. Adults $10, includes the house tour. 141 Cambridge Street. Telephone: (617) 227–3956.

Theater District. Five of Boston's opulent theaters from early in the century have been painstakingly restored and some of the best theater in the country plays in Boston either right before or just after a Broadway run. Not everything good comes from (or goes to) New York. The stages also feature locally mounted plays as well as dance and music productions. Check with the box office at each theater for schedule information and tickets. Colonial Theater, 106 Boylston Street; telephone: (617) 426–9366; Emerson Majestic Theatre, 221 Tremont Street;

telephone: (617) 824–8000; Shubert Theatre, 265 Tremont Street; telephone: (617) 482–9393; Wang Center for the Performing Arts, 270 Tremont Street; telephone: (617) 482–9393; and Wilbur Theatre, 246 Tremont Street; telephone: (617) 423–4008. For those willing to take pot luck, half-price tickets to same day productions are available from the **BOSTIX** booths in Faneuil Hall Marketplace, Copley Square, and Harvard Square in Cambridge. Tickets go on sale at 11:00 A.M. No credit cards accepted. No telephone.

ACTIVITIES

Biking the Emerald Necklace. Bostonians consider the 5-mile stretch of linked parks designed by Frederick Law Olmsted to rival, maybe even surpass, his other great landscape designs, including New York's Central Park. One of the best ways to get a sense of the sweep and scope of this great green path through the city is by bicycle. Back Bay Bikes and Boards rents bicycles for $20 per day. 333 Newbury Street. Telephone: (617) 247–2336.

Boston Harbor Islands. Few American cities can boast such a beguiling cluster of islands virtually adjacent to the downtown. Nine of Boston's harbor islands have been a state park for some time and were recently designated a National Recreation Area, administered by the National Park Service. Georges Island, dominated by a Civil-War era fort, is the "hub" of the system, reached by a forty-five-minute ferry ride. From Georges a free water taxi shuttles to several other islands, including Lovells, which has a swimming beach. Boston Harbor Islands Ferry. Long Wharf. Adults $8.00. The ferry operates from May through Columbus Day. Call for schedule. Telephone: (617) 227–4321.

Charles River Canoe and Kayak. The Charles River Basin, which flows between Boston and Cambridge, is a dynamic waterway with terrific city views from a boat. Just a short distance upriver and outside the metropolitan area, the Charles is a rural delight. The best way to experience the river's split personality is by canoe. Charles River Canoe and Kayak rents both for $10 to $12 per hour. Basin location is on Soldiers Field Road, Brighton. Upriver location is at 2401

Commonwealth Avenue, Newton. Telephone: (617) 965–5110.

TOURS

Duck Tours. Gaily painted WWII amphibious vehicles have become a common sight on Boston streets as they amble past the usual sites and then plunge into the Charles River. Adults $20. Telephone: (617) 723–3825.

Trolley Tours. Several trolley tour operations offer an efficient way to cover the sites, although you should take the accompanying narration with a grain of salt. Passengers can get on and off throughout the day, making the tours a good way to hop around the city. All have booths outside the Boston Visitor Information Center on Boston Common, including Beantown Trolley; telephone: (617) 986–6100; Minuteman Tours; telephone: (617) 876–5539; and Old Town Trolley; telephone: (617) 269–7010. Adults $15 to $20.

National Park Service Guided Tours. As many locals as visitors take advantage of the chance to bone up on city history on these informative outings led by NPS rangers. In addition to the continuous Freedom Trail and Charlestown Navy Yard tours, programs include the Black Heritage Trail and spring and fall weekend walks through the Emerald Necklace. Check for details at the Boston National Historical Park Visitor Center, 15 State Street. Telephone: (617) 242–5642.

FAIRS, FESTIVALS, AND EVENTS

Boston Marathon. The world's oldest continuously-run marathon covers the 26.2 miles from Hopkinton to Boston on the third Monday in April. Telephone: (617) 236–1652.

Boston Pops Annual Fourth of July Concert and Fireworks. The Charles River Esplanade is the scene of this patriotic extravaganza and of other free Pops concerts during the month of July. Telephone: (617) 266–1492.

Boston Harbor Islands

Bunker Hill Weekend. The commemoration of the Battle of Bunker Hill includes costumed reenactors (telephone: 617–242–5641) and a parade that has become a community celebration (telephone: 617–242–2646). All take place the weekend of or before June 17.

First Night. More than 130 other cities have adopted Boston's idea of an arty, multicultural New Year's Eve Party, but we think that the first remains the best. Telephone: (617) 542–1399.

Lilac Sunday. The stroll along Bussey Hill at the Arnold Arboretum on the third Sunday in May is a rite of spring. But the 400-plus lilacs—one of the most extensive collections in the world—actually begin blooming in early May and last well into June. Telephone: (617) 524–1717.

New England Spring Flower Show. The oldest annual flower exhibition in the country is held in mid-March. Telephone: (617) 536–9280.

Reenactment of the Boston Tea Party. Held on the Sunday closest to December 16, participants begin at the Old South Meeting House and march through the streets to the Tea Party Ship and Museum. Telephone: (617) 338–1773.

Religious Festivals. Boston is one of the few U.S. cities with elaborate festivals honoring the patron saints of Italian immigrants. They take place almost every weekend from mid-July through August in the North End. Telephone: (617) 635–4455.

SHOPPING

Filene's Basement. 426 Washington Street. Telephone: (617) 542–2011. Astute readers of this book may have guessed that we are not big fans of outlet malls. So where do we shop? This is it—where rubbing elbows with a Beacon Hill matron over a pile of off-season merchandise from Lord & Taylor or haggling with a punk rocker over the latest shipment of black clothing from Barneys is more sport than shopping. The Basement pioneered the "automatic markdown" in 1908 (25 percent reductions off already reduced prices every two weeks) and waiting out a markdown is still the city's best game of chance.

Cambridge, Massachusetts

For advance information, contact the Cambridge Office for Tourism, 18 Brattle Street, Cambridge, MA 02138. Telephone: (617) 441–2884.

LODGING

A Friendly Inn at Harvard Square. 1673 Cambridge Street. It's about a five-minute walk to Harvard Square from this well-kept B&B that attracts many foreign travelers. Telephone: (617) 547–7851. Inexpensive to moderate with breakfast.

Charles Hotel in Harvard Square. One Bennett Street. The modern rooms remain a little spare, even after 1998 renovations, but the location in the heart of Harvard Square can't be beat. Telephone: (617) 864–1200 or (800) 882–1818. Expensive to very expensive.

Inn at Harvard. 1201 Massachusetts Avenue. The library shelves in the soaring atrium should let you know that this small hotel is the property of Harvard University and is often used by university visitors. Guests have dining privileges at the Harvard Faculty Club. Telephone: (617) 491–2222 or (800) 222–8733. Expensive to very expensive.

Isaac Harding House. 288 Harvard Street. This historic home in mid-Cambridge was converted to top-notch bed-and-breakfast in 1997. Wheelchair accessible. Telephone: (617) 876–2888. Moderate to expensive with breakfast.

Royal Sonesta. 5 Cambridge Parkway. Located barely on the Cambridge side of the Charles River (near the Museum of Science), this hotel has superb views of the river and the skylines of Beacon Hill and Back Bay. It offers one of the best summer packages for families. Telephone: (617) 491–3600. Expensive to very expensive.

FOOD

Mr. Bartley's Burger & Salad Cottage. 1246 Massachusetts Avenue. Telephone: (617) 354–6559. Even Harvard has a student hangout where the sandwiches and gigantic burgers are named after celebrities and the tables are packed all day. Lunch and dinner. Inexpensive.

Casablanca. 40 Brattle Street. Telephone: (617) 876–0999. Local writers and other celebrities like to lounge beneath the Bogart murals. Appropriately enough, the French bistro food has definite North African colonial spicings. Lunch and dinner. Moderate to expensive.

Chez Henri. 1 Shepard Street. Telephone: (617) 354–8980. It's only a short walk out of Harvard Square to this stylish French bistro with a Cuban accent. Short on cash? Go for the fixed-price menu in the dining room or the Cuban sandwiches at the bar. Dinner. Expensive.

Rialto. The Charles Hotel, 1 Bennett Street. Telephone: (617) 661–5050. Chef Jody Adams was named top chef in New England in 1997 by the James Beard Foundation. This swank restaurant with upscale takes on trattoria and bistro food is worth the splurge. Dinner. Expensive to very expensive.

Toscanini's Ice Cream. 899 Main Street; telephone: (617) 491–5877; and 1310 Massachusetts Avenue; telephone: (617) 354–9350. A recent study revealed that Bostonians eat 20 percent more ice cream than the rest of the country. We suspect that these shops—with such hard-to-resist flavors as saffron, green tea, cardamom, and burnt caramel and a sneaky pricing policy that makes it much cheaper to get two or three scoops rather than just one—are the reason why.

Up Stairs at the Pudding. 10 Holyoke Street. Telephone: (617) 864–1933. Located over the Hasty Pudding Theatre, this is practically Harvard's unofficial restaurant. Dinner is an occasion for diners with deep pockets and hearty appetites for Italian-accented New American cuisine. But the Pudding also offers a great a la carte Sunday brunch and superb lunches on a beautiful, hidden, flower-laden deck. Sunday brunch, lunch, and dinner. Expensive to very expensive.

OTHER ATTRACTIONS

American Repertory Theatre. As befitting its partnership with Harvard University, the ART is one of the more avant-garde regional theaters in the country. Performances are held at the Loeb Drama Center, 64 Brattle Street. Telephone: (617) 547–8300.

Brattle Theater. They serve real butter on the popcorn at this repertory house that features classic and art films—a reminder of what it was like to go to the movies before the advent of the multiplex. 40 Brattle Street. Telephone: (617) 876–6837.

Club Passim. This legendary folk club (also once known as Club 47) gave Joan Baez her debut mike in 1959 and more recently helped launch the careers of such singer-songwriters as Suzanne Vega, Patty Larkin, Tracy Chapman, Nancy Griffith, and Shaun Colvin. 47 Palmer Street. Telephone: (617) 492–7679.

Harvard Museums of Cultural and Natural History. Extensive holdings include one of the most extensive collections of zoological type specimens in the world, mineralogical and geological specimens dating back to 1783, and the remarkable "glass flowers"—more than 3,000 scientifically accurate life-size glass models handblown and shaped by Leopold and Rudolph Blaschka between 1887 and 1936. Open Monday through Saturday from 9:00 A.M. to 5:00 P.M., Sunday from 1:00 P.M. to 5:00 P.M. Adults $5.00 (includes admission to Peabody Museum of Archaeology and Ethnology). 24–26 Oxford Street. Telephone: (617) 495–3045.

House of Blues. We're usually not crazy about chains, but this funky spot in Harvard Square started it all and continues to showcase top names in electric blues, performing amid a collection of Southern outsider art. The Sunday gospel brunch is a weekly sell-out. 96 Winthrop Street. Telephone: (617) 491–2583.

MIT Museum. The last time we checked they did indeed sell pocket protectors in the shop. But this small museum does a good job of providing some insight into the life of the university. Exhibitions range from a dead-serious history of the slide rule to accounts of ingenious pranks (called "hacks") perpetrated by students over the years. Science and art converge in the stunning holographic art and in Harold Edgerton's photographs that reveal events too fleeting for the eye to see—like beautiful splashes of drops of milk. Open Tuesday through Friday 10:00 A.M. to 5:00 P.M., Saturday and Sunday noon to 5:00 P.M. Adults $3.00. 265 Massachusetts Avenue. Telephone: (617) 253–4444.

Mount Auburn Cemetery. This 174-acre garden cemetery was on the outskirts of town when it was founded by the Massachusetts Horticultural Society in 1831, inspiring both the garden cemetery and public parks movements across the country. The cemetery welcomes visitors to appreciate its plantings (more than 300 species of trees and 130 species of shrubs and ground covers) and art work (including memorial art by Augustus Saint-Gaudens and Stanford White) and to visit the graves of its illustrious dead (including architect Charles Bulfinch, Christian Science founder Mary Baker Eddy, Isabella Stewart Gardner, Winslow Homer, and Henry Wadsworth Longfellow). The cemetery's rich plantings make it a sanctuary for urban wildlife and as many as 1,000 birds a day visit Mount Auburn during peak spring migration in mid-May. Open daily 8:00 A.M. to 5:00 P.M. Mount Auburn opens at 7:00 A.M. during daylight saving time. 580 Mount Auburn Street. Telephone: (617) 547–7105, ext. 821 for information about programs, extension 824 for birding hotline.

Peabody Museum of Archaeology and Ethnology. Founded in 1866, the Peabody was the first museum in America devoted exclusively to anthropology. Its holdings include Mayan objects, materials from predynastic Egypt, gold figures from Panama, and materials from the Lewis and Clark expedition. But the centerpiece exhibition, "Change and Continuity," addresses the interactions between indigenous peoples of North America and Europeans and the adaptations that occurred as a result of these encounters. Open Monday through Saturday 9:00 A.M. to 5:00 P.M., Sunday 1:00 to 5:00 P.M. Adults $5.00 (includes admission to Museums of Cultural and Natural History). 11 Divinity Avenue. Telephone: (617) 495–2248.

Regattabar. Touring headliners and top local acts make this spot in the Charles Hotel perhaps the premier jazz club in the area. 1 Bennett Street. Telephone: (617) 876–7777.

FAIRS, FESTIVALS, AND EVENTS

Cambridge River Festival. This multicultural celebration of the arts and city life takes place on the banks on the Charles River on the first Saturday after Labor Day. Telephone: (617) 349–4380.

Dragon Boat Festival. This race of intricately carved and painted boats takes place in early June and commemorates the life of Chinese poet-patriot Qu Yuan. Telephone: (617) 441–2884.

Head of the Charles Regatta. The largest rowing event in the world is held in mid-October. Telephone: (617) 864–8414.

SHOPPING

Bookstores. Harvard Square boasts one of the largest concentrations of bookstores in the world and any book that isn't available here probably isn't worth reading. **Wordsworth Books** (30 Brattle Street, telephone: 617–354–5201) alone stocks more than 100,000 discounted titles and the **Harvard Cooperative Society** (1400 Massachusetts Avenue, telephone: 617–499–3200) not only provides Harvard's textbooks but has recently refurbished its general books departments and added a nice cafe. **Harvard Bookstore** (1256 Massachusetts Avenue; telephone: 617–661–1515) isn't affiliated with the university, but it's often the shop of choice by literati; moreover, it carries an excellent line of remaindered and used books. Some of the smaller, quirkier spots really give the Square its character. The tiny **Grolier Poetry Book Shop** (6 Plympton Street, telephone: 617–547–4648) is packed from floor to ceiling with more than 15,000 volumes. **Schoenhof's Foreign Books** (76A Mount Auburn Street, telephone: 617–547–8855) carries books in dozens of languages. **James & Devon Gray Booksellers** (12 Arrow Street, telephone: 617–868–0752) specializes in books printed before 1700. **Pandemonium Books & Games** (36 JFK Street, telephone: 617–547–3721) features fantasy, science fiction, and horror, with subdivisions for werewolves or vampires. And should you need to plan your next trip, the **Globe Corner Bookstore** (28 Church Street; telephone: 617–497–6277) specializes in travel guides, maps, and travelogues.

Lexington and Concord, Massachusetts

For advance information on Lexington, contact the Chamber of Commerce Visitor Center, 1875 Massachusetts Avenue, Lexington, MA 02420. Telephone: (781) 862–1450. For advance information on Concord, contact the Concord Chamber of Commerce, 2 Lexington Road, Concord, MA 01742. Telephone: (978) 369–3120.

FOOD

Guida's Coast Cuisine. 84 Thoreau Street, Concord. Telephone: (978) 371–1333. Fresh seafood prepared Portuguese style is the specialty of this restaurant on the upper floor of the historic Concord Depot. Lunch and dinner. Moderate to expensive.

OTHER ATTRACTIONS

Additional Concord Literary Sights. The **Concord Museum** has Emerson's study and the world's largest collection of Thoreau artifacts. Open Monday through Saturday 9:00 A.M. to 5:00 P.M., Sunday noon to 5:00 P.M. Adults $6.00. 200 Lexington Road. Telephone: (978)

369–9609. Emerson wrote his first great book, *Nature,* at the Revolutionary-era **Old Manse,** where Nathaniel Hawthorne later spent his honeymoon. Open mid-April through October, Monday through Saturday 10:00 A.M. to 5:00 P.M., Sunday and holidays 1:00 to 5:00 P.M. Adults $5.00. 269 Monument Street. Telephone: (978) 369–3909. Louisa May Alcott penned her first published works at **The Wayside,** which became the only home Hawthorne ever owned and the domicile in which he lived out his days. Open May through October, Thursday through Tuesday 10:30 A.M. to 4:30 P.M. Adults $3.00. 455 Lexington Road. Telephone: (978) 369–6975.

Museum of Our National Heritage. Sponsored by the Scottish Rite of Freemasonry, this museum explores American history and popular culture. Its local treasure is the "Lexington Alarm," a call to arms penned on April 19, 1775, and dispatched to other Colonies. It's exhibited yearly on Patriots Day. Open Monday through Saturday 10:00 A.M. to 5:00 P.M., Sunday noon to 5:00 P.M. Free. 33 Marrett Road (Route 2A), Lexington. Telephone: (781) 861–6559.

ACTIVITIES

Minute Man Bikeway. A successful rails-to-trails conversion has made it possible to bike along the route of the minutemen as they chased the Redcoats back to Boston after the Battle of North Bridge in Concord. The 10½-mile paved path begins in Bedford (almost in Concord) and ends at the Alewife subway station in Cambridge. Marked with signs showing Paul Revere in tricorn hat riding a bicycle, the popular route is often filled with bicyclists, joggers, in-line skaters, and young parents trotting behind baby carriages.

4 · The North Coast

Introduction

You will probably drive a lot more miles than you expected on New England's North Coast. As the crow flies, it's less than 300 miles from the New Hampshire-Massachusetts border to Eastport, Maine. But if you could pull the ragged edges of the Maine coastline straight, it would stretch all the way from Boston to Los Angeles and well out into the Pacific Ocean. Cartographers joke that no one has ever been able to accurately calculate the exact distance covered by all the little jogs and coves and switchbacks and jetties of the Maine coast. Estimates start at 3,500 miles and some experts say that even that figure falls 1,000 miles short.

That is what we have called New England's North Coast—3,500 to 4,500 miles of shoreline in Maine and the snippet that is New Hampshire's coast.

The more often that you turn off the main road (usually Route 1) toward the water, the more of the North Coast you will see. You will find the historic old houses, the coves and piers where generations of men built sturdy boats and sailed them literally halfway around the world. In the little harbors you will find the fishermen who still go to sea—some of them the tenth or even twelfth generations of their families to do so. On those side roads toward the water you will find, even still, painters who draw their inspiration from the ocean's edge as surely as Fitz Hugh Lane and Winslow Homer did a century and more ago.

We've divided this chapter by the three distinct geographies of the region: southern crescent, peninsula country, and Downeast. A good highway system allows travelers who wish to bypass both the southern crescent and the peninsula country to simply zoom up I–95 to Augusta and swing east on Route 3 to head Downeast.

Hundreds of thousands of vacationers make the mistake (we think) of taking this precise route every summer as they descend on Acadia National Park. To truly savor the North Coast, it is far better to follow the venerable byway of Route 1 and its turn-offs (often Route 1A) until you reach Downeast Maine, where Route 3 heads down onto Mount Desert Island. This highway is the direct descendant of the old Colonial roads that linked coastal villages, and those Colonial roads were built on the old Native American trails that linked even earlier settlements. People have been touring the North Coast by Route 1 and its antecedents for thousands of years. We suggest that you follow suit.

With some local variations, towns along the three sections share a similar general history. Almost every place that Europeans ultimately settled was occupied first by Abenaki bands that took their tribal names from their principal encampments. They often fought with each other—and with the Micmacs who raided them from Nova Scotia and New Brunswick—but practiced the same mix of seasonal hunting and fishing as well as some light agriculture. (The growing season is too short, the temperatures too cool, and the soil too poor on much of the North Coast for corn-based farming to have become very important.)

Many of the larger offshore islands served at some point as base camps for European fishing and whaling vessels, in some cases well before the "official" discovery of the western hemisphere. Samuel de Champlain surveyed and mapped most of this coast in 1604–05, even planting a French colony on an island in Passamaquoddy Bay. (The colony soon moved to Nova Scotia, where it grew into the Acadian community there.) The English retaliated with a short-lived colony of their own at Popham, near the mouth of the Kennebec River.

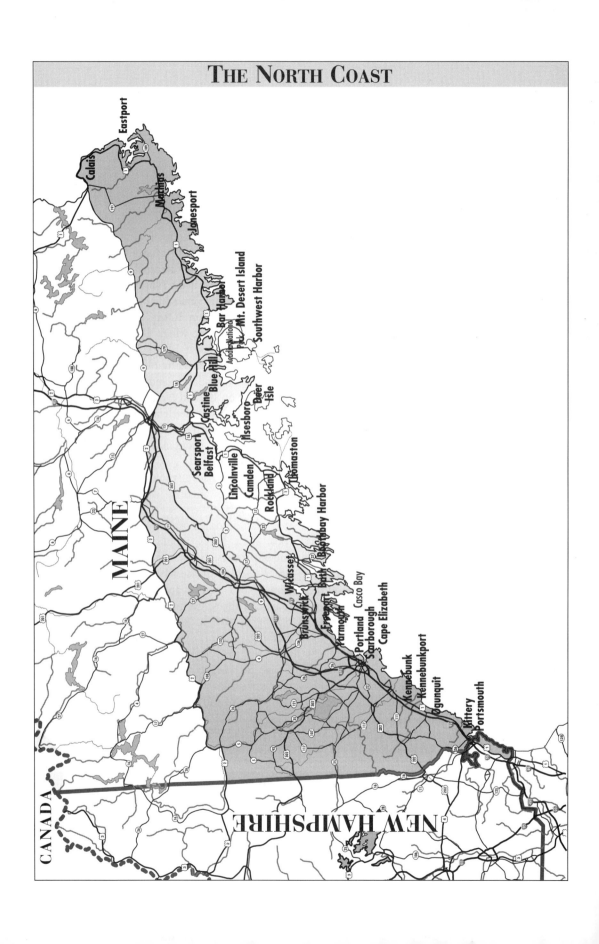

But it took the enthusiastic descriptions of Captain John Smith to seriously interest the English in this part of North America. During his voyage of 1614, he surveyed the coast from Massachusetts Bay to Penobscot Bay, and Smith's and Champlain's charts became blueprints for a series of seasonal trading posts at the mouths of the large rivers. English settlement of the coast began in earnest between 1620 and 1660. Some English villages sputtered and failed because the settlers had to fight off the Natives as well as the French (and sometimes Dutch and Flemish). But many took hold, especially at the southern end of the North Coast, where the Massachusetts Bay Colony provided military protection and a market for fish, fur, and timber.

In the eighteenth century, towns at the mouths of rivers evolved into shipbuilding centers, turning towering inland timber into tall ships. They led America in overseas trade in the years after Maine achieved statehood in 1820. The North Coast went into decline in the years after the Civil War. Many of the men who left to fight never returned—not necessarily because they were casualties of war, but because the West was opening and greater opportunity lay elsewhere. Those who stayed mostly turned away from the overseas trade, since diesel-powered steel ships made the graceful multi-masted sailing ships obsolete. In time, the fishing played out as well.

North Coast towns turned to textile and leather mills at the end of the nineteenth century, only to lose their livelihoods during the Great Depression when the mills moved south. With the exceptions of Portland and the Penobscot River city of Bangor, this relative poverty spared most towns the mistakes of mid-century "urban renewal." As a result, when tourism became a mainstay of employment in the 1960s, the Main Streets and old Victorian housing stock of most towns were still intact.

These boom and bust cycles of innovation and obsolescence have left the towns of the North Coast with a multilayered past, much of which is still preserved. Yet these towns never fade away. Newcomers discover them, as if for the first time, fall in love with the landscape and end up staying because personal roots go deep here. Their common history aside, each town has its distinct character and its ardent proponents. You could stop anywhere along the route and, given some patience and perseverance, spend weeks getting to know a place. Like their people, these towns are initially reticent and shy, but they grow increasingly garrulous on longer acquaintance.

Seeing the North Coast

The Southern Crescent of New Hampshire and Maine

The southern crescent, which includes the entire New Hampshire coast—all eighteen miles of it!—north to Cape Elizabeth, Maine, is a gentle coastal plain where marshlands creep down to sandy beaches punctuated by spits of upthrust rock. Many of the famous summer beach and resort communities line this stretch, where the high tide line is defined both by the strand of beach wash and the string of summer cottages. The far western edge of the Gulf Stream sometimes sweeps inshore, giving the beaches the warmest waters of northern New England.

Because of their proximity to Massachusetts Bay Colony, towns of the southern crescent have the longest and best-preserved Colonial histories. And because they still lie close to Boston, they are also the most heavily visited communities along the North Coast. This is a region to savor sandy beaches and historic house museums, to stay at Victorian B&Bs or honky-tonk beach motels.

New Hampshire's Beaches

From the Massachusetts border to Portsmouth, New Hampshire, the coastline consists of sandy beaches separated by rocky points. The place to begin a North Coast tour is **Hampton Beach,** where you can reach Route 1A from the New Hampshire Turnpike's exit 2.

Hampton Beach is one of the longest sandy stretches in New England and the sand is some of the finest. The beach town's proximity to Boston made Hampton something of a summer resort even before the automobile (a train used to run into the town of Hampton, about a mile inland), and with the advent of the automobile, Hampton became known as the French Canadian Riviera by virtue of being one of the closest ocean beaches to Montreal. The French Canadian influence, boosted by the large number of French Canadian mill workers from New Hampshire's Merrimack Valley who also vacation here, has given Hampton Beach a Quebecois quality that still persists. *Içi nous parlons français,* announce signs all over town. *Oui, nous aussi.*

In July and August, traffic slows to a crawl down Ocean Boulevard, and thousands of well-tanned bodies are out strutting their stuff, dining on fried dough and pizza, quaffing mugs of beer, and occasionally batting around a volleyball on the beach. If you have come for the day to sun and swim, you'll have to park at a pay lot a mile from the beach and walk. By night, the Hampton Beach bar scene gets into full swing, with a raucous good time had by all.

By late September or early October, the long, beautiful beach—by then swept clean by the high tides of the autumnal equinox—is virtually deserted and beachside parking is plentiful and free. Hampton Beach is the mayfly of North Coast summer places, living brightly, intensely, and briefly each year.

The character of New Hampshire's beaches changes radically once you leave Hampton's North Beach, which continues the brassy edge of Hampton State Beach after a rocky interstice. As you cross into North Hampton and then into Rye, most of the land within sight of the ocean is occupied by substantial private estates with luxuriant gardens.

To get a glimpse of this gardening impulse in full bloom, watch for a left-hand turn to **Fuller Gardens,** located at 11 Willow Avenue in North Hampton. Telephone: (603) 964–5414. The gardens are open daily from mid-May through October from 10:00 A.M. to 6:00 P.M. Admission is $5.00. Like many of the estate gardens on the New Hampshire coast, this one dates to the early and mid-twentieth-century fascination with English gardening as popularized in this country by the writings of Gertrude Jekyll. Except for a recent and lovely Japanese garden that makes a nice contrast, most of the grounds are planted as formal English gardens, with an emphasis on roses.

There is something about the light on this part of the North Coast that makes roses flourish. Route 1A is densely lined with wild roses all through North Hampton and Rye, especially on the cliffs overlooking the rocky parts of the coast. At Fox Head Point in North Hampton there is a large patch of the white single-flowered variant of the common beach rose. Called *Rosa rugosa alba,* it has a strong clove component to its scent. Found in greater profusion on Cape Cod, *alba* is also sometimes called the Salt Spray Rose because it thrives in sandy beach soil and has been widely encouraged by naturalists because it stabilizes shifting sand dunes.

Several public sandy beaches lie along the coast in Rye. The best of them for swimming is Wallis Sands State Park, which also has a pay parking lot, restrooms, lockers, and a seasonal snack bar. Before the road turns into Little Harbor and enters Portsmouth, you'll encounter **Odiorne Point State Park,** which is open daily from early May until late October. The entrance fee is $2.50 per automobile.

The park is the largest stretch of undeveloped shore on the New Hampshire coast, which is ironic as it was the site of the first settlement of what eventually grew into Portsmouth. Just one structure sits there now, a large stone house built in the 1920s when this was private land. It houses the **Seacoast Science Center,** which is open May through October daily from 10:00 A.M. to 5:00 P.M. Admission is $1.00. Telephone: (603) 436–8043. The center tells the entire geological and historical tale of this 327-acre property, which was appropriated by the federal government in World War II and fortified to protect Portsmouth harbor and the Portsmouth Naval Shipyard. A free map available at the center outlines several hiking trails, including a route along the shore that cuts through low wooded growth across a freshwater marsh to emerge next to an artificial hill that once concealed artillery. It loops out to Frost Point, where the view from the end of a stone jetty demonstrates precisely why the military installed gun emplacements here: Portsmouth harbor and the shipyard—critical to the war effort—lie dead ahead, open and vulnerable as a cracked walnut.

Piscataqua River Harbor, New Hampshire

Actually, three communities sit at the mouth of the Piscataqua River—Kittery on the Maine side and Portsmouth and New Castle on the New Hampshire side. From Odiorne Point heading north on Route 1A, turn right on Route 1B for a quick driving tour through the island community of New Castle. You will soon reach the remains of the once grand **Hotel Wentworth** on Little Harbor, where in 1905 the delegates to the Russo-Japanese peace conference celebrated the Treaty of Portsmouth that ended the Russo-Japanese War. A half mile farther is a road to Jaffrey's Point, the site of the **ruins of Fort Stark,** alleged to be the oldest defense works on the coast of the United States, built sometime between 1640 and 1682. The term "quaint" fits the village of **New Castle** more than any other town on the North Coast. Once the seat of colonial government, it endures as a fishing village of narrow, twisted streets, small saltbox cottages, and ancient churchyards.

The little village played a role in the American Revolution. On December 13, 1774, the ubiquitous Paul Revere delivered the news that the British colonial government had banned the export of gunpowder and arms to the American colonies. The next day 400 members of the Portsmouth Sons of Liberty surrounded **Fort William and Mary,** just east of the town square. Since there were only five guards and a commander inside, the Redcoats wisely capitulated. The arms seized that day were later issued to American soldiers on the eve of the Battle of Bunker Hill. The site is open for touring during daylight hours and goes by its post-Revolution name, **Fort Constitution.**

Badger's Island served as a shipyard for the fledgling Revolutionary Navy, when Commodore

Puddle Dock, 1890, Portsmouth, New Hampshire

John Paul Jones had his famous frigate, the *Ranger* and its companion, the *Raleigh,* built here in 1777. After the Revolution, the **Portsmouth Naval Shipyard** was established on neighboring Dennett's Island, with the first vessel, the seventy-four-gun frigate *Washington,* sliding down the ways in July 1815. The shipyard, which lies within the boundaries of Kittery, Maine, ultimately built many ships used by the U.S. Navy in the Civil War and the Spanish-American War. It still produces and outfits submarines.

The shipyard is most visible from Route 1B as the road circles New Castle and enters the oldest part of Portsmouth over a succession of small islands, an area known collectively as "Three Bridges." During the region's fishing years (1650–1850), the islands were used to dry fish, in part because they were downwind from the mainland settlement. The mainland begins at "Strawbery Banke," so named for the berries that once covered its shores. The settlement was named Piscataqua in 1631 by the governor of Plymouth Colony (who had never seen the place but had jurisdiction over it), but was quickly renamed Strawbery Banke by the first settlers. In 1653, the less imaginative Massachusetts General Court incorporated the town as Portsmouth.

Of all the sites around the mouth of the Piscataqua River, **Portsmouth** offered the most dry ground and the best farmland, and its early settlers flourished. Town fathers now gloss over some aspects of the early years, as Portsmouth was also notorious for its pirates—both the outlaws and the sanctioned privateers—who preyed on coastal shipping. Like other shipbuilding and mercantile centers, Portsmouth also had its share of slave traders and dealers in rum, but time has a way of laundering the early sources of wealth.

Portsmouth still deserves her nineteenth-century nickname, "Queen of the Piscataqua," in large part because the central city has changed little since its pre-Civil War mercantile heyday. **Market Square** remains the center of activity, with the shops, restaurants, and entertainments of the old port arrayed between the square and the waterfront, and the stately residential community stretching inland. Indeed, Portsmouth serves as the regional center for boutique shopping and fine dining and has become a bedroom community for professionals because it lies within an hour of Boston and minutes from the Maine coast.

Portsmouth has embraced historic preservation with the fervor of a civic religion. The city's pride is **Strawbery Banke Museum,** a sprawling ten-acre site in the Puddle Dock neighborhood. This historic waterfront area, first settled in the 1690s, went through many changes and by the 1950s consisted of block after block of decrepit housing and a large number of establishments frequented by sailors stationed at the Portsmouth Navy Yard. Logically enough, Puddle Dock was targeted for demolition under the banner of "urban renewal."

But in 1958 a group of preservation-minded Portsmouth citizens formed Strawbery Banke, Inc., to preserve the neighborhood and its history. Once largely focused on interpreting some of the fine mansions on its grounds, Strawbery Banke now deals with a full 300 years of history in the neighborhood. In fact, some of the more interesting buildings depict immigrant life in the early twentieth century and small-town life during World War II. Many of the 40 buildings are unheated, so Strawbery Banke closes during the winter. The museum is open from mid-April through October daily from 10:00 A.M. to 5:00 P.M. It re-opens for Home for Thanksgiving Weekend and for Friday and Saturday night Candlelight Strolls on the first two weekends of December. Adult admission is $12. The entrance to the museum is on Marcy Street across from Prescott Park. Telephone: (603) 433–1100.

Personal Narrative:
Portsmouth's Domestic Preserves

Strawbery Banke Museum has become so democratic in its focus that it's easy to overlook the extraordinary wealth of Portsmouth's West Indies traders and privateers two centuries ago. We've often noticed that those who made a good living by the sea liked to have a showplace home on shore and Portsmouth is certainly no exception. Fortunately, six of those manses, all built between 1716 and 1807, have been preserved as house museums.

The information kiosk in Market Square provides an excellent map, called the "Portsmouth Trail," to help visitors locate these time capsules in the midst of a modern city. Admission to any one house is $5.00, with a $1.00 discount at all subsequent houses. It's a good inducement, but only the most ardent fan of decorative arts and domestic lifestyles would even attempt to visit them all in one day. We opt to visit four so that we can roam the streets of this lovely small city at a leisurely pace. The houses are open from mid-June to mid-October, but on slightly different schedules.

From Market Square, we head down Market Street to the **Moffatt-Ladd House.** The narrow street comes nearly to the foundations of the house, and it's not until we climb the stone steps through the street-side gate that we can fully appreciate this magnificent in-town mansion, completed in 1763 by Captain John Moffat as a wedding gift to his son Samuel and

Samuel's bride, Sarah. By all accounts they were inordinately happy here—and we can see why. Captain Moffat spared no expense in building this house for the lucky couple. Records show it took a veritable army of framers, joiners, carvers, and turners 467 days to complete the building—and we are awed by the different carvings on the balustrades of the front staircase alone. Unlike many historic homes, the Moffat-Ladd House is practically filled with family antiques. Our guide explains that "the family saved everything and hid everything in the back of closets."

English damask roses are one of the highlights of the beautiful terraced gardens behind the house. As the family story has it, Sarah plucked a rose from her wedding bouquet to plant in the dooryard garden and although the family long since deeded the house to the Colonial Dames of America, descendants still come to celebrate their weddings and take a cutting from the rose bushes for their own gardens. The Moffatt-Ladd House at 154 Market Street is open Monday to Saturday from 10:00 A.M. to 4:00 P.M. and Sunday from 2:00 to 5:00 P.M. Telephone: (603) 436–8221.

From the Moffatt-Ladd House, we trace our steps back through Market Square and up Congress Street, turning left to Middle Street. We can't miss the **John Paul Jones House** because the square yellow structure appears frequently in paint advertisements. Jones did not own the house—he only lodged here. The gambrel-roofed home was built in 1758 by prosperous sea captain Gregory Purcell. In 1774, Purcell went down with his ship and his destitute widow turned the family home into a genteel boarding house. Says our tour guide, "In those days when you lost your ship, you lost everything."

John Paul Jones took a room at the house in 1777 when he was in town to supervise the construction of the *Ranger,* and again in 1781, when the *America* was being built. Jones, our guide explains, spent most of his adulthood at sea, but when he was on land, he liked the finer things. Although we're charmed by the tale of widow Purcell and the feisty John Paul Jones, we're more covetous of the heirloom peony plants in the front yard and learn that the museum sells cuttings in the fall every two or three years. The John Paul Jones House at 43 Middle Street is open Monday through Saturday from 10:00 A.M. to 4:00 P.M., Sunday from noon to 4:00 P.M. Telephone: (603) 436–8420.

We pass several colorful gardens as we turn left onto Court Street and then right onto Pleasant Street to the **Governor Langdon House,** a vast Georgian mansion erected for shipbuilder-merchant John Langdon in 1784. "One of the wonderful things about being a patriot at that time," our tour guide tells us immediately, "was that you could be a privateer. He made scads of money," mostly at the expense of the British merchant marine. When the Revolution was over, Langdon went into politics, serving two terms as governor of New Hampshire. The intricately carved woodwork was meant to impress visitors, and cavernous public rooms at the front of the house were planned with political entertaining in mind. George Washington came to dinner in 1789 (although he didn't sleep over) and, we're told, "wrote warmly of the house and its host."

The Governor Langdon House at 143 Pleasant Street is open Wednesday to Sunday from noon to 5:00 P.M. Telephone: (603) 436–3205.

After strolling through the one hundred-foot grape and rose arbor behind the Langdon House, we turn left on Pleasant Street, then left again on Hancock, walking down one side of the Strawbery Banke Museum complex and crossing Marcy Street beside the display gardens of Prescott Park. As the land slopes down on our right, we enter the **Point of Graves Burial Ground** through an old wrought-iron turnstile designed to keep out livestock. Captain John Pickering gave this patch of coastal farmland to the town as a cemetery in 1671. Because most of the stones are cut from durable local slate, the details of death's heads and angel wings have not been erased by time. Almost every cluster of graves includes one of a child less than five years old—a reminder of how fragile life was in the early days of settlement. Most of the graves date from the early eighteenth century, but the oldest legible stone here is from 1682.

Just around the bend on this little cove is

Mechanic Street, a formerly rundown neighborhood where the buildings now sport fresh paint as the rising tide of a flush economy lifts all boats. The **Wentworth-Gardner House,** a Georgian mansion built in 1760 for the younger brother of the last royal governor of New Hampshire, is the standout on the street. Yet it actually looks modest enough to inhabit without an army of servants and some of the details—including the intricately carved woodwork, the grand staircase, and the scenic wallpaper—are delightful. Antiquarian Wallace Nutting bought this house in 1915, restored it, and used it as a set for many of his photographs that helped spark the Colonial preservation movement. In 1918, he sold the house (at a nice profit) to New York's Metropolitan Museum of Art, which planned to move the house to Central Park. The Depression intervened and in 1940 a local association bought the property, which it maintains as a museum.

The Wentworth-Gardner House at 50 Mechanic Street is open Tuesday to Sunday from 1:00 to 4:00 P.M. Telephone: (603) 436–4406.

Old and new Portsmouth merge so well that we hardly miss a beat as we return to Market Square to recap our day's visits over espresso and homemade ice cream. We're glad that we have two more houses to look forward to on another day:

The **Warner House,** which dates from 1716, is one of Portsmouth's first brick houses and it harbors a real treasure in the murals on the walls and staircase landing. Possibly the oldest colonial wall paintings still in place, they depict Biblical scenes, animals, and Indian figures copied from European prints. The murals were restored in 1988 by artisans who also worked on the Sistine Chapel—and who believe that more original paintings lurk beneath the paint on the vaulted staircase ceiling. The Warner House at 150 Daniel Street is open Tuesday to Saturday from 10:00 A.M. to 4:00 P.M. and Sunday from 1:00 to 4:00 P.M. Telephone: (603) 436–5909.

The **Rundlet-May House,** built by textile importer James Rundlet in 1807, was filled with all the new-fangled house inventions of the day. It was the first home in Portsmouth

**Wentworth-Gardner House,
Portsmouth, New Hampshire**

with a coal-burning central furnace, an indoor well, a set kettle for doing laundry, and even a Rumford Roaster (a wall oven with integral rotisserie). Rundlet not only planned the details of the interior of his home, but he also laid out a series of terraces, banks, and walkways behind it. He tallied the costs to the penny, calculating that the roses, grapes, lilacs, and other shrubbery came to precisely $104—a hefty sack of change in 1807. The Rundlet-May House at 364 Middle Street is open Wednesday through Sunday from noon to 5:00 P.M. Telephone: (603) 433–2494.

Three bridges over the Piscataqua River link Portsmouth, New Hampshire, to Kittery, Maine. If you want to see other early fortifications at the mouth of the river—Fort McClary and Fort Foster on Kittery Point—the easiest way is to cross Memorial Bridge at the foot of State Street in Portsmouth. At one time this was the only bridge over the river and traffic would back up for miles when the drawbridge was lifted to permit ships to pass beneath.

Most drivers, however, are happy to bypass the forts in favor of the miles of outlet shopping along Route 1 in Kittery. If you are among them, take the tall I–95 bridge and watch for the Route 1 exit across the border in Maine. Route 1 soon leads to a series of villages known collectively as "the Yorks."

The Yorks, Maine

The oldest surviving European settlement on the North Coast, **York Village** was once the largest center of the Saco, an Abenaki people who took advantage of the mild coastal climate to grow corn. But by the time British settlers arrived in 1624, the Saco village had been ravaged by plague and abandoned.

York Village was much augmented in the 1640s by the arrival of Scottish military captives taken by Cromwell's army in the Battle of Dunbar and sold into servitude for periods of seven to twelve years. Most elected to stay behind when their terms expired. When Massachusetts took over the land grants of Sir Fernando Gorges in 1652, the settlement was incorporated as York and prospered as the capital of the Province of Maine. During the French and Indian War, the community was the frequent target of raids. The worst of the lot was the Candlemas Day (February 2) Massacre of 1692, when much of the town of York was burned and many of its residents were killed or taken captive to Canada.

Although there is very little physical evidence of this seventeenth-century history, the **Old York Historical Society** has managed to save six buildings that document eighteenth- and nineteenth-century history on the Maine Coast. Among the buildings, the museum maintains more than thirty period rooms and galleries filled with furniture, ceramics, glassware, paintings, and textiles.

Tours begin in **Jefferds Tavern,** a Colonial hostelry facing the Old Burying Yard. It was built in 1759 and features house "rules" admonishing guests to "abhor all oaths, curses and blasphemy." The **Old School House** has hard wooden benches and tiny windows. The **Old Gaol,** on the corner of Lindsay Street and 1A, is easy to recognize by the stocks on the hill out front. It is said to be the oldest public building in Maine and once served the entire province and then the state. Given the cramped and dank quarters, it is hard to believe that the Old Gaol housed prisoners until 1860. Along the riverfront, the **John Hancock Warehouse** (yes, *that* John Hancock) and **George Marshall Store** recall York's maritime heritage.

Possibly the most revealing building of the museum is the **Elizabeth Perkins House,** purchased in 1898 by Elizabeth Perkins and her mother and renovated in full-blown Colonial Revival style. The product more of the imagination of genteel house restorers than historians, the Perkins house presents a perfectly idealized picture of a bucolic, pre-Revolutionary America. Perkins was such an influential hostess in polite society that her ideas about how good British subjects lived in the New World became a kind of credo, and many estates from northern Massachusetts into Maine were "restored" in frank imitation.

The museum is open from mid-June through September, Tuesday through Saturday from 10:00 A.M. to 5:00 P.M. and Sunday from 1:00 to 5:00 P.M. Adults $6.00. The Jefferds Tavern Visitor Center is on Lindsay Road. Telephone: (207) 363–4974.

York Village is only one of four distinct communities within the York town boundaries. Two other centers, **York Harbor** and **Cape Neddick,** are principally private preserves of summer homes and yacht slips. Cape Neddick does have two rather secluded swimming beaches with severely limited parking: Harbor Beach and Passaconaway Beach.

If you seek beaches, it's better to head to brassy **York Beach,** where city dwellers have flocked for more than a century. Two extensive barrier beaches meet the Atlantic at York Beach. Long Sands (one and one-half miles long) has roadside parking and a bathhouse, while the smaller Short Sands, just a block from the village's shops and restaurants, is served by a large parking lot and a bathhouse.

Between the two beaches, the rocky peninsula of Cape Neddick juts out into the Atlantic. To reach one of the most photographed sites on the Maine coast, follow Nubble Road, which becomes Broadway at the tip, to Sohier Park. The park, which has limited parking and a visitor center, is a popular departure point for wetsuit scuba diving. (Even this far south, the waters are forbiddingly cold.) But most travelers come to see the rocky little island surmounted by **Nubble Light,** an 1879 structure also known as the Cape Neddick Light House. Farther out to sea is the beacon of Boon Island Light, subject of Kenneth Roberts' book *Boon Island.*

Ogunquit, Maine

Although we're leery of Algonquian place names translated by chambers of commerce, "beautiful place by the sea" sounds about right to us as an English rendering of "Ogunquit," a town dribbled out along three miles of wide, sandy beach and a mile of rocky headlands. And the landscape painters who began coming to Ogunquit in the late nineteenth century would almost certainly agree.

Not that you need to tote easel and brushes to visit Ogunquit. The town is laid out to be visitor friendly, with entrances to the sandy strand at Beach Street (the main beach) and two miles north at "the footbridge." Each area has a parking lot. The beach terminates on the south near a rocky point traversed by **Marginal Way,** a one and one-quarter mile elevated footpath above the ocean. The path leads through thickets of beach roses and is well equipped with benches from which to enjoy the view. It concludes at **Perkins Cove,** originally a fishing village and now a peculiar amalgam of artist colony and tourism center. If you'd rather not go on foot, a trolley makes the rounds from town to beach to Perkins Cove from mid-May through Columbus Day.

Because it is so tourist-friendly, Ogunquit can become rather overrun in the summer, and the stretch of Route 1 passing through the village inevitably snarls in the heavy traffic. But the village makes up for these inconveniences with a deft charm. It has long had a large gay summer population and has been a popular destination for sophisticated urbanites from both Boston and Montreal since before World War II. To some extent, Ogunquit's reputation as an art colony has helped it attract summer residents with cultural aspirations and refined tastes.

Such accomplished landscape artists as Thomas Doughty (a founder of the Hudson River school of painting) and Gloucester's leading light of luminism, Fitz Hugh Lane, scouted Ogunquit in the middle of the nineteenth century. But the town did not emerge as an art colony until the end of that century, when Boston impressionist Charles Woodbury began teaching summer art classes. He often directed his students to work among the fishermen in Perkins Cove, where some of the original buildings can still be seen.

But the area's artistic heyday extends from the mid-1920s into the 1950s. Walt Kuhn, one of the organizers of the breakthrough 1913 Armory Show in New York, began summering in Ogunquit in 1911 and bought a home here in 1920. His presence attracted such figures as Edward Hopper, Yasuo Kuniyoshi, and, finally, Marsden Hartley.

Ogunquit attracts land- and seascape painters of a certain sensibility. Hopper and Hartley soon moved on to paint on Monhegan Island and the rocky peninsula village of Corea, respectively. They were painters who saw the world in a hard-edged tumble of blocks, and their vision longed for something more substantial than Ogunquit's comparatively soft surfaces and graceful transitions. The light is more golden in Ogunquit, the air more full and quivering with light than it is on the rockier shores just a few miles north. Even today, Ogunquit's artists are less expressionistic and more impressionistic than their peers. They paint light and color, glorying in the soft twilight, the luminous noon, the marine inkiness of nightfall.

Perhaps the most fondly remembered of Ogunquit's artists is a man one critic called "a prominent American painter of the second rank," Henry Hyacinth Strater. Blessed with inherited wealth and a gift for friendship, he counted among his compatriots Ernest Hemingway, Ezra Pound, James Joyce, Marcel Duchamp, and Constantin Brancusi. To secure his legacy, Strater built the **Ogunquit Museum of American Art** in 1953 and served as its director until his death in 1987. When Strater received the Maine State Award on his 80th birthday, the citation mentioned his mastery of the "fissured and enduring rocks of the coast of Ogunquit, the blue delphiniums of his garden, or the variations of Adam's (and every man's) temptation." (Strater loved to paint voluptuous female nudes.)

The museum sits on landscaped grounds at Narrow Cove, overlooking the mouth of Perkins Cove just off Shore Road. The building's exterior exemplifies a kind of bland modernism of the 1950s, but its vaulted main gallery and three smaller exhibition rooms contain some striking treasures, including a half-dozen Marsden Hartley paintings, an excellent landscape by Charles Woodbury, and works by Walt Kuhn, Yasuo

Kuniyoshi, Bernard Karfiol, and Robert Laurent. The museum also owns literally hundreds of works by Strater. The Ogunquit Museum of American Art is open July through September, Monday through Saturday from 10:30 A.M. to 5:00 P.M. and Sunday from 2:00 to 5:00 P.M. Adults $4. Telephone: (207) 646–4909.

Wells, Maine

As you drive north on Route 1, Ogunquit passes almost seamlessly into the town of Wells, a community where the landscape and shore capture almost everything of allure on the southern crescent of the North Coast. Long a farming and fishing community, Wells exploded as a vacation mecca with the advent of auto touring. A seven-mile strand of sandy beach—really a one-time barrier island that has become attached to the mainland—attracts throngs every summer day to splash in the shallow waters and tan on the beach. Tacky souvenir shops—the kind that sell dozens of straw hats and scores of brands of suntan lotion—complete the picture.

But only a short distance from these seaside frolics are some of the most important wetlands in this part of New England and the headquarters of two organizations that helped preserve them. We'll grant that wetland appreciation is an acquired taste—best acquired with a lot of insect repellent—but once you learn to look closely, these environments teem with life you won't see elsewhere.

From the center of Wells, follow Route 1 north to the blinking yellow light and turn right on Laudholm Farm Road to reach the **Wells National Estuarine Reserve** at Laudholm Farm. Established in 1986, the reserve occupies an old saltwater farm with 1,600 acres of field, forest, wetlands, and beaches. Seven miles of nature trails lead through several ecosystems from old field (full of voles, mice, grouse, and the hawks that prey on them) to forest, from tidal river to ocean. The shoreline area hosts the endangered piping plover and the least tern along with more common seabird species.

Guided tours, offered April through October, focus on birds, wildlife, wildflowers, the marsh, the beach, or cultural history of the area. Visitors can participate in the bird-banding program from

June through August every Wednesday morning at 8:00 A.M. The Visitor Center is open all year, Monday through Saturday from 10:00 A.M. to 4:00 P.M. and Sunday from noon to 4:00 P.M. The trails are open daily from 8:00 A.M. to 5:00 P.M. Parking fee $2.00 per adult, $3.00 for nocturnal wildlife walk on nights of full moon. 342 Laudholm Farm Road. Telephone: (207) 646–1555.

Continue to the end of Laudholm Farm Road and you will be on Route 9 heading toward another cluster of villages called "the Kennebunks." In less than a mile you will come to Port Road on the right, the entrance to the **Rachel Carson National Wildlife Refuge** administered by the United States Fish and Wildlife Service. The refuge encompasses 4,800 acres of estuarine saltmarshes as well as upland habitats between Kittery and Cape Elizabeth. The headquarters parking lot gives access to the one-mile Rachel Carson Interpretive Nature Trail, which overlooks 1,600 acres of wetlands as well as a barrier beach. The refuge office has brochures showing the trail and offering wildlife spotting tips. Open daily from sunrise to sunset. Route 9 East. Telephone: (207) 646–9226.

The Kennebunks, Maine

The Kennebunks—Kennebunk, Kennebunk Beach, and Kennebunkport—are villages of the Town of Kennebunk nestled between the Mousam and Kennebunk rivers. Once famed for their shipbuilding, they are now better known for summer resident George Bush, the former president.

Kennebunk, the inland river village on Route 1, is perhaps the most picturesque of the three villages and Main, Summer, and several side streets have been declared a National Register Historic District. The village's commercial, religious, and residential buildings trace the evolution of popular architectural styles from Colonial, Federal, Queen Anne, and Greek Revival to Italianate. A bell cast by Paul Revere and Sons hangs in the First Parish Church's steeple, which was contructed from a Christopher Wren design.

The **Brick Store Museum** occupies an 1825 brick store and three adjacent nineteenth-century

buildings in Kennebunk's National Register District. The museum exhibitions focus on the maritime history of the Kennebunks as well as on fine and decorative arts of the area. Because the Bush family has had such an impact on the area, going back two generations before the president, temporary exhibitions often focus on some aspect of Bush activities. The Brick Store Museum is at the junction of Routes 1 and 35. It is open from mid-April through mid-December, Tuesday through Saturday from 10:00 A.M. to 4:30 P.M. From mid-December to mid-April, it is closed on Saturdays. Adults $3.00 or $5.00 with the Taylor-Barry House (see below). Telephone: (207) 985–4802.

The museum also maintains the **Taylor-Barry House,** last occupied by Edith C. Barry, an artist who painted in New York and Kennebunk. One of the four furnished rooms is set up as an early twentieth-century artist's studio. The Taylor-Barry House is at 24 Summer Street and guided tours are offered from June through September, Tuesday through Friday from 1:00 to 4:00 P.M. A good option for exploring Kennebunk in depth is to take a guided architectural walking tour of the historic district, led by a guide from the museum, which concludes with a tour of the Taylor-Barry House. The walking tours are offered mid-June through September on Wednedsay at 10:00 A.M. and Friday at 1:00 P.M. Adults $3.

Kennebunk Beach and **Kennebunkport** are both on Route 9, connected to Kennebunk by Routes 9A and 35. A trolley service also connects the villages. The long and broad sands of Kennebunk Beach, Mother's Beach, and Gooch's Beach are connected by sidewalks along (what else?) Beach Avenue, making this a favorite promenade for joggers, walkers, cyclists, and the occasional blader. (Given the level of country club decorum in the Kennebunks, in-line skaters are a distinct minority.) A resident parking permit is required to park anywhere near the Kennebunk beaches, so it's best to park in town and use the trolley to get to the sand.

Dock Square, the center of Kennebunkport, overlooks the Kennebunk River basin and has been a commercial center for two centuries. Once stocked with wares for local shipbuilders and traders, the waterside buildings now house bou-

Main Street, Kennebunk, Maine

tiques, restaurants, and art galleries serving those who live in the stately summer homes, including George and Barbara Bush.

George Bush usually shows up for the Memorial Day ceremony at the monument to "our soldiers and sailors" in the center of the Square. Locals still talk about the time when then-President Bush eluded his Secret Service detail to hike into town and shoot the breeze at the general store. The local police, we've been told, practically had a heart attack. When an officer asked where the Secret Service was, Bush explained laconically that it was no big deal for him to give them the slip. After all, he used to head the CIA.

If you follow Route 9 northeast of Kennebunkport, you'll come to the delightful and surprisingly old-fashioned working harbor of **Cape Porpoise.** Lobstermen, fishermen, and recreational boaters share the harbor, which is marked at its entrance by Goat Island lighthouse. Less than a mile farther along Route 9 is **Goose Rocks**—one of the best stretches of silver white sand on the East Coast. At low tide, you can see a barrier reef formation known as "Goose Rocks" just offshore. Local tradition has it that migrating geese use the formation as a navigational landmark. The sand dunes and beach grass are good nesting ground for piping plovers and lesser terns.

Route 9 detours up the shore of the Saco River to intersect with Route 1 in Saco, then wraps around the other side of the river down to the lobstering village of Camp Ellis and **Ferry Beach State Park,** a long sandy strand with free parking. Route 9 continues north into Old Orchard Beach after passing through the former camp-meeting village of **Ocean Park.**

Old Orchard Beach, Maine

Most people, however, drive into Old Orchard Beach from Route 1, and there's something fitting about this approach from the classic strip highway into the last of the genuinely sweet honky-tonk beach towns of New England. We have to be frank: Our more urbane friends think we have lost all sense of taste when we tell them that we love Old Orchard Beach. Too bad—we think they've lost all sense of fun.

Old Orchard Beach has been around a long time—the first settler, Thomas Rogers, established his "Garden by the Sea" here in 1657. Not long afterward, the hilltop rising above the long, sandy beach was planted in apple trees that provided a landmark for sailors and gave the area its appellation.

Old Orchard became an instant success as a summer resort as soon as people could reach it. In 1842 the first steam railroad connecting Boston to Portland had a station just two miles west of Old Orchard Beach. In 1853, the Grand Trunk Railroad connected Old Orchard Beach to Montreal, launching a history of French Canadian summer vacationers that continues to this day.

By the end of the century, Old Orchard was a booming playground. The first pier opened in 1898, the first arcade in 1902. Time and again Old Orchard's attractions have been destroyed by fire or weather, but it rises phoenix-like from every disaster.

Nature has been generous to Old Orchard. Its three-mile strand is the nucleus of seven miles of sandy beaches between Saco and Scarborough. That's seven miles of gentle waves lapping at a gradual shore, seven miles of healthy dunes anchored with sawgrass. It's all the room in the world for sunbathers and Frisbee throwers and strapping young men skimming the beach wash on boogie boards.

As a counterpoint to this natural playground, the **Palace Playland** amusement park features a

Pier at Old Orchard Beach, Maine

giant arcade, the Gondola Ferris wheel, the Galaxy Coaster, and a whole range of kiddy rides. It is open from Memorial Day to Labor Day daily.

There's something giddy about Old Orchard. It's the only place we know where we get overwhelming urges to eat fried dough, to play the pinball machines, to stand still for a (temporary) tattoo, to break beer bottles with a baseball so we can win a stuffed penguin. There's really nothing else like it in New England.

Old Orchard Beach is a family resort as democratic as they come. Good motels line the beachfront where posh hotels used to stand. In the summer they are mostly full and, compared to other beach areas, relatively inexpensive. Walk out the door, cross 20 feet over the dunes, and suddenly there you are—on a nearly empty sand beach. Pick one of the Grand Avenue motels, and the Atlantic Ocean is at your back door.

If you follow East Grand Avenue northward out of town (Route 9), you will discover some of the least-used public beaches of the area, **Grand Beach, Pine Point Beach,** and **Western Beach.** Taken together, they boast more than a mile of pure white sand beach with sheltered swimming.

Scarborough and Cape Elizabeth, Maine

Route 9 makes a 90-degree left turn at Pine Point to skirt the Scarborough River. At its mouth, the river is actually the confluence of more than a dozen brooks, streams, and small rivers—a remarkable estuarine system that is rare anywhere in New England north of Narragansett Bay. Bird-

watchers find the Scarborough Marshes, as the area has been known since the 1670s, one of the most rewarding places to visit in the Northeast. The **Scarborough Marsh Nature Center** covers more than 3,000 acres of tidal and freshwater marsh, salt creeks, and uplands. A boardwalk nature trail gives good access to the marshes, with some blinds set up for observing shy waterfowl. Walking and canoe tours are offered daily, and night canoe tours are given on the full moon and the night before and after the full moon. The center also rents canoes by the hour and the half day. The center is open mid-June through early September daily from 9:30 A.M. to 5:30 P.M. Parking free. Walking tours $4.00, canoe tours $9.00. Pine Point Road. Telephone: (207) 883–5100 or (207) 781–2330.

The town of Scarborough also encompasses the elite community on **Prouts Neck,** a knobby peninsula on the eastern side of the Scarborough River. If you're heading north on Route 9, turn right onto Black Point Road (Route 207), which terminates at Prouts Neck. Public parking is banned in the private community, so it's best explored on a bicycle or on foot after parking at Scarborough Beach State Park near the neck of the peninsula. Much of Prouts Neck is now dedicated as a bird sanctuary, with boardwalks through the woods and above the rocks.

If the rocks at Prouts Neck look familiar, it might be because they are featured in so many of the powerful late paintings of Winslow Homer, who grew up in Boston but spent the last 25 years of his life primarily working from his Prouts Neck studio. Although Homer died in 1910, his family still owns his studio and it remains off-limits to uninvited visitors. Homer would have liked that. He prized his privacy and even wrote on his 1899 painting *The Gulf Stream,* "Don't let the public poke its nose into my picture."

Stony Prouts Neck presages the coast to come after one brief, beachy interlude in Cape Elizabeth, the northern terminus of the North Coast's crescent of sandy beaches. The Cape Elizabeth peninsula is best reached from Prouts Neck by following Spurwink Road (Route 77) where it branches off to the right from Black Point Road as you return toward Scarborough village. The road changes its name several times within Cape Elizabeth, but is still marked as Route 77. It swings past **Higgins Beach** and **Crescent Beach State Park**—two rather lightly used but excellent swimming and sunbathing beaches.

The road continues to a place where two geographies intersect—the rocky points and sandy dunes of **Two Lights State Park.** The pair of nineteenth-century lighthouses that gave the park its name were favorites of Edward Hopper, who painted their stark desolation from several views in 1927 and 1929. While there is a housing development nearby, a zoning battle in 1987 preserved "Hopper's View" by stopping development from coming any closer to the lights. Somewhat less scenic is the nearby Cape Elizabeth Light. The sudden appearance of lighthouses signals the end of the southern crescent of New England's North Coast, as sand gives way to stone and the warm waters influenced by the Gulf Stream meet the frigid Labrador Current.

Maine's Peninsula Country

Between Casco Bay and Penobscot Bay, the coast fragments into rocky points of shale and slate, the shattered face of a continent snapped off in the last kiss goodbye between North America and Africa, then pummeled down and lifted up in succeeding glaciations. Probably half the miles of coastline of the region are found on these long narrow peninsulas that dribble like a wispy beard off the chin of the mainland. Two major (the Androscoggin and Kennebec) and several minor river systems flow into the ocean in peninsula country, and the dangerous offshore shoals are lit with many lighthouses. Maine has sixty-three lighthouses—more than any other state—and the majority of them are found here. Most were constructed in the nineteenth century by some of America's foremost architects and engineers, who prevailed over daunting challenges to build enduring structures on rocky wave-swept ledges and shifting sands.

As you round Cape Elizabeth, you cross a border that signs along the road don't even hint at.

The long barrier beaches of the southern crescent are by and large gone, and the shoreline turns dark and boulder-strewn. Even the type of rock changes from sedimentary shale and sandstone to the harder materials of basalt and granite. The legendary "rocky coast of Maine" begins at Casco Bay, which is signaled on its southern edge by **Portland Head Light.**

From Two Lights State Park, follow Route 77 north for about one mile, watching for signs to the turnoff to the right for the lighthouse and **Fort Williams State Park.** One of the most photographed lighthouses in the world, Portland Head is the oldest lighthouse in Maine, constructed in 1791 as part of Fort Williams. (The fort ruins and surrounding grounds are great places for flying kites and admission is free.) Portland Head's interior is now a lighthouse museum open June through October daily from 10:00 A.M. to 4:00 P.M., April, May, November, and December on Saturday and Sunday from 10:00 A.M. to 4:00 P.M. Adults $2.00. 1000 Shore Road. Telephone: (207) 799–2661.

Casco Bay and Portland, Maine

The main community of interest in Casco Bay is **Portland,** the largest and most prosperous city in Maine. Casco Bay has a deep channel that leads past an archipelago into a broad harbor at Portland. The islands of Casco Bay provide shelter from the brutish storms of the North Atlantic. As a result, the river-mouth harbors in Portland and South Portland have served as safe haven for large ships since the eighteenth century. Even today they are the major receiving ports of northern New England, and as you drive into South Portland you will pass massive petroleum and gas storage tank farms.

Most travelers to Portland either come up Route 1 through South Portland (Route 77 from Portland Head Light connects back to Route 1) or follow the I–295 spur from the Maine Turnpike. If you come by I–295, take the waterfront exit.

Portland is nothing if not persistent. The earliest English settlement (called Falmouth) did not fare well, as the entire community was destroyed in 1675 during King Philip's War. But settlers returned, building up substantial mercantile trade with England—which came to a sudden halt on October 18–19, 1775. Although Falmouth had initially taken a Loyalist stance in the Revolution, neighboring communities so riled the British officials that they demanded that Falmouth citizens turn in their arms. Many refused and a fleet of warships opened fire, bombarding the town through the night. By dawn some 400 buildings were reduced to rubble and ashes. Renamed Portland, the community rebounded after the Revolution as a commercial port and shipping center, only to burn down again in the Great Fire of 1866, which started during the Independence Day celebration. And still Portland bounced back. Not for nothing is the city's motto *Resurgam*—"I Shall Rise Again." With new building codes in place, Portland was rebuilt with brick in a distinctive Victorian style that persists throughout the city.

In fact, the area known as **West End** ranks among the best preserved Victorian residential districts in the United States. (Several of the homes now serve as B&Bs—see "Staying There.") The **Western Promenade** is a landscaped public walkway along the edge of a west-facing cliff. On a clear day, the White Mountains are visible in the distance.

The adjacent State Street district is lined with Federal and Greek Revival mansions. The grandest dame of them all is **Victoria Mansion,** built and furnished between 1858 and 1862 for Ruggles S. Morse, one of the first Mainers to go out into the world to make his fortune. Morse was a New Orleans hotelier, and when he decided to return to Portland, he was determined to make a splash. He hired the New Haven society architect Henry Austin to design an Italianate villa, then engaged New York operatic set designer Gustave Herter to dress up the interiors. Austin and Herter pulled out all the stops. Walls and ceilings were covered with trompe l'oeil, including imitation wood marquetry—ironic given that the Maine timber industry was at its height. Carved marble fireplaces, elaborate rosewood furniture, French porcelains, carpets woven in Scotland—nothing was too good for Morse. Amazingly, many of the original furnishings survive, making Victoria Mansion a must-see experience, if only because it stands in such contrast to the customary modesty of Mainers. Open May through

October, Tuesday through Saturday from 10:00 A.M. to 4:00 P.M. and Sunday from 1:00 to 5:00 P.M. Adults $5.00. 109 Danforth Street. Telephone: (207) 772–4841.

Congress Street serves as both the commercial heart and the transportation spine of the Portland peninsula. Its shops and office buildings sit cheek by jowl with civic structures and museums, including the **Portland Museum of Art** and the **Wadsworth Longfellow House.** The Portland Museum of Art occupies a handsome modernist building designed by the I.M. Pei firm and constructed in 1983, when Portland began to rebuild itself after decades of economic slump. The new museum building became a source of civic pride that helped galvanize other renovation and construction in the neighborhood. Its collections offer good cause for that pride. The American galleries are particularly strong in late nineteenth- and early twentieth-century artists who worked in Maine, including works by Winslow Homer, Andrew and N.C. Wyeth, Edward Hopper, and Rockwell Kent. The museum owns one of the world's best collections of Homer watercolors, but because they are fragile and sensitive to light, only part of the collection is shown at a time and then usually only during the summer. Open Tuesday through Saturday from 10:00 A.M. to 5:00 P.M. (Thursday until 9:00 P.M.) and Sunday from noon to 5:00 P.M. Adults $5.00. 7 Congress Square. Telephone: (207) 775–6148.

The **Wadsworth Longfellow House** seems modest by comparison with the Victorian homes of Portland, but it is nearly a century older. Built in 1786 by General Peleg Wadsworth with bricks brought in by boat from Philadelphia, it was a country home at the time. Poet, scholar, and translator Henry Wadsworth Longfellow (Peleg Wadsworth's grandson) grew up in the house and wrote some verse here. The house is maintained by the Center for Maine History, which also has a gallery with changing exhibits. Open June to October daily from 10:00 A.M. to 4:00 P.M. Adults $5.00. 485–489 Congress Street. Telephone: (207) 879–0427.

Many visitors to Portland spend all their time in the **Old Port Exchange** shopping and dining district. Many parts of the old port were razed during the craze for urban renewal, but construction funds ran out before the core of the area could be gutted. When the economy took an upturn, the Old Port was rediscovered and redeveloped, with boutiques, microbreweries, restaurants, and cafes occupying the former chandleries and warehouses.

And the port itself continues to operate, with sightseeing and whalewatching vessels berthed gunwale to gunwale with fishing boats. In fact, a substantial portion of Maine's catch is offloaded here and there's a public fish auction Monday through Thursday at 1:00 P.M. on Portland Fish Pier.

Casco Bay Ferry Terminal is located at the east end of Old Port Exchange and serves the island communities in the harbor. The ferry is a good way to see Casco Bay and maybe even mingle with the locals. Two routes, with stops at the islands of Cliff, Chebeague, Long, and Great Diamond, operate all year. Adults $9.50. There is also regular roundtrip ferry service to Peaks Island, a Portland bedroom community with a good beach. Adults $3.00. Several sightseeing cruises also operate during the summer. Commercial and Franklin Streets. Telephone: (207) 774–7871.

Freeport, Maine

As you drive north from Portland on Route 1, the urban sprawl soon gives way to more bucolic scenery. All cars (and a number of tour buses) seem to be headed for Freeport, site of one of the world's most popular outlet mall developments. Even if you despise outlet malls, there's good reason to stop: the store of legendary outfitter **L.L. Bean,** which started it all.

We can't help but wonder what Bean would think about the current merchandising extravaganza. Born in 1872, Leon Leonwood Bean learned at an early age to make a living from the outdoors, claiming in his memoirs to sell his first deer to disappointed out-of-state hunters in 1885. Ultimately he married a Freeport woman and, with his brother, opened the Bean Brothers store in Freeport in 1905. Frustrated by always having wet feet when he went hunting or fishing, he devised the Maine Hunting Boot in 1911. This one item—a leather last with rubber bottoms—remains a big part of the Bean empire.

The next year Bean put together a catalog of his outdoors gear and mailed it to everyone who had purchased a nonresident fishing or hunting license in Maine. It was the beginning of a mail-order empire that helped, to a great extent, to establish Maine's image as the quintessential outdoorsman's paradise.

For many years the L.L. Bean store has been open twenty-four hours a day—all the better to service the fishermen driving up from New York in the spring or the hunters coming from Boston in the fall. For those of us who drove long distances to and from Maine in the days before 1984 (when a vast new store was built), the funky old store was a welcome haven for hot coffee and good chat. It was the kind of place where you could stop at 3:00 A.M. the day before trout season opened and a clerk could tell you which flies were hatching up north near Grand Isle and steer you to the dry flies that would best imitate them.

With the popularity of preppie style (when did prepsters start dressing like hunters?), Bean has become more an apparel store these days. But the company still stocks the Maine Hunting Boot, fly fishing gear, canoes, tents, and practically anything you might need to light out for the territory. The store is at the corner of Main and Bow Streets—not that you could miss it.

Brunswick and the Harpswells, Maine

Peninsula country begins in earnest north of Freeport. The long necks and islands that string in a north-south line off the mainland are largely ridges of igneous rock that would have been highlands except for the last glaciation. The weight of the ice so depressed this land that it is still rising an inch or two each year even 12,000 years after the ice receded. All the soft, sedimentary rock between the ridges was gouged out by the ice sheet, leaving depressions where the rivers that drain the southeast flank of the White Mountains flow to the sea.

Brunswick is located at the falls of the Androscoggin River, about 15 minutes north of Freeport on Route 1. Although it is several miles upriver from the ocean, much of Brunswick's wealth was tied to the sea, as early residents engaged in coastal trade and floated timber down the Androscoggin to sell to shipbuilders. Grand sea captains' mansions fill its several National Historic Districts, but the community is dominated by the campus of Bowdoin College at the end of Maine Street (as the main street is called).

The college was chartered by Massachusetts (Maine was part of the Bay State until 1820) in 1794, but didn't open until eight years later, when absentee timberland landlord James Bowdoin III came through with the money to build much of the original campus. Some of its most famous graduates include Nathaniel Hawthorne and Henry Wadsworth Longfellow (both class of 1825), President Franklin Pierce (who gave Hawthorne all those government jobs that kept him going when his books didn't sell), and Arctic explorers Robert Peary and Donald MacMillan.

The **Peary-MacMillan Arctic Museum** pays homage to those two alumni and chronicles their Arctic explorations. Exhibits include the sled by which Peary and his African American colleague Matthew Henson reached the North Pole (if in fact they did), as well as the instruments Peary used to make the controversial observations that determined they were at the top of the world. Open Tuesday to Saturday from 10:00 A.M. to 5:00 P.M., Sunday from 2:00 to 5:00 P.M. Hubbard Hall. Telephone: (207) 725–3000.

If you follow Route 123 south from Maine Street in Brunswick, you will soon arrive at one of the most distinctive areas of the Maine coast—the town of **Harpswell,** which encompasses the communities of North, South, and West Harpswell as well as Harpswell Center, Cundy's Harbor, Orr's Island, Bailey Island, and some forty-five other specks of land surrounded by water. There are so many villages on this small spit of land because they grew up as independent fishing communities in the years before roads connected them.

Harpswell Neck, the west side of town, is a single peninsula—a thin finger of granite topped with pine trees and the occasional hardscrabble, saltwater farm. It provides an increasingly rare view of the old maritime Maine of lobster trapping and near-shore fishing with hand lines from small boats—a slow life that moves with the inexorable rhythms of the tides. The Neck's population includes literally scores of lobstermen, and you'll see their yards piled high with buoys in

Duck decoys, folk art

need of painting and traps in need of repair. They're not starving—they each have hundreds more traps resting on the offshore ledges. To the east are the three islands of Great, Orr's, and Bailey. They are joined by bridges, of which the Cribstone Bridge, linking Orr's and Bailey's, is said to be a unique example of a stone bridge constructed without mortar.

Bath and Below, Maine

Often mentioned in the same breath with Brunswick because they are so close together and form a regional economic unit, **Bath** lies at a peculiar spot on the Kennebec River where it becomes so broad and deep that some of the world's largest ships can come into its port. Bath may be a good 15 miles from the Gulf of Maine, but only because the long peninsulas and islands of Phippsburg, Arrowsic, and Georgetown intervene. The Kennebec is one of the territory's great logging rivers, since it drains northwestern Maine's timber country. The combination of upriver timber and an extremely sheltered deep water port helped create and sustain a centuries-old shipbuilding tradition in both Bath and its nearby peninsula country.

Shipbuilding began in this area in Georgetown, closer to the mouth of the Kennebec, but during times of hostilities, that island proved difficult to defend. Following the War of 1812, Bath emerged as the fifth largest seaport in the new nation, with shipbuilding as its largest industry. Nearly half the ships constructed in the United States between 1862 and 1902 were built in Bath and the shipyards of adjacent Kennebec River communities. The Bath Iron Works, which dominates the harbor, is a company of shipbuilders and engineers that dates back to 1884 and continues to produce vessels for the United States Navy.

The twenty-acre **Maine Maritime Museum** is one of the better places to get an overview of the historic and continuing interplay between Mainers and the sea. Five of the original buildings of Percy & Small Shipyard trace the process of building a wooden ship from preliminary designs through to launch. It's a sequence that the yard knew well: Between 1894 and 1920 Percy & Small constructed forty-one four-, five-, and six-masted schooners. In the summer, you can board a Grand Banks fishing schooner, the *Sherman Zwicker,* and get an idea of what life on board was like during the 1940s, while another exhibition room deals with onshore life through a diorama of workers preparing lobster meat for canning. The museum also has an extensive collection of paintings, figureheads, and ship models, and offers an excursion boat tour on the Kennebec River to give visitors a closer look at the museum's own historic boats (anchored in the river in the summer) and to let them see the Bath Iron Works in operation. Open daily 9:30 A.M. to 5:00 P.M. Adults $8.00. 243 Washington Street. Telephone: (207) 443–1316.

Long before the Europeans arrived, the islands and peninsulas due south of Bath served as summer encampments where Abenaki peoples dug shellfish, hunted seabirds, and harpooned seals and whales. When the Europeans came, the Pejepscots and Sagadahocs suffered the same fate as most New England Native peoples—decimation first by disease, then by war.

The Europeans came early. A stone with runic markings bearing the date 1018 was found at Popham Beach at the end of the Phippsburg peninsula. It is attributed to Norsemen, though it may have ended up here via trade, since there is no enduring evidence of Norse settlement in the region. (Keep in mind that the climate of the North Coast was much milder between A.D. 900 and A.D. 1300, making it more suitable to agriculture.)

French explorer Samuel de Champlain is believed to have mapped the lower reaches of the Kennebec River in 1605, and in 1607 (the same year as the Jamestown, Virginia, settlement), the English planted a colony at Popham. Either the

Maine coastal life or the absence of women didn't agree with its 100 settlers, and they returned to England a year later aboard the first English-built ship in the New World, the *Virginia of Sagadahoc.* The settlers managed to leave enough signs of their habitation behind to keep archaeologists busy for years, and the original settlement remains a closed archaeological site.

Two of Maine's best beaches bracket the end of the Kennebec River. **Popham Beach State Park,** which has extensive parking and more than 3,600 yards of powdery white sand, is used primarily by Mainers. Perhaps because it is a half-hour drive south on the peninsula, casual tourists rarely find it. This is one of the few places north of Cape Cod where the waves rolling in off the Atlantic are big enough for serious surfing. If you would rather stay out of the cold water (a good idea unless you have a wetsuit), the park also has extensive nature trails and dune walks. Striped bass fishing from the park's rocky headlands can be incredibly good. (This area of the coast sees mostly "schoolies"—bass in the five- to ten-pound range.)

Reid State Park lies equally far down the coast on the island of Georgetown. Cross the Kennebec River Bridge from Bath into Woolwich and take an immediate right at the end of the bridge onto Route 127. Near the end of the route, turn right onto Seguinland Road to reach the park. Reid is better known and more developed than Popham Beach, with a snack bar, bathhouses, and fireplaces. In addition to nature trails, Reid has two long sandy beaches—Mile Beach and Half Mile Beach. Depending on the previous winter's storms, these beaches sometimes have sandbars across them. When the tide goes out, it leaves behind sandy lagoons between the islands and the main beach where the water becomes as warm as a bath until the next high tide spills in and chills it down again.

Wiscasset, Maine

As you follow Route 1 north from Bath, you will lose sight of the water until you come abruptly into Wiscasset. With uncharacteristic braggadocio, Wiscasset calls itself "the prettiest village in Maine," and no other town has stepped forward to dispute it (to do so would be immodest). Disgruntled drivers sometimes refer to Wiscasset as "the prettiest little bottleneck on Route 1."

The courthouse, built in 1824, is the oldest operating courthouse in New England and Wiscasset's streets are a veritable museum of eighteenth- and nineteenth-century sea captains' homes. We recall the first time we brought an architect friend from New York to Wiscasset. He was awestruck—"like a textbook," he exclaimed. We spent hours just walking up and down the streets. Like many coastal communities, Wiscasset has just a few rather steep streets leading up and down the hills, and many cross streets where the houses are built to look down toward the water. This arrangement makes for long back yards, lots of green grass, and, because the town is so old, many majestic trees.

One of the more outstanding and interesting homes, the **Nickels-Sortwell House,** is open for tours, which include the period gardens. Built in 1807 by a prosperous ship owner and trader, it reflects the wealth and sophistication of the time. But the Embargo Act of 1807 and the War of 1812 caused many coastal families to lose their fortunes, and the Nickels family was among them. Around 1830 the house became a hotel. In 1895 the Sortwell family transformed it back into a summer residence, which they gave to the Society for the Preservation of New England Antiquities (SPNEA) in 1958. Open June through September Wednesday through Sunday. Tours offered on the hour from 1:00 to 4:00 P.M. Adults $4.00. Main and Federal Streets. Telephone: (207) 882–6218.

Not all of Wiscasset is quite so solemn or decorous, of course. The main street has its share of boutiques, antiques dealers, and craft stores. One of the enduring symbols of old-time Maine auto touring, **Red's Eats,** survives at the foot of Main Street at Water Street. It looks like a hot dog stand (and the hot dogs are pretty good), but Red's is better known for its lobster roll. The nearby harbor, which used to be dominated by the rotting hulks of two old schooners, is a vibrant, active place full of both fishing boats and recreational craft. Striped bass fishing off the bridge between Wiscasset and Edgecomb is particularly good in July and August, when the mean

tide runs nine and four-tenths feet and the stripers run upriver with the tides to feed on smaller fish. And commercial fishing still plays a role in Wiscasset's economy, as the tidal flats along the river yield a healthy harvest of clams and the deeper water is still rich with lobsters.

Boothbay Peninsula, Maine

If you follow Route 1 into Edgecomb and then turn south on Route 27, you will be touring the fabled Boothbay peninsula. Summer fishing grounds of late-fifteenth-century Basque fishermen, the region was settled by English seafarers and shipbuilders in the seventeenth century. Like so many other towns, Boothbay began building boats from the outset, using the tall pines of the peninsula as masts for its schooners. By 1700 these schooners were sailing to all the ports of the Atlantic. But Boothbay's scenic serenity soon overtook its utility as a trading and fishing port. As early as 1870, great resort hotels dotted the landscape, with guests arriving by passenger steamship. The resort hotels are gone, but in their place are private estates and condominium communities.

Boothbay Harbor, the chief community at the end of the peninsula, is a popular place for yachts cruising the north Atlantic to put in for a few days. You don't come here to do anything in particular—and that's the point. The headlands of the peninsula stand high above the water and the bays by the harbor are extraordinarily picturesque.

But you can also come by automobile, and the town's roads are lined with motels. The summer crush can be a bit overwhelming, but if you're willing to spend the extra money, quieter and more scenic lodgings are available on Southport Island in Newagen. (See "Staying There.") If you drive down to the tiny **Newagen Harbor,** you will see one of the greatest contrasts on the coast between a serene sheltered harbor and a titanic roiling ocean outside it. Ledges beyond the harbor explode with white geysers of water as the big ocean waves hit them.

Pemaquid Peninsula, Maine

The villages of **Newcastle** and **Damariscotta,** which face each other across the Damariscotta

River, elected to have Route 1 go around them. This bypass solution—one of the first places on the Maine coast where it was tried—has helped preserve the small-town feel of the communities while still leaving them easy to reach. Like Wiscasset, they're situated at the broadest harbor of a long tidal river, and both communities built many ships in their early years before the tall timber petered out.

For many years the ancient shell middens on both sides of the river were mined for fertilizer—until archaeologists realized that they represented a treasure trove of pre-contact native culture. More than one million cubic feet of oyster shells are contained in three layers going down thirty feet. Some of the oldest shells measure up to 20 inches across, and the top layer of shell deposits is intermixed with ancient fire pits and human artifacts, including stone implements that could only have been oyster knives. Archaeologists now believe that the coastal peoples of the region came to the Damariscotta River every summer for at least 2,000 years to fish and dig oysters, which they apparently smoked and dried as winter provisions. Oysters have not flourished here since the time of English settlement, but are on the rebound with the cleanup of the river.

Watch for the right hand turn to Route 130 south, which leads a dozen miles south on the Pemaquid Peninsula to the **lighthouse at Pemaquid Point.** You'll know it when you see it, for it is one of the three most photographed lighthouses on the North Coast (the other two are Portland Head Light and West Quoddy Light).

Pemaquid Point is a streaky lava outflow intermixed with granite. It freezes in stone the powerful forces unleashed when New England and Canada's Atlantic provinces separated from the British Isles and Scandinavia more than 200 million years ago. A swell of magma from the center of the planet rose to the surface when the separation of continental plates ripped a hole in the earth's mantle.

The Pemaquid light was erected in 1827 less as a warning of dangerous shoals than as a navigational aid for sailors making landfall from the east. The light has been automated for many years, so the keeper's house has become the **Pemaquid Fishermen's Museum.** The rocks below the light

Lighthouse at Pemaquid Point, Maine

are a favorite spot for weddings, and sometimes it seems like it's hard to view the scene for all the painters and photographers jostling for just the right angle. The museum is open more or less daily (it's staffed by volunteers) between Memorial Day and Labor Day from 10:00 A.M. to 5:00 P.M. Adults $1.00.

The actual villages of the peninsula sit on the east and west coasts. While they host many summer visitors, both **Pemaquid Harbor** (west) and **New Harbor** (east) are active, year-round fishing villages. Their charm is that they don't try to be anything they aren't (despite the souvenir shops and art galleries). Coming here is an escape to the "real Maine," albeit an economically upbeat corner of it.

English fishing boats first anchored in Pemaquid Harbor around 1600, and the small harbor offers a good view of Fort William Henry, a reproduction of the 1692–94 fort that was destroyed in 1696. Over the years, three additional forts stood on the site and were attacked and to some extent destroyed by the British, by pirates, by the Natives, by the French, and—finally—by the local citizenry during the American Revolution. Just south of the harbor along the west coast is **Pemaquid Beach Park,** which has a crescent-shaped white sand beach, picnic tables, and bathhouses.

Muscongus Bay, Maine

Follow Route 32 north from New Harbor up the east side of Pemaquid Peninsula for a pleasantly rural drive that passes through the fishing villages of Chamberlain, Round Pond, Bremen, and Broad Cove before rejoining Route 1 at **Waldoboro,** a town that veterans of Route 1 driving remember for two reasons: the speed trap at the bottom of the valley where Route 1 and Route 32 cross, and Moody's Diner, a Maine institution, near the top of the more northerly hill.

Waldoboro's two historic claims to fame are that the first five-masted schooner, the *Governor Ames,* was built here in the 1850s, and that the town was founded by German immigrants who were hoodwinked by an inflated description of New World real estate. The old **German Cemetery** next to the German Church on Route 32 on the south side of Waldoboro village contains a grave marker with this illuminating inscription: "This town was settled in 1742 by Germans who immigrated to this place with the promise and expectation of finding a prosperous city, instead of which they found nothing but wilderness."

Watch for the right turn onto Route 220, which takes you down the east coast of Muscongus Bay toward the village of **Friendship,** one of the most famous of Maine's boatbuilding communities. To see exhibits on the history of the Friendship sloop, stop at the **Friendship Museum** in the old brick schoolhouse on Route 220. Staffed by volunteers, it's open more or less from July through Labor Day from 1:00 to 4:00 P.M. No telephone. Admission is by donation.

The Friendship sloop, a modern cruising adaptation of the inshore fishing sloop, was developed specifically for the ragged coastline of Maine's peninsula country. The combination of hull and sail design give the Friendship sloop extraordinary maneuverability to work slowly along the ledges of the region's thousands of little coves, avoiding the shoals and threading the narrows.

Friendship has the advantage of an extremely sheltered harbor with quick access to deep water—the land snaps off and plunges to great depths just offshore. Historically, some of Maine's best mackerel runs are found here in July and August, along with bluefish and even, a little farther out to sea, tuna and swordfish. Fishing close to shore yields pollock and hake.

Thomaston and Monhegan Island, Maine

From Friendship, follow Route 97 northeast to the junction with Route 1, which leads into **Thomaston,** our nomination as the most handsome Federal-era town on the North Coast. Most travelers in a hurry to get Downeast on Route 1 bypass Thomaston and Rockland by driving Route 90 through Warren to reconnect with Route 1 in Rockport. But if you want to see a town where the seafaring heritage is writ large, don't sacrifice Thomaston, which calls itself "the town that went to sea."

A fortuitous combination of geology and geography determined Thomaston's early fortunes. Although most of the North Coast is composed of igneous rocks, Thomaston sits atop a vast limestone shelf—a piece of uplifted ocean floor. The town is sited at the head of a long, narrow inlet into which the St. George River drains, providing a safe harbor sheltered from all kinds of weather. During its 1790–1840 heyday, Thomaston concentrated on quarrying limestone and building ships to carry construction stone and slaked lime (lime that has been reduced in charcoal-burning kilns) around the world.

Much of the wealth generated by this activity found expression in splendid domiciles. Indeed most of the central town along Route 1 and side streets has been designated a National Historic District—mostly for the concentration of Greek Revival and Federal-era homes. In surprising contrast to these luxurious abodes is the Maine State Prison, built here many years ago because Thomaston was easily reached by water in an era when roads were poor.

The **Maine Watercraft Museum** occupies two acres that used to be home to many of the legendary shipyards on Thomaston's working waterfront. This museum has restored and now displays more than 100 antique and classic small craft built in Maine prior to 1960 in what the museum calls a "hands-on and in-the-water environment." Included are Kennebecs, Old Towns, Skowhegans, and such saltwater working boats as the peapod and the dory. The museum offers cruises on a 22-foot classic runabout or a 30-foot Friendship sloop, from $12 to $25. Open late May through September, Wednesday through Sunday 10:00

A.M. to 5:00 P.M. Adults $4.00. 4 Knox Street Landing. Telephone: (207) 354–0444.

Unfortunately, not a single example of the five-masted schooners that made Thomaston famous remains afloat. These were big, heavy working boats designed to haul limestone from Thomaston and granite from the Penobscot Bay islands down the eastern seaboard to build some of the grandest buildings of New York and Philadelphia. They usually ended their lives cut down to barges or beached to rot on a harbor island.

The St. George Peninsula extends south by southwest from Thomaston with a rugged and unpopulated coast on the west side along the St. George River, and a series of tiny but very productive fishing villages along the east side, which faces the Penobscot Bay. Follow Route 131 south to explore the peninsula. At the tip, where the road ends, is **Port Clyde,** which has a sheltered deepwater harbor between the mainland and Hooper Island.

Nowadays Port Clyde is a busy fishing harbor, an overnight anchorage favored by yachtsmen, and site of the main ferry to **Monhegan Island.** Monhegan Boat Lines operates both the venerable *Laura B.* and the more modern *Elizabeth Ann.* Sailings vary from three per week November through April to three per day in July and August. Adults roundtrip $25, plus $4.00 per day parking at Port Clyde. (Visitors aren't allowed to bring vehicles.) Advance reservations required. Telephone: (207) 372–8848.

Perhaps because it's 12 miles out to sea near the main shipping lanes, the spruce-tufted 700-acre Monhegan Island was "discovered" a number of times. It appears to have been a popular cod-fishing base for Basque, Portuguese, Spanish, and Breton fishermen for several decades before Columbus bumped into North America. John and Sebastian Cabot charted it in 1498; George Waymouth claimed it for England in May 1605; Samuel de Champlain claimed it for France two months later; and John Smith planted the English flag in 1614. The first permanent English settlement in 1654 was destroyed in 1689 by the French. The pirate Paulsgrave built shore dwellings and a prison here in 1717, using Monhegan as a base for capturing several vessels. Every so often someone starts digging on Monhegan for pirates' gold, though it's more likely that Paulsgrave took his booty with him instead of burying it. Fishermen moved onto Monhegan in 1720, and the modern community is descended from those hardy souls.

Monhegan has attracted artists ever since Robert Henri and his New York School of Art students—among them George Bellows, Edward Hopper, and Rockwell Kent—first came here around the turn of the century. Kent built a home in 1905 and offered art classes, but had to leave in disgrace in 1909 (something about another man's wife), not to return until the 1950s when everyone who cared was dead. Throughout the twentieth century, Monhegan has been a favorite retreat of many artists, including Marsden Hartley and many lesser lights. Nowadays you might spot Jamie Wyeth (son of Andrew, grandson of N.C.) perched on a headland with an easel propped in front of him. Wyeth owns the cottage that Kent built for his mother in 1908. As often as it's been painted, Monhegan's subject matter seems inexhaustible. As George Bellows aptly observed, "The island is only a mile wide and two miles long, but it looks as large as the Rocky Mountains."

There is truly something magical about the light that appeals to painters, and something about the pace as well. Monhegan barely belongs to the twentieth century. It's a place where you use cash instead of plastic, where the lodgings usually have shared baths, and where you walk everywhere because no place is that far and you're not in a hurry anyway. If you visit Monhegan, plan to stay overnight, as the ride each way is seventy minutes and the boat doesn't linger long before returning. You can spend your day walking the trails, especially those along the ocean, where you're likely to spot whales.

Monhegan is also an excellent place to watch birds, especially in May and again from late August into October. As the largest spot of land offshore, it attracts many migrating birds that have become tired or disoriented as they cross the Gulf of Maine. The huge ground-feeding woodpecker, the flicker, is common here, along with a flood of migrating vireos, warblers, sparrows, thrushes, and flycatchers. The smaller birds attract migrating raptors, especially peregrine falcons, sharp-shinned hawks, and merlins.

Don't plan on a lobster dinner unless you're visiting during the Monhegan lobstering season, which begins January 1 and ends at sunset on June 25. This self-governed season avoids taking lobsters during their molting season. Like other exoskeletal creatures, lobsters grow by shedding their shells each year and growing new ones. The molt usually takes place in July and August, and lobster aficionados avoid eating them until September or later because the flesh of a new molt cooks up watery and bland. By avoiding this season, Monhegan fishermen dominate the lobster trade in the brutal winter months, when prices become astronomical.

When you return to the mainland, head north on Route 131 for about seven miles to the village of St. George, where you should turn right onto Route 73 north toward Rockland, passing through the scenic villages of Spruce Head, South Thomaston, and **Owls Head.**

The summer village of Owls Head is home to an interesting transportation museum (see "Staying There") and **Lighthouse Park.** The park includes a small beach and walking trails, but exists mostly to offer unobscured access to Owls Head Light, which was built in 1825. The 20-foot-tall, white-brick conical tower stands 87 feet above the sea on the peak of the headland. From Route 73, take North Shore Drive to Owls Head and follow the signs to Lighthouse Park.

On a clear day—and there are many of them between July and mid-October—the view from the lighthouse penetrates some 16 miles to the far side of Penobscot Bay. Look carefully, and you'll see Monhegan to the southeast and the large islands of Penobscot Bay—Vinalhaven due northeast, Islesboro due north. Owls Head is the last of the major peninsulas you'll encounter until you head Downeast, for it sits at the mouth of Penobscot Bay, an ocean trench that penetrates into the center of Maine's coast and was believed by early explorers to be the fabled Northwest Passage to Asia. As you travel north up the western shore of the bay, the land will rise quickly on the inland side, dropping precipitously into the ocean. Less heralded than the fabled Downeast landscape near Acadia National Park, Penobscot Bay is a region of rare beauty and deep historical roots.

Rockland, Maine

Route 73 north becomes Main Street in Rockland, the southernmost of four important communities on Penobscot Bay's western shore. (The others are Camden, Belfast, and Searsport.) Rockland got its name from the limestone quarried here and shipped out on Thomaston's schooners. Until it separated from Thomaston, it was known as Shore Village. Travelers often give Rockland short shrift in favor of the picture-postcard village of Camden just a few miles up the coast.

But if Camden has a pretty face, Rockland has the more engaging personality. It is a working town, where the chief occupation has always been some form of fishing. For many years, cod fishermen landed their catch here and the entire town was covered with drying racks, leading to the old ditty, "Camden by the sea, Rockland by the smell. If you want to go to hell fast, go to Belfast." Rockland, to be blunt, smelled like fish.

Not any more. The cod industry is gone, and so too are the fishmeal plant and the sardine-packing industry. But Rockland continues to land more lobsters than any other port in the world, celebrating this distinction each August with the Rockland Lobster Festival. (See "Staying There.")

Maine offers both prime habitat for lobsters and the sheltered anchorages small lobster boats need. Lobstering was already profitable in these parts by the 1840s, but the "bugs," as lobstermen call them, were held in low regard by many locals. Until the middle of the twentieth century, lobster was considered fit food only for the poor or for the prisoners incarcerated in Thomaston. There are even stories of servants of the summer folk who demanded that they be fed lobster less often.

Times have changed. Biologists warn that current harvest levels are not sustainable because fishermen are catching females before they can breed. (Lobsters begin breeding at five to seven years and can live more than a century.) The National Marine Fisheries Service has advised a trap limit of 480, as opposed to the current Maine limit of 1,200 traps per license, and an increase in the minimum size of lobsters to avoid a crash in the lobster population akin to the population crash that destroyed the cod fishing industry in 1994.

Despite the dire predictions, Rockland's harbor is still a busy place. You can walk along the Breakwater to historic **Rockland Breakwater Lighthouse** (1888–1902), an 18-foot-square tower atop a fog signal house that offers a panoramic view of mountains, islands, Penobscot Bay, and the inner harbor. The harbor view is a remarkable sight: fishing boats of that peculiar Maine style with the small pilot house and large open decks for stacking lobster traps or nets, Coast Guard vessels, pleasure craft of every configuration, windjammer schooners, and bulky island ferries. While maintaining its crown as queen of the lobstering industry, Rockland has also become the windjammer capital of New England in recent years as boats have relocated to its ample wharves from Camden and other more crowded harbors.

While most windjammers tour Maine waters for a week at a time (see "Staying There"), one-night cruises are offered aboard the 67-foot schooner *Wendameen*. It sails daily at 2:00 P.M. and anchors in a quiet cove for the night, returning to port by 10:00 A.M. the next morning. $155 includes dinner and breakfast. Telephone: (207) 594–1751.

Or you can get out on the water via the ferry to Vinalhaven/North Haven or to Matinicus Island operated by the **Maine State Ferry** service. Sailings vary with season. Telephone: (207) 624–7777 or (207) 596–2202. Vinalhaven and North Haven are luxurious summer communities with very little for the casual visitor except some nice roads for bicycle touring, while tiny Matinicus has two populations: well-off summer folk and a few very hardy fishermen. The ferry route, however, is very scenic.

It's also worth strolling the streets of Rockland. Main Street is an historic district lined with commercial buildings in a handsome variety of Italianate, Mansard, Greek Revival, and Colonial Revival styles. Rockland also has two museums that justify spending a day or more in this unlikely destination. The **Shore Village Museum** is both Maine's lighthouse museum and a repository for memorabilia ranging from uniforms of local Civil War regiments to a giant lobster shell. It's one of those rare museums that *encourages* photographs. The museum aggressively pursued every scrap of glass, shard of wood or piece of equipment available when all the light-

houses along the Maine coast were automated between the 1950s and 1970s and now claims to have the largest collection of lighthouse and Coast Guard artifacts on display in the country. We'd be hard pressed to dispute it. Those items that can be displayed in active form are groaning foghorns, clanging bells, flashing lights. We're just glad not to face the glare from some of lenses that are six or more feet in diameter. Coast Guard exhibit rooms contain machinery from lighthouses, buoys, life-saving gear, and even search-and-rescue boats. And if you're a postcard collector, get out your checkbook. The museum shop has somewhere around 400 lighthouse postcards for sale. Open June through mid-October daily from 10:00 A.M. to 4:00 P.M. Donation. 104 Limerock Street. Telephone: (207) 594–0311.

It's not surprising to find this lighthouse collection on Penobscot Bay. On the other hand, you might not expect a top-flight art museum with works by some of the best-known artists of this century. But here it is: the **Farnsworth Art Museum and Wyeth Center,** which traces Maine's role in American art with a collection that spans three centuries in five downtown buildings, one of them an historic church. The museum owns works by Fitz Hugh Lane, Winslow Homer, George Bellows, Edward Hopper, Milton Avery, Fairfield Porter, Charles and Maurice Prendergast, John Marin, Childe Hassam, Rockwell Kent, and sculptor Louise Nevelson and continues to collect works by Maine's leading contemporary artists.

The two largest collections are the Wyeth family (N.C., Andrew, and Jamie) and the works of Louise Nevelson. The Nevelson collection, second only to the Whitney Museum of American Art, includes many of her early paintings.

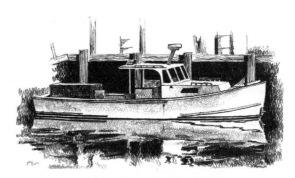

Lobster boat, Rockland, Maine

(Nevelson painted for nearly two decades before taking up sculpture.) Russian-born Nevelson actually grew up in Rockland, leaving as soon as she could and perhaps illustrating the point that the coast has more of a hold on figurative than abstract artists. Certainly the area has long had a strong attraction for the Wyeth artistic dynasty, and in 1998 the museum opened the Center for the Wyeth Family to house Andrew and Betsy Wyeth's personal collection of family art and archival materials.

And why not? In 1991 the Farnsworth was given the **Olson House,** a farmhouse in nearby Cushing where Andrew Wyeth studied and painted for more than three decades. Wyeth executed a series of drawings, watercolors, and temperas of the house and its residents, Christina Olson and her brother Alvaro. One of those paintings remains perhaps his most famous work, *Christina's World.* Wyeth once remarked, "I just couldn't stay away from there . . . . I'd always gravitate back to the house . . . . It was Maine." The house is open Memorial Day to Columbus Day daily from 11:00 A.M. to 4:00 P.M.

Admission to the museum also includes the Farnsworth Homestead, a circa 1850 Greek Revival home with original furnishings from the well-to-do merchant, William Farnsworth, for whom the museum is named. It is preserved—not restored, but preserved—as if the Farnsworth family had just stepped out circa 1870. The homestead is adjacent to the museum on Elm Street.

The Farnsworth Museum and the Wyeth Center are open from Memorial Day to Columbus Day daily from 9:00 A.M. to 5:00 P.M. During the rest of the year, they are open Tuesday through Saturday from 10:00 A.M. to 5:00 P.M., Sunday from 1:00 to 5:00 P.M. Adults $9.00. 352 Main Street. Telephone: (207) 596–6457.

Rockport and Camden, Maine

Route 73 rejoins Route 1 in the center of Rockland. If you follow Route 1 north for six miles, you'll see the turnoff on the right for the village center of **Rockport,** a harbor with all the picturesque scenery that Rockland's lacks. Framed on two sides by high rocks, it's really a narrow cove with an exposed beach at low tide that makes

boat launching a cinch. Because it's favored by many recreational sailors as a safe anchor, it also appeals to photographers in search of that quintessential harbor shot. Indeed, the Maine Photographic Workshop is located right next to the town landing. The harbor faces east, making for some beautiful sunrise shots through the forest of sailboat masts. Marine Park has a bronze statue of Andre the Seal, a celebrity of sorts in the 1980s when he made an annual swim here from his winter home at Boston's New England Aquarium. (In the movie version of his biography, Andre is played by a sea lion, not a harbor seal!) If you happen to get to Rockport harbor at low tide, some of the last of the old lime kilns are visible at the water's edge.

Route 1 continues north two miles into **Camden,** Wiscasset's rival for Route 1's most scenic bottleneck. The first tourist who came here, Captain John Smith in 1614, described the setting as "under the high mountains of the Penobscot, against whose feet the sea doth beat." He had a point: The Camden Hills come so close to the water that they look far taller than their mere 800 or so feet. Camden's harbor lies at the base of a natural amphitheater, used at various times since the nineteenth century as an outdoor stage. The harbor is virtually circled by land, offering complete shelter from the weather; as a result, it is a very popular anchorage for expensive cruising vessels.

Moreover, the town is simply downright pretty, with many sprawling Victorian houses on the hills above the harbor. All this scenic beauty has its price: All throughout the summer months Camden is mobbed with visitors trying to get past each other on the narrow sidewalks lined with shops and restaurants. It is possible to escape the crush by either getting out on the water or up into the hills.

While Camden remains the home port for a substantial windjammer fleet whose ships offer sails of three to six days, there are some shorter jaunts available as well. For example, to simply try sailing aboard a schooner, two-hour trips are available from late May through mid-October aboard the 75-foot *Olad* and the 55-foot *North Wind.* Adults $15–$20. Both berth in Camden Harbor. Telephone: (207) 236–2323.

A more intimate way to see Penobscot Bay

from a boat deck is to sign up for a cruise aboard the *Lively Lady Too*. The captain, a former biology teacher and lobsterman, offers fishing and sea life nature cruises, and he keeps a touch-tank on board so customers can handle various forms of undersea life. The *Lively Lady Too* also does a six-hour cruise on Penobscot Bay, with lunch on board. Several routes are offered, but you'll pass by seven or eight lighthouses on each of them. There's also a three-hour late afternoon and early evening cruise to an uninhabited island for a lobster and clam bake, with a grand view of sunset over Camden Hills on the return trip. Prices begin at $20. Bayview Landing. Telephone: (207) 236–6672.

You can drive or hike to the summit of Mount Battie in **Camden Hills State Park** on Route 1 north of the village center. The summit offers a poet's view and then some—Camden Harbor, Penobscot Bay, inland lakes, and mountains. On a clear day, Cadillac Mountain on Mount Desert Island looms in the distance. The park has 30 miles of hiking trails, several of which are maintained for snowmobiles in the winter. The Mount Battie Auto Road is open May through October. Telephone: (207) 236–3109. Automobiles $3.00, plus $2.00 per person.

Lincolnville and Islesboro, Maine

The views just keep coming as you drive north from Camden along Route 1, with broad vistas opening on Penobscot Bay over long hilly meadows. Suddenly, in six short miles, you will descend Ducktrap Hill (which locals justifiably call Speedtrap Hill) into the genial wide spot in the road known as **Lincolnville Beach.** One of the rare sandy beaches this far north, it draws hordes of local residents during July and August. The beach is so gradual that the water is very warm at high tide as it flows over long sand flats that have been heated by the sun. That warmth and the fact that the water is rarely more than three feet deep makes the beach a popular swim-and-splash spot for families with small children.

The beach exists largely because sand has accumulated at the mouth of the Ducktrap River in the lee of the large island of **Islesboro,** 1.5 miles offshore. The Islesboro Ferry runs all year from Lincolnville Beach, with frequent crossings in the summer and twice-daily service in the winter. Telephone: (207) 789–5611. The scene shown on the cover of this book is just north of the ferry landing.

The village of Islesboro, at the midpoint of the east side of the long skinny island, is one of the few Penobscot Bay island communities closely linked to the mainland, making it possible for islanders to commute to work and school. It's a quiet little place with a decent general store and a small harbor full of lobster boats.

The other village, Dark Harbor, lies on the south half of the island and is one of the least ostentatious of Maine retreats for persons of great wealth. Their homes tend to be modest by mansion standards and so secluded that you might not see them except from a boat. Some Dark Harbor residents do not bother with automobiles, preferring to come and go by yacht to their private moorings.

Islesboro does not advertise for summer visitors, so if you decide to tour the island, be respectful of people's privacy. A bicycle is one of the best ways to tour the 10 miles of roads. The town beach on the south end of the island has stunning scenery, sea birds, and a rather large colony of gray seals. If you bark at them, they'll likely bark back.

To see some of Islesboro from the water, **Ducktrap Sea Kayak Tours & Rentals** offers guided tours along the coast and islands where you're likely to encounter seals, loons, and (sometimes) dolphins. The seals and loons will keep their distance from your kayak. The dolphins are more curious and more playful and have been known to swim up next to small boats. Reservations required. Lincolnville Beach. Telephone: (207) 236–8608.

Belfast, Maine

Route 1 continues another 10 miles north along an inland route toward Belfast, which is swiftly becoming one of the more desirable summer retreats along Penobscot Bay, thanks to a huge boost to the economy a few years ago when the credit card company MBNA moved into town. (Now you know why those credit card solicitors have such thick accents.)

Incorporated in 1773 and burned twice—by the British in 1775 and in a massive town-wide fire in the 1880s—Belfast became the shire town of Waldo County in 1853. The name was determined by a flip of a coin between John Mitchell of Londonderry, New Hampshire, who discovered the area, and Jim Miller of Belfast, Ireland. The winner is pretty obvious.

During the nineteenth century, Belfast's eleven boatyards built some 360 ships, and many of the town's finest homes were constructed for sea captains. Because the city perches high on a hill, these grand homes had a clear view of the harbor and most sea captains' homes were crowned with a widow's walk—a railed observation platform on the roof where the lady of the house could watch for her husband's return. While many of these buildings burned in the Great Fire, which razed the town from the waterfront to High Street, several elegant Federal and Greek Revival houses remain.

When David was growing up here in the 1950s and 1960s, the last spinster daughters of the old sea captains were passing on, leaving these homes and their contents to distant relatives. At least once a summer one of the large international auction houses would dispose of the contents of a captain's home, usually to distant bidders registering their offers by telephone for the exquisite Oriental porcelain, rugs, paintings, and furniture.

Belfast underwent bleak times after World War II, when the chicken processing industry dominated the town and the byproducts were unceremoniously dumped in the bay at the mouth of the Passagassawakeag River. (Hence Belfast's ranking below Rockland in the regional ditty.) The advent of the Environmental Protection Agency spelled the end of that practice and with it, the end of profitability for the poultry industry. After decades of severe recession, the city has returned to relative prosperity, cleaning up the waterfront (now filled with pleasure craft) and converting the old houses into B&Bs. For the moment, Belfast is the scenic bargain on Penobscot Bay—a secret that David's parents swore him not to divulge until they moved out of town. But now you're in on the secret.

Searsport, Maine

Searsport, just seven miles north on Route 1, was the great *international* seafaring town of the entire Maine coast. (Belfast built more ships, but they were mostly coasting schooners.) Incorporated in 1845, Searsport was the home port of a full ten percent of the U.S. Merchant Marine captains in the 1870s and 1880s. Eleven boatyards here built more than 200 deepwater ships of various rigs between 1810 and 1890, Searsport's shipping heyday.

It is one of the mysteries of human history why a small community should come out of nowhere to make its name known across the world. Searsport was—and still is—a modest community of about 2,000 souls. While it does have the advantage of an astonishingly deep harbor (at one point rivaling New York and Boston for shipping tonnage), there's little explanation why it should have captured such a disproportionate segment of American trade.

But Searsport had a system—several able shipwrights, cheap timber floated down the Penobscot River, and enough capital and daring to risk everything. Typically a captain and his father-in-law and one or two other investors would put themselves in hock to build a ship, which the Searsport master would sail around Cape Horn, trading the whole way, and across the southern seas to India and China. They were engaged in the same Far Eastern trade as the sailors of Salem and Boston, but remained more successful at it for longer.

One reason was that deep Searsport harbor. Searsport shipwrights pioneered the Downeaster—a vessel built along the lines of the extreme clippers of the 1850s but larger. In fact, they were among some of the largest sailing ships ever constructed, and they could haul large cargoes swiftly for great distances, even competing with steamships in the late nineteenth century.

Searsport's brief era as master of the seven seas is captured in the town's superb **Penobscot Marine Museum,** where you'll find a wall with portraits of nearly 300 Searsport deepwater captains. Mostly formal renderings of solemn men with beards or outrageous sideburns, to a man they look uneasy at having to sit still on the orders of the painter or photographer. After all, those who lived long enough (many died young and tragically) were grizzled veterans of the Cape Horn passage.

The museum offers an all-encompassing view of life on the Penobscot Bay, but no matter how good the exhibits on lobster fishing or brick-carrying schooners might be, the more fascinating story lies in those faces and the exploits of their owners—their amazing transects from Liverpool dead on to the Falkland Islands, their truck in spices and rugs and silks. More than any place we've ever visited, this museum captures the audacity and adventure of the last great Age of Sail.

The curly-headed, blue-eyed boys on the wall brought their immense square-riggers through the tempests and 30-foot swells around Cape Horn. They commanded ships of wood and cloth, where 100-mile-per-hour winds—said to be "cold enough to freeze the marrow in your bones"—whipped the canvas and roiled the sea and battered man and boat alike in a harrowing ordeal. It's little wonder that so many commanders left the sea to embrace the land by the age of 40, filling their grand houses with the booty of their sailing days.

A surprising number of these homes still stand, often as inns or B&Bs. If you visit one of them—the A.V. Nickels Inn is a good example—it's easy to walk into the parlor, sit down by the fireplace, and imagine the "old man" with his pipe and his brandy, surrounded by his Oriental furniture, his vases, and screens, holding forth on the adventures of his youth. The rewards of investment, he would tell potential partners, are all around you. Subscribe to the venture, and you can become a wealthy man as well. It's said that a ship could be financed in an evening.

In all, there are nine historic buildings in the museum complex on Church Street and Route 1 with twenty-five galleries of furnishings, ship models, paintings, photographs, China Trade art and artifacts, and small craft. Open from Memorial Day weekend through mid-October, Monday through Saturday from 10:00 A.M. to 5:00 P.M., Sunday from noon to 5:00 P.M. The library is open to researchers throughout the year; call for hours. Adults $6.00. Church Street.

Telephone: (207) 548–2529.

As you continue north on Route 1 for another 11 miles, you are approaching the mouth of the Penobscot River, a mighty waterway that early explorers dearly hoped was the fabled Northwest Passage. Just before you reach the high bridge over the Penobscot, there is a "scenic" pullout that hasn't had much scenery for the last generation, at least not since the trees here grew so high that they block all views of the river. But you can park here and walk toward the bridge for a breathtaking, if dizzying view down into the gorge where Verona Island sits at the mouth of the Penobscot. Eagles and ospreys often fish these waters, riding the thermal currents at about the height of the road, then plunging several hundred feet in spectacular dives to seize fish from the tidal river below the dam. A fish ladder here, combined with the end of log drives and cleanup of industrial waste on the Penobscot, has meant the return of the Atlantic salmon migration. It's hard to tell who benefits more—the fishermen or the eagles.

The Penobscot River is a border of sorts. For nearly a century it divided the coast between English and French spheres of influence, and while its once mighty flow has been tamed by dams, it's still an impressive divide between the peninsula country you are leaving behind and the land Downeast to which you are headed.

Downeast Maine

The "rocky coast of Maine" that begins in peninsula country assumes grander and more heroic proportions as you move Downeast from Penobscot Bay. The term "Downeast" is often applied haphazardly to the entire state of Maine, but most Mainers reserve it for the section of the Maine coast from the east end of Penobscot Bay to the Canadian border. Prevailing winds sailing out of Penobscot Bay come from the west-northwest off the mainland, enabling a competent sailor to skirt the rocks between Deer Isle and Isle au Haut. When the ship finally threads its way through this archipelago, prevailing winds shift to come out of the west-southwest, allowing a coasting vessel to simply sail down the wind northeastward. Hence, despite the number of small (and at one time uncharted) islands off this stretch of coast, a sailor could travel "down the wind," even without a chart, and keep within a mile of the shore.

The peninsulas, bays, and islands of Downeast Maine make photographers' shutter fingers itchy. It's hard to resist trying to capture a massive swell rolling in from the ocean to crash on boulder-strewn beaches and high slate ledges. One branch of the Appalachian Mountain chain spills into the sea here, creating Mount Desert Island and its justly famed vistas within Acadia National Park. Farther east, the land levels off to the grassy headlands known aptly as blueberry barrens until, at Passamaquoddy Bay, Maine ends and New Brunswick begins.

The Penobscot River marks the beginning of Downeast Maine. Most summer vacationers going to and from Bar Harbor skip over the peninsulas between Penobscot Bay and Mount Desert Island by continuing on Routes 1 and 3 to Ellsworth. In the process, they miss some of the prettiest scenery and most bountiful inshore fisheries in New England. The area's laconic style tends to attract more summer residents than short-term visitors, which translates into fewer frills at the inns and restaurants but also smaller crowds.

Castine, Maine

After crossing the bridge over the Penobscot, you'll go about two miles to the junction with Route 175, where you should turn right to drive toward Castine. The roads on the peninsulas on the east side of Penobscot Bay are very confusing. In some places two or more roads carry the same

route number and in other places "north" on a road is actually bearing south by the compass. To help you thread your way through this maze (maybe another reason tourists bypass the area), we're giving fairly detailed driving directions here. If you're planning to spend a lot of time exploring the back roads, we suggest purchasing *The Maine Atlas and Gazetteer,* an invaluable resource that's rescued us more than once from the classic Maine situation of "you can't get there from here."

Route 175 veers to the left at a fork in about eight miles, but continue straight on Route 166. In about two miles, the road divides again between 166 and 166A. Both lead to Castine, but 166A passes saltwater farms and a rocky coast punctuated by long tidal flats. Along this frost-heaved blacktop road you'll also see many abandoned apple orchards and tiny, overgrown cemeteries. If you stop to read the stones, their stories could make you weep. This part of Maine suffered heavy losses in the Civil War, and you'll see many markers for the Union dead and their widows, who survived another fifty years.

Route 166A emerges on Castine's Battle Avenue, where British troops soundly drubbed the upstart Americans in 1779, holding the town until 1783. When the Americans won their independence, many of Castine's Loyalists relocated to New Brunswick, putting their dwellings on barges and setting them on new foundations at St. Andrews by the Sea. From Battle Avenue, turn left to descend Main Street.

Main Street is a gallery of domestic architecture circa 1800. Midway up the hill, Court Street leads to the Wayside Pulpit church on the old town square with its historic schools and monument to the sailors and soldiers killed in the "The Great War, 1861–1865."

The town sponsors a summer festival and Art Walk on the last Saturday in June, but artists abound in Castine at all seasons, and the galleries along Main Street represent many of them. Many pleasure boats anchor in Castine's harbor, though the big attraction (if it happens to be in port) is the **T.V. *State of Maine,*** the 500-plus-foot training vessel of the Maine Maritime Academy. The vessel spends most of the year at sea, but when she's in port, a schedule of public tours is posted. Telephone: (207) 326-4311. The academy, which trains officers for the United States Merchant

Lobster dinner

Marine fleet, dominates much of the village, but there's really nothing open for public viewing.

Just up from the dock, you can walk (or drive) Perkins Street to the Dyce Head Foot Path beside the decommissioned lighthouse. This short trail leads down a bluff and wooden steps to a spectacular rocky crag overlooking treacherous waters.

Penobscot Peninsula and Deer Isle, Maine

Leave town by Route 166 north, turning right in 4.1 miles onto Route 199 to the town of Penobscot. Three main buildings here offer everything a small town needs: the post office, the church, and a seafood shack that specializes in crab rolls—a treat that most Mainers prefer to lobster. If you sit at the single picnic table in back you will discover a million-dollar view over a long pasture to the northern bay of the Bagaduce River, which is really just an arm of Penobscot Bay that penetrates far inland.

Continue straight on 199N and 175S, staying on 175 when they split. Route 175 is joined by Route 15 south at Caterpillar Mountain. Pull over at the road's high point for an extraordinary view of Downeast Maine in microcosm: a foreground of blueberry barrens, a middle ground of ocean dotted with spruce-covered islands, the peaks of the Camden Hills in the distance.

At the stop sign in Sargentville, turn right onto Route 15 toward Deer Isle, crossing a narrow little suspension bridge to Little Deer Isle, then a causeway to Deer Isle proper. The island has two villages on it—Deer Isle, which is next to the famous Haystack Mountain School of Crafts, and Stonington. Deer Isle has some nifty shops selling crafts and photography (see "Staying There"), but **Stonington,** a fishing and stone quarrying village, is probably the more interesting of the two.

Walking the village of Stonington will give you a hint of the unromantic life of an inshore fisherman, though the gallery scene is creeping in too. Locals treat tourists as a passing amusement, and may pull your leg by acting "quaint" and talking with the "Maine" accent affected more by bad television actors than the real residents. In another touch of local humor, some shops sell

"tourist traps"—wooden lobster traps too worn for fishing but fit for souvenirs. In truth, most lobstermen now fish with wire traps, so wooden traps are getting hard to find. Don't even think about touching one you see washed up on a beach. It's a crime called "molesting a trap" and carries a $50 fine. A lobsterman suggested to us once that if you really want a trap, stop at a house where you see lots of them piled up in the yard. Then, "ring the bell and talk to the wife. She'll be glad to unload one for a buck and pocket the cash."

You'll note that the Stonington harbor contains very few pleasure boats, as this is truly a working port of lobstermen and scallop dredgers. Not surprisingly, the Maine Lobsterman's Association is headquartered here in Stonington. As of 1998, Maine's 7,300 licensed lobster fishermen were fishing about two million traps, and in 1997 landed about half the nation's 84-million-pound catch.

Even the **ferry to Isle au Haut** is a work boat—it operates mostly to carry the mail to the several inhabited islands just offshore. A large part of Isle au Haut (pronounced *aisle-ah-HOE*) is preserved under the auspices of Acadia National Park. The boat makes four trips a day in the summer, three a day in spring and early fall, and two trips a day Monday through Saturday in the winter. Adults $24 roundtrip. The Isle-au-Haut Boat Company dock is at the end of Seabreeze Avenue. Telephone: (207) 367–5193.

Blue Hill, Maine

To see some stunning ocean scenery along the edge of Blue Hill Bay, retrace your steps to the suspension bridge over Eggemoggin Reach and turn right onto Route 175 (Reach Road). Follow it around as its hews close to the coast, passing through the villages of Sedgwick, Haven, Brooklin, and North Brooklin. This last—which doesn't show up on most maps—is where E.B. and Katherine White retired in 1957 after her days as fiction editor of the *New Yorker*. E.B. had bought a farm in 1933 and lived there from 1938 to 1943, gathering inspiration for his children's classic, *Charlotte's Web*. This is the hard and scrubby soil that Katherine described gardening in her own classic, *Onward and Upward in the Garden.*

Continue north (just keep the ocean on your right) and Route 175 will rejoin Route 15 in the town of Blue Hill, founded in 1762. Blue Hill prospered in the early nineteenth century with shipbuilding, sea trading, and mining for copper and granite, but like so much of this part of Maine, lost many of its menfolk to the Civil War. With seventy houses on the National Historic Register, Blue Hill has become a summer retreat and a year-round cultural center for Downeast Maine. In fact, one of the first Maine landscape paintings was a panorama of the village by parson Jonathan Fisher in 1824. Today, Blue Hill is known for the pottery made from local clay (see "Staying There").

At the little rotary that passes as the center of Blue Hill, look for Route 172 north toward Surry and Ellsworth. We've been telling you to slow down and take it easy rather than rushing toward Mount Desert Island and Acadia National Park. But now is the time to drive straight through Surry and Ellsworth, following Route 3 as it splits from Route 1 and shoots south to Mount Desert Island.

Mount Desert Island, Maine

When Samuel de Champlain ran aground on the island in 1604, he called it *Ile des Monts Deserts* (island of bare mountains), making this one of the few natural features in Maine without an Algonquian name. Champlain's "bare mountains" (or rocky balds, as hikers call them) are technically monadnocks—non-volcanic swellings of magma from the Acadian orogeny that have been scraped clean of topsoil by glaciers. The cragged cliffs and stony coves of the island give fresh meaning to the hoary tourism cliché, "rocky coast of Maine." At 108 square miles, Mount Desert Island is Maine's largest island and its chief destination for summer tourism.

Not surprisingly, Mount Desert's operatic landscape attracted American painters almost as soon as they learned of it. Among the first artists to visit the region were several Hudson River school painters who arrived in the middle of the nineteenth century to try to capture the shattered

landscape of mountains that plummet into the sea, of walls of granite rising from the ocean that dwarf the tall masts of ships sailing next to them. By 1850, Mount Desert was established as an essential destination for any painter of heroic American landscape worth his salt. And, in a pattern familiar throughout New England, wealthy summer people followed on their heels.

By the 1880s, America's titans of industry and finance gathered each summer on Mount Desert Island in a roster that reads like an antitrust suit—Rockefeller, Carnegie, Vanderbilt, Pulitzer, Astor, Morgan, Ford. And, as they did in Newport and the Berkshires, this moneyed gentry built fabulous mansions that they called "cottages," where they partied and entertained lavishly. Little Mount Desert Island became a world-famous watering hole for the new class of Americans who were famous for being rich. The ocean frontage from the town of Bar Harbor to Salisbury Cove was known as "Millionaire's Row."

This era of lavish consumption lasted through World War I, with around 200 mansions being built before the advent of income tax and the stock market crash put a dent in new construction. Many of the estates perished in an apocalyptic fire in 1947 that was reported in news around the world. More than 10,000 acres of the island was consumed by flame, and many families of old wealth never returned to Mount Desert.

But the well-to-do rusticators left an enduring legacy in **Acadia National Park,** which accounts for about 35,000 acres on Mount Desert Island and another 5,000 acres on nearby islands and peninsulas. When it was established in 1919, Acadia became the first national park east of the Mississippi. Neither carved out of public lands nor purchased with public funds, the park was created from lands donated by individuals who recognized the unique beauty of the region and had the wherewithal to preserve it for the future. George Dorr, scion of a wealthy Boston family, led the effort. In 1901 he established a corporation "to preserve points of interest for the perpetual use of the public."

One of the park's most generous donors was John D. Rockefeller, Jr., who gave almost one-third of Acadia's acres, including the stretch from Sand Beach to Otter Point, along Ocean Drive, a road that he had rebuilt during the 1930s. This area, perhaps the most scenic part of Acadia, is the most heavily visited portion of the park today. Not content to donate land alone, Rockefeller also constructed more than 50 miles of beautiful carriage roads to enable visitors to fully enjoy the scenery.

Mount Desert Island is shaped like a lobster claw and is divided roughly in half by the only fjord on the east coast of the United States, Somes Sound, with Somesville at its head. The eastern lobe of the island contains the biggest and busiest town, Bar Harbor, with the bulk of the island's tourist accommodations, as well as the smaller community of Northeast Harbor, which chiefly serves a wealthy summer clientele. The western lobe (or "quiet side") contains Southwest Harbor, a string of tiny villages along the southwest coast, and several large and beautiful lakes. While the towns of the western lobe offer some tourist amenities, their principal livelihood comes from fishing.

You will have to make a quick decision. As you cross the bridge onto Mount Desert Island, you are immediately faced with a fork in the road. The left fork (Route 3) heads to Bar Harbor and the Hulls Cove Visitors Center of Acadia National Park. The right fork (Route 102) leads due south to the western lobe and Southwest Harbor, the island's second largest town.

Western Lobe of Mount Desert

Southwest Harbor continues to make its living through commercial fishing (the catch is the tenth largest in Maine) and boatbuilding. If you park in town and walk down to the harbor, you will see dozens of barnlike buildings that house boat-building operations. Some of the eastern seaboard's finest yachts are constructed here, along with power boats, fishing trawlers, and recreational sailboats. Its location on the southwest side of Somes Sound, protected at the mouth by Greening Island, makes Southwest Harbor a superb anchorage for small craft.

From the harbor, **Cranberry Cove Boating** operates ferries to three of the Cranberry Islands: Great Cranberry, Little Cranberry (Islesford), and Sutton Island. Telephone: (207) 244-5882. All three islands are fishing communities, but

Islesford also has a small historic museum run by the National Park Service. Truthfully, the main reason to visit them is to enjoy the boat ride.

Leaving the harbor, the road south (Route 102) is called Manset Road until it reaches **Seawall,** a major campground of Acadia, at which point it becomes Seawall Road into Bass Harbor, looping back to Southwest Harbor as Bass Harbor Road. This scenic loop road around the Bass Harbor peninsula is also marked (now and then) as Route 102A.

Bass Harbor is a favorite of photographers who try to capture the essence of this fishing village, but, to be honest, it is not particularly pretty, nor is it picturesque. It is too poor to be elegant and too well off to be quaint. Yet there is something of an enduring appeal in its very plainness. Probably the most photogenic scene near Bass Harbor is the **Bass Harbor Light,** off Route 102A. Built in 1858 and now privately owned, it remains a prominent landmark for local sailors.

Plenty of people live offshore from Mount Desert, and the **Maine State Ferry Service** operates regular boats from Bass Harbor to Swan's Island and to Frenchboro on Long Island. Telephone: (207) 244-3254. Like the Cranberry Isles, these are small fishing communities with few amenities for visitors. But the boat ride through this archipelago is stunning.

Eastern Lobe of Mount Desert

The eastern lobe of Mount Desert Island is far more extensively visited than the western lobe. It contains the communities of Northeast Harbor on the east side of Somes Sound, Bar Harbor on the east side of the island, and the most trafficked sections of Acadia National Park in between. As you come onto the island, Route 3 branches to the left, continuing down the east side of Mount Desert, then looping along the south coast until it joins Route 198 at Asticou, a village just north of Northeast Harbor. The loop swings north to the top of Somes Sound. Route 198 continues north back to the bridge you crossed to get onto Mount Desert in the first place. Route 233, a winding mountain road, crosses the eastern lobe between Somesville and Bar Harbor. We realize that these road directions sound confusing, but they are fairly clear on a map and you will need to use all the roads to get around the island.

Northeast Harbor was a simple fishing village until it was discovered by the first rusticators around 1870. It soon became (and remains) a summer place, principally for wealthy urbanites, and its harbor is famous as a yachting center. The 1947 fire did not reach Northeast Harbor, which helps explain why so many gracious nineteenth-century homes remain.

Route 3 loops around the island from Northeast Harbor to **Bar Harbor.** For the first 125 years of settlement, the town was called Eden, which tells you something about its location. Later it was renamed for the prominent sandbar that accumulated in the bay.

East of Eden lies Frenchman Bay, dotted with the Porcupine Islands. From an elevated view these rounded islands bristled with hemlock and spruce really do resemble a family of behemoth porcupines out for a swim, and they illustrate the type of spruce-fir-hemlock forest that covered the northeast side of Mount Desert Island before the fire of 1947. This same type of mature forest is found on the western lobe as well, but the seeds that sprang from the ashes of the fire were largely of deciduous trees. It took nearly two decades to cover the scars of the fire, but now the area around Bar Harbor in the adjacent portion of Acadia National Park is a lovely woodland dominated by birch, aspen, and pin cherry with an undergrowth of low-bush blueberries, firebush, and red sumac.

One effect of the fire was to clear much of the oceanfront outside of town near Bar Harbor (fire-fighters managed to save most of the downtown property), leaving open space where farsighted developers soon built motels. As a result, Bar Harbor is a compact community of late nineteenth- and early twentieth-century buildings surrounded by a brief strip of tourist services built in the early 1950s. It is de rigueur to decry the crowding on the streets and sidewalks in July and August, but it is an unfortunate fact that paradise doesn't have much elbow room in the height of the season.

The center of Bar Harbor consists of four chief streets. Main Street parallels the eastern shore from the town pier at the north end of town down to Cromwell Harbor. West Street parallels the north shore of town from Route 3 to the town pier. Cottage Street is the next parallel street south of West and home to many small restaurants. Broad Mount Desert Street (Routes 3 and 233) is the road most drivers use to enter town. Virtually all the restaurants, shops, and many of the lodgings in Bar Harbor are found on these four streets. (Some of those lodgings, by the way, are erstwhile summer mansions converted to B&Bs.) A number of boat excursions and sailing trips leave from the town pier, and, over the summer, several ocean cruise ships sit at anchor just offshore for a day and send their passengers into town on launches.

From our perspective, the best way to see Bar Harbor is to circumnavigate it by literally pacing the periphery. The **Shore Path** is a delightful walking route that runs along the cliffs at the water's edge from Agamont Park (adjacent to the town pier) southward to Wayman Lane. It's not a long path—less than a mile—but it has great views on both sides. Frenchman Bay is filled with small and large sail craft, and the oceanfront homes are a sight to behold in themselves. Another good walk is out Bridge Street at low tide to Bar Island, the sandbar that gave Bar Harbor its name.

ACADIA NATIONAL PARK, MAINE

Although there are dozens of roads into Acadia National Park, it's best to enter through the Hulls Cove Visitors Center so you can pick up a map and pay for your usage pass. Automobile passes are $5.00 per day, $10 for four days, or $20 for the year. Four-day passes for cyclists and pedestrians are $3.00.

This entrance leads directly to the **Park Loop Road,** a drive of 27 hilly miles that gives you a sample of the interior and many of the highlights of the park's coast. We like to think of the Loop Road as Acadia Light—an abridged version of the park that acquaints you with this unique landscape.

One of the first stops, **Sieur de Monts Spring,** has a nature center and specimen gardens that label about 300 plant species found throughout the park. Several walking trails provide good access to the woodlands for birders. Among the species nesting near the spring are black-billed cuckoos and rose-breasted grosbeaks. This stop is also the site of the **Abbe Museum,** which is devoted to chronicling 10,000 years of Native American culture and history in the immediate region. One exhibition, "Indians in Eden," explores the last 200 years of interaction between the Abenaki and the EuroAmericans on Mount Desert Island. There's special emphasis on the craft goods made for the tourist industry, especially baskets (of which the Abbe has a superb collection). Adults $2.00. Open mid-May, June, September, and October daily from 10:00 A.M. to 4:00 P.M., July and August daily from 9:00 A.M. to 5:00 P.M. Telephone: (207) 288–2179. The Abbe plans to open a branch in downtown Bar Harbor.

Probably the most popular part of Acadia is the southeast coast of the island, much of which was the gift of John D. Rockefeller. Park Loop Road takes you directly to **Sand Beach,** where the hearty can brave the cold ocean for swimming while everyone else simply enjoys the sun on the coarse sand. Nearby across some spectacular ledges is **Thunder Hole,** which gets its name from the occasional thunderclaps made by wave motion inside the hollow rocks. It only occurs at a three-quarter rising tide with rough seas, but that doesn't stop people from hoping. If you stop and the spot is quiet, walk on the ledges to take in the spectacular views. Keep in mind that the early landscape painters endured weeks of difficult travel to see this very sight.

The next stop on Park Loop Road, **Otter Cliff,** offers a vision of pounding surf and wonderful waves while nearby **Otter Point** is a great place for exploring the rich life of tidepools at low tide. The Loop Road turns inland and passes Jordan Pond, where the **Jordan Pond House,** a tea house on the site of a former farm, is surrounded by beautiful gardens. The civilized custom of afternoon tea is a holdover from the Gilded Age.

A separate parking lot gives access to Jordan Pond itself, which is circled by a very pleasant walking trail through the woods and along the shore. There's a dramatic view here of the **Bubble Erratics,** though the trail up to these geological anomalies is very steep from the pond. Use the Erratics parking lot instead for a much easier climb. As you round the Loop Road, a spur winds three and one-half miles up to the summit of **Cadillac Mountain.** At 1,530 feet, Cadillac is the

Otter Point, Acadia National Park, Maine

highest of Mount Desert's seventeen peaks and the highest mountain on the east coast of the Americas north of Brazil. The summit offers 360-degree views of interior mountains and of the bays and islands surrounding Mount Desert, but for the best sunsets, park at the Blue Hill parking lot, about three-quarters of the way to the top.

Park Loop Road won't satisfy you if you're after the experience of uncrowded wilderness, but Acadia is laced with more than 120 miles of hiking trails and 57 miles of car-free carriage roads, parts of which still remain in Rockefeller family hands. (Bicycles are banned on those stretches ever since noisy cyclists spooked one of Abby Rockefeller's carriage teams.) If you'd like a feel for the lifestyle of the folks who built these roads for their own pleasures, we strongly suggest a **horse-drawn carriage tour** of the park. It's a little pricey but many people find it one of their fondest memories of Acadia. Contact Wildwood Stable, one-half mile south of Jordan Pond House. Telephone: (207) 276–3622.

Another excellent way to explore the park is to

join the free guided hikes and walks offered by the National Park Service rangers. A schedule is listed in the *Beaver Log,* published by the National Park Service and available in the Visitors Center. These outings run the gamut from strolls along carriage roads and easy trails to strenuous hikes across headlands and up mountain peaks. The Park Service also offers several sea cruises and bus tours for which fees are charged.

Personal Narrative:
Learning to Look at Acadia National Park

Acadia National Park may be one of the smallest national parks, but there is still a lot to see in its 40,000 acres (35,000 of them on Mount Desert Island). With only a couple of days to spend, we often rush around trying to see and do too much.

On a recent visit, we decide to slow down and look at the park closely with the guidance of a professional photographer and naturalist. Paul Johnson is a representative of the Kodak Photographic Programs, which place photographers in four national parks (Acadia is the only one in the East) to give tips to amateur photographers and encourage them to shoot more film. It seems a fair exchange for a variety of free programs that are listed in the *Beaver Log.*

At 8:30 on a chilly August morning we join a group assembled in the parking lot above Jordan Pond, one of more than a dozen glacier-carved ponds and lakes in the park. Paul looks us over and sizes up the camera gear hanging around our necks—anything from the simplest point-and-shoots to $2,000 Leicas. "The compliment that a photographer least wants to hear is 'oh, isn't that pretty,'" he says. "I'm going to show you stuff you can do to make any picture better."

We walk beneath a bower and emerge at the bright shoreline of Jordan Pond. A pair of rounded mountains—North and South Bubble—rise steeply on the north shore of the lake. They are among the most photographed sites in Acadia and for our group they are the object of some of our most important lessons.

"I'm tempted to say that the only difference between professional and amateur photographers is branches," Paul jokes. "Pros always add branches to their photos for depth and dimension." He lifts his camera and composes an image of the Bubbles framed by tree branches. "Amateurs take them out." But not us: We aim and focus in exactly the same direction.

As we stroll along the pondside path, Paul stops and studies a jumble of rocks in the shallow water at the shoreline. "The foreground is the most neglected part of most people's pictures," he says, pointing out how the small rocks echo the shape of the Bubbles. Using a wide angle lens, he fills the foreground of his picture with the rocks, relegating the Bubbles to the horizon at the top of the frame. It's a much more dramatic view.

The same lessons apply on an afternoon walk across the sandbar that connects the town of Bar Harbor to the first of the Porcupine Islands in Frenchman Bay. The 8– to 12–foot tide means that the sandbar is fully revealed at low tide, allowing walkers to make their way across its rocky surface.

From this vantage point, the harbor seems like a mirage: Boats at anchor mark the line where the deep blue ocean ends and the deep blue sky begins. How could any photographer fail to capture a great image with such raw material? But Paul cautions us to avoid the picturesque harbor scene that we can buy on hundreds of postcards. For a different look he tells us to keep the sky either high or low—we shouldn't cut our image in half at the horizon.

Veterans of Paul's walks know about framing with the all-important tree limb. The closest thing available on this rocky shore is a gnarled piece of sun-bleached driftwood that has been polished by wind and water to a silvery sheen. Paul approves. The driftwood makes an unusual vertical frame for the harbor scene—and people in the foreground add even more interest.

Paul reminds us that it is easy to be overwhelmed by the big view and miss the telling details. He points at a rusting chain on a stone anchor to make his point. Later he takes out his tripod to focus closely on soft gray and black rocks punctuated with a line of barnacles. "Show a picture like this to your friends," he says, "and you'll get brain engagement."

One of the most dramatic walks is along the rocky cliffs at Otter Point, perhaps the quintessential rocky coast. Paul surprises our group by shooting vertical images while most of us shoot horizontals. Sure enough, he has isolated a more riveting slice of the overpowering view. "We're managing the foreground to give the picture more dimension," he says. To make sure that our entire image—both foreground and background—will be sharp, Paul tells us to focus about a third of the way into the picture. Think of it as a guideline, he says, admitting that he usually does it by the seat of his pants.

The climb along the ledges is a bit tricky, but at least we don't miss interesting details as we constantly check our footing. Simultaneously we all spot a solitary yellow flower growing from a crevice and squat down to capture this tenacious survivor. Stand up, Paul commands. A downward view will capture a more sweeping image.

The hardest lessons come one evening when a group gathers for a sunset shoot at the Blue Hill Overlook on Cadillac Mountain. The overlook is 30 feet lower than the summit, but at 1,500 feet, it still offers panoramic views of the Penobscot and Sargent mountains, the Bubbles, Eagle Lake, Blue Hill Bay, and offshore islands. It also has a better orientation than the peak for viewing sunsets.

Unfortunately, a gloriously clear day conspires against us. "Broken clouds with holes in them are the ideal conditions for sunset," Paul says, explaining that the color comes from the sun reflecting off the clouds. "If you want any red color in the sky, you've got to have clouds." A few fair-weather cumulus clouds dot the horizon when we arrive at about 6:45 P.M. As sunset approaches around 7:30 P.M., the clouds evaporate. "Happens all the time," Paul shrugs.

The brightness of the sun against the darkness of the ground presents a tricky technical challenge, Paul tells us as we scan the horizon. "You have to accept the fact that the land will be dark if you have color in the sky."

"So, Paul, when's the best time to shoot?" someone asks.

"If you like it, take a picture." Good advice, we decide, as the shutters on our cameras click almost in unison.

Blueberry Country, Maine

The Downeast coast keeps going for many miles after Mount Desert Island. We call this region "blueberry country" because that's what it is. The soils are so thin and acidic in this part of Downeast Maine that little will grow except the splendid wild blueberry, which thrives in profusion and which Mainers consider far superior to its cultivated high-bush cousin. So landlubbers here earn their meager living from the blueberry barrens and canning factories, while the fishermen tap the declining resources of the sea.

You'll have to backtrack from Mount Desert Island to Ellsworth to continue the journey Downeast. Make a sharp right onto Route 1 north and follow it through the villages of Hancock and the Sullivans. If you've come this far, it's worth turning right in the village of West Gouldsboro to drive toward Winter Harbor and make the seven-mile loop drive through **Schoodic Point,** a non-contiguous part of Acadia National Park. The 2,080 acres of the park have striking views of Frenchman Bay and Mount Desert Island. It's also a good place to get out of the car and hike some of the trails on the cliffs above the water. The lighthouse you see off to the west is Winter

North and South Bubble from Jordan Pond, Acadia National Park, Maine

Atlantic Puffin, Machias Seal Island, Maine

Harbor Light, built in 1856.

The park's loop road will deliver you back to Route 186, which reconnects with Route 1 in Gouldsboro, home of a fruit winery. Continue on Route 1 through the picturesque village of Columbia Falls (see "Staying There") until you see the sign for Jonesport to the right (Route 187).

Jonesport and Beals Island, fishing communities joined by a bridge at the end of this peninsula, boast the largest lobster fishing fleet in Downeast Maine, and Jonesport remains famous for the quality of its lobster boats. Many fishermen from other parts of Maine and even New Brunswick and Nova Scotia come here to have boats built for them. The fellows in gum boots pretty much ignore visitors, but take a spin around Beals Island to see the closest thing to a nineteenth-century fishing community still surviving in New England. A causeway connects Beals to Great Wass Island, home of the 1,540-acre **Great Wass Island Preserve,** maintained by the Maine chapter of the Nature Conservancy. The three and one-half miles of trails cross exposed headlands and raised coastal peat bogs. The preserve is habitat for eider ducks and scoters and the surrounding waters are heavily fished by eagles and ospreys. Telephone: (207) 729–5181.

To do some serious bird watching, make arrangements with Norton of Jonesport to visit **Machias Seal Island.** The family that runs this service has been in Jonesport since 1760, so you can be sure they know these waters well. The twenty-five-acre island, managed by the Canadian Wildlife Service, lies 10 miles from the mainland.

In clear weather, the boat trip of nearly two hours is an excellent opportunity to view seals and (sometimes) whales. Seabirds abound—cormorants, storm petrels, shearwaters, gannets, guillemots, and jaegers. When you reach the island, you'll land by rowboat and immediately be bombarded (at least in July and August) by Arctic terns who are trying to keep you away from their nests. The big attraction here is the population of Atlantic puffins, a cute bird once hunted to near extinction but now making a comeback thanks to restoration programs. You can watch them from behind blinds. The island also hosts the nesting grounds of endangered razorbill auks and common murres. The maximum stopover is limited to three hours. $50 per person. Reservations required. Sawyer's Square Road. Telephone: (207) 497–5933.

Route 187 loops northeastward from Jonesport along the shores of Englishman Bay to rejoin Route 1 at Jonesboro, which in turn continues east to **Machias,** the wild blueberry capital of Maine. The area is surrounded with low bush wild blueberries—covered with white blossoms in spring, blueberries in summer, and day-glo foliage in autumn. The local processing plant offers tours in the summer.

The Daughters of the American Revolution maintain the **Burnham Tavern** as a museum for good reason—the hotheads of Machias jumped the gun on the rest of the American colonies and planned the first naval battle of the American Revolution here. The "battle" was a rather minimal skirmish that amounted to seizing a moderately armed British schooner on June 12, 1775, for reasons that were more a matter of local rather than revolutionary politics. Based on this event, the people of Machias call their town "the Lexington of the Sea." Ultimately the rebels also seized two other ships, and the British burned down Portland as reprisal. And in 1777, the British fleet returned to Machias to destroy the little community because they feared (correctly) that the fort there was to be used to stage an attack on Nova Scotia. At the last minute, the British withdrew under heavy fire from the colonists and their Penobscot, Passamaquoddy, and Maliseet allies. The historical museum is open June through September, Monday through Friday from 9:00

A.M. to 5:00 P.M. Adults $3.00.

About 15 miles east of Machias, Route 1 turns northward, but most travelers choose to follow Route 189 to **Lubec,** the easternmost town in the United States. As you're entering town, watch for the signs to **Quoddy Head State Park** and the right turn onto South Lubec Road. In three miles, turn left onto West Quoddy Head Road to reach the park. It's not a huge park—481 acres—but the 200-foot cliffs give it a drama that few spots can match. A boardwalk over a seven-acre peat bog offers a great opportunity to observe rare plants (including the carnivorous sundew and pitcher plants). Both fin and minke whales abound in the waters around Quoddy Head, and you will have great views of both Campobello and Grand Manan islands. The park is open daily from Memorial Day to Labor Day and on weekends until November 1. Telephone: (207) 733-0911. Next to the park is the candy-striped West Quoddy Head Light, built in 1858 to replace the 1807 lighthouse built on orders of Thomas Jefferson. The only red-and-white lighthouse on the Maine coast, its beacon is visible for 18 miles out to sea.

Back in Lubec, you pass through Customs on a bridge to Campobello Island, New Brunswick, site of **Roosevelt Campobello International Park.** The thirty-four-room "cottage" was the summer home of Franklin Delano Roosevelt and is surrounded by nature trails. Extensive interpretive exhibits tell of Roosevelt's life and the friendly relations between the United States and Canada. Open May through mid-October from 10:00 A.M. to 6:00 P.M. (Atlantic Time). Free.

Cobscook Bay is surrounded by land in the shape of the letter "C," with Lubec on the lower lip and Eastport on the upper. Although they are separated by about a mile of water, they are divided by nearly 40 miles of road. If you are determined to make it to the end of the coast at Eastport, backtrack on Route 189 to Route 1 and resume the northerly drive. In about three miles you will come to the entrance to **Cobscook Bay State Park,** worth a stop to watch the tides come in or out. "Cobscook" is a Passamaquoddy word meaning "boiling tides," and it's absolutely accurate. The mean tide here is 24 feet.

Route 1 continues through the small villages of Dennysville and Pembroke, but at Perry, you should make a right onto Route 190 to head through **Pleasant Point,** the reservation of the Passamaquoddy tribe. These people once ranged all up and down both sides of the St. Croix River but have resided on this reserve since 1886. The settlement of federal land claims in the 1970s has helped the local economy, as the tribe elected to invest its settlement into businesses that would produce good jobs. The tribe's traditional Ceremonial Day, usually August 1, features a pageant of tribal history, canoe races, and crafts exhibitions. Tribal offices telephone: (207) 853-2551.

Eastport is the end of the line, but don't expect something momentous. This pleasant little town was the birthplace of the sardine canning industry in 1875, when Julius Wolfe invented canning machinery. At one time the town had eighteen canneries, and the waste products provided an olfactory "welcome" to Eastport that kept most people away. But the sardine industry tanked in the 1970s and the town is now rebounding nicely, becoming one of the largest producers of farmed Atlantic salmon in North America. The salmon business is much easier on the environment, far more aesthetically pleasing, and much less seasonal than sardines.

The Maine coast ends with a final dramatic flourish. Eastport has the distinction of the highest tides in the United States—measuring up to 40 feet at the extremes. This strong tidal flow often conflicts with the strong current from the St. Croix River. Between the city shoreline and Dog Island, the river and the tides create the "Old Sow," one of the world's largest whirlpools.

West Quoddy Head Light, Maine

Staying There

The Southern Crescent of New Hampshire and Maine

New Hampshire's Beaches

For advance information, contact the Hampton Beach Area Chamber of Commerce, 836 Lafayette Road, Hampton, NH 03842. Telephone: (603) 926–8717 or (800) GET–A–TAN.

LODGING

Rock Ledge Manor B&B. 1413 Ocean Boulevard, Rye. This relaxed seaside manor has four guest rooms and one of the best porches on the New Hampshire seacoast for following the tides of the Atlantic Ocean, right across the street. Telephone: (603) 431–1413. Moderate with breakfast.

CAMPGROUNDS AND RV PARKS

Hampton Beach State RV Park. Route 1A, Hampton. Located along the tidal Hampton River and part of Hampton Beach State Park, this is the only RV park directly on the New Hampshire coast. There are twenty sites in a prime spot south of the main part of the beach, with miles of sandy beaches, a park store, and saltwater fishing. Telephone: (603) 926 8990. The campground is open mid-May to mid-October and begins accepting reservations in January; telephone: (603) 271–3628.

FOOD

The Ice House. 115 Wentworth Road (Route 1B), Rye. Telephone: (603) 431–3086. This summer institution set in a stand of pines along the road to New Castle is a local favorite for ice cream and seafood suppers, in that order. Inexpensive.

FAIRS, FESTIVALS, AND EVENTS

Fireworks Displays. On Wednesday evenings in July and August there are spectacular fireworks displays at Hampton Beach. Telephone: (603) 926–8717.

The Piscataqua River Harbor, New Hampshire and Maine

For information on Portsmouth and the surrounding area, contact the Greater Portsmouth Chamber of Commerce, 500 Market Street, Portsmouth, NH 03801. Telephone: (603) 436–1118.

LODGING

Inn at Strawbery Banke. 314 Court Street, Portsmouth, New Hampshire. When it was built in 1800, this home was close to the waterfront and it is still in the heart of the earliest settlement, much of which is now incorporated into the Strawbery Banke Museum. The inn's wide floorboards and sloping floors give you a good feel for the area's historic houses. Telephone: (603) 436–7242 or (800) 428–3933. Moderate with breakfast.

The Oracle House Inn. 38 Marcy Street, Portsmouth, New Hampshire. Another little piece of history, this eighteenth-century Colonial is right next door to Strawbery Banke Museum. With three charming guest rooms with fireplaces, the house was once the home of an officer in the British Navy and the site of the publication of the first daily newspaper (*The Oracle*) in New Hampshire. Telephone: (603) 433–8827. Moderate with breakfast.

Sise Inn. 40 Court Street, Portsmouth, New Hampshire. This 1881 Queen Anne home was built by a prosperous businessman in a modernized American Empire style. Before being turned into an elegant B&B, the building led a varied life as apartments, a health center, business offices, a dress boutique, and a beauty parlor. Fortunately, all its occupants preserved the striking golden oak interior. The thirty-four guest rooms and public areas are decorated in the Victorian style with antiques and period reproductions. Telephone: (603) 433–1200. Moderate with breakfast.

FOOD

Dolphin Striker. 15 Bow Street, Portsmouth, New Hampshire. Telephone: (603) 431–5222. The white plaster walls, beamed low ceilings, and dark wooden tables and chairs give a colonial feel to this local institution right across from the tugboat dock. The kitchen emphasizes continental treatments for fish and meats. Lunch and dinner. Moderate to expensive.

Dunfey's Restaurant. Moored under Memorial Bridge near Strawbery Banke. 1 Harbor Place, Portsmouth, New Hampshire. Telephone: (603) 433–3111. This restaurant aboard the MV *John Wanamaker,* the last active steam tug in U.S. coastal waters, has indoor dining rooms as well as tables outside on the upper deck, making it a good choice in any weather. Open May through mid-October. Lunch and dinner. Moderate.

Lindbergh's Crossing. 29 Ceres Street, Portsmouth, New Hampshire. Telephone: (603) 431–0887. This site was the famed Blue Strawberry for many years, possibly New Hampshire's most innovative restaurant. It recently changed hands, and the New American bistro menu keeps up the high standards with the added advantage of an a la carte menu. Dinner. Moderate to expensive.

The Line House. Route 1, Kittery, Maine. Telephone: (207) 439–3401. This tiny side-of-the-road restaurant about a three-minute drive north of Kittery's factory outlet malls has simple old-fashioned road food. The franks and beans—Maine's traditional Saturday night supper—are always good and the fish and chips plate is one of the best we've eaten on the Maine coast. Breakfast, lunch, and dinner. Inexpensive.

Oar House. 55 Ceres Street, Portsmouth, New Hampshire. Telephone: (603) 436–4025. This fairly old-fashioned New England seafood restaurant offers the occasional surprise like bouillabaisse or rack of lamb. For a light meal on a nice day, find a seat on the outdoor deck overlooking the harbor, right next to the dock for the harbor cruises. Lunch and dinner. Moderate to expensive.

Warren's Lobster House. Route 1, Kittery, Maine. Telephone: (207) 439–1630. Perched on pilings above the Piscataqua River right across the bridge to downtown Portsmouth, New Hampshire, the rambling white structure is a local gem. Diners arrive by boat and by car for such traditional favorites as Warren's Crabmeat Casserole and Shrimp Scampi or the Downeast Shore Dinner—chowder, steamed mussels, and fried or steamed clams. Warren's has been going strong for more than a half century and the kitchen knows how to handle fish. Among the variations on lobster are baked stuffed lobster tails, a baked stuffed lobster tail served with three boiled claws, or a pile of five claws served with butter. Lunch and dinner. Moderate.

OTHER ATTRACTIONS

USS **Albacore.** Built in 1952 as an experimental prototype for modern submarines, the *Albacore* continued to set underwater speed records into the late 1960s, thanks to its innovative hull design. It continued to be a test prototype for new developments in sub technology until 1973. Open daily 9:30 A.M. to 5:30 P.M. Adults $4.00. Albacore Park (I–95 exit 7, then two-tenths of a mile east off Market Street), Portsmouth, New Hampshire. Telephone: (603) 436–3680.

FAIRS, FESTIVALS, AND EVENTS

Annual Bow Street Fair. Portsmouth's longest running arts festival has been staged for more than three decades. This outdoor music showcase is held for two days in late July along the historic waterfront in Portsmouth, New Hampshire. Telephone: (603) 433–4793.

Candlelight Stroll. For two weekends before Christmas, Strawbery Banke in Portsmouth, New Hampshire, sponsors a stroll through the Christmas decorations of eight period houses that range from the 1700s to 1950s. Hosts and hostesses in period costume offer refreshments. Telephone: (603) 433–1100.

Grand Old Portsmouth Brewer's Festival. Held for two days in late September, this event recreates the 1870s with period games and entertainment and provides the opportunity to sample some of New England's finest microbrews. Held at Strawbery Banke Museum, Portsmouth, New Hampshire. Telephone: (603) 433–1100.

SHOPPING

Kittery Trading Post. Route 1, Kittery. Telephone: (207) 439–2700. This outfitter has been in business since 1938 and has grown to be one of the largest in New England. Along with the predictable outerwear and footwear, the Trading Post has equipment for camping, backpacking, rock climbing, archery, fishing, winter sports, and water sports. In early September, the Post holds demonstrations and classes on outdoors skills.

Outlet Malls. One hundred twenty brand name outlet stores—one of the largest concentrations in the United States—occupy a one-mile stretch of Route 1 in Kittery. Telephone: (888) KITTERY.

The Yorks, Maine

For information about York Beach, Cape Neddick, York Harbor, and York Village, contact

Nubble Light, Cape Neddick, Maine

The Yorks Chamber of Commerce, P.O. Box 417, York, ME 03903. Telephone: (207) 363–4422.

LODGING

York Harbor Inn. Route 1A, York Harbor. The inn opened its doors more than 100 years ago and features thirty-five rooms with fine antiques or period reproductions. The inn overlooks the harbor and some rooms have ocean views. All guests can enjoy the location: Nubble Light is just down the street and the innkeepers can give directions to a fine and uncrowded beach just a short stroll away. Telephone: (207) 363–5119 or (800) 343–3869. Moderate.

CAMPGROUNDS AND RV PARKS

Camp Eaton. Route 1A, York Harbor. This facility within walking distance of Long Sands Beach has RV hookups and wooded tent sites. Telephone: (207) 363–3424.

Libby's Oceanside Camp. Route 1A, York Harbor. Directly on the ocean and adjacent to a sandy beach, this site has RV hookups only. Telephone: (207) 363–4171.

FOOD

Goldenrod Restaurant. Railroad Road and Ocean Avenue, York Beach. Telephone: (207) 363–2621. This turn-of-the-century landmark has a restaurant section finished in classic oak with a cobblestone floor as well as an old-fashioned soda fountain. In truth, its biggest business is nostalgic—saltwater taffy made on the premises. Breakfast, lunch, and dinner. Inexpensive.

York Harbor Inn. Route 1A, York Harbor. Telephone: (207) 363–5119. The main dining room with spectacular ocean views is a place where you "dress for dinner." More casual is the Wine Cellar, an English-style pub. Lunch and dinner. Expensive.

FAIRS, FESTIVALS, AND EVENTS

Lighting of Nubble Lighthouse. One of the more original Christmas holiday events on the Maine coast is the lighting of the lighthouse in late November. Telephone: (207) 363–1040.

York Days. This nine-day event begins in late July and features the usual summery mix of road races, crafts displays, dances, concerts, parades, and fireworks. Telephone: (207) 363–1040.

Ogunquit, Maine

For information, contact the Ogunquit Chamber of Commerce, Route 1 South, Box 2289, Ogunquit, ME 03907. Telephone: (207) 646–2939.

LODGING

Above Tide Inn. 26 Beach Street. With nine simply furnished guest rooms, the inn is located at the mouth of the Ogunquit River. Decks on pilings over the water help you enjoy the ocean view, which includes great sunsets. Telephone: (207) 646–7454. Inexpensive to moderate, with breakfast.

Beachmere Inn. 12 Beachmere Place. The fully renovated and modernized Victorian inn and a snappy 1950s classic two-story motel sit on a broad grassy lawn on the water's edge. A gate puts you right on the Marginal Way or lets you descend to secluded bathing coves. Rooms have kitchenettes and cable TV and many have balconies or decks. Telephone: (207) 646–2021 or (800) 336–3983. Inexpensive to expensive.

Chestnut Tree Inn. 93 Shore Road. This 1870 yellow clapboard Victorian has been an inn for more than a century, but its twenty-two guest rooms offer modern amenities of air conditioning and cable TV. Sixteen rooms have private baths. The large front porch overlooks the chestnut tree in the front yard. No smoking. Telephone: (207) 646–4529 or (800) 362–0757. Inexpensive to moderate with breakfast.

Juniper Hill Inn. 196 Route 1. Juniper Hill Inn sits on five acres north of town, with plenty of room for two heated pools, sauna, fitness center, sun decks, and colorful gardens. A private path leads to the beach. Telephone: (207) 646–4501 or (800) 646–4544. Inexpensive to expensive.

Riverside Motel. Shore Road. The name is too modest for this motel with a great view of the fishing harbor and art colony of Perkins Cove—to which it's connected by a wooden pedestrian drawbridge over the harbor. In addition to the motel rooms, there are also rooms in the white clapboard 1874 house on the grounds. Some rooms have private patio, all have air conditioning, cable TV, and refrigerator. Telephone: (207) 646–2741. Inexpensive to moderate with breakfast.

FOOD

Arrows. Berwick Road. Telephone: (207) 361–1100. If you want to splurge, this modest, gray eighteenth-century farmhouse surrounded by beautiful gardens has one of the finest restaurants in the state. The owners grow their own organic produce and create elegant New American dishes with a hint of Asian influence. Open from late April through Thanksgiving. Dinner. Very expensive.

Bread & Roses Bakery. 28A Main Street. Telephone: (207) 646–4227. When we're driving up the Maine coast, we always stop here for cookies to tide us over until we reach the mecca of cookies in Camden. This friendly bakery also offers a variety of vegetarian lunch specials such as homemade soups, pizza, and roll-up sandwiches.

Hurricane. Perkins Cove. Telephone: (207) 646–6348. This casual restaurant on Perkins Cove at the end of Marginal Way has a great ocean view. The fare is updated New England and the house specialty is Maine lobster chowder. Lunch and dinner. Moderate to expensive.

OTHER ATTRACTIONS

Ogunquit Playhouse. The big white theater building with ample green lawn is a famed venue of professional summer theater and offers three musicals and two plays during each ten-week summer season. Route 1 South. Telephone: (207) 646–2402 or (207) 646–5511.

ACTIVITIES

Finestkind. On-the-water tour options include a cruise to Nubble Lighthouse or a lobstering trip to see lobster traps hauled. Prices start at $8.00 per adult. From May through mid-October. Barnacle Billy's Dock, Perkins Cove. Telephone: (207) 646–5227.

FAIRS, FESTIVALS, AND EVENTS

Capriccio. A nine-day arts festival in early September features performances by the Portland Ballet and local theater groups as well as folk, blues and chamber music concerts, poetry readings and storytelling. Telephone: (207) 646–7055.

SHOPPING

The Blacksmith's Mall. Route 1. Telephone: (207) 646–9643. Route 1 from Kittery to Arundel is one of our favorite stretches to look at antiques and collectibles. This group shop of about sixty-five dealers is one of the best of its kind along Route 1. Telephone: (207) 646–9643.

Wells, Maine

CAMPGROUNDS AND RV PARKS

Pinederosa Camping Area. 128 North Village Road. There are 152 large wooded or field sites at this camping area that is only two miles from the beach and has its own swimming pool. Telephone: (207) 646–2492.

FOOD

Maine Diner. Route 1. Telephone: (207) 646–4441. The vegetable garden out back supplies ingredients for many of the menu offerings. This large, custom-made diner is wheelchair accessible. Breakfast, lunch, and dinner. Inexpensive to moderate.

SHOPPING

Lighthouse Depot. Route 1 North. Telephone: (207) 646–0608. The publicity brochure for this shop may have you thinking that it is housed in a lighthouse. But even stranded by the side of the road, this two-floor gift shop probably is true to its claim to have the largest collection of lighthouse gifts ever assembled.

The Kennebunks, Maine

For information about Kennebunk, Kennebunk Beach, and Kennebunkport contact the Kennebunk/Kennebunkport Chamber of Commerce, P.O. Box 740, Kennebunk, ME 04043. Telephone: (207) 967–0857.

LODGING

The big old nineteenth-century houses of the Kennebunks have found new life in one of the largest and most interesting concentrations of B&Bs in historic properties anywhere in New England. Showpiece homes in their day, they are elegantly styled, comfortably furnished, and offer pretty much anything you could ask for a romantic getaway on the Maine coast.

Captain Fairfield Inn. Corner of Pleasant and Green Streets, Kennebunkport. The inn occupies a Federal-style mansion built circa 1813 and is named for James Fairfield, a sea captain and privateer who lived here in the early 1800s. (You can see his portrait in the Brick Store Museum.) The inn has nine large guest rooms, three with working fireplaces, and the grassy lawn shaded by large trees overlooks the Green River. Telephone: (207) 967–4454 or (800) 322–1928. Moderate to expensive with breakfast and afternoon tea.

1802 House. 15 Locke Street, Kennebunkport. This small, informal, and quiet inn overlooks the Cape Arundel Golf Club where George Bush plays and is about a ten-minute walk to Dock Square. The six guest rooms have been recently updated and most have four-poster beds, working fireplaces, and sitting areas. Some have double whirlpool baths. Non-smoking. Telephone: (207) 967–5632 or (800) 932–5632. Moderate to expensive with breakfast.

Fontenay Terrace Motel. 128 Ocean Avenue, Kennebunkport. This eight-room motel is a good choice for those who want to enjoy the natural attractions of the area rather than the commercial ones. It sits at the edge of a tidal inlet with a beach just 300 yards away. The public fishing wharf, where lobster boats unload their catch, is across the street. All rooms have mini-refrigerator, cable TV, and outside sitting area facing the shaded lawn. Non-smoking. Telephone: (207) 967–3556. Inexpensive to moderate.

The Maine Stay. 34 Maine Street, Kennebunkport. This is a versatile property for a variety of travelers. A big white inn with a sweeping front porch (with rocking chairs) holds four guest rooms and two deluxe fireplace suites. Also on the grounds are cottages decorated in English country style with kitchens and connecting doors to accommodate big families. Several cottages also have fireplaces. Telephone: (207) 967–2117 or (800) 950–2117. Moderate to expensive with breakfast and afternoon tea.

Rhumb Line Motor Lodge. Ocean Avenue, Kennebunkport. In a wooded setting about a mile from George Bush's place on Walker Point, this sixty-room motor lodge is probably a better bet for families with kids who might not enjoy the daintier pleasures of the historic inns. There are heated indoor and outdoor pools, a spa and sauna, and occasional lobster bakes. It's a short walk to the ocean. Rhumb Line is one of the stops on the Intown Trolley. Telephone: (207) 967–5457. Inexpensive to moderate with breakfast.

White Barn Inn. Beach Street, Kennebunk Beach. This Relais & Chateaux property is a superb choice for those who want a luxury experience with more privacy than a B&B can offer. The former farmhouse has small, antique-furnished rooms, and the new addition boasts capacious modern suites with fireplaces and whirlpool baths. Telephone: (207) 967–2321. Moderate to very expensive.

FOOD

Port Lobster. Ocean Avenue, Kennebunkport. Telephone: (207) 967–5411. This seafood market was established in 1953 and specializes in shipping lobster nationwide via Federal Express. They also offer a takeout lunch menu of clam or lobster chowder, crabmeat, shrimp, or lobster rolls. *Down East Magazine* says their lobster rolls are among the best in the state, which means they're always fresh and not too heavy on the mayo.

White Barn Inn. Beach Street, Kennebunk Beach. Telephone: (207) 967–2321. The seasonal menu in this elegant dining room draws heavily on local produce, meat, and fish to produce what could be argued is the finest gastronomic experience available on the Maine coast inside a beauti-

fully restored, two-level barn. In the winter, the view through the large dining room window on the back resembles a Christmas card. The superb New American cuisine is matched by an excellent wine list. Dinner. Expensive.

Windows on the Water. 12 Chase Hill Road, Kennebunk. Telephone: (207) 967–3313. The Kennebunks are blessed in having yet another fine dining venue, albeit somewhat less trend conscious. From a relaxed setting overlooking the river, Windows offers everything from a hamburger to lobster ravioli, rack of lamb, lobster bisque, or their "world famous" lobster-stuffed potato. Lunch and dinner. Moderate to expensive.

OTHER ATTRACTIONS

Seashore Trolley Museum. You can see more than 200 trolleys from around the world and watch volunteer craftsmen restoring nineteenth and early twentieth-century models before taking demonstration rides around the grounds. Open mid-June through September, daily 9:30 A.M. to 6:00 P.M. (museum) and 10:30 A.M. to 4:00 P.M. (trolley rides). Call for spring and fall hours. Adults $7.00 for museum admission and unlimited rides. 195 Log Cabin Road, Kennebunk. Telephone: (207) 967–2800.

ACTIVITIES

Indian Whale Watch. The trip is narrated by an experienced whale researcher collecting data for the Cetacean Research Unit. Adults $25. Offers a morning cruise July through September and also sunset whale watches in July and August. Departs from Arundel Wharf Restaurant, Ocean Avenue, Kennebunkport. Telephone: (207) 967–5912.

Nautilus Whale Watch. This operator claims to have a 99 percent sighting record since 1986. Morning and sunset cruises have trained naturalists on board. Adults $25. Kennebunkport Marina. Telephone: (207) 967–0707.

TOURS

Intown Trolley. A forty-five-minute narrated tour gives the history of Kennebunkport and drives by the beaches, Blowing Cave, Spouting Rock, and

President Bush's estate. Adults $6.00. One fare is good all day. Telephone: (207) 967–3686.

FAIRS, FESTIVALS, AND EVENTS

Christmas Prelude. This ten-day event has a lot more community spirit than commercial hype. Events include holiday and crafts fairs, a tree lighting, caroling, hand bell choir concerts, a festival of trees at the Brick Store Museum, all sorts of special suppers (fish chowder, beef stew, lobster, chili), and open houses at the historic bed-and-breakfasts. Telephone: (207) 967–0857.

Arundel, Maine

SHOPPING

Arundel Antiques. Route 1. Telephone (207) 985–7965. This two-level shop bursting with merchandise calls itself "Maine's busiest antiques mall." It's one of the few that provides restrooms for its patrons.

Old Orchard Beach, Maine

For information contact Old Orchard Beach Chamber of Commerce, P.O. Box 600, First Street, Old Orchard Beach, ME 04064. Telephone: (207) 934–2500 or (800) 365–9386.

LODGING

There may be more motels and cabins in Old Orchard than year-round private homes. As a general rule, the least expensive and oldest are found on the road leading into town from Route 1, while the entire beach is lined on both sides of Grand Avenue with motels that mostly date from the 1950s. Note that because so much of Old Orchard's business traditionally comes from Quebec, excellent bargains are available when the Canadian dollar is depressed and the Quebecois are staying home.

Atlantic Birches Inn. 20 Portland Avenue. This property on a quiet tree-lined corner is a short walk from the pier. Ten guest rooms are divided between a 1903 Victorian and a 1920s bungalow. There's an outdoor swimming pool and a front porch shaded by white birch trees. Telephone:

(207) 934–5295 or (888) 934–5295. Moderate with breakfast.

The Edgewater. 57 West Grand Avenue. The classic Old Orchard Beach accommodation is a two-story motel at the water's edge. The Edgewater is nicely maintained, has a good pool, and is an easy walk from the center of town. Telephone: (207) 934–2221 or (800) 203–2034. Moderate to expensive.

The White Lamb. 3 Odessa Avenue. For a quieter experience, these efficiency units are surrounded by a white picket fence and sit under "restful pines" in a seaside location at the south end of the strand. Telephone: (207) 934–2231. Moderate.

FOOD

Joseph's. 55 West Grand Avenue. Telephone: (207) 934–5044. Old Orchard is the absolutely best place on the Maine coast to indulge in junk food. But when you've had enough (if you've had enough), Joseph's lets you enjoy real food in an attractive dining room or on the garden patio. Breakfast and dinner. Moderate to expensive.

FAIRS, FESTIVALS, AND EVENTS

Annual Beach Olympics. Family fun is the watchword at this three-day event in mid-August with beach games, prizes, and entertainment. Telephone: (207) 934–2500.

Fireworks. From late June until Labor Day there are fireworks over the beach near the Pier every Thursday evening.

Scarborough and Cape Elizabeth, Maine

LODGING

Black Point Inn Resort. Prouts Neck. It's no surprise that Winslow Homer used to paint this stunning rocky outcrop of granite and shale between the barrier beaches. This turn-of-the-century beachfront resort features eighty rooms in the main inn or cottages—many with ocean views. Guests have use of the Prouts Neck summer colony's yacht club and golf course, as well as tennis, health club, pools, nature trails, and miles of sandy beach. For those who like their fun with a formal atmosphere. Telephone: (207) 883–4126 or (800) 258–0003. Very expensive with breakfast and dinner.

CAMPGROUNDS AND RV PARKS

Bailey's Pine Point. Route 9, Scarborough. Tent, trailer, and RV sites are available and there is a shuttle bus to beaches. Telephone: (207) 883–6043.

FOOD

Two Lights Lobster Shack. Two Lights Road, Cape Elizabeth. Telephone: (207) 799–1677. Edward Hopper painted here, and we bet he would have been glad to enjoy a lobster roll between brushstrokes with a grand view of the craggy shore from an oceanside picnic table. Lunch and dinner. Inexpensive to moderate.

Maine's Peninsula Country

Portland, Maine

For information about Portland and the surrounding area, contact the Convention and Visitors Bureau of Greater Portland, 305 Commercial Street, Portland, ME 04101. Telephone: (207) 772–4994.

LODGING

The Danforth. 163 Danforth Street. This erstwhile silver merchant's home passed through many uses before it was rescued from near-decay in 1994 and transformed into an elegant nine-room B&B (seven rooms have working fireplaces). Telephone: (207) 879–8755. Moderate to expensive with breakfast.

Pomegranate Inn. 49 Neal Street. Well-selected antique furnishings and bold wall paintings by a local artist give this B&B near the Western

Promenade a one-of-a-kind flair. There are eight guest rooms in the 1884 Italianate main house and a carriage house. Telephone: (207) 772–1006 or (800) 356–0408. Moderate to expensive with breakfast.

Portland Regency. 20 Milk Street. The historic armory building in the center of the Old Port has been made into posh hotel. The location is convenient but can seem a little loud on summer weekends. Telephone: (207) 774–4200 or (800) 727–3436. Moderate to expensive.

West End Inn. 146 Pine Street. This circa 1871 brick Victorian features elegant public spaces and five guest rooms with canopy beds and wallpaper that befits the Victorian penchant for color and pattern. Telephone: (207) 772–1377 or (800) 338–1377. Moderate to expensive with breakfast.

CAMPGROUNDS AND RV PARKS

Wassamki Springs. 855 Saco Street, Westbrook. One of the nearest campgrounds to Portland for tent, trailer, and RV camping sits on a private thirty-acre lake. Telephone: (207) 839–4276.

FOOD

Fore Street. 288 Fore Street. Telephone: (207) 775–2717. Chef Sam Hayward is a fanatic about superb local ingredients and treats them to the stylish and craftsmanlike preparations they deserve. "Fire" is the key word here, as most entrees are either roasted on a spit or in a wood oven with apple wood. Be sure to reserve ahead as this spot is extremely popular with local and visiting foodies. Dinner. Moderate to expensive.

Katahdin. 106 High Street. Telephone: (207) 774–1740. Katahdin's easy-going insouciance brings New England cooking up to date in a funky, eclectic decor that attracts Portland's upmarket Bohemians as well as many of its foodies. Lunch and dinner. Inexpensive to moderate.

Miss Portland Diner. 49 Marginal Way. Telephone: (207) 773–3246. This meticulously maintained Worcester Diner from 1949 made a cameo appearance in the Mel Gibson film *Man Without a Face.* Try old-time New England cooking such as a plate of meatloaf and mashed potatoes. Breakfast, lunch, and dinner. Inexpensive to moderate.

Street & Company. 33 Wharf Street. Telephone: (207) 775–0887. A good bet for informed, even elegant cooking, Street & Company prepares fish in any number of creative, innovative ways and matches the plates with a cozy atmosphere and friendly, helpful service. Dinner. Moderate to expensive.

The Village Cafe. 112 Newbury Street. Telephone: (207) 772–5320. This casual spot consistently wins local polls for Portland's best fried clams. Lunch and dinner. Moderate.

Zephyr Grill. 653 Congress Street. Telephone: (207) 828–4033. Although the grilled food is similar to Fore Street's, Zephyr is often less expensive and a lot less crowded. It also features several vegetarian dishes in addition to grilled meats and fish. Dinner. Moderate to expensive.

OTHER ATTRACTIONS

Portland Pirates. A minor-league hockey team affiliated with the Washington Capitals plays from early October to early April at the Cumberland County Civic Center on Spring Street. Telephone: (207) 828–4665.

Portland Sea Dogs. A minor-league baseball affiliate of the Florida Marlins, the Sea Dogs plays to enthusiastic crowds at 6,000-seat Hadlock Stadium from early April to early September. 271 Park Avenue. Telephone: (207) 874–9300 or (800) 936–3647.

Portland Stage Company. The largest professional theater company in northern New England performs at the Portland Performing Arts Center, 25A Forest Avenue. Telephone: (207) 774–0465.

Portland Symphony Orchestra. City Hall Auditorium is the venue for classical, pops, and chamber concerts. 389 Congress Street. Telephone: (207) 773–8191.

ACTIVITIES

Eagle Tours. There are a number of ways to get out on the ocean, including harbor and seal-watching cruises, a cruise to Portland Head Light, or an excursion to Eagle Island, summer home of Admiral Robert Peary. Adults $7.00 to $16.50. Long Wharf. Telephone: (207) 774–6498.

Olde Port Mariner Fleet. Cruise options include deep sea fishing, whale watching, and lobster trap hauls as well as harbor tours. Adults $8.50 to $45.00. Long Wharf. Telephone: (207) 775–0727 or (800) 437–3270.

Palawan. This 58-foot yacht makes morning, afternoon, or day-long sails from the Old Port. Adult fares start at $20 and a minimum number of passengers is required. Telephone: (207) 773–2163.

FAIRS, FESTIVALS, AND EVENTS

Aucocisco. This nine-day festival held in April celebrates life on Casco Bay with environmental and historical exhibits, performances, and tours of some of the working boats of the region, such as a Coast Guard cutter and Maine Maritime Academy's training vessel. Telephone: (207) 772–6828.

First Night. Portland's New Year's Eve celebration takes place in the downtown arts district with afternoon events for families, a parade, evening performances in a variety of locations, and fireworks at midnight. Telephone: (207) 772–9012 or (800) 639–4212.

Maine Boat Builder's Show. This three-day event in mid-March signals spring for every wannabe sailor for hundreds of miles around. It's a great place for dreaming. . . . Telephone: (207) 774–1067.

SHOPPING

Most of the best shops, galleries, and boutiques are found in the Old Port area bounded by Commercial, Franklin, Congress, and Union Streets.

Abacus. 44 Exchange Street. Telephone: (207) 772–4880. This excellent craft gallery has a range in work in all media from craftspeople all over the country.

Carlson & Turner Books. 241 Congress Street. Telephone: (207) 773–4200. Portland has a number of used and antiquarian book dealers. This one has an interesting collection of titles about Maine.

Cross Jewelers. 570 Congress Street. Telephone: (207) 773–3107. A 3.5-million karat find of the pink and green semi-precious stone in 1972 put Maine on the map as one of the world's great tourmaline centers. The stone has become the gem of choice for Maine jewelers, and Cross has an especially good selection. Open only on weekdays.

L.L. Bean. 542 Congress Street. Telephone: (207) 865–4761. Maine's most famous outdoors gear retailer operates a factory store in Portland with overstocks, discontinued items, and returns. If you're a serious Bean buyer, head north to Freeport.

Maine Potters Market. 376 Fore Street. Telephone: (207) 774–1633. This cooperative gallery handles many of the state's best ceramic artists.

Nancy Margolis. 367 Fore Street. Telephone: (207) 775–3822. Another superb craft gallery with work in all media, Nancy Margolis carries a bit more jewelry and more local artists than Abacus.

Thomas Moser Cabinetmaker. 415 Cumberland Avenue. Telephone: (207) 774–3791. Handcrafted, Shaker-influenced furniture is displayed in an elegant showroom. Moser has a strong following across the U.S. and Canada, and you will likely have to order a piece based on the display samples.

Stein Gallery. 20 Milk Street. Telephone: (207) 772–9072. Stein represents about 65 of the best glass artists working throughout the United States.

Freeport, Maine

LODGING

Harraseeket Inn. 162 Main Street. It just keeps getting bigger and bigger, though the 1989 and 1996 additions keep the spirit of the late nineteenth-century structure that lies at the center of this modern hotel complex. Despite the faux rusticity, Harraseeket's large guest rooms are tasteful and comfortable. Telephone: (207) 865–9377 or (800) 342–6423. Moderate to expensive.

CAMPGROUNDS AND RV PARKS

Flying Point Campground. Flying Point Road. This campground on the ocean west of town has thirty-eight sites for tents and RVs, with swimming, boating, and fishing. Telephone: (207) 865–4569.

FOOD

Harraseeket Inn. Telephone: (207) 865–9377. The main dining room of this hotel is decorated in a New Yorker's idea of Maine rustic, but the food is fabulous New American with bounteous help from nearby gardens. Breakfast, lunch, and dinner. Moderate to expensive.

Harraseeket Lunch & Lobster. On the docks, South Freeport. Telephone: (207) 865–4888. As respite from the outlet malls, escape to Harraseeket Lunch for dockside dining on Maine's favorite crustacean. Lunch and dinner. Inexpensive to moderate.

OTHER ATTRACTIONS

Desert of Maine. A glacier that slid along the coast about 12,000 years ago left behind sand and mineral deposits that have been turned into one of Maine's more quirky attractions. The site features nature trails, gift and souvenir shops, sand paintings, a world sands collection, and a museum with antique farm tools. (In the late eighteenth century, hay and potatoes were grown here until soil erosion exposed the "desert.") Open early May to mid-October, daily 8:30 A.M. to 7:00 P.M. Adults $6.75. Desert Road. Telephone: (207) 865–6962.

SHOPPING

L.L. Bean. Main and Bow Streets. Telephone: (207) 865–4761. Maine's most famous outdoors gear retailer was here long before the outlet malls. Open around the clock across the calendar.

Outlet Malls. There are more than 110 outlet stores throughout town, each within walking distance of the next. Telephone: (207) 865–1212.

Brunswick and the Harpswells, Maine

For information about Bath, Brunswick, and the surrounding region, contact the Bath-Brunswick Region Chamber of Commerce Tourist Information Center, Route 1 North, Bath, ME 04530. Telephone: (207) 443–9751.

FOOD

Cook's Lobster House. Garrison Cove Road, South Harpswell. Telephone: (207) 833–6641. ***Estes Lobster House.*** Route 123, South Harpswell. Telephone: (207) 833–6340. The Harpswell peninsula supports many fishermen and they supply these two huge seafood houses. Cook's has a nice view of the Cobwork Bridge. Estes offers a triple lobster plate with french fries and butter. Lunch and dinner. Inexpensive to moderate.

Miss Brunswick Diner. 101 Pleasant Street, Brunswick. Telephone: (207) 729–5948. This diner has undergone a lot of changes, but is still worth a stop. The exterior has been covered with clapboard and the back bar was pushed back to make room for tables in addition to stools. Oddly enough, the menu features "Mexican" (Tex-Mex) food among the entrees. Breakfast, lunch, and dinner. Inexpensive.

FAIRS, FESTIVALS, AND EVENTS

Maine Festival of the Arts. This four-day celebration of Maine creativity was founded in 1977 by the late Maine humorist Marshall Dodge (the "I" of the "Bert and I" duo). Held for four days in early August in Brunswick, it features more than 1,000 artists from Maine and away, music, theater, dance, visual arts, crafts, literary arts, folk arts, storytellers and comedians, and Maine-made products. Telephone: (207) 772–9012 or (800) 639–4212.

Thomas Point Beach Bluegrass Festival. In late August or early September, Brunswick hosts a festival of world class entertainers and field pickin'. Telephone: (207) 443–9751.

Bath and Below, Maine

For information about Bath, Brunswick, and the surrounding region, contact the Bath-Brunswick Region Chamber of Commerce Tourist Information Center, Route 1 North, Bath, ME 04530. Telephone: (207) 443–9751.

LODGING

Grey Havens Inn. Seguinland Road, Georgetown. This classic shingled summer hotel is set on a rocky bluff overlooking the ocean. In keeping with tradition, Grey Havens has a covered porch and deck chairs on the bluffs so that guests can enjoy the view. Telephone: (207) 371–2612. Moderate to expensive with breakfast.

FOOD

Five Islands Lobster Co. Flag Rock Road, Five Islands. Telephone: (207) 371–2990. This classic of Maine dining sits beside a tidal river, with views of spruce-studded islands. Enjoy the view and your meal at picnic tables or take your lobster to go. Lunch and dinner. Inexpensive.

Georgetown Fisherman's Co-op. Route 127, Five Islands. Telephone: (207) 371–2950. The fellows in gum boots on this working wharf may well have trapped your dinner. Locals swear by the Co-op's onion rings. Lunch and dinner. Inexpensive to moderate.

FAIRS, FESTIVALS, AND EVENTS

Heritage Days. This three-day celebration in early July in Bath features fireworks, of course, as well as historic walking tours and boatbuilding demonstrations that commemorate Bath's position in shipping and shipbuilding. Telephone: (207) 443–9751.

Wiscasset, Maine

FOOD

Sea Basket. Route 1. Telephone: (207) 882–6581. Lobster stew is one of the specialties at this unpretentious diner. Lunch and dinner. Inexpensive to moderate.

OTHER ATTRACTIONS

Musical Wonder House. We don't know that we've encountered a sea captain's mansion put to more unusual use. In this case, an 1852 mansion with impressive flying staircase and classical moldings is the showcase for a collection of restored mechanical musical instruments, such as music boxes and player pianos. They are shown and played on guided tours daily from late May through Labor Day from 10:00 A.M. to 6:00 P.M. Tours start at $6.50 for adults. 18 High Street. Telephone: (207) 882–7163.

FAIRS, FESTIVALS, AND EVENTS

Annual Strawberry Festival and Auction. Held in late June, this old-fashioned fair at St. Phillip's Church, with strawberry shortcake and sundaes and a country auction, has been a village staple since the early 1950s. Telephone: (207) 882–7825.

Boothbay Peninsula, Maine

For information about the Boothbay region, contact the Boothbay Harbor Region Chamber of Commerce, Route 27, P.O. Box 356, Boothbay Harbor, Me 04538. Telephone: (207) 633–2353.

LODGING

1830 Admiral's Quarters Inn Bed & Breakfast. 71 Commercial Street, Boothbay Harbor. A renovated sea captain's home, the Admiral's Quarters is within easy walking distance of shops, restaurants, and piers. The six guest rooms have individual entrances and decks overlooking the harbor. When the wind is chilly, enjoy the solarium. Telephone: (207) 633–2474. Moderate with breakfast.

Five Gables Inn. Murray Hill Road, East Boothbay. The fifteen guest rooms of this last remaining summer hotel in East Boothbay, built in the 1870s, overlook Linekin Bay from the crest of a hill. Rooms under the gables are cozy and eccentric and the property offers old-fashioned hospitality. Telephone: (207) 633–4551 or (800) 451–5048. Moderate to expensive with breakfast.

Linekin Bay Resort. 92 Wall Point Road, Boothbay Harbor. If you want to take full advantage of the coastal location, this resort at the water's edge overlooking Linekin Bay includes sailing instruction and use of Rhodes 19-foot sailboats in its rate. There's also canoeing in the protected waters of Linekin Bay, as well as fishing from a dock or boat. The resort consists of five lodges on the water and thirty cabins in the piney woods. Open from late June through late August. Telephone: (207) 633–2494 or (413) 584–4554 (winter). Moderate with three meals.

Newagen Seaside Inn. This secluded complex of buildings on Southport Island, six miles from Boothbay Harbor, offers modern comforts, great views, and six wonderful miles between you and the Boothbay day trippers. Telephone: (207) 633–5242 or (800) 654–5242. Moderate to expensive with breakfast.

Spruce Point Inn. Grandview Avenue (Atlantic Avenue Extension). This turn-of-the-century inn sits on fifteen oceanside acres at the entrance to Boothbay Harbor. Accommodations include grand suites, modest rooms in the main house, private cottages, and condominiums. Clay tennis courts, a heated spa, a saltwater pool at ocean's edge, and a heated freshwater pool complete the sybaritic package. Telephone: (207) 633–4152 or (800) 553–0289. Very expensive with breakfast and dinner.

FOOD

Boothbay Region Lobstermen's Co-op. Atlantic Avenue, Boothbay Harbor. Telephone: (207) 633–4900. We're partial to cooperative lobster pounds, since the fishermen tend to make a better profit on their catches. You can watch them come and go here, and see your dinner hauled right from the boats. Indoor and outdoor seating. Lunch and dinner. Moderate.

Cabbage Island Clambake. Fisherman's Wharf, Boothbay Harbor. Telephone: (207) 633–7200. We're not certain whether to consider this dining or an activity. You take a cruise to Cabbage Island, where a feast of lobsters, clams, corn on the cob, new Maine potatoes, and onions is steamed under a bed of seaweed. The island has beautiful views and ocean trails to explore. Daily from late June to mid-September. Adults $37.50.

Crumps. 34 McKown Street, Boothbay Harbor. Telephone: (207) 633–7655. This English-style tea room serves traditional pub lunches and afternoon teas.

Ebb Tide. 67 Commercial Street, Boothbay Harbor. Telephone: (207) 633–5692. This diner is known for its thick chowders and homemade pie. We love places like this where the breakfast menu is available all day. Breakfast, lunch, and dinner. Inexpensive to moderate.

King Brud. This cart near the intersection of McKown and Commercial Streets in Boothbay Harbor has been selling hot dogs since 1943.

Spruce Point Inn. Atlantic Avenue, Boothbay Harbor. Telephone: (207) 633–4152. The cuisine ranks among the finest in Maine and the dining room has a spectacular ocean view. Reservations and proper dress (jacket, no jeans)

New England Farmland

are required. Dinner. Expensive.

OTHER ATTRACTIONS

Boothbay Railway Village. The highlight of this re-creation of a historic New England village is a ride on a narrow gauge steam train. There are also more than fifty antique automobiles. Adults $7.00. Open mid-May through early June on weekends, early June through mid-October daily from 9:30 A.M. to 5:00 P.M. Route 27, Boothbay. Telephone: (207) 633–4727.

ACTIVITIES

Appledore. Two and one-half hour cruises to the outer islands aboard the 64-foot windjammer *Appledore* pass several lighthouses. Passengers almost always see seals sunning on the rocks. Adults $20. Fisherman's Wharf. Telephone: (207) 633–6598.

Balmy Days *Cruises.* Take a harbor tour, night cruise, or supper cruise aboard the *Balmy Days* for $8.00 to $22.00 for adults. If you prefer the snap of canvas to the rumble of a motor, sightsee from the sea on a one and one-half hour sail aboard the *Bay Lady,* a 31-foot sloop, for $18. *Balmy Days* also makes a 9:30 A.M. run to Monhegan Island in the summer. Pier 8, Boothbay Harbor. Telephone: (207) 633–2284.

Cap'n Fish's Whale Watch and Scenic Nature Cruises. The captains are Boothbay Harbor natives who love and understand the sea. All cruises emphasize the rich natural life of the area—from puffin, seal, and whale watch cruises, to the popular cruise to Pemaquid Point Lighthouse. Adults $10–$15. Pier 1, Boothbay Harbor. Telephone: (207) 633–3244.

FAIRS, FESTIVALS, AND EVENTS

Fisherman's Festival. This three-day festival in Boothbay Harbor in mid-April gets a jump on the summer season with an old-fasioned fish fry, fish chowder contest, lobster crate race, Miss Shrimp Princess pageant, a boat parade, and the Blessing of the Fleet. Local fishermen compete in net-mending, fish filleting, clam shucking, shrimp picking, and even lobster eating. Telephone: (207) 633–2353.

Windjammer Days. Two-day festival in late June includes an antique boat parade, street parade, concerts, shipyard open houses, and fireworks. The highlight, however, is the arrival and departure of the windjammers in Boothbay Harbor. Telephone: (207) 633–2353.

Pemaquid Peninsula, Maine

For information about the Pemaquid region, contact the Damariscotta Region Chamber of Commerce, P.O. Box 13, Main Street, Damariscotta, ME 04543. Telephone: (207) 563–8340.

LODGING

Mill Pond Inn. Mill Pond Road, Newcastle. This secluded retreat with six comfortable rooms sits on a little peninsula in Mill Pond, which is actually a wide spot in the Damariscotta River before it opens into 15-mile-long Damariscotta Lake. Guests can use the inn's canoes to paddle around the lake—or even enjoy the warm freshwater (well, warm compared to the nearby Atlantic). There are Adirondack chairs on the dock, hammocks in the yard. Telephone: (207) 563–8014. Moderate with breakfast.

Newcastle Inn. River Road, Newcastle. Three of the fifteen rooms in this renovated Federal-style inn on the Damariscotta River have fireplaces, some have river views. Telephone: (207) 563–5685 or (800) 83-BUNNY. Moderate to expensive.

FOOD

Salt Bay Cafe. Main Street, Damariscotta. Telephone: (207) 563–1666. A reasonable choice for family-style dining, Salt Bay has especially good crab cakes. Lunch and dinner. Inexpensive to moderate.

The Sea Gull Shop. Pemaquid Point. Telephone: (207) 677–2374. We could have listed this under shopping, since they sell a lot of touristy souvenirs. But it's a good place for blueberry French toast for breakfast or lobster pie and fried clams for dinner. Breakfast, lunch, and dinner. Inexpensive to moderate.

Shaw's Fish and Lobster Wharf Restaurant. New Harbor. Telephone: (207) 677–2200. We fear that someday Hollywood will discover Shaw's, film a movie here and ruin everything. It's almost too good to pass up—a picturesque view of the working harbor, a deck lined with picnic tables, and a full menu of well-prepared fin and shellfish. Cover yourself with a bib, grab a mallet, and enjoy those crustaceans. If you squint, you might see Monhegan Island on the horizon on a clear day.

SHOPPING

Edgecomb Potters. Route 27, Edgecomb. Telephone: (207) 882–6802. With more than 20 years experience, the potters have perfected their technique of creating richly glazed, deeply colored, high fire porcelain. The showroom also displays the work of other Maine artists, including Richard Fisher's cast bronze bells.

Muscongus Bay, Maine

FOOD

Moody's Diner. Route 1, Waldoboro. Telephone (207) 832–7468. Founded in 1944 and in the same family ever since, Moody's continues to turn out good road food at reasonable prices. That probably explains why the parking lot is always full. No smoking. Breakfast, lunch, and dinner. Inexpensive to moderate.

SHOPPING

The Roseraie at Bayfields. If you get lost, just roll down your windows. The proprietor says you will smell the sweet aroma of the roses before you see the place. The Roseraie offers species, old garden, modern shrub, and climbing roses. The garden, called a "catalog in the ground" is planted with more than 300 varieties. The peak bloom is the fortnight bracketing July 1. But there is much to see from early June to early October. Route 1, Waldoboro. Telephone: (207) 832–6330.

Thomaston Peninsula, Maine

LODGING

Craignair Inn. Clark Island, Spruce Head. This

lodging has a facinating history. It was built in 1928 to house workers from the nearby quarries and there are still many reminders of that era on the island—quarry workers' homes, the Union Hall, the chapel where quarry workers and their families worshipped, and several stone wharves. Craignair was converted to an inn in 1940 and sits on a granite ledge on four acres of shorefront crossed by several walking paths. Guest rooms in the main building share baths and are furnished simply—quilts on the beds and hooked rugs on the floors. Guest rooms in a separate annex all have private baths and are furnished with antiques. Telephone: (207) 594-7644 or (800) 320-9997. Inexpensive to moderate with breakfast.

FOOD

Miller's Lobster Company. Wheeler's Bay, Route 73, St. George. Telephone: (207) 594-7406. Another classic lobster shack, this one sits smack among the boats of St. George's gorgeous little harbor. Lunch and dinner. Inexpensive to moderate.

OTHER ATTRACTIONS

Owls Head Transportation Museum. There are many surprises along the Maine coast—not the least of which is this collection of more than 150 World War I-era vehicles, including aircraft, automobiles, motorcycles, bicycles, and carriages. Adults $6.00. Open April through October daily from 10:00 A.M. to 5:00 P.M., and November through March daily from 10:00 A.M. to 4:00 P.M. The museum is located on Route 73, two miles south of Rockland. Telephone: (207) 594-4418.

FAIRS, FESTIVALS, AND EVENTS

Transportation Rally and Aerobatic Show. The Owls Head Transportation Museum has an ambitious schedule of special weekend activities, including this two-day event in early August that includes antique autos, high-wheel bicycles, aircraft, and a World War I airshow. Telephone: (207) 594-4418.

Monhegan Island, Maine

LODGING

Island Inn. Huge by Monhegan standards (it accommodates fifty-five guests), the Island Inn actually has some rooms with private baths. It also has a great ocean view and a cozy common room with jigsaw puzzles for rainy days. Telephone: (207) 596-0371. Moderate to expensive with breakfast and dinner.

Monhegan House. The dormitory-style bathrooms down the hall and lack of closets in this venerable (since 1870) lodging house set the tone: This feels like another, earlier century. With thirty-two rooms, Monhegan House sits right in the middle of the village. Telephone: (207) 594-7983 or (800) 599-7983. Inexpensive.

Trailing Yew. This hillside compound of cabins and cottages *really* isn't in the modern age—some of the facilities lack electricity, though all the (shared) bathrooms have lights. (If your room is unelectrified, you'll be issued a kerosene lantern.) A very informal and rustic place—summer camp for adults, really—Trailing Yew is popular with birders and hikers. Moreover, the community table is surprisingly good, especially if you remember always to take the fresh fish option. Telephone: (207) 596-0440. Moderate with breakfast and dinner.

Rockland, Maine

For regional information, contact the Rockland-Thomaston Area Chamber of Commerce, Harbor Park, P.O. Box 508, Rockland, ME 04841. Telephone: (207) 596-0376 or (800) 562-2529.

LODGING

Captain Lindsey House Inn. 5 Lindsey Street. Operated by the same folks who own the schooner *Stephen Taber* and the motor cruiser *Pauline*, this circa 1837 nine-room B&B offers special packages with the boats. Telephone: (207) 596-7950 or (800) 523-2145. Inexpensive to moderate with breakfast.

Old Granite Inn. 546 Main Street. Located right across from the island ferry dock, the Old Granite

Inn is a comfortable, smoke-free lodging with eleven rooms, most with private baths, in walking distance to the Farnsworth and the central shopping district. Telephone: (207) 594–9036 or (800) 386–9036. Inexpensive to moderate with breakfast.

Food

Cafe Miranda. 15 Oak Street. Telephone: (207) 594–2034. This hot spot among local gourmets offers a constantly changing Mediterranean menu. If you're lucky, you might snag an outdoor patio table. Lunch and dinner. Inexpensive to moderate.

Activities

Windjammer Excursions. Rockland has become the windjammer capital of America's Atlantic coast, eclipsing nearby Camden, Rockport, and Boothbay Harbor. Trips aboard these schooners— some old, some rather new—typically run for a week during the main season, with boarding on Sundays and return to port on Saturdays. Shorter trips of three and four days are offered during the shoulder seasons of June and September. Accommodations vary, but these are not luxury liners. The repeat customers find a windjammer sail to be exhilarating. Non-repeat customers grumble about sleeping quarters as narrow as a coffin and the decidedly crude toilet facilities. You know who you are: If camping out on a wooden deck (or below deck when it rains) suits you fine, then the schooners can be the most exciting way to tour the Maine coast. If you like hot showers, flush toilets, and queen-size beds, you'll be happier staying ashore. Rates vary with the season and with the amenities a given ship offers, but range from $500 to around $1,000 a week for room and board and all the salt spray you can sniff. Weeks in July and August book up early. Contact the individual boats for details.

American Eagle, 92 feet, twenty-eight passengers. Telephone: (800) 648–4544.

Angelique, 95 feet, thirty-one passengers. Telephone: (207) 236–8873 or (800) 282–9989.

Heritage, 94 feet, thirty-three passengers. Telephone: (800) 648–4454.

Isaac Evans, 65 feet, twenty passengers. Telephone: (800) 648–4544.

J&E Riggin, 90 feet, twenty-six passengers. Telephone: (207) 594–2923 or (800) 869–0604.

Kathryn B, 80 feet, twelve passengers. Telephone: (800) 500–6077.

Nathaniel Bowditch, 82 feet, twenty-four passengers. Telephone: (207) 273–4062 or (800) 288–4098.

Stephen Taber, 68 feet, twenty-two passengers. Telephone: (207) 236–3520 or (800) 999–7352.

Summertime, 53 feet, seven passengers. Telephone: (800) 562–8290.

Timberwind, 75 feet, twenty passengers. Telephone: (207) 236–0801 or (800) 759–9250.

Victory Chimes, 132 feet, forty-five passengers. Telephone: (207) 594–0755 or (800) 745–5651.

Fairs, Festivals, and Events.

Maine Lobster Festival. The classic of Maine events—more than fifty years old—highlights the fact that more lobsters are landed at Rockland than the rest of the state. This four-day event early in August is a fixture in the community and includes the arrival of King Neptune, the crowning of the Lobster Queen, a parade, boat rides, lobster buoy race, and lobster dinners cooked almost continuously. Telephone: (207) 596–0376.

Schooner Days. This three-day event in mid-July features a schooner race in Rockland Harbor, a parade of schooners, live music, marine demonstrations, and seafood. Telephone: (207) 596–0376

Rockport and Camden, Maine

For regional information, contact the Rockport-Camden-Lincolnville Chamber of Commerce, Public Landing, P.O. Box 919, Camden, ME 04843. Telephone: (207) 236–4404 or (800) 223–5459.

Lodging

Blackberry Inn. 82 Elm Street, Camden. There

are ten guest rooms as well as elegant parlors in this colorfully painted Victorian home within walking distance of downtown Camden and the harbor. Some rooms feature fireplaces and whirlpools and some are wheelchair accessible. Telephone: (207) 236–6060 or (800) 388–6000. Moderate to expensive with breakfast.

Edgecomb-Coles House. 64 High Street, Camden. This property sits on a quiet hillside overlooking Penobscot Bay. It's a short walk to Camden harbor, or the innkeepers will lend you bicycles, which you might prefer for touring Camden Hills State Park, just a mile away. Telephone: (207) 236–2336 or (800) 528–2336. Moderate to expensive with breakfast.

High Tide Inn. Route 1, Camden. This seven-acre property rests at the foot of Mount Megunticook and slopes gradually down to the sea. There are a variety of lodging choices ranging from lodge rooms to motel units to cottages. But all guests enjoy the lawns and lounge chairs, the views of Penobscot Bay, and 250 feet of private beach. Telephone: (207) 236–3724 or (800) 778–7068. Inn rooms and motel rooms: Inexpensive to moderate with breakfast (high season only).

Lord Camden Inn. 24 Main Street, Camden. Right on Main Street amidst the shops and restaurants, this clean and well-kept hotel offers the freedom to come and go that's hard to exercise at a B&B. Telephone: (800) 336–4325. Moderate to expensive.

Swan House. 49 Mountain Street, Camden. This 1870 Victorian home at the foot of Mount Battie has been a bed-and-breakfast since 1983. There are six guest rooms with private baths and a number of comfortable public areas—from the parlors to the sun porch to the gazebo in the backyard. Telephone: (207) 236–8275 or (800) 207–8275. Moderate with breakfast.

Whitehall Inn. 52 High Street, Camden. This handsome Colonial Revival inn is where Edna St. Vincent Millay debuted her poem "Renascence." Telephone: (207) 236–3391. Moderate to expensive.

CAMPGROUNDS

Megunticook by the Sea. Route 1, Rockport. Camping cabins are available as well as eighty wooded sites on the ocean. Facilities include a heated pool. Telephone: (207) 594–2428 or (800) 884–2428.

FOOD

Lobster Stu's. Sharp's Wharf, Camden. Telephone: (207) 236–8763. Here's where you can get simple lobster in a town where frou-frou preparations are more likely. Lunch and dinner. Inexpensive to moderate.

Mama & Leenie's. 27 Elm Street, Camden. Telephone: (207) 236–6300. This is our cookie mecca. This tiny cafe has good soups, salads, and sandwiches and, we have to admit, better cookies than Mom ever made.

Sea Dog Brewing Co. 43 Mechanic Street, Camden. Telephone: (207) 236–6863. Camden's entry in the statewide surge of brewpubs has good beer in the Pacific Northwest style and conventional pub grub. Lunch and dinner. Inexpensive to moderate.

ACTIVITIES

Despite Rockland's dominance of the windjammer trade, Camden also retains an active fleet.

Maine Windjammer Cruises is a cooperative booking agent for three ships. Telephone: (207) 236–2938, or (800) 736–7981. Its boats are the schooner *Grace Bailey,* 81 feet, twenty-nine passengers; the schooner *Mercantile,* 82 feet, twenty-nine passengers; and the sloop *Mistress,* 46 feet, six passengers.

Lewis R. French, 65 feet, twenty-two passengers. Telephone: (207) 236–9411 or (800) 469–4635.

Mary Day, 90 feet, thirty passengers. Telephone: (207) 236–2750 or (800) 992–2218.

Roseway, 112 feet, thirty-six passengers. Telephone: (207) 236–3520 or (800) 225–4449.

FAIRS, FESTIVALS, AND EVENTS

Arts and Crafts Shows. In mid-July and mid-October, Camden hosts juried shows with about

100 artists and craftspeople displaying their wares in Camden Amphitheater, Harbor Park, and along Atlantic Avenue. Telephone: (207) 236–4404.

Bay Chamber Concerts. Rockport's 1891 opera house is the setting for performances by acclaimed local, national, and international talents, primarily during July. Pre-concert lectures and post-concert receptions enhance the experience. Telephone: (207) 236–2823.

Windjammer Weekend. For three days in early September Camden celebrates the windjammer industry with live music, performances, nautical demonstrations, crafts, and a parade of sail. Telephone: (207) 236–4404.

Lincolnville and Islesboro, Maine

LODGING

The Mount Battie. Route 1, Lincolnville. Four miles north of Camden on Route 1, this twenty-one-room motel has beautiful views of Penobscot Bay from the decks. The proprietors encourage guests to enjoy the umbrella-topped tables on the deck or the hammock hung between two birch trees. There's even a barbecue on the deck for guest use. Telephone: (207) 236–3870 or (800) 224–3870. Inexpensive to moderate with breakfast.

The Spouter Inn. Route 1, Lincolnville Beach. Lincolnville is often overlooked between the more tourist-oriented towns of Camden, Belfast, and Searsport. But this is a good place to stop if you are planning to take the ferry to Islesboro or just want a low-key place along Penobscot Bay. All rooms have a view of the ocean, some have fireplaces and Jacuzzis. Telephone: (207) 789–5171. Moderate to expensive with breakfast.

FOOD

Lobster Pound Restaurant. Telephone: (207) 789–5550. Tempting as it is to dine al fresco next to the sandy strand of Lincolnville Beach across from the Islesboro Ferry Terminal, you'll enjoy your lobster, clams, and fries more in the interior dining room away from the mendicant gulls. Moderate to expensive.

The Lobster Pound Restaurant, Lincolnville Beach, Maine

Ducktrap River Fish Farm. 57 Little River Drive, Lincolnville. Telephone: (207) 338–6280. Ducktrap ships all over the world, but you can stop in to stock up for a gourmet picnic of wild and farm-raised fish naturally smoked over northern hardwoods and fruit woods. They also sell seafood pâtés and sauces.

OTHER ATTRACTIONS

Kelmscott Farm. This working farm is dedicated to the conservation of endangered livestock breeds such as Cotswold sheep, Gloucestershire Old Spots pigs, Nigerian dwarf goats, Kerry cows. There is also an heirloom garden. Open Tuesday through Sunday from 10:00 A.M. to 5:00 P.M. in the summer; closes at 3:00 P.M. in the winter. Adults $5.00. Off Route 52, about four miles north of Lincolnville Center. Telephone: (207) 763–4088.

Belfast, Maine

For information contact the Belfast Area Chamber of Commerce, 31 Front Street, Belfast, ME 04915. Telephone: (207) 338–5900.

LODGING

Belfast Bay Meadows Inn. 90 Northport Avenue (Route 1). Bay Meadows offers a retreat from the summer hubbub on the seventeen-acre grounds of what used to be a lovely saltwater farm just south of town. The meadows are landscaped now and make pleasant strolling (with paths to the shore) and there are additional paths through the surrounding woods for rustic walks. The nineteen guest rooms are divided between the historic main house and hotel-type lodgings in a converted barn. Telephone: (207) 338–5715 or (800) 335–2370. Inexpensive to moderate.

Harbor View House of 1807. 139 High Street. This restored Federal house amid a row of sea captain's houses that survived the Great Fire has spectacular views of Penobscot Bay. There's also an antiques shop on the premises. Breakfast might feature lobster and eggs. No smoking. Telephone: (207) 338–2244. Inexpensive to moderate with breakfast.

Jeweled Turret Inn. 16 Pearl Street. This 1898 Queen Anne Victorian is a striking reminder that Belfast used to have traders with a lot of money and time on their hands to spend it. The inn is named for the stained-glass turret inset with gemstones that encases an oak spiral staircase. Among other unique architectural details are a fireplace built with rocks and semi-precious stones from every state in the Union, four parlors with ornate fireplaces and beautiful woodwork, and two rubble-stone verandas. Telephone: (207) 338–2304. Moderate with breakfast.

Food

Belfast Bay Brewing Company. 100 Searsport Avenue. Telephone: (207) 338–2662. Located in East Belfast by the side of Route 1, Belfast Bay is home base for Maine's best master brewer, Dan McGovern. It's worth stopping for a bitter or an IPA (India Pale Ale), and you can get the usual pub fare to accompany the suds. Lunch and dinner. Inexpensive to moderate.

Belfast Bay Meadows Inn. 90 Northport Avenue (Route 1). Telephone: (207) 338–5715. The main dining room overlooks Penobscot Bay and the New American menu, with a strong emphasis on grilled meat and fish, is nearly as good as the view. Dinner. Moderate to expensive.

Young's Lobster Pound. Mitchell Avenue (off Route 1). Telephone: (207) 338–1160. Young's

buys most of the catch of the Searsport, Belfast, and Stockton Springs lobstermen, so you can be sure that the lobster you get here is very local. Right on the shore in East Belfast, Young's will steam some up to go or you can sit down at the tables and crack them there if you don't mind the rather industrial harbor view. Lunch and dinner. Moderate.

Activities

Ace Aviation. Scenic flights over Penobscot Bay take in the panoramic sweep of land and sea and also the details of the lighthouses, islands, and Camden hills. From $25. Belfast Municipal Airport. Telephone: (207) 338–2970.

Belfast & Moosehead Lake Rail Road Company. Steam locomotive or diesel trains travel from Penobscot Bay through woodlands and fields and past charming villages. Or you can cruise the bay on the riverboat *Voyageur.* $12 adults for either, with a discount for both. Telephone: (207) 948–5500 or (800) 392–5500.

Fairs, Festivals, and Events

Belfast Bay Festival. This five-day event in mid-July with chicken barbecue, live entertainment, midway amusement rides, parade, and fireworks is held in Belfast City Park. Telephone: (207) 338–5719.

Shopping

Bennett's Down to Earth Gems & Minerals. Route 1. Telephone: (207) 338–5530. The resident gemcutter and goldsmith makes interesting jewelry, including one-of-a-kind pieces with Maine gemstones such as pink and green tourmalines, purple amethysts, and cool blue aquamarines. Bennett's also sells mineral specimens, including many from Maine, that range from common and inexpensive to rare and pricey.

Monroe Salt Works. Route 1. Telephone: (207) 548–0046. Like many of the tiny towns of Waldo County just inland from Belfast, Monroe attracted a lot of back-to-the-land counter cultural folks in the 1960s and 1970s who knew bargain properties when they saw them. Many of these new homesteaders took up pottery, learning the salt glaze technique that dominated this area's pottery a century earlier. Monroe Salt Works, relocated to Belfast, was the most successful of the companies to emerge from that time, and their work features fruit, floral, and fish designs.

Searsport, Maine

For information, contact Searsport & Stockton Springs Chamber of Commerce, Main Street, P.O. Box 139, Searsport, ME 04974. Telephone: (207) 548–6510.

LODGING

Captain A.V. Nickels Inn. Route 1. A photograph of the mutton-chopped Captain Nickels hangs in the Penobscot Marine Museum. His 1874 home has a big front porch, rolling lawns, and ocean frontage on Penobscot Bay that includes a 300-foot beach that's a great spot for bonfires and cookouts. The grand ballroom hosts many weddings. On our last stay, one other guest was a wedding planner on vacation who pronounced the entire property perfect. Telephone: (207) 548–6691 or (800) 343–5001. Inexpensive to moderate with breakfast.

Colonial Gables. Route 1. This nicely kept-up late 1940s motel and housekeeping cottage complex sits on ten acres overlooking Penobscot Bay. It has its own private beach. Telephone: (207) 338–4000 or (800) YES–MAINE. Inexpensive.

Thurston House B&B Inn. 8 Elm Street. This rather modest circa 1831 Colonial home located in the village recalls the years before Searsport became such a force in overseas trade. It's within easy walking distance of the Penobscot Marine Museum. Of the four guest rooms, two have private baths and two have bay views. Telephone: (207) 548–2213 or (800) 240–2213. Inexpensive with breakfast.

CAMPGROUNDS

Searsport Shores. 216 West Main Street. This vast campground in former hayfields bills itself as a "camping resort" because it has a private beach, lobster bakes, and variety of daytrip itineraries. Tent and RV sites are available. Handicapped accessible. Telephone: (207) 548–6059.

FOOD

Jordan's. Main Street. Telephone: (207) 548–2555. This dairy bar cum clam shack is a local favorite for fried fish, meatloaf buried in gravy, soft-serve ice milk, and root beer floats. Swing by on a Friday or Saturday night to see the kids from the area out on dates in a distant echo of *American Graffiti.* Lunch and dinner. Inexpensive.

Nickerson Tavern. Route 1. Telephone: (207) 548–2220. Practically every building of note in this area is a former sea captain's home, and that's true as well of the Nickerson Tavern. It also happens to serve outstanding contemporary American cuisine with an emphasis on garden vegetables and fresh fish and a refreshing absence of foodie pretension. Dinner. Moderate to expensive.

Periwinkles Bakery. 227 West Main Street. Telephone: (207) 548–9910. With a specialty in European pastries and breads, this spot is a good choice for a lunch of soup, salads, quiches, and sandwiches.

SHOPPING

BlueJacket Ship Crafters. Lighthouse Place, Route 1. Telephone: (207) 548–9970 or (800) 448–5567. We can't think of a better location for a shop offering cast metal fittings, model making supplies, and kits to build model wooden ships. For inspiration, completed models are on display—and finished scale models are for sale.

Searsport Antique Mall. Route 1. Telephone: (207) 548–2640. Searsport used to call itself the "antiques capital" of Maine, but most of the fanciest goods from the Far Eastern trade have since been sold. The wares now emanate from more modest homes and attics, but Searsport remains a good place to poke around for antiques and collectibles at shops that range from junk heaps to others that wouldn't be out of place on Manhattan's Upper East Side. This particular multi-dealer shop cuts across all ranges and interests. If you're going to choose just one place to browse, this is the best.

Downeast Maine

Castine, Maine

LODGING

Castine Inn. Main Street. The rambling old inn in the center of town has twenty comfortable rooms, some of which overlook the harbor. Number twelve is small and has its private bath across the hall, but it has the best view over the inn's colorful gardens and across the bay. An interesting mural of local scenes gives you something to marvel at when you sit down to dinner. Telephone: (207) 326–4365. Moderate with breakfast.

FOOD

Dennett's Wharf. Sea Street. Telephone: (207) 326–9045. Something of a yachtsman's bar, this restaurant in the heart of the harbor is a good place to purchase a simple seafood dinner. In warm weather you can eat on the deck over the water. Lunch and dinner. Inexpensive to moderate.

Penobscot Peninsula and Deer Isle, Maine

LODGING

Inn on the Harbor. Main Street, Stonington. You can't get any closer to the water without climbing aboard a boat. The casual lodging sits right in the midst of the briny atmosphere. Its remarkable deck commands the harbor. Telephone: (207) 367–2420. Moderate.

FOOD

Bayview Market & Takeout. Route 199, Penobscot. Telephone: (207) 326–4882. More a clam shack than a lobster shack, Bayview has a few picnic tables so you can chow down on a clam roll and enjoy the view of broad fields, the salty Bagaduce River and, off in the distance, Penobscot Bay. Lunch and dinner. Inexpensive to moderate.

Bay View Restaurant. Seabreeze Avenue, Stonington. Telephone: (207) 367–2274. This is what a Downeast down-home restaurant is like—darn little fuss and good, simple food. Try Nellie's Sauteed Lobster Meat a la Nova Scotia on toast points—an old family recipe. Lunch and dinner. Inexpensive to moderate.

Eaton's Lobster Pool. Blastow Cove, Little Deer Isle. Telephone: (207) 348–2383. Nearby Stonington is headquarters for the Maine Lobstermen's Association and many members sell their catch directly to Eaton's. While the main business is for steamed lobster to take home, you can also get shore dinners to eat at the picnic tables. Lunch and dinner. Inexpensive to moderate.

Fisherman's Friend. School Street, Stonington. Telephone: (207) 367–2442. Yet another place where the fellers in gum boots eat (as the name suggests); you're best off with the fried fish or the lobster stew positively swimming with chunks of meat. BYOB (Bring your own "bee-uh"). Lunch and dinner. Inexpensive to moderate.

SHOPPING

Blue Heron Gallery and Studio. Deer Isle Village. Telephone: (207) 348–2940. For a small town, really just a bend in the road, Deer Isle Village has several galleries of photography, arts, and crafts. The Blue Heron specializes in contemporary crafts and features work by faculty members of Haystack Mountain School of Crafts, many of whom have national and even international reputations. The gallery is open from June to September.

Maine Crafts Association Retail Shop. 6 Dow Road, Deer Isle Village. Telephone: (207) 348–9943. This organization is the glue that holds the state's artisans together. More than seventy members show their work in this shop.

Blue Hill, Maine

LODGING

Blue Hill Farm Country Inn. Route 15. Homely and moderate, this farmhouse inn is exactly as described—country lodging for the summer folk. The best and largest rooms can be found in the renovated barn. Telephone: (207) 374–5126. Moderate.

Blue Hill Inn. Union Street. As befitting a hostelry dating from 1840, the decor in this Federal style inn is colonial, but with a touch of whimsy. This is the usual choice for big-city folks who've heard about Blue Hill by reading E.B. or Katherine White and want to see for themselves. Guests in the eleven rooms are perfectly situated for exploring the town by foot. No smoking. Telephone: (207) 374–2844. Expensive with breakfast and dinner.

John Peters Inn. Route 176 East. A bit out of town, John Peters Inn compensates by having twenty-five acres of land on the shore. The four-teen guest rooms of this 1810 manor are decorated with antiques and nine of them have fireplaces. That's a welcome amenity, as evenings get chilly next to the water in Maine, even in the hottest part of August. No smoking. Telephone: (207) 374–2116. Moderate to expensive with breakfast.

Food

Blue Hill Inn. Union Street. Telephone: (207) 374–2844. The French provincial style of the inn's dining room combines with a dogged com-mitment to local, organic produce, meat, and fish to create some memorable meals at prices that are high by local standards but a steal compared to urban restaurants. Each night there's a three- or five-course fixed price menu with a few choices under each course. Northern France is a lot like Maine, so the recipes translate seamlessly. Expensive to very expensive.

Firepond. Main Street. Telephone: (207) 374–9970. Perhaps a tad overdecorated, Firepond's eclectic inter-national menu reflects the chef's former life in the heady competition of Manhattan fine dining. The former blacksmith's shop, situated along a stream, is a delightful setting, and the inventive dishes are expert-ly prepared. Dinner. Moderate to expensive.

Left Bank Bakery and Cafe. Route 172. Telephone: (207) 374–2201. Like peace, man . . . . The sixties (and seventies) live on in this local institution that features fresh breads, soups, salads, and naturally sweetened muffins and desserts. Acoustic musicians perform several nights a week. Breakfast, lunch, and dinner. Inexpensive.

Fairs, Festivals, and Events

Blue Hill Fair. Locals love this traditional coun-try fair in early September for its agricultural exhibits, pig scramble, blueberry pie eating con-test, oxen pulls, livestock shows, fireworks, large midway, grandstand entertainment, and auto thrill shows. Telephone: (207) 374–3701.

Kneisel Hall Summer Music School and Festival. World-renowned faculty offer chamber music concerts on Friday evenings and Sunday afternoons throughout the summer. There are also children's concerts, master classes, student con-certs, and open rehearsals. Telephone: (207) 374–2811.

Shopping

Rackliffe Pottery. Route 172. Telephone: (207) 374–2297. The artisans who established this pot-tery trained at Rowantrees (see below). The Rackliffe family also uses local clay and their own lead-free glazes, creating functional wares that are ovenproof and dishwasher safe. Located in a shady grove overlooking Blue Hill Bay.

Rowantrees Pottery. Route 177. Telephone: (207) 374–5535. Blue Hill is known for its pot-ters and Rowantrees in the best-known of the bunch. Founded in 1934 as a philanthropic and social experiment, Rowantrees is one of the oldest surviving art potteries in the United States. The functional pieces are made from local clay and local minerals are used in many of the glazes.

Ellsworth, Maine

Shopping

Big Chicken Coop. Route 1. Telephone: (207) 667–7308. The chief industry in this part of Maine from World War II to about 1975 was rais-ing broiler chickens, and this rambling monstros-ity was one of the larger outfits. Now it's filled to the rafters with antiques, collectibles, and used books.

Trenton, Maine

Food

Oak Point Lobster Pound. Off Route 230.

Telephone: (207) 667–8548. On the mainland about a mile from crossing onto Mount Desert Island, this fancy lobster pound (they have waiters, for goodness sake!) serves a rather broad menu that includes shore dinners, lobster stew, lobster roll, and shrimp scampi as well as plain old boiled lobster with melted butter. Lunch and dinner. Moderate.

Mount Desert Island, Western Lobe (Bass Harbor and Southwest Harbor, Maine)

LODGING

Bass Harbor and Southwest Harbor are less than a half-hour drive from Bar Harbor and even closer to many parts of Acadia National Park. They're also a lot quieter and less expensive than Bar Harbor, making them a good base for exploring Mount Desert at your leisure.

Bass Harbor Inn. Shore Road, Bass Harbor. The innkeepers have totally restored this 1832 house, creating a variety of lodging options. Several rooms overlook the harbor; others face Mount Desert's peaks. Telephone: (207) 244–5157. Inexpensive to moderate with breakfast.

The Claremont. Claremont Road, Southwest Harbor. Mount Desert's oldest summer resort hotel overlooks Somes Sound. Amid the genteel atmosphere, guests play croquet on the lawn and sip cocktails in the boathouse. Telephone: (207) 244–5036 or (800) 244–5036. Moderate to expensive with breakfast.

The Inn at Southwest. 371 Main Street, Southwest Harbor. The nine guest rooms of this downtown Victorian were recently redecorated with a handsome touch, but we'd rather spend our inn time rocking on the fabulous wrap-around porch. Telephone: (207) 244–3835. Moderate with breakfast.

Penury Hall Bed 'n' Breakfast. Main Street, Southwest Harbor. Character is the byword at Penury Hall, which is comfortably rumpled and delightfully casual. The three guest rooms share two baths and the owners love to chat. It's a favorite with Brits doing the fall tour and with

young European hikers. Telephone: (207) 244–7102. Moderate with breakfast.

CAMPGROUNDS

Bass Harbor Campground. Route 102A, Bass Harbor. With 112 sites—including separate RV and tenting areas—this campground is a ten-minute walk from the ocean. Telephone: (207) 244–5857 or (800) 327–5857.

Smugglers Den Campground. Route 102, Southwest Harbor. This well-located campsite has 100 sites for tents and RVs and oceanfront camping. There's a heated pool on the site and Echo Lake Sand Beach in Acadia National Park is only a twenty-minute walk away for the island's best freshwater swimming. Telephone: (207) 244–3944.

FOOD

Beal's Lobster Pier. Clark Point Road, Southwest Harbor. Telephone: (207) 244–3202. The thing that's truly special about Beal's, especially since it's on Mount Desert, is that there's nothing special. No frills. No dopey signs. Eat your lobster here, where all they care about is lobster. Lunch and dinner. Inexpensive to moderate.

Keenan's. Route 102A, Bass Harbor. Telephone: (207) 244–3403. Louisiana bayou country goes Downeast—much to the delight of the locals as well as aficionados of backroads restaurants. If you order the seafood sampler, you'll have enough fish that you'll be ordering chicken the rest of your stay in Maine. Dinner. Inexpensive to moderate. No credit cards.

Preble Grill. 14 Clark Point Road, Southwest Harbor. Telephone: (207) 244–3034. With a Mediterranean take on fresh local fish and shellfish (they make a fine bouillabaisse), Preble also does grilled steaks and chops and offers a long menu of microbrewery beers. Dinner. Moderate to expensive.

OTHER ATTRACTIONS

Wendell Gilley Museum of Birdcarving. Southwest Harbor native Wendell Gilley has a national reputation as a carver of birds and this museum features his work as well as changing wildlife art exhibits and daily demonstrations of carving. Open June to October Tuesday through Sunday from 10:00 A.M. to 4:00 P.M., except during July and August when it is open until 5:00 P.M. Open May, November, and December Friday through Sunday from 10:00 A.M. to 4:00 P.M. $3.25 adults. Wheelchair accessible. Main Street and Herrick Road, Southwest Harbor. Telephone: (207) 244–7555.

ACTIVITIES

Dive Maine. This operation rents snorkeling and SCUBA equipment and provides morning, afternoon, and night dive trips with a captain who has more than two decades of experience in Maine's coastal waters. Route 102A, Bass Harbor. Telephone: (207) 244–5751.

Island Cruises. Cruises traverse the islands of Blue Hill Bay, an area rich in wildlife. One good option is the lunch tour that goes to Frenchboro, a 170-year-old fishing village on Long Island. Bass Harbor docks. Adults $17. Telephone: (207) 244–5785.

Mount Desert Island, Eastern Lobe (Bar Harbor and Northeast Harbor, Maine)

For information on Bar Harbor, contact the Bar Harbor Chamber of Commerce, 93 Cottage Street, P.O. Box 158, Bar Harbor, ME 04609. Telephone: (207) 288–5103.

LODGING

The Atlantic Eyrie. Route 3 north of Bar Harbor. This property has an eagle's eye view of Frenchman Bay and offers some units with kitchens. Telephone: (207) 288–9786 or (800) HABA–VUE. Moderate to expensive.

Aurora Motel. 51 Holland Avenue, Bar Harbor. Located on a side street at the edge of town, this neat but modest ten-room motel is within easy walking distance of shops and restaurants. Telephone: (207) 288–3771 or (800) 841–8925. Inexpensive to moderate.

Edenbrook Motel. 96 Eden Street, Bar Harbor. About a fifteen-minute walk north of town on Route 3, this was the first motel in Bar Harbor. It is well-kept with modern amenities. Telephone: (207) 288–4975 or (800) 323–7819. Moderate.

Holbrook House. 74 Mount Desert Street, Bar Harbor. One of the grand cottages from the late nineteenth century features twelve guest rooms, a sun room, and the perfect porch to enjoy a summer day. No smoking. Telephone: (207) 288–4970. Moderate to expensive, with breakfast.

Manor House. 106 West Street, Bar Harbor. There are fourteen rooms in this nineteenth-century "cottage" set back from the road on deeply shaded grounds. West Street is where the 1947 fire stopped, so many nice homes survive here. Telephone: (207) 288–3759 or (800) 437–0088. Moderate to expensive, with breakfast.

Mira Monte Inn. 69 Mount Desert Street, Bar Harbor. Lush perennial gardens surround this 1864 Victorian style cottage. The fifteen guest rooms are furnished with antiques and many have fireplaces and balconies. Telephone: (207) 288–4263 or (800) 553–5109. Moderate to expensive with breakfast.

CAMPGROUNDS

Barcadia Campground. Off Route 198 near the top of the island, Barcadia has 200 oceanfront and ocean view sites facing west toward sunset. Use the private beach for fishing or access for canoeing and kayaking. Barcadia also runs shuttle buses to Bar Harbor. Reservations accepted—and practically essential in July and August. Route 198, Bar Harbor. Telephone: (207) 288–3520.

Bar Harbor Campground. Route 3, Bar Harbor. There are 300 sites in this campground, also close to Acadia National Park. There is a heated pool and ocean view. Telephone: (207) 288–5185. Does not accept advance reservations.

FOOD

Acadia Restaurant. 62 Main Street, Bar Harbor. Telephone: (207) 288–4881. With chipped Formica booths and bilious fluorescent lighting, you'd hardly expect Acadia to serve such good fish chowder. This is real Maine food as eaten by real Mainers who prefer "dinnuh" at 11:30 and "suppuh" at 4:30. Absolutely no concession has been made to the tourist trade, even though Acadia is in the middle of Bar Harbor's busiest street. So enjoy the turkey sandwiches, meatloaf, macaroni and cheese, and that luscious chowder. Breakfast, lunch, and dinner. Inexpensive.

George's. 7 Stephens Lane, Bar Harbor. Telephone: (207) 288–4505. Much as we like the traditional plain seafood so characteristic of this part of Maine, it's also nice to discover a classy little hideaway like George's, where the current fine-dining trend toward a pan-Mediterranean menu puts a little spice and a little finesse into the excellent local provender. Dinner. Expensive to very expensive.

Jordan's. 80 Cottage Street, Bar Harbor. Telephone: (207) 288–3586. You want to know what's *really* going on in Bar Harbor? Who's been seeing whom? What that New York feller's asking for his cottage? Come to breakfast at Jordan's, a coffeeshop where the most important meal of the day is served from 5:00 A.M. to 2:00 P.M. Breakfast and lunch. Inexpensive.

Maine Coast Brewing Company Tap Room & Grill. 21A Cottage Street, Bar Harbor. Telephone: (207) 288–4914. Another in an increasingly long line of Maine brewpubs with excellent suds and fairly conventional pub grub. Lunch and dinner. Inexpensive to moderate.

Porcupine Grill. 123 Cottage Street, Bar Harbor. Telephone: (207) 288–3884. There's nothing bristly about the deftly prepared New American food at Porcupine, where the flavors are bold and the prices are reasonable. Least expensive are the pasta dishes. Dinner. Moderate to expensive.

West Street Cafe. West and Rodick Streets, Bar Harbor. Telephone: (207) 288–5242. The look is slicker than the execution, which is fairly old-school Maine. But West Street always offers a great package price on the quintessential Downeast meal: fish chowder, french fries, lobster, and blueberry pie. Lunch and dinner. Moderate to expensive.

OTHER ATTRACTIONS

Criterion Theatre. There are rainy day matinees at 2:00 P.M. in this 1932 art deco theater—with a Dolby Stereo Surround Sound system. 35 Cottage Street, Bar Harbor. Telephone: (207) 288–3441.

Natural History Museum. The College of the Atlantic has exhibits of plant and animal life on the island and a self-guided nature trail. Turrets Building, Route 3, Bar Harbor. $2.50 adults. Open mid-June to early September daily 9:00 A.M. to 5:00 P.M., and early September to mid-October daily 10:00 A.M. to 4:00 P.M. Telephone: (207) 288–5015.

St. Saviour's Church. This Episcopal Church, the oldest, largest, and tallest public building on Mount Desert Island, was completed in 1878. It has forty-two beautiful stained-glass windows covering more than a century of craftsmanship (1886–1992), including ten windows by Louis Comfort Tiffany. Free tours daily in July and August and year-round by request. 41 Mount Desert Street, Bar Harbor. Telephone: (207) 288–4215.

ACTIVITIES

Acadia Bike & Coastal Kayaking. For independent exploring, this shop rents mountain bikes, local Old Town canoes, and touring kayaks. They also offer a guided sunrise bicycle descent of Cadillac Mountain and guided sea kayak tours. 48 Cottage Street, Bar Harbor. Telephone: (207) 288–9605 or (800) 526–8615.

Bar Harbor Bicycle Shop. Rents mountain bikes and accessories. 141 Cottage Street, Bar Harbor. Telephone: (207) 288–3886.

Beal & Bunker. This family-run operation has been providing year-round mail boat ferry service to the five Cranberry Isles for more than forty years and stops at Great Cranberry, Islesford (also called Little Cranberry), and Sutton (summer only). Most island residents make their living by lobster fishing or boat building and repair. Islesford is also the summer home of a number of artists and craftspeople. $10. Municipal Pier, Northeast Harbor. Telephone: (207) 244–3575.

Harbor Boat Rentals. If you've a hankering to do a little inshore fishing, head here to rent a 13- or 17-foot Boston whaler. 1 West Street, Bar Harbor. Telephone: (207) 288–3757.

Historic Vessels. Offers morning, afternoon, or sunset sails aboard the *Margaret Todd,* a 151-foot four-masted schooner (the first four-master to sail in Maine in more than fifty years); *Young America,* a 130-foot topsail schooner that replicates a nineteenth-century merchant sailing vessel; or the 84-foot *Sylvina W. Beal,* which was built in 1911 and worked as a fishing vessel until 1980. Prices begin at $20 for adults. Bar Harbor Inn Pier, Bar Harbor. Telephone: (207) 288–4585 or (207) 288–2373.

The Islesford Ferry Company. This service has also been operating for more than forty years and offers several cruise options including a scenic island cruise with a lunch stopover on Little Cranberry Island or a cruise to Baker Island narrated by a naturalist from Acadia National Park. Adults $11. Town Marina, Northeast Harbor. Telephone: (207) 276–3717.

National Park Sea Kayak Tours. This operation enjoys introducing people to the sport of kayaking with small group tours in stable and comfortable two-person kayaks. 137 Cottage Street, Bar Harbor. Telephone: (207) 288–0342.

Sea Princess Cruises. Cruise choices include a morning cruise of the Great Harbor and Somes Sound and a shorter, late-afternoon cruise in Somes Sound alone. All the trips emphasize wildlife and geology and always have a naturalist on board, including some from Acadia National Park. Cruises start at $12 for adults. Town Marina, Northeast Harbor. Telephone: (207) 276–5352.

Whale Watcher, Inc. Offers nature cruises for eagles, porpoises, seals, and other marine mammals, and birds; whale watching cruises, and sails aboard the 85-foot schooner *Bay Lady.* Prices begin at $15 for adults. Corner of West and Main Streets, next to Town Pier, Bar Harbor. Telephone: (207) 288–3322.

TOURS

Bus Tours. Jolly Roger's Trolley passes some of the mansions and takes in the Cadillac Mountain summit in a one-hour tour. Adults $10. The 2.5-hour National Park Bus Tour can cover more of the highlights of Acadia. Tickets are sold at Testa's Restaurant, 53 Main Street, Bar Harbor. If you have your own vehicle, you're better off with the Acadia Tape Tour.

Down East Nature Tours. Birdwatching tours at different proficiency levels are led by naturalists who are also familiar with local flora. Telephone: (207) 288–8128.

A Step Back in Time. One-hour walking tours of the downtown Bar Harbor area are led by guides in Victorian-era costumes who will regale you with tales of Bar Harbor at the turn of the century, when it was the most exclusive resort in the world. $10 adults. Purchase tickets at Acadia Bike and Canoe, 48 Cottage Street or Acadia Outfitters, 106 Cottage Street, Bar Harbor. Telephone: (207) 288–9605.

FAIRS, FESTIVALS, AND EVENTS

Arcady Music Festival. The College of the Atlantic in Bar Harbor is one venue for a performance series that ranges from Renaissance rondos to ragtime and runs from mid- to late-August. Telephone: (207) 288–3151.

Bar Harbor Music Festival. Bar Harbor Congregational Church is the primary location for a variety of musical events from string orchestra to jazz and pops. But there's also a tea concert at Breakwater 1904 mansion and a free concert at Blackwoods Campground Amphitheatre at Acadia National Park. Events take place from early July to early August. Telephone: (207) 288–5744 (July and August), (212) 222–1026 (year-round).

Mount Desert Festival of Chamber Music. National and international artists perform chamber music concerts on Tuesday evenings in July and August at the Neighborhood House, a restored historic building with excellent acoustics. Main Street, Northeast Harbor. Telephone: (207) 276–3988 or (207) 288–4144.

SHOPPING

Acadia Outfitters. 45 Main Street, Bar Harbor. Telephone: (207) 288–5592. This downtown shop has a full and well-priced line of outdoor gear. If you forgot to buy something at L.L. Bean, you can probably find it here.

Sherman's Books & Stationery. 56 Main Street, Bar Harbor. Telephone: (207) 288–3161. Local-interest books published by limited-distribution publishers are one of the great strengths of Sherman's, which is an old-fashioned bookstore combined with an old-fashioned stationer's.

Acadia National Park

Acadia National Park Headquarters, on Route 233 near the northern edge of Eagle Lake, serves as the park's visitor center from November through April. For advance information, contact P.O. Box 177, Bar Harbor, ME 04609. Telephone: (207) 288–3338.

Hulls Cove Visitor Center, just off Route 3 at the head of Park Loop Road, is open during the busy season. To help visitors get the most from this extraordinary natural site, there is an introductory film, maps of roads and trails, and full schedule of ranger-led programs. Stickers to indicate you've paid your park usage fee can be obtained here. Automobile passes are $5 per day, $10 for four days or $20 for the year. Four-day passes for cyclists and pedestrians are $3. General park information: (207) 288–3338.

CAMPGROUNDS

There are more than 500 woodland campsites in Acadia National Park, but no RV hookups. **Blackwoods Campground,** six miles east of Bar Harbor on Route 3, has 310 sites, which must be reserved in advance from mid-June through mid-September by telephone only. Contact Destinet at (800) 365–2267. The 200-plus sites at **Seawall Campground,** four miles south of Southwest Harbor on Route 102A, are offered on a first-come, first-served basis.

FOOD

Jordan Pond House. Park Loop Road. Telephone: (207) 276–3316. It's a classic experience to have afternoon tea and popovers on the lawn of the Pond House while enjoying the view of the pond itself. Lunch, tea, and dinner. Inexpensive to moderate.

ACTIVITIES

Acadia Tape Tour. This is a much better option for overview touring of Acadia than any of the bus tours. The tape gives directions for a 56-mile driving tour of Park Loop Road in Acadia National Park and Northeast Harbor and enables you to proceed at your own pace. Available at Hulls Cove Visitor Center for rental or purchase.

Ranger Programs. The Beaver Log publishes a full schedule of free ranger-led programs, including nature walks, more strenuous hikes, and evening programs in outdoor amphitheaters at both campgrounds. In addition, a variety of bus tours and sea cruises are available for fees ranging from $7.00 to $20.00. These programs are without question the best way to learn about the unique history, geology, flora, and fauna of Acadia. Telephone: (207) 288–5262 for information and reservations.

Blueberry Country, Maine

For information on Machias, contact the Machias Bay Area Chamber of Commerce, Route 1, 23 East Main Street, Machias, ME 04654. Telephone: (207) 255–4402.

LODGING

Bayviews Bed and Breakfast. 6 Monument Street, Lubec. This restored 1894 Victorian home is within walking distance of Campobello Island and has great views of the bay that can be enjoyed from the deck, the lawn, or a hammock. Because proprietor Kathryn Rubeor lives in Manhattan during the school year, where she teaches art in Chinatown, the B&B is only open July through Labor Day. The public areas and four guest rooms are full of antiques and collectibles assembled with an artist's eye. Maine is a great place for antiques hunting and you might very well get the bug from Kathryn if you don't have it already. Telephone: (207) 733–2181. Inexpensive with breakfast.

The Bluff House Inn. Route 186, South Gouldsboro. Perched above Frenchman Bay, this eight-room inn has a panoramic view that includes spectacular sunsets. It's a good base for exploring Schoodic Peninsula, the less visited part of Acadia National Park, and for those who are interested in hiking or kayaking or canoeing (you can launch your craft from the shore of the inn). Telephone: (207) 963–7805. Inexpensive with breakfast.

Riverside Inn & Restaurant. Route 1, Machias. This restored sea captain's home on the banks of the East Machias River holds two guest rooms, with two more in the carriage house. No smoking. Telephone: (207) 255–4134. Inexpensive to moderate with breakfast.

OTHER ATTRACTIONS

Historic Ruggles House. This 1818 house has little changed over the years. It's especially fortunate that the beautiful handcarved moldings and graceful flying staircase have been preserved. The work is of such skill and delicacy that villagers were said to have believed that the carver's knife was guided by the hand of an angel. Open June through mid-October, Monday through Saturday from 9:30 A.M. to 4:30 P.M., Sunday from 11:00 A.M. to 4:30 P.M. Donation. Main Street, Columbia Falls. No telephone.

ACTIVITIES

Tidal Trails Eco-tours. Dedicated to helping people explore and appreciate the hundreds of miles of shoreline of the Cobscook and Passamaquoddy bay area, Registered Maine Guides lead a variety of tours ranging from whale watching and canoeing to tide pool biology and charter fishing. They also rent sea kayaks, canoes, mountain bikes, and clam gear. Local gossip and fish tales are free. Leighton Point Road, Pembroke. Telephone: (207) 726–4799.

**Flying Staircase,
Thomas Ruggles House, Columbia Falls, Maine**

FAIRS, FESTIVALS, AND EVENTS

Wild Blueberry Festival. Machias is the shire town of blueberry country and the site of the first naval battle of the American Revolution, both of which are honored in this two-day festival in mid-August. In addition to numerous blueberry eating opportunities, a craft fair, fish fry, and rubber duck race, the original musical, *Red, White and Blueberry* is performed. Telephone: (207) 255–4402.

SHOPPING

Columbia Falls Pottery. Main Street, Columbia Falls. Telephone: (207) 483–4075 or (800) 235–2512. A restored 1865 country store is the studio and showroom for the work of Columbia Falls Pottery. Their location off the beaten path in a small town (population 525) gives the artists plenty of time to appreciate Maine's natural beauty—look for lupine, blueberry, or beach rose designs painted by hand on a variety of functional objects.

5·Up Country

Introduction

This chapter deals with three separate mountain groups—the White Mountains of New Hampshire (and Maine), the Green Mountains of Vermont, and the Berkshire Hills of western Massachusetts. We admit that these New England peaks aren't as towering and majestic as the Rockies, but they have an undeniable drama as they rise abruptly from near sea level. It's little wonder that they have been the subject of some of the most purple prose ever penned about the sublime beauties of Nature. Moreover, the mountains loom large in New England culture and history, attracting some of the earliest tourists and, later, wealthy rusticators, and providing the topography that launched downhill and cross-country skiing in the United States.

What they might lack in stature, our mountains make up for in age. They are millions of years older than the brash peaks of the American West. Most of the rocks of New England's western mountains are at least 600 million years old. At that time, the Taconic range of the Berkshire Hills and both eastern and western forks of the Green Mountains were the shallows near the shore of a warm sea. The lapping of ocean waves broke up rocks and pebbles into sand, which built up in layers to become compressed into sandstone. Coral beds formed in the ancient seas and as these marine animals died, their shells became limestone.

This seashore was crunched about 500 million years ago during the Taconic Orogeny (a word geologists use to describe mountain-building events). When continental plates collide, their edges crumple like an automobile fender in a traffic accident. In the Taconic Orogeny, the continents that would become northern Europe and North America collided, causing highlands to rise at the margins. The pressure of land masses hitting each other squeezed some rocks, turning limestone into marble in the Green Mountains and into quartzite in the Berkshires. These highlands once rose 25,000 feet or more, but almost immediately, wind and weather began to cut them down, washing their lofty tops down the western slopes to fill the murky swamps of what would become the Midwest.

As the proto-continents receded from each other after the collision, their movements opened the floor of the ocean between them—the area that would eventually become the Atlantic Ocean. Magma swelled from the center of the planet, in most cases halting before it reached the open air as lava. Cooling slowly under pressure for thousands of years—plenty of time to form crystal patterns—it solidified as granite. The magma that reached the surface formed basalt, the nearly black and featureless rock so familiar in New England.

The White Mountains are a little younger than the Green Mountains or the Berkshires. About 400 million years ago, North America and North Africa bounced against each other in what scientists call the Acadian Orogeny, pulling apart from each other about 200 million years ago. Again, the rocks of the ocean floor were buckled and compressed and lifted up—raising those igneous rocks of the ocean floor to the towering heights of the White Mountains.

That's why you'll find very different kinds of rocks in the mountains of western New England and in the mountains of eastern New England. Rocks throughout the Berkshires and much of the Green Mountains tend to be sedimentary. They are shales and sandstone, limestone and marble. As such, they support slightly different flora because the soil is more alkaline than the rest of New England. Great fern colonies are found in the Berkshires, for example.

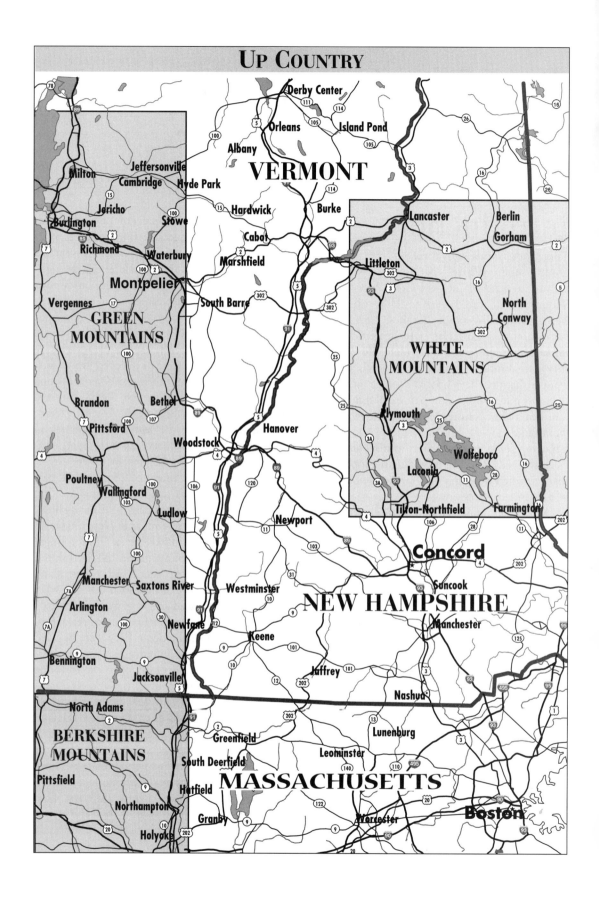

UP COUNTRY

VERMONT

Derby Center · Orleans · Island Pond
Albany
Jeffersonville · Hyde Park
Milton · Cambridge
Jericho · Hardwick · Burke
Burlington · Stowe
Richmond · Waterbury · Cabot · Lancaster · Berlin · Gorham
Montpelier · Marshfield · Littleton
Vergennes · South Barre · North Conway

GREEN MOUNTAINS

WHITE MOUNTAINS

Brandon · Bethel
Pittsford · Hanover · Plymouth
Woodstock · Wolfeboro
Poultney · Laconia
Wallingford · Tilton-Northfield · Farmington
Ludlow · Newport

Concord

Manchester · Saxtons River · Westminster · **NEW HAMPSHIRE** · Suncook
Arlington · Manchester
Newfane · Keene
Bennington · Jaffrey
Jacksonville · Nashua

North Adams · Lunenburg
BERKSHIRE MOUNTAINS · Greenfield · Leominster
South Deerfield
Pittsfield · Hatfield · **MASSACHUSETTS** · Boston
Northampton · Granby · Worcester
Holyoke

The rocks of the White Mountains and the highlands that continue up into central Maine are mostly igneous rocks—granite, basalt, feldspar, even some flint and the volcanic glass known as obsidian. The soils are highly acidic, best suited to evergreen conifers, and because the rocks are harder than those farther west, the landscape is more jagged.

In both cases, the rocks have been eroded over eons and were finally polished clean and smooth by the glaciers that retreated less than 15,000 years ago, leaving behind the rounded mountains and hills we see today. But for picturesque beauty and the fascination of human history, the allure of New England's Up Country is as old as the hills.

Seeing Up Country

New Hampshire's White Mountains

The White Mountains are one of New England's most prominent geological features. They are visible on a clear day from the tip of Cape Cod, from the hilly neighborhoods of Portland, Maine—even from western Vermont. Out at sea, they are a beacon of landfall: In 1508, when explorer Giovanni da Verrazano sailed off what would be later named the New Hampshire coast, he recorded seeing "high mountains within the land."

He probably sighted the so-called Presidential Range, the central and highest section of the White Mountains. The Whites are relatively stunted compared to the Rocky Mountains, having endured an additional 260 million years of erosion. But they are the highest peaks in New England and the highest in the Appalachian chain north of the juncture of North Carolina and Tennessee. Their grandeur—and their visibility—results from rising so abruptly from the land around them. Mount Washington, for example, measures more than 5,000 feet from base to summit. Most of the White Mountains rise from a base between 500 and 1,000 feet above sea level. Eight are more than a mile high, and another twenty-two rise more than 4,000 feet above sea level. Providing passage between ridges and peaks are some nine "notches," as New Englanders call the deep defiles often known as "gaps" in other American mountain ranges.

All in all, the White Mountain range covers an area of more than 1,200 square miles, mostly in north-central New Hampshire but with some spillage into western Maine. Most of the mountain group lies within the boundaries of the 773,000-acre White Mountain National Forest created in 1911 to preserve and manage a semi-wilderness of forested hillsides, more than one hundred waterfalls, dozens of remote lakes, and hundreds of miles of small brooks and streams. An elaborate network of recreational hiking trails, the oldest dating from 1819 and many others from the late nineteenth century, weaves throughout the region.

Native and English names are in accord about the range. The Algonquian speakers of the region referred to the mountain range as Waumbek Methna, or White Rocks, and the Englishmen followed suit, observing that from a distance, the mountains gleam white against the sky.

Early Colonial sources claimed that the tribes

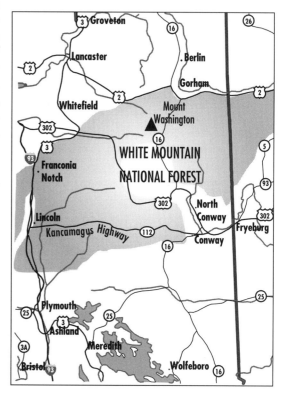

The White Mountains

**Foliage in the White Mountains. Sugar Maple (1);
red maple (2); striped maple (3); large toothed
aspen (4); pin cherry (5); yellow birch (6); Northern
red oak (7); sumac (8); basswood (9); American
mountain ash (10); American beech (11);
witch hazel (12); speckled alder (13);
white birch (14); white ash (15); tupelo (16);
quaking aspen (17).**

rarely ventured into the mountains. According to John Josselyn, writing in 1672 in *New England Rarities Discovered,* "These martial tribes of hardy and adventurous men lived for ages within sight of the mountains and within a day's march of the deer-hunting glens and teeming brooks, but were restrained from visiting them by the ineffable awe which taught them to believe that such visits would be invasions of the shrine of the Great Spirit." Josselyn went on to suggest that warriors who actually went into the White Mountains would be doomed to wander forever "among the gloomy ravines, whence their despairing shrieks were borne from time to time to the valleys on the wings of stormy winds." While there's no doubt that these peaks are awe-inspiring, archaeological

excavations of campsites and tool-making sites call Josselyn's theories into question.

In practice, touring the White Mountains means visiting the New Hampshire towns along the roads that encircle the White Mountain National Forest. Route 16 runs along the eastern edge of the forest between Conway and Gorham. Route 3 and I–93 run along the western edge between Thornton on the south and Bethlehem on the north. The two sides are connected by three east-west routes: Route 2 north of the mountains between Gorham and Lancaster, Route 302 through Crawford Notch between Glen and Bethlehem, and Route 112 (the Kancamagus Highway) through the forest's southern flank between Conway and Lincoln. The far eastern flank of the White Mountains (and 50,000 acres of the White Mountain National Forest) lies over the border in the state of Maine, accessed most easily by a loop that extends east from Gorham, New Hampshire, on Route 2 for 12 miles to Gilead, Maine. Route 2 goes another 10 miles to Bethel, Maine. Or, at Gilead, Route 113 (the Evans Notch Road) goes south for 31 miles to Fryeburg, Maine, where Route 302 connects westward to Conway, New Hampshire. Route 113 is closed during the winter due to the difficulty of maintaining this remote mountain road.

Mount Washington, New Hampshire

Just as the White Mountains are the greatest of the New England highlands, Mount Washington is far and away the grandest of the Whites. At an elevation of 6,228 feet, it stands head and shoulders above its fellows in the Presidential Range. Any rock so prominent on the horizon was bound to attract the attention of adventurers, so it's not surprising that Mount Washington was one of the first major peaks scaled in New England. In late spring of 1642, Darby Field of the settlement of Pascataquack (now Exeter, New Hampshire) was led by two Pequawket Indian guides to the summit, apparently to search for precious gemstones on what he called "Chrystall Hills."

According to an entry in the journal of Massachusetts Bay Colony Governor John Winthrop, Field's journey took eighteen days.

The escapade inspired two magistrates from Maine, Thomas Gorges and Richard Vines, to follow his example. They sped up the process by canoeing up the Saco River and climbing from there, reaching the summit in August. These two great adventures seem to have satisfied Colonial curiosity about Mount Washington, and the records show no organized visits until 1725, when Colonial bounty hunters who had come looking for scalps touched off a brief frontier war.

But water power and the lure of timber eventually drew colonists inland. And the beckoning peak of Mount Washington (still unnamed) drew their attention. In 1765, Conway, New Hampshire, became the first town in the mountain region to gain a charter.

More than two centuries later, **Conway** and its former north village, **North Conway,** serve as the gateways to the eastern end of the White Mountains heading north on Route 16. At Conway you can opt to go west toward Franconia on the scenic Kancamagus Highway (see below) or continue north on Route 16 to the most developed and best known section of the White Mountains. North Conway anchors the Mount Washington Valley with its clutch of lodgings, restaurants, and bars. Route 16 is lined with factory outlet stores and the old railroad station is headquarters for the **Conway Scenic Railroad,** a particularly charming way to view foliage (see "Staying There").

In **Glen,** just north of North Conway, the northern route branches to go around Mount Washington through two different mountain passes: **Crawford Notch** to the west (Route 302) and **Pinkham Notch** to the east (Route 16). Both notches link the north country to the seacoast, and both offer approaches to the summit of Mount Washington. As such strategic points, Crawford and Pinkham notches were sites of intensive development from the earliest years of settlement.

Crawford Notch and the Cog Railway

Crawford Notch, well known by the tribes who hunted these mountains, was discovered by white hunter Timothy Nash in 1771 when he climbed a tree to look for a moose he had wounded. He made his way through the notch from the north and proceeded to Portsmouth, where he informed Governor John Wentworth of his discovery.

A decade later, Abel Crawford and his family built a house near what is now the town of Fabyan and became the first European settlers in the notch area. Crawford soon sold the property to his father-in-law, Eleazar Rosebrook, and moved 12 miles farther south. In 1803 when the New Hampshire Turnpike was chartered to build a commercial road between the coast and the north country, Rosebrook built a two-story house with lodgings for travelers—the first hotel in the White Mountains.

Rosebrook died in 1817 and his property passed to Abel Crawford's older son, Ethan Allen Crawford, a nearly mythical figure in White Mountain lore. Ethan certainly looked the part. Nathaniel Hawthorne described him as "a sturdy mountaineer of six feet two and corresponding bulk, with a heavy set of features such as might be molded on his own blacksmith's anvil, but yet indicative of mother-wit and rough humor."

But he more than earned his fame—channeling his considerable energy into opening the White Mountains to visitors. In 1819, Ethan Allen Crawford, helped by his father Abel, cut the first walking trail to the summit of Mount Washington. The following year, Ethan improved his trail and constructed a bridle path most of the way to the summit. Called the Crawford Path, it's the oldest continuously used recreational trail in the country and the only tangible reminder of Crawford's entrepreneurial activities. It leaves from the Appalachian Mountain Club (AMC) Information Center just north of Crawford Notch State Park and ventures eight sometimes difficult miles to the summit.

About the same time, Abel opened an inn at Crawford Notch to provide overnight lodging and meals to the teamsters who were driving freight between the coast and the north country. The Crawfords soon discovered that a notable portion of their trade consisted not of rough teamsters but of genteel tourists—the pioneers of recreational mountain climbing in America—and, over the years, they constructed a succession of evergrander hotels to serve this new trade. (The shuttered and decaying Crawford House on Route 302 is an 1859 incarnation erected by Colonel Cyrus Eastman after the Crawfords were out of the tourism business.)

By 1827 Ethan was advertising lodgings and guide services in the Boston and New York papers. By 1832, when Nathaniel Hawthorne came through to write a sketch for *New-England Magazine,* the Crawfords' inn was a de rigueur stop for scenic tourists. Hawthorne noted among his fellow guests a doctor, a geologist, two newly-wed couples from Massachusetts, a pair of gentlemen from Georgia, and a young man with opera glasses and a penchant for spouting Byronic verse about the glories of mountain landscape. The Crawfords' guest books also record many luminaries of the age, among them Ralph Waldo Emerson, Henry David Thoreau, Charles Sumner, James Russell Lowell, and Washington Irving.

Other hotels sprang up on the west slope and the tourism business took off—making Mount Washington second only to Niagara Falls as a natural wonder that every well-bred American was expected to see. By 1850, the golden age of White Mountain tourism and hotel-building had begun. Construction raged for half a century. By 1900 there were more accommodations for travelers to the White Mountains than there are today—even the smallest community had at least fifty rooms. Only the last of the grand dames among White Mountain resorts, the **Mount Washington Hotel,** constructed in 1902, stands in fully restored glory as a reminder of those halcyon days. (See "Staying There.")

A large stretch of Route 302, the road that passes through Crawford Notch, became **Crawford Notch State Park** in the 1920s, and just north of the park the Appalachian Mountain Club maintains an information center as well as its dormitory-style Crawford Hut (see "Staying There"). Several hiking trails leave from the headquarters parking lot and the AMC can offer advice and printed guides about others. About 3.5 miles south of park headquarters is a parking lot for the **Arethusa Falls Trail**—a popular and relatively easy (but steep) walk of about a mile and a quarter into the woods to one of the highest waterfalls in the Northeast—about 200 feet.

The Crawford family may have opened Mount Washington for hikers, but it lay to Sylvester Marsh to combine technology and tourism to bring the masses to the mountain. Enamored of the views when he climbed Mount Washington in 1852, Marsh hatched the idea of building a cog railway to the summit and in 1858 presented a small working model to the New Hampshire Legislature, at which point one legislator is said to have cracked that he might as well build a railroad to the moon. The Civil War intervened before he could begin construction, but by 1866 Marsh had an engine and base station ready and over the next three years built the rail line all the way to the summit.

When Marsh's first train arrived at the summit on July 3, 1869, he had accomplished what was deemed impossible. The mechanics are brilliantly simple: The engines always stay on the downhill side of the cars, pushing them up the mountain and slowing their descent. The key to the system is that the wheels are locked to a gear system in the rails—a straightforward but effective way to guarantee traction and control speed. Indeed, Marsh's innovation served as the model for Swiss engineers who built cog railways in the Alps.

Other than adding double cogs to the engine wheels, little has changed about the **Mount Washington Cog Railway** since. It still operates from early May through October, taking about seventy-five minutes to climb 3,700 feet over 3.2 miles of track from the base station to the summit. The average grade is 25 percent, but at the steepest point, Jacob's Ladder, it is more than 37 percent. Fares begin at $21 and advance reservations are usually necessary. The access road is at Fabyans Station, Route 302, Bretton Woods. Telephone: (603) 278–5404, or (800) 922–8825.

By 1875 the long-distance rail lines had converged on the west side of Mount Washington at Fabyans and a year later, the Boston, Concord and Montreal built a spur from Fabyans to within a half mile of the Cog Railway base station. Marsh promptly extended his railway to meet it, and for many years thereafter it was possible to board a train in Boston and travel by rail to the summit of Mount Washington.

The Mount Washington Cog Railway, New Hampshire

Pinkham Notch and the Auto Road

Although Route 302 is heavily traveled for sightseeing, the main modern route through the White Mountains remains Route 16, which goes up the east side of Mount Washington through Pinkham Notch. **Gorham,** at the head of the notch, was granted in 1771 as the "Shelburne Addition" when the recipients of the original Shelburne grant complained that their land was untillable. At the confluence of the Peabody and Androscoggin Rivers, Gorham lay at the northern end of the valley that extended southward through Pinkham Notch. Road construction through this wilderness began in 1774 and in 1778, Benjamin Copp and his family pioneered the region, settling in what would

become the town of Jackson. The Copps were joined in 1790 by Joseph Pinkham and his family. The notch was ultimately named for Joseph's son Daniel. Legend has it that the Pinkhams brought in their worldly goods during the winter of 1790 on a sled pulled by a trained pig.

The eastern side of Mount Washington got a jump on mass development when the Atlantic & St. Lawrence railroad began passenger service to Gorham in 1851. Hotels sprang up through the valley southward to **Glen,** which quickly became a resort area to rival Crawford Notch on the other side of Mount Washington. Sensing a potential bonanza, in 1853 a group of investors formed to build a carriage road to the summit of Mount Washington. They went bankrupt, but their successors opened the Carriage Road on August 8, 1861. On opening day, some 200 people reached the summit and watched as a six-pound cannon was fired to celebrate the occasion.

It was the world's first mountain toll road—charging two cents per mile for walkers, three cents per mile for travel on horseback, and five cents per mile for each person in a carriage. The eight-mile-long road rises 4,600 feet, with average grade of 12 percent.

The first motorized ascent of the toll road came on August 31, 1899, when F.O. Stanley (of the famous twin inventors) and his wife, then residents of Newton, Massachusetts, drove all the way up in a steam-powered Locomobile, the Stanley Steamer not having yet come to market. (It may have been the last time a car going up the road didn't have to worry about overheating.) In 1908, the Carriage Road was finally opened to automobiles.

Nicely paved and well maintained, the road still functions as the **Mount Washington Auto Road.** It is open to private cars from 7:30 A.M. to 6:00 P.M. during the summer, with shorter hours in the spring and fall. (The season, weather permitting, runs from mid-May until late October.) The rates have risen a bit: They are now $15 for vehicle and driver plus $6.00 for each adult passenger. Plan on driving in low gear and allow a half hour to forty minutes going each way. There are many turnoffs along the road to get water for overheated radiators. The drive is taxing to many vehicles, hence the souvenir bumper sticker, "This

Car Climbed Mt. Washington." If you'd rather not drive, guided tours in vans are also available from 8:30 A.M. until 5:00 P.M. for $20 per adult. The guided trip is about an hour and a half, including a half hour at the summit. Route 16, Glen. Telephone: (603) 466–3988.

A few miles south of the entrance to the Auto Road on Route 16 is the **Pinkham Notch Scenic Area** visitors center, operated by the Appalachian Mountain Club (AMC). The center offers weather and hiking trail information all year round and operates free guided walks and evening lectures in the summer. Telephone: (603) 466–2721. A handout from the USDA Forest Service available here outlines several short hikes suitable for families with small children. Most take less than one hour roundtrip. Among the highlights are routes to three different waterfalls, a walk through the woods to a beaver pond, and a trail that winds to the top of a rocky ledge with spectacular views of Mount Washington and Pinkham Notch. Trails leave from the AMC parking lot or from nearby parking areas.

One of these, the **Tuckerman Ravine Trail,** is a huge draw in the spring for daredevil skiers. The large glacial cirque, or bowl, on the southeast side of Mount Washington, fills up with snow driven off the mountain by fierce winter winds. Since 1926, expert skiers with a death wish (someone dies here almost every year) have hiked their way to the top—a rise of 4,200 feet—and skied down the steep (35 to 55 degree pitch) run. The prime skiing season for the ravine is late March into May, although skiers have been known to venture the icy run into July. Because the cirque lies in shade most of the day, snow lingers into September—a hint of the next glaciation to come.

The **Wildcat Mountain Gondola Tramway** also has its base on Route 16 in Pinkham Notch. These two-passenger gondolas take about twelve minutes to climb 4,010 feet to the summit of Wildcat, east of Mount Washington, where there is excellent winter skiing from November until May and excellent hiking from June into October. From Memorial Day until mid-June the tramway is open for sightseeing from 10:00 A.M. until 4:45 P.M. on weekends only; from mid-June through October it keeps the same hours daily; adult fare is $9.00.

The Summit of Mount Washington

If you're traveling by car or railway to the summit of Mount Washington, plan to bring a warm jacket or sweater—even in the middle of the summer. (Hikers need much more gear and should consult the AMC or Forest Service rangers before setting out.) The record high temperature is a modest 72 degrees Fahrenheit, recorded in August 1975, and conditions at the summit differ radically from those in the valley below. On one of our visits on a beautiful day in early October, temperatures hovered between the upper 50s and low 60s at the base of the mountain, but only reached the low 40s at the summit. At the same time, winds ranged from five to fifteen miles per hour in the valley, but gusted from thirty to fifty miles per hour at the peak.

Although Darby Field climbed Mount Washington in 1642, the summit was little visited until after the American Revolution. In 1784 the Reverend Dr. Jeremy Belknap of Dover, New Hampshire, and the Reverend Manesseh Cutler of Ipswich, Massachusetts, led the first "scientific" expedition to the summit. Belknap never made it to the top, but Cutler and several others did, making quick observations before fog closed in around them. Cutler's drawings and descriptions of alpine plants found on Mount Washington were for many years the standard scientific reference. In the ensuing decades a number of natural historians followed, including Dr. Jacob Bigelow, Francis Boott, William Oakes, and Edward Tuckerman—all of whom have geographical features named for them.

Their interest is understandable since the White Mountains comprise an ecological zone unique in New England, particularly the upper elevations where plants are closely related to species found in arctic regions farther north. Some seventy-five higher plant species (along with mosses and lichens) are found in the alpine zone (4,800–5,200 feet above sea level), including several known to live only in this area. The alpine species—small plants with relatively large flowers—bloom predominantly from early June to early July while snow still fills some of the ravines and covers the easterly slopes. The Mount

Washington Auto Road provides especially good access to many bloom areas.

Beginning with the first Summit House in 1852, a succession of hotels and other lodgings were erected at the summit of Mount Washington. So popular was mountain tourism that the summit became known as "City Among the Clouds." But that all changed in June 1908, when fire scoured the summit clean of human interlopers, leaving only the remote hotel known as the **Tip Top House.** Built in 1853 and recently restored, it's the only structure on the summit that dates to frontier days.

The **Sherman Adams Summit Building,** which opened in 1980, promises to be the most long-lasting of summit buildings. Its massive steel and concrete frame (more like a bridge than a dwelling) is set into the north side of the mountain just below the summit. Engineering specifications call for it to withstand winds up to 250 miles per hour. The building is open from Memorial Day to Columbus Day daily from 8:00 A.M. to 8:00 P.M., weather permitting. (See "Staying There" for winter tours to the summit.) Designed to serve both hardy trekkers on the Appalachian Trail as well as more casual visitors, the Adams Building houses an information center, restrooms, a cafeteria, a gift shop, first aid room, a post office (Mt. Washington, 03589), as well as separate restroom and packroom facilities for hikers.

Cool temperatures and the mountain's position at the convergence of weather systems combine to envelop the summit with fog—actually, clouds—about 60 percent of the time. But weather changes frequently, with fog dissipating or settling in within minutes. When the weather cooperates, there are superb views of the northern peaks of the Presidentials through large windows on the main floor of the Adams building and from the roof. A walkway from the rooftop observation deck leads the rest of the way to Mount Washington's summit.

The west end of the Adams building houses the **Mount Washington Observatory.** Although the main quarters and observation tower are closed to the public, you can visit the small **Mount Washington Summit Museum** (adults $1.00) on the lower level that relates the moun-

tain's human and natural history through dioramas, photographs, and artifacts.

Following a tradition of meteorological observations from Mount Washington that began in 1852, the Mount Washington Observatory was established in 1932 to provide weather observations and radio communications. The Observatory has since evolved into one of the leading mountain weather stations in the world, conducting research projects for industry, federal government, and educational institutions. Over the years, Mount Washington observers have studied cosmic radiation, the physics of icing, the physical composition of clouds, and the behavior of atmospheric electricity.

They work in an extraordinary environment—often termed the most severe combination of wind, cold, and icing at any permanently inhabited place on earth. The mountain lies smack dab in the middle of one of North America's major storm tracks, where fronts coalescing on the Great Lakes, riding up the Eastern Seaboard and sliding down from the Arctic across the Laurentian shield all converge. As a result, Mount Washington records some of the most severe weather on the planet outside of the polar regions. (The record low temperature, recorded in January 1934, was 47 degrees below zero. The winter snowfall record of 566.4 inches—that's more than 47 feet—was set during the winter of 1968–69.)

Because the mountain rises steeply from the surrounding landscape, it suffers from the Bernoulli effect. As winds strike the mountain and flow up its slopes, they become compressed and speed up. The average wind speed atop Mount Washington is thirty-five miles per hour and gusts greater than one hundred miles per hour occur in every month of the year. The highest reliably measured wind gust on the planet—231 miles per hour on April 12, 1934—occurred here. (Reports of 236-mile-per-hour winds during a December 1997 typhoon in Guam were withdrawn as inaccurate by the National Weather Service.) The 1934 observation was made by using a stopwatch to count clicks transmitted by a telegraph from a heated bronze anemometer. The clicks were then calculated with a slide rule to yield the actual wind speed. The original journal entry, written by meteorologist Sal Pagliuca, notes, "'Will they believe it?' That was our first thought."

The observatory takes eight readings each day, and those who decide not to venture to the summit can listen to live weather reports each morning from radio stations WBNC-AM (1050 kHz) in Conway and WMOU-AM (1230 kHz) in Berlin.

A Sidetrip into Maine

The White Mountain National Forest continues over the state border into Maine, and the mountain ranges themselves continue well beyond the borders of the National Forest. The little village of **Bethel,** Maine, 22 miles east of Gorham, New Hampshire, on Route 2, was founded in 1774 but in more recent years has evolved into a summer and winter sporting center. Access to trails and campgrounds on the less crowded eastern portion of the National Forest makes for splendid hiking in this area. The **Evans Notch Visitor Center** of the White Mountains National Forest provides hiking maps and camping information. Telephone: (207) 824–2134.

Bethel is a splendid little New England town arranged around a classic green dominated by the Bethel Inn & Country Club. (See "Staying There.") But probably the greatest draw to Bethel is **Sunday River Ski Area and Mountain Bike Park,** where a young management trainee named Les Otten arrived in 1975. By 1980 he had bought the resort—the first acquisition in what became the ski resort empire of the American Skiing Company in the 1990s. Telephone: (207) 824–3000 or (800) 543–2754.

The **Evans Notch Road,** Route 113, is something of an antidote to the commercialization of most roads through the White Mountains. Some five campgrounds are located near the road and some last-minute tent sites tend to be available even during July and August. This deeply wooded, narrow mountain road is truly beautiful, so it's worth taking advantage of the many turnouts to simply look at the scenery. The road concludes in **Fryeburg,** where a right turn onto Main Street (Route 302) heads west to Conway, New Hampshire.

Personal Narrative:
October on the Kancamagus Highway

The US Forest Service had good reason to designate the Kancamagus Highway, the 34.5-mile stretch of Route 112 between the Saco River in Conway and the Pemigewasset River in Lincoln, as one of its "Scenic Byways." In any season it is a spectacular if sometimes curving and narrow road that rises and falls through the mountains. During the fall foliage season, the "Kanc" (as it's known locally) changes from merely spectacular to downright stunning.

While this extraordinary foliage viewing means that the Kanc gets a lot of traffic during late September and early October, a surprising number of leaf peepers simply drive straight through to hit North Conway's factory outlet stores, completing the route in 45 minutes. We choose to travel east to west and make a day of it by exploring the turnouts and trails along the route.

The Kanc is a relatively new road for New England. The first white settlers in the region came via the Swift River around 1790 and built the village of **Passaconaway,** named after "Child of the Bear," the chieftain who united seventeen tribes of central New England into the Penacook Confederacy in 1627 and ruled until his death in 1669. (The road and nearby Mount Kancamagus are named for his grandson, "Fearless One," who was the third and final sagamore of the confederacy. He ended up going to war with the English and fleeing to Quebec in 1691.) The small farming and logging community was joined to Conway by a town road in 1837. A century later, under the Civilian Conservation Corps and the Works Progress Administration, the road was extended from Passaconaway west and from Lincoln east. World War II intervened, but the sections were finally completed and opened to through traffic in 1959, although the final stages weren't paved until 1962. Lack of a viable road system during the era of New England settlement has kept the area fairly wild, although signs of long-ago logging exist all along the river. In fact, without logging, the Kancamagus would be lined entirely by a climax forest of conifers and would look the same in foliage season as during the rest of the year.

We make our way on Route 16 north from coastal New Hampshire (where it's called the Spaulding Turnpike) to Conway. At the junction with Route 112 we stop at the **White Mountain National Forest Saco Ranger District Office and Information Center.** Telephone: (603) 447–5448. We are after one of the handy folding maps of the Kancamagus Highway that names the surrounding mountain peaks and shows where the various public facilities lie. The station also sells detailed trail maps for back country hiking on the established mountain trails that cross the Kancamagus Highway. We dutifully pay $3.00 for a usage fee pass that we place on the windshield. (The permit program is on a trial run that may expire at the end of 1999.)

The road closely follows the bed of the Swift River, climbing steadily for the first six miles until it reaches the turnoff for **Covered Bridge Campground and Lower Falls.** The

Swift River has cut a narrow but deep cleft through the metamorphic rock in the 10,000 years since the glaciers receded. The Lower Falls area—really a long series of cascades—is lined with hiking paths and picnic tables on both sides. The predominant trees of this part of the Kancamagus are Norway (or swamp) maples, which turn a glorious deep red during September and October.

The effects of glaciation on the landscape are especially vivid on the **Boulder Loop Trail,** a moderately strenuous three-mile walk that climbs about 1,000 feet and takes two to two-and-a-half hours to complete. The trail leaves from the Covered Bridge Campground parking lot. Because the terrain is rocky and the footing sometimes loose, sturdy hiking boots are a definite help. The Forest Service provides a nice trail map with a series of interpretive stops.

We walk through the **Albany Covered Bridge,** constructed in 1858 and renovated in 1970. As we look out through the sides of the bridge a family that is fishing on a concrete pier near the far end takes our picture. The trail shines bright yellow ahead of us, mostly from the birch and aspen leaves, although flecks of

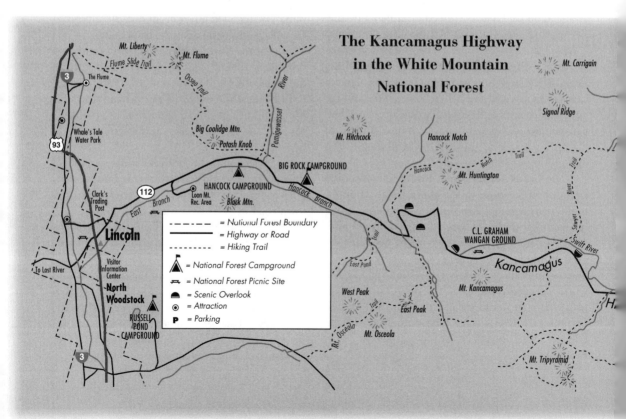

red from the leaves of scrubby pin cherry and young swamp maples also glint through. The first of eighteen marked stops quickly appears—a little nature lesson about lichens, the symbiotic colony of algae and fungus that look like dead leaves on the rocks. The fungus absorbs and stores water, which the algae processes with sunlight to make food for both plants. The fungus also secretes an acid that crumbles the surface of the rock so that the plants can hold on. Along with wind and water erosion, lichen activity has been one of the chief steps in producing soil above the barren rock in the White Mountains.

As we continue toward the Ledges, we begin to rise out of the deciduous forest into a mixed forest, where spruce trees intermingle with the birches and maples. About twenty minutes into our hike we get our first reward of an exquisite overview of the Swift River Valley and the Kancamagus Highway below. The patchwork of color sweeps down into the valley, where it is brightest yellow and orange from the maple leaves mixed with birch and beech, and up the far hillside, where we see the peaks of Blue Mountain, Three Sisters, and Mount

Chocorua in the distance.

The trail re-enters forest and continues to climb over the next twenty minutes as we approach the Ledges. As we walk down on the Ledges there is a disconcerting "hollow" sound underfoot, caused (we learn from Forest Service information) by joint fractures in the underlying bedrock. The rock offers safe footing, but we keep back from the edge of the Ledges for good reason: a 200-foot drop.

It is a quicker walk around the rest of the trail because we are heading downhill and the views are more obscured. The day is still young and we have much more to see.

We drive three more miles before stopping at the aptly named **Rocky Gorge Scenic Area** to make photographs along the stretch of falls and rapids. Granite forms a natural bridge across the river to a short, rustic wooden bridge where we gaze down into the gorge carved over the centuries by rushing water. The trail continues through a tall stand of red pine to tiny Falls Pond, where we meet an elderly man fishing for brook trout. He is not having much luck, this being the end of the season, but owns up to having caught a 12-inch trout in this pond in

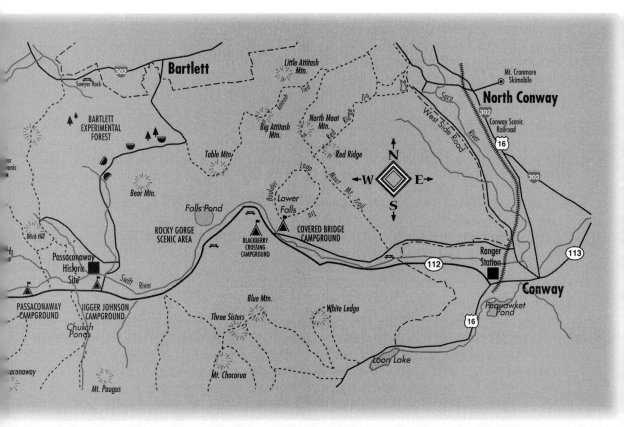

the spring. When we tell him we are playing hooky for the day to go leaf-peeping, he claims that the foliage around this pond can't hold a candle to the show the maple trees are putting on at Crystal Lake and Long Pond, both south of Conway on Route 153. We are headed the other way, so we have to take his word for it.

After driving another four and a half miles, we come to the **Russell Colbaith House,** built in the early 1800s. It is open for tours during the peak summer months but closed in October. It's the centerpiece of the **Passaconaway Historic Site,** which also has a campground and is the trailhead for hikes that can range from an hour to a day or more. Some of the foot trails have been in use since the earliest days of settlement. The easiest trail here—accessible for wheelchairs and strollers—simply goes a half mile along the river.

But we are looking for the little parking lot and picnic area on the left (south) side of the road that accesses the trail for **Sabbaday Falls.** The National Forest Service grades this trail as wheelchair accessible, but even on a perfect day when there has been no rain, the terrain is tricky for all but the most rugged chairs. We observe one family give up when they cannot push one member's chair up the grade.

The rangers advised us that the walk through the woods would be as spectacular as the falls themselves, and they are right. The trail rises a bit through deep mixed forest of pine trees, oaks and a few maples and beeches. It follows the stream at the base of the falls and we are overwhelmed with the smells of autumn—the pine scent, the rotting leaves. A steady soundtrack of rushing water completes the scene. The falls themselves are a series of granite pans where the water shoots straight out—fun to see but not as dramatic as the quaint country name led us to expect.

Finally, we make our last stop of the drive at the picnic area at **C. L. Graham Wangan Ground,** a wooded glade beside the river. The water here is shallow as it burbles over a stream bed filled with boulders and we hop from rock to rock, following the lead of several fishermen.

The highway continues to climb until it crosses the 2,860-foot **Kancamagus Pass** and begins a swift descent into the Pemigewasset River valley. Two miles from the end is **Loon Mountain Park.** Entry to the park, which has a number of displays and attractions, is free. The gondola here operates all year, providing scenic views of the White Mountains most of the year and access to ski trails in the winter. Adults $10. (See "Staying There.")

The Western Edge and Franconia Notch, New Hampshire

The Kancamagus Highway concludes at **Lincoln,** which, with its sister community across the Pemigewasset River, **North Woodstock,** serves as the southwestern gateway to the White Mountain National Forest. Travelers coming directly to this area from Boston or elsewhere in southern New England generally drive up I–93 to the Route 3 exit in North Woodstock.

Like so much of the upland interior of New England, the towns along this passage between mountain ranges were granted as payment to soldiers and officers who had fought in the French and Indian War. Thus, North Woodstock was granted in 1763 to Eli Demerit by the Colonial governor, Benning Wentworth, but not settled until the eve of the American Revolution. Franconia, farther north, was granted in 1764, but was little developed until iron ore was discovered in 1790. (The New Hampshire Iron Factory Company flourished here until the close of the Civil War.)

Between the two towns lies this area's real claim to fame—the eight-mile-long passage called **Franconia Notch** between Cannon Mountain and the Franconia Range. Known first as "Profile Notch," it was settled in the 1780s by David Guernsey (or Garnsey—sources differ in the spelling). In 1807, he and others repulsed an attack by a band of Abenaki Indians, most of whom they killed. The surviving members of the band fled north to Quebec.

Sources disagree on which white settler discovered each of the Notch's various scenic attractions, specifically the Flume and the Old Man of the Mountains, but by the early nineteenth century the area was just as established a tourist mecca as Crawford and Pinkham notches to the east. Many grand hotels—all since burned—stood along the slopes of the Notch to accommodate the annual influx of travelers determined to see what God and Nature had wrought. In fact, the writer and lecturer most responsible for popularizing the White Mountains, Boston Unitarian minister Thomas Starr King, wrote of Franconia Notch in 1860 that the region "contains more objects of interest to the mass of travelers than any other region of equal extent within the compass of the usual White Mountain tour."

Almost the entire Notch is now taken up by Franconia Notch State Park, a 6,000-acre park that was originally a commercial enterprise but was purchased over the years by the state with substantial private donations. A 10-mile, two-lane parkway, marked both as Route 3 and I–93, cuts through the middle of the park, making it possible to drive between the scenic points of interest.

The Flume, at the southern end of the Notch, is an 800-foot-long gorge of a tributary to the Pemigewasset River on the western flank of Mount Liberty. Its steep, moss-covered walls rise 90 feet in places and at some spots the gorge is a mere 12 feet wide. A sturdy boardwalk with some steep spots traverses the quarter-mile gorge. There are also two covered bridges inside the Flume. Admission to the visitor center, which is a good place to pick up information about Franconia Notch State Park and surrounding attractions, is free. It has a modest restaurant, an extensive gift shop, and a free movie that explains that the gorge, once a canyon filled with lava, was eroded away by water over the millennia. The Flume is open from mid-May until late October, daily from 9:00 A.M. until 4:30 P.M. Adult admission is $6.00. Telephone: (603) 745–8391.

A smaller version of the same geological phenomenon may be seen for free at **The Basin,** a mile and a half north of the Flume. The basin itself, reached by a short walk from the roadside parking lot, is a 30-foot-diameter glacial pothole at the bottom of a waterfall. Below the Basin, the Pemigewasset River tumbles through the Baby Flume.

Three miles north is **Profile Lake,** a small body of water once fancifully called "the Old

The Flume, Franconia Notch State Park, New Hampshire

Man's Washbowl." Profile Mountain rises almost straight up from the lake, and near its summit is the famous rock formation known variously as the **Profile, the Old Man of the Mountains, or the Great Stone Face.** Perhaps best known in the version featured on the New Hampshire license plate, the actual formation often proves disappointing to travelers who have come a great distance to see what amounts to speck of a thing 1,500 feet up the hill.

The Visitor Center for this spectacle is surrounded by a massive parking lot with many long slots for the tour buses that flock here in the fall. At the downhill corner of the lot stands a small sign with an arrow pointing to "Old Man Viewing." (Many wives photograph their husbands in front of this sign, which must be one of the most popular photo ops in the White Mountains.) The trail eventually leads to the eastern edge of Profile Lake, which indeed offers an

**Old Man of the Mountains,
Franconia, New Hampshire**

likeness on the precipice. There was the broad arch of the forehead, a hundred feet in height; the nose with its long bridge; and the vast lips, which, if they could have spoken, would have rolled their thunder accents from one end of the valley to the other."

But the most quoted observation, often attributed to Daniel Webster with slightly more mellifluous wording, appeared in 1856 in *Incidents in White Mountain History* by Benjamin Willey: "Men put out signs representing their different trades; jewelers hand out a monster watch; shoemakers, a huge boot; and, up in Franconia, God Almighty has hung out a sign that in New England He makes men."

Just a half mile north of the Old Man is the **Cannon Mountain Aerial Tramway,** where eighty-passenger gondola cars ascend 2,022 feet in just seven and one-half minutes to the Summit Observation Platform. On a clear day this aerie provides views of parts of Maine, Vermont, and even the distant Taconic range of eastern New

excellent, if distant, view of the Profile. (A 300mm or longer lens is required to produce the photograph reproduced on postcards.)

The head, which measures forty feet high, consists of five separate ledges anchored with iron pins since 1916 because the formation is crumbling away. The Profile was probably "discovered" in 1805 by two road workmen, Francis Whitcomb and Luke Brooks, who were washing their hands in the lake and looked up with astonishment to see what they perceived to be the profile of their president, Thomas Jefferson. A great deal of hyperbole attended this natural phenomenon in the nineteenth century, leading Swedish novelist Fredericka Bremer to assess it in 1851 as not quite as advertised. "It has not any nobility in its features, but resembles an old man in a bad humor and with a nightcap on his head," she wrote.

Writing from a possibly more chauvinistic perspective, Nathaniel Hawthorne described the formation in *Twice-Told Tales*: "It seemed as if an enormous giant, or Titan, had sculpted his own

**Cannon Mountain Aerial Tramway,
Franconia Notch State Park, New Hampshire**

York. During ski season the same tramway and six other lifts service the Cannon Mountain ski trails—the longest developed vertical drop in New England. (Tuckerman Ravine is even longer than Cannon's 2,146 feet, but you have to walk to the top.) Sightseeing on the tramway costs $8.00 round-trip. The tram is open daily from 9:00 A.M. until 7:00 P.M. in July and August, until 4:30 P.M. in the spring and fall.

Vermont's Green Mountains

"Vermont" literally means "green mountain," and in the Green Mountain State, geology has to a great extent, determined destiny.

The mountain chain by the same name runs from the Massachusetts border to northern Vermont on a north-south axis, with an eastern and western range from Mount Pico (east of Rutland) north. In practice, the Green Mountains divide Vermont into two valleys—the Champlain on the west and the Connecticut River on the east (covered in another chapter)—with a few high east-west mountain passes, mostly along riverbeds, between those two areas.

In the pre-contact era, the Iroquois inhabited the land west of these ranges, and the Algonquian-speaking Abenaki inhabited the lands to the east. Neither native population used the mountains for much more than hunting grounds. When English Colonists began to settle these rugged uplands after the French and Indian War, they stuck to the valleys where at least a marginal agriculture was possible. The geographic isolation fostered a spirit of independence and self-reliance that remains to this day the bedrock of Vermont character.

Once Vermont became the fourteenth state in 1791, the legislature sought to link up the two population centers. Beginning in 1796, Vermont granted monopolies to construct private turnpikes across and through the mountainous interior, but it lay to the railroads to open the Green Mountains to the outside world. When the last spike was driven in the Rutland and Burlington Railroad connecting Burlington and Boston on December 18, 1849, Green Mountain tourism was on its way, with first Camel's Hump (south of North Duxbury) and then Mount Mansfield (near Stowe) experiencing an influx of sightseers in a pattern similar to the White Mountains. "Vermont in summer" was soon touted as "the Almighty's noblest gallery of divine art."

The train hasn't been the favored mode of transportation in the Green Mountains for many years now, but travelers generally follow the old train routes—paralleling the Connecticut River on I–91 from New York, or following the Boston & Burlington tracks along I–89 from eastern New England. Ultimately, one must cross the mountains, and Montpelier, Vermont's state capital, is generally the most convenient place.

Most traditional towns and villages still lie along mountain river valleys, while development of the mountains themselves is a twentieth-century phenomenon born of the interests of mountain hikers and—to an overwhelming extent in some places—of skiers.

Montpelier, Vermont

With only 8,800 people, Montpelier is the smallest state capital, which seems fitting, since Vermont is the least populated (565,000) and most rural state in the nation. Montpelier is an unusual small town, though. Because it is the seat of government and home office of several insurance companies, it has the highest per capita population of lawyers of any municipality in the nation. A sizable percentage of its residents are also chefs, thanks in large part to the New England Culinary Institute (NECI) headquartered here.

Montpelier was a latecomer, even by Vermont standards. It wasn't organized as a town until 1791. In 1805, Montpelier beat out Burlington to serve as the state capital, in good measure because its residents were willing to donate land for the State House and help pay for its construction.

Pragmatism may have dictated the choice of Montpelier as the capital, but it was also a fine aesthetic choice. Located near the geographical center of Vermont, Montpelier is almost an ideal valley town. Wooded hills cup the village, which lies at the low spot on one of the chief east-west passes in the Green Mountains. Unlike some of the similarly sized communities farther south, Montpelier does not suffer from the New York

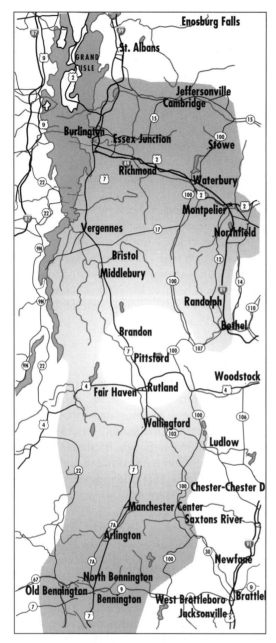

The Green Mountains

Downtown Montpelier—essentially State and Main Streets—is compact and unusually handsome. The brick buildings, most constructed in the 1870s, are finished with nice architectural details. Restaurants abound, and thanks to the presence of NECI, they are definitely a cut above the usual fare you'd expect in a city so small. "You can eat your way through this town," we have been told more than once. (See "Staying There.")

The dominant landmark of Montpelier is the **State House.** Finished in 1859, the current building is the third—two early wooden versions burned, although the granite columns on the portico date from the second incarnation. Many a Green Mountain foliage photograph features its large golden dome set against green conifers intermixed with colorful deciduous trees. The State House is open for public tours Monday through Friday from 8:00 A.M. to 4:00 P.M. It is also open Saturdays from 11:00 A.M. until 3:00 P.M. from early July until mid-October. Tours are free. Telephone: (802) 828–2228.

Inside the State House is a museum of Vermont's political and military history. The Cedar Creek Room has an enormous mural depicting a War of 1812 naval battle fought on Lake Champlain. From June through August, there are band concerts every Wednesday at 4:00 P.M. on the State House lawn.

The **Vermont Historical Society Museum,** a looming brick presence at 109 State Street near the State House, resembles an old mountain hotel. It is a treasure trove of state paraphernalia, important records, and what amount to oddities and souvenirs of Vermont's past. Photographs and historic documents vie for attention with such peculiar objects as a stuffed catamount, the once-native Vermont mountain lion, of which this example is said to be the final specimen. Because Vermonters left the state in droves in 1816, the year in which all the crops failed when a foot of snow fell in June and smaller snowstorms hit in July and August, many midwesterners can trace their family histories to Vermont. As a result, the historical society's library sees extensive use for genealogical research. The museum is open for tours Tuesday through Friday from 9:00 A.M. until 4:30 P.M., Saturday until 4:00 P.M., Sunday from noon until 4:00 P.M. Adults $2.00. Telephone: (802) 828–2291.

country gentleman syndrome. It is peopled largely by native Vermonters or folks from "away" who have assumed the protective coloration of native Vermonters. A tinge of Woodstock Nation is still discernible in the updated head shops, the emphasis on hand crafts, the vegetarian menus, and the New Age emporia, but even bohemianism has acquired an air of permanence.

Vermont State House, Montpelier

The 180-acre **Hubbard Park** rises from the downtown and creates the hillside backdrop for the State House. The park's extensive hiking trails do double duty in the winter for cross-country skiing and snowshoeing. The 50-foot stone observation tower, built in 1900, is a terrific example of late nineteenth-century thinking about landscape architecture. Its turret was left incomplete to simulate a medieval ruin and thus enhance the picturesque qualities of its setting. The observation deck commands a panoramic view over the Winooski River valley and the mountain ranges that ring Montpelier.

Mount Mansfield, Vermont

The route circles from Montpelier north to Mount Mansfield, the tallest of the Green Mountain peaks, and then southward into Stowe, the ski capital of the East. At Stowe it picks up Route 100, which runs north-south along the Green Mountain chain practically to the Massachusetts border. (An optional route continues from Waterbury to Burlington, then south through the Champlain Valley to the Massachusetts border on Route 7.)

Leaving Montpelier, continue out Elm Street on Route 12 north, following the river past its source to Morrisville, 21 miles away through a lovely, bucolic mountain valley. At Morrisville, take Route 15 west for 16 miles to Jeffersonville, a once sleepy town awakened in recent years by the extensive development of nearby **Smuggler's Notch Ski Area** (see "Staying There"). Follow the signs in Jeffersonville for Smuggler's Notch and Stowe, both of which are reached on Route 108. Fly fishermen may wish to take a few breaks in this scenic drive. The Brewster River near Jeffersonville has particularly good fishing for brown trout, while the same river about two miles farther toward Mount Mansfield (before you come to the Brewster River Gorge) is heavily populated with brook trout.

This 18-mile stretch of Route 108 between Jeffersonville and Stowe was born in 1815 as the Mansfield Turnpike but soon acquired the nickname of "Smuggler's Notch Road." Smugglers used this notch extensively during the American embargo on British trade (1807–12) to move goods between Canada and Boston. A deep cleft between Mount Mansfield and the Sterling Mountains, the notch had two advantages for clandestine trade: It lay far off the main roads watched by revenue officers and the hillsides are pocked with convenient storage caves. There are those who claim the notch reverted to its old tricks during Prohibition.

Narrow and twisting **Smuggler's Notch Road** is closed during the winter, but makes a spectacular scenic drive in every other season. The notch begins about five miles south of Jeffersonville. About three miles after passing Morse's Mill, the road begins to climb steeply. Watch for a roadside turnout where you can park and get a sense of some of the special features of this geology. A chasm on the northwest side of the turnout is sometimes called the "natural refrigerator" because the cold air issuing from it stays a constant 48 degrees even during the warmest part of the summer. Nearby is Smuggler's Cave—not so much a true cavity as a room constructed by the accidental deposition of boulders by glaciers. Other turnouts in the next mile are marked for various rock formations that someone at some point thought looked vaguely recognizable (Smuggler's Face, Singing Bird, Hunter and His Dog, etc.).

Cresting at 2,162 feet, Smuggler's Notch Pass separates two of Vermont's highest peaks, Mount Mansfield (4,393 feet) and Spruce Peak (3,320 feet). Over the crest is **Smuggler's Notch State Park.** One of Vermont's designated Natural Areas, the park is lined in places by cliffs rising 1,000 feet beside the road. Within the park it is possible to connect to the Long Trail to hike up the side of Mount Mansfield to tundra-like terrain usually associated with territory many hundreds of miles farther north. The notch is one of the prime nesting areas for the peregrine falcon, and sharp-eyed travelers may see them zooming overhead in swift and acrobatic flight. (They feed mostly on songbirds, taking their prey on the wing.)

Access to Mount Mansfield's principal summit is possible from the **Mount Mansfield Toll Road** on the Stowe side of Smuggler's Notch. Now improved to something approaching modern standards, this five-mile-long road was completed as a carriage trail to the top of Mount Mansfield in 1869. Brute force of will pushed the road through, as the terrain dictated long stretches at steep inclines across the face of mountain slopes. One 100-yard section of the road was built of logs that hung over the edge of a precipice. It was noted at the time that many a faint-hearted visitor who endured the ride never repeated it. Now covered with gravel, the present four-and-a half-mile road makes sharp, steep curves as it winds around heavily forested slopes. Be sure your vehicle is in good repair. The road is open daily from Memorial Day to Columbus Day from 10:00 A.M. until 5:00 P.M. Toll is $12 for a private car, $7.00 for a motorcycle. Telephone: (802) 253–3000.

A somewhat less harrowing way up to Mount Mansfield is to take the **Stowe Gondola,** which takes at least thirty minutes but delivers you to the summit where you can explore hiking trails. The gondola operates daily from Memorial Day until late October from 10:00 A.M. until 5:00 P.M. The round trip ticket is $9.00. Telephone: (802) 253–3000.

Mount Mansfield, it should be noted, consists of a clump of peaks on a rather sprawling mountain. Viewed from just the right angle, these peaks create a profile of a supine man's head; as a result, some of the rocky upthrusts have acquired such colorful sobriquets as the Adam's Apple, the Chin, the Nose, etc. You'll rarely hear these terms used by local residents, who simply don't see the mountain that way, but they survive on many maps.

Stowe, Vermont

As Mountain Road (Route 108) descends into Stowe, scenic vistas give way increasingly to roadside development. Stowe was promoted as early as 1859 as a premier destination for mountain sightseeing and evolved in the twentieth century as the skiing capital of the East.

Skiing was imported from Europe, and the story goes that it was first introduced in Stowe in 1912, when several Swedish families moved to town and began to use skis to get around. In 1914, the Dartmouth College librarian skied down the Mount Mansfield toll road and piqued many sportsmen's curiosity. But the sport really gained momentum in 1933 when a group of 25 men working for the Civilian Conservation Corps forged the first ski trails at Mount Mansfield State Forest. Soon after the trails were built, Stowe formed the Mount Mansfield Ski Club and by 1936 had established its own ski patrol. The following season, a rope tow powered by a Cadillac engine was rigged from the base camp to the top of the longest trail—five miles. The tow cost 50 cents per day or $5.00 per season. In 1940, Stowe introduced the first single chair lift in the United States.

Perhaps because Stowe became committed to skiing when sport, rather than real estate development, was still the point, it remains a village with deeply rooted character rather than just another ski country clone. Well equipped with small but distinctive lodgings and a fair number of surprisingly good restaurants, it makes an excellent base for outdoor activities both summer and winter.

In addition to the forty-seven slopes and trails of the Stowe Mountain Resort, the town boasts a network of more than 200 miles of cross-country ski trails. One of the most pleasant walks from spring into fall is the 5.3-mile **Stowe Recreation Path,** which follows a mountain stream from the center of the village toward Mount Mansfield. It begins behind the Stowe Community Church and passes beside fields and woodlands and even a few swimming holes. Access points are also found at Weeks Hill Road, Luce Hill Road (across from the Stonybrook condominiums), and at the trail's conclusion at Brook Road. Luce Hill Road has a parking lot. No motorized vehicles are allowed on the path, but walkers may find themselves sharing the lane with bicyclists and bladers in the summer or cross-country skiers in the winter. Snowshoers should stop by the Green Mountain Club headquarters for a list of recommended trails.

Personal Narrative: Snowshoeing in Stowe

All the money that alpine skiing has pumped into the Vermont economy tends to obscure the fact that snowshoeing was Vermont's leading winter sport until the 1930s. Now it's on the way back. Already known for its alpine skiing and, thanks to the Trapp family of *Sound of Music* fame, cross-country skiing, Stowe has also steadily developed into one of the premier snowshoeing centers.

Snowshoes became widespread in Vermont in the early 1900s as a practical means to get back uphill after sliding down on a toboggan. Vermonters developed regional snowshoe styles—one with a short tail for crossing brushy terrain, another longer-tailed version for open snowy terrain.

The Stowe-based Tubbs Snowshoe Company essentially reinvented the snowshoe in the late 1980s. By using an aluminum frame in place of bent wood and plastic decking in place of rawhide lacing, Tubbs created a snowshoe that would hold up to wet conditions and did not need constant readjustment. Crampons on the bottom made it a simple matter to go up and down hills.

Having seen these radically different snowshoes in the store, our curiosity is piqued. So we arrange to spend some time at the **Inn at Turners Mill,** run by Mitzi and Greg Speer. Greg grew up snowshoeing in Stowe, and although he enjoys alpine skiing and teaches telemark and cross-country skiing at Stowe Mountain Resort, Greg's passion remains snowshoeing. Every winter day he heads out his back door and follows Notch Brook upstream.

Greg outfits us with some Tubbs shoes (a half-day snowshoe rental comes with the lodging). When we visited the Tubbs factory, they warned us that the hardest part of snowshoeing is getting the bindings on. We definitely need some help to pull them tight across the toes and then loop the rear strap around the ankles. But the strapping provides great lateral stability, and the pivoting bindings make walking in snow almost as easy as walking on pavement. Moreover, the crampons allow us to easily go up and down grades without slipping or having to go sideways.

We quickly learn to walk normally with our legs slightly farther apart and to take short strides so that we won't step on our shoes. We also use a cross-country ski pole as a stabilizer—really, a walking stick—for steadying ourselves on grades. It takes a half mile of walking on slanted ground to learn to trust that the crampons will keep us from sliding. We learn to put more weight on the front of our feet going uphill, more on the back going downhill.

Greg gives us a lecture about our clothing, which is all of the wrong sort. He emphasizes wearing several layers of anything but cotton.

Snowshoes

The best fabric next to the skin is polypropylene fleece because it wicks away the moisture, but wool or silk will do. Waterproof boots are a good idea, especially if you go through ice into water or if the snow is wet or slushy. At any rate, warm boots are essential.

One of the nice things about snowshoeing is that the equipment requires no special treatment or technique, unlike serious cross-country skis, which should be waxed with different types of waxes depending on snow conditions. With snowshoes you end up walking on the surface of wet snow. In dry fluffy snow you sink an inch or two.

We begin by walking up Notch Brook with Greg and his Bernese mountain dog, Otto, as far as we can toward Bingham Falls. The overland distance is about a mile each way with a rise in elevation of about 500 feet. It is late in the season, so soft ice makes walking on Notch Brook too chancy. Instead we make our way through an open forest of fir, hemlock, birch, and beech trees along the banks of the brook. Our trail ranges from about 20 feet above the water to about 80 feet by the time we reach the falls.

At points we have to traverse narrow passages or cross small streams running down the hill from hillside springs. We go up and down the hillsides many times to find flat paths through the forest. Along the way we see cabins, the site of a sawmill and blacksmith shop, and several stone cellar foundations that probably were dwellings at some point. This section of Stowe was once logging country, but the forest has reclaimed the homesteads—at least until some condo developer discovers how beautiful the stream overlook can be.

It takes us about an hour and twenty minutes to reach Bingham Falls, where we are rewarded with the sight of a narrow, deep-woods cascade that drops fifty feet or more. The return trip—downhill—is even faster. Going both ways, we see deer tracks and even spot a doe and a yearling. Greg shows us where black bears have made claw marks on beech trees as they try to reach the beech nuts. Otto keeps running ahead in sheer jubilation but, like the herding animal he is, he circles back to try to move us along. We understand some of his joy because snowshoes suddenly give us access to the winter woods that would be impossible without them.

Green Mountain Club and the Long Trail

Route 108 meets Route 100 in Stowe village, and the eastern slope of the Green Mountains lies due south. Turn right in the village and drive toward Waterbury.

If you have any interest whatsoever in the outdoors, stop at the **Green Mountain Club headquarters** on Route 100 between Stowe and Waterbury. The offices are open until around 4:30 each day. The club is perhaps Vermont's leading advocate of outdoor recreation, with an emphasis on mountain hiking. It was founded in March 1910, when James P. Taylor, a lover of hiking and the associate principal of Vermont Academy at Saxtons River, gathered twenty-three kindred spirits at the Van Ness Hotel in Burlington. At the time, only eight mountains in Vermont had trails to their summits, and the new Green Mountain Club set about changing that. The parent organization spawned several semi-independent regional clubs that built trails in the mountains nearest their communities, acting on the joint goal "to make . . . the Vermont Mountains play a larger part in the life of the people." It took a generation to finish the job, but in 1931 the 265-mile Long Trail was completed from the Massachusetts border to the Quebec border. At the time it was the longest continuous footpath in the United States. In the 1930s, Vermont rejected an offer by the federal government to construct a skyline highway along the footpath—preferring its wilderness without asphalt. Undisturbed to this day by motor traffic, 122 miles of the Long Trail do double-duty as the Vermont segment of the Appalachian Trail. In addition to the basic rustic footpath along the crest of the Green Mountains, the GMC maintains 175 miles of side trails as well as sixty-two rustic cabins and lean-tos that provide overnight shelter. (See "Staying There.")

The headquarters has an excellent information center with GMC guidebooks, maps, and related publications, including the essential *Guide Book of the Long Trail* and the *Day Hiker's Guide to Vermont*. The *Guide Book* provides a complete description of the Long Trail, its side trails and shelters. It also includes detailed trail information on the Appalachian Trail in Vermont. In addition to critically important topographical maps, it gives detailed directions to trailheads and offers suggested hikes. The *Day Hiker's Guide,* complete with thirty-nine topographical maps, covers more than 150 suggested short hikes. If you're not a hearty hiker who plans to spend a week on the trails, consider picking up the free *Day Hiker's Vermont Sampler,* a folder with a Vermont map and descriptions of several hikes. It is also free by mail if you send a self-addressed, stamped legal size envelope to the GMC, RR1, Box 650, Waterbury Center, VT 05677. Telephone: (802) 244–7037.

Waterbury, Vermont

Because Waterbury is both an Amtrak stop and an exit from I–89, there are perhaps more stores here than full-time residents. (We exaggerate, but not by much.) The main reason to stop beside the road on Route 100, however, is to embark on the **Ben & Jerry's Ice Cream Factory Tour.** Think of it not as another factory tour but as a slice of one form of Vermont culture, where good milk and good deeds converge with a playful rhetoric. (The company donates 7.5 percent of its pretax profits to support social change.) The tongue-in-cheek tour begins with a silly movie about how the firm got started (as an ice cream scoop shop in Burlington in 1978 after Ben and Jerry took a $5.00 correspondence course) with a few quick highlights of the speedy growth. Visitors are then herded to a mezzanine where they can watch ice cream being made at a pace of 180,000 pints per week on two shifts that operate from 8:00 A.M. until midnight, Monday through Saturday. Some 500 family farms milk 40,000 cows just for Ben & Jerry's. The tour saves the best for last: the tasting room, where visitors often get to try experimental flavors, especially in the summer. As you might guess, there's also a gift shop. Among the ice-cream-label T-shirts, the Chubby Hubby shirt comes only in Large, X-Large, and XX-Large. Ben & Jerry's has a fiercely loyal work force, maybe because each worker is allowed to take home three pints a day. Tours are given daily from 10:00 A.M. to 5:00 P.M., and from 9:00 A.M. until 8:00 P.M. in

July and August; adults pay $2.00, children under 12 free. Telephone: (802) 244–TOUR.

A Fork in the Road

Reaching Waterbury calls for a driving decision, which may be determined by season and interests. Route 100 continues south through peak ski country along the eastern side of the Green Mountains. But if hiking, shopping, and American history are of greater interest, then continue northwest on I–89 to Burlington to begin a tour of the west side of the Green Mountains.

Vermont's East Slope: Ski Country

THE MAD RIVER VALLEY

Route 100 south of I–89 seems to simply wind through the countryside with occasional detours for small villages. The bucolic simplicity is misleading, as the rustic-looking dairy farms along the roadway are, more often than not, private retreats and second homes owned by salaried executives from the megalopolis to the south. The villages of Waitsfield, Warren, and Fayston have charms even for the traveler passing through. You might stumble across a polo match on the weekends at the Waitsfield polo grounds, and you'll likely want to stop for provisions at the Warren Store Deli (see "Staying There").

But the reason most people visit the Mad River Valley is because they own a timeshare at **Sugarbush** or a piece of the action at **Mad River Glen,** the two striking ski areas a few miles west of Route 100 on Route 17. The two areas could not be more different.

Mad River Glen began attracting skiers around 1947, when early patrons built New England's first trailside homes. The ski area first cranked up its "now famous" single chair in 1948. Founder Roland Palmedo envisioned a ski area where sport, rather than profit, would rule and made Truxton and Betsy Pratt, who purchased the area in 1972, swear to that philosophy. When Truxton died in 1975, Betsy worked hard to maintain Palmedo's vision, and when she finally decided to sell, she sold Mad River Glen to the only people she could trust—its skiers. On December 5, 1995, Mad River Glen became the only cooperatively owned ski area in America, bucking the strong trend toward homogenization under large corporate umbrellas. Each share costs $1,500 and shareholders must also make an annual pre-purchase of $200 per season that can be applied to almost any product or service on the mountain. Betsy Pratt's marketing motto still rules, though: "Mad River Glen: Ski It if You Can."

Sugarbush was the prototype of the tony ski resort when its first lift ticket was sold on Christmas Day 1958. Co-founders Damon and Sarah Gadd were a prominent New York City couple and Sugarbush soon began to attract the "jet set." Into the early 1960s, on a given Saturday morning one might see band leader Skitch Henderson, actress Kim Novak, designer Oleg Cassini, and many other fashion models and now-forgotten celebrities on the slopes. Dubbed "Mascara Mountain," Sugarbush was the place to be seen. In the early 1960s, Sugarbush built the region's first bottom-of-the-lift village. But the jet set party soon moved on to Los Angeles and resorts like Aspen and Tahoe, and Sugarbush went through several owners, unable to build giant condos and install massive snowmaking capacity thanks to Vermont development laws. Ironically, by the early 1990s, other ski resorts were trying to recapture the retro character that Sugarbush never lost.

KILLINGTON AREA, VERMONT

Poor little Sherburne, Vermont! This once-sleepy lumbering village near the headwaters of the Ottauquechee River has been thoroughly overshadowed by the year-round recreational community within its borders. Killington Peak, the second highest pinnacle in the Green Mountains at 4,235 feet, was the site of some of the earliest tourism development in the state. Prompted by the success of Mount Mansfield—which was, after all, pretty much in the middle of nowhere—the town of Rutland built a road to the summit of Mount Killington in 1879 and constructed a lavish summit house. Publicists for Killington advertised "a fine road leading east from the village" and a view from the top "far surpassing in extent and beauty that obtained from any other mountain in Vermont" and "even regarded more attrac-

tive than that from Mount Washington, being less a scene of desolation and of greater pastoral beauty, presenting to the beholder a sea of mountains clothed to their summits with verdure, their sides dotted with nestling lakes and fertile farms."

They were right.

Given such a head start—and the fact that it is just enough closer to New York than Stowe—Killington has blossomed into Vermont's largest outdoors center, with skiing in the winter at **Killington Basin Ski Area** and **Pico Peak Ski Area** (see "Staying There") and hiking in the summer and fall. The Long Trail continues north from Sherburne Pass while the Appalachian Trail turns east toward the White Mountains. The other junction of note here is Route 100 with the east-west road, Route 4, which goes east to Woodstock (see "Connecticut River Valley") and west to Rutland.

Pico was one of the earliest well-developed ski mountains, dating from a then-amazing 800-foot ski tow along Route 4 constructed in the late 1930s. By 1940, local developers James and Brad Mead had built a T-bar with the highest lift capacity in the world. Pico can also boast the oldest continuously registered ski safety patrol in the national ski patrol system.

Summer visitors, in particular, are struck by the fact that the Killington area never really developed a base village, even though it ranks as one of the largest ski areas in the East. Part of the reason is that skiing is spread across six separate mountains. More than 20,000 beds are available in the area, but they are spread out in small pockets of intense development. This dispersion has two effects: The rugged countryside is less blighted by large-scale development than one might expect, and everyone who goes to Killington has to drive, making traffic surprisingly dense during foliage and ski seasons.

PLYMOUTH AND LUDLOW, VERMONT

Just south of Killington is Plymouth, a hamlet whose chief claim to fame is that President Calvin Coolidge was born here in 1872 and was visiting in 1934 when he was sworn in as successor to President Warren G. Harding. The **Plymouth Notch Historical Site** on Route 100A includes the birthplace, boyhood home, and grave of

Killington Basin Ski Area, Killington, Vermont

Coolidge. Within the historical site, the **Calvin Coolidge Visitors Center** has a small museum that chronicles the thirtieth president's life. It is open daily from Memorial Day until the weekend after Columbus Day from 9:30 A.M. to 5:30 P.M. Adult admission is $5.00. Telephone: (802) 672–3773. Also at the site is the **Plymouth Cheese Factory,** built in 1890 by Coolidge's father, John. This operating factory sells its cheeses Monday through Saturday. Admission is free.

A former woolen mill town conveniently situated on the freight train line, Ludlow got its second wind in the 1980s when new owners decided to develop **Okemo Mountain,** and now the ski resort business dominates everything. (See "Staying There.")

Lower Vermont Ski Country

Ski culture has pretty much taken over the remaining 62 miles of Route 100 to its juncture with Route 9, the Molly Stark Highway. This is

not a bad thing, although rampant development along this route prompted strict environmental and zoning laws to make sure the process wasn't replicated elsewhere in the state. Vermont's environmental protection law, Act 250, is the toughest environmental standard in the United States.

Londonderry is the gateway to **Stratton Mountain** (where snowboarding was invented) and **Haystack. West Dover** supplies access to **Mount Snow. Wilmington,** where Routes 100 and 9 cross, is often favored as a base for skiing several mountains.

Mount Snow opened in 1954 as the opening salvo of Walter Schoenknecht, whom everyone remembers as an eccentric genius. In 1953 he purchased Mount Pisgah from farmer Reuben Snow and renamed the ski area after the farmer, selecting the area because it was close to New York. Snow's farm was transformed by ski lifts and trails, lodges, a skating rink, and an immense floodlit geyser. Ski lodges mushroomed for miles around. Schoenknecht is often considered the first American ski resort operator to embrace a "total resort" concept, although many of his ideas now seem either corny or quaint.

Until Stratton stole the show, Mount Snow was the hottest place for singles to hang out in the 1950s and 1960s. In 1958 Schoenknect introduced the first outdoor swimming pool (heated to 110 degrees) at a ski area. He also had an indoor skating rink and tropical plants, including bananas, in the base lodge. Moreover, he introduced the world's first skis-on gondola—a progenitor of today's detachable chair lifts. Skiers would sit in the chair, the shell would be closed around them, protecting them from the wind, the chair would be attached to the cable, and guests would ride up the mountain.

Schoenknecht was frustrated in realizing one dream: He petitioned the Atomic Energy Commission to explode an underground nuclear bomb to create back-bowl skiing and more vertical drop for a ski mountain. But, nonetheless, in 1960 the *Boston Globe* claimed that Mount Snow was the world's largest ski area. The resort had thirty-five trails and eight lifts. And the Snow Lake Lodge hadn't even been built yet. When it opened in 1962, the Japanese Dream Pools—two soaking pools (one hot, one cold) surrounded by huge tropical plants—became a hot site for fashion magazine shoots and bikini contests.

The ski business no longer has room for characters like Walter Schoenknecht, but he is remembered at Mount Snow in the "Thanks Walt" trail—a winding cruiser off the Sunbrook slopes.

Vermont's Champlain Valley

To get to Burlington from Waterbury, continue northwest on I–89 for 28 miles.

BURLINGTON, VERMONT

The great explorer, Samuel de Champlain, first plied the waters of the lake that bears his name in July 1609, inadvertently setting the stage for the French and Indian War by terrifying the Iroquois when he fired on a small band with an arquebus. The Iroquois never forgave the French for causing them to lose face, and readily aligned themselves with the English in subsequent battles for the rich lands of North America.

Covering about 490 square miles, Lake Champlain is the sixth largest body of fresh water in the United States. It is 108 miles long, 12 miles across at its widest point and has a maximum depth of 399 feet. Flowing northward from Whitehall, New York, it drains eventually into the St. Lawrence River via the Richelieu River in Quebec. In 1998 there was considerable debate about whether or not Champlain could be called a Great Lake. Immense as it may be, the lake is only a fraction the size of the inland seas that bear that name, although they all share similar geological origins. For purposes of funding environmental research, Congress decided Champlain could join the club, but with a lower-case "g."

At various points in the geological record, Champlain was an inlet of the ocean, as a fossilized whale skeleton found in nearby Charlotte attests. There are those who insist that Lake Champlain has a sea monster in its depths, known affectionately in the tourism trade as "Champ." This presumed cousin to the Loch Ness monster was allegedly seen in July 1984 by seventy passengers aboard the *Spirit of Ethan Allen II,* a tour boat that sails from Burlington.

Set directly on the shore of Lake Champlain, Burlington was founded in 1775 but largely abandoned during the Revolution because it was too close to the massed British military forces in Montreal. Settlement resumed in the 1790s, and the University of Vermont was founded here in 1791. Now the largest city in Vermont (population 39,100), Burlington is also the economic center for the state and the chief shipping port on Lake Champlain. A large student population defines much of the town's character—it is loaded with inexpensive restaurants and coffee bars and many stores offering outdoor gear and clothing with a decidedly youthful flair. (It is often said that Vermont is to skiing what Indiana is to basketball.) Burlington makes an excellent base for exploring the Champlain Valley region to its south.

The four-block pedestrian **Church Street Marketplace** is the principal historic district, lined with handsome three-story brick buildings from the late nineteenth century and the occasional marble or granite oddity employing native Vermont stone. More than 160 shops, restaurants, and summer street vendors offer their wares here. The broad street also serves as a venue for events and festivals throughout the year.

Battery Park, the waterfront district centered on the old artillery battery, offers a pleasant eight-mile bicycle path as well as train rides and a children's science center. This area also holds the various boat docks, where you can book a vessel to see a bit of Lake Champlain. The ferry boat *Champlain* makes several crossings per day from late May to mid-October between Burlington and Port Kent, New York, for a roundtrip fare of $23.00 for a car and driver and $5.75 per adult passenger. (A bicyclist pays $6.75.) The excursion vessel *Essex* also makes three trips daily from early summer through foliage season at 11:30 A.M., 2:00 and 4:00 P.M. These excursions include a narrated history of the lake and its lore. Rates start at $7.95. For information, contact Lake Champlain Transportation Company, King Street Dock. Telephone: (802) 864–9804.

Shoreline cruises on the *Spirit of Ethan Allen II* depart from Burlington Boathouse on College Street. Cruise options on the three-deck sightseeing boat range from scenic cruises (one and one-half hours), sunset cruises (two and one-half hours) to a variety of dinner cruises. The captain tells about Revolutionary naval battles, local history, and never fails to mention the elusive

Champ. Rates start at $7.95. Wheelchair accessible. Telephone: (802) 862–8300.

SHELBURNE, VERMONT

Route 7 leaves the south side of Burlington through a long patch of gas stations and strip malls before it breaks into open country in South Burlington and finally into farm vistas at Shelburne. The alluvial soils of the Champlain Valley are at their richest and deepest in Shelburne, just seven miles south of Burlington. And while the growing season is short, thanks to the northerly latitude, farming developed here on the northern European model, with a strong emphasis on animal husbandry. Perhaps the most extraordinary monument to Vermont's farming heyday is the working farm museum called **Shelburne Farms.** William Seward Webb, who had made a fortune in the railroad business (and had married Lila Vanderbilt), decided to live the life of a country squire here in Shelburne and in 1886 began to build the farm. His good taste and considerable wealth enabled him to engage Frederick Law Olmsted, then in the midst of creating the Boston park system, to design the grounds and Gifford Pinchot, who would later found the U.S. Forest Service, to consult on the tree plantings. As a demonstration of modern farm practices, Webb built a five-story, turreted Farm Barn and an even more massive Breeding Barn, where he strove to perfect the hackney horse.

But Henry Ford put the buggy whip—and the hackney horse—out of business and Webb's grand farm faded, only to be revived in the 1970s as a farm museum. The immense barns have been reborn, and the cheese business alone could keep the place afloat. (Large-scale production of Vermont cheddar doesn't get any better than this.) The sixty-room manor house has been converted to the Inn at Shelburne Farms (see "Staying There"). Touring the working farm is a delight for children and adults alike. The Visitor Center is open daily all year from 10:00 A.M. to 5:00 P.M. The grounds and farm buildings are open from the end of May to mid-October, with tours given up to five times a day. Adult admission with tour is $9.00, day pass $5.00. Telephone: (802) 985–8442.

The New York-based Webb family continued making big impressions on Shelburne. The **Shelburne Museum** is the extraordinary legacy of Electra Havemeyer Webb, who with her husband, J. Watson Webb, began collecting Americana shortly after World War II. Some Americana collectors acquire dolls or political posters or folk carvings and so did the Webbs. But they also collected virtually everything else imaginable, from decorative arts to entire New England buildings that they moved to their Shelburne property. It's a good thing that the admission pass is valid for two consecutive days, because it's almost impossible to tour the entire forty-five-acre, thirty-seven-building site in one day.

The Shelburne Museum has one of the most impressive collections of vintage American quilts, for example, as well as one of the leading collections of carved duck decoys. An entire, albeit small, building is devoted to miniature circuses, some of which are animated. Whole pieces of the New England past are preserved here—a Lake Champlain lighthouse, an 1890 train station, even the 220-foot steam ship *Ticonderoga*. On one hand, the entire museum is a demonstration that properly funded nostalgia knows no bounds. Yet the intelligent interpretation and often exhaustive collections succeed in accomplishing what nostalgia never can—the preservation of genuine, indigenous cultural roots. You leave the Shelburne Museum with a deeper understanding of the New England frame of mind. Shelburne Museum is open mid-May until late October daily from 10:00 A.M. until 5:00 P.M. Adults $17.50. Route 7. Telephone: (802) 985–3346.

VERGENNES, VERMONT

Continue driving south on Route 7 through the village of Charlotte (where a whale skeleton was unearthed in one of the lake banks) to Vergennes, once the major shipbuilding center on Lake Champlain. During the War of 1812, young America faced formidable British forces on its northern border, and the Champlain Valley became a significant battleground. An invading British army of 14,000, half of them veterans of the Napoleonic wars of France, was driven back by New York militiamen and Vermont volunteers in and around Plattsburgh, New York, on the western shore of Lake Champlain about 10 miles away. The British forces nonetheless outnumbered the Americans, and many Vermonters and upstate New Yorkers feared it was just a matter of time before their lands were annexed by British Canada. The shipbuilders of Vergennes, however, constructed a fleet of American warships, which Commodore Thomas Macdonough used to defeat the British fleet in the most decisive naval battle of the war in Plattsburgh Bay.

MIDDLEBURY, VERMONT

Middlebury appears almost as a mirage on Route 7 as the perfect little town in the middle of a hollow. Everything looks so bright and well-scrubbed that it could be a movie set, but it's merely the look of prosperity. Since it was chartered in 1800, Middlebury College has dominated the town, and you'll find that dining options tend to favor inexpensive fast food, while lodging options cater either to well-heeled visiting parents or to cyclists and hikers.

Middlebury has a history of wilderness appreciation that can be traced back to Joseph Battell, who began visiting the Green Mountains on his doctor's advice in the 1860s. He looked eastward from Middlebury and purchased a farm on the slopes of Bread Loaf Mountain, where he built the Bread Loaf Inn. With his inherited wealth and investment dividends, Battell maintained what many visitors of the time called a "fabulous table." Known for his broad-ranging intellectual interests in horse breeding, mathematics, physics, photography, and cartography, Battell proved to be a pioneer of land conservation. He sought to protect the Bread Loaf scenery for posterity by purchasing hundreds of acres—including most of Monastery Mountain, Worth Peak, Boyce Peak, Bread Loaf, Camels Hump and Roosevelt, Grant and Lincoln Mountains—that have since been incorporated into the Green Mountain National Forest.

This grant by Battell (who also helped save Middlebury College from insolvency) is now part of what the National Forest Service calls the **Bread Loaf Wilderness.** Covering 21,480 acres, it is the largest wilderness area in the Green Mountain National Forest. All vehicles and machines are banned, making this a perfect area

to recapture the mountain experience of more than a century ago.

Access to the Bread Loaf Wilderness Area is principally on the 17-mile section of the Long Trail that links up the mountain peaks like beads on a chain. Copies of the Bread Loaf map are available from the ranger station on Route 7. Drive east from Middlebury on Route 125 to skirt the southern end of the wilderness area, connecting to Forest Road #59, which borders the west side. Several parking lots are located at trail heads. Depending on the time of year, be watchful on the trails for black bear and moose, as both are plentiful in the area. (Trees scratched by bears are everywhere along the trails.)

SHOREHAM, VERMONT

Rather than continue directly south on Route 7, drive south on Route 30 and then Route 74 to Shoreham. Beautiful rolling hill country full of second-growth forests flattens out to broad pasturelands as you approach the Champlain Valley. No wonder these roads rank as one of the most popular cycling routes in New England—although we can remember riding here and ending up not with tired legs, but with sore arms from pushing our bicycles uphill. (We were riding from the valley to the mountains rather than the more sensible downhill route.)

Route 74 will take you to the **Ticonderoga Landing,** where in 1775 Ethan Allen and Benedict Arnold took joint command of the Green Mountain Boys and captured Fort Ticonderoga, a few hundred yards across Lake Champlain. Leave New England for a few minutes and take the six-minute ferry ride over to see the restored fort. Ironically, Ticonderoga was virtually impregnable if properly garrisoned, as the French had shown in 1758 when 3,500 troops under Montcalm repulsed and decimated 15,000 British soldiers. But on May 10, Ethan Allen and the boys clubbed a single British sentry senseless, rousted the sleeping British commander, and informed him that the fort was taken. He surrendered without a shot. British cannon from the fort were then hauled overland and delivered to General Washington in Cambridge, who positioned them at Dorchester Heights and drove the British fleet from Boston harbor, literally under their own guns.

Circle back to Route 7 via Route 73 east (19 miles) and return to tracing the main route of settlement along the west side of the Green Mountains. In 19 miles you will pass through the major center of Rutland, where Routes 7 and 4 cross, and several small villages with excellent cross-country skiing before you come to Manchester in another 32 miles. Just north of town you're offered the choice of Route 7 (a highway) and what the locals persist in calling **"Historic Route 7A"** (although the Vermont highway people just mark it 7A). Ignore Robert Frost's advice (though he did live around here at one point) and take the road more traveled by, 7A.

MANCHESTER, VERMONT

Manchester always has been a resort and probably always will be. Although it has a handsome town green and many a white house with green shutters, it belongs less to a bucolic era of hardscrabble mountain farming than to the last quarter of the nineteenth century, when wealthy Americans began to rusticate and seek relief from the sweltering cities.

The strongest evidence of the Gilded Age rusticators lies in Manchester Village at the mighty **Equinox** hotel, where green wooden rocking chairs line the long porch supported by Greek Revival columns. (See "Staying There.") Even the sidewalks are slabs of white marble. The village was also the home of Charles Orvis, whom many credit as the father of fly fishing in America (he started selling flies and rods in 1856). Orvis's home is now a small inn that is part of the Equinox complex.

Many a celebrity came to fish with Orvis, and though his company is still headquartered in Manchester, his legacy seems most alive in **The American Museum of Fly Fishing.** This small museum is dedicated to the legacy of fly fishing around the world and contains an encyclopedic collection of flies, rods, reels, and other paraphernalia. It is open from May through October daily from 10:00 A.M. to 4:00 P.M., and from November through April on weekdays from 10:00 A.M. to 4:00 P.M. The museum is located at the corner of Seminary Avenue and Route 7A. Telephone: (802) 362–3300. Admission is $5.00.

One of the rusticators who withdrew each summer to Manchester was Robert Todd Lincoln, son of the slain president. His magnificent twenty-four-room Georgian Revival mansion in a vast estate on the south side of the village off Route 7A was inhabited by his descendants until 1975, when it became a house museum. The driveway into **Hildene** is nearly a mile long, unpaved and shaded by bowers. You clank along the hardpack, waiting for your muffler to drop and wondering if this trip was such a good idea—and suddenly, from the middle of the woods, you emerge into a hidden estate that looks for all the world like an English lord's mansion transplanted to Vermont. The disorder of the forest gives way to manicured lawns and formal gardens.

Lincoln built the estate in 1903, so it incorporates modern devices like electric lighting into the faux eighteenth-century design. Many of the original plantings survive, and the house is filled with original furnishings and family memorabilia. One item of particular interest is the 1908 Aeolian organ with 1,000 pipes. It is played on each tour. Guided tours are given mid-May through October daily on the half hour from 9:30 A.M. to 4:00 P.M. During the winter, twenty-one groomed cross-country trails totaling 15 kilometers are open for woodland and meadow ski touring. Telephone: (802) 362–1788. Guided tours are $7.00. Ski trail fees range from $7.00 on weekdays to $9.00 on weekends.

Manchester was also one of the birthplaces of alpine skiing in Vermont. After traveling in

**Hildene, the Lincoln Family Home,
Manchester, Vermont**

Europe to perfect his skiing technique, Fred Pabst of the Pabst Brewing Company decided to develop the sport in America. In 1934, he chose Vermont for his ski resort because—amazingly—he encountered less governmental red tape here than in the western states. Vermont, he also reasoned, was closer to major population centers.

In 1936 Pabst purchased a seventeen-acre parcel in Manchester Center and eventually turned his full attention to developing **Bromley Mountain,** which is technically in the town of Peru but is reached from Manchester. He is widely credited with making skiing a user-friendly sport by contouring his trails, grooming the surface and texture of the snow, and constructing the landscape to check against erosion. In 1949–50, Pabst began to roll snow so that it would stay flat on the trails.

The ski area maintains that user-friendly, rather old-fashioned feel. (The hotshots are all over at Killington.) Unlike most Vermont ski areas, Bromley faces south, making it a pleasant place to ski even when the weather is extremely cold. The terrain is all novice and easy intermediate (as Pabst intended)—just the thing for occasional skiers who want an excuse to stay at the Equinox and shop Manchester's designer outlet malls. Lift rates range from $35 to about $46, depending on season and day of the week. Bromley is located on Route 11 in Peru, six miles east of Manchester. Telephone: (802) 824–5522 or (800) 865–4786.

The same mountain also provides an excellent summer outlook from the **Bromley Alpine Slide and Scenic Chairlift,** which each cost $5.00.

Route 7A is lined with small antiques and used book dealers between Manchester and Bennington, which makes for an interesting, if frequently interrupted, drive. The historic route and the newer highway rejoin just north of the historic village of Bennington, continuing southward into the Berkshire Mountains or eastward over the Molly Stark Trail, Route 9, toward Wilmington and Brattleboro.

BENNINGTON, VERMONT

Bennington consists of two almost separate villages—the town of Bennington, with most of the shops and restaurants, and the historic section known as Old Bennington, where most of the attractions are located.

Old Bennington is popularly considered the site of the Revolutionary War battle on August 16, 1777, when General John Stark's American troops defeated an expedition by British General John Burgoyne, thus securing New England's northwest flank from further attack. Actually, Stark's troops were stationed here, but the fighting took place just across the border in Wallomsac, New York. Nonetheless, the **Battle of Bennington** is marked by a 306-foot granite monolith on a tall bluff in Old Bennington. It was the tallest battle monument in the world when it was erected in 1891 and is still the tallest structure in Vermont, affording a terrific view of the surrounding landscape. The monument is at the end of Monument Avenue, a half mile west of Route 7 via West Main Street. The elevator fee is $1.50. The Bennington Battle Monument is open from mid-April through October daily from 9:00 A.M. to 5:00 P.M. Telephone: (802) 447–0550.

At the other end of Monument Avenue is **Old First Church,** one of the most beautiful and classical of New England white Congregational houses of worship. Even older than the 1805–06 church building is the adjacent **Old Burying Ground,** which contains the graves of many of Bennington's founders, five governors of the state of Vermont, and (more recent) the poet Robert Frost. The burying ground is a veritable forest of striking tombstones, many executed in carved slate with eighteenth-century death's heads and similar iconography. Frost's stone is a recumbent slab, marked with the epitaph, "I had a lover's quarrel with the world."

As you return to modern Bennington on West Main Street, you'll pass the site of the **Catamount Tavern.** In the days when Ethan Allen and the Green Mountain Boys were terrorizing the New York Tories (Allen was known variously as the "Robin Hood of Vermont" as well as "the Anti-Christ" by his foes), they plotted many of their sorties here over a pint. The building is not open to the public, but the spot is marked by a handsome statue of a catamount, the Vermont name for the (probably) extinct eastern mountain lion. (Allen had put a stuffed catamount out front to show his ferocity toward all Tories and New Yorkers, this being the era when New York

Bennington Battle Monument, Bennington, Vermont

The Berkshire Hills of Massachusetts

The Taconic and Hoosac ranges of western Massachusetts are usually called the Berkshire Hills—not the Berkshire Mountains—and that seems fair enough. Although the Berkshires are a virtually seamless extension of the southern Green Mountains, they lack the drama of the peaks and ridges farther north in Vermont and New Hampshire. But the Berkshire hill country has a gentle beauty of its own that attracted the wealthy rusticators of the late nineteenth and early twentieth centuries and continues to draw travelers who seek a tame but scenic outdoors and some of the summertime high points of American performing arts.

The Berkshires as a region generally connotes the broad valley between the Taconic Range on the northwestern flank and the Hoosac range that divides the region from the Connecticut River Valley to the east. The valley is punctuated by the occasional peak, and at 3,491 feet, Mount Greylock in the northwest corner of Massachusetts is the highest.

In a sense, Mount Greylock had the advantage of lucky positioning and articulate admirers. Many higher and more majestic peaks lie but a few miles north, but it was to Greylock, the highest point on the Berkshire horizon, that the literati of nineteenth-century New England flocked to behold the sublime and cogitate on the profound spiritual aspects of natural wonders. In part, Greylock was simply convenient. One of the earliest east-west roads between Boston and Albany passed along its northern flanks because a passable, if difficult, notch is situated there.

When Nathaniel Hawthorne explored the region in 1838, he wrote in *American Notebooks* that "Every new aspect of the mountains, or view from a different position creates a surprise in the mind." Hawthorne may have inspired his Concord neighbor, Henry David Thoreau, to make his 1844 journey to the summit of Mount Greylock, walking up the mountain alone carrying only some sugar, rice, fresh clothes, and a few travel books.

Herman Melville could see it from the window of his study in Pittsfield where he wrote

landowners were seeking to annex all of Vermont.)

Farther down the hill, appropriately halfway between Old Bennington and the newer town, is **Bennington Museum,** a top-flight local museum. Probably the most famous holdings are several paintings and extensive memorabilia of the folk artist Grandma Moses. Most of the Grandma Moses exhibits are shown in the schoolhouse she attended as a child. But the collections are even more interesting from the point of view of local history and decorative arts. More than 5,000 pieces of pressed, cut, or engraved glass and art glass are on display, along with extensive collections of folk art, toys, and country furniture. The museum also owns a nearly complete collection of every production line ever produced by the Bennington Pottery. One notable exhibit is the Bennington 1776 Stars and Stripes flag, one of the oldest extant American flags. Admission is $5.00. The museum, located on West Main Street, is open June through October daily from 9:00 A.M. to 6:00 P.M.; it closes at 5:00 P.M. the rest of the year. Telephone: (802) 447–1571.

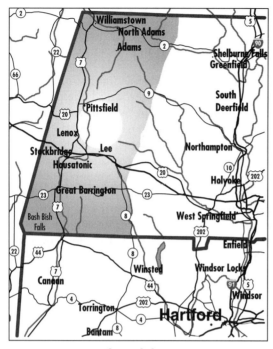

The Berkshires

Moby-Dick and it remains a popular conceit to assume that the snow-covered shape of the mountain inspired the famous white whale. In any event, like the other authors, Melville paid homage to the mountain, dedicating his novel *Pierre* to "Greylock's Most Excellent Majesty."

Melville's journey to the summit of Mount Greylock in 1851 was much more convivial than Thoreau's. Among their supplies, he and his eleven traveling companions carried brandied fruit, champagne, port, cognac, and Jamaican rum. As Avery A. Duyckinck, one of the climbers, explained in a letter to his wife, "With this and a party of very good natured people—and a pack of cards so you can get through the night."

This commingling of artistic sensibilities and the appreciation of natural beauty—combined with the determination to do it in style—continues to characterize the Berkshires today. The region's early history is a common story—farming by the Mohican and Hoosac tribes; warfare with the Iroquois in the sixteenth and seventeenth centuries; exploration by English, Dutch, and French fur traders; then settlement by the English in the eighteenth century. Farming was limited during the French and Indian War, and rebuilding in the

nineteenth century favored the application of the region's many streams to millworks.

By the time the railroad made its way through the mountains to the Berkshire valley in the late nineteenth century, the region was already evolving as a tourist destination and a refuge for wealthy New Yorkers and Bostonians who built lavish summer "cottages." By the end of the nineteenth century, Lenox and Stockbridge were dotted with about seventy-five cottages and the Berkshires became known as the "Inland Newport." In 1913 the inauguration of a Federal income tax put something of a brake on grandiose real estate development, but three of these extravagant cottages are open to the public and remain much as they were when their original residents lived in them. Others have been transformed into lodgings and restaurants.

Wealthy summer residents encouraged the performing arts in the Berkshires, giving root to a grand tradition in music, theater, and dance that continues unabated. Three of the oldest surviving institutions are the Tanglewood Music Festival (established more than fifty years ago), the Berkshire Theatre Festival (established in the late 1920s), and Jacob's Pillow Dance Festival (established in the 1930s). They are joined by a whole range of other theatrical and musical organizations. This patronage has also extended to the visual arts, particularly painting, and the artistic milieu combined with a low cost of living in the hill towns, has helped the Berkshires become a center for workers in fine crafts.

The character of the Berkshires today remains stamped by a century of wealthy rusticators. Although it is possible to visit the region as a daytripper, there are so many things to see and do in such a small area that a fleeting visit is bound to prove frustrating. This is a region to enjoy the natural beauty, fine arts, and resonant history by day and partake of the performing arts by night.

North Adams, Massachusetts

North Adams bills itself as the "Gateway to the Berkshires," which presumes that one is approaching from the east along Route 2, which crosses much of the Hoosac range between the Berkshires and the Connecticut River Valley. This is a particularly fine way to approach North Adams, especially since the road makes a 180-degree turn as its descends into town—the aptly named Hairpin Turn memorialized on thousands of postcards printed during the early days of auto touring. Drivers are no longer allowed to park on the turn, which has some very dramatic views. Travelers can also approach North Adams from the Green Mountains by Route 8 from Vermont, which joins Route 2 just east of the North Adams town center.

North Adams is a former mill town and manufacturing center that is rebuilding from a shattered manufacturing economy. With a vibrant local college, a smattering of computer-related businesses, and a contemporary art museum occupying one of the larger abandoned mills, it is a town with a great deal of promise. **Massachusetts Museum of Contemporary Art,** in the works for more than a decade, expects to open with its first exhibitions before the turn of the millennium. MassMoCA, as it's called, plans to make use of its cavernous spaces in the former Sprague Electric factory at 87 Marshall Street to specialize in large-scale art that other museums cannot accommodate. Telephone: (413) 664–4481.

Reuse is a recurring theme in North Adams, and **Western Gateway Heritage State Park** has transformed a group of railroad freight buildings into a multimedia railroad exhibit and history museum of this Victorian industrial center. The most dramatic exhibits at the park concern the Hoosac Tunnel, which opened the Berkshires to short-term visitors and helped establish the tourism industry.

Prior to the 1870s horses, wagons, and stagecoaches could traverse the Hoosac Range, albeit precariously, but trains could not manage the grades. As the economic behemoths of their age, the railroad companies decided that what they could not go over, they would go through. So the Boston & Albany Railroad undertook the construction of the four-and-three-quarter-mile Hoosac Tunnel, which was the longest bore in the world when it opened in 1875. Engineers constructed a series of lining huts atop Hoosac Mountain, taking careful sightings and elevations to guide the workers below, who tunneled from both ends. When they met with a final blast of dynamite on November 27, 1873, the error in

alignment proved to be less than one inch in 25,000 feet. Finishing the tunnel for train travel took another three years and the entire project came to a staggering $14 million. The Hoosac Tunnel remains in steady use and was expanded in the mid-1990s to create enough headroom for double-deck freight cars. Western Gateway Heritage State Park is open daily from 10:00 A.M. to 5:00 P.M. Admission is free and the visitors center is wheelchair accessible. The park is on Route 8 just south of the center of North Adams. Telephone: (413) 663–6312.

Even before the railroad came in, intrepid tourists had begun to visit North Adams for the scenery. The author of a popular 1870 guidebook, *From the Hub to the Hudson,* observed that "all men and women who have stout shoes . . . and a love of the beautiful may find, by climbing any hill road or mountain path in the region, a prospect that will delight the eye."

To delight your own eye, follow Route 2 west from town until you see a small sign pointing toward **Mount Greylock Reservation.** This is Notch Road, and the summit is eight miles away. (Rockwell Road in Lanesboro is the southern access and is reached from Route 7. It joins Notch Road about four miles from the summit.) The **Mount Greylock Reservation Visitors Center** is on Rockwell Road and is open from mid-May to mid-October daily from 9:00 A.M. to 5:00 P.M. Telephone: (413) 499–4262.

Established in 1898, the 12,500-acre Mount Greylock State Reservation is the oldest park in Massachusetts. Its centerpiece is Mount Greylock, which affords views of the Taconic and Hoosac ranges of up to 100 miles on a clear day. According to the authors of *Most Excellent Majesty,* a volume published on the ninetieth anniversary of Mount Greylock Reservation, the mountain serves as a barometer of weather and season for the people who live below it: "In the valleys below, people look to Mount Greylock at the beginning of winter as if it were a general leading them into battle. The first snows, usually in October, rest on its shoulders, as do the last snows of spring. And in April and May valley dwellers watch breathlessly as the green 'leafing-out' line slowly creeps up the mountain slopes."

There are a number of trails for people to ascend the slopes as well. The Bellows Pipe Trail (so-called for the sound made by high winds in the rock formations) that Thoreau walked still exists, though it now has a crushed stone surface and is designated for mountain bike usage. Rated as a moderate to expert trail, the Bellows Pipe Trail departs from Notch Road at an elevation of about 1,540 feet and climbs to the 3,491-foot summit over four and two-tenths miles. During the spring, the trail is lined with trilliums, ramps (wild leeks), and, in boggy spots near Notch Reservoir, the tight coils of fiddlehead ferns. During the summer, day lilies planted by early settlers continue to bloom and even the occasional ancient and craggy apple or cherry tree is visible from the path.

The Appalachian Mountain Club rates an average time for ascent of Bellows Pipe Trail at three hours and ten minutes. Thoreau took the mountain at a more leisurely pace, spending the better part of a day climbing, sleeping overnight beneath the Williams College weather observatory platform, and returning to North Adams the next day. As he noted in his description of the journey in *A Week on the Concord and Merrimack Rivers,* "Even country people, I have observed, magnify the difficulty of traveling in the forest, especially among mountains. They seem to lack their usual common sense in this. I have climbed several higher mountains without guide or path, and have found, as might be expected, that it takes only more time and patience commonly than to travel the smoothest highway."

Modern hikers have it even easier. More than 45 miles of marked trails crisscross the reservation, including eleven and one-half miles of the Appalachian Trail. Some short loops near the summit can be traversed in an hour or less. This entire area was once farmland (though the annual crop of rocks apparently persuaded most farmers to find another place to dig), so dense forest is not an obstacle. But the mountain has been untilled and uncut long enough that a startling variety of flora are found and the protected status of reservation land has proven a welcome nesting habitat to more than a hundred bird species.

The 93-foot granite War Memorial Tower was erected at the summit in 1932. Its beacon can be seen for 70 miles. There is no external observation deck, but a winding interior staircase offers views through narrow slits in the upper walls. The view,

however, is nearly as good from the platform at the base. The summit closes one-half hour after sunset. Should you prefer, like Thoreau, to spend the night, the Appalachian Mountain Club maintains a lodge at the summit and the state offers access to camp sites. (See "Staying There.") Intrepid mountaineers may also ski or snowshoe in the reservation in the winter. Winter camping is permitted and there is also a lean-to for snowshoe backpackers without tents.

Williamstown, Massachusetts

Just west on Route 2 is Williamstown, where Route 7 also descends from Bennington, Vermont. Both the town and Williams College are named for Colonel Ephraim Williams, who met his demise in 1755 in the French and Indian War. Colonel Williams left a bequest to be used toward establishing and supporting "a Free School forever in the township west of Fort Massachusetts, called West Hoosac, provided it be given the name of Williamstown."

West Hoosac was still a frontier community, and the political and social upheavals of the next few decades kept the school from getting off the ground until 1790. It was finally chartered by the state in 1793 as Williams College. Just as Dartmouth College overwhelmed Hanover, New Hampshire, Williams soon overwhelmed Williamstown and even today the town feels like an adjunct to the campus.

The college has been linked with Mount Greylock from its earliest years. One of the first trails up the western summit was built by Williams college faculty and students in 1830 and the college also established the first observation center at the summit in 1831. In 1863, Professor Albert Hopkins founded the Alpine Club, the first mountain-climbing club in the country. Ironically, most of the members were ladies, even though Williams was an exclusively masculine domain at the time. The Alpine Club was nonetheless the forerunner of the Williams Outing Club, which continues to help maintain Greylock's trails.

When Thoreau climbed Mount Greylock, he wrote that Greylock was a mighty asset to the college: "It would be no small advantage if every college were thus located at the base of a mountain,

**War Memorial Tower,
summit of Mount Greylock, Massachusetts**

as good at least as one well-endowed professorship. . . . Some will remember, no doubt, not only that they went to college, but that they went to the mountain."

Just as the mountain is an asset to the college, the college is an asset to the town. Williamstown's Main Street is a steady procession of proud buildings in an assortment of nineteenth and twentieth-century styles, marching along on the raised hillsides above the street. Two of these buildings are of significant interest to the nonstudent.

During the summer, **Williamstown Theatre Festival** occupies the red brick, four-columned Adams Memorial Theatre. This tremendously popular summer theater broke with tradition by offering many new plays in the 1950s and 1960s, featuring playwrights such as Tennessee Williams when his work was still considered risky and avant garde. WTF also broke with the tradition of

employing journeymen stage actors and faded Broadway stars to feature film and television actors, many of them marquee names. (Christopher Reeve was a frequent player here, for example.) This practice continues, making WTF's productions among the hottest tickets in the Berkshires. WTF presents a mix of classical plays and newer plays (often by screenwriters) on the Mainstage and more experimental new plays on the smaller Nikos Stage. Its season runs from June through August and also includes some free performances and cabaret. The theaters are both wheelchair accessible. 1000 Main Street. Telephone: (413) 597–3400.

Also on Main Street is the **Williams College Museum of Art,** which emphasizes modern, contemporary, and non-Western art. The building is distinguished by its neoclassical rotunda and modern addition by Charles Moore. In addition to an in-depth collection of some 400 works by Maurice and Charles Prendergast, the museum has samplings from other "big names," such as Juan Gris, Fernand Léger, Picasso, Andy Warhol, and Edward Hopper. (Hopper's masterpiece, *Morning in a City,* is here.) And like many college museums, it mounts frequent temporary exhibitions. It is open Tuesday through Saturday from 10:00 A.M. to 5:00 P.M., Sunday from 1:00 to 5:00 P.M. Free. Main Street. Wheelchair accessible. Telephone: (413) 597–2429.

Williamstown's village center along Spring Street is perhaps of more interest to residents and students than to travelers, as it is essentially a commercial adjunct to the campus. Its collection of eateries, bakeries, and shops proffer what passes as essentials if you are eighteen to twenty-two years old.

Route 2 continues westward through the campus to the junction with Route 7. Follow the road toward Route 7 south to the **Sterling and Francine Clark Art Institute,** arguably one of the best small art museums in the United States. Sterling Clark had the good fortune to be the grandson of a partner of Isaac Singer, inventor of the sewing machine. After receiving a degree in engineering from Yale, he entered the army, serving in the Philippines and China during the Boxer Rebellion, and later led a scientific expedition into remote northern China. But in 1912, at the age of thirty-five, he settled down in Paris and began to collect art. Early on, he concentrated on Old Masters, but his French wife, Francine, soon won him over to nineteenth-century French painting, which became the core of the Clark family collection.

The Clarks were astute collectors who paid little heed to fashionable taste. They cared not a whit that the critics of their day frowned on Pierre Auguste Renoir—they purchased more than thirty of his paintings and sculptures. Claude Monet was briefly out of favor, and they purchased seven of his paintings, including one of the stunning Rouen Cathedral series. They bought Winslow Homer (ten oils, dozens of works on paper) when no one wanted his representational work, John Singer Sargent when he was condemned by critics as little more than a parlor portraitist. The Clarks acquired several of J.M.W. Turner's atmospheric land- and seascapes in the days when he was dismissed as a dabbler in colored fog. The list of out-of-favor artists whose works they championed is extensive, including Corot, Degas, Mary Cassat, and Toulouse-Lautrec.

The Clarks divided their time between Paris and New York and decided that their personal art collection should have a permanent home of its own. After considering a number of sites, they chose Williamstown in 1950, had the handsome main building constructed of white Vermont marble in an appropriate neoclassical style, and in 1955 the Sterling and Francine Clark Art Institute opened to the public.

The Clark has grown since, adding buildings and augmenting the collection, which ranks among the foremost in the United States in French Impressionism and nineteenth-century English landscape painting. One condition of their bequest was that museum admission remain free. The grounds of the museum are dotted with picnic tables and a footpath leads to the crest of Stone Hill, which gives a very pleasant scenic overview of Williamstown. The Clark is open September through June Tuesday through Sunday from 10:00 A.M. to 5:00 P.M., July and August daily from 10:00 A.M. to 5:00 P.M. Free. Wheelchair accessible. 225 South Street. Telephone: (413) 458–2303.

From the Clark, turn south on Route 7 (South Street) and the land will slope away down before you. Williamstown lies at one of the few high east-west ridges linking the Hoosac and Taconic ranges, and south of town the landscape descends into long, gentle grades into a river valley. Most of these valley hillsides are hay fields and pastures, where big-eyed brown Guernsey cows graze placidly in the sun.

About three miles south, at the juncture of Sloan Road, Route 7, and Route 43 is what remains of the village of South Williamstown—mostly a general store with good picnic fixings. Turn right onto Sloan Road and drive one mile to visit **Field Farm** (see also "Staying There"), a fascinating property owned by the Trustees of Reservations. Lawrence and Eleanore Bloedel built their striking modern home on this 296-acre estate in 1948. The house, now a B&B, is a model of modest modern design and the landscape in which it sits is a tribute to the conservation movement. Approximately four miles of foot trails wind through cropland, pasture, marsh, and forest, with spectacular views of Mount Greylock and the Taconic Range. In addition to a plethora of wildflowers, rare maidenhead and walking ferns flourish in the lime-rich soil. Cross-country skiing is permitted on the trails in the winter. 554 Sloan Road. Telephone: (413) 458–3135.

Return to Route 7 and resume the drive south. You'll note at the intersection that Route 43 west leads to the town of Hancock, but don't take this route to visit Hancock Shaker Village. The Pittsfield State Forest divides the town in two, with the tiny village center on the north side (Route 43) and Hancock Shaker Village on the south side, which is reached from Route 20.

Pittsfield, Massachusetts

All major roads of the Berkshires converge in Pittsfield, by far the largest community in the region. Pittsfield flourished in the late nineteenth and early twentieth centuries as a manufacturing center, with General Electric dominating the economy until its gradual withdrawal in the 1970s and 1980s. Faced with an unstable economic base, it is now a community in transition.

Even as early as the mid-nineteenth century, Pittsfield showed substantial vigor. Author Herman Melville lived here at **Arrowhead,** a 1780s farmhouse, from 1850 to 1863. He wrote *Moby-Dick* here in 1850–51, and worked on several other books in this bucolic setting outside of town. But Melville was a better writer than businessman, and eventually lost Arrowhead and returned to New York. The house is operated as a "Melville-related site" by the Berkshire Historical Society—a designation that wisely doesn't claim too much for the building. It is furnished in Melville-era furniture, but owns very few of the author's personal belongings. Still, the building seems to echo with the writer's fervor, and it is easy to understand his dark broodings over an unknowable God if you look out his study window and imagine the lush landscape blasted by winter, with only the great fleshy white hump of Mount Greylock looming over everything. Arrowhead is open from Memorial Day through Labor Day daily from 10:00 A.M. to 5:00 P.M. After Labor Day through October it is open Friday through Monday from 10:00 A.M. to 5:00 P.M. Adults $5.00. The downstairs exhibits are wheelchair accessible. 780 Holmes Road. Telephone: (413) 442–1793.

More of Melville's own possessions and associated memorabilia can be found at the Pittsfield public library, the **Berkshire Athenaeum,** where the Herman Melville Memorial Room displays some of his personal books, pictures, and letters as well as his writing desk. The library is open from September through June, Monday through Thursday from 9:00 A.M. to 9:00 P.M., Friday 9:00 A.M. to 5:00 P.M., and Saturday from 10:00 A.M. to 5:00 P.M. During July and August it is open Monday, Wednesday and Friday from 9:00 A.M.

to 5:00 P.M., Tuesday and Thursday from 9:00 A.M. to 9:00 P.M., and Saturday from 10:00 A.M. to 5:00 P.M. Free. Wheelchair accessible. 1 Wendell Avenue. Telephone: (413) 499–9480.

At the traffic circle in downtown Pittsfield, get on Route 20 west to drive five miles over the town line into Hancock to reach **Hancock Shaker Village.** The Hancock Shakers called their community "City of Peace," and even today the tidy village, simple buildings, whitewashed fences, neat gardens, and rolling pastures embody a commanding sense of order and tranquility. Hancock was one of the most enduring Shaker settlements, inhabited by members of the celibate, communal religious sect from 1790 to 1959. Although Shaker communities once stretched from Maine to Indiana, Hancock and the nearby New Lebanon, New York, villages were the nerve centers of the Shaker network, and Hancock's architecture strongly influenced many non-Shaker builders throughout New England.

Twenty buildings constructed between 1790 and 1916—along with 1,200 acres of land the Shakers once farmed, quarried, and lumbered—have been preserved as a living history museum. (For a site that was active into the 1990s, see Canterbury Shaker Village in "The Lakes.")

Early Shakers considered their founder, Mother Ann Lee, to be the female personification of God and equal in their eyes to Christ. It followed logically that both the spiritual and temporal leadership of Shaker communities was shared by men and women—although the sexes

Hancock Shaker Village, Pittsfield, Massachusetts

did not mix. The five-story 1830 Brick Dwelling is a reminder of that separate but equal status. About 100 brothers and sisters lived on separate sides of the building—each side the mirror image of the other right down to the entrance doors, staircases, and peg rails for hats and cloaks.

An early Shaker eldress declared "There is no dirt in heaven," and throughout the buildings you will notice peg rails for hanging clothes, tools, chairs, and mops, along with tall built-in cupboards and chests that you would not have to sweep under. The Dwelling's kitchen was the epitome of modernity in its time—with running water, efficient ovens, and wood-fired appliances for boiling, steaming, deep-frying, and grilling.

The Brick Dwelling and other buildings house the largest collection of Shaker furniture and artifacts in an original Shaker site. Most of the artifacts are in room settings where interpreters explain the lives of the people who made and used the objects. The interpreters do not pretend to be Shakers, but create reproductions of nineteenth-century Shaker goods to the standards set forth by Shaker founder Mother Ann Lee: "Do all your work as if you had a hundred years to live and as if you were to die tomorrow."

Officially known as the United Society of Believers in Christ's Second Coming, the Shakers at Hancock worshipped in the gambrel-roofed Meetinghouse. The whitewashed, blue-trimmed interior is rimmed with built-in benches for visitors and possible converts who came to observe the Shakers sing and dance praises to God. Because the Hancock community was rich in land, it took in a large number of refugees from the world—widows and orphans, especially—and it was not uncommon for older couples to join the sect, taking vows of celibacy and moving into the separate men's and women's quarters.

Staff farmers maintain specimen herb and vegetable gardens at the Village and raise livestock of breeds common to western Massachusetts in the mid-nineteenth century, when Hancock Shaker Village was at its zenith. Hancock's agricultural success is symbolized by the extraordinary Round Stone Barn. The community built the structure in 1826 to stable fifty cattle in stanchions radiating from a central haymow like spokes of a wheel. This practical design made it easy to feed, milk, and clean up after the animals.

Now long empty, the building seems an exemplary work of art to worship God through daily labor—which was, in the final analysis, the point of Shaker life. Hancock Shaker Village is open from Memorial Day to late October daily from 9:30 A.M. to 5:00 P.M., and during April, May, and November daily from 10:00 A.M. to 3:00 P.M. Adults $12.50 (good for ten days). Evening tours and candlelight dinners on most Saturdays July through October are $38 per person. Junction of Routes 20 and 41. Telephone: (413) 443–0188.

From Hancock Shaker Village, backtrack to Route 7 and continue south toward Lenox.

Lenox, Massachusetts

Prior to the establishment of a federal income tax, Lenox was one of the Eastern Seaboard's playgrounds of the rich, many of whom built summer "cottages" here between 1890 and 1910. Today it is as close as the southern Berkshires get to a nerve center for the summer social season that revolves around the Tanglewood Music Festival. Although still quite small, Lenox has more boutiques, more restaurants, more upscale lodgings than any of the other communities in its area. It is also marginally more expensive than surrounding towns.

Before visiting the village center, stop at the junction of Routes 7 and 7A to see one of those fine Berkshire cottages, **The Mount.** It was the home of Edith Wharton, the first woman to win the Pulitzer Prize—for *The Age of Innocence,* a chronicle of her own class and lifestyle. Wharton was born Edith Jones to the family for whom the phrase "keeping up with the Joneses" was coined. Never formally schooled, she nonetheless had enormous talent, rock-solid self-assurance, and audacious ambition. So sure was Wharton of her taste that her first published book was *The Decoration of Houses,* issued in 1897 when she was all of twenty-five. Having published her ideas about home design and decoration, she proceeded to put them into practice by building The Mount, which she conceived as a complete revolt against the stuffy Victorian house. She modeled the house on a country estate she had visited in Lincolnshire, England, and adapted bits of French and Italian architecture where it suited her, probably driving her architects insane in the process. Nonetheless, the classical mansion was completed in 1902 on a stunning 130-acre lakeside property and she lived in it with her husband for a decade before she decided to divorce him. She left for France and never returned.

Like so many Berkshire estates, The Mount has changed hands several times and went through some dark days after World War II. It is now owned by the Edith Wharton Restoration, a nonprofit organization that aims to restore both interior and exterior to Wharton's era in time for The Mount's centennial in 2002.

The guided tour of the building (which Wharton paid for with the proceeds from her successful novel, *The House of Mirth*) is a must for fans of architecture and followers of the lifestyles of the rich and famous. The tour combines the literary, historical, biographical, and design aspects of Wharton's career. The Mount is open for tours on weekends in May and from Memorial Day through October from 9:00 A.M. to 3:00 P.M. (last tour at 2:00 P.M.). Adults $6.00. Corner of Plunkett Street and Route 7. Telephone: (413) 637-1899.

Shakespeare & Company ranks among the world's great companies devoted principally to the works of the Bard. Led by artistic director Tina Packer, the company uses the carriage house and stables and four sites on the property of The Mount as outdoor stages. Shakespeare's plays are featured on the main stage, which is the natural amphitheater behind the mansion, and other playwrights are relegated to the adjunct stages. Although it is absolutely essential to virtually bathe in insect repellent before going to one of these evening performances, they invariably ignite a kind of magic that can transform Shakespeare haters into lifelong fans. The company uses no gimmicks like modern dress or adapted speeches. They perform straight Shakespeare that is full of life and all the mirth or terror the playwright intended. The entire season stretches from mid-May through October, with a whirlwind of activity from late June through August, when one-act plays adapted from the works of Edith Wharton are also performed inside the house. Telephone: (413) 637-3353.

Another summer estate that has been turned over to artistic purposes is **Tanglewood,** the summer home of the Boston Symphony Orchestra for more than fifty years and the site of the Tanglewood Music Festival of chamber music, jazz, and contemporary artists. Except for an hour before and during concerts, the 500-acre estate with ancient evergreens and formal gardens overlooking Stockbridge Bowl lake is free for strolling. When concert-goers speak of "the Shed," they are referring to the open auditorium (with overhead roof) built in 1938 that seats 5,000 people.

The Tanglewood concert scene is as much about the gestalt of the whole experience as it is about the music. Tens of thousands of people purchase lawn tickets and spread out their blankets, quilts, bedspreads or, in some pretentious cases, Oriental carpets to enjoy the music under the stars. Since getting a spot even somewhat close to the stage means arriving early, the lawn sitters also bring dinner in the form of wonderful picnics. (Many caterers and restaurants will assemble Tanglewood boxed dinners.) We have actually seen people set up silver dishes with caviar on a bed of ice for hors d'oeuvres before moving on to an entire roasted duck. Of course, some of us pack sandwiches and potato salad to eat on beach towels.

Also on the grounds is the mansion of the original owner of the site, William Aspinwall Tappan, and a replica of a cottage that Hawthorne rented in 1851, called at the time the Little Red Shanty. Hawthorne spent a year and a half there and completed *The House of Seven Gables*. The replica is used for practice studios. Tanglewood's performance season runs from the end of June through Labor Day, with the Boston Symphony Orchestra concerts beginning in July and con-

The Mount, Edith Wharton's home, Lenox, Massachusetts

cluding near the end of August. Wheelchair accessible. Route 183, West Street. Telephone: (413) 637–5165 (summer) or (617) 266–1492 (off-season).

Lee and Jacob's Pillow, Massachusetts

Most of the southern Berkshires still glitter from association with the Gilded Age, but the Midas touch never really brushed the town of Lee, about four miles southeast of Lenox on Route 20. Lee's principal business used to be a paper mill; now it is the tourist business that spills over from the more glamorous towns of the region. Nonetheless, Lee manages to hold on to a small-town charm that other places have lost. Its drugstore—just a few doors down from an old fashioned 5&10—still has a working soda fountain, and Joe's Diner on the north end of town has hardly changed a whit since Norman Rockwell used it as a setting for a *Saturday Evening Post* cover of a runaway boy and a policeman. Lee is strategically located at one of the two Berkshire exits from the Massachusetts Turnpike. It's also on the road from the rest of the Berkshires to the isolated hilltop site of **Jacob's Pillow Dance Festival** in Becket.

A century ago, Becket was a bustling, if rural industrial community with a silk mill, tanneries, and woodworking plants. The industry has vanished, and now this mountainous village is a quiet retreat where artists of many sorts pursue their work.

Modern dance pioneer Ted Shawn bought the hilltop site of a former family farm in 1930 as a retreat at a time when he and his wife and partner, Ruth St. Denis, were considered America's first couple of modern dance. Their Denishawn Dance Company had popularized a new form of expressive dance that was rooted in the theatrical and in ethnic dance traditions. In the process, they blazed a trail for the generation of dancers and choreographers who would establish modern dance as a bona fide expression of the twentieth century. (Martha Graham, for example, was a Denishawn dancer.)

St. Denis and Shawn separated in 1931 and in 1933 Shawn realized his dream of legitimizing

dance as an athletic expression for men to challenge the "sissy" image of male dancers. He recruited eight men and forged a new, muscular style, performing "tea lecture demonstrations" at the Pillow. The first audience of forty-five for Ted Shawn and His Men Dancers grew to hundreds by the end of the summer. The troupe went on to tour for seven years in the United States, Canada, England, and Cuba, dissolving when the dancers enlisted in the armed forces for World War II.

Other summer dance programming at the Pillow during the early war years demonstrated that a following for modern dance existed in the Berkshires, and in 1942 a committee raised enough money to lift the debt from the property and installed Shawn as director of the Jacob's Pillow Dance Festival, a position he held until his death in 1972.

"The Pillow" (as everyone calls it in the Berkshires) soon became the touchstone of modern dance in America—blending the cerebral urban styles with folk dance, mime, modern ballet, and a range of uncategorizable forms. That eclecticism remains a hallmark of the dance programs today. The Ted Shawn Theatre (the first theater in the United States designed specifically for dance) is the main venue for the headliners, and the setting couldn't be more dramatic, as the back opens to the outdoors where the trees behind the stage are lit with floodlights.

There's an undeniable magic about the setting. The Pillow lies at the end of a twisty mountain road heavily overhung with branches, but the complex is on the top of a hill amid manicured lawns dividing wooded glens.

It's possible to visit almost any day during the nine-week season and see free outdoor performances of emerging artists, hear lectures, watch demonstrations or master classes, or participate in critiques of choreography in progress. That many of these free events take place on an outdoor stage in the middle of the woods simply adds to the allure—one almost expects nymphs and satyrs to materialize from the trees and join the movements. The Jacob's Pillow Dance Festival runs from late June through late August, with performances or other activities occurring Tuesday through Sunday each week. George Carter Road off Route 8. Telephone: (413) 243–0745.

Stockbridge, Massachusetts

If you skip Lee and Becket and simply continue south on Route 7 from Lenox, you will quickly arrive in Stockbridge. Even if you have never visited before, you might have a déjà vu experience as you drive in on Main Street. The cheerful, well-scrubbed, prosperous small town is an archetype of rural America. No wonder it attracted illustrator Norman Rockwell, who lived and worked here for several decades at the end of his life. Stockbridge's Main Street has barely changed since Rockwell painted it more than a half century ago: a thin strip of clapboard and brick buildings all in a line with the **Red Lion Inn** at the end.

The Red Lion functions as the social center of the town. An inn of one sort or another has welcomed travelers to Stockbridge since 1773, although this incarnation dates from 1897 with a couple of more recent additions. Rockwell lunched at the inn every Thursday, and virtually every visitor to the town spends at least a little time sitting in one of the rockers on the huge porch to watch the summer pass.

Given the ubiquity of Norman Rockwell's images, you might find you recognize a number of places in Stockbridge. The old Stockbridge Firehouse on Elm Street was the subject of *The American LaFrance.* On top of Theresa's Cafe and Bev's Ice Cream on Main Street (the big sign out front says "Stockbridge General Store") is the site of Rockwell's first studio in Stockbridge. The setting for the *Post* cover, *Marriage License,* is the former town office building, also on Main Street and now inhabited by Yankee Candle. Shanahan's Market on Elm Street still serves ice cream, burgers, and ice cream sodas at the soda fountain counter featured in Rockwell's *After the Prom.* Rockwell loved to feature locals in his paintings. He once remarked, "Every time I go to town meeting or some other public affair, I fairly drool over the models I have so far missed."

The **Corner House,** a Georgian-style white clapboard building on the corner of Main and Elm Streets, was the first site of a Norman Rockwell Museum, and Rockwell and other community activists saved the building from demolition. But it proved inadequate for the number of visitors and a new museum was made possible in large part by a donation from Stephen Spielberg, a big admirer of Rockwell.

To get to the **Norman Rockwell Museum,** simply follow the signs to Route 183 west of the town center. The thirty-six-acre hillside site has a long view north across an ox-bow bend of the Housatonic River to the Berkshire Hills dotted with mansions. Rockwell and his third wife Molly lived in town (at 8 South Street, a private home) and liked to ride bicycles for exercise. One of their favorite routes was this road west from town that leads to the museum, which they helped to establish.

Rockwell spent the last twenty-five years of his life in Stockbridge and the museum has the largest collection of his original art. He was certainly prolific, creating more than 4,000 recorded works of art and 321 covers for the *Saturday Evening Post* alone. During his six-decade career, Rockwell chronicled the introduction into American life of the telephone, radio, electrical lighting, television, airplane travel, and manned flights to the moon. Skylit galleries display Rockwell's works—and his sheer output seems all the more amazing if you visit the room that follows a single work through a painstaking process from idea to thumbnail sketch, to a detailed charcoal drawing from a model, to a color study, to the finished painting, and finally the reproduction. The galleries include his first *Post* cover in 1916 as well as his final magazine cover in 1976 for *American Artist.*

As the Rockwell era of illustration fades into history, it is worth reflecting on what a powerful influence his imagery was on popular culture. His paintings of the *Four Freedoms* occupy a skylit rotunda gallery of their own. He cast Franklin Delano Roosevelt's speech in concrete terms immediately comprehensible to all Americans, showing freedom of speech, freedom of worship, freedom from want, and freedom from fear in the faces of everyday people. The original paintings toured the country in 1943, raising $143 million for the war bond effort. And while there is no denying the sentimentality and flag-waving political naiveté of much of Rockwell's work, it's also notable that when he severed ties with the ultra-conservative *Post* in the 1960s, he turned to putting a human face on racial issues in a manner that influenced many Americans.

In addition to the main museum (which has a predictably excellent gift shop, which includes signed Rockwell prints among its merchandise), the grounds also hold Rockwell's final studio, moved from its original location in the center of town and restored to its appearance during his life. It overlooks a bend in the Housatonic River—a spot Rockwell would have loved had he been a landscape painter. Because it is unheated, the studio is only open from May through October. The grounds are very pleasant and picnicking is permitted. The Norman Rockwell Museum is open May through October daily from 10:00 A.M. to 5:00 P.M., November through April Monday through Friday from 11:00 A.M. to 4:00 P.M. and Saturday and Sunday from 10:00 A.M. to 5:00 P.M. Adults $9.00. Wheelchair accessible. Route 183. Telephone: (413) 298–4100.

While Rockwell tapped into the small-town charm of Stockbridge, the village (originally founded as a mission to the Mohican tribe) was Lenox's near rival as a retreat for the elite of America's Gilded Age.

Less than a mile farther south on Route 183 from the Rockwell Museum, in the Stockbridge village of Glendale is **Chesterwood,** the summer estate of Daniel Chester French. From May through October for thirty-four years, French came here to enjoy the landscape and work on his sculpture commissions, including his most famous, the *Seated Lincoln* in the Lincoln Memorial in Washington. In New England, French is perhaps better known for one of his first commissions, the Concord Minute Man.

The house at Chesterwood was built in 1901 in the Colonial Revival style, reflecting French's translation of a traditional New England landscape into a gentleman's estate. The studio predates the house by three years, and demonstrates the sculptor's ingenuity. Not only is it well lit by windows, but barn doors open at one end and railroad tracks extend out into the open air. Periodically French would use a railroad hand cart to roll his works in progress outdoors to study them in natural light.

It's hard to see how French could be so enormously prolific at this site. A wisteria-trimmed porch on the back of the studio offers almost too much of a distraction, and French himself said that he considered the 122-acre estate nothing

Chesterwood Studio, Stockbridge, Massachusetts

short of "heaven." The National Trust for Historic Preservation operates the property now, and mounts yearly outdoor sculpture exhibitions on the extensive lawns. Chesterwood is open May through October daily from 10:00 A.M. to 5:00 P.M. Adults $7.50. 4 Williamsville Road, off Route 183. Telephone: (413) 298–3579.

Chesterwood is something of a special case among the Berkshire estates, but to see another of the striking nineteenth-century "cottages," simply drive up Prospect Hill to **Naumkeag.** The residence of Joseph Choate, an attorney who served as ambassador to England from 1899 to 1905, this twenty-six-room mansion was designed by Stanford White in 1886. It lives up to its name, which means "haven of peace" in Algonquian. The original furnishings have been preserved and they include an outstanding collection of antique furniture, Chinese porcelains, rugs, and tapestries. The gardens were designed by Fletcher Steele and include a peony garden, a Chinese garden, and birch walk. Naumkeag is open Memorial Day to Columbus Day daily from 10:00 A.M. to 5:00 P.M. Adults $7.00, gardens only $5.00. Prospect Hill Road. Telephone: (413) 298–3239.

Stanford White, perhaps the leading American architect of the Gilded Age, also designed the main playhouse used by the **Berkshire Theatre Festival,** now in its eighth decade and one of the oldest summer theaters in the nation. For many years BTF has produced its own plays, although it was once one of the stops on the barnstorming summer theater circuit. BTF has hosted many famous names on its boards, from Katharine Hepburn and James Cagney to Joanne Woodward and Dustin Hoffman. In addition to American classics, light romances, and comedy revivals on the main stage, BTF also produces more experimental work on its Unicorn Stage and children's theater under a large tent. The season runs from mid-June through August. Wheelchair accessible. Main Street. Telephone: (413) 298–5536.

West Stockbridge, Massachusetts

The village of West Stockbridge lies just four miles west of Stockbridge on Route 102, heading toward the New York border. It is also the western gateway to the Berkshires for travelers coming from the New York Thruway and getting off the Massachusetts Turnpike at exit 1. The Shaker Mill Pond and Williams River weave their way along Main Street, where the world's first hydro-electric dam was constructed. Notably less tony than Stockbridge itself, West Stockbridge has emerged from a funky counter-cultural identity in the 1960s and early 1970s to embrace a genteel artiness. Both sides of the Williams River in the village center—Main Street and Harris Street—are lined with small shops selling clothing and jewelry (Main Street) or crafts and art (Harris Street). Harris Street is dominated by several crafts studios of artisans working in glass, stained glass, leather, and wood and the end of the street contains some of the village's better restaurants. New construction and renovation have created several lodging options as well.

Great Barrington, Massachusetts

If you head into Great Barrington by driving south on Route 7, you'll pass the trailhead for **Monument Mountain** just three miles south of Stockbridge center.

This topographic hiccup is hardly monumental, but its 1,735-foot peak overlooks the hills and valleys of southern Berkshire County and the hike to the top is a pleasant walk. The easy Indian Monument Trail is about one and one-quarter miles and the steeper Hickey Trail is about three-quarters of a mile. The landscape is thick with mountain laurel, white pines, and hemlocks. Both trails take about forty-five minutes to climb.

The famous nineteenth-century poet William Cullen Bryant, who lived in Great Barrington, wrote a poem that much impressed his peers about the legend attached to Monument Mountain. Herman Melville and Nathaniel Hawthorne began their friendship in August 1850, when Oliver Wendell Holmes introduced them and they all climbed Monument Mountain in a thunderstorm. At the top they drank a toast to William Cullen Bryant with Heidsieck champagne from a single silver mug. Then they proceeded to read Bryant's poem about an Indian maiden who threw herself off the mountain after she was forbidden to marry a member of a hostile tribe—a primitivist take on the Romeo and Juliet story. The trails are open daily and are free. Route 7. Telephone: (413) 298–3239.

The town of Great Barrington is everything West Stockbridge aspires to be—a vibrant multicultural community with a dynamic mix of artists and artisans, businesspeople, New Agers, and just plain folks. Incorporated in 1761, Great Barrington is the largest town in the southern Berkshires and was the site of the last attempt of the British government to hold court in America—and of the freeing of the first slaves under due process of law. One of the great figures of African American history, W.E.B. DuBois, was born in Great Barrington and the town has a history of progressivism. William Stanley pioneered the use of alternating current for street lights here and then sold his patent rights to the present General Electric Company. In 1886 Great Barrington became one of the first communities in the world with electric street lights and electric lights in its homes.

Main Street parallels the Housatonic River, and the Great Barrington Land Conservancy has created a fascinating trail along the riverbank. Although Great Barrington industries much abused the river, the conservancy and hundreds of volunteers have begun the arduous process of reclaiming the river for its scenic beauty. They have removed more than 210 tons of debris so far. The Housatonic River Walk begins behind the Riverbank House on the north end of Main Street at Cottage Street. Follow the signs through the gate to a pleasant, if short, walkway behind the Main Street businesses. The project, which has another half-mile to go, is often cited as a model of citizen environmental action.

The town center is very different from the genteel burgs only a few miles to its north. The counter culture is still very much alive here, as evidenced by shops proffering mystical books and paraphernalia, but there is also a sense of whimsy to many of the establishments. This is a good place to begin looking seriously at antiques and collectibles—and not a bad spot at all to get a bite to eat. If you are camping or have rented a cabin, note that Great Barrington is one of the few places in the southern Berkshires with a full-fledged supermarket.

The houses and barns on both sides of Route 7 south of Great Barrington are handsome, and you have to read the signs to tell which are antiques dealers, which are B&Bs, and which are private residences. Close to forty antiques dealers line the main roads of Great Barrington and the two towns to its immediate south, Egremont and Sheffield.

Sheffield and Egremont, Massachusetts

By a slim margin, Sheffield has the most dealers in antiques, which seems appropriate since it was the first town settled in Berkshire County. When Sheffield was established in 1725 on a floodplain beside the Housatonic River, it opened the way for settlement of the entire Housatonic Valley north to Pittsfield. The village center is tiny; Sheffield is mostly open agricultural land still under till.

Neighboring Egremont and its hamlet of South Egremont (on Routes 23 and 41) more closely resemble an old-time village. They lie on the old stagecoach road about halfway between Hartford and Albany, which made Egremont a handy place to stop for the night at the Egremont

Inn (see "Staying There"). Some of the most striking and upscale antiques to be found in the southern Berkshires are sold by Egremont's dealers. Rather like all the new Oregonians who want to close the border with California now that they have moved, Egremonters often grumble about all those New Yorkers who have moved to town to open shops and be innkeepers. If you're patient, you'll soon learn how many years it has been since *they* left Manhattan.

From Egremont it is a short drive southwest to the town of Mount Washington, which as close as we can tell does not really have a town center but does have the magnificent Mount Washington Forest (telephone: 413–528–0330) and Bash Bish Falls State Park.

Personal Narrative: To the Falls

We have never heard of anyone actually visiting Bash Bish Falls, but one June day when we have had our fill of antiquing in Egremont, we decide to check them out since the falls are alleged to be the most dramatic in Massachusetts.

Our directions are what might be charitably called vague: "Drive out to Mount Washington from South Egremont. . . ." Fortunately, it turns out that the road is well marked. From the village of South Egremont we follow Route 41 south about 100 yards past the point where Route 23 splits off to the west. Following the signs, we turn right on Mount Washington Road, heading west across this beautiful valley bottomland full of old farms, many of which are still under till with corn.

The road is marked for slow passage—25 miles per hour—and it doesn't take long to see why. As we round a turn, a whitetail doe bounds out in the road, the flag of her tail pointing straight up, and crosses into a woodland thicket. Less than a mile later, we spot another doe in a field behind a farmhouse and we slow down and stop without making any noise. She is turned broadside to us and stares, her big ears at full alert. As we watch, it looks like a large rabbit is bounding through the grass toward her. No, it's not a rabbit—it's her fawn.

The fawn bounds up to the doe and nuzzles beneath her to nurse. We have seen hundreds of white-tail deer over the years, but have never witnessed this scene. But the doe is nervous about our presence and she pulls away and wades through the grass into denser cover of an alder thicket with the fawn following.

After seeing three deer in such quick succession, we are very careful about how we drive along this road. The property is posted on both sides against hunting, fishing, and trespassing. This part of the town of Mount Washington is a patchwork of state forest and private land, and the private landowners seem zealous about guarding their property rights. No wonder the deer are so bold! The roadsides, especially on the north-facing hill on our left, are lined with immense thickets of mountain laurel, both white and pink. We know that mountain laurel is the state flower of Connecticut, but it appears to be profusely native to this part of Massachusetts.

We continue to a well-marked junction at the Mount Washington Town Hall and an unusual church building with a square belfry and vertical siding. A sign tells us that Bash Bish Falls is four miles to the right. Soon the road begins to descend around one of the peaks of Mount Washington, wrapping around it to follow the small river to the falls.

There is a parking lot marked for Bash Bish Falls, which has a short but very steep trail down to the falls. The trail is made somewhat easier by wooden steps cut into the embankment, but this is a path for people equipped with walking sticks and hiking shoes—neither of which we've brought. But about a mile down the road (and we do mean "down"), we pass over the border to New York State and come to another parking lot. It appears that the state park is a dual state park, and the New York side has some rental cabins. More to the point, it has a very promising trailhead toward the falls—a woodland road that is steep in only a

few places and offers good footing the whole way.

The trail follows the river upstream for about a mile along a long sequence of shallow rapids—really a mile-long falls with a drop of maybe 150 feet. Suddenly it rises rather sharply and we're at the spot where the Massachusetts trail comes out—right at Bash Bish Falls.

The final waterfall of Bash Bish Falls is an eighty-foot drop where the river divides around a huge basalt boulder perched in the middle of a cataract. As promised, it is perhaps the most dramatic falls in Massachusetts, roaring down into a basin and then flowing past a collection of glacial boulders of at least three different kinds of rock before the river regains its coherence below.

There's only one other person at the falls, a woman perhaps in her late sixties or early seventies who is sitting at the top of the steps looking down at the falls. She asks if we know how the falls were named, and when we express curiosity, she tells us that Bash Bish was an Indian maiden who was paddling in her canoe above the falls when trappers came after her. She fled downstream, and her canoe became entangled in the rocks at the head of the cataract. Rather than face capture, she dove down into the basin and was never seen again—except when she appears as an apparition on moonlit nights.

The woman then says, a little shyly, "I have a story of my own." She and her husband vacationed every summer here with their children and continued to come even after the children were grown, staying at the cabins on the New York side. When her husband died, he was cremated and they scattered his ashes at the base of Bash Bish Falls. She has purchased a summer vacation home and comes to the falls every morning.

As for her husband, "I know what's he's doing on moonlit nights," she smiles.

Staying There

New Hampshire's White Mountains

For information about White Mountains lodging, dining, and attractions, contact White Mountains Attractions, P.O. Box 10, North Woodstock, NH 03262. Telephone: (603) 745–8270 or (800) 346–3687. The White Mountains Visitor Center is located at exit 32 off I–93 in North Woodstock.

For a listing of some of the region's lodgings, contact Country Inns in the White Mountains. Mailing address: P.O. Box 2025, North Conway, NH 03860. Telephone number for central reservations service: (800) 562–1300. Two other sources of information will be indispensable for active outdoors enthusiasts.

For advance information about the **White Mountain National Forest,** contact the central office: 719 Main Street, Laconia, NH 03247. Telephone: (603) 528–8721; TTY (603) 528–8722. Visitors centers are located throughout the park. The **Saco Ranger Station** is located at 33 Kancamagus Highway, just west of Route 16. Telephone: (603) 447–5448. The **Androscoggin Ranger Station** is located at 80 Glen Road in Gorham. Telephone: (603) 466–2713. The **Ammonoosuc Ranger Station** is located on Trudeau Road in Bethlehem. Telephone: (603) 869–2626. The **Evans Notch Ranger Station,** located on Route 2 just north of Bethel, Maine, covers the Maine portion of the White Mountains. Telephone: (207) 824–2134.

The National Forest also operates **campgrounds** throughout the White Mountains. The sites range considerably in size and extent of services and include some that are accessible for people with disabilities. **Dolly Copp Campground,** north of Pinkham Notch on Route 16 is one of the largest, with space for more than 1,000 campers. This particular campground is named for Dolly Emery Copp, a pioneer woman who married Hayes Copp in 1827 and moved to a

cabin at this site. They took in travelers for the next four decades. On their golden anniversary, Dolly declared that fifty years was long enough to live with any man, and the couple divided the farm and household and both moved away. For complete information about camping, contact the central office listed above. To reserve a campsite, call (800) 280–2267; TTY (800) 879–4496.

Another essential source of information for hikers is the Appalachian Mountain Club, 5 Joy Street, Boston, MA 02108. Telephone: (617) 523–0636. The AMC operates two visitors centers in the White Mountains. The **Pinkham Notch Visitor Center and Lodge** is located ten miles north of Jackson on Route 16. Telephone: (603) 466–2727. The **Crawford Notch Station Information Center** is on Route 302. Telephone: (603) 466–7774. *The AMC White Mountain Guide* should be in the backpack of anyone who starts off on a hike in the White Mountains.

The AMC also operates a **network of eight huts,** stretching for 56 miles along the Appalachian Trail. Some are above the tree line and access to each hut is rated by difficulty of the hike. Each hut has bunk-bed accommodations and running water. Seven of the eight offer full-service lodging, with breakfast and dinner and various scheduled walks and programs. "Base camp" lodging with more amenities is also available. The **Joe Dodge Lodge** at the Pinkham Notch Visitor Center has bunk rooms, private rooms, hot showers and flush toilets. The **Crawford Hotel** offers bunkhouses, pay showers, and a self-service kitchen. Some of the lodgings are open year-round, while others are closed during the winter. Telephone: (603) 466–2727. Inexpensive.

For advance information on the towns in the Mount Washington Valley, contact the Mount Washington Valley Chamber of Commerce, P.O. Box 2300G, North Conway, NH 03860–2300. Telephone: (603) 356–3171 or (800) 367–3364.

Center Conway, New Hampshire

ACTIVITIES

Saco Valley Canoe Trips. This company provides new, state-of-the-art Old Town Canoes as well as shuttle service for the route of your choice. The staff can recommend a number of trips that range from four to almost fourteen miles and feature good fishing spots, sandy swimming beaches, and the opportunity to paddle under covered bridges. Route 302. Telephone: (603) 447–2444 or (800) 447–2460.

North Conway, New Hampshire

LODGING

Cranmore Mountain Lodge. 859 Kearsarge Road. The most famous visitor to this country inn was Babe Ruth, who vacationed here when the property was owned by his daughter. Eleven rooms in the main house are supplemented by four rooms in the barn loft. Telephone: (603) 356–2044 or (800) 356–3596. Moderate with breakfast.

Old Red Inn & Cottages. Route 16/302. This 1810 home has beautiful gardens and mountain views. In addition to seven rooms in the inn itself, there are also two-bedroom cottages, some with fireplaces and kitchenettes. Telephone: (603) 356–2642 or (800) 338–1356. Moderate with breakfast.

Scottish Lion Inn. Route 16. The eight guest rooms in this bed-and-breakfast feature a mix of Scots and early American decor. Telephone: (603) 356–6381. Inexpensive to moderate with breakfast.

Stonehurst Manor. Route 16. This Victorian stone-and-shingle mansion, the former summer estate of carpet tycoon Erastus Bigelow, sits above Route 16 on thirty-three acres with beautiful views. The fourteen rooms in the mansion itself give the best sense of the privileged lifestyle of the estate's first inhabitants. The ten rooms in the 1952 wing are certainly comfortable but less evocative. A pool and Jacuzzi are available, but many guests use the manor as a point of departure for walking, hiking, and cycling. In the winter, sixty-five kilometers of free cross-country ski trails begin at the back door. Telephone: (603) 356–3113 or (800) 525–9100. Moderate to expensive with breakfast and dinner.

FOOD

Scottish Lion Inn. Route 16. Telephone: (603) 356–6381. As you would expect in dining rooms where both the walls and the waitstaff are clad in tartans, the menu features finnan haddie and Highland game pie and the bar stocks more than sixty single malts. But this restaurant also offers American and international dishes. Lunch and dinner. Moderate to expensive.

Stonehurst Manor. Route 16. Telephone: (603) 356–3113. Four dining rooms and a screened patio (in summer) offer a full dinner menu (expensive) or a variety of creative wood-fired pizzas (inexpensive to moderate). Dinner only.

OTHER ATTRACTIONS

Conway Scenic Railroad. Trains played a big role in opening up the White Mountains and this railroad recalls that tradition. From North Conway's 1874 Victorian station, a steam locomotive travels through Mount Washington Valley to Conway and on to Bartlett. This "lowlands" trip journeys through fields and woodlands and crosses the Saco and a number of other rivers. Adult fares range from $8.00 to $16.50. A diesel locomotive also makes the round-trip of five and one-half hours through Crawford Notch to Fabyan Station, taking in some of the most spectacular of the White Mountains scenery: sheer bluffs, steep ravines, wide mountain vistas, and panoramic views of the Mount Washington Hotel and Presidential Range. Adult fare $31.95 to $39.95. Route 16/302 in North Conway center. Telephone: (603) 356–5251 or (800) 232–5251.

Mount Washington Observatory Resource Center. If you don't have time or stamina to make it to the summit, this free facility on Route 16 relates the details of Mount Washington's weather and history. Open mid-May to mid-October daily; weekends year-round. Telephone: (603) 356–8345.

ACTIVITIES

Cranmore Mountain. Set within walking distance from downtown North Conway, this resort is the oldest operating ski area in New England and it retains that old-fashioned feel. Most trails are best suited for beginner and intermediate skiers but there are four new glade trails for all abilities as well as a tubing park, ice skating rink, and snowshoe rentals. Skimobile Road. Telephone: (603) 356–5544.

North Conway Country Club. Established in 1895, this classic 6,300-yard, eighteen-hole course situated along the Saco River provides views of Mount Washington and the Moat Range. Telephone: (603) 356–9391.

TOURS

Mount Washington Observatory Edutrips. Winter overnight trips to the summit of Mount Washington are among the more unique experiences in the region—but only for people in excellent physical condition who are properly equipped to hike safely in extreme cold. The Observatory information says it all: "Those who are prepared for sub-zero cold, hurricane force winds, and whiteout conditions are occasionally privileged to enjoy remarkable vistas of snow-covered peaks, the setting sun slipping behind ranges 130 miles distant, and other breathtaking experiences known only to the winter mountaineer." Mailing address: Mount Washington Observatory, Main Street, P.O. Box 2310, North Conway, NH 03860–2310. Telephone: (603) 356–8345. $350.

FAIRS, FESTIVALS, AND EVENTS

Annual Railfans Day. For more than twenty years, this full day of railroading activities (such as special runs, equipment demos, and a flea market) has been held in mid-October at Conway Scenic Railroad. Telephone: (603) 356–5251.

SHOPPING

League of New Hampshire Craftsmen Shop. 2526 Main Street. Telephone: (603) 356–2441. One of seven League shops throughout the state, this collection of artisan-made fine crafts provides a particularly nice contrast to the mass produced merchandise featured in the area's outlet shopping.

Outlet Malls. Route 16 between North Conway and Conway is lined with outlet shopping, which

flourishes in part because New Hampshire has no sales tax. Among the highlights is Chuck Roast Mountainwear, purveyor of locally made Polartec fleece outerwear for children and adults, at the Mount Washington Outlet Center. An L.L. Bean Outlet is also nearby.

Bartlett/Lower Bartlett, New Hampshire

ACTIVITIES

Attitash Bear Park. Attitash has more than 200 acres of terrain on two interconnected mountains and recently introduced a new summit trail, a Kachina triple chairlift, and a new snowboard park. Lift tickets are also valid at Cranmore. Attitash has access to cross-country ski trails and an expanded program of guided snowshoe tours. In the summer, there are alpine slides, water slides, a scenic chairlift to an observation tower at the summit as well as mountain biking and horseback riding. Route 302. Telephone: (603) 374–2368 or (800) 223–7669.

Bear Notch Ski Touring Center. Based in a 200-year-old farmhouse, the center offers cross-country skiing and snowshoeing, with a number of riverside trails and spectacular mountain views. Route 302. Telephone: (603) 374–2277.

FAIRS, FESTIVALS, AND EVENTS

Attitash Bear Park Equine Festival. Show jumpers from all over the globe demonstrate their skills and compete for $150,000 in prize money. This five-day annual event is held in late August.

BankBoston Celebrity Ski Classic. New England sports and TV personalities are part of this event to raise money for the Genesis Fund, which supports children with genetic and birth defects. Events include races, a barbecue, and gala awards banquet each year in late January at Attitash Bear Park.

Ski for the Cure. This annual benefit race raises money for the New England Cystic Fibrosis Foundation. The weekend of events takes place in mid-March at Attitash Bear Park.

Jackson, New Hampshire

LODGING

Eagle Mountain House. Carter Notch Road. This five-story wooden hotel in a secluded valley outside Jackson dates from the pre-automobile days of White Mountains sightseeing but was fully renovated in 1986. The ninety-three guest rooms have country pine decor, but everybody's favorite spot is in a rocking chair on the wide front porch with views of the mountains beyond. Amenities include golf, tennis, swimming, a health club, and, in the winter, cross-country skiing. Like most Jackson inns, it's linked to Jackson's network of trails. Telephone: (603) 383–9111 or (800) 966–5779. Moderate to expensive.

Inn at Thorn Hill. Thorn Hill Road. Lodgings at this pricey but classy property are spread among an inn designed by Stanford White, a carriage house, and cottages. Located in a wooded spot just outside of town, the inn has nineteen guest rooms and two parlors, one with a woodstove, piano, and perfect view of Mount Washington. It also boasts an outdoor hot tub. Telephone: (603) 383–4242 or (800) 289–8990. Expensive to very expensive with breakfast and dinner.

The Wentworth. Route 16A. Sitting in the center of Jackson Village, this survivor from the Gilded Age has been brought up to date and garnished with an outdoor pool and eighteen-hole golf course. Some of the rooms feature fireplaces and/or Jacuzzis. Telephone: (603) 383–9700 or (800) 637–0013. Expensive.

FOOD

Eagle Mountain House. Carter Notch Road. Telephone: (603) 383–9111. If it's steamship round or roast turkey you're looking for at dinner time, look no farther. The Eagle Mountain House's dining room focuses on the New England classics. Lunch (June through October) and dinner. Moderate to expensive.

Inn at Thorn Hill. Thorn Hill Road. Telephone: (603) 383–4242. Other resort-style lodgings in the area stick to the old-fashioned New England basics, but the dining room of the Inn at Thorn

Hill assumes a more sophisticated palate for its New American offerings with a continental touch. Reservations essential. Dinner. Expensive to very expensive.

The Wentworth Dining Room. Telephone: (603) 383–9700. The dining room of this resort hotel serves regional American cuisine, with an emphasis on healthy eating. Dinner. Moderate to expensive.

ACTIVITIES

Black Mountain. One of the pioneer ski slopes dating back to the 1930s, Black Mountain has 1,100 feet of vertical drop with four lifts. Thirty trails range from gentle learning slopes to traditional trails winding through scenic splendor to double black diamond trails. Black Mountain's modest size makes it good for families and beginners. There is also a run on Whitney's Hill exclusively for snow tubers. Route 16A. Telephone: (603) 383–4490 or (800) 475–4669.

Jackson X-C. Regularly rated as one of the five top cross-country ski centers in the country, Jackson has 157 kilometers of groomed and ungroomed trails that weave throughout the village and lead into the surrounding mountains. Main Street. Telephone: (603) 383–9355 or (800) 927–6697.

Wildcat Mountain. With what many skiers believe are the best scenic views of any ski area in the White Mountains, Wildcat looks down on the White Mountain National Forest with a great view of Tuckerman Ravine and the summit of Mount Washington. It was first carved up for "ski running" by Civilian Conservation Corps crews in 1933 and their handiwork survives in the namesake 1.5-mile trail. One of the ski area's cofounders set the record on this trail (1 minute, 55.8 seconds) in 1955—and it still stands. There's a high speed detachable quad to the 4,062 summit where you can choose from forty-three trails, with a maximum vertical drop of 2,100 feet. The beginner Polecat Trail is the longest ski trail in New Hampshire. The newly expanded glade skiing area covers more than twenty-five acres and snowboarders have been allotted a new snowpark. The gondola also operates weekends late May to early June and then daily until mid-October for sightseeing. Rides to the summit are $9.00 adults. At the top, you can follow self-guided nature trails with striking vistas of Mount Washington. Several waterfalls are also within easy hiking distance from the base of the mountain. Route 16, Pinkham Notch. Telephone: (603) 466–3326 or (800) 255–6439.

Pinkham Notch, New Hampshire

ACTIVITIES

Great Glen Trails. Surrounded by Mount Washington and the Presidential Range, the wide, gently sloping trails are well-suited for all-season activity. In the winter, they support cross-country skiing (including adaptive programs for skiers with disabilities), snowshoeing, kicksledding, and ice skating. Spring, summer, and fall find biking and hiking, as well as fly-fishing clinics and other activities. Route 16, Pinkham Notch. Telephone: (603) 466–2333.

FAIRS, FESTIVALS, AND EVENTS

Mount Washington Road Race. This footrace to the summit of Mount Washington, held in mid-June, has been an annual event for almost forty years. Telephone: (603) 466–3988

Glen, New Hampshire

LODGING

The Bernerhof Inn. Route 302. Nine guest rooms (six with double Jacuzzis) occupy the gabled and turreted Victorian inn, situated off Route 302 on the way to Crawford Notch. As suits such an architecturally interesting building, the guest rooms also feature odd corners and angles, accented with a restrained country decor. Telephone: (603) 383–9132 or (800) 548–8007. Moderate with breakfast.

CAMPGROUNDS AND RV PARKS

Glen-Ellis Family Campground. From the junction of Routes 16 and 302, go one-quarter mile west on Route 302 for one of the best commercial campgrounds in the White Mountains. Glen-Ellis

has 200 sites, river swimming, fishing, and canoeing. Telephone: (603) 383–4567.

FOOD

Bernerhof Inn. Route 302. Telephone: (603) 383–9132. The inn hosts the Taste of the Mountains Cooking School and has a reputation for the Central European cuisine of its dining room. The adjacent pub has a fireplace, golden oak paneling, a bearskin on the walls, and more than sixty varieties of beer. Lunch and dinner. Moderate to expensive.

Bretton Woods, New Hampshire

LODGING

Bretton Arms Country Inn. Route 302. On the same property as the Mount Washington Hotel, this property is open year-round so that in addition to summer and fall activities, guests can enjoy alpine skiing next door at Bretton Woods Ski Area or walk out the door to ninety kilometers of cross-country trails. Lacking the resort formality of the Hotel, it's a cozier place to return after a day of physical activity. Built as a private home in 1896, the Bretton Arms was first opened to guests in 1907. Closed since 1973, it was restored and reopened in 1986 with thirty-four rooms and suites. Telephone: (603) 278–1000 or (800) 258–0330. Moderate to expensive.

Bretton Woods Motor Inn. Route 302. The most casual lodging of the Bretton Woods group (across the street from the Mount Washington Hotel), the motor inn still enjoys the same great location and views and is open year-round. Telephone: (603) 278–1000 or (800) 258–0330. Moderate.

Mount Washington Hotel & Resort. The only surviving grand hotel from the "Gilded Age" may also be the area's greatest attraction after its namesake mountain. Threatened with demolition, the "white elephant" was purchased in 1991 by a group of local business people who are steadily renovating and improving the property. But they can't improve on its location. The red roofed, white clapboard inn standing out against the Presidential range is an incredible sight as you come around a curve in the road. In a style called

"Spanish Renaissance," but that we think of more as "Mountain Elegance," the flamboyant hotel opened in 1902 after more than two years of work by 250 master craftsmen. The mile-long driveway leads past broad lawns and gardens and the eighteen-hole putting green. The 900-foot white-railed veranda is one of the best spots in the region to simply gaze transfixed by the mountains.

Displays throughout the hotel evoke the past, but the ornately restored lobby—with its crystal chandeliers, Tiffany stained glass, gilded antique mirrors, and rich carpeting—does more to recapture the bygone era than any memorabilia. The opulent Main Dining Room, where an orchestra serenades diners, has beautiful views. It is shaped as an octagon so that no guest would feel slighted by sitting in a corner. The more restrained— almost austere—furnishings of the guest rooms are a welcome contrast. TVs are available on request, but it's far more fun to join other guests in the TV lounge. One October we watched the World Series with several baseball fanatics from Japan.

The hotel stays true to its origins as a destination for "rusticating." Its grounds include two PGA championship golf courses, plus the putting green situated around the hotel's flower gardens. There are indoor and outdoor pools and a dozen red clay tennis courts. Horses are available for sashaying along the bridle paths of the White Mountain National Forest, and there are dozens of trails for hiking or cycling as well as good fishing holes in mountain streams.

Telephone: (603) 278–1000 or (800) 258–0330. Expensive to very expensive with breakfast and dinner. A variety of packages are usually available. Although the hotel plans to open for the winter in the new millennium, it now closes from early November into May.

FOOD

Bretton Arms Country Inn. Route 302. Telephone: (603) 278–1000. The formal, fireside dining room serves some of the more polished continental cuisine in the region. Dinner. Expensive.

Fabyans Station. Route 302 at the Cog Railway

The Mount Washington Hotel and Resort, Bretton Woods, New Hampshire

access road. Telephone: (603) 278–2222. Originally built as a railroad station in the Victorian period when tourists came to Mount Washington literally by the trainload, Fabyans Station has been completely done over in a faux Gay Nineties style (right down to ersatz stained glass). It's more playful than deceitful, though, and the family-friendly menu of American standards like ribs, chicken, and pasta is one of the less expensive choices in the area. Lunch and dinner. Moderate.

ACTIVITIES

Bretton Woods Ski Area. Every mountain resort hotel needs a ski area, and this one is owned by the Mount Washington Hotel. It's relatively uncrowded, five lifts serving thirty-two ski trails, a snowboard half-pipe, and 1,500 vertical feet of drop. Even better, the area has a 100-kilometer cross-country trail network groomed for both traditional and skate skiers. You can ski on the grounds of the Mount Washington Hotel or take a chair lift to the Mountain Road cross-country ski trail, which winds down the mountain for five miles, offering spectacular views of Mount Washington. Route 302. Telephone: (603) 278–5000 or (800) 232–2972. For cross-country ski information: (603) 278–5181.

FAIRS, FESTIVALS, AND EVENTS

Annual Native American Cultural Weekend.
Held over three days in mid-July, this gathering of
Indian nations highlights the Indian people of
New England and Hawaii. Telephone: (603)
444–2329.

Hart's Location, New Hampshire

LODGING

Notchland Inn. Route 302. This 1860s granite
mansion sitting on one hundred acres boasts
views of Crawford Notch and the surrounding
mountains. The twelve rooms and suites have
working fireplaces. Arts & Crafts buffs will find
the front parlor, designed by Gustav Stickley,
especially interesting. Telephone: (603) 374–6131
or (800) 866–6131. Expensive to very expensive
with breakfast and dinner.

CAMPGROUNDS AND RV PARKS

Dry River Campground. There are thirty primitive tent sites available at the state-run site in
Crawford Notch State Park. The campground
also serves as a central base camp for a variety of
trails in the park and White Mountain National
Forest. For information, contact New Hampshire
Division of Parks and Recreation, P.O. Box 1856,
Concord, NH 03302–1856. Telephone: (603)
271–3556; TTY Relay NH (800) 735–2964. For
reservations, contact the central reservation center: (603) 271–3628. Direct line to campground:
(603) 374–2272.

Bethel, Maine

For information, contact the Bethel Area
Chamber of Commerce, Train Station, Cross
Street, P.O. Box 439, Bethel, ME 04217.
Telephone: (207) 824–2282. The office is open
for visitors Monday through Friday from 9:00
A.M. to 5:00 P.M.

LODGING

Bethel Inn & Country Club. Occupying 200
acres at the edge of Bethel Common, the Inn's
buildings are easily identified by their yellow
color. The facility was constructed in 1913 to
house the patients of Dr. John Gehring, who
treated nervous disorders with healthy living and
exercise in the fresh air. The emphasis is still on
fitness, with a fitness center, outdoor pool, golf
course, tennis courts, and, a short drive away, a
small lake for swimming. There are twenty-five
miles of cross-country ski trails for the winter. The
original rooms are rather small, but comfortable
with country antiques. There are also suites in the
original building. Modern condominium lodging
is also available but it doesn't have the same character. Telephone: (207) 824–2175 or (800)
654–0125. Expensive to very expensive with
breakfast and dinner, except in April and
November when meals are not served.

Holidae House. Main Street. About a five-minute
walk from Bethel Common, this century-old
home has seven guest rooms, each of which is furnished with Oriental rugs and antiques. Some
have ceiling murals and whirlpool tubs. Given the
flair of the decor, it's not surprising that the
innkeeper also has an antiques shop in the
barn out back. Telephone: (207) 824–3400.
Inexpensive to moderate with breakfast.

FOOD

Iron Horse Bar and Grill. Cross Street.
Telephone: (207) 824–0961. Two vintage rail
dining cars at the new Bethel Station complex
right outside town serve as a lounge car and a dining car, the latter with a vaguely Art Deco feel. In
addition to the predictable steak, chicken, and
seafood, Iron Horse also offers a selection of game
dishes. Lunch and dinner. Moderate to expensive.

Moose's Tale. Route 2 at the Sunday River access
road. Telephone: (207) 824–4243. This local
microbrewery has the usual pub food to accompany some very good beers for quaffing next to
the stone fireplace in the main dining room.
Lunch and dinner. Inexpensive.

Mother's. Upper Main Street. Telephone: (207)
824–2589. This homey and casual restaurant in a
gingerbread-trimmed Victorian has several small
dining rooms, but in the summer aim for a table
on the front deck. Lunch and dinner. Moderate.

ACTIVITIES

Sunday River Ski Area & Mountain Bike Park.
Sunday River is an American success story. In 1958, it consisted of little more than a T-bar and a couple of trails. And it had grown very little in 1972 when the then-owners of Killington bought it and, in 1975, sent young management trainee Les Otten over to work there. Otten purchased the area in 1980 and made it his launch platform for the American Skiing Company empire of eastern and western ski resorts. Following a period of expansion, Sunday River now encompasses interconnected mountain peaks, 126 trails, 654 acres, and seventeen lifts (including four high-speed quads), providing a great variety of skiing from steep descents to glade skiing to wide intermediate trails. Locke Mountain offers a scenic view of the town of Bethel nestled in the valley. The summit of Jordan Bowl offers a choice of views of Mount Washington in one direction, the Mahoosucs in another, and Sunday River valley in another. In the summer, mountain bike trails and hiking trails are accessible from the base by lift. Rates vary for hikers or cyclists and include access fees. Call for details. Located six miles north of Bethel, off Route 2 in Newry. Telephone: (207) 824–3000 or (800) 543–2SKI.

Fryeburg, Maine

FAIRS, FESTIVALS, AND EVENTS

Fryeburg Fair. The largest agricultural fair in Maine—and one of the most traditional—takes place over eight days in late September and early October. Telephone: (207) 935–3268.

Lincoln, New Hampshire

For advance information about the Western White Mountains, contact Mountain Country, P.O. Box 559, Lincoln, NH 03251.

LODGING

Kancamagus Motor Lodge. Main Street. This thirty-four-room motel with in-room steam baths and beautiful mountain views is a good budget choice. Telephone: (603) 745–3600 or (800) 346–4205. Inexpensive.

FOOD

Cafe Lafayette Dinner Train. Hobo Rail Station, Route 112. A 1952 Pullman dome car, the Granite Eagle, makes a two-hour journey along the banks of the Pemigewasset River, where you are likely to spot moose or deer while dining on a five-course meal. The train runs Saturday through Wednesday from late June through the end of October, with sporadic service in May, early June, and December. Adults. $38.95. Telephone: (603) 745–3500 or (800) 699–3501.

The Common Man. Route 112 and Pollard Road. Telephone: (603) 745-3463. Pretense is at a minimum here, but hearty New England cooking is at a maximum—good seafood, prime rib, and rich desserts. Great Barn Lounge has a huge stone fireplace. Lunch and dinner. Moderate.

ACTIVITIES

Loon Mountain. Located in White Mountain National Forest off the Kancamagus Highway, Loon's 43 trails are spread out on 250 acres that offer a 2,100-foot vertical drop. Loon currently has the largest snowboard park in the East and serves as the site of many of the region's snowboard competitions. Kancamagus Highway. Telephone: (603) 745–8111.

Loon Mountain Cross Country Center. Thirty-five kilometers of groomed and tracked cross-country ski trails replace the Loon hiking trails for the winter. There's also a lighted skating rink. On the Kancamagus Highway. Telephone: (603) 745–6281.

FAIRS, FESTIVALS, AND EVENTS

Annual New Hampshire Highland Games. This three-day celebration of Scottish culture in mid-September is the largest Scottish festival in the Northeast, with music, athletics, country and highland dance, genealogy, and crafts. Telephone: (800) 345–SCOT

Bavarian Fall Foliage Festival. Timed to peak foliage during the first two weekends in October, this annual event features German beer and food, crafts, a Bavarian band and dancers. It is held at Loon Mountain. Telephone: (603) 745–8111.

Mid-Summer Arts & Crafts Fair. More than thirty years old, this annual event has become one of the largest and liveliest juried arts and crafts fairs in New England. Loon Mountain Park plays host in mid-July. Telephone: (603) 745–6281.

Music in the White Mountains Summer Festival. From mid-July to mid-August, North Country Chamber Players, one of New England's foremost chamber ensembles, performs a series of concerts in the Lincoln area. Telephone: (603) 869–3154.

Professional Lumberjack Festival. This annual competition includes such timber-related sports as axe throwing, springboard chop, supermodified and stock chainsaws as well as tree climbing and birling demonstrations. The event takes place in late August at Loon Mountain. Telephone: (603) 745–8111.

North Woodstock, New Hampshire

LODGING

Woodstock Inn. Main Street. Not to be confused with the Woodstock (Vermont) Inn, this white Victorian hostelry with black shutters features nineteen guest rooms in the main house and two other buildings on the property. The rooms with shared bath cost less and have more country character. Telephone: (603) 745–3951 or (800) 321–3985. Moderate with breakfast.

FOOD

Clement Inn and *Woodstock Station.* Owned by the Woodstock Inn, the Clement Inn offers elegant fine dining on its enclosed porch. Dinner. Expensive. Woodstock Station, part of the Clement Inn operation, is the more informal brewpub housed in an old train station. Decor is themed to old winter gear. Typical pub food can be washed down with the porters, stouts, and ales of the craft brewery, also on the premises. Lunch and dinner. Telephone: (603) 745–3951. Moderate.

Peg's Family Restaurant. Main Street. Telephone: (603) 745–2740. You can stop in as early as 5:30 A.M. for an order of flapjacks in this friendly local spot that serves breakfast and lunch until 2:30 P.M. and offers specials from 99 cents.

OTHER ATTRACTIONS

Lost River Gorge. This gorge was created when glaciers ground their way across North America. A self-guided tour, which takes about one hour, along boardwalks and bridges allows you to follow the river as it appears and disappears through the narrow, steep-walled gorge over tumbled granite, crevasses, caverns, and falls. In addition to a picnic area, there are geological displays and a lovely waterfall and a garden with more than 300 varieties of native flowers, ferns, and shrubs. Open early May through mid-October. Adults $4.50. Route 112. Telephone: (603) 745–8031.

Franconia and Franconia Notch, New Hampshire

LODGING

Franconia Inn. 1300 Easton Road. Families are especially welcome at this pleasant thirty-two-room country inn with a nice big parlor and a basement gameroom for the kids. It's a good spot to kick back and be bucolic, with tennis courts, a pool, riding stable, and cross-country ski trails. Telephone: (603) 823–5542 or (800) 473–5299. Moderate.

CAMPGROUNDS & RV PARKS

Cannon Mountain. Route 18, off exit 3 of I–93. This state-run RV park is located near Echo Lake in Franconia Notch State Park, making it a good choice for those who want to hike, bike, fish, swim, or ski. For information, contact New Hampshire Division of Parks and Recreation, P.O. Box 1856, Concord, NH 03302–1856. Telephone: (603) 271–3556; TTY Relay NH (800) 735–2964. To make reservations at Cannon Mountain, call (603) 823–5563.

Lafayette Campground. Also within Franconia Notch State Park, this ninety-seven-site campground is located along the main highway corridor, I–93/Route 3. Reservation center: (603)

271–3628. Direct line to the campground: (603) 823–9513.

FOOD

Franconia Inn. 1300 Easton Road. Telephone: (603) 823–8078. The smoke-free dining room serves a very broad menu based on American standards with the occasional sauced dish available. It has great views of the mountains. Dinner. Moderate.

OTHER ATTRACTIONS

The Frost Place. "R. Frost" still graces the mailbox at the famous poet's humble farm homestead, which is filled with memorabilia and manuscripts. There's also a bookstore and a nature trail through the woods out back. Open Memorial Day to Columbus Day daily from 1:00 P.M. to 5:00 P.M. Adults $3.00. Ridge Road. Telephone: (603) 823–5510.

The New England Ski Museum. This free museum at the base of Cannon Mountain traces the history of skiing with one hundred years of skis and ski gear and equipment ranging from chair lifts to snowmaking machines. The gift shop has reproductions of vintage posters and apparel. The museum is open Memorial Day to Columbus Day daily from noon to 5:00 P.M., December 31 to March 31 Thursday through Tuesday. Telephone: (603) 823–7177 or (800) 639–4181.

ACTIVITIES

Cannon Mountain. Located in Franconia Notch, this state-run ski area was one of the first ski resorts in New England. It has the most vertical feet (2,146) in New Hampshire and is known for its challenging runs. There are thirty-eight trails, a snowboard park, and an eighty-passenger enclosed aerial tramway that reaches the summit in eight minutes. The tramway also operates from mid-May through mid-October. Adults $9.00. There is also an eight-mile paved recreation path for hiking and mountain biking, as well as swimming at Echo Lake Beach (adults $2.50), where canoes and paddleboats are also available. On I–93. Telephone: (603) 823–5563. Snowphone: (800) 552–1234.

Franconia Cross Country. This 65-kilometer trail system offers spectacular views of Franconia Notch along with ten stream crossings and a waterfall. Telephone: (603) 823–5542 or (800) 473–5299.

Franconia Soaring Center. With the only sailplanes in the area, this soaring center takes full advantage of the thermals rising off the White Mountains. At Franconia Airport on Route 116. Telephone: (603) 823–8881.

Bethlehem, New Hampshire

LODGING

Adair. Old Littleton Road. This 1927 Georgian Revival home opened as an inn in 1992. The beautifully landscaped grounds include a patio, tennis court, and swimming pool. The first-floor sitting room with fireplace and comfortable chairs is for refined lounging. The downstairs Granite Tap Room (with a VCR) is more casual. The eight guest rooms are furnished with a mixture of antique and reproduction furniture. Telephone: (603) 444–2600 or (800) 441–2606. Moderate to expensive with breakfast.

Hearthside Village. Route 302. This property halfway between I–93 and the village of Bethlehem calls itself a "cottage motel" and claims to be the first motel court built in New Hampshire. At any rate, its sixteen steep-gabled cottages dating from the 1930s and 1940s are unique. Many feature fireplaces and kitchenettes, all are simply furnished. This place is especially nice for families, with a pool, an indoor playroom for young children, and a recreation room with video games and Ping-Pong for their older brothers and sisters. Telephone: (603) 444–1000. Inexpensive.

Mulbern Inn. Route 302. This property, built by the Woolworth heirs in 1913, was originally called the Ivie Estate and much of the original elegance has been preserved. The oak staircases and stained glass windows make a nice backdrop to the relaxed and friendly inn. Telephone: (603) 869–3389 or (800) 457–9440. Moderate with breakfast.

FOOD

Tim-Bir Alley. Old Littleton Road. Telephone: (603) 444–6142. Drawing its name from its proprietors, Tim and Biruta Carr, this restaurant in the elegant dining room of the Adair Inn has become one of the favorite spots in the northern White Mountains. Dinner. Moderate.

OTHER ATTRACTIONS

The Rocks Estate. It seems only appropriate that there would be Christmas tree farms in Bethlehem, including one at The Rocks, former summer estate of John Jacob Glessner, one of the founders of International Harvester. Named for the boulders left behind from the last glaciation, the estate is now the northern headquarters for the Society for the Protection of New Hampshire Forests. Admission to The Rocks is free, although there are small fees for some of the programs. The 1,300-acre estate has picnic areas and about three miles of trails for hiking or cross-country skiing. The working farm has 50,000 Christmas trees. In the autumn, visitors can tag a tree and return to pick it up or have it shipped to them at holiday time. The estate is located just west of Bethlehem on Route 302. Telephone: (603) 444–6228.

SHOPPING

Over the past few years, Bethlehem has developed a reputation as an antiques center. Ten shops along a short stretch of Main Street offer a variety of wares, from estate furniture to old woodstoves to pottery and glass.

FAIRS, FESTIVALS, AND EVENTS

Annual Craft Fair. This display and sale of the work of North Country craftspeople has been held for more than twenty years. Where better to do a little early Christmas shopping than at this mid-October event? Telephone: (603) 869–2806.

Annual Quilt Show and Sale. North Country quiltmakers show the labors of a long winter at this two-day event in early May. Telephone: (603) 869–3364.

Flea Market. For those who prefer to get as close as possible to the source in their search for

antiques and collectibles, Bethlehem holds a flea market on the town green every Saturday from June through October. Telephone: (603) 869–2151.

Sugar Hill, New Hampshire

LODGING

Sunset Hill House. Sunset Hill Road. This circa 1882 inn stands on a 1,700-foot ridge, which means great views of both the Presidential Range and the Green Mountains of Vermont—the latter serving as backdrop for the sunsets of the inn's name. The Victorian Country style inn has twenty-four guest rooms, a nine-hole golf course, and heated pool. Telephone: (603) 823–5522 or (800) 786–4455. Moderate to expensive with breakfast.

FOOD

Polly's Pancake Parlor. Hildex Farm, 672 Route 117. Telephone: (603) 823–5575. This very popular spot is open from 7:00 A.M. until 3:00 P.M. on weekdays and until 7:00 P.M. on Saturday and Sunday from mid-May to mid-October. The pancakes are made from homeground flour, but you can also opt for soup, quiche, and homemade bread.

Littleton, New Hampshire

LODGING

Thayer's Inn. Main Street. It's a real treat to find a surviving small-town hotel. This 1843 inn has seen a variety of famous guests, including President Ulysses S. Grant, who addressed a crowd from one its balconies. Its forty guest rooms are spread out on four floors and the octagonal cupola offers great views. Telephone: (603) 444–6469 or (800) 634–8179. Inexpensive.

FAIRS, FESTIVALS, AND EVENTS

Annual Art Show & Sale, Antique Car Show & Parade. A variety of activities bring visitors to town during foliage season. Telephone: (603) 444–6561.

Littleton Trout Tournament. This annual, family-oriented fishing contest held for three days in late June offers $10,000 in prizes. Telephone: (603) 444–6561.

Berlin, New Hampshire

For advance information about the Northern White Mountains, contact the Northern White Mountain Chamber of Commerce, 164 Main Street, P.O. Box 298, Berlin, NH 03570. Telephone: (603) 752–6060 or (800) 992–7480.

Gorham, New Hampshire

CAMPGROUNDS & RV PARKS

Moose Brook State Park. Jimtown Road off Route 2. This fifty-six-site campground includes pull-through and remote sites and has excellent trout fishing in many nearby streams. For information, contact New Hampshire Division of Parks and Recreation, P.O. Box 1856, Concord, NH 03302–1856. Telephone: (603) 271–3556; TTY Relay NH (800) 735–2964. Reservation center: (603) 271–3628. Direct line to the campground: (603) 466–3860.

ACTIVITIES

Mount Washington Sky Adventures. Two passengers can join a pilot to soar near the summit of Mount Washington in a three-seat Schweizer glider. Flights are also offered in a 1942 Stearman biplane or a six-passenger twin-engine Piper Aztec. Located just off Main Street on Routes 2 and 16. Telephone: (603) 466–5822 or (888) 353–2893.

TOURS

Moose Tour. The northern White Mountains have the largest moose population in the state. Local guides know the best places to search for moose and offer interesting history and lore along the way. Tours depart at sunset at the Gorham Information Booth and take place from Memorial Day through the end of October. Adults $15. Telephone: (603) 752–6060 or (800) 992–7480.

FAIRS, FESTIVALS, AND EVENTS

Climb to the Clouds, Mount Washington Auto Road Hill Climb. This three-day event in late June, featuring a race to the summit of Mount Washington, is the oldest motor-sports event in America. There are also car shows, concerts, and a barbecue. Telephone: (603) 466–3988.

Mount Washington Auto Road Bicycle Hill Climb. More than a quarter-century old, this hill-climb is one of the toughest in the United States. It takes place in late August. Telephone: (603) 447–6991.

Shelburne, New Hampshire

LODGING

Philbrook Farm Inn. 881 North Road. This inn offering what has been called the "ultimate Currier & Ives experience" is perfectly situated between Wildcat in New Hampshire and Sunday River in Maine and is still run by the same family that opened it in 1861. Telephone: (603) 466–3831. Moderate with breakfast (homemade doughnuts) and dinner.

Waterville Valley, New Hampshire

LODGING

Valley Inn. Tecumsah Road, two-tenths of a mile off Route 49. This four-story motor inn with fifty-two rooms is the only non-condo lodging in the Waterville Valley ski and outdoor recreation area. Located 11 miles east on Route 49 from I–93, exit 28, in the southwest corner of the White Mountain National Forest. Telephone: (603) 236–8336 or (800) 343–0969. Inexpensive to moderate.

FOOD

Mountain View. Tecumsah Road. Telephone: (603) 236–8336. The Mountain View dining room of the Valley Inn presents New American cuisine with surprising finesse amid casual country decor. Dinner. Moderate,

ACTIVITIES

Waterville Valley. At 4,000 feet, Mount Tecumseh supports fifty trails and twelve lifts on 255 acres. The longest run, with a 2,020-foot vertical drop, is three miles. The ski area is engaged in a long-term expansion project that will conclude sometime around 2002. During the summer, mountain biking takes the fore here. Located 11 miles east on Route 49 from I–93, exit 28, in the southwest corner of the White Mountain National Forest. Telephone: (603) 236–8311.

Base Camp Adventure Center. Both cross-country skiers and snowshoers use the seventy kilometers of tracked and thirty kilometers of backcountry trails through the White Mountain National Forest. Town Square. Telephone: (603) 236–4666.

Vermont's Green Mountains

For advance information about the Green Mountain National Forest, including camping, contact: Forest Supervisor, Green Mountain National Forest, 231 North Main Street, Rutland, VT 05701. Telephone: (802) 747–6700; TTY (802) 747–6765. In addition to main office, there are several ranger stations throughout the forest. The **Manchester Ranger District** is located at Routes 11 and 30 in Manchester Center, telephone: (802) 362–2307. The **Middlebury Ranger District** is located on Route 7 in Middlebury, telephone: (802) 388–4362. The **Rochester Ranger District** is on Star Route 100 in Rochester, telephone: (802) 767–4261.

Montpelier, Vermont

LODGING

Betsy's Bed & Breakfast. 74 East State Street. This fully restored Queen Anne has lace curtains, antique furnishings, a formal parlor with fireplace, and all the Victorian-style country wallpapers and upholstery you could ask for. It's only three blocks from the center of town, which makes it a good base for strolling. Telephone: (802) 229–0466. Inexpensive to moderate with breakfast.

Capitol Plaza Hotel & Conference Center. 100 State Street. This 1930s brick hotel underwent a full renovation in 1994. It emphasizes meetings and conferences and the location one block from the State House makes it lobbyists' hotel of choice. Its forty-six rooms include several large suites. Telephone: (802) 223–5252 or (800) 274–5252. Moderate.

The Inn at Montpelier. 147 Main Street. The nineteen rooms of this historic country inn, several with fireplaces, are located in two Federal-style buildings from the early 1800s that have been augmented in the typical New England way. The large wraparound porch in Colonial Revival style, something of a landmark, is not a bad spot to sit and watch the pace of things in easygoing Montpelier. Telephone: (802) 223–2727. Moderate to expensive with breakfast.

FOOD

Horn of the Moon Cafe. 8 Langdon Street. Telephone: (802) 223–2895. The cafe claims to be the oldest vegetarian natural foods restaurant in New England, and we've yet to hear anyone dispute it. The cavernous coffeehouse format is a distinct throwback to the 1960s, but then, so is much of Montpelier, and many people swear by their food. This is veggie with an emphasis on meat substitutes—especially various soy analogs to meat. Lunch and dinner. Inexpensive.

La Brioche Bakery & Cafe. 89 Main Street. Telephone: (802) 229–0443. Head to the counter in the back for morning muffins and croissants or lunchtime soups, sandwiches, quiches, and the like. One of the training areas for students of the New England Culinary Institute (NECI), La Brioche aims for the highest standards in contemporary light dining—and hits them. You'll hear people on the street at noontime say, "Oh, let's just go to La Brioche for a sandwich," the (correct) implication being that it's a good place to get quality light food in casual surroundings. Breakfast and lunch.

Main Street Grill & Bar. 118 Main Street. Telephone: (802) 223–3188. At lunchtime the NECI students cook, and at dinner they both cook and serve. The informal style is a nice fit with Montpelier and the light contemporary American cuisine is uniformly good. Lunch and dinner. Moderate.

Chef's Table. 118 Main Street. Telephone: (802) 229-9202. Serving the same lunch menu as Main Street Grill & Bar, the Chef's Table gets more formal in the evening with a three-course, fixed price menu. Lunch and dinner. Moderate to expensive.

Oscar & Zeke's. 11 Main Street. Telephone: (802) 229-1019. Simple and stylish in a down-home kind of way, Oscar's and Zeke's is where you'll head for meatloaf and other "homestyle" food, as well as some vaguely Southwestern fare (chicken-chili burrito). The meatloaf recipe comes from the grandmother of one of the owners, served with "Gram's secret sauce" and garlic mashed potatoes. Lunch and dinner. Inexpensive.

OTHER ATTRACTIONS

Sugar Houses. The maple sugaring season begins in mid-February and often lasts into April. During this "sweet season" you can observe the "boiling down" at area sugar houses. **Morse Farm** is located 2.5 miles northeast of Montpelier on County Road. The Morse family has been sugaring for eight generations and many of their trees date back to the nineteenth century. In addition to the sugar shack, Morse Farm has a sugaring museum, country store, and walking trail. Morse Farm is open daily 9:00 A.M. until 5:00 P.M., from 8:00 A.M. until 8:00 P.M. during the summer. Telephone: (802) 223-2740 or (800) 242-2740. **Bragg Farm** is located seven miles east of Montpelier on Route 14 North in East Montpelier and is open daily year-round from 8:30 A.M. until 6:00 P.M. The Braggs have only been farming here for five generations. . . . This is one place to catch a look at the old-fashioned way of sugaring—collecting in buckets (rather than plastic tubing) and boiling down the sap with wood fires. Telephone: (802) 223-5757.

SHOPPING

The Artisans' Hand. 89 Main Street. Telephone: (802) 229-9492. This cooperative crafts gallery features work of 125 Vermont craftspeople. You'll find everything from folk-art coat hooks depicting cats, cows, moose, fish, and dogs to exquisite pottery and glass work as well as an excellent range of weaving and other good fiber arts.

Windstrom Hill. 32 State Street. Telephone: (802) 229-5899. Folk artist Ruth L. Pope hand-paints furniture, landscapes, portraits, clocks, birdhouses, and pretty much anything that will stand still. The effect is not as commercial as it sounds—in fact, it's pretty folksy.

Jeffersonville, Vermont

FOOD

Le Cheval d'Or. Main Street. Telephone: (802) 644-5556. Chef-proprietor Yves Labbe is from the Loire Valley and has brought country-French cooking to ski country. Now that "French" food is no longer so exotic, Labbe's venison roast, wine-infused stews, and so forth verge on being mainstream—you could say Vermont has come around to seeing food his way. Dinner. Very expensive.

ACTIVITIES

Smugglers' Notch. This essentially self-contained resort located halfway between Jeffersonville and Mount Mansfield is considered one of the best for families. More than 1,000 acres (the largest skiing and snowboarding acreage in Vermont) are criss-crossed by sixty trails with a maximum total vertical drop of 2,610 feet. One of the three mountains is dedicated entirely to new skiers and snowboarders (though not on the same trails). The Notch has a variety of programs for children, divided by age level, that are consistently rated very high by *Snow Country* magazine. There are also extensive child care programs. In addition to day and night skiing during the winter the resort has evening tube sliding, 23 kilometers of cross-country trails, snowshoeing, ice skating, indoor tennis, and an indoor pool. From Christmas until early April, intermediate and expert skiers and snowboarders can connect to Stowe Mountain Resort on a trail that leads to Spruce Peak. A one-day lift ticket to Stowe is free with packages of two or more days. (You can also drive around the mountain—which takes at least an hour in the winter.) Summer and fall activities include mountain biking, horseback riding and carriage rides, tennis on outdoor courts, swimming, a water slide, as well as guided hikes and walks. Route 108. Telephone: (802) 644-8851 or (800) 451-8752.

Stowe, Vermont

Unlike Smuggler's Notch, Stowe is a real village dotted with dozens of different kinds of lodgings, ranging from motels to tiny B&Bs to ski chalets, small lodges, and full-scale resorts. For information on Stowe and the central reservations service, contact the Stowe Area Association, Box 1320, Stowe, VT 05672. Telephone: (802) 253–7321 or (800) 247–8693. The information office is located on Main Street in Stowe Village.

LODGING

Green Mountain Inn. This circa 1833 inn is located right on Main Street in the center of Stowe Village at the end of Mountain Road (junction of Routes 100 and 108). Not all of the inn dates so far back, but the property qualifies as a member of the Historic Hotels of America and includes sixty-four rooms and suites spread over four buildings. The decor re-creates prosperous America of the nineteenth century, with reproduction stenciling on the walls and period antiques and reproductions. Some rooms have canopy beds, fireplaces, or Jacuzzis and there is a complimentary health club. Telephone: (802) 253–7301 or (800) 786–9346. Moderate to expensive.

Inn at the Mountain. 5781 Mountain Road. The Inn is the motel/hotel of Stowe Mountain Resort, as opposed to the more upscale condo accommodations. One nice amenity is the steam bath in each unit, as well as cable TV and refrigerator. A few rooms actually do permit you to ski in and out from your door. Telephone: (802) 253–3000 or (800) 253–4754. Moderate to very expensive.

The Inn at Turner Mill. 56 Turner Mill Lane. You can't get any closer to the Stowe lifts without staying in the accommodations of Stowe Mountain Resort. Set amid pines and maples on ten acres bordering Notch Brook at the foot of Mount Mansfield, this inn was built in 1936 and retains the early rustic style and simple enthusiasm for the mountain lifestyle. That's not to say there haven't been some nice modernizations (like heat). Options vary from one, two, or four-bedroom setups, each with a kitchen. Some also have

or share a fireplace. During the hiking (rather than skiing) months, the four-bedroom apartment becomes several separate rooms that share a common library, kitchen, living room, porch, and two bathrooms. Rustic log furniture is found throughout—the handiwork of innkeeper Greg Speer. The Inn at Turner Mill is situated to take advantage of all the summer and winter outdoors activities of the area, with knowledgeable hosts who can point you in the right direction. Greg is a real snowshoeing enthusiast and gives guided tours (a half-day snowshoe rental comes with the room). Telephone: (802) 253–2062 or (800) 992–0016. Moderate with breakfast (summer only).

Innsbruck Inn. 4361 Mountain Road. One of the many Stowe hostelries in the style of the Austrian Tyrols, the Innsbruck has twenty-four rooms, some with fireplace, as well as sauna and whirlpool and outdoor pool for guest use. All rooms come with coffeemakers and refrigerators and a few units have full efficiency kitchens. Innsbruck sits streamside and has stunning summer gardens. It's just outside Stowe Village, on the Stowe Recreation Path, and connects directly to three cross-country trail networks. Telephone: (802) 253–8582 or (800) 225–8582. Moderate to expensive.

The Siebeness, a Country Inn. 3681 Mountain Road. This warm and relaxing place for families (kids are usually in ample evidence) has twelve rooms and an outdoor hot tub. Some suites have Jacuzzis and mountain views. The inn serves a highly acclaimed hearty country breakfast. Telephone: (802) 253–8942 or (800) 426–9001. Moderate to expensive with breakfast.

Spruce Peak Inn. 6992 Mountain Road. This hostel-style lodging for hard-core hikers and ski bums has bunk beds in men's or women's dorms. This is where the CCC crew that carved out Mount Mansfield's first ski trails crashed at night and it is definitely on the Spartan side. On the other hand, it's close to the slopes and mountain trails and the inn bursts with camaraderie. You can reserve a bunk only or a bunk with breakfast and dinner. Reservations by mail only. Mailing address: Spruce Peak Inn, Vermont State Ski

Dorm, 6992 Mountain Road, Stowe, VT 05672. Telephone: (802) 253–4010. Inexpensive, even with the meals.

Topnotch at Stowe Resort and Spa. One of only a handful of spas in New England, this luxury property offers a laundry list of treatments. The ninety-two rooms and suites, as well as larger condominiums, are nestled on 120 beautiful acres, with views of Mount Mansfield. In the summer there are hiking and cycling, an equestrian center, and tennis to augment the spa treatments. In the winter, 15 miles of cross-country ski trails, ice skating, and horse-drawn sleigh rides keep guests busy. The indoor pool is open all year. *Condé Nast Traveler* called Topnotch "one of the best places to stay in the world." They may be right, but it comes at a price. Telephone: (802) 253–8585 or (800) 451–8686. Expensive to very expensive.

Trapp Family Lodge. 42 Trapp Hill Road. Is there anyone who doesn't know the story of the Baron and Baroness von Trapp and their ten children as sketched in *The Sound of Music*? In 1942 they bought a hillside farm and converted it into an Austrian-style home and began welcoming guests in the summer of 1950. In 1968, Johannes von Trapp designed the first cross-country ski center in America with 100 kilometers of groomed and back country cross-country skiing trails. Today, the family enterprise includes ninety-three guest rooms (seventy-three in the main lodge), one hundred guest houses, two restaurants, and meeting facilities. It's all situated on 2,200 acres with great views of the Green Mountains. In the summer, guests can hike, ride mountain bikes, play tennis, or swim in the pools. Telephone: (802) 253–8511 or (800) 826–7000. Moderate to expensive. It is very expensive during foliage and ski season, but the rate includes breakfast and dinner.

CAMPGROUNDS AND RV PARKS

Gold Brook Campground. Located on Route 100, 7.5 miles north from exit 10 off I-89, the campground has a beautiful lawn on Gold Brook and offers good access for swimming, hunting, fishing, hiking, and snowmobiling from its one hundred sites for tents and RVs. Open year-round. Telephone: (802) 253–7683.

Smugglers' Notch State Park. The park is located at the base of Mount Mansfield and the campground is on the Stowe side of the notch across from the Mount Mansfield gondola. Built by the CCC in the 1930s, this campground has twenty-one tent/trailer sites and fourteen lean-tos. Open mid-May to Columbus Day. Telephone: (802) 253–4014 (summer) or (802) 479–4280 (winter).

FOOD

The Blue Moon Cafe. 35 School Street. Telephone: (802) 253–7006. Around the corner from the main drag in Stowe Village, this cozy and stylish eleven-table bistro features local artwork on the walls and contemporary American cuisine on the menu. Think of Blue Moon as Vermont gourmet: French lentil soup with Vermont feta cheese, alder smoked duckling breast with spinach and raspberries, braised rabbit with foraged mushrooms and wild leeks, or pan-seared sea scallops with skillet salad and herb glaze. Dinner. Moderate.

The Cliff House. Telephone: (802) 253–3665. Dinner at the top of Mount Mansfield, which you can reach only on the high-speed two-person gondola, is another treat where the menu leans toward Vermont gourmet, but without the emphasis on game. The sophisticated, candlelit tables here are likely to be set with smoked salmon, potato pancakes, and American freshwater caviar or black and white crusted pork tenderloin with crispy noodle spring roll. Lunch is inexpensive. The fixed-price fancy dinner, offered Thursday through Saturday in the winter, daily in the summer, is very expensive.

Harvest Market. 1031 Mountain Road. Telephone: (802) 253–3800. This gourmet store has delicious sandwiches, soups, and baked goods for lunch. If you're staying at a place with a kitchen, pick up some of the excellent prepared entrees (chicken pot pie, Indonesian ginger chicken) to take back to the room and heat up for dinner.

Isle de France. Mountain Road. Telephone: (802) 253–7751. The modest frame building doesn't prepare you for the sumptuous interior (chandeliers, mirrors, white linen tablecloths) of this superb restaurant. Chef Jean Lavina has lightened up the classical cuisine of his native France with Vermont supplies, but the wine list still leans heavily on the old country. Dinner. Expensive.

Pie in the Sky. 492 Mountain Road. Telephone: (802) 253–5100. One of the hot New England food trends finally made it to the mountains: Pizza and pasta prepared in a wood-fired oven. You can eat in or take out. You get to make a lot of choices for your pizza. Traditional or whole-wheat crust? Thick or thin? Then there are thirty-seven toppings to "create your own," or you can select from traditional or non-traditional specialty pizzas. Lunch and dinner. Inexpensive.

Restaurant Swisspot. Main Street. Telephone: (802) 253–4622. This local favorite in Stowe Village offers three types of cheese fondue as well as beef fondue. You can also get quiches, sandwiches, and burgers in this room with a cheery alpine feel enhanced by all the varnished wood, checked curtains, and posters of Swiss scenes on the walls. It could easily be the Alps instead of the Green Mountains, and that's the point. Lunch and dinner. Inexpensive to moderate.

The Shed. Mountain Road. (802) 253–4364. This brewpub produces five standard ales and one special ale, that might be raspberry wheat, pumpkin, or spiced Christmas ale. The menu is stock pub grub—sandwiches, burgers, beef, seafood, chicken—but food is given as much attention as beer. Lunch and dinner. Inexpensive to moderate.

Siebeness Inn. 3681 Mountain Road. Telephone: (802) 253–8942. Non-guests may stop by for the highly regarded four-course breakfast, which includes fresh baked goods, fresh fruit plate, and choice of several main dishes such as buttermilk pancakes or cinnamon French toast (both with pure Vermont maple syrup) and beverage.

Trapp Family Lodge Austrian Tea Room. 42 Trapp Hill Road. Telephone: (802) 253–8511. The Tea Room has its own cute little building away from the main lodge, with panoramic mountain view. The lunch offerings (no dinner) include soups, sandwiches, homemade wursts, and imported German beers. But people really come for the pastries—the best of Austria meets Vermont: linzertorte, sachertorte, Vermont maple cream pie. Open from 10:30 A.M. to 5:30 P.M.

ACTIVITIES

The Fly Rod Shop. This very friendly shop has an extensive line of fly-fishing supplies and gives free two-hour casting classes on Wednesday afternoons and Saturday mornings, spring ("as soon as the ice melts") through fall. They also rent equipment and offer a guide service. You can fish for rainbow, brook, or brown trout in the Lamoille and Winooski Rivers. On Route 100, two miles from Stowe Village. Telephone: (802) 253–7346.

The Mountain Bike Shop. This year-round outfitter rents mountain bikes in the summer and snowshoes and cross-country skis in the winter. They also offer guided snowshoe tours. On Mountain Road near Stowe Village. Telephone: (802) 253–7919.

Stowe Mountain Resort. There are bigger mountains and more developed resort areas, but Stowe remains the sentimental favorite as the capital of skiing in the East. Mount Mansfield and adjoining Spruce Peak form a grand panorama defined by the rugged cliffs of Smugglers Notch. Mount Mansfield offers 2,360 vertical feet, while Spruce is a little milder. The whole resort has forty-seven total trails with thirty-nine miles of skiing. The longest trail is 3.7 miles and, in general, Stowe permits skiers to keep going longer on a run than most places. The Front Four are considered the longest cruising runs in the East and offer very challenging terrain. But more than half the trails are intermediate and Spruce Peak offers more acreage for beginning skiers than the total area of many ski resorts. In 1998, Stowe Mountain opened a mountain biking center, offering lift-served mountain biking on both Mount Mansfield and Spruce Peak. It's located at the Spruce Peak base area. About twenty trails on Mount Mansfield have intermediate and advanced terrain for bikers, while Spruce Peak has twelve beginner and intermediate trails. In addition, the gondola takes hikers and sightseers to the summit of Mount Mansfield in less than eight minutes. Spruce Peak has the region's only alpine slide. 5781 Mountain Road. Telephone: (802) 253–3500 or (800) 24–STOWE.

Umiak Outdoor Outfitters. Umiak rents canoes and kayaks and offers instruction and guided tours. Rentals begin at $8.00 (kayak) and $10.00 (canoe) per hour. In the winter, Stowe Snowmobile Tours is based at Umiak and offers rentals and tours. Route 100, south of Stowe Village. Telephone: (802) 253–2317.

The greater Stowe area is the largest Nordic network in the East, with more than 200 miles of interconnected cross-country ski trails and four Nordic centers:

Edson Hill Manor Ski Touring & Riding Center. Just up the hill from Topnotch, this more small-scale operation lies directly across the valley from Mount Mansfield and provides skiers with incredible views. There are 25 kilometers of trails and access to Vermont's Catamount Trail as well as to other Stowe touring centers. During the snowfree season, there are riding stables. 1500 Edson Hill Road. Telephone: (802) 253–7371 or (800) 621–0284.

Stowe Mountain Cross-Country Touring Center. A pass to the Nordic center also allows use of the Toll House chairlift to access back country and touring trails closer to the top of Mount Mansfield. 5781 Mountain Road. Telephone: (802) 253–3000 or (800) 253–4SKI.

Topnotch. There are 20 kilometers of groomed and ungroomed trails through a variety of terrain. Skiers can immediately access Stowe's Recreation Path, a relatively flat trail that leads to Stowe Village and offers broad vistas of the mountains. Intermediate trails connect to the Trapp Family Lodge and Stowe Mountain. Mountain Road. Telephone: (802) 253–8585 or (800) 451–8686.

Trapp Family Lodge. In 1968 Maria von Trapp's son Johannes opened the ski center at the Trapp Family Lodge—the first commercial cross-country ski center in the United States. It's still Stowe's leading center with 55 kilometers of groomed trails and 45 kilometers of back-country trails. Some of Stowe's oldest ski paths date back to the 1920s and are now back-country trails that wind their way along the curved inner face of the mountain—linking Trapp's trails with the Stowe Mountain Resort's cross-country center. 42 Trapp Hill Road. Telephone: (802) 253–8511 or (800) 826–7000.

FAIRS, FESTIVALS, AND EVENTS

Stowe Derby. Held in mid to late-February, this one-day event is the country's oldest combination downhill and cross-country event. It draws international competitors but is open to amateurs. The race goes from the top of Mount Mansfield to Stowe Village. Advance registration is required. Telephone: (802) 253–7321.

Stowe Winter Carnival. The Stowe Winter Carnival began with a modest group of winter activities in 1921 and grew in popularity until it was suspended during World War II, languishing until 1974. It includes a Stowe-Sugarbush Downhill Ski Challenge, snow sculpture competition, downhill, cross-country, snowshoe and snowboard races, church suppers, and even a snow-golf competition. All the festivities are packed into about a week in late January and early February. Telephone: (802) 253–7321.

SHOPPING

Vermont Furniture Works. Depot Building, Main Street. Telephone: (802) 253–5094. If you fall in love with the country style, this company handcrafts furniture in the fashion typically found in rural New England during the late eighteenth and early nineteenth centuries in cherry, maple, and tiger maple. All furniture is constructed with traditional carpentry methods such as mortise and tenon joinery, dovetail drawers, and hand-applied finish.

Waterbury, Vermont

The Green Mountain Club is one of the best resources for information about year-round outdoor activities along the Long Trail and throughout the Green Mountains. Headquarters is located on Route 100 between Waterbury and Stowe. They publish the *Guidebook of the Long Trail* and many useful maps and pamphlets, including suggested hiking and snowshoe trails. It's always wise to check in with local experts before heading out on unfamiliar terrain. The Waterbury headquarters also has campsites and shelters for hikers. Telephone: (802) 244–7037. (See "Seeing Vermont's Green Mountains.")

LODGING

Inn at Blush Hill. Blush Hill Road. This circa-1790 Cape Cod sits on a hilltop off Route 100 with beautiful mountain views. But most guests tend to remember the breakfast of waffles, pancakes, or French toast topped with Ben & Jerry's ice cream. There are five guest rooms with down comforters: one with a mountain view, one with a Jacuzzi, another with a fireplace. Telephone: (802) 244–7529 or (800) 736–7522. Inexpensive to moderate with breakfast.

OTHER ATTRACTIONS

Cold Hollow Cider Mill. Walk through the bakery and the gourmet food and gift shop and you'll find the cider press that's operated year-round and always makes enough for free samples. Vermont cheese samples are also often available. Route 100. Telephone: (802) 244–8771.

Waitsfield, Vermont

For advance information about the Sugarbush Valley area, contact the Sugarbush Chamber of Commerce, Route 100, Box 173, Waitsfield, VT 05673. Telephone: (802) 496–3409 or (800) 828–4748.

LODGING

Inn at Mad River Barn. Route 17. This rustic 1948 ski lodge is run by Betsy Pratt, who purchased Mad River Glen ski area with her husband in 1972 and ran it from his death in 1975 until selling it as a cooperative. Many of the fifteen rooms have a queen-size bed and two singles, making the inn a good choice for families. There are also a pub and a restaurant on the property as well as an outdoor pool for summer use. Telephone: (802) 496–3310 or (800) 631–0466. Inexpensive to moderate with breakfast.

Inn At the Round Barn Farm. East Warren Road. The eleven guest rooms, with features such as Jacuzzi tub and steam showers and fireplaces, are located in a large, white clapboard farmhouse with an extension. Guests ski free at the inn's cross-country ski center. Telephone: (802) 496–2276. Moderate to very expensive with breakfast.

Lareau Farm Country Inn. Route 100. This restored farmhouse with sixty-seven acres beside the Mad River has the real country look engendered by antiques galore and handmade quilts. The thirteen rooms include a suite with a Jacuzzi. Telephone: (802) 496–4949 or (800) 833–0766. Inexpensive to moderate with breakfast.

FOOD

Bridge Street Bakery. Bridge Street. Telephone: (802) 496–0077. Stop at this extremely friendly place for breakfast muffins or bagels or a lunch of the soup of the day with self-serve salad bar and fresh baked bread.

R.V.S.P. Bridge Street. Telephone: (802) 496–RSVP. The initials stand for Richard's Very Special Pizza. This storefront dishes out pizza that is equally popular with locals and with visitors who have it flown in when they need a fix.

ACTIVITIES

Clearwater Sports. Year-round outfitter offers many imaginative programs. In winter, they rent snowshoes, sleds, back-country skis, and organize an eight-kilometer snowshoe race, a full-moon snowshoe trip, and two- to four-hour snowshoe trips in the Mad River Valley. In summer, they rent canoes, kayaks, mountain bikes, inner tubes, and camping gear. They also offer canoe and kayak instruction and guided tours, including a special program for children and several guided tours for women only. From mid-June through mid-September they offer Full Moon Canoe Cruises to a secluded spot in the Waterbury Reservoir where a gourmet meal is served. Route 100. Telephone: (802) 496–2708.

Mad River Glen. Mad River Glen first cranked up its now-famous Single Chair in 1948. In 1995, Mad River Glen became the only cooperatively owned ski area in America, dedicated to resisting the homogenization that some feel is harming the experience at other mountains. Mad River Glen is famous for its legendary expert terrain which gives skiers 2,000 vertical feet of true Black Diamond skiing. But there are varied trails for beginners and intermediate skiers as well. The extensive trail system follows the contours of General Stark

Mountain to a single base area, making it easy for skiers of different ability to ski together. Thanks to the antiquated lift, the slopes are uncrowded and snowboarders are banned. Mad River Glen is the official home of the North American Telemark Organization and the North American Telemark Festival in early March, the oldest and largest gathering of Telemark skiers. Mad River Glen also sponsors Environmental Programs to help people learn about the alpine environment. In the winter these might include guided snowshoe treks or cross-country skiing tours. In the summer and fall there are guided hikes and a children's Nature Camp. Telephone: (802) 496–3551.

The Round Barn Cross-Country Ski Center. Round Barn offers 25 kilometers of groomed trails for classical and skate skiing and snowshoeing in the heart of Sugarbush Valley. Trails lead through sugar maple forests and over rolling hills with scenic views of the Green Mountains. East Warren Road. Telephone: (802) 496–6111.

Sugarbush. The original rugged mountain of Sugarbush has some striking terrain now enhanced by improved snowmaking and much better lifts after being taken over by American Skiing Company in 1995. The ski area has extended over the years to include six interconnected mountain areas, peaks up to 4,000-feet, 112 trails, and 2,650 vertical feet of drop. Hotshots gravitate to Killington to the south, so Sugarbush tends to attract more mature skiers for its "classic terrain and character." The eighteen lifts include seven quads and even snowboarders have some new facilities with the improved Mountain Rage Snow Park and a Pipe Dragon-cut half pipe. The back country ski center, called "Out Back in the Bush," is located at Lincoln Peak in Sugarbush. Telephone: (802) 583–3333 or (800) 537–8427.

Vermont Icelandic Horse Farm. These purebred horses are considered to have the most comfortable gait in the world. Riders can test the claim on a number of trails of varying lengths, open all year. The Common Road. Telephone: (802) 496–7141.

Warren, Vermont

LODGING

The Pitcher Inn. Main Street. The theme at this elegant inn might be called "trompe l'oeil," after the term for paintings that fool the eye. Although it occupies exactly the same footprint as a nineteenth-century inn in the center of the village, it's all new construction in the old style, complete with the gigantic stone hearth in the dining room. The seven guest rooms are all created with a great sense of whimsy and high style deserving of the pages of *Architectural Digest*. They range from the rather simple Chester Arthur room (named for the president born not far away) furnished in his late nineteenth-century period to the Mallard Room, a duck hunter's fantasy. Telephone: (802) 496–6350 or (888) TO–PITCH. Expensive to very expensive.

FOOD

Chez Henri. Telephone: (802) 583–2600. This French bistro sits at the base of Sugarbush and has been offering classic French cuisine for more than 30 years. Lunch and dinner. Moderate.

The Pitcher Inn. Main Street. Telephone: (802) 496–6350. A NECI-trained chef produces Vermont gourmet dining—salmon, venison, quail—augmented in warm months by an extensive kitchen garden. Lunch and dinner. Expensive.

The Warren Store Deli. Main Street. Telephone: (802) 496–2864. There's an old-fashioned feel to this upscale deli that caters to urban tastes with salads and soups, sandwiches made on freshly baked bread, pastries and cookies. There are a few tables and everything is available for takeout.

ACTIVITIES

Ole's Cross-Country Ski Center. The 50-kilometer trail network is groomed daily for classical and skating techniques. Snowshoers are also welcome on the trails. This center is connected to the Round Barn Cross-Country Ski Center in Waitsfield, making even more trails available for ambitious skiers. Located at the Sugarbush-Warren Airport. Telephone: (802) 496–3430.

Sugarbush Soaring Association. A variety of scenic glider rides are offered over Mad River Valley and Sugarbush. Telephone: (802) 496–2290 or (800) 881–7627.

FAIRS, FESTIVALS, AND EVENTS

Sugarbush Brewers Festival. Live music and food accompany the display and sampling of products from New England brewers. The two-day event takes place in mid-September. Telephone: (802) 583–2381.

Killington Area, Vermont

For advance information contact The Killington & Pico Areas Association, P.O. Box 114, Killington, VT 05751. Telephone: (800) 337–1928.

LODGING

Cortina Inn. Route 4. Close to Killington and Pico slopes, Cortina has ninety-seven rooms with TV and air conditioning. In the summer there are eight tennis courts, mountain biking, and heated pool, as well as saunas, spa, and a fitness center to ease muscles strained by summer or winter outdoor activities. Telephone: (802) 773–3331 or (800) 451–6108. Moderate to expensive with breakfast.

Inn at Long Trail. Route 4. Situated at 2,250 feet, the Inn at Long Trail claims to be New England's first ski lodge and has the style and pedigree to support that assertion. The rustic inn was constructed in 1938. The common room features a fieldstone fireplace and tree trunks supporting the beams. A Precambrian quartz outcropping juts through the wall in the pub and dining room. There are fourteen guest rooms on the second and third floors and a wing with six suites with fireplaces. Situated on the highway crest of Sherburne Pass, the inn overlooks the Pico Peak base lodge. The live Irish music and singalongs at McGrath's Irish Pub (on the premises) are very popular. Telephone: (802) 775–7181 or (800) 325–2540. Inexpensive to expensive. During foliage weekends, meals must be taken with the room.

Inn of the Six Mountains. Killington Road. This relatively new property located near the sixth green of the Killington Golf Course is a good bet for families. The 103 rooms have spectacular views, flexible sleeping arrangements, mini-refrigerators, and cable TV. Also on the premises are indoor and outdoor pools and hot tubs, sauna, and exercise room. Telephone: (802) 422–4302 or (800) 228–4676. Inexpensive to expensive.

The Summit Lodge. Killington Road. The Summit, one of the older lodges in the area, calls itself a classic four-season resort in an area where winter is clearly king. Set above and somewhat insulated from the main traffic arteries on Killington Road, the lodge has forty-five rooms with mountain views. Amenities include five tennis courts, two racquetball courts, an outdoor heated pool, a duck pond, manicured gardens as well as a Jacuzzi and saunas. Telephone: (802) 422–3535 or (800) 635–6343. Moderate to expensive.

The Vermont Inn. Route 4. An 1840s farmhouse set on a knoll above Route 4, the inn has eighteen guest rooms and a cozy living room, making it a different and perhaps more personal option than larger properties in the Killington area. The six-acre site features extensive perennial gardens, pool, and tennis court. Telephone: (802) 775–0708 or (800) 541–7795. Moderate to expensive with breakfast. Breakfast and dinner arrangements are available at higher rates.

FOOD

Churchill's Restaurant. Route 4, Mendon. Telephone: (802) 775–3219. If gourmet fare has got you down, drive west on Route 4 to check out Churchill's for moderately-priced American food, such as seafood, steaks, and prime rib. There is also a children's menu. Churchill's is famous for its reasonably priced roast turkey dinner. Lunch and dinner. Inexpensive to moderate.

Hemingway's. Route 4. Telephone: (802) 422–3886. Always in the top rankings of the Green Mountain State's restaurants, Hemingway's gives you three dining room choices—a formal room with chandeliers and vaulted ceiling, a more casual room that looks out on an herb garden, or an intimate stone-walled wine cellar. Based on classical French cooking, Hemingway's helped pioneer gourmet dining with a Vermont caste, using local game, cheeses, and produce, and in many cases, helping purveyors build their businesses. The wine cellar may be the best in Vermont. Several fixed-price meal options are available as well as an a la carte menu. Hemingway's is closed in November and from mid-April to mid-May. Dinner. Very expensive.

Maple Sugar & Vermont Spice. Route 4, Mendon. Telephone: (802) 773–7832. A bit west of Killington, this rustic replica of a sugarhouse has a gift shop downstairs and a restaurant with small tables and a counter upstairs. It's widely known for huge pancake and waffle breakfasts, with local syrup, sausages, and bacon. Open daily from 7:00 A.M. to 2:00 P.M., the restaurant serves breakfast all day, as well as lunch.

The Vermont Inn. Route 4. Telephone: (802) 775–0708. The Vermont Inn is one of those rare restaurants that will satisfy granny, the kids, and your finicky big-city gourmet cousin. The food is derived from traditional New England cuisine, so it's familiar, but the executions emphasize freshness and the presentation has real flair. In the winter, you might even get a table next to a roaring fire. Lunch and dinner. Moderate.

ACTIVITIES

Green Mountain National Golf Course. Vermont's newest course features beautiful mountain views and superb design. Barrows-Towne Road, two miles north of Killington Road on Route 100. Telephone: (802) 422–GOLF.

Killington. Killington was the first major resort to invest in broad scale snowmaking and now has the East's most extensive snowmaking system. Since being acquired by American Skiing Company, there has been a continual and continuing upgrade—new lifts, new trails, increased snowmaking capacity. Killington has some of the most loyal skiers anywhere. There are 212 trails that can accommodate any level of expertise, although expert and beginner slopes outnumber intermediate trails. At this writing there are thirty-three lifts and more are in the works. Introduced in 1995, the Killington High Country Touring Center uses the Skyeship—the world's fastest and first heated eight-passenger lift—to bring guests to the top of 3,800-foot Skye Peak. From there, guests can take snowshoe walks guided by staff naturalists. The same lift offers stunning views of the six surrounding mountains during foliage season. For the part of the year known as "hard sledding" (the other Vermont season besides winter), there are twenty hiking trails totaling about 50 miles. Killington operates a mountain biking center in the summer with 41 miles of trails, with mountain access via the Killington Chairlift beginning on weekends in late May and then daily from June through mid-October. At the junction of Routes 4 and 100 in Sherburne. Telephone: (802) 621–MTNS or (800) 621–6867. Mountain Bike Center: (802) 422–6232.

Killington Snowmobile Tours. The operators use "the newest high tech snowmobiles" from Polaris and offer several options in Calvin Coolidge State Forest. The "Tame Terrain Tour" travels through tall timbers to a breathtaking view of the Killington and Pico Mountain Range. For the less tame, there are trips up steep mountain trails at speeds up to 50 miles per hour. On Route 4 at the foot of the Killington Access Road. Telephone: (802) 422–2121.

Mountain Meadows Ski Touring Center. There are 60 kilometers of trails, some meandering through old-growth evergreen forests, some stretching across open fields, and some backcountry trails. Three kilometers of skating and classic terrain are treated to snowmaking. The cafeteria in the trailside base lodge features food from some of the best local restaurants. Route 4. Telephone: (800) 221–0598.

Pico. Pico Peak Ski Area was "rescued" from potentially permanent Chapter 7 closure by neighboring Killington and was scheduled to be interconnected with its savior in 1999 now that both are under the American Skiing Company umbrella. This is the place for intermediate skiers to head for cruising runs on the lower peak and glade skiing near the top. Sherburne Pass, Rutland. Telephone: (802) 775–4345 or (800) 898–7426.

Vermont Ecology Tours. Whenever we've been out looking for wildlife, we've been surprised how much more we can see with a local guide who really knows the terrain. This outfit organizes trips to look for birds (endangered peregrine falcons, red-tailed hawks, woodpeckers, etc.) or mammals such as moose and beaver. Many of the trips involve lesser-known trails and roads of the Green Mountain National Forest. Glazebrook Center, Killington Road. Telephone: (800) 368–6161.

FAIRS, FESTIVALS, AND EVENTS
Foliage Crafts Show. For those who prefer the mountains in the fall, a juried crafts show is held for three days in early October at Sunrise Mountain Lodge. Telephone: (802) 422–3783.

The Killington Music Festival. This annual festival born in the early 1980s brings prestigious musicians from around the world to Vermont to teach young artists in a summer residency program. The highlight is a series of world class chamber concerts performed by the faculty and guest artists. Concerts are held at the Killington Skyeship Base Station. For schedule and further information, telephone: (802) 773–4003.

Summer Crafts Show. The Pico Base Lodge is the site of a three-day juried crafts show, sponsored by the Vermont Crafts Expo, in late July. Telephone: (802) 422–3785.

Vermont Sheep and Wool Festival. Two-day festival in early October has sheepdog and wool-spinning demonstrations and workshops on topics ranging from felting and knitting to shepherding techniques and pasture maintenance. Held at Snowshed Base Lodge at Killington Ski Resort. Telephone: (802) 457–2049.

Ludlow, Vermont

LODGING
Governor's Inn. 86 Main Street. This 1890 Victorian country house has eight guest rooms presided over by one of New England's best-known innkeeping couples, Charlie and Deedy Marble. Telephone: (802) 228–8830 or (800) GOVERNOR. Expensive with breakfast and dinner.

FOOD
The Governor's Inn. 86 Main Street. Telephone: (802) 288–8830. Ranking right up there with Vermont's best dining, Governor's Inn offers complimentary hors d'oeuvres before dinner in the formal dining room. There's only a single, fixed-price seating per night, but the lucky few dine in great style at tables set with silver, Waterford crystal, and antique bone china. The apple pie—almost certainly on the menu during foliage season—won best of New England honors from *Yankee* Magazine. Closed November and April. Dinner. Very expensive.

ACTIVITIES
Okemo Mountain Ski Area. Okemo is for families who simply like to ski without all the posturing, fancy clothes, and high-hormone pizzazz of the conglomerate-owned resorts. This is one of Vermont's last family-run ski areas, with a friendly base area and a surprisingly good range of beginner, intermediate, and advanced trails. Telephone: (802) 228–4041 or (800) 786–5366.

Londonderry/ Stratton Mountain, Vermont

ACTIVITIES
Stratton Mountain. Southern Vermont's highest peak has 563 acres of terrain and twelve lifts including New England's first high-speed, six-passenger chairlift. Conceived in faux-alpine style when it opened in the 1960s, Stratton now appeals to boarders with an attitude. It's not a surprise. Local bartender Jake Burton supposedly invented snowboarding here in the late 1970s, so Stratton is viewed by some of the gnarly set as The Source. Telephone: (802) 297–2200 or (800) 843–6867.

Newfane, Vermont

FAIRS, FESTIVALS, AND EVENTS
Heritage Festival. This juried crafts show offers something a little different with the inclusion of Vermont products, collectibles, a raffle, supper, and Morris dancers. It is held in mid-October on Newfane Common. Telephone: (802) 365–7855.

West Dover, Vermont

LODGING

Inn at Sawmill Farm. Route 100. This Relais & Chateaux property—pretty much a guarantee of sumptuous luxury at a price—has been operated for more than twenty-five years by Rod and Ione Williams—an architect and interior designer respectively, whose tastes and sensibilities are obvious throughout. Telephone: (802) 464–8131. Very expensive.

FOOD

Inn at Sawmill Farm. Route 100. Telephone: (802) 464–8131. The parents host, the son cooks. And it's hard to fault the haute American-Continental cuisine prepared by chef and co-owner Brill Williams. The two dining rooms feature exposed beams, antiques, and the innkeepers' collection of copper and brass. The wine cellar is justly famed for its 35,000 bottles, with a heavy emphasis on French wines. Dinner. Very expensive.

ACTIVITIES

Mount Snow Resort and Haystack. Mount Snow has 130 trails, a 1,700-foot vertical drop, and 767 total skiable acres with twenty-six lifts serving five mountain faces. The North Face has the most challenging terrain and offers the best views. In 1998, a new high-speed quad made it easier to reach Carinthia, an area of nice, long cruising trails that was underused because it was served by an old, slow double chair. Mount Snow established the first snowboard park in the East and now boasts one of the most active snowboard cultures in the country. The Gut is the East's longest illuminated halfpipe. There are also "Family Fun" centers with sledding, ice skating, and other activities. Haystack, a 10-mile drive away, is joined to Mount Snow under the American Skiing Company corporate umbrella. With much shorter lift lines and more traditional New England runs, it's a far less hairy scene for serious skiers. Route 100. Telephone: (802) 464–3333 or (800) 245–7669.

Wilmington, Vermont

CAMPGROUNDS AND RV PARKS

Molly Stark State Park. 705 Route 9 East. The 150-acre park includes twenty-three tent/trailer sites and eleven lean-tos, with a choice of private wooded sites or open grassy sites. The campground is located at the base of Mount Olga and a trail leads to the fire tower on the summit for a great view. Telephone: (802) 464–5460 (summer) or (802) 886–2434 (winter).

FOOD

Skyline Restaurant. Route 9, the Molly Stark Trail, near the border of Wilmington and Marlboro. Telephone: (802) 464–5535. Famous for waffles and griddlecakes with Vermont maple syrup, the Skyline is possibly even better known for its 100-mile view.

Burlington, Vermont

LODGING

For such a good-sized town, Burlington is not an easy place to find a room with character. There are a number of chain motels along Route 7 south of town. The city itself is loaded with small B&B homestays—some in the historic district and some near the lake. The Lake Champlain Regional Chamber of Commerce will provide a listing. Mailing address: 60 Main Street, Burlington, VT 05401. Telephone: (802) 863–3489.

The Inn at Essex. 70 Essex Way, Essex. About a quarter-hour drive from Burlington, the inn is another part of the New England Culinary Institute mini-conglomerate. Many of its ninety-seven rooms have fireplaces. Special Culinary Weekends are one of the big draws here. Telephone: (802) 878–1100 or (800) 727–4295. Moderate to expensive.

Willard Street Inn. 349 South Willard Street. Built in the late 1880s for a prominent businessman, this brick house with marble details, slate roof, and a striking marble outdoor staircase that descends from the solarium to the English-style gardens offers fifteen guest rooms, ten of which have private baths. Telephone: (802) 651–8710 or (800) 577–8712. Moderate to expensive with breakfast.

CAMPGROUNDS AND RV PARKS

North Beach Campground. 80 Institute Road. With one hundred sites on the shores of Lake Champlain, this campground has all the usual amenities plus a sandy beach. It's owned and operated by the Burlington Parks and Recreation Department and is within walking distance of the Burlington Bike Path. Telephone: (802) 862–0942 or (800) 571–1198.

FOOD

Al's French Frys. Williston Road (Route 2), South Burlington. Telephone: (802) 862–9203. This may look like just another burger joint to you, but to Ben Cohen and Jerry Greenfield (the Ben & Jerry's ice cream moguls), it's french fry heaven. The diner-ish establishment is always busy, but if you're only getting fries (they have hot dogs, hamburgers, and chicken patties, too), go to the head of the line. Open daily from 10:30 A.M. until 11:00 P.M. Inexpensive.

Butler's Restaurant. 70 Essex Way, Essex Junction. Telephone: (802) 879–1100. This fine restaurant at the Inn at Essex is the showcase of NECI's best students and the NECI style, touted as a "bold rethinking of American and European cuisines with an emphasis on regional ingredients." Much of the menu is also available in the less dressy tavern. Dinner. Moderate.

Carbur's Restaurant & Lounge. 115 St. Paul Street. Telephone: (802) 862–4106. Every college town has a place that prides itself on a giant menu of sandwiches—in this case one hundred combinations. Wash them down with any of eighty beers from around the globe. Lunch and dinner. Inexpensive.

Cheese Outlet Fresh Market. 400 Pine Street. Telephone for catalog: (800) 447–1205. If you're assembling a picnic, camping, or have accommodations with cooking facilities, this is the best place in Burlington to purchase cheeses (including several locally handcrafted goat and cow cheeses), as well as gourmet goods, fresh bakery items, and ready-to-heat meals. They also have a good selection of microbrewed beers and California and imported wines. Open daily.

Ice House. 171 Battery Street. Telephone: (802) 864–1800. This is probably the best place in town to watch the sun set over Lake Champlain while sipping a cocktail or dining on casual contemporary American fare. Lunch and dinner. Moderate.

Leunig's Bistro. 115 Church Street. Telephone: (802) 863–3759. Leunig's is something of a fixture in Burlington. Good, true bistro fare seasoned with recorded jazz or classical music gives that vaguely European ambience college-town dining rooms so often strive for without succeeding so well. Lunch and dinner. Inexpensive to moderate.

NECI Commons. 25 Church Street. Telephone: (802) 862–6324. The New England Culinary Institute expanded in 1997 from Montpelier into Burlington with this striking remake of one of the historic Church Street buildings into a combination dining-education center. The street level features a great casual bakery-cafe in the front, with a neo-Deco styled dressy casual dining room farther back in the deep building. The upstairs bar with very high ceilings and drop-dead swank styling is *the* place to be seen in Burlington. The whole operation is one big practice lab for the NECI students, and as such, offers good value for excellent, up-to-the-minute contemporary American cuisine. Like every NECI operation, the diner gets a card to grade the food, presentation, menu, waitstaff, overall dining experience, and value. Reservations are not accepted for dinner, but you can call ahead to get on the wait list. Lunch and dinner. Moderate.

Shanty on the Shore Restaurant and Fish Market. Just up from the Lake Champlain ferry dock, Shanty on the Shore blithely ignores the fact that it sits on freshwater rather than salt. The menu is heavy on haddock, swordfish, shrimp, clams, and oysters. Basically, it's a good spot to enjoy an unpretentious fish dinner with a cold beer without feeling a pinch in the pocketbook. 181 Battery Street. Telephone: (802) 864–0238. Lunch and dinner. Inexpensive.

OTHER ATTRACTIONS

Ethan Allen Homestead. Ethan Allen was one of Vermont's most colorful founders. Leader of the Green Mountain Boys before and during the American Revolution, Allen and his men captured Fort Ticonderoga and Crown Point and at one point Allen was the benevolent dictator of Vermont. Said one of his detractors when he died, "On this day Ethan Allen died and went straight to hell." The Homestead was his last dwelling—a farm high above the Winooski *(onion)* River. The site is a mix of modern historical museum with multimedia exhibit, walking trails on several acres, and the restored wood frame farmhouse. It's also a great spot for scenic picnics. The Homestead is open from mid-May to mid-June daily from 1:00 to 5:00 P.M., from mid-June to mid-October Monday through Saturday from 10:00 A.M. to 5:00 P.M., Sunday from 1:00 to 5:00 P.M. Adults $3.50. To get to the Homestead from downtown Burlington, take Route 7 north. Turn left on Pearl Street, then right on North Champlain Street. Turn left at the end, then make an immediate right onto Route 127 north. Take the first exit ("North Avenue Beaches") and make the first right at a small green sign. Telephone: (802) 865–4556.

Robert Hull Fleming Museum. This art-history survey museum at the University of Vermont not only has Greek, Roman, and Egyptian antiquities, but it also shows American and European artists with a special emphasis on twentieth-century painting by Vermont artists. Admission by donation. Open from the day after Labor Day through April from Tuesday through Friday 9:00 A.M. to 4:00 P.M., Saturday and Sunday from 1:00 to 5:00 P.M. From May through August the museum is open Tuesday through Friday from noon until 4:00 P.M. and on Saturday and Sunday from 1:00 to 5:00 P.M. Colchester Avenue on the University of Vermont campus. Telephone: (802) 656–0750.

ACTIVITIES

Boat Rentals. Go along for the ride on a captained day sail or take the helm of a sloop to explore Lake Champlain yourself. Sea Doo jetskis and inflatable boats are also available for rental. Day sails occur three times daily on changing schedule between May and October. Adults $20. Boat rentals vary from half-hour jetski rental for $35 to four-hour rental of smallest sloop at $87 up to eight-hour weekend rental of 40-foot sloop for $324. Call Winds of Ireland for details and reservations. Burlington Community Boathouse. Telephone: (802) 863–5090.

Sea Kayak Tours. True North Kayak Tours offers separate kayak trips for beginners and advanced kayakers that cover different areas of Lake Champlain. Beginner and advanced technique sessions are also available. Day tours are out from 10:00 A.M. until 5:00 P.M. and cost $55. Sunset tours, offered on Wednesday and Friday for two hours, cost $25. Call for details and reservations. Telephone: (802) 860–1910.

TOURS

Vermont Town Tours. Ninety-minute narrated tours of Burlington and the surrounding area, including the University of Vermont and the local wood-chip power generating plant, depart three times daily from historic Union Station (the Amtrak station) at the junction of Battery and Main Streets. Adults $12. Telephone: (802) 434–4250.

FAIRS, FESTIVALS, AND EVENTS

Champlain Valley Fair. Vermont's largest fair is held in adjacent Essex Junction late August through early September, with major grandstand shows, a giant midway, horse shows, agricultural exhibits, and competitions. Telephone: (802) 878–5545.

Discover Jazz Festival. This six-day festival in early June presents jazz, gospel, Latin music, and blues in more than fifty locations around the city including City Hall Park, Church Street Marketplace, clubs, buses, and beaches. Telephone: (802) 86–FLYNN.

First Night Burlington. This December 31 celebration, like others throughout the region, welcomes in the New Year with a variety of arts activities and performances. Telephone: (802) 863–6005 or (800) 639–9252.

Lake Champlain International Fishing Derby.
This event is not confined to Burlington, but
encompasses all of the lake. It's a multi-species
tournament open to all levels of anglers who compete for cash prizes in a friendly event. For three
days in mid-June. Telephone: (802) 862–7777.

Vermont Craft Workers. They do things on a
grand scale in little Essex, also the site of the
region's largest craft show, with more than 400
juried exhibitors from the U.S. and Canada, featuring traditional, contemporary, and country
crafts. The exhibition takes place in late October.
Telephone: (802) 878–4786.

SHOPPING

Bennington Potters North. 127 College Street.
Telephone: (802) 863–2221. Three levels of a
century-old building hold Bennington's dinner-
ware, cookware, and flower pots, as well as other
complementary "nesting" goods.

Essex Outlet Fair. 21 Essex Way. Telephone:
(802) 657–2777. The only designer factory outlet
in Northern Vermont.

Lake Champlain Chocolates. Top quality chocolate makes for excellent fudge, dipped fruits, and
chocolates. You can watch fudge being made at
the shop on the pedestrian mall (61 Church
Street; telephone: 802–862–5186) or view the
whole candymaking operation from behind a
glass window at the factory (431 Pine Street; telephone: 802–864–1808) where a small selection of
discount items is available.

Vermont State Craft Center/Frog Hollow. 85
Church Street. Telephone: (802) 863–6458. The
work of more than 300 Vermont craftspeople is
displayed in three galleries around the state,
including this one on the Church Street pedestrian
mall.

Shelburne, Vermont

LODGING

The Inn at Shelburne Farms. Harbor Road. This
1890s manor built by William Seward Webb and
Lila Vanderbilt Webb overlooks Lake Champlain
and is surrounded by a 1,000-acre operating farm.
There are twenty-four guest rooms, most of which

have private baths. You approach up a winding
drive, with grounds bearing the stamp of
Frederick Law Olmsted. If you've been roughing
it in the Green Mountains or keeping to the budget by staying in inexpensive motels, treat yourself
to a night here. Telephone: (802) 985–8498.
Moderate to very expensive.

FOOD

Harrington's of Vermont. Route 7. Telephone:
(802) 434–3411. Harrington's is well-known for
its hams and turkeys that have been smoked with
corn cobs. Choose either for a sandwich in this
gourmet store/deli.

The Inn at Shelburne Farms. Harbor Road.
Telephone: (802) 985–8498. The restaurant continues the high style of the inn. The marble-
floored main dining room overlooks Lake
Champlain, while a smaller room has a pasture
view. Produce and cheeses from the farm find
their way into the kitchen and onto the
Continental-Vermont menu, which is likely to
feature Vermont game birds or elegant desserts
like a frozen blackberry mousse. The restaurant
serves breakfast and dinner from mid-May to
mid-October. Expensive.

OTHER ATTRACTIONS

Vermont Teddy Bear Factory. Tours are offered
daily year-round and visitors can create their own

Shelburne Farms, Shelburne, Vermont

bears. Adults $1.00. Route 7. Telephone: (802) 985–3001, ext. 1800 or (800) 829–BEAR.

FAIRS, FESTIVALS, AND EVENTS

Shelburne Farms Harvest Festival. This one-day event in mid-September features a children's farmyard, crafts demonstrations, environmental workshops sponsored by the Green Mountain Audubon Society, and free hayrides around the grounds designed by Frederick Law Olmsted. Harbor Road. Telephone: (802) 985–8686.

Shelburne Museum Lilac Festival. Of the many activities the museum sponsors throughout the year, one of our favorites is this festival from late May to early June when 400 lilac bushes are in bloom. Route 7. Telephone: (802) 985–3346.

Charlotte, Vermont

OTHER ATTRACTIONS

The Cook's Garden. Vegetable gardeners (as opposed to flower gardeners) will find the demonstration gardens behind the headquarters of Shep and Ellen Ogden's mail-order seed company fascinating. The Ogdens carefully select varieties well-suited to northern New England and complementary to the offerings of larger seed companies. Off Riverside Road on old U.S. Route 7. Telephone: (802) 824–3400.

The Vermont Wildflower Farm. At the largest wildflower seed center in the eastern United States, you can "browse" the six acres of wildflowers before selecting seeds in the shop. Adults $3.00. Open May through late October daily from 10:00 A.M. to 5:00 P.M. Located on Route 7, 12 miles south of Burlington and 5 miles south of the Shelburne Museum. Telephone: (802) 425–3500.

FAIRS, FESTIVALS, AND EVENTS

Lake Champlain Balloon Festival. This three-day event in early June calls itself the largest balloon festival in New England. It features fifty hot air balloons and other sky-oriented activities such as skydivers and fireworks as well as the usual arts and crafts, food, and entertainment. Telephone: (802) 425–4884.

Middlebury, Vermont

For advance information about central Vermont and for lodging referrals to small B&Bs in and around Middlebury, contact the Addison County Chamber of Commerce, 2 Court Street, Middlebury, VT 05753. Telephone: (802) 388–7951 or (800) 733–8376.

LODGING

Inn on the Green. 19 South Pleasant Street. Graceful National Historic Landmark house from 1803 on the village green offers ten rooms with private baths and period decor. Telephone: (802) 388–7512. Inexpensive to moderate with breakfast.

Middlebury Bed and Breakfast. Washington Street. Within walking distance to town, this B&B appeals to hikers, cyclists, and college students visiting friends. Telephone: (802) 388–4851. Inexpensive with breakfast.

Middlebury Inn. Every prosperous town had a prestigious inn at one time. This was, and still is, Middlebury's entry in the Historic Hotels of America. Perhaps the lodging of choice for parents who visit their offspring at Middlebury College, the inn offers posh country comfort. There is also an adjacent motel. Telephone: (802) 388–4961 or (800) 842–4666. Inexpensive to expensive. Meal plan available.

Swift House Inn. Route 7 at Stewart Lane. For more of a country (rather than town) experience with all the amenities, the Swift House Inn offers rooms with fireplaces and double whirlpool tubs in this 1815 estate of a former Vermont governor. Telephone: (802) 388–9925. Moderate to expensive with breakfast.

OTHER ATTRACTIONS

Otter Creek Brewing. Perhaps the best established of the western Vermont microbreweries, Otter Creek offers free daily tours of the facility capped by a visit to the tasting bar and the brewhouse gift store. 85 Exchange Street. Telephone: (802) 388–0727 or (800) 473–0727.

University of Vermont Morgan Horse Farm. The Morgan, said to be the first American horse

Morgan horse farm, Middlebury, Vermont

breed, is Vermont's state animal. You'll see these handsome animals at pasture and in corrals here, depending on season and time of day. The facility presents a good guided tour about the history and lineage of the breed. It's also a picturesque spot to bring a picnic. Adults $3.50. Tours and videotape presentations are given from May to October daily on the hour from 9:00 A.M. to 4:00 P.M. Route 23. Telephone: (802) 388–2011.

SHOPPING
Vermont State Craft Center at Frog Hollow. 1 Mill Street. Telephone: (802) 388–5020. This is the site of the original Frog Hollow gallery, in a historic mill building next to Otter Creek Falls in downtown Middlebury.

Shoreham, Vermont

LODGING
Shoreham Inn & Country Store. Shoreham Village. Shoreham is little more than a wide spot in the road, but Cleo Alther has been welcoming cyclists and hikers for decades to this very casual, family-style lodging in a cheerfully funky 1790 inn next door to the general store and within spitting distance of the post office. Shoreham Inn

tends to be a stopover between Fort Ticonderoga and Middlebury for casual cyclists. Because bicycle tour groups use the inn extensively, be sure to check on availability of a room. Most share baths. Telephone: (802) 897–5081 or (800) 255–5081. Inexpensive with breakfast.

Brandon, Vermont

LODGING
Churchill House Inn. Near both the Catamount Trail and the Green Mountain National Forest, this 1871 inn operated by the Jackson family proudly shows its lineage with simple and comfortable rooms and a bounteous table at mealtime. It's a good location for summer hikers and winter cross-country skiers. Each of the eight rooms has a private bath and some have whirlpools. Telephone: (802) 247–6851 or (800) 838–3301. Summer: Moderate with breakfast. Winter: Expensive with breakfast and dinner.

Rutland, Vermont

FAIRS, FESTIVALS, AND EVENTS
Vermont State Fair. More than 150 years old, this classic fair is held over nine days from late August into early September, with horse, ox, and pony pulling, draft horses, pari-mutuel harness racing, and a big midway. Also on site are a sugarhouse, dairy building, and milking parlor. Telephone: (802) 775–5200.

Manchester, Vermont

LODGING
The Equinox. Manchester Village. One of the last great mountain resorts, the Equinox has been around since 1769 and lays claim to 2,300 acres and commanding views. Over the years, the Equinox has expanded and modernized to the point where the once fairly humble inn and tavern have been dwarfed by nineteenth and twentieth-century additions. The 183 guest rooms have antique furnishings, luxury fabrics, and Audubon prints on the walls. But you needn't settle for a room. You can also rent townhouses with fireplaces, kitchens, porches, and mountain views. The resort facilities include a golf course, tennis

courts, falconry school, fitness center, and outdoor pool. Telephone: (802) 362–4700 or (800) 362–4747. Expensive to very expensive, with a wide range of packages available.

Equinox Mountain Inn. Skyline Drive. Equinox Mountain, which is in the Taconic range rather than the Green Mountains proper, looms on Manchester's west. The road to the summit is a toll road and the inn at the top is a scenic wonder. As New England's last remaining mountaintop inn (at 3,835 feet), this seventeen-room aerie is surrounded by 8,000 private, mostly forested acres. Pets and children under twelve are barred, but this is more an outdoorsperson's place than a family getaway. It is open May through October. Telephone: (802) 362–1113 or (800) 868–6843. Moderate.

Inn at Ormsby Hill. Historic Route 7A. This restored circa-1764 country manor house sits high on a hill surveying the surrounding landscape, with especially good views of the Green Mountains. This is the place to book to feel like a country squire in a bedroom with canopied bed, romantic touches, two-person Jacuzzi baths, and slightly overwrought decor. Telephone: (802) 362–1163 or (800) 670–2841. Moderate to expensive with breakfast.

Food

Chantecleer. Route 7A. Telephone: (802) 362–1616. Chef Michael Bauman turns out elegant mountain resort cuisine (well, he's from Switzerland) at this top-rated restaurant located in a converted nineteenth-century barn that still has the silo attached. Bauman makes good use of seasonal local produce for this restaurant that remains open only in summer and fall. House specialties include Dover sole and rack of lamb. Dinner. Expensive.

The Equinox. Manchester Village. Telephone: (802) 362–4700. The formal Colonnade dining room of the Equinox resort features upscale contemporary cuisine. Breakfast, Sunday brunch, dinner. Expensive. The Marsh Tavern, once a hangout of Ethan Allen and the Green Mountain Boys, serves more traditional New England fare—pot roast, veal chops, pan-seared swordfish—in atmospheric rooms with wooden tables and Windsor chairs. Breakfast, lunch, and dinner. Moderate.

Up for Breakfast. 710 Main Street, Manchester Center. Telephone: (802) 362–4204. A good spot for gourmet breakfast fare such as banana crepes, Up for Breakfast is an excellent alternative to the fancy B&B breakfast. Breakfast.

Activities

Gleneagles Golf Course. This eighteen-hole championship-level course, which belongs to the Equinox, was originally built in 1927 by Walter Travis. Renowned golf course architect Rees Jones supervised a $3.5 million restoration and update in 1992. Greens fees begin at $43 for players who are not guests of the hotel. Telephone: (802) 362–3223.

Shopping

Factory Outlets. We still haven't figured out why outdoorsy places like L.L. Bean and Orvis seem to attract designer factory outlets. But Manchester's conglomerate of factory outlet malls at least features small stores with sterling names: Movado watches, Armani, Baccarat, Coach, Tommy Hilfiger, and Polo-Ralph Lauren, for example. They're in an unmissable row along Route 7.

Orvis. The main sales room of this purveyor of outdoor gear (especially for fly fishing) is on Historic Route 7A. Telephone: (802) 362–3750. There is also a shop for discontinued merchandise from the catalog on Union Street in the downtown center. Telephone: (802) 362–6455.

Arlington, Vermont

Fairs, Festivals, and Events

Ethan Allen Days. This Revolutionary War re-enactment is held on Father's Day weekend. Telephone: (802) 447–3311.

Bennington, Vermont

For information on Bennington and the surrounding area, contact the Bennington Area Chamber of Commerce, Veterans Memorial Drive, Bennington, VT 05201. Telephone: (802) 447–3311.

LODGING

Kirkside Motor Lodge. 250 West Main Street. This motor lodge right in the heart of historic Bennington is within walking distance of the Bennington Museum and Battle Monument. The twenty-three guest rooms are decorated in a colonial, country style. Telephone: (802) 447–7596. Inexpensive to moderate.

Molly Stark Inn. 1067 East Main Street. This 1890 Victorian country home is on the Molly Stark Trail, a bit out of town center. There are six guest rooms and a private guest cottage. The rooms all vary in size and decor, but in general, they are "relaxed country" with antiques, handmade quilts, claw-foot tubs. No smoking. Telephone: (802) 442–9631. Inexpensive to moderate with breakfast.

Paradise Motor Inn. 141 West Main Street. Also right in historic Old Bennington and within walking distance of the attractions. Some of the seventy-six rooms have private balconies, patios, and saunas, and there are tennis courts and a heated pool on the grounds. Telephone: (802) 442–8351. Moderate.

CAMPGROUNDS AND RV PARKS

Woodford State Park. Located on a mountain plateau about 11 miles east of Bennington, this park is surrounded by the Green Mountain National Forest. There are 103 campsites as well as a small beach and hiking trails. Naturalist programs are presented throughout the summer. Telephone: (802) 447–7169 (summer) or (802) 483–2001 (winter). Reservations are accepted beginning the first Tuesday in January.

FOOD

Paul's Fish Fry. Corner of Washington and Main Streets. No phone. Calling itself "Famous since 1965," Paul's specializes in fried fish and fried fish dinners, including shrimp, oysters, haddock, clams, and chicken. You can also get hamburgers and hot dogs. Drive-in to order at the window, or eat on site at picnic tables or in the dining room. Lunch and dinner. Inexpensive.

FAIRS, FESTIVALS, AND EVENTS

Antique Car Show and Swap Meet. Hundreds of antique cars, motorcycles, and tractors are displayed at this three-day event in mid-September. There are also swap-meet vendors, contests, food, and entertainment. Telephone: (802) 447–3311.

Bennington Battle Day. This mid-August event includes a parade, food, children's activities, and fireman's competitions. Telephone: (802) 447–3311.

SHOPPING

Bennington Potters Yard. 324 County Road. Telephone: (802) 447–7531. There is a free tour of the largest production art pottery in the Northeast. The showroom includes some discounted kiln runs.

The Berkshire Hills of Massachusetts

For information about the Berkshires, contact Berkshire Visitors Bureau, Berkshire Common, Plaza Level, Pittsfield, MA 01201. Telephone: (413) 443–9186.

Mount Greylock

LODGING

Bascom Lodge. This Appalachian Mountain Club property at the summit of Mount Greylock was built by the Civilian Conservation Corps and offers co-ed dormitory bunk rooms and four private rooms for through-hikers and short-term visitors. Open from mid-May to late October. Telephone: (413) 743–1591 for current week reservations, (413) 443–0011 for advance reservations. Inexpensive.

CAMPGROUNDS AND RV PARKS

Mount Greylock State Reservation. Headquarters: Rockwell Road, Lanesboro, Massachusetts. Thirty-five campsites are located near Sperry Road. Telephone: (413) 449–9426.

North Adams, Massachusetts

FOOD

Appalachian Bean Cafe. 67 Main Street. Telephone: (413) 663–7543. This bright and airy spot on the corner of a downtown block has a variety of sandwich choices as well as baked goods. Breakfast and lunch.

OTHER ATTRACTIONS

Natural Bridge. The only water-eroded natural bridge in North America shares a modest interpretation area with an abandoned marble quarry and a beautiful marble dam. Parking fee $2.00. Route 8. Telephone: (413) 663–6312.

FAIRS, FESTIVALS, AND EVENTS

La Festa. This three-day Italian street fair in mid-June has fireworks, ethnic foods, craft exhibits, and nationally known entertainers. Telephone: (413) 66–FESTA.

Williamstown, Massachusetts

LODGING

Field Farm Guest House. 554 Sloan Road. Offering a change of pace from the Victorian and country decor of most B&Bs, Field Farm is a Modern style house built in 1948, with much of the original owners' collection of Scandinavian modern furniture and American modern art still in place. As a bonus, the home sits on 296 acres of forests, fields, and wetlands, with four miles of trails and great views of Mount Greylock and the Taconic range. Telephone: (413) 458–3135. Moderate with breakfast.

Four Acres Motel. Route 2. This two-story brick motel has thirty rooms and is just a short drive out of town. Telephone: (413) 458–8158. Inexpensive to moderate with breakfast.

Maple Terrace Motel. 555 Main Street (Route 2). Fifteen motel rooms are attached to a handsome Federal-style home, next door to a horse farm and within driving distance of the Williamstown downtown. Telephone: (413) 458–9677. Inexpensive to moderate.

Northside Motel. 45 North Street (Route 7). There are thirty rooms in this attractive and comfortable motel within walking distance of the museums, shopping district, and Williams College campus. Telephone: (413) 458–8107. Inexpensive to moderate.

FOOD

Papa Charlie's Deli. 28 Spring Street. Telephone: (413) 458–5969. The presence of the Williamstown Theatre Festival adds a certain panache to the typical college-town sandwich shop. Here, the sandwiches are named for the stars: Christopher Reeve, Richard Thomas, Mary Tyler Moore, and Gilda Radner.

Robin's Restaurant. Foot of Spring Street. Telephone: (413) 458–4489. The food and decor are casual bistro style. In nice weather, the tables on the outdoor deck provide a view of all the comings and goings on Main Street. Lunch and dinner. Moderate to expensive.

The Store at Five Corners. Routes 7 and 43. Telephone: (413) 458–3176. Located on a busy intersection, this country store dates back to 1770 and is a convenient place to pick up sandwiches and baked goods.

Wild Amber Grill. 101 North Street (Route 7). Telephone: (413) 458–4000. People come here

**Field Farm Guest House,
Williamstown, Massachusetts**

for the contemporary American cuisine and for the lively cabaret performed by artists associated with the Williamstown Theatre Festival. Lunch and dinner. Moderate.

Pittsfield, Massachusetts

CAMPGROUNDS AND RV PARKS

Pittsfield State Forest. Cascade Street. The top of Berry Mountain provides a nice panoramic view, but the most spectacular thing in this forest is the bloom of sixty-five acres of wild azaleas in June. There are thirty-one campsites, boat ramps, hiking trails, and streams for canoeing and fishing. Telephone: (413) 442–8992.

OTHER ATTRACTIONS

Berkshire Museum. The art and furniture collections of the small-town museum reflect the often provincial tastes of its early twentieth-century donors. More fascinating are the artifacts of everyday Berkshire County life and the collection of oddities and gee-whiz articles. The natural history exhibits on the first level also have a certain old-fashioned charm. For nearly a half century, the museum has also screened foreign and American independent films in the Little Cinema. Museum admission: Adults $6.00. Open Tuesday through Saturday from 10:00 A.M. to 5:00 P.M., Sunday from 1:00 to 5:00 P.M. Also open Monday during July and August. 39 South Street (Route 7). Telephone: (413) 443–7171.

Berkshire Opera Company. During July and August, the Koussevitsky Arts Center at Berkshire Community College is the setting for fully staged operas in their original languages with a supertitle system to display the English translations. On West Street off the Park Square Rotary. Telephone: (413) 528–4420.

Silvio O. Conte National Archives and Records Administration. Opened in 1994, this archive library has become an important stop for amateur genealogists who want to peruse a variety of materials that include soldiers' records and pension documents from the Revolutionary War, census data going back to 1790, Supreme Court documents, immigration and naturalization records,

and passenger lists from the thousands of ships bringing immigrants to New York, Boston, and Philadelphia. More than seventy volunteers have been trained to help visitors. Open Monday, Tuesday, Thursday, and Friday from 8:00 A.M. to 4:00 P.M. and Wednesday from 8:00 A.M. to 9:00 P.M. 100 Dan Fox Drive. Telephone: (413) 445–6885, ext. 26.

South Mountain Concerts. From late August into early October, the South Mountain Concert series presents chamber music and recitals at the South Mountain Concert Hall, two miles south of town on Route 7. Telephone: (413) 442–2106.

FAIRS, FESTIVALS, AND EVENTS

Festival Americana. The highlight of this patriotic festival is one of the largest Fourth of July parades in the country. Telephone: (413) 499–3861.

Festival of Trees. From mid-November through early December, this much-anticipated event features more than 300 creatively decorated trees set up in nine galleries at the Berkshire Museum. Telephone: (413) 443–7171.

Lenox, Massachusetts

LODGING

Birchwood Inn. 7 Hubbard Street. When it's hot in the village, there's a cool breeze on the porch of this inn situated on the top of a hill overlooking the town. The location is also a plus for its proximity to the hiking, biking, and cross-country ski trails of Kennedy Park. A 1767 farmhouse, with library and parlor, forms the core of the property, which has been enlarged over the years. Telephone: (413) 637–2600 or (800) 524–1646. Moderate to expensive with breakfast.

The Gables Inn. 103 Walker Street. Easily the most fanciful building in town, the 100-year-old Queen Anne style "cottage" was the home of Edith Wharton's mother-in-law and the refuge of her husband Teddy after Edith divorced him. The lavish public areas and nineteen guest rooms are decorated with period antiques and fine art. The grounds include a tennis court and indoor swimming pool (in season). Telephone: (413) 637–

3416. Moderate to expensive with breakfast.

The Kemble Inn. 2 Kemble Street. The Kemble, with its three grand halls on the ground floor and dramatic staircase, would do a Georgian gentleman proud. This 1881 "cottage" sits on a big lot and has incredible mountain views from its back porch. The fifteen guest rooms are named for authors associated with the Berkshires; some have fireplaces and Jacuzzis. Telephone: (413) 637–4113 or (800) 353–4113. Moderate to expensive with breakfast.

The Village Inn. 16 Church Street. This 1771 inn is right in the heart of the shopping and dining district of downtown Lenox and its front porch is a great place to take a break and survey the scene. The thirty-two guest rooms are furnished with country antiques. Telephone: (413) 637–0020 or (800) 253–0917. Inexpensive to expensive.

Walker House. 64 Walker Street. The owners of the Walker House have named their guest rooms after composers. The atmosphere in this 1804 Federal home is relaxed and friendly, with cats on the back porch and stuffed animals and other quirky collections throughout the grand parlor and other public spaces. Telephone: (413) 637–1271 or (800) 235–3098. Moderate to expensive with breakfast.

FOOD

Cafe Lucia. 80 Church Street. Telephone: (413) 637–2640. The covered wooden deck is the best spot in town for outdoor dining. It may be called a cafe, but the food is more what you'd expect at a good northern Italian trattoria, with an emphasis on grilled meats and fish. Dinner only. Moderate to expensive.

Church Street Cafe. 65 Church Street. Telephone: (413) 637–2745. Don't let the white linens fool you—this is casual dining without the muss and fuss of some haughty Lenox restaurants. A solid New American menu is nicely executed in the contemporary culinary-school style. Lunch and dinner. Moderate to expensive.

Roseborough Grill. 71 Church Street. Telephone: (413) 637–2700. Offering a contemporary New

Tanglewood, Lenox, Massachusetts

American menu similar to its neighbor, Church Street Cafe, Roseborough Grill opts for a country provincial decor, with pink and green sponged walls. Alternately, you can choose to dine at a table on the porch. Lunch and dinner. Moderate to expensive.

OTHER ATTRACTIONS

Stockbridge Summer Music. Seven Hills Inn, a Berkshires "cottage" filled with antiques, is the setting for a July and August music series of popular, chamber, and jazz recitals. 40 Plunkett Street. Telephone: (413) 443–1138.

SHOPPING

Michael Charles Cabinetmakers. 50 Church Street. Telephone: (413) 637–3483. Handcrafted furniture in the Shaker tradition is made of solid hardwoods with traditional joinery techniques. If you can't afford a desk or four-poster bed, there are also mirrors, trays, and stools.

Hoadley Gallery. 21 Church Street. Telephone: (413) 637–2814. The husband of the shop owner is a ceramist and she has assembled an outstanding assortment of ceramic work by artists from throughout the country.

Ute Stebich Gallery. 69 Church Street. Telephone: (413) 637–3566. Unlike any other gallery we have encountered in the Berkshires, this spot features exceptional contemporary art by local, national, and international artists.

Stone's Throw Antiques. 51 Church Street.

Telephone: (413) 637–2733. In an area known for its oversized cottages, this nicely arranged shop features glass, silver, and small-scale furniture that wouldn't be out of place in more manageable homes.

Lee, Massachusetts

LODGING

Chambery Inn. 199 Main Street. This small European-styled hotel used to be a parochial school and is named for the hometown of the French nuns who organized it. An impeccable job of renovation has preserved such unique features as the boys' and girls' staircases and wall-mounted blackboards while creating comfortable standard guest rooms and spacious suites. Telephone: (413) 243–2221 or (800) 537–4321. Moderate to very expensive with breakfast.

FOOD

Joe's Diner. 85 Center Street. Telephone: (413) 243–9756. Standard diner fare is available in this unpretentious spot immortalized as the setting for Norman Rockwell's painting *The Runaway.* Breakfast, lunch, and dinner. Inexpensive.

SHOPPING

Berkshire Outlet Village. Route 20. Telephone: (413) 243–8186. More than sixty outlet stores featuring clothing and housewares, including locally based Crane & Company, are located within walking distance of each other.

Stockbridge, Massachusetts

LODGING

Four Seasons on Main B&B. 47 Main Street. There are only three rooms in this attractive home in the village center and they are named for three of the four seasons. The wicker-furnished front porch has a great view of the main drag and the Old Corner House. Telephone: (413) 298–5419. Moderate to expensive with breakfast.

The Inn at Stockbridge. Route 7. This 1906 country inn is set on twelve acres just about a mile from downtown Stockbridge and recently added a cottage house with four junior suites to complement the seven guest rooms in the original house. Telephone: (413) 298–3337. Moderate to very expensive.

Red Lion Inn. 30 Main Street. Established as a stagecoach stop in 1773 and rebuilt in 1897, the Red Lion Inn is one of the few remaining American inns in continuous use since the eighteenth century. Huge as it is, the rooms have been kept immaculately up to date, with individual air conditioning and eclectic furnishings in the elegant country style also promulgated by the owners' Country Curtains store. Many corporate

The Red Lion Inn, Stockbridge, Massachusetts

groups come here on retreat, and the Red Lion is popular with travel agents booking clients into the Berkshires. And, yes, some upscale bus tours overnight here as well. The Red Lion remembers the days when men wore vests and ladies wore hats, and though both fashions are gone, the establishment maintains a decorum worthy of that more genteel age. Telephone: (413) 298–5545. Moderate to expensive.

The Taggart House. 18 Main Street. This former Berkshire "cottage" is set back from the street with a big lawn, massive trees, and a wisteria-draped entry portico. This luxury property takes its cues from the country manor house style of grace and comfort. With the downtown location and the cottage mystique, it invites a certain level of make-believe. Telephone: (413) 298–4303. Very expensive.

FOOD

Red Lion Inn. 30 Main Street. Telephone: (413) 298–5545. The dining room menu of the Red Lion has evolved over decades to present meals approximating a dinner you could imagine in a Norman Rockwell painting: carved roasted turkey with cornbread dressing, grilled tenderloin of beef, pork chop stuffed with an apple and bacon hash, grilled salmon, and so on. (Rockwell ate here every Thursday.) Every so often the chef sneaks in something different, such as a vegetarian entree of oven-braised artichokes with red lentils. The dining room is semi-formal—jackets for men but ties optional—but similar Anglo-American fare is also available in the casual Widow Bingham's Tavern and an even more casual menu (burgers, shepherd's pie) in the Lion's Den Pub, which is ensconced in the cool, dark cellar. Breakfast, lunch, and dinner. Expensive to very expensive.

Theresa's Stockbridge Cafe. Main Street. Telephone: (413) 298–5565. This venerable hippie cafe was once the site of Alice's Restaurant, immortalized in the Arlo Guthrie song of the same name. Even with a new name, Theresa's is a fun, counter-cultural cafe with a range of vegetarian food and a lot of Massachusetts Mexican on the menu. Lunch and dinner. Inexpensive to moderate.

Daily Bread Bakery. Main Street. Telephone: (413) 298–0272. The house specialty, sourdough French bread, is the base for a variety of sandwich fillings.

OTHER ATTRACTIONS

Berkshire Botanical Garden. Located about two miles from Stockbridge center, self-guided trails lead past a variety of herb, vegetable and perennial gardens, fruit trees, a pond garden, and a primrose walk. Wheelchair accessible. Adults $5.00. Open May through October daily from 10:00 A.M. to 5:00 P.M. Routes 102 and 183. Telephone: (413) 298–3926.

FAIRS, FESTIVALS, AND EVENTS

Main Street at Christmas. This three-day event has house tours and a crafts marketplace, but what makes it unique is the re-creation of Norman Rockwell's painting, *Stockbridge Main Street at Christmas,* complete with sleigh rides. Telephone: (413) 298–5200.

SHOPPING

Country Curtains. At The Red Lion Inn. Telephone: (413) 298–5565. Stepping into this shop is like stepping into the pages of their well-known catalog of curtains, bedding, and gift accessories.

West Stockbridge, Massachusetts

LODGING

Shaker Mill Inn. Village Center. Modern rooms and suites in a converted Shaker house include patios or balconies and small kitchens. Several rooms can be connected for large families. Telephone: (413) 232–8596. Moderate to very expensive with breakfast.

FOOD

La Bruschetta. 1 Harris Street. Telephone: (413) 232–7141. The kitchen has all the flair of a contemporary big-city trattoria with the added advantage of being close to the source for its ingredients. Much of what appears on the plates hasn't traveled far: they're using the local goat cheese, the local lamb, the local eggplant, the local lettuce. . . . The fish dishes are good enough to make us give up prejudices about eating seafood more than 50 miles from the coast and the wine list ranks among the best in the Berkshires. Dinner only. Expensive.

SHOPPING

Berkshire Center for Contemporary Glass. 6 Harris Street. Telephone: (413) 232–4666. Visitors can watch pieces being made in the hot-and-cold-glass working studios before looking at finished work in the adjacent gallery. The artist-owners feature their own work and a well-considered selection of work by other artists. There are a number of glass studios in the Berkshires, but as far as we know this is the only one that lets you try your hand at making a paperweight.

New England Stained-Glass Studios. 5 Center Street. Telephone: (413) 232–7181. Approaching glass from an entirely different perspective, Raymond Dorazio makes exquisite reproductions of Tiffany stained-glass lampshades.

Great Barrington, Massachusetts

LODGING

Days Inn. Main Street. We rarely recommend lodging chains, preferring places with more local character. But we make an exception for this well-located motel on the main shopping and dining drag that received a full makeover when it was acquired by Days Inn in 1998. Telephone: (413) 528–3150. Moderate.

FOOD

Castle Street Cafe. 10 Castle Street. Telephone: (413) 528–5244. Funky Great Barrington has its upscale sybarites as well, and Castle Street serves them well with a dynamic and constantly changing New American menu that takes full advantage of produce from the Housatonic Valley's organic and specialty farmers. Dinner only. Moderate.

Old Barn Club—Roadside Grill. If you're driving Route 7 south of town and Fido is with you,

be sure to stop for a Pooch Platter—a hamburger, chicken breast, dog bone, and water served in a doggie dish for $2.00. For humans, the usual grill choices are supplemented by ostrich burgers. Humans and canines can enjoy their treats on a grassy lawn under big shade trees. People even get to sit at picnic tables. Lunch and dinner. No phone. Inexpensive.

Union Bar and Grill. 293 Main Street. Telephone: (413) 528–6228. With an industrial chic styling that verges on the nineties' answer to Art Deco, Union projects a hipper-than-thou image, but the world-trotting dishes, which favor the flavors of Asia and the American Southwest, are surprisingly competent. Lunch and dinner. Moderate.

OTHER ATTRACTIONS

Aston Magna Festival. Baroque and classical chamber music are performed on period instruments in the intimate setting of St. James Church on Route 7 during July and early August. Telephone: (413) 528–3595 (summer), (203) 792–4662 (off-season).

FAIRS, FESTIVALS, AND EVENTS

Annual Monument Mountain Climb. This one-day event in early August commemorates the picnic and climb up Monument Mountain in 1850 when Herman Melville and Nathaniel Hawthorne met. Telephone: (413) 442–1793.

Great Josh Billings Runaground. For this triathalon in late September, participants make their way from Great Barrington to Lenox via bicycle, canoe, and on foot. Telephone: (413) 298–4992.

SHOPPING

Birdhouse Gallery. 87 Railroad Street. Telephone: (413) 528–0984. Animal carvings, primitive paintings, pottery, and game sets are among the offerings in this gallery specializing in twentieth-century American folk art.

The Emporium. 319 Main Street. Telephone: (413) 528–1660. This large group antiques shop in the heart of town is one of the better places in the southern Berkshires to look for fine jewelry, china, silver, glass, and other domestic items.

Sheffield, Massachusetts

LODGING

The Berkshire 1802 House. 48 South Main Street. This 200-year-old home in the village has seven guest rooms, open and screened porches, and two acres of grounds for relaxing. Telephone: (413) 229–2612. Moderate with breakfast.

Race Brook Lodge. 864 South Under Mountain Road. This informal lodge is housed in a restored 1790s timber-peg barn and offers both guest rooms and suites. Telephone: (413) 229–2916. Moderate to expensive with breakfast.

FOOD

Mystery Cafe. 137 Main Street. Telephone: (413) 229–0075. While you wait for your sandwich to be prepared, you can browse a few shelves of household antiques and used mystery books.

OTHER ATTRACTIONS

Barrington Stage Co. This adventurous company focuses on contemporary drama and musicals, including premieres and also offers a Monday night cult film festival. Nursery facilities are available for children ages two to eight. Performances are held from late June through early August at the Consolati Performing Arts Center, Berkshire School Road. Telephone: (413) 528–8888.

Berkshire Choral Festival. Two hundred choristers are joined by renowned conductors and soloists for an exploration of great choral works from Mozart and Bach to Gershwin and gospel. Performances are held in July and August in the Rovensky Concert Shed at Berkshire School on Route 41. Telephone: (413) 229–3522.

SHOPPING

Centuryhurst. Route 7. Telephone: (413) 229–8131. The owners have an exquisite selection of Wedgwood and also display similar quality collections from other dealers. For example, the selection of tin and lead soldiers and other antique fig-

ures is one of the best we've seen. Some excellent buys can be had on twentieth-century Midwestern art pottery as well.

Fellerman & Raabe Glassworks. 534 South Main Street (Route 7). Telephone: (413) 229–8533. The artists work in the back and the showroom features their work, plus perfume bottles, vases, paperweights, lamps, jewelry, and sculpture from other glass artists.

Ole TJ's Antique Barn. 649 South Main Street. Telephone: (413) 229–8382. A good place to look for country furniture and old tools.

Sheffield Pottery. 995 North Main Street (Route 7). Telephone: (413) 229–7700. It's worth stopping if you are looking for planters or gardenware as this showroom has good selections from manufacturers around the country. The clay mined out back is shipped all over New England to other potters.

Ashley Falls, Massachusetts

OTHER ATTRACTIONS

Bartholomew's Cobble. This 277-acre reservation preserves an ecosystem that is rare in New England. The "cobble" is a rock outcrop of marble and limestone with ribs of quartzite that protects the softer stone from erosion. The alkaline soil produced by these rocks supports one of the most diverse concentrations of fern species and allied plants in North America and unusually diverse flora abound in the reservation—more than 800 species of vascular plants, including some rare ones such as the tulip tree and the hackberry. Wildflowers blanket the reservation in late April and early May. Minks, river otters, beavers, and muskrats are common along the Housatonic River banks in the reservation and the cobble is a flyway for more than 240 bird types. The grasslands on the reservation are home to some of the largest nesting populations of the endangered eastern bluebird. To get to Bartholomew's Cobble, follow Route 7 south for 1.6 miles from Sheffield Center. Go right on Route 7A for 0.5 mile. Turn right at the railroad tracks onto Rannapo Road and drive 1.5 miles to Weatogue Road on the right. The entrance and parking lot are about 100 yards up the road on the left. Open mid-April to mid-October daily 9:00 A.M. to 5:00 P.M. Weatogue Road. Telephone: (413) 229–8600. Open year round. Trail fee $3.00.

Egremont/South Egremont, Massachusetts

LODGING

Baldwin Hill Farm. 121 Baldwin Hill Road, Egremont. This hilltop Victorian farm has been in the same family for three generations and features four spacious guest rooms (two have private bath). The 450-acre site has spectacular views in every direction and is great for hiking, bird watching, and cross-country skiing. Telephone: (413) 528–4092. Moderate with breakfast.

The Egremont Inn. Old Sheffield Road, South Egremont. Moved to its present location sometime around the War of 1812, the Egremont Inn practically oozes antique authenticity. With nineteen rooms and suites in a variety of configurations, it offers the best of two worlds: contemporary beds and plumbing with old-time country architecture and setting. You might find yourself wondering when the stagecoach to Albany leaves. Telephone: (413) 528–2111 or (800) 859–1780. Moderate to expensive with breakfast.

The Weathervane Inn. Route 23, South Egremont. A small cluster of buildings on ten acres of land holds eleven guest rooms. Telephone: (413) 528–9580 or (800) 528–9580. Moderate to expensive.

FOOD

Egremont Inn. Old Sheffield Road, South Egremont. Telephone: (413) 528–2111. With an eighteenth-century tavern and early nineteenth-century dining room, you'd expect traditional New England fare here, and you'd be right. But it's prepared with care and surpasses expectations. There's nothing "fancy" about it except the quality. Breakfast, brunch, and dinner. Moderate to expensive.

SHOPPING

Red Barn Antiques. Route 23, South Egremont. Telephone: (413) 528–3230. This shop has an excellent selection of restored kerosene, gas, and early electric lighting.

Splendid Peasant. Route 23, South Egremont. Telephone: (413) 528–5755. This exquisite shop features folk art antiques in museum-like settings at—unfortunately—auction house prices. We like to study the pieces before we head elsewhere in hopes of finding such treasures in the rough at prices we can afford.

6 · The Lakes Region

Introduction

A band of more than 273 lakes lies nestled in a broad belt beneath the bulging belly of the White Mountains, cutting a swath across the Granite State from the Connecticut River Valley to the Piscataqua River Valley. But these waterlands do not end at the Maine border. Indeed they march northeastward all the way through the Pine Tree State into the province of New Brunswick, following a line south of the Appalachian Mountains. From late Colonial times until the present, this wet streak along New England's underside has been where summer dwells—a landscape of indolent dragonflies by day and the manic call of loons by moonlight.

Like so many features of the New England landscape, the lakes were created by the glaciers of the Laurentide ice sheet, which last retreated from the Northeast about 12,000 years ago. The lakes fill gouges left in the earth by the crushing blanket of ice that reached a depth of up to 200 feet. When the climate warmed, the southern edges of the ice sheet began to melt and the leading edge retreated northward.

The warming periods were sporadic. For several years the ice would melt rapidly, then slow to a creep. Periods of rapid melt were marked by large deposits of rock and mud that the ice had scraped up on its way south—debris that formed a band of hills a short distance inland from the New England coast. Water from later melts was trapped in the hollows between these glacial moraines on the south and the mountains of the Appalachian chain on the north. The result was the band of lakes from the White Mountains to New Brunswick.

Archaeological sites in the nearby White Mountains show that the archaic inhabitants of New England, the so-called "Red Paint people,"

were gathering flint-like stones there to make tools 8,000 to 10,000 years ago—shortly after the glaciers receded. In all likelihood, they were also exploiting the resources of the lakes, but soil conditions and changing water levels have obliterated evidence of habitation before around A.D. 1300, by which time the Algonquian-speaking bands had picked up many of the tool- and pottery-making practices of their relatives to the south and west. But a hunter-gatherer lifestyle suited the inhabitants of the interior woodlands of northern New England better than settled agriculture, and they found the lakes ideal as winter hunting grounds and summer fishing areas. For centuries they had the lands to themselves, aside from the occasional trapper or missionary who ventured into the wilderness from the European coastal settlements after 1630.

Then, around 1750, lumbering crews arrived in search of tall timber for the sailing ships being built along the coast. Lakes Sunapee and Winnipesaukee in New Hampshire and Sebago in Maine soon saw their shores stripped, opening the land for farming. The transformation from wilderness was swift. We think of Colonial America as a time of hard work, scant resources, and real deprivation. But on the eve of the American Revolution, the seaside cities and towns had their own moneyed classes in search of leisure and inclined to emulate the country squires of their homeland who were flocking to England's Lakes District. Even before all the timber was cut on the shores of New England's more accessible lakes, the summer vacationers began to arrive. The shores of Sunapee, Winnipesaukee, and Sebago became resorts almost before they had working towns.

In 1763, the colonial governor of New Hampshire, John Wentworth, set the tone for the region by constructing his summer home about 500 feet from the shore of a small lake east of Lake

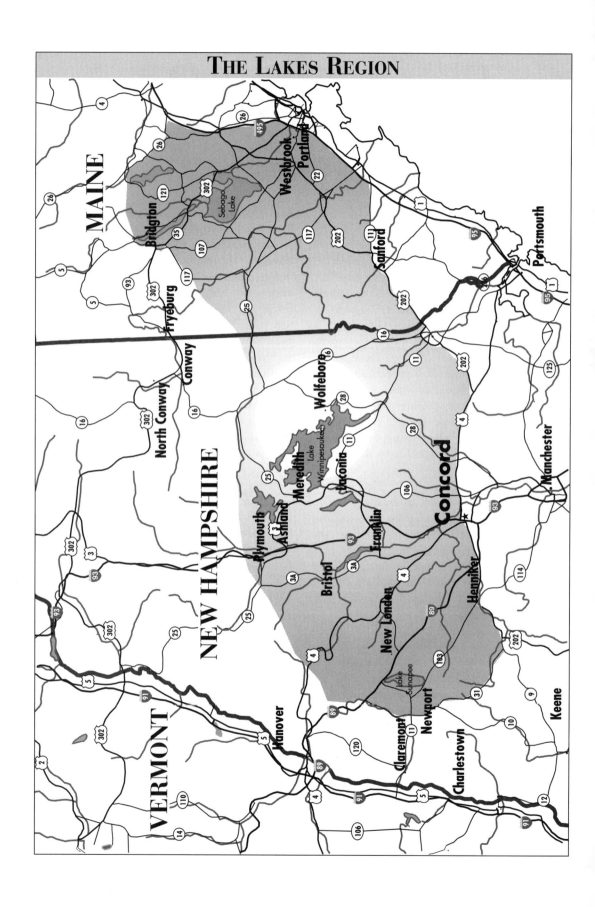

THE LAKES REGION

MAINE

VERMONT

NEW HAMPSHIRE

Portland

Westbrook

Bridgton

Sebago Lake

Fryeburg

Conway

North Conway

Sanford

Portsmouth

Wolfeboro

Meredith

Lake Winnipesaukee

Laconia

Ashland

Plymouth

Franklin

Bristol

New London

Concord

Manchester

Henniker

Lake Sunapee

Newport

Claremont

Charlestown

Keene

Hanover

Winnipesaukee that eventually was named after him. One of the few royal governors to escape the American Revolution with his life and property intact, Wentworth is perhaps best known as the first of the "summer people," giving credence to Lake Winnipesaukee's later claim as America's first summer resort.

Wentworth did things bigger than life. His "summer house" plans called for a palatial structure 100 feet long, 40 feet wide, and two stories high. The windows were each six feet high and the key to the front door was reported to weigh a pound and a half. His grandiose plans were never completely realized, but Wentworth moved into the unfinished estate in 1770 and managed to corral enough royal tax funds to construct a road from Portsmouth 45 miles north to his new summer dwelling. A year later, he had another road constructed westward to Hanover, New Hampshire, to reach the upper Connecticut Valley. Apparently Wentworth didn't hire the best of roadbuilders, as a 1780 letter written by Mrs. Wentworth lamented the bumps from Portsmouth to their summer home: "I dread the journey, from the roughness of the carriage, as the roads are so bad . . . ." Later travelers were more fortunate. By the early 1850s they could arrive at Lakes Sunapee, Winnipesaukee, and Sebago by train, and journey around Sunapee and Winnipesaukee on ferries, first powered by horses on a treadmill, then by steam engines. Sebago had its steamers, too, but barges outnumbered them, as Sebago quickly became a waterway between Portland and the eastern edge of the White Mountains.

But however rough the beginnings of the summer experience, Wentworth and those who flocked in his wake established what has become a paradigm of the New England vacation: spending a week or two (or, for the most fortunate, a month or two) of lazy days on the lake shore, soaking in the alpine sun by day, enjoying the crisp cool air of the evenings. And this classic vacation has never gone out of style. These lakes continue to serve as getaways for New Englanders and for city dwellers all up and down the eastern seaboard, and as you circumnavigate their shores you will see summer homes that range from imposing old estates to lavish European-style chalets to modest small cottages.

But the Lakes Region also serves the traveler who is only passing through and may stop for just a day or two. Some of the large lakeside hotels survive from their Gilded Age heyday, and many more colonies of lakeside cabins have been converted to short-term stays. The "Seeing" section of this chapter deals primarily with the areas surrounding Lakes Sunapee and Winnipesaukee in New Hampshire and Lake Sebago in Maine where the casual traveler can sip at the well of leisure where so many "summer people" drink their fill.

Seeing the Lakes Region

Lake Winnipesaukee, New Hampshire

New England is dotted with place names adopted from local Indian dialects of the Algonquian language group, and Lake Winnipesaukee exemplifies the complexities of rendering one language into another. There were 132 different spellings for the lake on record until the present one was established by an act of the New Hampshire Legislature in 1931 and approved by the U.S. Geographical Board in 1933. Nor can anyone seem to agree what the word "Winnipesaukee" means. Poetically minded tourism boosters of the nineteenth century offered such explanations as "beautiful water in a high place" and "the smile of the Great Spirit" for the Algonquian word. (The first "translation" is certainly true—a rare example of place that lives up to its hype. The second "translation" goes with a fanciful tale about a Romeo-and-Juliet love affair between offspring of two warring tribes that ended with a happy marriage.) The rather less elegant "large pour-out place," referring to the fish runs at the outlet to the Winnipesaukee River, seems most plausible if least romantic.

Whatever the name means, Winnipesaukee denotes New Hampshire's largest lake—20 miles long at its longest and 1 to 12 miles wide. The lake is a series of drowned valleys with a central bowl, having three bays on the west, one on the north, and three more on the east. Its deepest measured point is around 300 feet and its surface covers seventy-two square miles. Yet the lake rarely looks as big as it is because the 186-mile shoreline bends and folds and the opposite shore is never out of sight. Moreover, the lake is dotted with islands, the popular conceit being that there is one for each day of the calendar year. The state

claims that 274 of the islands are large enough to be habitable, though only a handful support even seasonal dwellings.

The shores of the lake were occupied by several different bands of Abenaki (one of the largest of the Algonquian-speaking groups in New England) who left behind artifacts ranging from arrowheads to the elaborate fish traps, or weirs, visible well into the twentieth century at the site of the Abenaki village of Aquedotan, next to the narrow passage between huge Lake Winnipesaukee and tiny Lake Paugus. This site is now completly obscured by the village of Weirs Beach.

The first Europeans known to have seen the lake were members of a surveying party sent north in 1652 by Governor John Endicott of Massachusetts to establish the colony's northern boundary line, which they marked by chiseling their initials and the date into a rock on the shore at Aquedotan. (The site is now under water.) The boundary held until the division of the Massachusetts and New Hampshire colonies in 1740. The earliest settlement by colonists on Winnipesaukee's shores was Alton Bay, the chief inlet of the lake, in 1770, followed quickly by Meredith on the west, Moultonborough on the north, and Wolfeboro on the east.

It may have taken the colonists a while to discover Lake Winnipesaukee, but after the French and Indian War ended, they began building on its shores. New Hampshire Colonial governor John Wentworth constructed the first summer getaway here on the east side of the lake, and other colonists followed him quickly from Portsmouth to enjoy the pristine lake environment. Early real estate and tourism promoters lauded Winnipesaukee not so much as a sight to tour, but as a place to escape the crowded cities (builders couldn't keep up with the housing needs of new immigrants) and the bustle of the mill towns that were proliferating across New England in the first half of the nineteenth century. Winnipesaukee was touted as a gentle wilderness.

Ironically, this promotional campaign was successful enough to nullify its claims. The arrival of the railroads in the late 1840s and early 1850s suddenly made Winnipesaukee more accessible than the Portsmouth Road (Portsmouth to Wolfeboro) and the College Road (Hanover to Wolfeboro via Meredith) ever had. The Boston, Concord & Montreal Railroad reached the west side of Lake Winnipesaukee in 1847, opening the lake to large numbers of travelers. At the same time, the Atlantic & St. Lawrence Railroad was finished between Portland, Maine, and Montreal, bringing service to Wolfeboro by way of North Conway in the White Mountains. But the Boston traffic was always the heavier, and the west side of the lake quickly grew up as the louder, brighter, busier tourism destination. The east side, by contrast, became the sedate spot where people came to spend the entire season.

As "America's first resort" (a claim Wentworth made possible), **Wolfeboro** is a good place to begin a tour of Winnipesaukee. Summertime passes in undulating rhythms measured less by the clock than by the weeks between hayings, the sequence of larval hatches watched so closely by fly fishermen, or the succession of wild fruits at the edges of fields. Alpine strawberries ripen in June, red raspberries in July, and wild blackberries in August.

Route 28 leads to Wolfeboro over rolling countryside from the Merrimack Valley on the west or down sharply dropping hills from the White Mountains on the north. Even as you drive in, Wolfeboro's charm is evident in a glance: the lake, the woodsy shore, and the genial country architecture.

Approaching from either direction delivers you to the bottom of a hill where the lake suddenly stretches out for nearly 20 miles. This is Wolfeboro's compact center, a lakeside rim of pastel and brick buildings housing souvenir shops, sporting goods retailers, restaurants, and ice cream stands. A taciturn dockside sign proclaims: "WOLFEBORO. ESTABLISHED 1770. POPULATION 4807." Steam locomotives used to bring passengers right to the docks to board cruising

Sailboat on Lake Winnipesaukee, New Hampshire

steamships. And the old **train depot** is the best place to begin exploring this quiet side of Lake Winnipesaukee. The trains have been gone for many years, but the renovated station serves as a local information center, complete with brochures and a town map.

Every crossroads in New England seems to have a historical society and only the most ardent lover of local history would visit them all. But the **Wolfeboro Historical Society** is more than worth your time. For one thing, you can marvel at a model of John Wentworth's mansion, which burned in 1820 and has served as a valuable archaeological site in recent decades. Samples of pottery and other household goods excavated from the cellar hole are among the historical society exhibits. And you get a sense how little the twentieth century has touched Wolfeboro. A turn-of-the-century postcard displayed in the historical society could have been written last week: *This is a pretty place but decidedly quiet. Wish you and Mabel were here. We play 'Bridge' and I am try-*

ing to learn to swim. Old dogs, new tricks.—Nell
Nell might branch out today to add deepwater diving or lakeshore kayaking to augment that basic, do-little vacation, but the essence of the easygoing vacation still pervades Wolfeboro. The historical society buildings are open in July and August from Monday to Friday from 11:00 A.M. to 4:00 P.M. and Saturday from 11:00 A.M. to 2:00 P.M. The site is on South Main Street at the Old Town Green. Telephone: (603) 569–4997.

The **dock** is town's nerve center—home to a smattering of casual restaurants, a tiny waterside park, and stops for the trolley and tour buses. Just behind the picnic tables of the inevitable waterside snack bar, the largest town landing reaches out into the lake.

Twice each day and once each evening in July and August a great blast from the horn of the **M/S Mount Washington** startles the dock to announce a forthcoming cruise. The behemoth vessel—first built for service on Lake Champlain in the 1870s, moved to Winnipesaukee in 1940, and cut apart and expanded in 1982—shuffles between brassy Weirs Beach and demure Wolfeboro, crossing and re-crossing the lake with a narrative patter about the islands, the bays, the coves. The 230-foot ship is only the latest in a series of such vessels. The first steamboat plied Winnipesaukee's waters in 1833, the *Belknap*, and *Lady of the Lake* cruised from 1848 until 1893. Schedule and rates vary for **M/S Mount Washington** cruises depending on the season, though they begin at $15. Call for details or stop at the town dock ticket booth. Telephone: (603) 366–2628.

Five public areas in Wolfeboro offer access to the shore. Next to the main dock is a little green area known as **Cate Park,** a lovely spot for a picnic and the site of a community band concert every Wednesday night in July and August. Public swimming beaches number four—one just north of the village center (**Brewster Beach**), one south of the village (**Carry Beach**), and one north of town on Lake Wentworth (**Allen H. Albee Beach**). These lake beaches are remarkable for their sheer simplicity: a parking lot, sand, warm water that gently tapers to diving depth, bath houses at Carry and Brewster, a lifeguard stand, a float anchored in the deep end of a roped-off swimming area. A drive eastward out of town on

M/S *Mount Washington* on Lake Winnipesaukee, New Hampshire

Route 109 will deliver you full circle, historically speaking, to **Wentworth State Beach** near the site of Wentworth's mansion.

It's also worth driving west on Route 109 to see the little lakeside cottages of New Hampshire rusticators that line this part of Winnipesaukee. When you reach the junction with Route 171 in 15 miles, turn right for 2 miles to visit the Lucknow Estate, now developed as a tourism destination under the moniker **Castle in the Clouds.** Eccentric millionaire Thomas Plant built this oddball mansion—a little Highland Gothic, a little Spanish Mission—in 1913, demonstrating a flair for the medieval chic affected by wealthy industrialists of his day. (Compare Higgins Armory in Worcester. See "Seeing the Midlands.") The entrance road is narrow and winding but offers plenty of turnouts for scenic views. If you feel compelled to snap some images—and you will, especially during foliage season—do so on the way up, as the view from the exit road is not as dramatic and there is no place to stop. Castle Springs bottles the spring water that issues from the rocks here, and you can take a free tour of the bottling plant and spring site if you're so inclined. The 5,200-acre estate is crisscrossed with bridle paths and if you reserve ahead, the stables will save you a horse.

Castle in the Clouds is open weekends mid-May through mid-June and Labor Day through the weekend after Columbus Day, daily from mid-June through Labor Day. It opens at 9:00 A.M. and closes at 5:00 P.M. from May into September, then at 4:00 P.M. the rest of the season. General admission to the grounds is $4.00; admission with castle tour is $10. Horseback rides are $25 per hour and require advance reservations. Telephone: (603) 476–2352 or (800) 729–2468.

From Castle in the Clouds return to Route 171 west through Moultonborough (4 miles) and pick up Route 25 west for 4 more miles through Moultonborough Falls to Center Harbor—originally known as Senter Harbour, after the Senter family that founded the town. If you're interested in seeing tranquil **Squam Lake,** the body of water that starred in the Fonda-family tearjerker, *On Golden Pond,* follow signs to Holderness (7 miles). Two boat tour companies offer tours of various movie locations. (See "Staying There.") Otherwise you can continue on for 5 miles to **Meredith,** a key town on the northwest end of Winnipesaukee.

Meredith is a study in the "new" New Hampshire. It's always been something of a tourism destination, though mostly for bass fishermen, as this arm of the lake is warm enough to support large populations of the spiny-backed small-mouth bass, perch, and sunfish. If swimming is more your bent, the sandy beach on Waukewan Street offers glorious mountain views from the shores of Lake Wauwewan, a puddle adjacent to Winnipesaukee. A rather large shopping center has been developed in the mill complex beside Lake Winnipesaukee, and a handsome motel with its own dock sits at the head of the bay. The most important attraction in Meredith, however, is the **Winnipesaukee Scenic Railroad,** somewhat south of what's now the main town center, just off Route 3. Composed of a rather broad variety of rolling stock that served northern New England at one time or another, the "railroad" is really a labor of love—kind of a personal collection of old train cars that keeps rolling to provide its own upkeep. During July and August, one- and two-hour scenic rides between Meredith and Weirs Beach are offered daily. In May, June, September, and October the train follows a more relaxed schedule, rolling down the line if enough people are interested. Special fall foliage tours are offered between Meredith and Plymouth. Trips begin at $8.50. Telephone: (603) 279–5253 in season, (603) 745–2135 at other times.

The 4-mile trip by automobile south on Route 3 to **Weirs Beach** is much faster than by train, delivering you swiftly into the honky-tonk pleasures of a beachside resort. Technically part of the town of Lakeport (which used to be part of the city of Laconia), Weirs has been the most popular human habitation on Lake Winnipesaukee since long before the European colonists arrived. Jet skis, motorboats, and the human crush make

Harbor in Meredith, New Hampshire

fishing impossible here now, but this area once ranked among New England's richest fishing grounds because it sits at the lake's outlet to the Winnipesaukee River, which flows into the Merrimack, which empties into the Atlantic Ocean. Migratory fish—notably Atlantic salmon, sea-run trout, eels, and shad—all passed through the narrows on their way to spawn, and the early inhabitants took advantage of this behavior to trap the fish in weirs. The industrial mills built on the Merrimack in the early nineteenth century made the rivers impassable for fish spawns, but those same species of fish are still found in the lake along with brook trout, hatchery-raised rainbow trout, smallmouth bass, and several varieties of perch.

Small fry still splash in the shallows at **Endicott Beach,** but they're more likely human than piscine. Public parking is cheaper than the pay lots, but you have to arrive early to secure a spot. The beach, which came into its own in the Victorian period, still has an old-fashioned **boardwalk** that leads into the Weirs Beach town center. Access roads around Weirs Beach are lined with high-energy attractions—a waterslide with three increasingly challenging levels, an amusement park with all the electronic jangle even the most hormone-challenged teenager can handle, and a "fun park" of go-karts, batting cages, and the like. Yes, it is tacky and unseemly—sort of in the league with a risqué tattoo—but this sort of honky-tonk is fading fast in New England, and the flashing lights and buzz of sound at Weirs Beach has an undeniable appeal. A warning, though—you might find the razzle-dazzle a bit too chaotic in mid-June, when 150,000 motorcycle aficionados descend on the region for **Motorcycle Week.** Although the races, held since 1939, have moved south to the Louden Speedway, many of the leather-vested, long-bearded outlaws with tattooed knuckles still like to visit Weirs Beach for beer-filled parties.

A retreat to the natural world is only 4 miles away at **Gunstock Recreation Area** and **Ellacoya State Park,** both in Gilford. The state park has a public beach and extensive RV camping facilities. Gunstock, also state-operated, has intermediate-level alpine skiing and nordic skiing in the winter, turning the trails over to hikers and horseback rid-

ers in the summer. Besides its easy access from Boston via I–93, Gunstock's chief appeal is the view from its slopes over Lake Winnipesaukee to the White Mountains.

Personal Narrative:
A Day Trip to Canterbury Shaker Village

Like a lot of Americans, we're fascinated—and a little mystified—by the nearly defunct religious sect known as the Shakers. The group called themselves the United Society of Believers in Christ's Second Coming, but they've always been known to the outside world as Shakers (originally, "Shaking Quakers") for the shaking and trembling some members experienced during worship services. As a religious group, they have all but vanished, but their legacy of simplicity in thought and design persists. Whenever we are near one of the communities—now mostly operating as museums—we make a point of visiting.

It's a brilliant June day when we leave I–93 at exit 18 north of Concord, New Hampshire, and head east, following the signs about 7 miles to Canterbury Shaker Village. We're in the high country south of Lake Winnipesaukee amid a line of glacial hills, and we're struck by the verdant lushness of the countryside. The last time we visited was in the autumn, and the narrow country roads passed through brilliant arching bowers—golden birch leaves, red and orange maple leaves, the stolid bronze of the oaks. There are few long vistas because the road keeps twisting and turning, rising to small hilltops, sinking into gulleys and streambeds. Stone walls are half hidden by the resurgent roadside trees, for the fields in this part of New England that were so assiduously tilled in the first half of the nineteenth century were abandoned in the second half when better land beckoned farther west. It seems as if life almost stopped in these parts sometime before the Civil War. When we pass through the village of Canterbury, it's almost a postcard image of a town hall (dated

1736), country store, white clapboard church, graveyard—and little else.

A mile later we pull into the parking lot of Canterbury Shaker Village, which looks to be a prosperous hilltop farm. Signage here is plain and excellent, so we find our way easily to the desk of the Trustees Office to pay our admission and pick up a map of the community. Appropriately enough, this 1831 building was where the Shakers did their business with "the world," as they referred to everything outside their community.

Willa O'Rourke soon greets us and a dozen other visitors, leading us across the road to a broad pasture in front of the Meeting House. We stand beneath the high, arching branches of venerable sugar maples, which Willa explains were planted in the mid-nineteenth century for orphan children raised by the community—one for each child to tend. Those children have long since grown old and died, but the majestic trees still serve as their living markers.

Willa recounts some basic Shaker history—how Mother Ann Lee led a small band of followers to America in 1774, founding a celibate communal religious sect at Watervliet, New York, that was devoted to creating a kind of heaven on earth in devotion to God. From that base, the Shakers proselytized across New England, and by 1784, when Mother Lee died, had established several communities. The origins of the Shakers, Willa explains, is tied to the beginnings of the Industrial Revolution. People attracted to the sect were often those left behind and cast aside by social upheaval. In effect, she says, the Shakers were Protestant monks and nuns—a concept that finally gives us some insight to the appeal of these communities. They functioned as refuges from the world, much as monasteries and nunneries did in the Middle Ages.

Canterbury became a Shaker community when the farmer who owned the property invited the Shakers in 1782 to share the farm. In 1792 a covenant was signed and the Shaker brothers and sisters systematically replaced all the buildings with Shaker structures. Willa gestures uphill to the Meeting House, built in 1792, as an example of a "Shaker" structure. It

Canterbury Shaker Village, Canterbury, New Hampshire

has two entrances—one for men, the other for women. Although the sexes lived side by side, they lived separately, even using different doors to enter a common building.

We all traipse inside, some of us following the gender distinction of the doors, some not. The interior is one large, open room with pegs all around to hang clothing and furniture during the worship service, for the Shakers sang and danced their prayers. We're directed to look closely at the floorboards, where iron and copper markers are embedded. These were "stops" to indicate where everyone would stand during a dance. Willa sings "Simple Gifts," the best-known Shaker song ("'Tis a gift to be simple, 'tis a gift to be free . . .") and points out that the words contain dance directions like the calls in a square dance.

At its height around the time of the Civil War, Canterbury Shaker Village had a population of about 300 people and 100 buildings, including several mill buildings on the seven large, hand-dug ponds at the rear of the property. The present museum property is down from 4,000 to 694 acres and twenty-four buildings. Ever practical, the Shakers took down buildings as the community shrank.

As we walk through a few more buildings Willa keeps up a running commentary on Shaker life. She contrasts them to the Amish, for Shakers welcomed labor-saving inventions. Canterbury, she tells us, had its own electric lights before the rest of New Hampshire and its own telephone system. The Shakers owned (communally, of course) some of the first automobiles in the area and generally used the most up-to-date technology available. Brother David Parker invented an industrial washing machine for use in Canterbury in 1858, and the community then manufactured and sold it to resort hotels from Mount Washington south to Florida. Likewise, Shakers invented the flat broom and manufactured them by the thousands.

Willa explains that the Shakers—at Canterbury and elsewhere—paid particular attention to herbal medicine as practiced by the New England Indian tribes, and by the early nineteenth century were well known for their herbal remedies. From herbs to seeds was a simple step; Mount Vernon, New York, Shakers invented the paper seed packet and soon all the Shaker communities were selling seed to gardeners. (Canterbury's gift shop still does.) Canterbury was known for its textiles, particularly the "Dorothy cloaks" that became fashionable as opera cloaks for women. They would take orders at resort hotels and make each one to a customer's specifications. The Canterbury sisters also operated knitting machines, knitting the varsity sweaters for Dartmouth, Harvard, and Yale.

The schoolhouse speaks volumes about both the life and death of the Canterbury community. The Shakers often took in orphans and abandoned children or women with young children, and they were great believers in basic education. They built the first school in Canterbury in 1823, then added a story to it in 1863. A Shaker education was so prized that the town of Canterbury contracted with the Shakers to educate its children, and this schoolhouse operated well into the 1930s.

But most of the children raised in Shaker communities did not stay. (One had to make a choice at age 21 or older to become a Shaker.) Although the Shakers were a long-lived bunch, the Canterbury community began to dwindle. When just thirteen sisters remained, they made provisions to incorporate as a museum with a clause that allowed the remaining members to

live out their days. The last sister died in 1992.

When the tour concludes, we stay around to simply walk the property a bit. Other Shaker villages have a museum quality that this one lacks, perhaps because it is so modest. Yet the broad green fields reaching out to hardwood forest seem peaceful, tranquil, and timeless. If we close our eyes we can almost imagine a line of Shaker brothers with their ten-foot-long seeding trays marching across the field in time to a hymn, seeding hay as a form of worship.

Canterbury Shaker Village is open May through October daily from 10:00 A.M. to 5:00 P.M. During April, November, and December it is open on Saturday and Sunday from 10:00 A.M. to 5:00 P.M. Admission is $9.00. The Creamery Restaurant serves an a la carte lunch of traditional New England fare and the Bakery is usually open from 10:00 A.M. to 2:00 P.M. with snacks. Cafeteria-style service is available in the Summer Kitchen from June through August. Telephone: (603) 783–9511.

Lake Sunapee, New Hampshire

The Penacook people who dominated what is now southwestern New Hampshire referred to Lake Sunapee as "Wild Goose Water," probably in reference to the Canada geese that made good use of this 9- by 3-mile body of water conveniently situated along their migratory path. Although the Penacooks hunted here, there is no evidence of permanent encampments. The first year-round dwelling on Lake Sunapee's shores seems to date from 1762, when Zephaniah Clark built his house at the foot of the lake in what is now the town of Newbury. The king's surveyors knew of the lake, however, and it began to appear on maps around 1750, spelled as either "Sunope" or "Sunipee."

Unlike Winnipesaukee, where large areas were given as land grants, Sunapee developed from a series of very small grants, many as payment to soldiers in the French and Indian War. They cleared the thick forests and began to farm the

Sailboats on Lake Sunapee

thin soil of the glacial moraines (rubble dumps) that surround the lake. Life was hard, and weather was no help—a severe tornado that struck in 1821 served as the basis for a Charles Dickens short story, "The Fishermen of Sunapee." But life went on in the hunkered-down frontier fashion until 1849—when the railroad reached Newbury and changed everything. In short order the shores of Lake Sunapee became, like the Winnipesaukee region before them, a refuge for summer rusticators. "City" folk from Concord built summer cottages at Pine Cliff (Newbury) and other colonies soon followed, the largest being at Blodgett Landing on the eastern shore.

The eastern shore of the lake has remained as a private preserve, but the western shore soon developed into a major summer recreational center. The Sunapee House was built in the town of Sunapee in 1855 as a year-round lodging. The first summer hotel, the Lake View House, was built in 1875 at Burkehaven, now also part of Sunapee. Over the next thirty years, the summer hotel business rose to its peak. Commercial transportation on the lake began in 1854 with a horse-boat with a capacity of one hundred passengers. It ran for eight years. The first steamboat on the lake, the *Surprise,* was launched in 1859, but went out of business when its owner enlisted in the Civil War. Like many parts of New England, Sunapee was slow to recover from the depopulation that followed the war, but by 1876, a number of steamboats began to crisscross its waters.

Because it is so much smaller than Lake Winnipesaukee, Lake Sunapee is defined by just a

few communities and one major mountain. On the south is the sleepy hamlet of Newbury, notable chiefly as the gateway to Mt. Sunapee State Park. On the west is the town of Sunapee, where most of the lake attractions are found, and on the northeast is the substantial village of New London.

Most travelers approach Lake Sunapee from I–89, taking exit 11 at **New London,** which lies a few miles from the lake itself. Home of Colby-Sawyer College, New London is the de facto economic and social center of Lake Sunapee. If you're staying in the Lake Sunapee region, you may well find yourself in New London to shop for groceries (look for the excellent local Nunsuch Dairy goat cheeses), to attend a summer stock production at the Barn Playhouse, or to dine at the New London Inn.

But the summer life of the lake really centers on the town of **Sunapee** and its village of **Sunapee Harbor**, situated on Route 103B on the west side of the lake. The grand hotels of the last century are gone, but this village still has the most lodging for short-term visitors. (Cabins and summer homes are often rented years in advance.)

During the summer, you'll likely find a volunteer sitting in the doorway of the **Sunapee Historical Society Museum** in Sunapee Harbor (free, hours by chance; no telephone). Although it takes only a few minutes to tour this homey collection of local memorabilia, it's well worth your while for the evocation of Lake Sunapee as it was in the Gilded Age when the rich arrived by train and journeyed to their summer estates via steam launches. The museum contains wonderfully naïve photographs, a pilot house salvaged from one of the ferries, and fading pages of a *Saturday Evening Post* feature on harvesting ice from Lake Sunapee. A sign on the roped-off stairs to the second floor warns, "No admittance unless you want to help us clean the attic." One of the lesser-known claims of Sunapee is that Enos M. Clough invented a horseless carriage here in 1869. Although Clough drove it as far as St. Johnsbury, Vermont, the Sunapee town fathers forbade its operation in town because it scared the horses. Disgusted, Clough sold it to a Lakeport, New Hampshire, man who promptly ran the vehicle into a fence and destroyed it.

You can rent canoes and kayaks here at the harbor, but a better way to see Lake Sunapee—especially during the summer when motorboat traffic can make paddling a little chancy—is by taking a leisurely cruise aboard the **M.V. *Mount Sunapee II.*** While the boat is more of a modest pleasure cruiser than a turn-of-the-century steamer, the captain's narration lets you imagine Sunapee's heyday as he points out where the grand hotels and sprawling country estates used to stand. There are two tours daily from mid-June to Labor Day, one tour on Saturdays and Sundays only from mid-May to mid-June and from Labor Day to mid-October. Adults $10. Telephone: (603) 763–4030.

One of those estates, located almost directly across the lake on the east side on Route 103A is called The Fells. Now the **John Hay National Wildlife Refuge at The Fells Historic Site,** it was built in 1883 by author and statesman John Hay, who accumulated 1,000 contiguous acres of farmland over the next seven years to serve as a summer retreat for his family and friends. Hay was President Lincoln's private secretary during the Civil War, wrote a ten-volume biography of Lincoln, served as assistant secretary of state under President Hayes, and as secretary of state under Presidents McKinley and Theodore Roosevelt. He was also ambassador to Great Britain during the Spanish-American War.

Between 1914 and 1940, Clarence Hay (John's son) and his wife, Alice Appleton Hay, transformed rocky pastureland into rolling lawns and a series of flower and shrubbery gardens that reflected the successive waves of gardening fads in the early twentieth century. The most amibitious of these was the alpine garden, which Clarence constructed between 1929 and 1935. It blends rockeries, shrubbery, water gardens, and fruit orchards with views of both Lake Sunapee and Mt. Sunapee.

The old estate was broken up in 1960, when Clarence Hay deeded 675 acres to the Society for the Protection of New Hampshire Forests (you'll see the SPNHF signs along the road to the site), then sold off other portions. The remaining 163.5 acres—which included the core of the estate along with the lake frontage—was deeded to the U.S. Department of Fish & Wildlife, becoming the John Hay National Wildlife Refuge when Alice Hay died in 1987.

Relatively little has been done to the site since Alice's death, but the grounds hold some delightful hiking trails. The easiest and most immediately rewarding is the one-mile loop of the nature trail (complete with twenty-seven interpretive stations) that leads from the house down to Lake Sunapee and back through hillside meadows.

The estate house at The Fells is open for tours June through October, and the grounds are open to hikers daily from dawn to dusk. Call the volunteer group, the Friends of the John Hay National Wildlife Refuge, for tour hours and fees. Telephone: (603) 763–4789.

Another excellent hiking area is Mt. Sunapee, the 2,473-foot peak at the heart of **Mt. Sunapee State Park,** which has swimming in the summer and skiing in the winter. The **scenic chairlift ride** operates from Memorial Day weekend through late June and Labor Day through mid-October on weekends only, and Wednesday through Sunday from late June through Labor Day. It reopens during the ski season. A network of hiking and mountain biking trails leads from the Summit House. This large park also has the best swimming beach on Lake Sunapee; the 1,800-foot sandy beach and its parking lot are some distance from the mountain. Note that parking in the lot just off Route 103 can be hard to find on a hot day in July or August. Mt. Sunapee State Park is open daily throughout the year. The beach opens for weekend use on Memorial Day weekend, and is open daily from mid-June through September 1. Beach admission for adults is $2.50. Canoes and paddleboats are rented by a concessionaire; telephone (603) 763–5436 for details. The chairlift ride during the summer for adults is $5.50 round trip or $4.50 one way. Lift-assisted mountain biking carries a fee of $8.00. Call for information on other fees and seasonal amenities. Telephone: (603) 763–2356.

Sebago Lake, Maine

This striking body of water is shaped rather like the continent of Africa. Sebago Lake is the second largest lake in Maine (Moosehead Lake is the largest—See "Seeing the North Country"), covering some forty-six square miles and reaching depths up to 400 feet. It is a principal reservoir for the city of Portland and surrounding areas.

You'll sometimes hear people speak of the "Sebago Lakes," meaning the entire chain of Maine lakes from the southeast side of the White Mountains down to the Presumpscot River, which flows to the sea between Portland and Falmouth. The construction of Songo Lock between Long Lake and Brandy Pond in 1830 allowed barges to traverse the entire length from the headwaters of Long Lake in Harrison, Maine, down to Naples, through Sebago Lake and into the Presumpscot to carry timber from the heavily forested interior to the shipyards of Portland. Literally hundreds of 65-foot boats traveled this waterway on a regular basis between 1830 and 1850, when the arrival of the railroad obviated the need for the canal system. It is still possible to travel 30 miles by boat from the upper end of the system at Harrison through the Songo Lock in Naples into Sebago Lake. Alas, the canal system below Sebago has fallen into ruin.

By the time the last commercial ships passed through the Sebago lock system in 1872, the area had become a lively "wilderness" retreat for Portland lumber barons and even for Bostonians, who would travel overnight by packet to Portland and head upriver to the cabins and hotels around the lake. Among those who extolled the pleasures of Naples were Henry Wadsworth Longfellow and Nathaniel Hawthorne. One of the attractions was fishing for landlocked salmon, or "togue," as they are known in Maine. The species was once designated as *salmonis sebago* until biologists realized that, aside from its migratory habits, it was identical to the Atlantic salmon.

The shores of most of the Sebago system are lined with private cottages, and access to the lake is limited. The exception to that rule is the town of Naples, which sits on the Songo Lock between Long Lake and Sebago Lake. To get to Naples, take Route 302 northwest from Portland, Maine, or east from the White Mountains outpost of Conway, New Hampshire. **Sebago Lake State Park** has extensive sandy beaches with excellent swimming, boating, and fishing as well as pleasant hiking trails through the surrounding woods. During the summer you can also rent boats here for excursions on the lake.

But the main action is found on the Causeway between Long Lake and Brandy Pond, where a confluence of recreational opportunities creates a gentler version of Winnipesaukee's Weirs Beach. Rental and ticket kiosks line the Causeway, offering a day of kitschy fun on the water where a 1950s ethos meets 1990s technology. We have never seen a place in New England that young children enjoy quite as much.

The most sedate approach to the water is to take a cruise on the *Songo River Queen II*. The boat makes one-hour sightseeing tours of Long Lake. Perhaps more interesting is the two-and-a-half-hour cruise that passes through the Songo River lock system. The one-hour cruise is $7.00, the longer cruise $10.00. Telephone: (207) 693–6861. For a quieter trip, you can rent a canoe from **Long Lake Marina.** Telephone: (207) 693–3159.

But the quirkier attractions are the ones that kids really seem to like: large, plastic pedal boats called Aqua-Bikes; bumper boats, which are whirling powered inner tubes that amount to bumper cars on water; and Seadoo-brand jet-skis. Thrill-seeking teens—assuming their guardians will sign the requisite release forms—are particularly taken with parasail rides that carry them a few hundred feet above the lake. And who can blame them? The parasail rises and rises until the spectacle of summer on the lake lies far below, spread out like a world in miniature.

Staying There

Lake Winnipesaukee, New Hampshire

For advance information on the towns surrounding Lake Winnipesaukee, contact the Lakes Region Association. Mailing address: P.O. Box 589G6, Center Harbor, NH 03226. Telephone: (603) 253–8555 or (800) 60–LAKES.

Wolfeboro, New Hampshire

Wolfeboro Chamber of Commerce, located in the Depot Building on Depot Street where steam locomotives used to arrive with their visitors, has a good supply of brochures and offers free maps. P.O. Box 547, Wolfeboro, NH 03894. Telephone: (603) 569–2200. The Chamber also operates an **Information Booth** on the town common on South Main Street during the summer.

LODGING

Allen "A" Motor Inn. Route 28. While this older motel may lack some of the pizzazz of in-town lodging, the forty-three smallish rooms in three buildings are well maintained. The property is about two miles north of Wolfeboro village but is only a two-minute walk to Allen A. Albee Beach on Lake Wentworth. Telephone: (603) 569–1700 or (800) 732–8507. Moderate.

Brook & Bridle Summer Homes and Inn. Roberts Cove Road. This lakeside retreat 4 miles south of Wolfeboro off Route 28 consists of a thirty-acre site with eleven summer homes and a pine-paneled inn with eleven guest rooms. The guest rooms, available only September through May, are an excellent choice for fall foliage viewers. (Rooms one and three through six have lake views.) In some ways, this lodging shows Winnipesaukee's best qualities—former bridle trails for walking, good swimming and boating access, superb fishing at the mouth of the brook. Telephone: (603) 569–2707. Moderate.

The Lake Motel. Route 28. This motel on Crescent Lake (one of the waterways connecting Lakes Wentworth and Winnipesaukee) maintains its own beach, lawn games, and an array of small watercraft for guest use, making it almost an in-town mini-resort. Telephone: (603) 569–1100. Moderate.

The Tuc' Me Inn. 118 North Main Street. This intimate bed-and-breakfast in an 1850 Federal house a few doors uphill from the Wolfeboro Inn is the place to turn for a friendly and relaxed atmosphere. One of the innkeepers operates a scroll saw as a hobby, so window casings and light fixtures are all framed in fretwork to complement the country Victorian decor. Of the seven guest rooms, three come with private bath. The Libby and Douglas rooms share a second-floor porch, making them a good choice for couples traveling together. Telephone: (603) 569–5702. Moderate with breakfast.

The Wolfeboro Inn. 44 North Main Street. Parts of the inn, which is the "fancy" place in town, date from 1812, although the landmark white clapboard house has been stretched back toward the water with additions both this century and last. Most of the forty-four rooms are quite new, and even the old ones have been very recently refinished. The extensively manicured grounds on a prime bit of downtown real estate are disappointing only in that beach access is minimal. But from late June to early September, guests get a free one-and-one-half hour sightseeing cruise on the M/V *Judge Sewall,* which the Wolfeboro Inn owns and operates. Telephone: (603) 569–3016 or (800) 451–2389. Moderate to expensive.

CAMPGROUNDS AND RV PARKS

Wolfeboro Campground. Route 28. Located about 6 miles north of town, this campground offers fifty wooded sites for tents and trailers with hookups. Telephone: (603) 569–9881.

FOOD

Bittersweet Restaurant and Lounge. Route 28 north. Telephone: (603) 569–3636. A reminder of the area's farming heritage, the bright red former barn building has a commanding presence on high ground overlooking broad fields. The rough-hewn interior with half-round timbers and old wagon wheels as light fixtures creates a rustic setting appropriate to the roasts, steaks, and chops. The subterranean lounge is dark and cool, except for a charming little patio encircled by an ancient stone wall. Lunch Tuesday through Saturday June through August, dinner Tuesday through Saturday and Sunday, brunch all year. Moderate.

1812 Room. This is the Wolfeboro Inn's fancier restaurant—where you get roast beef instead of burgers, Dover sole instead of fish and chips. Lunch and dinner. Moderate to expensive.

P.J.'s Dockside. Telephone: (603) 569–6747. Every port town has one—the casual restaurant at the community dock. P.J.'s happens to be better than most, in that the burgers and fries are excellent and the atmosphere inside makes everything taste like summer. Settle into a wooden booth and snuggle up to the paneled walls for breakfast, lunch, or dinner through the tourism season. Inexpensive to moderate.

Pop's Doughnuts. 45 Center Street, Wolfeboro Falls. Telephone: (603) 569–9513. Stop by at night at this twenty-four-hour eatery and ask for whatever happens to be still warm. Alternatively, it's a fine spot for a high-calorie breakfast at the counter or at one of a few tiny tables.

Wolfetrap. 118 North Main Street. Telephone: (603) 569–1047. During the summer you get a waterfront view of "Back Bay" to enjoy good seafood and a strikingly good raw bar for a landlocked town. Lunch and dinner. Moderate.

Wolfe's Tavern. Wolfeboro Inn. Telephone: (603) 569–3016. You could imagine that Governor Wentworth and his merry band might have stopped here for a pint—at least that's the impression that the low ceilings, exposed beams, and hanging beer mugs give. Breakfast, lunch, and dinner. Inexpensive to moderate.

OTHER ATTRACTIONS

Wright Museum. There's a certain schizophrenia about this museum, which gives equal time to a collection of war machinery from World War II and what amounts to a civic attic of artifacts chronicling life on the home front during the war. Open daily 10:00 A.M. to 4:00 P.M. Adults $5.00, discount for seniors and military veterans. 77 Center Street. Telephone: (603) 569–1212.

ACTIVITIES

Dive Winnipesaukee. Wrecks abound in Winnipesaukee's sometimes turbulent waters. This dive outfitter rents scuba equipment to certified divers and arranges trips to sunken ships. 4 North Main Street. Telephone: (603) 569–8080.

Wolfeboro X-C Ski Association. Wolfeboro has two grades of well-developed groomed nordic skiing trails—the challenging "Abenaki" trails and the family-oriented "Lakeview-Nordic" trails—that cross a lot of private lands. Passes are required to use them and can be purchased at Nordic Skier Sports at the north end of Main Street. A one-day pass is $5.00, a season pass $15.00. All funds support grooming equipment and trail improvement. NSS also rents cross-country and telemark skis. Telephone: (603) 569–3151.

TOURS

Molly the Trolley. This open-air trolley offers a narrated forty-five-minute tour of the small downtown and travels past many of the luxurious summer houses around the lake. All-day pass $3.00 adults. Runs July and August daily 10:00 A.M. to 4:00 P.M. Tickets are available at the town dock. Telephone: (603) 569–5257.

FAIRS, FESTIVALS, AND EVENTS

Lakes Region Open. About fifty or sixty of New England's best waterskiers compete for trophies in slalom, tricks, and jumping categories in late July. Telephone: (603) 569–3017.

SHOPPING

League of New Hampshire Craftsmen Shop. 64 Center Street, Wolfeboro Falls. Telephone: (603) 569–3309. The studio craftspeople of the Granite State are some of the best organized in the country. This store is one of seven League shops throughout the state featuring traditional and contemporary crafts.

Moultonborough, New Hampshire

FOOD

Famous Baked Bean Suppers. Bean suppers have been a tradition in Moultonborough for four decades, serving two kinds of beans, hot dogs, slaw, potato salad, homemade brown bread, and pies, tea, coffee, and lemonade. At the United Methodist Church on Main Street almost every Saturday during July and August. Inexpensive.

The Woodshed. Lee's Mill Road, off Route 109. Telephone: (603) 476–2311. This rustic adaptation of a barn and farmhouse to a grand country dining spot is worth a side trip for a good meal. All the dining rooms are handsomely decorated in the barn theme, but be sure to ask specifically for a table in the barn when you make a reservation. The exposed beams and soaring roofline create a dramatic setting for decidedly hearty fare—escargot, prime rib, steaks, roast pork. Dinner and Sunday brunch. Moderate.

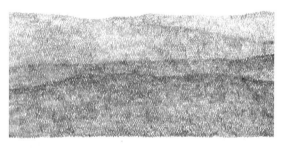

Castle in the Clouds,
Moultonborough, New Hampshire

Center Harbor, New Hampshire

LODGING

Red Hill Inn. Route 25B. Set on a sixty-acre estate atop a hillside at the junction of Route 25B and College Road between Lake Winnipesaukee and Squam Lake, this century-old three-story brick mansion is furnished in country Victorian style. The twenty-one guest rooms are scattered among five buildings, including an 1850s farmhouse and sections of a barn. In the mansion itself, the Kancamagus and Passaconaway rooms are the prime spots in the front. Two flanking suites have views of Winnipesaukee from rustic-paneled sitting rooms. Telephone: (603) 279–7001 or (800) 5–REDHILL. Moderate to expensive.

SHOPPING

Keepsake Quilting. Inside the Shops at Senter's Marketplace on Route 25B. Telephone: (603) 253–4026. Keepsake claims to be "America's largest quilt shop." We can't verify the claim, but they do have more than 6,000 bolts of cotton, shelves of quilting books, patterns, stencils, tools, and other supplies. For instant gratification, choose from an exceptional selection of handmade quilts.

FAIRS, FESTIVALS, AND EVENTS

Winni Derby. For three days in mid-May, some 3,500 anglers vie for $65,000 in prizes in one of New England's biggest fishing derbies. The grand prize, given to the angler who catches the largest salmon, is a boat, motor, trailer, and all the gear to fish to his or her heart's content. Entry fees are $30, $20 for children under age sixteen. Telephone: (603) 253–8689.

Holderness, New Hampshire

LODGING

The Manor on Golden Pond. Route 3. This circa 1903 stucco-and-timber manor (they call it an English estate) has seventeen bedrooms, a six-bedroom carriage house, and four housekeeping cottages. Most of the bedrooms in the main house have wood-burning fireplaces, some have whirlpools. The fourteen pine-wooded acres overlook Squam Lake. There's swimming at the lake or pool, a clay tennis court, canoes, paddle boat, and all the usual amenities for semi-resort rustication. During the winter you can ski cross-country or snowshoe. Telephone: (603) 968–3348 or (800) 545–2141. Expensive to very expensive with breakfast, afternoon tea, and full dinner.

TOURS

The Original Golden Pond Tours. This two-hour tour on an all-weather pontoon boat departs from the movie boathouse, passing through scenic Squam River to Golden Pond, visiting other movie locations along the way. Tour operates from Memorial Day through foliage season. Adults $10. Departs from the Squam Boats Dock, Route 3 at the bridge in downtown Holderness. Telephone: (603) 279–4405.

Squam Lake Tours. Also offering two-hour tours on all-weather pontoon boats, this company emphasizes the local scenery over the movie sites. Adults $10. The company also arranges guided fishing trips for one to three persons. On Route 3, one-half mile south of Holderness center. Telephone: (603) 968–7577.

Meredith, New Hampshire

For information on the area around Meredith, contact the Meredith Chamber of Commerce on Route 3. P.O. Box 732, Meredith, NH 03253. Telephone: (603) 279–6121. The Chamber also operates an **information booth** on Route 3 halfway between the village center and Bay Point from late May to mid-October.

LODGING

The Inn at Bay Point. Bay Point. Set at the edge of a lakefront park, all twenty-four modern rooms of the inn have views of Lake Winnipesaukee. Some have small balconies, fireplaces, or whirlpools. Telephone: (603) 279–7006 or (800) 622–6455. Moderate to expensive.

Olmec Motor Lodge. 95 Pleasant Street. Rustic lakeside lodgings with access to all forms of boating. Telephone: (603) 279–8584. Moderate.

CAMPGROUNDS AND RV PARKS

Clearwater Campground. Route 104. This full-service tent and trailer campground has wooded campsites and a lake beach with fishing and boating. From I–93, take exit 23, then proceed 3 miles east on Route 104. Telephone: (603) 279–7761.

Meredith Woods 4Season Camping Area. Route 104. As the name suggests, this RV park is set up for year-round camping, with a sandy beach for fishing and boating as well as snowmobile trails. Welcome winter amenities include an indoor pool and a hot tub. From I–93, take exit 23 and proceed 3 miles east on Route 104. Telephone: (603) 279–5449.

FOOD

Boathouse Grille. The Inn at Bay Point. Telephone: (603) 279–7006. Classy restaurant serving steaks, chops, and grilled fish overlooks Winnipesaukee. During mild weather it's possible to dine on the screened porch. The restaurant has its own dock, and some customers arrive by boat. Breakfast, lunch, and dinner. Moderate to expensive.

George's Diner. Plymouth Street. Telephone: (603) 279–8723. The cuisine is hardly haute—in fact, it's about as close to family casual as you can find. The big attraction is the rotating selection of all-you-can eat specials. Lunch and dinner. Inexpensive.

Hart's Turkey Farm Restaurant. Route 3. Telephone: (603) 279–6212. About the only thing that makes Hart's seem like a "farm" restaurant is that the dining area is as big as a barn. It's definitely a New Hampshire institution, serving more than a ton of turkey on a busy day. You can also get fried fish, steaks, and the like. Dinner. Moderate.

OTHER ATTRACTIONS

Lakes Region Summer Theatre. This professional summer stock company performs the time-honored frothy summer fare—musicals and light comedies—Tuesday through Sunday. Route 25. Telephone: (603) 279–9933.

ACTIVITIES

Meredith Marina & Boating Center. The bass fishing is good on this end of the lake; this is where you can rent powerboats by the day, week, or month. Bay Shore Drive. Telephone: (603) 279–7921.

Wild Meadow Canoes & Kayaks. Located between Meredith and Center Harbor on Route 25, Wild Meadow sells, rents, and repairs canoes and kayaks. Telephone: (603) 253–7536 or (800) 427–7536.

FAIRS, FESTIVALS, AND EVENTS

Fine Arts and Crafts Festival. For two days in late August, Meredith hosts what many consider the highest quality arts and crafts show in the Winnipesaukee region.

SHOPPING

Annalee Dolls. At the end of Reservoir Road off Route 3 or Hemlock Drive off Route 104. Telephone: (800) 433–6557. Annalee Thorndike first created her highly collectible flexible felt dolls in the early 1960s. This is "where it all began"—complete with gift shop, doll museum, the complete doll line, and doll decorating accessories.

Burlwood Antique Center. Route 3 near the junction of Route 104. Telephone: (603) 279–6387. Open daily from May through October, Burlwood's 170 dealers carry a wide variety of country antiques, collectibles, and attic finds.

League of New Hampshire Craftsmen Shop. 279 Daniel Webster Highway, Route 3 South. Telephone: (603) 279–7920. One of seven League shops throughout the state featuring traditional and contemporary crafts.

Weirs Beach, New Hampshire

For information on the Weirs Beach area, visit the Greater Laconia/Weirs Beach Information Center at 11 Veterans Square in adjoining Laconia. Telephone: (603) 524–5531 or (800) 531–2347.

LODGING

Weirs Beach has the greatest concentration of lodging on Lake Winnipesaukee, most of it older motels in the moderate range. Many of the smaller properties change hands with some frequency, so contact the Information Center for the most current listings.

Grand View Motel. Route 3. Location, location, location. The motel rooms and tiny housekeeping cottages (at almost the same rate) live up to the name with a grand view from Route 3 of Lake Winnipesaukee and the White Mountains. Telephone: (603) 366–4973. Moderate.

FOOD

Kellerhaus. Route 3. Telephone: (603) 366–4466. There was a time when summer meant saltwater taffy and other gooey sweets. It still does at the Kellerhaus—along with an ice cream buffet and even a Belgian waffle breakfast.

OTHER ATTRACTIONS

Daytona Fun Park. Technologically assisted "fun" is the theme of this park with go-carts, mini-golf, and batting cages. Route 11B. Telephone: (603) 366–5461.

Funspot. New Hampshire landmarks form the theme for this 1960s miniature golf course, a paean to the more bizarre side of American inventiveness. Route 3. Telephone: (603) 366–4377.

New Hampshire Antique & Classic Boat Museum. During the summer you can see a number of the classic small boats always so popular on Lake Winnipesaukee. Open Monday through Saturday from 10:00 A.M. until 6:00 P.M., Sunday from 10:00 A.M. until 4:00 P.M. Adults $4. Dexter Shoe Complex, Route 1B at the Weirs Bridge. Telephone: (603) 524–8989.

The Surfcoaster. Vacationers for whom the mere lake is insufficient can frolic in wave pools and on waterslides. Route 11B. Telephone: (603) 366–4991

Weirs Beach Waterslide. Human otters can cavort on four slides. Route 3. Telephone: (603) 366–5161.

Weirs Drive-In Theater. Drive-ins may be an endangered species, but this megaplex of drive-ins shows double bills all summer on four screens. Route 3.

ACTIVITIES

Thurston's Marina. For those who want to buzz around the lake on their own, Thurston's rents ski boats, pontoon boats, water-ski equipment, and two-person jet-skis. At the Route 3 bridge. Telephone: (603) 366–4811.

TOURS

Sightseeing Boats. Three boats that dock at Weirs Beach are *Sophie C,* a U.S. Mail boat that runs mid-June through early-September, Monday through Friday (adults $12); *Doris E,* which cruises the northern end of Winnipesaukee and Meredith Bay daily June to early September (adults $8.00 for one-hour cruises, $12.00 for two-hour cruises); and the M/S *Mount Washington* (adults $13.00 for two-hour cruises, $15.00 for two-and-a-half hour cruises). Telephone: (603) 366–2628.

Gilford, New Hampshire

LODGING

Ames Farm Inn. 2800 Lake Shore Road. The "inn" is really a self-contained summer community of efficiency apartments and lakefront cabins that have their own individual boat slips. A vast grassy yard stretches all the way to the water. Accommodations rent only by the week during July and August. Telephone: (603) 293–4321 or 742–3962. Moderate.

CAMPGROUNDS AND RV PARKS

Ellacoya State RV Park. Route 11. The park has thirty-eight sites with full hook-ups right next door to Ellacoya State Beach on Winnipesaukee's southwest shore. Telephone: (603) 293–7821 (June through mid-October), (603) 271–3627 (January through May).

Gunstock Campground. Route 1A. Gunstock has 250 year-round sites on its 2,000 acres. Telephone: (603) 293–4344.

FAIRS, FESTIVALS, AND EVENTS

Octoberfest. Every year since 1982, Gunstock Recreation Area has celebrated all things German on a mid-October Saturday and Sunday. The big attractions by day are the food—wursts, schnitzel, sauerbraten. Evening performances feature oompah bands, alpine horn players, and folk dances. Route 1A. Telephone: (603) 293–4341.

SHOPPING

Pepi Herrmann Crystal. 3 Waterford Place. Telephone: (603) 528–1020. Hermann claims to be "one of the few Master Crystal Cutters in the world." You can tour the studio and its associated museum, which includes early American, ancient, and contemporary glass. Then, of course, they'll be delighted if you visit the gift shop.

Lake Sunapee, New Hampshire

For advance information, contact the Lake Sunapee Business Association, P.O. Box 400, Sunapee, NH 03782. Telephone: (603) 763–2495 or (800) 258–3530.

Sunapee/Sunapee Harbor, New Hampshire

LODGING

The Burkehaven. 179 Burkehaven Hill Road. On the ridge road above the lake, this recently renovated motel has a pretty upland view, pool, and tennis courts. Some units come with kitchen. Telephone: (603) 763–2788. Moderate.

Dexter's Inn & Tennis Club. Stagecoach Road. Slick contemporary lodgings suit Dexter's role as a summer tennis getaway. Telephone: (603) 763–5571 or (800) 232–5571. Expensive.

The Inn at Sunapee. Located on the ridge road above Lake Sunapee, this establishment has sixteen rooms (including five "family suites") scattered about in an 1875 farmhouse and other buildings on the property. Lest you forget that this is also farming country, when you stare out the window at breakfast, you might see milk cows staring back from the pasture across the road. There's also a small pool and a tennis court. Telephone: (603) 763–4444 or (800) 327–2466. Moderate with breakfast.

FOOD

The Anchorage. Telephone: (603) 763–3334. The only restaurant perched directly on Lake Sunapee's shoreline at Sunapee Harbor is appropriately casual and features a light American menu. You can even tie up your boat while you get a bite to eat. Lunch and dinner. Inexpensive.

Woodbine Cottage. Sunapee Harbor. Telephone: (603) 763–2222. Unless you're one of those people who'd rather shop than eat, you can pass through the gift shop to the pine-paneled lodge-style dining room where you can enjoy comfort food of eggs, pancakes, or muffins (at breakfast), or roast turkey and pot pie at lunch or dinner. They make their own ice cream and sauces as well as fresh fruit pies. The butterscotch buns are so popular that they are available by the pan if ordered in advance. Open from May through mid-October, Woodbine Cottage serves Sunday brunch, lunch, and afternoon tea. Dinner is served only on Friday and Saturday. Moderate.

ACTIVITIES

Alden of Sunapee. To explore Lake Sunapee's big island and innumerable coves, rent a canoe or kayak here at the Harbor. Telephone: (603) 763–3177.

Newbury, New Hampshire

LODGING

Best Western Sunapee Lake Lodge. 1403 Route 3. Near both the Sunapee state beach and the Mt. Sunapee ski slopes, this fifty-five-room lodge built in 1995 offers the comfort of familiar surroundings (it *is* a Best Western, after all) in a good location for the annual crafts show. Telephone: (603) 763–2010, or (800) 606–5253. Moderate.

FAIRS, FESTIVALS, AND EVENTS

League of New Hampshire Craftsmen's Annual

Craftsmen's Fair. This nine-day event, held in early August, is the oldest crafts fair in the United States, dating from the 1930s. More than 170 craftspeople display their work. Held at Mt. Sunapee State Park. Telephone: (603) 224–3375.

New London, New Hampshire

LODGING

The New London Inn. Main Street. This 1792 landmark in a college village is an old country inn with authentic, untouched character. The boxy rooms are brightly lit by large windows—the airiest and brightest accommodations are on the second floor facing Main Street. A wicker rocker on the first- or second-floor arcade porch is the best spot to watch the slow pace of country life. Telephone: (603) 526–2791 or (800) 526–2791. Moderate.

FOOD

The New London Inn. Main Street. Telephone: (603) 525–2791. Variations on traditional New England fare make up the menu. If any dish uses the goat cheese from local Nunsuch Dairy, be sure to try it. The dining room has been refurbished, but in nice weather, ask if you can sit on the front porch and watch the world go by (ever so slowly). Breakfast, lunch, and dinner. Moderate.

Baynham's Country Store & Café. 180 Main Street. Telephone: (603) 526–8070. The cafe serves three meals a day, seven days a week, but the grocery aisles are the real prize—including a good supply of Nunsuch Dairy cheeses.

OTHER ATTRACTIONS

Mt. Kearsage Indian Museum. Most easily reached from exit 8 off I–89, this young museum certainly has good intentions. Collections run the gamut from souvenirs made by some of the Eastern Woodlands tribes in the early twentieth century to items from the Wild West. For all the shortcomings of a museum constructed around limited private collections, it's worth the half-hour sidetrip to see artifacts from the New England and eastern Canadian tribes. The clothing, miniature canoes and sometimes exquisite quill- and beadwork speak poignantly of the last vestiges of aboriginal cultures. By way of contrast, see the museums at the Connecticut casinos. (See "Touring the South Coast.") A wooded trail on the grounds is signed with plaques explaining the medicinal uses of many native plants. Open May through October, Monday through Saturday from 10:00 A.M. to 5:00 P.M., Sunday from noon to 5:00 P.M. Tours are given on the hour, with the last tour at 4:00 P.M. Adults $6.00. Kearsage Mountain Road, Warner. Telephone: (603) 456–2600.

The New London Barn Playhouse. Founded in 1933, the Barn claims to be the oldest consecutively operating summer theater in the state. Performances run from mid-June to Labor Day. Main Street. Telephone: (603) 526–4631.

ACTIVITIES

Norsk Cross-Country Ski Center. Located at the New London Country Club, Norsk offers rentals and access to twenty-four trails covering 50 miles. Trail fees range from $7.00 to $11.00, depending on day of week and time of day. Telephone: (603) 526–4685 or (800) 42–NORSK.

Sebago Lake, Maine

Naples, Maine

For information on the Naples area, stop by the Naples Business Association on Route 302 north of town from late June to early September. Route 302, Naples, ME 04055. Telephone: (207) 693–3825.

LODGING

The Augustus Bove House Bed & Breakfast. Routes 302 and 114. The former Hotel Naples was one of the first summer hotels in the area. It overlooks Long Lake at the Causeway, and remains a handsome hostlery despite losing some of its grounds over the years to Routes 302 and 114, which join in front of the porch. Telephone: (207) 693–6365 or (800) 693–6365. Moderate with breakfast.

Inn at Long Lake. Lakehouse Road. Only steps from the Causeway, this sixteen-room manse is a bargain for its combination of elegance and convenience. Telephone: (207) 693–6226 or (800) 437–0328. Moderate to expensive with breakfast.

West Shore Motel. Route 302. The motel is only the tip of the iceberg. Down the hill behind it is a cabin community, and farther still is the compound's beach on Long Lake, one mile west of the Causeway. Telephone: (207) 693–9277. Moderate.

CAMPGROUNDS AND RV PARKS

Bay of Naples Family Camping. Route 11/114. Don't take the witty name *too* seriously—this is Maine, not the Mediterranean. Nonetheless, it's a pleasant campground with sandy beaches. Telephone: (207) 693–6429 or (800) 348–9750.

Four Seasons Camping Area. Route 302. These campsites near a natural sandy beach on Long Lake sit in tall pines and birch groves 3 miles west of Naples. Telephone: (207) 693–6797.

FOOD

Bray's Brewpub. Junction of Routes 32 and 35. Telephone: (207) 693–6806. You can enjoy traditional New England fare at the tables, but the real appeal are the sharp, light ales brewed on premises in the style popularized a few miles away in Bethel. Lunch and dinner. Inexpensive.

Charlie's on the Causeway. Route 302. Telephone: (207) 693–3826. Mainers tend to appreciate "bee-ah," so Charlie's carries a long line of microbrews on tap to complement its fried seafood. If you're skipping the suds, you can order takeout from the window on the side, then repair to the deck overlooking the seaplane dock. Lunch and dinner. Moderate.

OTHER ATTRACTIONS

Steamboat Landing Mini-Golf. Carved out of a woodsy area on Route 114 about a quarter mile from the Causeway, this zany mini-golf center features nineteen holes themed to Maine tourism, including a lobster trap, the Casco Bay ferry, and the Maine Turnpike. Route 114. Telephone: (207) 693–6782.

Bridgton, Maine

Located near the head of Long Lake, Bridgton is more a summer resident town than a base for visitors. But because it is a real year-round place, you're likely to visit here for such activities as grocery shopping or doing the laundry. For information on the Bridgton area, contact the Bridgton-Lakes Region Chamber of Commerce, Route 302, P.O. Box 236, Bridgton, ME 04009. Telephone: (207) 647–3472 (June to mid-October), (207) 647–2533 (mid-October to May). The Chamber operates an **information booth** on the town common from late May until mid-October.

LODGING

Grady's West Shore Motel. This conventional motel has a private beach on Highland Lake. Telephone: (207) 647–2284. Moderate.

Tarry-a-While Resort & Restaurant. Situated on a twenty-five-acre hillside with private beach on Highland Lake and views of lake and mountains, Tarry-a-While has been in operation since the first tourism boom of the 1890s. Accommodations vary, but everyone shares such amenities as bicycles and boats. Telephone: (207) 647–2522. Moderate to expensive with breakfast.

OTHER ATTRACTIONS

The Bridgton Drive-In. Located on Route 302 at the west end of town, this drive-in is one of a vanishing breed of outdoor movie theaters.

7 · The Midlands

Introduction

It's too bad that so many travelers to New England overlook what we call the Midlands—the hardworking interior between the mountains and the Atlantic Ocean where bucolic villages surrounded by farmland alternate with mill towns on the banks of the rivers that drain the upland plateaus. Admittedly, the Midlands aren't the flashiest part of New England. They don't have the drama of the mountains, the fecundity of the Connecticut River Valley, the freshness of the lakes region, or the primal lure of the coastline. But they sure can spin a yarn about the growth of a nation and the ingenuity of a people.

Back at America's beginning, the Midlands were the breadbasket of New England and, to a great extent, of New York. The fruit industry began here in the late seventeenth century, when the first orchards of the Nashoba Valley were planted in the western wilderness inland from Boston. Even today, horticulture remains one of the specializations of this part of New England, attested by the greenhouses of eastern Connecticut, where so many of America's houseplants are developed.

But farming took a back seat to industry once the mill wheels were wed to the power loom. America's version of the Industrial Revolution got its start on the streams and rivers of interior New England. The tumble of falling water drove the rattling, whirring machinery of the nascent textile industry and transformed sleepy river villages into mighty mill towns. Wherever the power of a waterfall could be harnessed, the machines of central New England pounded out the heartbeat of America's first industrial economy.

If you're willing to invest some time and pay close attention to detail, you'll be repaid with remarkable stories of pluck, luck, and ambition.

Across the area, entrepreneurs with money in their pockets from overseas trading turned mere prosperity into great fortunes. Mill girls left failing family farms to become America's first class of independent women. Immigrants, some of them literally starving when they arrived in America, parlayed their hard work and a knack for machinery into middle-class prosperity.

The funny thing is that these stories were almost lost. The mill towns have been going downhill for a long time—some since the end of the Civil War—and life in the mills was a chapter that most communities were happy to forget. A century ago New England made much of the world's textiles; now it produces only a scant percentage of specialty fibers. The silk, cotton, and woolen mills fell silent—many of them preserved as they stood, their mighty machines seized by rust and time.

The historic preservation movement came along just in time to salvage this piece of history while some mill workers were still alive. And the towns that were once ashamed of the mills have come to value the past, honoring it with small museums, historic sites, and interpretive centers.

If you want to recapture the brawny energy that built a nation and its economy, all you need to do is step inside some of these exhibits and visit the artifacts of an age when the power of the machine was new and wondrous. Fill your ears with cotton and venture inside Lowell's Boott Mill, for instance, and you'll quickly learn that the machines are not so silent after all. In fact, their thundering vibrations shake the earth. If they no longer weave the fabric of a nation, they still have the power to weave a compelling tale.

By Yankee standards of distance (surely the phrase "country mile" wasn't coined here), the Midlands encompass a long loop that covers dozens of valleys that drain the eastern face of New England. This area of mill towns and farm

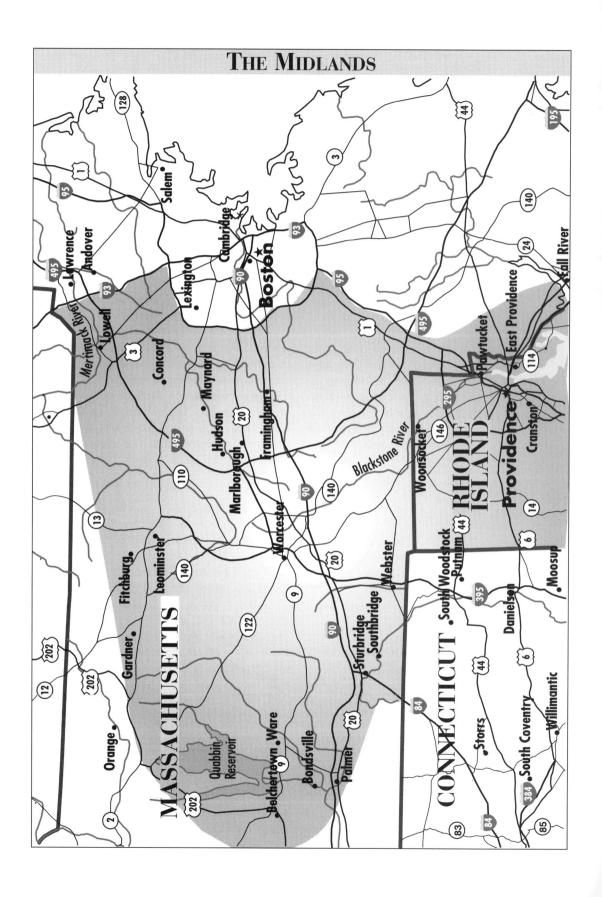

THE MIDLANDS

villages stretches from eastern Connecticut and northern Rhode Island through central Massachusetts to the Merrimack River Valley. We've arranged it so you can base yourself in a succession of convenient spots and venture out to explore surrounding areas.

The living-history museum of Old Sturbridge Village (OSV), located at the intersection of Interstate highways 84 and 90 (the Massachusetts Turnpike), is a good place to begin. The authentic New England town called Sturbridge, Massachusetts, is largely overshadowed by the sprawling museum of New England country life of the 1830s. Unlike, say, the Shaker villages, OSV isn't an intact survivor from the long-ago time. It's a highly successful re-creation of how central New Englanders lived during the Federal period. OSV spares no detail—from children playing games on the town common to the blacksmith forging barrel hoops to folks tending cattle and minding the store.

Because OSV has become an important tourist destination, the immediate area is rich with travelers' amenities, making Sturbridge a logical base for exploring. To the northwest is New England's most accessible wilderness area, the Quabbin Reservoir. It is a manmade lake and watershed inhabited by eagles, bears, deer, coyotes, wild turkeys, and other abundant wildlife. To the southeast lies the Blackstone River Valley, a region of mill towns flowing downstream to Providence, Rhode Island, a vibrant cultural center undergoing a remarkable economic renaissance.

The "big city" of the Midlands is Worcester, Massachusetts, once an industrial powerhouse and Boston's gateway to the west. The interstate highways make it so easy to bypass Worcester that most casual travelers do exactly that—which is too bad, since this handsome city is a major cultural capital in its own right. From Worcester, it is an easy drive northeast to Lowell, where America's Industrial Revolution came to fruition. Built as a factory town to employ farmers' daughters at spinning jennys, Lowell became so successful that it drew immigrants from French Canada and eventually from all over the world. Even in its early days, Lowell was such a marvel that visitors came from around the world to see the future. Now the city derives much of its living from

tourism that looks to the past, yet it remains a magnet for immigrants and a cradle of industries that rely more on the microchip than the mill wheel.

History: Cut from American Cloth—An Industrial History of the Midlands

The last time we visited Slater Mill in Rhode Island, our guide was a Pawtucket native too young to remember when the town's textile mills were still operating. After a thorough explanation of the sites—including a demonstration of hand and machine spinning—he stopped and reflected, "You look around at all these inventions and all the work that went into this place, just to make thread, and you want to say, 'big deal!' Right?'

"But," he continued "once the mills came you didn't have to spend all your time making cloth."

And that's the heart of the Industrial Revolution in a nutshell. We forget that producing cloth was one of the single most time-consuming chores of the pre-industrial household. Raising, gathering, and processing the fiber was the least of it. Then someone had to comb it out into strands, spin it into coarse thread or yarn ("homespun"), and finally weave (or less often, knit) it into fabric. Considering all the stages involved, it's little wonder that the production of textiles gave birth to the Industrial Revolution. And New England, with its abundant water power and close links to Europe, was a natural place for power manufacturing to begin in America.

Like old England, colonial New England was awash with little streams and rivers, so the use of water power came naturally to the earliest colonists. The basic principles of the water-powered mill had been known in Europe, by the Roman period, and the English brought that knowledge with them to the New World.

The earliest mills in New England harnessed water to power the saw blades that cut the vast forests into lumber, the grinding stones that turned grain into meal and flour, and the triphammers of forges that fabricated iron. In fact, you can see modern replicas of these mills at Old Sturbridge Village. All three began with the same mill setup. The mill builder would first create a dam at a site where a river or stream dropped several feet. From the mill pond behind the dam, he would construct an open conduit called a "mill race" to feed water to the mill wheel. The simplest wheels, little more than flat blades spun by the force of falling water, produced adequate torque to operate a drop forge's triphammer, but they tended to jam when turning millstones or saw blades.

The solution was the heavier and more complex breast wheel, sometimes built into the dam itself. Water fills the spaces between blades of a breast wheel and the weight of the water sets the heavy wheel in motion. That motion is transmitted by gears or pulleys linked by leather belts to a spinning shaft that operates the saw blade or the grindstone. By the mid-1700s, breast wheels dominated New England riverscapes.

In a move that hinted of the textile manufacturing revolution to come, some of these breast wheels were used to operate carding mills—machines that combed out raw wool, beaten flax, or bolls of cotton into straight fibers for hand spinning into thread or yarn.

English inventors were the first to figure out how to mechanize the more complex processes of turning raw fiber into cloth. The invention of the flying shuttle in 1733 by John Kay allowed weavers to literally double their output, leading to an increased demand (and higher prices) for cotton yarn for weaving. Although planters in the southern American colonies gladly obliged by stepping up cotton production, it took several decades before anyone figured out how to mechanize spinning. In 1767 weaver and carpenter James Hargreaves invented the spinning jenny, permitting a worker to operate eight spindles at once. Two years later, wigmaker Richard Arkwright developed the "water frame," a machine to spin cotton with rollers operated by water power. In 1779, spinner Samuel Compton patented his "spinning mule"—a device that wed Arkwright's and Hargreaves' inventions to produce a finer, stronger thread. Since spinning mules were large and heavy machines, it quickly became the practice to power them with water mills. Arkwright built entire factory districts to manufacture cotton thread and, with Edmund Cartwright's invention of the first practical power loom in 1785, cotton cloth. The fully industrialized textile industry was born.

England vaulted ahead of the rest of Europe in textile production and the British government effectively declared mechanical knowledge a state trade secret, passing laws that forbade skilled mechanics from emigrating. That didn't stop Samuel Slater. Born in Derbyshire, he was apprenticed at the age of fifteen to a factory that produced textile machinery and rose swiftly to become the supervisor. Attracted by American bounties for textile mechanics, at age twenty-one Slater lied about his occupation and shipped off to America to make his fortune, landing in the employ of Moses Brown in Providence, Rhode Island, in 1789.

Like his fellow Yankee traders, Brown had endured extensive losses while the American Revolution made shipping impossible. Born to a family with a penchant for the mechanical, he had already bankrolled the Almy and Brown textile firm. He set Slater to redesigning their machinery, and Slater was able to faithfully reproduce from memory the specifications for the Arkwright machines. The first water-powered spinning mill in America was up and running by 1790. By 1793, Slater Mill in Pawtucket, Rhode Island, was a reality. But when Slater left England, Arkwright hadn't incorporated weaving into his mills, so Slater didn't know how to fabricate a power loom. The new machines of Almy, Brown and Slater (as the firm was renamed) could only spin cotton. Cloth production was still farmed out to cottage weavers.

It fell to a scion of Boston's codfish aristocracy to complete the cycle. Francis Cabot Lowell, born to the class of shipping merchants who flourished from Newburyport to Boston, was a leading importer of English textiles at the

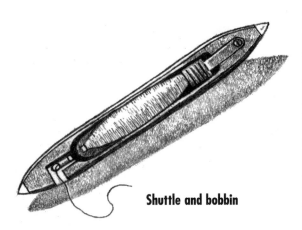

Shuttle and bobbin

dawn of the nineteenth century. His business, however, suffered a setback when Thomas Jefferson declared an American embargo on British goods in the years leading up to the War of 1812. Lowell could see that money could be made in textile manufacturing on American soil but he was leery of the social ills visited on British factory towns.

In 1810 he took his family to England, ostensibly to recover his health, using the occasion to oh-so-coincidentally visit the textile mills of Manchester. Lowell was a quick study and memorized the working of the power looms. He returned home when war broke out between Britain and the U.S., and set to work with master mechanic Paul Moody to replicate the British power looms. Along with fellow Bostonians Patrick Tracy Jackson and Nathan Appleton, Lowell formed the Boston Manufacturing Company and built a $400,000 mill on the Charles River in Waltham, Massachusetts, in 1814. It was the first site in the western hemisphere to bring all the processes of manufacturing textiles under a single roof—and it was an instant financial success.

The Waltham mill generated so much cash that its owners—and other investors from their social circle—sought a new and larger site with a larger falls to power more machinery. They settled on the mile-long falls of East Chelmsford on the Merrimack River, renaming the community for Lowell, who died before the mills were built. Also in deference to the far-sighted Lowell, the Boston Associates attempted to create a paternalistic industrial utopia where the workers would spend a few years bettering themselves before moving on to other lives. In the beginning, the mills were staffed by young women from the countryside living supervised lives in clean boardinghouses and earning better wages than a school teacher or nurse of the era.

Lowell, too, was a success, and the Boston Associates expanded to Chicopee, Massachusetts, on the Connecticut River and down the Merrimack to new towns such as Lawrence, Massachusetts. Competitors seized on their model, and even by 1850, the output of the Merrimack River milltowns was dwarfed by the miles of cloth flowing from other mills, notably those in Fall River, Massachusetts, only a few miles from Pawtucket, Rhode Island, where the textile industry had begun.

Competition led to price cuts, and mill owners across New England cut wages, sped up machinery, and turned to new sources of labor. If the daughters of Yankee yeoman farmers did not like the new working conditions, longer hours, and lower wages, then refugees from the Irish famine were happy to have the jobs. The cycle continued into the early twentieth century with successive waves of immigrants from Quebec, from Italy, from Greece, from Baltic Europe, from the eastern Mediterranean.

Yet by the Civil War, the Boston capitalists had secured their place in American business. They had constructed several Boston railroads, built immense personal fortunes, and created financial institutions to manage that money. They soon abandoned manufacturing for money management and investment, just as they had abandoned merchant shipping for manufacturing. But before their exit from industry, they created an enduring feature of the New England landscape: the ubiquitous red-brick mills. Wherever you go in New England, every river town seems to have one or more of the nineteenth-century structures along the river. Some have been converted to warehouses, others to luxury housing, many to shops and boutiques. And many more continue to crumble by the riverbank, reminders of a time when New England was the industrial heart of America.

Seeing the Midlands

The Rustic Midlands

Sturbridge, Massachusetts

You'll probably want to spend a full day at **Old Sturbridge Village** (OSV). With more than forty buildings on 200 acres, it's the largest living history museum in the Northeast, re-creating town and farm life and work in a typical New England village of the 1830s. OSV illuminates the farming and early industrial history of this region, providing useful perspective for exploring nearby villages and towns.

As you might recall from your U.S. history, during the era depicted at OSV America stood poised at the edge of the Industrial Revolution and the opening of the western frontier. Rural New Englanders had no idea how quickly their lives would change. But you can still get a good sense of that vanished way of life by visiting the village and town common, the mill district, and the traditional family farm—all staffed with interpreters dressed in period costume and going about their daily tasks.

The **Common** itself closely resembles the center of many a New England hamlet even today—one of the pleasures of exploring New England is stumbling on these little gems of central greenery surrounded by historic architecture. Here at OSV, however, horse-drawn wagons pass by and you might spy children in knickers and vests playing a game of rounders, a stick-and-ball ancestor to Mr. Doubleday's baseball.

Around the Common, **four houses,** each furnished with antiques and carefully reproduced country furniture, represent a cross-section of domestic lifestyles—a tradesman's temple of domesticity, a behind-the-times home of an elderly widow and her unmarried daughter, the cluttered quarters of the parsonage, and the elegant architecture and fine furnishings of a prosperous merchant and scientific farmer. At the other end of this grassy green from the Greek Revival **Center Meetinghouse** stands the **Bullard Tavern,** where visitors can sample the flavors of traditional Yankee cookery.

Behind the tavern, a tree-lined path continues through a covered bridge over the Quinebaug River and around the perimeter of the mill pond. As was typical of New England villages in the Federal period, a **sawmill** and a **gristmill** stand at the outlet of the pond. The nearby **carding mill** is a hint of the industrialization to come: its water-powered machinery pulls out well-washed fleece into long fibers for spinning. At the **blacksmith shop,** the smith works at his hearth with hammer and tongs, pounding out metal parts for the mills, repairing iron-link chains and wagon parts and shaping the all-important shoes for horses and oxen.

New England is a region that moves with the rhythm of the seasons, and nowhere are they more evident than at the **Freeman Farm** just over the mill stream bridge from the the mill district. Each spring the lambs and calves are born and the farmers plan their plantings. Across the summer they labor in the fields with hoes, stooping to weed and pick off pests.

Just outside the farmhouse door is the farm in miniature: the **kitchen garden** of potatoes and onions, beans and squashes so central to the country diet of the era. Take special note of the seed-saving bed, where plants are set out to go to seed for next year's crop. (You can buy these heirloom variety seeds, by the way, at the gift shop at the Visitors Center.)

Come fall, OSV pretenders begin their labors in earnest, gathering the harvest before the first hard frost, and preserving it for the winter. Ox-drawn wagons lug pumpkins from the fields, and even the youngsters help gather root crops for underground winter storage. Inside the farm-

Street scene in Old Sturbridge Village, Sturbridge, Massachusetts

sells traditional goods such as tin ovens, redware beanpots, and rolling pins, as well as a full line of heirloom seeds, OSV cookbooks and reference pamphlets, and various foodstuffs.

Old Sturbridge Village is located on Route 20 off the junction of I–84 and I–90 in Sturbridge, Massachusetts, a little more than an hour's drive from Boston, Providence, or Hartford. OSV is open throughout the year, but is closed Mondays during November and December and from mid-February through late March. From January through mid-February, OSV is open only on Saturdays and Sundays. Adult admission is $16, valid for two consecutive days. About half of the historic buildings are wheelchair accessible. A sign language interpreter is available on the third Saturday of the month, April through December. Telephone: (508) 347–3362 (extension 325 for reservations and information about events, extension 282 for the Access Coordinator), or (800) SEE–1830; TTY: (508) 347–5383.

house, cooks cut and trim apple and pumpkin slices, which are dried at the hearth and stored for winter pies. Cattle and horses spend the winter months feeding on hay gathered from the fields during two, sometimes three summer cuts.

If you're visiting on a September or October weekend, you may be able to catch the community cider pressing. OSV's unusually large press was recently restored, and it's a wonder to see it in operation. The gear-driven, horse-powered crusher grinds apples; then the mill operator builds a "cheese" of alternate layers of ground apples and straw. When the screws are tightened on the cheese, apple juice flows through a straw sieve into a barrel. Although old-time farmers usually let their cider ferment to provide a warming beverage for winter, OSV sells the whole pressing before the wild yeasts get to it.

In addition to routine activities, OSV presents many special workshops and other events that range from garden planning sessions to re-creations of holiday festivities. (Thanksgiving dinner, for example, books up months in advance, but the Fourth of July activities, which feature an old-fashioned parade and bona fide Oration as well as a reading of the Declaration of Independence, have plenty of room for all comers.) The Museum Shop in the Visitors Center

Personal Narrative: The Winter Village

One of the nice things about OSV is that it's open all year—including the "dead of winter," a term that surely originated in central New England. Candlelight dinners, roaring fireplaces, and horse-drawn sleighs may make for a romantic outing these days, but they were everyday fare for New Englanders in the 1830s. And during February, when many attractions go into hibernation, OSV offers a series of "Village by Candlelight" evenings that capture both the good and the bad about the good old days of the 1830s.

What finally attracted us to sample OSV on a cold February night was that we could stay in modernized lodgings—specifically, the **Oliver Wight House,** which was built around 1789 and served as a tavern and roadside lodging for many years beginning in the 1790s. Now it's part of a lodging complex right at the entrance to the village. The Wight House has ten rooms with updated comforts (like heat, lights, indoor plumbing, and nice furniture) within a distinctly Federal-era structure. (See "Staying There.")

The Village by Candlelight events—a wholesome Big Night Out, circa 1835—take place Friday evenings. We check in to our room early and bundle up with warm clothes, knowing from past experience that while fireplaces and metal stoves warm many of the OSV buildings, the side of your body turned away from the heat can get plenty chilled.

Come 6:00 P.M., we follow the candle lanterns set into snowbanks along the path from the Visitors Center to the Center Meetinghouse for musical selections on the 1830s pipe organ. It's a mix of popular and church music in this stately old Congregational church, where the Puritan heritage is amply evident in the plain lines and hard seats. When the organist takes a break, we meander down the path to the Knight Store for nonstop story-telling of period New England tales. Once we've heard a few ghost tales and an account of a horse trader who outwitted the devil himself, we wander out to take a horse-drawn sleigh ride around the Common.

In the clear air of a nippy February night, the sky overhead is a tapestry of stars perfectly visible here miles from city lights. Constellation-gazing in the cold, though, whets our appetites and about 8:00 P.M. we head to the Bullard Tavern for a hearty dinner rather like the fare the Yankee farmers of Sturbridge might have enjoyed. On this night, OSV is offering clam chowder, a choice between chicken stew or *tourtière* (a French Canadian meat turnover), and gingerbread or apple-pear cobbler for dessert. After we dine, we join other visitors in the tavern for a Punch-and-Judy puppet show, a little fast card gambling action, and a magic show replete with jokes older than the OSV antiques.

By the time we pad back to our lodging around 10:00 P.M.—it's close enough to walk—we're warm from the hearty food and high times. And when we get back to the room, we don't even switch on the TV for the late news. Why return so soon to the present when the 1830s seem so close and so real?

Center Meetinghouse, Old Sturbridge Village, Sturbridge, Massachusetts

A Day in the Quabbin Wilderness, Massachusetts

By slaking Boston's thirst, civil engineers produced a remarkable "accidental" wilderness in the middle of Massachusetts—the Quabbin Reservoir watershed, just a short distance northwest of Sturbridge. "Reservoir" conjures up images of small manmade lakes surrounded by fringes of pine trees, but the Quabbin is an epic landscape where wilderness continues to overtake the towns that dotted its acres until the 1920s.

The Quabbin is wild, majestic, and mysterious. Stretching 18 miles north to south, the lake covers thirty-nine square miles of a drowned valley almost exactly midway between Worcester, Massachusetts, and the Connecticut River. The surrounding watershed comprises 56,000 acres, of which more than 40,000 are open to public use. Eagles soar overhead and the manic call of the loon echoes in the myriad of coves along the 181-mile shoreline of the lake and its more than sixty islands (all of them former hilltops). The Quabbin woods are populated with deer and coyote, bobcat and moose. Its streams and brooks are home to mink, beaver, and otter. Feisty snapping turtles and red-eared turtles share the waters with bass and perch, salmon and trout. Yet this wilderness is surprisingly accessible, with more than forty gates opening to trails, dirt roads, and even a few paved roads of the towns of Dana, Prescott, Enfield, and Greenwich that were inundated as the reservoir filled.

From Sturbridge drive 13 miles west on Route 20 to North Monson and the junction with Route 32. Follow Route 32 north for 10 miles to the junction of Route 9 in Ware and turn left (west) on Route 9. In 4 miles, the Quabbin Park Cemetery appears on your left. Continue 3 miles to the **Quabbin MDC Visitors' Center** at Winsor Dam, where displays tell the tale of the Quabbin's construction.

By the late nineteenth century, metropolitan Boston was running out of drinking water, sparking the search for an area where a reservoir might be built. The Swift River Valley soon emerged as a natural, since the deep and wide glacial valley was surrounded by high hills and three branches of the Swift converged here. ("Quabbin" is a Nipmuck word meaning "where the waters come together.") From the brink of the twenty-first century, we look back on the creation of the Quabbin with a sense of marvel at the engineering feats and an awe for the wilderness that has sprung up around the reservoir. But there was also a human toll. The small towns of Dana, Prescott, Enfield, and Greenwich were literally wiped off the map. Their 2,500 citizens were evacuated; 7,500 burials in small cemeteries were relocated and the villages were leveled and burned. On April 28, 1939, the towns officially ceased to exist. A year later two massive earthen dams at the south end of the valley were completed and the reservoir slowly filled, reaching its 412-billion-gallon capacity in 1946.

When it was constructed, the Quabbin Reservoir was the largest man-made domestic water supply system in the world and it remains one of the largest unfiltered water supplies in the world, supplying 300 million gallons of water each day for use by nearly half the population of Massachusetts. The Quabbin MDC Visitors Center at 485 Ware Road, Belchertown, is open Monday through Friday from 8:30 A.M. to 4:30 P.M. and weekends from 9:00 A.M. to 5:00 P.M. Telephone: (413) 323–7221.

The **Quabbin Park** recreational area near the visitors center encompasses 9 miles of paved roads and another 20 miles of trails and dirt roads for light hiking and walking. It also has some of the reservation's few picnic areas and toilets with running water. (A few portable toilets for use by fishermen are scattered at designated boat beaching areas on the shoreline.) The lookout tower on Quabbin Hill, about 400 feet above the shoreline elevation, gives a stunning view of the waters stretching away from massive Winsor Dam nearly to the horizon. And there's a fair dose of second-hand nostalgia to be had by visiting the Quabbin Park Cemetery, where each of the four towns has its own area, complete with Civil War monument and other memorials from the village commons and parks. This is the tame side of Quabbin, although in the winter you sometimes see bald eagles feeding on deer who have been stranded on the ice above Winsor Dam.

Routes 9, 202, 122, and 32 box in the Quabbin Reservation, and from these highways, there are more than forty gates to paths, trails, or roads leading through the woods to the water. This is our favorite way to experience some of the wildness of the Quabbin, far from the crowds. Our favorite gate is **Gate 15** off Route 202 on the

Northern maidenhair fern

Yellow lady's slipper

Pelham-Shutesbury town line. From the visitors' center, continue west on Route 9, then north on Route 202. This road, the Daniel Shays Highway (named for the leader of Shays Rebellion) follows the high ridges separating the Connecticut River valley from the Swift River Valley. The Quabbin occasionally flashes into view as a blue bowl of water far below on the right. The town of Pelham appears in 8 miles—recognizable only by a gas station and restaurant on the corner of Amherst Road (the sign for that left says "Amherst 7"). Two miles farther north on the right is a turnout with limited vehicle parking for Gate 15. We only made the mistake of parking directly in front of the gate once. When we came back, the Metropolitan District Commission rangers who patrol the Quabbin had towed our car away.

This particular entrance to the Quabbin follows the remains of an old dirt road that used to connect the villages of Shutesbury, which still exists, and Prescott, which occupied the large peninsula that divides the east and west arms of the reservoir. (Prescott is still dry land but is off-limits to public use because it harbors several scientific and wildlife management research programs.) The 1.5-mile trail down to the water has been reverting to wilderness for six decades, and the footing can be tricky, especially where it crosses Atherton Brook—depending on whether or not beavers have flooded the road with one of their dams! (The beavers are best seen around

dusk.) The elevation drops about 500 feet.

Maidenhair ferns grow along the tiny brook that trickles by the road—in the spring they form the highly prized fiddleheads. The road branches a few hundred yards from the gate. The right branch passes several dwellings discernible mostly by the flowers that their owners left behind. In the spring daffodils still bloom in clumps where doorsteps used to be, and during the summer roses mysteriously bloom in the woods. This right branch quickly peters out, but the left branch continues downhill.

The marshy area under a canopy of hardwood trees at the brook is rife with both the native ladyslipper orchid and a more obnoxious bloomer, skunk cabbage. As the road rises to bend around a large granite outcrop, the edge of the trail is lined with checkerberry, aka wintergreen, beneath the stand of three tall white birches nicknamed "the three graces" by poet Gibbons Ruark.

We try to step carefully and quietly through this path down to the water, watching the surrounding woods closely for a flicker of white that will be followed by a crashing sound in the brush. That's a white-tailed deer giving us a wide berth. Over the years we have seen beaver, porcupine, red and gray squirrels, coyote, and deer along this trail, and have spotted bobcat tracks in soft mud around some of the springs and bear tracks near some of the blackberry thickets. Legend has it that an Eastern cougar (allegedly extinct) also roams this wildlife sanctuary, though proof is scant. Some 250 bird species have been recorded in the Quabbin, including wild turkey, great-horned owls, saw-whet owls, red-headed and pileated woodpeckers, blackbilled cuckoo, northern shrike, and many different warblers.

Swimming is forbidden in Quabbin waters, but fishing is permitted from mid-April to mid-October with a state license. Where this road meets the water is not especially good fishing, but many trout and salmon have been taken a hundred yards north across Cobb Brook, where there are deep-water holes. Fishermen may find that they have avian competitors. Bald and golden eagles nest here and, along with osprey, often appear on this arm of the Quabbin circling overhead, then suddenly swooping down to grab fish in their talons. The bald eagles are a recent re-introduction by scientists, who raised young eagles from hatchlings here, releasing them to the wild with the Quabbin imprinted as their home. And each year they come back to nest—wild spirits reclaiming the wilderness from humankind.

Rhode Island Spinners

Providence, Rhode Island

Rhode Island's capital city, Providence, is arguably the most livable city its size in New England. Few municipalities of 170,000 people can claim such a wealth of fine bookstores, truly great restaurants, excellent museums and galleries, and good theater. Many a Boston-area foodie thinks nothing of driving an hour to Providence just to have dinner.

Most travelers approach Providence on I–95 from the south along the coastal route or from the north from Boston. From Sturbridge, the simplest approach is more scenic. Drive east on Route 20 to I–395 south. Continue to Route 44 in Connecticut (exit 97) and head east through rolling countryside to Providence. You might even want to stop at the halfway mark in Chepachet to see Brown & Hopkins, which was established in 1809 and claims to be the oldest country store in continuous existence.

Whichever route you take into Providence you'll find a city that has recently regained the good looks it boasted during its economic heyday a century ago. New highways finally make it easy to get into and around the city (rather than just out of it). A revitalized waterfront has replaced a stinking underground sewer with a sequence of delightful open-air parks. And reconstruction of the downtown has created a pleasant shopping and business district instead of a gully between the attractions of College and Federal Hills on the east and west sides of the city, respectively.

To get the most out of today's Providence (and fully comprehend its 350-year rivalry with Boston), it helps to know a little about the city's history. Roger Williams, a liberal cleric who ran afoul of the Massachusetts Bay Colony authorities, founded the community in 1636 when he

escaped from Salem one step ahead of the law. Naming it for God's guidance, Williams planned Providence as a "lively experiment" in religious liberty and the separation of church and state. His site selection proved providential indeed—the community rose where two major rivers meet and flow as one into the head of Narragansett Bay.

Providence remained a sleepy community of farmers and fishermen until the 1675–76 Native American uprising known as King Philip's War, in which many tribes across New England joined forces to attempt to drive the Europeans from their land. Although Williams had scrupulously purchased the property rights for Providence from the Narragansetts, his old friend, the sachem Canonicus, had died in 1647 and Providence was drawn into the war. In March 1676, a Narragansett band invaded the town and put twenty-nine of its seventy-five buildings to the torch. The official records of the early colony were preserved when the town clerk (who was also the miller) threw them into his mill stream. All but a handful of pages were retrieved after the raid and are now in city archives.

Providence recovered quickly from the devastation. Budding entrepreneur Pardon Tillinghast constructed Providence's first wharf in 1680, and within fifty years the small town exploded into a major force in the "triangle trade" in slaves, rum, and molasses among New England, Africa, and the West Indies. By the mid-eighteenth century, Providence's aristocracy of wealth was well established, headed by four scions of the Brown family: John, Joseph, Nicholas, and Moses. Along with other merchant princes, they endowed schools and hospitals, built art-filled mansions along Benefit Street and generally ran the show.

Although Boston patriots get most of the ink in the history books, Providence's gentry did their part in the American Revolution as well. John Brown conspired with other leading citizens to torch the *Gaspee,* a British revenue vessel that had run aground outside neighboring Warwick harbor. And on March 2, 1775, Providence held a tea party that put Boston's to shame. Patriots assembled a huge pile of tea in Market Square, poured a barrel of tar over it, and set it afire to the huzzahs of a large crowd. Led by Providence firebrands, Rhode Island declared its independence from British rule on May 4, 1776, a full two months before the signing of the Declaration of Independence in Philadelphia.

Thanks to a head start from Samuel Slater's cotton thread mill established in 1790 in adjacent Pawtucket, by 1830 Providence had become the most industrialized municipality in the most industrialized state in the union. The shipping aristocracy swiftly shifted its capital to manufacturing, enabling Providence to figure prominently in machine tools, cotton textiles, woolen textiles, and jewelry and silverware manufacturing until the Great Depression ended a century of economic prosperity.

The factory system that developed in Providence demanded more labor than the surrounding communities could supply, and the city became a magnet for immigration—first by the Irish, then the Italians and French Canadians. When the textile industry headed south, Providence was left destitute, wallowing in poverty and decay until well after World War II. Its rebirth has resulted, in part, from a new service-based economy as a center for health care and higher education.

Two well-established institutions deserve much of the credit for the pleasing face Providence presents these days: Brown University and the Rhode Island School of Design. Brown began in 1764 in Warren, Rhode Island, as Rhode Island College, then moved to Providence in 1770. When Moses Brown (of the Brown brothers) made a large bequest to the school in 1804, it assumed his name. RISD (pronounced locally as RIZ-dee) was created in 1877 by a group of Providence socialites as a centennial project to raise the level of commercial design. Many of the same women were instrumental in establishing Pembroke College at the hitherto all-male Brown University in 1897. Brown crowns College Hill, and RISD clings all around to its skirts.

Walking the Past in Providence

Probably the first building that catches your eye when you come into Providence is the looming **State House** perched on a promontory overlooking the city. Its massive marble dome is said to be second in size only to the one on St. Peter's Basilica in Rome. To our minds, there are only two compelling reasons to get any closer than the highway view. If you're a fan of ancient documents, the state's Charter of 1663 granted by Charles II is framed outside the Senate chambers. Or if you're a fan of Gilbert Stuart, a Rhode Island boy who became America's first great portraitist, you might want to see his full-length portrait of George Washington. (Stuart also painted the Washington portrait that appears on the $1.00 bill.) The State House, on Smith Street between Francis and Gaspee Streets, has free guided tours Monday through Friday from 8:30 A.M. to 4:30 P.M. Telephone: (401) 277-2357.

Like most New England cities, Providence is best toured on foot. One of the newest promenades recaptures the city's waterfront along the Providence River and the old industrial canals. **Waterplace Park** is a four-acre natural amphitheater, dedicated in 1994, framed by mile-long cobblestone and brick walkways along the river. The park area surrounding a one-acre pond serves as the city's chief venue for summertime outdoor entertainment—free concerts, fireworks, and outdoor theater. Fire sculptures called "Waterfire" light up the river from sunset to midnight with burning cauldrons on selected nights, creating a primitively stirring spectacle that one local describes as "neolithic."

If you like old homes of the rich and once-famous, you'll love **Benefit Street,** the leafy ridgetop street of College Hill overlooking the Providence River. Known as the "Mile of History," Benefit boasts the most impressive collection of historic homes in Providence, which in turn has the most original Colonial and Federal-era structures in America. To avoid a strenuous walk up College Hill (its incline would bring a smile to a Swiss goatherd's face), take a taxi to the beginning of Benefit Street, where it merges with North Main Street, and walk down the historical mile. Many of the homes on College Hill are either chocolate brown or a brownish pink—colors that have been used here for centuries and are characteristic of the neighborhood. Most of the buildings on Benefit are private and even some that are publicly owned are not open for touring, but the walk is a pleasant one, if only to admire the facades and the striking views of the State House, which keeps appearing between the dwellings.

Along with functioning as the "Main Street"

of College Hill, Benefit Street also has strong associations with the macabre side of American literature. Number **88 Benefit** was the home of Sarah Helen Whitman, the young widow whom Edgar Allan Poe courted, only to be spurned shortly before his death because her family objected to his dissolute habits. Poe dedicated two of his best poems, "To Helen" and "Annabel Lee," to Whitman, who was something of a poet in her own right. Behind her house is the **Cathedral of St. John Episcopal Church.** Poe often walked in the tiny tree-shaded church graveyard for inspiration, as did his twentieth-century admirer and emulator, horror-fiction author H.P. Lovecraft. (The walkway around the graveyard may be reached through the front of the cathedral or from the parking lot between North Main Street and Benefit Street.) The graveyard predates the church by a century, and the 1810 church itself, with its Neo-Gothic decorations, is the oldest Episcopal parish in Rhode Island. It was co-founded by a member of the Brown clan, of course.

The private, yellow-clapboard house at 135 Benefit, the **Stephen Harris House,** was built in 1764 on the site of a graveyard. Local legend holds that when the dead were disinterred and reburied elsewhere, the workman mistakenly left behind the remains of a French couple. By the nineteenth century the house was shunned—Lovecraft wrote a short story about it called "The Shunned House"—because of dire doings and terrifying screams in French that emanated from the structure at night. The occasional midnight walking tours by Lovecraft fans called "Lovecraft Lurk-Ins" conclude in tiny Mary Elizabeth Sharpe Park next to the Shunned House (now beautifully restored and maintained) with readings from the horror meister's hideous verses.

On a somewhat brighter note, after passing the Old State House at 150 Benefit and continuing for another block, you'll spy the graceful spire of the **First Baptist Meeting House** on the corner of Main and Waterman Streets. Every village in New England has a "First Church" but this 1775 structure is the place of worship for what is literally the *first* Baptist church in America—the congregation was founded in 1638. One of its co-founders was Roger Williams, who promptly quit the church a year later and spent the rest of his life

Rhode Island State House and Waterplace Park, Providence

as a religious "seeker," belonging to no denomination. The building is atypical of Baptist churches of the period, as the Baptist fellowship in those days frowned on steeples and bells. The Providence congregation erected its steeple nonetheless and hung a bell bearing this inscription:

> "For freedom of conscience the town
>   was first planted,
> Persuasion, not force, was used by
>   the people:
> This church is the eldest and has not
>   recanted,
> Enjoying and granting bell, temple
>   and steeple."

It probably shouldn't be a surprise that the architect was Joseph Brown, one of the quartet of Brown merchant brothers. Joseph was the rich trader with a bent for science and engineering, making his mark as an astronomer and philosopher as well as amateur architect. The church interior has a fabulous Waterford crystal chandelier dating from 1792. The building is open for self-guided tours between 9:00 A.M. and 3:00 P.M. on weekdays; a guided tour is given at 12:15 on Sundays.

The **Rhode Island School of Design Museum of Art** occupies much of the next block. This small museum owns some of New England's best collections of fine and decorative arts, all condensed in a fashion that makes a walk-through seem like a tour of the greatest hits of world art. Although affiliated with RISD (you'll see students sitting and sketching for hours on end), it serves as the de facto city art museum in Providence, and its wide-ranging holdings reflect the wealth of the Providence merchant families who have been patrons for many years. The art works span the centuries and the world, ranging from Greek and Roman statuary to Renaissance masters to a quite good selection of impressionism. If your interest runs to decorative arts, the Pendleton wing features an outstanding collection of nineteenth-century American furniture and silver. If you prefer a bit more pizzazz, head for the Daphne Farago wing, which displays contemporary art in all media. The museum, at 224 Benefit Street, is open Wednesday, Thursday, Saturday, and Sunday from 10:00 A.M. to 5:00 P.M., Friday from 10:00 A.M. to 8:00 P.M. Adult admission is $5.00. Wheelchair accessible. Telephone: (401) 454–6500; TTY: (800) 745–5555.

Legend has it that Poe and Whitman carried on their courtship in the stacks of the **Providence Athenaeum** at 251 Benefit Street at the corner of College Street. Admission is free. The library, which occupies a handsome 1838 Greek Revival building, is open Monday through Friday from 8:30 A.M. to 5:30 P.M., Saturday from 9:30 A.M. to 5:30 P.M. The library is closed on Saturdays during the summer; during the winter it is also open Sundays from 1:00 to 5:00 P.M. Telephone: (401) 421–6970. The library owns some key pieces of evidence of the Poe-Whitman romance: a December 1847 issue of *Colton's American Review* containing the anonymous poem "Ulalume." When Whitman showed the poem to Poe and admitted how much she admired it, he affixed his signature to the page. An oil painting of Whitman and a daguerreotype of Poe are hung together in one of the library's reading rooms.

The self-educated Lovecraft also frequented the Athenaeum and many of his characters go there to discover some tidbit of ancient and horrible lore. Lovecraft's own letters and memorabilia, by the way, are held in special collections at the John Hay Library at Brown University, a few blocks away at the corner of Prospect and College Streets.

The huge brownstone and brick structure whose grounds occupy an entire block is the **John Brown House,** the 1786 home of the merchant patriot who spurred the burning of the *Gaspee.* Built by this pioneer China trader, another member of Providence's first family, it is a treasury of fine furniture and chinoiserie. John Quincy Adams described the three-story Georgian as "the most magnificent and elegant mansion I have ever seen on this continent." The house museum is particularly noted for its magnificent collection of eighteenth-century Rhode Island furniture. Enter at 52 Power Street for guided tours Tuesday through Saturday from 10:00 A.M. to 5:00 P.M. and Sunday from noon to 4:00 P.M. (During January and February weekday tours are by appointment.) Adult admission is $6.00. Telephone: (401) 331–8575.

The next block is occupied by the tall yellow-clapboard **Nightingale-Brown House.** The largest wood-framed Federal mansion in Providence, it was built for a China Trade merchant and acquired by one of the Brown family. This in-town manse at 357 Benefit served as the family home of the Browns (for whom the university is named) for five generations before it was extensively rehabilitated and restored in the 1980s, a project funded by the $11-million proceeds from the sale of a single heirloom desk. Now owned by Brown University, it houses the John Nicholas Brown Center for the Study of American Civilization but is open for tours on Fridays from 1:00 to 4:00 P.M. Telephone: (401) 272–0357.

The "Mile of History" continues down Benefit Street another six blocks past some very impressive Georgian and Federal homes until it reaches **Wickenden Street,** a lively commercial street of small boutiques, restaurants, coffee shops, and the like, and one of Providence's best areas for light shopping. Several streets ascend College Hill from Wickenden. One of them, **Thayer Street,** functions as the main thoroughfare for Brown and RISD closer to the top of the hill. Both Wickenden and Thayer are great places for shopping (more than 100 boutiques), casual dining, and people-watching.

A Half-Day Visit to Pawtucket, Rhode Island

The people of Pawtucket, Rhode Island, are very careful not to overstate their case, but they'd like their fair share of recognition too. This small city cheek by jowl with Providence marks the spot where the American Industrial Revolution began—where water power enabled manufacturers to make more thread for cloth in a day than a hand spinner could make in a year. It's worth spending a half day here to soak in the history and get some background that will put the achievements of Lowell, Massachusetts, into perspective. You'll want to start at the beginning—the **Slater Mill Historic Site.**

To get to Slater Mill from Providence, follow I–95 north to exit 28, School Street in Pawtucket. Turn left at the bottom of the ramp and continue straight through the light to follow the road that goes downhill. At the light after crossing the river, turn right onto Roosevelt Avenue. The first right on Roosevelt enters the historic site's parking lot ($1.00 donation).

Pawtucket rests on both banks of the Blackstone River, which flows 46 miles from its source north of Worcester, Massachusetts, to Narragansett Bay. Along that route the Blackstone falls 438 feet, with the largest drop being the 17½-foot natural falls in Pawtucket (a name that means "rapids" or "falls" in the various dialects of Algonquian). The thunder of these falls was too much for aspiring engineers to ignore—all that power! No wonder Pawtucket became first among equals on the Blackstone.

As early as the seventeenth century the Blackstone River powered sawmills and gristmills. By the late nineteenth century, it had become America's first industrial river, lined by textile and machine shops and surrounded on its banks by company mill towns. By 1880 it was deemed "the hardest working river" in America. The Slater Mill Historic Site, a pleasant, parklike spot near Pawtucket's Main Street and its now-dammed falls, condenses this century of explosive growth into a tale told by three buildings.

Following an orientation film, the guided tour begins at the oldest structure on the site, a gambrel-roofed cottage owned by Sylvanus Brown (no relation to the wealthy Browns of

Providence). The cottage was built in 1758 and was restored and reset on its present foundation in 1973. Brown was a carpenter and millwright who died in 1820, leaving furnishings valued at $97 (of which a wooden case clock was valued at $25).

The interpretation here, though, focuses on how households went about making their own cloth in pre-industrial days. The guide demonstrates how to card wool, spin it on a spinning wheel (the woman of the house would walk one-hundred miles a year spinning wool on a "walking wheel"), and then how to weave rough cloth on a hand loom (usually the man's job). The guide also demonstrates how to beat long flax reeds to separate the fibers before carding and spinning them into linen. Early New Englanders generally made either woolen or linen cloth, since cotton could not be raised reliably in the short growing season.

Samuel Slater revolutionized the making of cloth, eliminating much of the tedious hand labor almost overnight. In modern parlance, Slater would be called an industrial spy. He had worked in the Arkwright textile mills in England—truly the beginning of the Industrial Revolution—and was familiar with how textile manufacturing machinery worked. The British government at the time recognized that the country's advantage in world trade depended on maintaining its technical edge, so British law made it illegal for people like Slater to leave the country, lest they set up shop someplace else.

Knowledge knows no borders, and just as the

Slater Mill, Pawtucket, Rhode Island

Breast wheel typical of a rural mill

Wooden crown gearing off waterwheel

British feared, Samuel Slater arrived in America in 1789 looking for a way to capitalize on his expertise. Moses Brown, the Providence merchant, introduced Slater to Sylvanus Brown in Pawtucket. They set up in a tailor's shop—a place designed for making patterns—and together they duplicated British water-powered spinning, picking, carding, and roving machines. With financial backing from Moses Brown and his friends, they built America's first successful water-powered cotton spinning mill.

The yellow-clapboard Slater Mill looks more like a barn than a factory, but when it was built in 1793, Pawtucket carpenters had a lot of experience making barns. They'd never built a factory before. Amazingly enough, this mill continued to produce cotton thread until it finally closed in 1905. In the early years of operation, all the workers were children aged seven to fourteen, who were small enough and nimble enough to dodge in and around the exposed working parts to tend the machines. ("I'm certainly glad they have schools these days," a young guide from Pawtucket declared, providing a little twentieth-century perspective.)

As the need for workers expanded, the children were joined by women in what came to be called the Rhode Island System of Manufacture, widely copied elsewhere in Rhode Island and adjoining parts of Massachusetts and Connecticut. A half hour before dawn each day the factory bell would ring to alert the workers. If they did not arrive at the factory by the second bell, which rang at dawn, they were fired.

America's first strike took place here over the problem of timekeeping, and the company built a clock tower to show the hours. The Rhode Island system, it might be noted, was often denounced as inhumane by mill owners who followed the Lowell system.

Apart from the Rhode Island System, Slater's main achievement was technological—building machines that put a strong and consistent twist on the cotton fibers to make strong thread. Initially, these spools went out to hand weavers to finish into cloth, for the great weaving innovations made in Lowell had not yet begun. (Although they date from much later than the rest of the factory, a few power weaving looms are also shown here.)

The third building on the site is the stone structure of the 1810 Wilkinson Mill, which is dedicated to showing the technological innovations of David Wilkinson. Wilkinson, who was Slater's brother-in-law, is considered the father of machine tools in America.

The mill is powered by a huge "gravity" wheel, which is turned by the weight of the water that catches in its blades rather than by the speed of the flow. The Slater staff don't let this wheel run all the time because it is out of balance and extremely noisy. But before bringing a group into the mill, the guide will raise the water gate, which is sealed in mud, to let the river flow onto the mill wheel's blades. It makes a monstrous croaking and creaking as the wheel begins to turn, powered by 4,000 pounds of water catching in its blade to spin the 16,000-pound breast wheel. The energy of the wheel is conveyed through massive gears and leather pulleys to the power tools on the floors above. It seems a bit like a Rube Goldberg scheme, given its complexity, but all that power made it possible to perform precision machine work in metal. Wilkinson invented the screw cutting lathe and his workers—skilled male master craftsmen and apprentices, as opposed to the women and children at the mill next door—produced the first commercially successful power looms in America.

Wilkinson was a better inventor than businessman, and his company went belly up around 1830, although the site continued as an active machine shop into the twentieth century. Most of the tools in the machine shop now actually date from the late nineteenth century. But thanks to Wilkinson's innovations, Pawtucket became the first major machine building center in the country. "We were legendary for our mastery of machine technology," our guide says with a touch of native pride.

Slater Mill Historic Site, at 3 Roosevelt Avenue, is open June through October, Tuesday through Saturday from 10:00 A.M. to 5:00 P.M. and Sunday from 1:00 to 5:00 P.M. From March through May and during the first three weeks of December, the site is open Saturday and Sunday from 1:00 to 5:00 P.M. Adults $6.00. Telephone: (401) 725–8638.

After looking over the Slater Mill Historic Site, it's worth spending a few minutes to stroll some of the main streets of Pawtucket to see the evidence of a mid-nineteenth-century city flush with success and embarked on a great building spree. Pawtucket has fallen on hard times since its heyday, but from 1850 to 1900 it was a boom city full of optimism and civic pride.

In the park downriver from Slater Mill is a particularly good view of Trinity Church, built of native stone in imitation of the Gothic style of an English country church, and of the Romanesque Revival style Pawtucket Congregational Church. Summer Street, a block away, has two other, somewhat later buildings that show Pawtucket's chest-puffing pride at the turn of the century. The 1897 Beaux Arts building at the corner of Summer and Maple Streets was built as a post office. Farther up the street, the 1902 public library building is literally a temple to learning—

an Ionic temple in white granite. Six pure white marble reliefs on the face mark great moments in literature and history.

Machine-Age Massachusetts

An Interlude in Worcester, Massachusetts

Worcester (pronounced WUSS-ster) calls itself "the heart of the Commonwealth," and it does indeed sit smack dab in the middle of Massachusetts. Until World War II it was also the leading manufacturing city in New England and remains the second-largest metropolis in the region. While Worcester has a great deal to offer its residents—especially lovely parks and fine colleges—travelers through the Midlands are apt to go from Sturbridge straight on to Lowell without stopping. But there's more than enough to occupy a day in Worcester, and these attractions are interesting enough in their own right to justify a roundabout route from Providence to Lowell via Worcester.

The simplest approach from Sturbridge is to head east on Route 20 for 12 miles to the junction with I–290 north. I–290 cuts right into the heart of Worcester. From Providence, head northwest on Route 146 for 35 miles until it meets I–290 in downtown Worcester.

Exit 18 from I–290 leads around a hillside to the parking lot of the **Worcester Art Museum,** a good general art museum with more than 30,000 objects covering fifty centuries of mostly Western culture from dynastic Egypt and ancient Rome to Pop Art. Nineteenth-century European academic painting is a strong suit at WAM, but far more charming is the untutored colloquial style of portraitist Ralph Earl, a Tory who returned home to Worcester after the Revolution. His 1796 *Looking East from Denny Hill* is the earliest painted view of the city. It's always interesting to see how personal connections can influence collections. Founding director Stephen Salisbury III (you'll see the name "Salisbury" all over Worcester) roomed with a rich young Mexican at Harvard, and their friendship resulted in WAM acquiring one of New England's most interesting collections of pre-Columbian art, including a stunning Olmec jade were-jaguar. Located at 55 Salisbury Street, the Worcester Art Museum is open Wednesday through Friday from 11:00 A.M. to 4:00 P.M., Saturday from 10:00 A.M. to 5:00 P.M., and Sunday from 11:00 A.M. to 5:00 P.M.; closed on major holidays. Adults $6.00; free Saturday 10:00 A.M. to noon. Telephone: (508) 799–4406.

To get to Worcester's most idiosyncratic museum, head north again on I–290 to the junction with I–190. The **Higgins Armory Museum,** the big shiny building just off the first exit, proves that boys will be boys. John Woodman Higgins, proprietor of Worcester Pressed Steel, grew up on tales of days of old when knights were bold. As a steel products manufacturer, he was enamored of early metallurgy and became enthralled by the world of steel armor. He wrote a friend in the 1920s that he longed for one "real good genuine suit." Before he was done collecting, he had acquired more than a hundred. Now that remarkable private collection of armor from medieval and Renaissance Europe, feudal Japan, and ancient Greece and Rome is open for public viewing. Many of the suits of armor are set up as if going to battle. It's a bit like an Arthurian legend come to life. Located at 100 Barber Avenue, Higgins Armory is open Tuesday through Saturday from 10:00 A.M. to 4:00 P.M. and Sunday from noon to 4:00 P.M. Adults $4.75. Telephone: (508) 853–6015.

Perhaps less highbrow than the museums, Worcester has **an outstanding collection of about a dozen working diners,** mostly arrayed on Routes 9, 12, and 122 north and east of the downtown. The diner wasn't born here—that distinction belongs to Providence—but Worcester was the heart of the diner-building industry from the end of the nineteenth century until the famous Worcester Diner Co. closed its doors in 1961. (See "Staying There.")

Lowell, Massachusetts

When Europeans first started touring America in significant numbers in the 1840s, the two biggest attractions were Niagara Falls and the city of Lowell—the wonders wrought by the hand of God and those by the hand of man, as one Scotsman observed. Those curious Europeans came hoping to see a grand experiment in the model industrial city, for even then Lowell was perceived as the cradle of America's Industrial Revolution—an industrial revolution with a human face.

Only a small agricultural village stood on the banks of the Merrimack River before a group of investors known as the Boston Associates constructed a canal system to harness the power of an abrupt drop in the river's elevation and proceeded to build factories and boardinghouses around the river and canals. Consequently Lowell is one of the few cities in Massachusetts without a significant colonial history. More than any other place in New England, Lowell was imagined whole out of the landscape. When those first European visitors came, they found a brawny brick city of towering mills—all surrounded by farmland.

To see Lowell with those eyes takes a bit of imagination today because the city has splashed well up the riverbanks as wave after wave of immigrants built houses, shops, and churches. Stalwart, brick-milled Lowell is better viewed from up close, where its nineteenth-century mills loom larger than life. All the phases of textile production were brought together in Lowell, and though surpassed by other New England mill towns, the city remained a titan in the American textile industry into the twentieth century.

But by the early 1970s, Lowell epitomized the saying that "the bigger they are, the harder they fall." Lowell had lost the advantage of its water power when most of the textile industry shifted to steam turbines in the 1880s, and the attrition of orders and jobs accelerated as the industry moved to the low-wage South after World War I. The last of Lowell's large mills closed in the 1950s, and the economy, as in so many New England mill communities, stagnated. Now the city has recovered, partly through new technologies that brought new jobs, and partly by establishing the Lowell Heritage State Park, Lowell Historic Preservation District, and Lowell National Historical Park. Don't even try to separate the various entities, for their jurisdictions often overlap. Among them they have brought the mill industries back to life for new generations of travelers.

To approach Lowell from Worcester, follow

I–290 to I–495 north and take the Route 3 "Lowell Connector." From Providence, follow I–95 north (which becomes Route 128 near Boston) to Route 3 North ("Middlesex Turnpike). At the Lowell Connector, take exit 5N ("Thorndike Street") and follow the signs for "Lowell National and State Park Visitor Parking." This route eventually leads to a large free lot off Dutton Street behind the Visitor Center.

The sheer enormity of the Lowell mills strikes you as you enter the National Historic Park Visitor Center in the 1902 brick textile mill complex of the Lowell Manufacturing Company, now called Market Mills. Many of these buildings now contain offices and warehouse space, but at one time they hummed with the production of thread, yarn, and cloth. The central courtyard of the complex gives you the full effect of being surrounded by a world of aspiration in brick. If America chose in the early nineteenth century to worship Progress, then these industrial structures were our first cathedrals.

The Visitor Center is the logical place to start a Lowell tour—or at least to pick up excellent maps of the historic sites and downtown Lowell. You can also make reservations for free guided tours on foot or bicycle and purchase tickets for the various canal tours. (See "Staying There.") The Center is open daily from 8:30 A.M. to 5:00 P.M., with extended hours on weekends and in the summer (closed Thanksgiving, Christmas, and New Year's Day). It is at 67 Kirk Street. Telephone: (978) 970–5000; TDD: (978) 972–5002. Admission is free.

Whatever else you decide to do in Lowell, do not miss the introductory video presentation at the Visitor Center, "Lowell: The Industrial Revelation." This entertaining and intelligent history of the city puts everything else into perspective.

Pawtucket Falls made Lowell possible. No, not the Pawtucket Falls at Slater's Mill in Rhode Island. "Pawtucket" simply means "rapids" or "waterfall" in all the dialects of the Algonquian language, so there were "pawtuckets" all over eastern New England. This particular "pawtucket" is a one-mile stretch where the Merrimack River loses 32 feet of its elevation. At first the rough water was simply a nuisance to navigation. In 1796 a canal was completed to circumvent the

Mills and canal system, Lowell, Massachusetts

falls and permit the easy passage of timber from the White Mountains down to the shipbuilders in Newburyport at the mouth of the river. But it was not long before industrialists saw the potential lurking in the "pawtucket."

Starting in 1821, the Boston Associates built a series of industrial canals to tap the energy of that 32-foot fall of millions of gallons of water. And along these power canals they constructed the city's first textile mills. Director Kirk Boott ran the city-building operation with an iron hand, determined to transform the farming village of a dozen homes into a model industrial community. The construction of the canal network made Lowell the "Venice of America," and much of the city still sits on islands surrounded by canals and the Merrimack River. A parallel network of waterside walkways connects the remaining mills and other historic sites, letting you walk down the same paths the workers took on their way to the spinning jennys and the looms in the pale pre-dawn light. (In the summer, there is also a free electric trolley, modeled on a 1901 streetcar, connecting several sites.) Lowell's ambitious public art program has filled many of the plazas and squares along the route with heroic sculpture. For example, "The Worker," set where Market Street crosses the Merrimack Canal, memorializes the Irish laborers who dug the canals by hand in the 1820s and 1830s.

The **Boott Cotton Mills,** with its handsome 1864 clock tower, is perhaps the best surviving example of early mill architecture in Lowell, exemplifying the breakthrough that the Boston Associates made in combining all the operations of making cloth into an integrated system. Slater's Mill and others that quickly followed made thread or yarn that was turned into cloth by weavers working in their homes. In an incredible leap of efficiency, the mills of Lowell were designed from the outset as integrated cloth-making facilities. (Lowell takes it name from the man responsible, Francis Cabot Lowell. In 1812 he visited Manchester, England's textile factories and observed the operations of the British power looms. He and master mechanic Paul Moody replicated the machinery for use in America.)

Organized in 1835, the Boott company was one of the longest-lived mills, hanging on until the bitter end of New England textiles in the 1950s. Now converted into a museum, the historic structure maintains an operating 1920s weave room on the first floor while interpretive exhibits fill the second. Located on John Street but hard to miss if you walk along the canals, Boott Cotton Mills Museum is open daily (except Thanksgiving, Christmas, and New Year's Day) from 9:30 A.M. to 5:00 P.M.; adults $4.00. Telephone: (978) 970–5000.

Before you enter the Boott's weave room, a park ranger will hand you a pair of ear plugs, for which you will be immediately grateful. The old textile mills were notoriously noisy, and the volume here is, at best, a dull roar as volunteers operate a few of the power looms to make souvenir dish towels (available in the gift shop). At any one time they run only a dozen or so of the eighty-eight looms on the floor, but even so, the noise is so intense that you feel the air vibrate on your skin.

The early workers apparently did not wear earplugs, but one of the more famous of the mill girls, Lucy Larcom, wrote in her 1889 memoir, *A New England Girlhood,* that "I discovered, too, that I could so accustom myself to the noise that it became like a silence to me. And I defied the machinery to make me its slave. Its incessant discords could not drown the music of my thoughts if I would let them fly high enough."

Just across Boardinghouse Park from the mill is the **Mogan Cultural Center,** where the "Working People Exhibit" in a former Boott Mills

boardinghouse makes the daily lives of the mill girls seem more tangible. While American industrialists were only too happy to adopt British textile technology, they sought to establish a more humane system of employment. English mills typically employed entire families at low wages, but the Lowell mills—at least initially—hired only young women from the surrounding countryside, providing them with clean boardinghouses, fair wages, and moral instruction. The idea was that these daughters of yeoman farmers would work at the mills a year or two, make some money for a dowry or to pay the family mortgage, and return home. In practice, this system created the first class of working women in America.

Thirty to forty young women would occupy one of these boardinghouses, sleeping two to a bed on the upper level, while the first floor was devoted to the keeper's quarters, the kitchen, and the dining hall. Since the women worked thirteen to fourteen hours a day ("only" eight hours on Saturday), they were allowed to return to the boardinghouse for breakfast and again for the big meal of the day at noon. The keeper kept a close eye on the women, who could lose their jobs for improper behavior or failing to attend church on Sunday. Historians have teased out a tantalizing composite of the mill girl as a rural young woman, usually between fifteen and twenty-six, who came to the city determined not only to make money but to better herself by reading and attending lectures. While many of them returned home with their savings after a year or two, many others worked to become financially independent—no small feat on the wages of a mill worker.

Not only were the mill girls America's first class of independent women, they were among the first workers to organize. The early paternalistic system collapsed as soon as Lowell's mills had competition, and the mill girls staged strikes for better pay and working conditions as early as 1834 and several times petitioned the Massachusetts Legislature for relief from exploitation. The mill owners responded by cutting wages and speeding up machines—and by hiring entire families of immigrants to work the mills. Precisely what Lowell had abhorred about the English system had come to pass: Lowell, too, was a place of "dark, satanic mills," as poet William Blake damned the British factories.

Exhibits in the Mogan Cultural Center also chronicle the social changes brought by the immigrants who stepped in to take the low-paying jobs left by the women. First came the Irish, beginning after 1845, then the French Canadians in the 1860s and 1870s. The Greeks, Poles, and other eastern Europeans followed in the 1890s and early 1900s—giving Lowell the ethnic diversity that produced both Paul Tsongas (Greek) and Jack Kerouac (French Canadian).

Boardinghouse Park pays more than lip service to this diversity by serving as the site of a summer evening concert series and one of the popular stages during the Lowell Folk Festival, which recognizes all the city's diverse cultural backgrounds (see "Staying There"). Immigrants no longer come to work in the mills, but Lowell has other opportunities now, and since the 1960s, the city has welcomed a large number of immigrants from Cambodia, Vietnam, and Latin America.

It's worth crossing Bridge Street here for a detour to pay homage to the man who perhaps loved Lowell most dearly. The **Jack Kerouac Commemorative** stands in the park in front of the old Massachusetts Mill, now a housing complex. Born in the Centralville part of Lowell to French Canadian immigrant parents in 1922 as Jean-Louis Kerouac, little Ti-Jean spoke French until the age of seven and had an illustrious career as a high school athlete before leaving to attend Columbia University on a football scholarship in 1939. Football didn't last and neither did Columbia. Jack became a writer—one of the central figures of the Beat generation—and didn't live in Lowell again until 1967. He died in Florida in 1969 while watching the *Galloping Gourmet* television show.

But Kerouac never forgot the city and its brawny industry, which he described as "Galloway" in the 1950 autobiographical novel, *The Town and the City.* "The textile factories built in brick, primly towered, solid, all ranged along the river and the canals, and all night the industries hum and shuttle. This is Galloway, milltown in the middle of fields and forests." He went on to set four other novels in thinly disguised versions of Lowell: *Dr. Sax, Maggie Cassidy, Vanity of Duluoz,* and *Visions of Gerard.* Smart, sentimental, self-consciously tragic—even in memory Kerouac remains a distinct Lowell type.

And Lowell remains loyal to Jack. The Commemorative is a small plaza with eight polished granite columns inscribed with excerpts from his writings. Each fall, there's a small festival that honors Kerouac and carries the torch for his Zen hipster vision of the city. (See "Staying There.") If you've a mind to visit his grave, get directions from the Visitors Center to Edson Cemetery off Gorham Street. He's buried in the Sampas family plot (his last wife was Stella Sampas, sister of a childhood friend). The flat stone has a simple inscription:

> "Ti Jean"
> John L. Kerouac
> Mar. 12, 1922–Oct. 21, 1969
> –He Honored Life–

After this literary interlude (or in lieu of it, if you're not a Kerouac fan), you might want to see a few other sites in Lowell that flesh out the industrial and textile history.

If you have a technical frame of mind, make a point of visiting the **Suffolk Mills Turbine Exhibit,** which is a bit out of the way on Father Morrissette Boulevard; the easiest way to get there is on the free park trolley. The exhibit occupies two levels of the former Suffolk Manufacturing Company, a cotton cloth producer that was organized in 1832. The floor is cut away between two levels to reveal a functioning, nineteenth-century water turbine and to expose the pulleys, belting, and shafting that transferred the power to the textile machines on the floor above. The water turbine was another innovation of the Boston Associates' organizer Francis Cabot Lowell working in conjunction with his master mechanic Paul Moody. Earlier mills in America, such as Slater's Mill in Pawtucket, Rhode Island, had depended on spinning breast wheels that tapped only a fraction of the power of falling water. The turbine was far more efficient, capturing more power from a smaller water drop.

Two other attractions are located closer to the National Park Service Visitor Center.

The **American Textile Museum,** which relocated to Lowell in 1997, helps put Lowell into a broader perspective. The first thing that grabs your eye when you enter the refurbished mill building is a procession of spinning wheels at

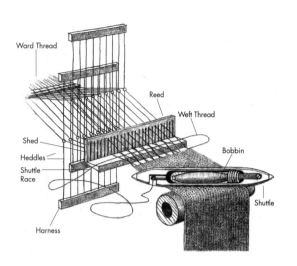

Ward Thread

Reed

Weft Thread

Shed

Heddles

Bobbin

Shuttle Race

Shuttle

Harness

Power loom with hand-operated shuttle

mezzanine height—a motif continued through the museum. (There are more than 300 on display.) This institution has a remarkable collection of artifacts, including 1,000 pre-industrial tools and more than 300 industrial machines. The chronologically arranged galleries follow cloth-making in America from the earliest hand spin-

ning and weaving to computer-controlled looms. There are also displays of old fabrics, bed covers, and antique clothing. The museum, located at 491 Dutton Street, is open Tuesday through Friday from 9:00 A.M. to 4:00 P.M. and on Saturday and Sunday from 10:00 A.M. to 4:00 P.M. It is closed on Thanksgiving, Christmas, and New Year's Day. Admisson is $5.00. Telephone: (978) 441–0400.

The **New England Quilt Museum** occupies the building that once housed the Lowell Institute for Savings, where many of the mill girls kept whatever they could set aside from their wages. The museum has a small but excellent permanent collection of both historic and contemporary quilts. In addition to exhibitions featuring the collection, the museum also mounts several exhibitions of contemporary quilts throughout the year. The museum shop is a good resource of books and other sewing and quilt-related items. Located at 18 Shattuck Street, the New England Quilt Museum is open all year Tuesday to Saturday from 10:00 A.M. to 4:00 P.M. From May through November it is also open on Sunday from noon to 4:00 P.M. Admission is $4.00. Telephone: (978) 452–4207.

Staying There

The Rustic Midlands

Sturbridge/Old Sturbridge Village, Massachusetts

Route 20 is Sturbridge's Main Street, and this strip is where you will find most lodging, dining, and shopping. In fact, most everything is clustered on the section of Route 20 near the entrance to Old Sturbridge Village, the living history museum that overwhelms the modern town. Route 131 also crosses Sturbridge; the town common sits on Route 131 about a half-mile south of the intersection of the two roads.

For more information on Sturbridge and the surrounding area, contact the Sturbridge Information Center, 380 Main Street, Sturbridge, MA 01566. Telephone: (508) 347-7594 or (800) 628-8379.

LODGING

Old Sturbridge Village Lodges and Oliver Wight House. Route 20 west. The Wight House was built around 1789 and, starting in the 1790s, served for many years as a tavern and roadside lodging. Now owned by OSV, it's part of a lodging complex right at the entrance to the village from Route 20. The ten rooms of the Wight House have comforts such as heat, lights, indoor plumbing, and good-quality colonial-style furniture that make the lodging a far cry from the public house it was in its early Federal days. The less expensive Village Lodges consist of forty-seven new motel-like units, stacked in compact two-story buildings. There's a single pool for the complex. Telephone: (508) 347-3327. Moderate.

The Publick House. This complex on the town common (Route 131, a half-mile south of the junction with Route 20) combines a few rooms in the historic inn (complete with slanting floors), a bed-and-breakfast cottage, and several motel units. The full-service facilities often attract bus tour groups. Telephone: (508) 347-3313. Inexpensive to moderate.

Quality Inn Colonial. Offering particularly good value, this exceptionally well-maintained single-level motel is on Route 20 east of the highway exits into Sturbridge. It sits back from the road and has two tennis courts on the premises. Telephone: (508) 347-3514. Inexpensive to moderate.

Sturbridge Country Inn. 530 Main Street. This 1840s farmhouse has been modernized with some romantic touches, including gas-log fireplaces and whirlpool baths in each of nine rooms. Telephone: (508) 347-5503. Moderate.

CAMPGROUNDS AND RV PARKS

Yogi Bear's Sturbridge Jellystone Park. There are 399 sites at this facility, which is the closest campground to OSV. Take exit 2 off I-84 and follow the signs. As the name suggests, the park offers a lot of activities—a pool, a waterslide, a lake for swimming, a petting zoo—that provide a nice change of pace from the more "grown-up" fun of OSV. Telephone: (508) 347-9570.

FOOD

La Petite France. 413 Main Street. Telephone: (508) 347-2730. Heavenly puff pastries, feathery croissants, and chewy baguettes head the choices at this French bakery.

Le Bearn. 12 Cedar Street. Telephone: (508) 347-2321. For travelers who would rather be in Burgundy than the New England Midlands, Le Bearn offers many of the classics of French country bistro cooking. Dinner. Expensive.

The Publick House. Town Common (Route 131 a half-mile south of the junction with Route 20). Telephone: (508) 347-3313. Three restaurants and a tavern as part of the lodging complex serve ultra-traditional American fare that seems to please the bus tours who stay here. Breakfast, lunch, and dinner. Moderate.

Thistle Inn. Country Village Complex, 420 Main Street. Telephone: (508) 347-5822. Perhaps a bit more in the Martha Stewart mode (in keeping with the householdy nature of the shops around it), the Thistle Inn offers an outstanding British (well, Scottish) style ploughman's lunch of cheese, chutney, relishes, and fresh breads at quite moderate prices. Lunch and dinner. Moderate.

Whistling Swan. 502 Main Street. Telephone (508) 347–2321.Once known as one of the better outposts of continental fare in central New England, Whistling Swan has kept up with the times and offers a menu that might be better called New American—fresh, light, and based on local ingredients. Dinner, Sunday brunch. Expensive. Upstairs from the Swan in the former hayloft of this circa 1855 barn are more casual surroundings of ***The Ugly Duckling.*** Dinner. Moderate.

FAIRS, FESTIVALS, AND EVENTS

Most holidays and changes of the seasons bring special events at Old Sturbridge Village. See "Sturbridge/Old Sturbridge Village."

Brimfield Outdoor Antiques and Collectibles Shows. Collectors from throughout New England—and many from New York and other points on the eastern seaboard—converge on the fields around rural Brimfield (eight miles west of Sturbridge on Route 20) three times a year to wheel and deal. Major shows take place in May, July, and September. Telephone: (413) 283–6149.

SHOPPING

Old Sturbridge Village Museum Shop. Old Sturbridge Village Road. Telephone: (508) 347–3362. In addition to "old-timey" items like rolling pins and bean pots, the Museum Shop has an extraordinarily good book selection on flower and vegetable gardening. It also sells a number of seeds of heirloom flowers and vegetables raised on the premises.

The Shaker Shop. 454 Main Street. Telephone: (508) 347–7564. A haven of refined good taste with its beautiful reproduction furniture, stencils, and decorating supplies, it's one of the few places we know that carries the modern versions of the old Shaker milk-based paints.

Showcase Antique Center. Junction of Route 20 and Old Sturbridge Village Road. Telephone: (508) 347–7190. In an area where there are many antiques dealers, this group shop stands out for its range of small and expensive collectibles.

Sturbridge Antique Shops. 200 Charlton Road (Route 20 east of intersections with I–90 and I–84). Telephone: (508) 347–2744. The seventy-five dealers at this group antiques and collectibles shop tend to be among the saner pricers in the region.

Rhode Island Spinners
Providence, Rhode Island

For more information on Providence and the surrounding area, visit the Providence-Warwick Convention and Visitors Bureau Information Center at Waterfront Park (The Pavilion, 2 American Express Way). The CVB's mailing address is 1 West Exchange Street, Providence, RI 02903. Telephone: (401) 751–1177 for the information booth; (401) 274–1636 or (800) 233–1636 for the offices.

LODGING

Days Hotel on the Harbor. 220 India Street. This six-story lodging is easy to reach from I–195, but you'll have to drive to most of the points of interest in Providence. Half of the 136 large and comfortable rooms overlook the harbor, although the interstate highway separates the hotel from the water. Telephone: (401) 272–5577. You can often get a better rate by calling the chain's reservation system, (800) 325–2525. Moderate.

C.C. Ledbetter Bed & Breakfast. 326 Benefit Street. Located in a 1790s house in the Benefit Street historic preservation district, this quirky B&B is a good bet for the artistically minded. Of the five rooms, one has a private bath and the other four share two baths. Narrow, old stairways are not for the unsteady and you should like dogs, as a pair of friendly spaniels have the run of the house. Guests often have connections with nearby Brown University and the Rhode Island School of Design, making for some lively conversations at the morning breakfast table. Telephone: (401) 351–4699. Moderate with breakfast.

Old Court Bed & Breakfast. 144 Benefit Street. Old Court offers yet another opportunity to stay on Benefit Street, this time in an 1863 Italianate home with ten rooms decorated in a variety of styles from rococo to Victorian. Telephone: (401) 751–2002. Moderate with breakfast.

Providence Biltmore Hotel. Kennedy Plaza. This Art Deco hotel was built in 1922 and underwent three years of renovations that were completed in 1997, returning to its status as the grande dame of Providence hotels. The lobby will remind you that once upon a time America built hotels that seemed spacious, glamorous, and romantic. The Kennedy Plaza site is a good downtown location at the central basin between College Hill and Federal Hill and adjacent to Waterplace Park. Telephone: (401) 421–0700 or (800) 294–7709. Moderate.

State House Inn. 43 Jewett Street. Near the State House and a bit removed from downtown, the State House offers good parking and some of the ten rooms have canopy beds or fireplaces. There's a substantial breakfast, and good in-room amenities that you don't always find in a B&B such as cable TV and hair dryers. Guests have access to a fax and copy machine, so a certain percentage of the guests tend to be businesspeople. Telephone: (401) 351–6111. Moderate with breakfast.

FOOD

Al Forno and Provincia. 577 South Main Street. Telephone: (401) 273–9760. Proprietors Johanne Killeen and George Germon have become celebrities since giving up visual art for culinary art. They introduced grilled pizza to Providence and spread it throughout New England. Patricia Wells, cookbook author and restaurant columnist for the *International Herald Tribune,* picks Al Forno as the best casual restaurant in the world. Having established casual Italian fare, Killeen and Germon moved on to do the same for Provençal cuisine in 1998, when they established a second restaurant on the premises. Dinner. Expensive.

Leon's on the West Side. 166 Broadway. Telephone: (401) 273–1055. Specializing in Mediterranean cuisine and known for their pasta, Leon's often wins "best brunch" in the annual *Rhode Island Monthly* polls. Served Saturday and Sunday, brunch includes French toast, pancakes, and omelets in a casual, if fairly hip atmosphere. At dinner, the best bets are pastas and grilled specials. Dinner, weekend brunch. Moderate.

Pot au Feu. 44 Custom House Street. Telephone: (401) 273–8953. This French outpost in a largely Italian/New American scene has been innovating for more than two decades. The stone-walled bistro in the downstairs is casual—offering omelets, soups, salads, and crepes, as well as the full dinner menu. The upstairs salon is more formal, dressier, and pricier. Dinner. Moderate to expensive.

Spike's Junkyard Dogs. 273A Thayer Street. Telephone: (401) 454–1459. These all-natural grilled hot dogs, typically served with a red pepper and onion relish and a side of "Poodle Fries," were voted best hot dog in Rhode Island by readers of *Rhode Island Monthly.* If you're hungry late at night, they're open until 2:00 A.M. on Wednesday and Thursday, until 3:00 A.M. on weekends. Lunch and dinner. Inexpensive.

Gourmets should not miss Providence's Italian food. Plan to spend part of a day wandering **Atwells Avenue** and adjacent streets on the west of town on **Federal Hill.** The attractions are principally culinary in Providence's Little Italy. De Pasquale Square, a little pocket plaza, is a good bet for sitting and watching the passersby. Besides, it's only steps to Pastiche Bakery cafe and Tony's Colonial Food Store.

Christopher's on the Hill. 245 Atwells Avenue. Telephone: (401) 274–4232. Christopher Turner is a Johnson & Wales grad and cooked in some of Providence's best-known kitchens before setting off on his own in this bright, elegant dining room that makes a welcome contrast to more casual East Side eateries. The well-rounded French/ Italian menu features pastas and wood grilled meats. Dinner. Expensive.

L'Epicureo. 238 Atwells Avenue. Telephone: (401) 454–8430. The owners belong to one of

Providence's most established families of butchers, so you'd expect the wood-grilled meats to be great and you'd be right. But so are the fish, and the house signature dish is actually clam and angel hair pasta with fresh tomato and garlic olive oil. Dinner. Moderate.

Pastiche. 92 Spruce Street. Telephone: (401) 861–5190. This great dessert spot on Federal Hill is just around the corner from the DePasquale Plaza. Chocoholics swear by the *torta di cioccolata*, a bittersweet chocolate torte with a hint of almond butter, though it's hard to pass up either the chocolate layer cake filled with chocolate ganache and covered with chocolate buttercream or the lemon mousse cake, which consists of layers of chiffon sponge and lemon mousse, all covered with lemon butter cream.

OTHER ATTRACTIONS

AS220. This alternative arts performance studio and living space holds poetry readings, stages performances, and mounts gallery exhibits. 115 Empire Street. Telephone: (401) 831–9327.

Johnson & Wales University Culinary Archives and Museum. Perhaps the most complete collection of gastronomy in the world, this small museum has been called the "Smithsonian Institution of the food service industry." The collection of more than 400,000 artifacts contains cooking and dining implements from 3,000 B.C. to present, including a wide variety of hotel and restaurant silver. Culinary students give the guided tours. Adults $3.00. Open Monday through Friday from 9:00 A.M. to 5:00 P.M., Saturday 10:00 A.M. to 5:00 P.M. 315 Harborside Boulevard. (401) 598–2805.

Providence Bruins. This American Hockey League team is the top development affiliate of the Boston Bruins. The Bruins play at the Providence Civic Center. Ticket information telephone: (401) 273–5000.

Roger Williams Park Zoo. The zoo, which has been undergoing major expansion and refurbishment throughout the 1990s, is located within the 430 green Victorian acres of Roger Williams Park. (The park also has beautiful for-

mal gardens, a pond with paddle boats, a planetarium, and a carousel.) The zoo has the African plains exhibit, polar bear and penguin exhibits, and tropical rain forest area found at most good, modernized zoos. We're fond of one of the more inventive exhibits, the Marco Polo Trail. This two and one-half-acre biopark trail traces Polo's sojourn through Asia, beginning with a Venice Plaza re-creation, complete with a watery canal and a full-sized reproduction of a thirteenth-century trading vessel. You encounter animals native to areas Polo visited—camels, the Himalayan black bears believed to have inspired the Tibetan legend of the abominable snowman, and the beautiful snow leopards. At this writing the trail stops short of Polo's journey into China, though zoo officials hope to complete the trail once sufficient funds are raised. Adults $5.00. Open April through October Sunday through Thursday from 9:00 A.M. to 5:00 P.M., Friday and Saturday from 9:00 A.M. to 6:00 P.M. From November through March the zoo closes daily at 4:00 P.M. 1000 Elmwood Avenue. Telephone: (401) 785–3510.

Trinity Repertory Theatre. Trinity Rep is one of America's leading regional live theater companies, with a history of developing new American plays. Performances take place on the two stages of the former Majestic Movie House in the heart of downtown Providence. Call for schedule. 201 Washington Street. Telephone: (401) 351–4242.

ACTIVITIES

Ferry. Passenger ferry (no vehicles) operates from India Street Wharf to Newport and on to Block Island from late June through Labor Day. Newport same-day round trip $5.90, Block Island same-day round trip $10.65. Call Interstate Navigation Company for schedule and reservations. Telephone: (401) 783–4613.

TOURS

Gray Line. Daily sightseeing tours of historic Providence and out to Newport, Blackstone Valley, or Foxwoods Casino are offered mid-April through mid-October. Telephone: (401) 658–3400.

Historic walking tours. From June into October,

Providence Preservation Society gives regular tours of historic areas of Providence. Adults $10. Call for schedule. Telephone: (401) 831–7440.

Lovecraft Lurk-Ins. Aficionados of the macabre writings of H. P. Lovecraft hold occasional tours of spots featured in his creepy stories. Telephone: (401) 943–2176.

FAIRS, FESTIVALS, AND EVENTS

Festival of Historic Houses. Home and garden tour sponsored by the Providence Preservation Society during the second weekend of June highlights the city's amazing concentration of original Colonial homes on and near Benefit Street. Friday night is a candlelight tour. Saturday focuses on houses and gardens. Sunday features tour of a neighborhood in process of revitalization. Each tour takes in eight to ten houses. Adults $20 per tour; discounts for more than one tour. Telephone: (401) 831–7440.

First Night Providence. Borrowing from Boston, Providence celebrates an alcohol-free New Year's Eve with ice sculptures, live performances, and fireworks.

Rhode Island Spring Flower and Garden Show. The flower show is held the third weekend in February at the Rhode Island Convention Center. Telephone: (800) 766–1670.

Waterfront Festival. This early September downtown festival celebrates Providence's revived waterfront parks with five entertainment stages, harbor tours, sailboat and rowing rides and races, and arts and crafts. Telephone: (401) 785–9450.

SHOPPING

The Arcade. Dating from 1828, the Greek Revival-style Arcade on Westminster and Weybosset Streets was the heart of the mart in downtown Providence in the nineteenth century. It was updated with specialty shops and small restaurants in the 1970s. As the nation's oldest indoor marketplace, it is recognized as a National Historic Landmark. The Arcade predated the modern shopping mall by more than a century.

ArTrolley. Thanks to RISD and relatively rational rents, Providence has an unusually large number of working artists. The free ArTrolley makes twelve stops near art galleries on the third Thursday of each month from 5:00 to 9:00 P.M. Galleries on the tour that represent large numbers of local artists are Gallery Flux at 260 Weybosset Street; telephone: (401) 274–9120; and Bert Gallery at 540 South Water Street; telephone: (401) 751–2628.

Pawtucket, Rhode Island

OTHER ATTRACTIONS

Pawtucket Red Sox Baseball. From April through August (and sometimes into September), this AAA International League affiliate of the Boston Red Sox plays at McCoy Stadium, 1 Columbus Avenue. Telephone: (401) 724–7300.

Machine-Age Massachusetts
Worcester, Massachusetts

For more information on Worcester and the surrounding area, contact the Worcester Area Chamber of Commerce. Mailing address: 33 Waldo Street, Worcester, MA 01608. Telephone: (508) 753–2924.

LODGING

Beechwood Inn. 363 Plantation Street. This modern brick building contains fifty-eight rather large rooms, four of which have gas fireplaces for a $20 supplement. Refrigerators and exercise bikes are available for a small fee. Telephone: (508) 754–5789 or (800) 344–2589. Moderate.

Crowne Plaza Worcester. 10 Lincoln Square. What this massive convention hotel (243 rooms) lacks in character it makes up for with such amenities as coffee-makers in all the rooms, fitness center, and indoor and outdoor pools. Telephone: (508) 791–1600. Moderate.

FOOD

El Morocco. 100 Wall Street (off Route 122S). Telephone: (508) 756–7117. Worcester residents have flocked to El Morocco since the Aboody family opened it in 1945. The menu is Lebanese and the food comes with a scenic overview of the city. Famous clients include Al Pacino and Dustin Hoffman. The lamb chop is so large that you should ask to have it cut in half before it's served. Lunch, dinner, Sunday brunch. Moderate.

Worcester used to be the center of the diner-construction industry. About a dozen diners are still in operation, concentrated on the east and north sides of the city center on Routes 9, 122, and 12.

Boulevard Diner. 155 Shrewsbury Street (Route 9). Telephone: (508) 791–4535. With a neon clock on the roof, this well-maintained diner is considered by diner aficionados to be one of the most photogenic in existence. Breakfast, lunch, and dinner. Inexpensive.

Miss Worcester Diner. 300 Southbridge Street (Route 146). Telephone: (508) 752–4348. This barrel roof diner is in very good condition, but the vintage booths have been replaced with nondescript contemporary booths. Breakfast, lunch, and dinner. Inexpensive.

Parkway Diner. 148 Shrewsbury Street (Route 9). Telephone: (508) 753–9968. Although the exterior has, sadly, been remodeled, the interior is in original shape. This diner features Italian specialties and has been run by the same family since the 1930s. Lunch and dinner. Inexpensive.

Lowell, Massachusetts

For more information on Lowell and surrounding areas, contact the Greater Merrimack Valley Convention & Visitors Bureau, 22 Shattuck Street, Lowell, MA 01852. Telephone: (978) 459–6150 or (800) 443–3332.

LODGING

Courtyard by Marriott. 37 Industrial Avenue East, off exit 3 of the Lowell Connector. This three-story, 120-room budget motel is favored by junior executives during the week, by families on weekends. A little out of the way, it does have a coffee shop. Telephone: (978) 458–7575 or (800) 321–2211. Moderate.

Sheraton Inn Riverfront. 50 Warren Street. Conveniently located right in the Lowell National Historic Park, this nine-story, 259-room hotel is popular with bus groups and high-tech conventions. The marble-floored lobby filled with comfy couches and overstuffed chairs looks out on the Pawtucket Canal. Workout opportunities include indoor and outdoor pools, Jacuzzi, sauna, and a full fitness center. Telephone: (978) 452–1200. Moderate to expensive.

Stonehedge Inn. 160 Pawtucket Boulevard, Tyngsboro. If you'd like to use the Lowell area as a base and want to pamper yourself, try this horse country setting along the Merrimack River a few miles outside of Lowell, about a mile off Route 3 in Tyngsboro. The resort is modeled after small European luxury hotels favored by its owner, a local real estate developer. The hotel portion contains thirty suites, the least of which are merely extremely nice double rooms. The pool and spa are in their own glass-enclosed building, and the thirty-three-acre property overlooks white-fenced pastures where thoroughbred horses graze. Telephone: (978) 649–4400 or (800) 648–7070. Expensive to very expensive.

FOOD

Four Sisters Owl Diner. 244 Appleton Street. Telephone: (978) 453–8321. This semi-streamliner-style diner is a Lowell institution that used to serve the mill workers. It still offers one of the best breakfasts in the Northeast. Breakfast and lunch.

La Boniche. 143 Merrimack Street. Telephone: (978) 458–9473. This truly French restaurant is in the 1892 Bon Marché Building, formerly Lowell's grand department store, built in the ornate Beaux Arts style with green trim on yellow brick, leaded glass, and faux columns. If you enter from the UMass/Lowell Barnes & Noble bookstore you'll come to the take-out counter with a few tables. A luxurious bar area leads into the main dining room, where yellow textured walls, white linens, and dark woodwork help create the European bistro atmosphere. Lunch and dinner. Moderate to expensive.

Old Worthen House. 141 Worthen Street. Telephone: (978) 459–0300. Lowell's oldest tavern and restaurant occupies an 1830s building with original woodwork and pressed tin ceiling. The fare is modest pub grub, but all meals are well under $10. Local tradition holds that Jack Kerouac carved his name into one of the tables here, but we've yet to find it. Lunch and dinner. Inexpensive.

Silks. At the Stonehedge Inn (see Lodging). The French menu with English translations suggests the level of impressive continental fare that Silks aspires to—and reaches. The wine list is one of New England's best, with 600 active selections. Unlike some places with long lists, Silks actually stocks all 600 in their own cellars—along with about 10,000 other bottles aging until they've reached their peak. The food will put a significant dent in your wallet, but the wine prices are very low for the quality. To get better wine for the money, you'd have to eat at home. Expensive to very expensive.

Southeast Asian Restaurant. 343 Market Street. Telephone: (978) 452–3182. The first Southeast Asian restaurant in Lowell and one of the most popular, this spot was opened in 1985 by Joseph Antonaccio and his Laotian-born wife, Chanthip Antonaccio. They feature the open-air market cuisines of Thailand, Laos, Cambodia, Vietnam, and Burma, making for a menu that borders on overwhelming. One good choice is the weekday luncheon buffet for $5.95, which offers about fifteen items. For groups of four or more at dinner, there are three different "mini-banquets" at $14.95 per person. Moderate.

OTHER ATTRACTIONS

Lowell Lock Monsters. Lowell's large French Canadian population considers hockey its "national" sport, and the Monsters enjoy fervent local support. This American Hockey League team plays in the Paul E. Tsongas Arena, which opened in January 1998. Telephone: (978) 458–PUCK (7825).

Lowell Spinners. This New York-Penn League affiliate of the Boston Red Sox baseball team plays at the new (1998) Edward LeLacheur Park on the banks of the Merrimack River. Lowell has had many different minor league baseball teams over the years, and whenever one goes bust, another moves in. Telephone: (978) 459–1702.

Merrimack Repertory Theatre. A fine example of the regional theater movement, Merrimack Rep performs contemporary dramas and popular musicals in its own theater in Memorial Auditorium, a former exhibition hall in the center of town at 50 East Merrimack Street. Telephone: (978) 454–3926.

TOURS

Downtown Tour. A 30–minute tour with a National Park ranger covers downtown Lowell, beginning at the Visitor Center and ending at the Boott Cotton Mills Museum. Tour themes vary and no reservations are required. Call for schedule. Telephone: (978) 970–5000; TDD: (978) 972–5002.

Canal Tours. During the spring, summer, and fall, National Park rangers conduct a number of boat tours on Lowell's canals. During the school year they often focus on environmental issues or conservation, while summer tours are more often oriented to history. Among the most interesting and most frequent is "Harnessing the Merrimack," which travels the Pawtucket Canal through Guard Locks and explores the Pawtucket Gatehouse to see how the river was diverted and controlled to power Lowell's mills. All tours are $4.00 for adults and depart from the National Park Visitor Center at 67 Kirk Street. Call for schedule. Telephone: (978) 970–5000; TDD: (978) 972–5002.

Suffolk Mill Waterpower Tour. This 90-minute tour of the Suffolk Mill Turbine Exhibit follows the transmission of waterpower from the Northern Canal through an operating nineteenth-century turbine to an operating power loom. The free tour leaves from the National Park Visitor Center at 67 Kirk Street. Call for schedule. Telephone: (978) 970–5000; TDD: (978) 972–5002.

FAIRS, FESTIVALS, AND EVENTS

Bread and Roses Labor Day Festival. This multi-ethnic labor festival commemorates the workers who participated in the 1912 strike that marked the highwater mark of the populist labor movement dominated by the International Workers of the World. In Lawrence, a twenty-minute drive away. Telephone: (508) 682–1863.

Lowell Celebrates Kerouac. In early October, Lowell-based fans of Jack Kerouac throw the kind of civic party that would have pleased Ti-Jean—complete with poetry readings, music, tours of sites featured in his books, and other events. Even some of the surviving hipsters from his New York-San Francisco days show up to help pay tribute. Telephone: (978) 458–1721.

Lowell Folk Festival. Held the last full weekend of July, the Lowell Folk Festival has become a major stop on the national tours and the largest free folk festival in the United States. Traditional musicians range from bluegrass to jazz, and all of the city's many ethnic cultures are celebrated by dancers, storytellers, craft demonstrations, ethnic food vendors, and parades. Telephone: (978) 970–5000

SHOPPING

American Textile History Museum Gift Shop. 491 Dutton Street. Telephone: (978) 441–0400. Large gift shop features quilts, weaving, and other arts and crafts items from contemporary craftspeople and artists. We particularly like Iro Design's hand-painted silk scarves and canvas totebags made from the paint-saturated dropcloths.

New England Quilt Museum Gift Shop. 18 Shattuck Street. Telephone: (978) 452–4207. Comprehensive selection of historic, art, and how-to books about quilting and many other sewing and quilt-related items.

8 · The Connecticut River Valley

Introduction

The Connecticut River can't hold a candle to continent-spanning waterways like the Missouri or Mississippi—it doesn't even have its own song. (Try rhyming "Connecticut.") Yet from the time that human beings began to inhabit New England—around 12,000 years ago—the river has been a principal transportation route and, for the last half millennium, its valley has produced the region's richest crops.

The Connecticut ranges across New England from north to south, stretching all the way from the subarctic boglands of northern New Hampshire southward to Long Island Sound. It divides New Hampshire from Vermont and bisects Massachusetts and Connecticut. In the course of 406 miles, the Connecticut River drains a total of 11,260 square miles—about a third each of New Hampshire, Massachusetts, and Connecticut, and about 40 percent of Vermont's land mass.

Closed in on the west by mountains and the east by a high plateau, the Connecticut River Valley has evolved its own culture, related to but distinct from the rest of New England. Until the 1600s, the valley was home to several Algonquian tribes who grew corn, squash, and beans in the valley bottomlands. Early European settlers came waving Dutch, English, and French flags. Through the nineteenth and twentieth centuries, the Connecticut River Valley attracted successive waves of immigrants from central Europe and Asia, resulting in one of the most ethnically and culturally diverse rural regions in the Northeast.

Look to the "South Coast" chapter for coverage of the Connecticut River Valley south of Wethersfield, Connecticut. That part of the river is far more closely allied geologically, culturally, and economically with the coastal towns and cities than with the rest of the Connecticut. This chapter deals with the river's heart—the great cultural and industrial centers of Hartford and Springfield, the fabulous soils of the Pioneer Valley, and the quirky but beautiful upper river towns of Vermont and New Hampshire. It follows the riverside roads, mostly Route 5, as it presses south to north, paralleling the direction of settlement.

Part of the Connecticut River Valley's story is a poignant one, for the region served as the frontier of Anglo-European settlement for more than a century. The English farmers who settled here were drawn by the land's fecundity but terrified by their isolation on a hostile frontier. Some of the most tragic encounters between Europeans and Native Americans were played out along the valley.

Unlike the coastal regions, the Connecticut did not appear on the maps drawn by early European explorers such as Giovanni da Verrazano, who completely missed the river when he sailed past in 1508. Dutch explorers finally discovered the mouth of the Connecticut in 1614, although they too nearly missed it because the mouth was blocked by a large sand bar that made navigation difficult. But once the river was on the map and it was clear that the Connecticut penetrated deep into the inland wilderness, European settlement proceeded upriver quickly, with the Dutch from Manhattan and the English from Plymouth and Massachusetts Bay squabbling over which group had the rights to develop fur trade on the river. All three groups set up fortified trading posts, but the English knew that the only way to secure the land was to settle on it.

In 1634 Englishmen from Dorchester, Cambridge, and Watertown in the Massachusetts Bay Colony planted a community at Wethersfield—and made the land their own by planting the first European-sown crops in the

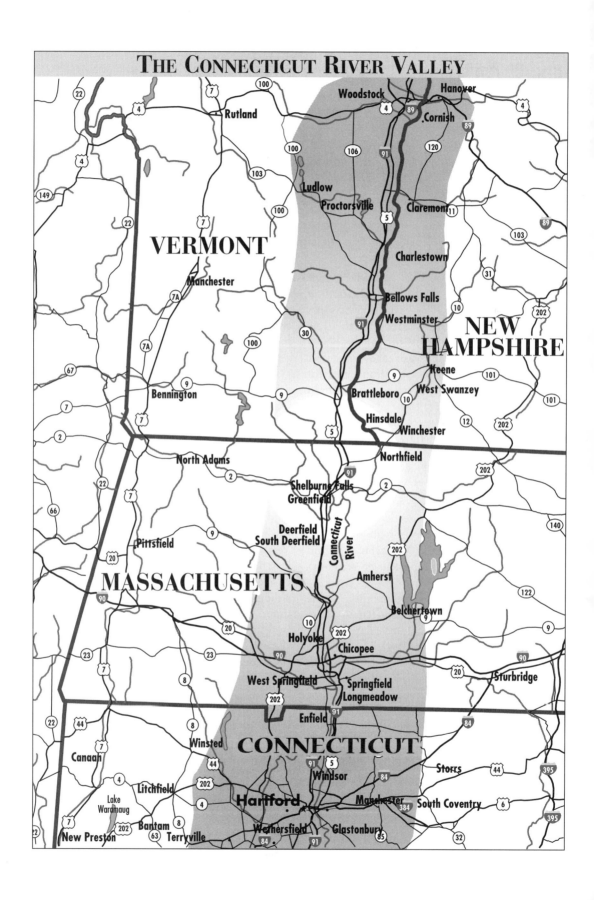

THE CONNECTICUT RIVER VALLEY

valley. Once the dam of Native resistance was breached, English settlers flooded into the valley. America's first "westward expansion" was underway.

This particular juncture of the Connecticut River was a key location. Until 1692, the river made a bend, creating a deep harbor that would be a key shipping transfer point between the coast and the communities that would be established inland and upriver. Unknown to the colonists, they had selected an area that had deep geological significance as well. Wethersfield was the southern reach of the vast glacial lake that filled the Connecticut River Valley until it breached a dam of glacial debris just south at Rocky Hill and emptied out in a torrential flood. And even earlier, the area had been the fertile swampy feeding grounds for dinosaurs of the early Jurassic Period. In several senses, the history of the Connecticut River Valley begins here.

History:
New England's
First Peoples

There's a common misperception that the Native peoples of New England are extinct, although even a cursory glance at census figures reveals that more than 50,000 New Englanders identify as members of one of the historical tribes. But even with a gradual population rebound in the twentieth century, Native culture plays only a small role in contemporary New England identity. For the most part, the original peoples of the area have assimilated almost entirely into mainstream American culture and traditional crafts and ceremonial practices are revivals based on historical records. Memories of the first inhabitants of the region persist most strongly in place names, including the Commonwealth of Massachusetts and the State of Connecticut. And though only the Mohawk Trail of western Massachusetts has a name that reveals its origin, many of the major roads of New England actually follow well-established trade routes. Route 7, which runs from southwestern Connecticut to Lake

Champlain, is one example. Route 20 between Boston and Albany is another. (The Massachusetts Turnpike and New York Thruway later followed Route 20 through the same mountain passes and river fords.)

At the time of European contact, the 100,000 to 150,000 inhabitants of New England were almost entirely of Algonquian stock. The Algonquian peoples represent one of the major waves of population of North America, possibly one of the earliest migrations from Asia over the Bering Straits. Algonquians are distributed throughout the eastern United States and Canada and, in the case of the Cree, throughout the northernmost forests and tundra of North America east of the Rocky Mountains to Labrador.

The New England peoples spoke different variants of a common language, a linguistic situation not unlike medieval western Europe, where local variants of Latin gradually evolved into the Romance languages. Their religious and ceremonial practices were remarkably similar, with some variations in the southern New England tribes attributable to their extensive trade links with peoples of the Ohio River Valley.

Archaeologists suspect that New England was settled from two directions by two branches of Algonquians. One group appears to have come from Nova Scotia and New Brunswick northeast of New England to inhabit Maine, New Hampshire, and the upper reaches of the Connecticut River Valley. The other, perhaps larger, migration came from the Great Lakes and Ohio River Valley southwest of New England and moved up the coast and river valleys to populate the areas of western Vermont, Massachusetts, Connecticut, and Rhode Island.

This view of the peopling of New England differs from assumptions by earlier archaeologists that a mysterious hunter-gatherer culture sometimes called the Red Paint People were the first inhabitants of New England after the glaciers receded and that the Algonquians had displaced them in relatively recent times. Scientists now believe that the Algonquians are the direct descendants of the first New Englanders who entered the region about 12,000 years ago, following the game herds into a landscape where the ice sheet was just beginning to retreat.

Indeed, the discovery in June 1998 of an encampment near Eliot, Maine, sheds some interesting light on these first human inhabitants of New England. The camp—uncovered while laying a natural gas pipeline—dates from 12,000 to 13,000 years B.P. (Before Present). Among the items found here were scrapers fashioned from red flint identified as originating near Munsungan Lake in what is now northern Maine—roughly 150 miles away across what would have been tundra at the time. This is consistent with a number of other archaeological finds that show Munsungan Lake and other northern Maine flints distributed throughout early sites in New England. This "flint mine" was probably surrounded by glaciers, suggesting that peoples who hunted on the ice might have roamed New England even when it was still glaciated.

Few of the very early sites have survived because the first peoples of New England lived mainly on the ice-free coastal plain that was submerged when the glaciers melted and the seas rose. We do know that, like their counterparts in Europe and Asia, they tended to follow the migrations of large food animals—mastodon and woolly mammoths, giant beaver, caribou, and moose.

About 10,000 years ago the massive Ice Age mammals began to die off—perhaps from overhunting—and the Native peoples switched to hunting smaller, non-migratory animals such as deer, as well as migratory waterfowl, fresh and saltwater fish, and marine mammals. As they became less migratory, they were able to set up semi-permanent seasonal encampments. By 6,000 years ago, there is evidence of rudimentary pottery in New England, suggesting that New Englanders were also processing nuts and seeds as food stores.

New England peoples always traded with other cultures, especially to their southwest, and through this trade it appears that corn was introduced to New England via the Ohio Valley around A.D. 1000. This signaled a major change in cultural patterns, as a dependable agricultural food source allowed them to establish permanent settlements and forced them to defend agricultural land. Over the next four centuries, villages began to spring up all over what is now Connecticut, Massachusetts, Rhode Island, and the Atlantic coast up as far as Casco Bay. These were places where flint corn would grow to maturity—essentially the area modern agronomists identify as zones five and six.

The coastal tribes were the most settled of New England peoples, as they had the advantages of both good agricultural land and the bounty of the sea to sustain them throughout the year. Inland tribes still depended more on hunting and maintained seasonal villages. The northernmost tribes were perhaps the most migrant of all, as they could grow squash and beans in small gardens at their summer camps but depended on preserved meat and fish to endure the winters.

Settlement brought its own problems. Tribes began to squabble over territory and, despite the common culture, small-scale warfare became endemic. Only the invasion of the Iroquois peoples into the Hudson Valley around A.D. 1400 galvanized the Algonquian tribes to organize into loose confederations to fend off their common enemies. Population grew swiftly during this period, especially in southern New England, as village life became established as the norm.

Although there had been sporadic contact between Europe and North America for at least 500 years, Europeans began to visit New England in significant numbers around 1500, making first contact with the northern tribes. Most of the initial visitors were fishermen, who established some seasonal shoreline camps to process fish and butcher whales. Europeans began to come in larger numbers a century later, seeking to trade manufactured goods for furs. Much of the original contact between the Native tribes and the Dutch, English, and French involved the fur trade.

At this point—around 1600—fewer than a dozen tribal confederations dominated the New England landscape, and each of these confederations was made up of several smaller tribal units. In the north were the **Abenaki** in Maine, the **Penacook** in much of New Hampshire, and

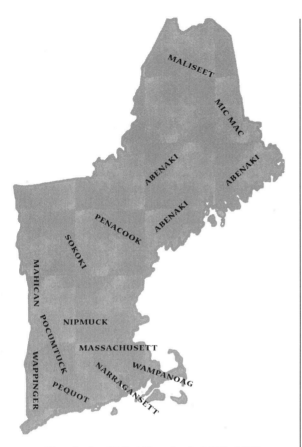

New England Tribal Homelands 1600–1750

the **Sokoki** along the upper reaches of the
Connecticut River Valley. The Housatonic
River Valley and the Lower Champlain Valley
(western Vermont south to the Connecticut
border) was the territory of the **Mahican.** The
Pocumtuck dominated the main portions of
the Connecticut River Valley in Massachusetts,
while the **Nipmuck** peopled the central high-
lands. The **Massachusett** were dominant in
eastern Massachusetts around Boston. The
Wampanoag held sway over much of
Narragansett Bay, Cape Cod, and the islands of
Nantucket, Martha's Vineyard, and the
Elizabeth Islands. Connecticut and Rhode
Island were dominated by the **Wappinger** on
the eastern side of the Hudson River Valley, the
Pequot everywhere east of the Litchfield Hills,
and the **Narragansett** throughout Rhode
Island. Displaced in the territorial battles
between the French and English, bands of

Maliseet and **Micmac** also inhabited parts of
Maine by the middle of the eighteenth century.
The rise of the fur trade tended both to increase
tribal warfare and to strengthen the larger confederations as tribes enlisted each other's aid
against their enemies.

In early decades of the seventeenth century,
the English also began to establish agriculture-
based settlements in New England, a development that brought European and Native cultures into much closer and more prolonged
contact. The Natives were suddenly exposed to
diseases for which they had no immunity; the
results were devastating. Smallpox, the common
cold, typhus—they all took their toll. When the
Pilgrims set down in Plymouth in 1620, they
greeted a people who had been decimated three
years earlier by an epidemic.

Perhaps one of the most poignant cases is
the man known as Squanto. He was one of several Nauset and Pawtuxet men kidnapped along
the shores of Massachusetts Bay by English
adventurers in 1614 and sold into slavery in
Spain. Squanto escaped to England, where he
learned English and explained his plight, and
was repatriated by an English ship in 1619.
When he returned, all of his Pawtuxet tribe had
died of European diseases. When the Pilgrims
arrived a year later, Squanto introduced them to
Massasoit, sachem (or leader) of the
Wampanoag people who had moved into the
abandoned area.

Our popular version of the Pilgrim
Thanksgiving, with Englishmen and
Wampanoags sitting down to feast together, is
obviously idealized, but relations between
Natives and Europeans were relatively civil for
the first few decades—especially since the
Natives outnumbered the immigrants, even
after the epidemics. But it was only a matter of
time before frictions between the original settlers and the European immigrants came to a
head. The first outright warfare occurred over
the richest farmland in New England in a campaign that the victors called the Pequot War.

The Pequots were a strong tribe, and they
held most of what is now Connecticut from
west of the Connecticut River east to the land
of the Narragansetts. Many smaller tribes also

lived in this territory, and the Pequots forced most of them to pay tribute. When English settlers began planting crops on the Connecticut River at Enfield, Hartford, and Wethersfield, the Pequots began to attack outlying farms.

In 1637, the English men of these settlements banded together, declared war on the Pequots and enlisted the aid of the Connecticut Mohegans, who made common cause on the principle that their enemy's enemy was their friend. With the superior force of cannon and musket, the English drove the main Pequot forces to a palisaded village at the site now known as Mystic, Connecticut. The English set the fort on fire, slaughtered those who fled, and sold the few survivors into slavery in Barbados. Many other Pequots who were not inside the fort fled north, where they were absorbed into other tribes. Those who remained were confined to a small reservation as English wards. The Pequot War reached a satisfactory closure for the Connecticut River colonists, with disastrous results for the tribe they had quashed. It was a harbinger of fiercer conflicts to come.

Ironically large-scale confrontation in Massachusetts and Rhode Island—where English and Native were in closest proximity—was avoided for several decades, in part because epidemics destroyed entire villages and left fresh land for the English to settle. John Eliot, "Apostle to the Indians," sought with some success to convert the tribes neighboring the Massachusetts Bay Colony, blunting calls by some Boston and Salem clerics to make war on the heathen. Several "Praying Towns" were established near Boston and Eliot had the Bible translated into the Massachusett dialect of Algonquian. Farther south, the Narragansetts continued to inhabit marshes and swamps that the English did not covet, thereby escaping the general epidemics and growing into the strongest nation in New England. They had their hands full, however, waging war with the Wampanoags over the islands of Narragansett Bay.

Englishman Roger Williams arrived in what would become Rhode Island in 1636, one step ahead of the Massachusetts Bay Colony authorities who wished to imprison him for suggesting, among other things, that the colonists should buy their lands from the Natives. Williams served as a go-between, helping the Narragansetts and Wampanoags make peace. In return, he secured title to large portions of land from Canonicus, sachem of the Narragansetts. (A sachem was the political leader of large tribal units or confederations. As leaders of the individual communities, sagamores were subject to the sachems.)

But by the time that Wampanoag sachem Massasoit died in 1662, colonists' attitudes toward the Natives had begun to shift. Immigration from England required more and more land, and Puritan clerics preached that God-fearing Englishmen had more right to the land than godless heathens. Frontier skirmishes became increasingly common—Natives attacking outlying farms, Englishmen raiding Native villages.

The regionwide struggle for dominance exploded in 1675 in a conflict that came to be known as King Philip's War. No distant European monarch, "King Philip" was the English name adopted by Metacom, sachem of the Wampanoags and son of Massasoit, the leader who had greeted the Pilgrims. More than three centuries later, the events that precipitated the war remain shrouded in controversy. Philip's brother, Wamsutta, had been killed under suspicious circumstances. Chroniclers of the time suggest that Philip was preparing to make war against the English and that the Massachusetts Bay Colony beat him to the punch before he could assemble his troops. Other sources suggest that the rumors of war were a pretext to exterminate the Natives.

Fighting broke out in June 1675 when Philip attacked Swansea in Massachusetts Bay Colony. The war that ensued was the most brutal and catastrophic conflict ever fought on New England soil. Whatever strategic aims the English or Philip had at the outset devolved into a genocidal struggle on both sides. Philip sought to drive the English from the continent. His troops ravaged the inland settlements and the English returned the favor. All-out war did not stop with simply killing troops or even the complete massacre of communities. In a blood frenzy, both sides took to mutilating bodies and posting heads on posts along the trails.

The body count was horrific—up to half the population killed on both sides. Entire English and Native communities were wiped out. Christianized Natives suffered perhaps the worst, as the English confined them to starve on the Boston harbor islands. War raged for two years, spreading throughout New England as English and Native neighbors turned on each other. Communities that had coexisted in relative harmony fell to slaughtering each other.

When Quaiapen, leader of the Narragansetts, was killed in battle, and Philip was hunted down in a swamp, shot, and beheaded, the tide turned against the leaderless Natives, winding down in the fall of 1676. Most Native villages were destroyed, and survivors from southern New England fled north to join tribes in Maine and Quebec. Many of the survivors who stayed in southern New England were sold into slavery in the Caribbean. The English effectively had New England to themselves.

Beginning as early as 1690, however, the surviving tribes were pulled into the so-called "French and Indian War" that kept North America in conflict until 1763. The Algonquian peoples of New England were traditional enemies of the Iroquois in New York, and when the Iroquois made strong political alliances with England, the colonial governments presumed all enemies of the Iroquois were therefore allied with the French. It was never that simple, of course, but many of the surviving New England peoples found themselves heading north to French Canada for safety. Those who wished to ally with the English had no choice but assimilation into English culture.

There were exceptions to this general pattern. The Passamaquoddy and Penobscot peoples of Maine managed to stay out of the French and Indian War as much as they could, sometimes serving as scouts and guides, and when the American Revolution took place, they fought side by side with the colonists against the British. The Micmacs of Maine and the maritime provinces of Canada were, in fact, the first sovereign people to recognize the new country. (The Iroquois weren't far behind.)

Settlements reached with state and federal governments in the 1960s and 1970s have given some new life to the remaining Native populations, especially those who have managed to keep their tribal status alive over the last three centuries. Maine's Passamaquoddy tribe turned a settlement into shrewd business investments designed to make jobs in their region for Passamaquoddies and non-Passamaquoddies alike. The Pequots and Mohegans of Connecticut have been successful beyond all dreams with gaming operations on their tribal lands—a model that the surviving Wampanoags of Massachusetts have been trying to emulate.

The Pequots and Mohegans have also established new tribal museums at their casino sites, a welcome addition to a few excellent museums elsewhere in New England. In this chapter, the Institute for American Indian Studies in Washington, Connecticut, is an excellent resource for learning more about the traditional ways of the peoples of southern New England. The Abbe Museum in Bar Harbor, Maine (see "The North Coast"), is particularly strong on the Abenaki people of northern New England.

Seeing the Connecticut River Valley

The Lower Valley, Connecticut

Wethersfield, Connecticut

The sleepy village of Wethersfield, so enamored of its early English settlement history, lies due south of Hartford, and can be reached from Route 99 from Hartford's Charter Oak Bridge or, coming either south from Hartford or north from the Connecticut coast, by taking exit 26 from I–91. Upon leaving I–91, follow signs for the Webb-Deane-Stevens Museum to reach the village center.

Wethersfield was settled in the spring of 1634 by a large party of Englishmen from Watertown in Massachusetts Bay Colony, who claimed the land by being the first European settlers to plant crops along the Connecticut River. They were followed almost simultaneously by settlers upriver at Hartford and Windsor. The communities were barely settled when the men from the three towns went to war in 1637 against the Pequot tribes of the region. In a fierce but brief war that decimated both sides, the Englishmen succeeded in quashing the most powerful Native alliance of southern New England. Angry that Massachusetts Bay was of no assistance in their war, they gathered in Hartford and in January 1639 the leading men of the three settlements signed a document called the Fundamental Orders that effectively created their own "publike State or Commonwealth." Connecticut was no longer an outlier of Massachusetts.

Wethersfield was the smallest of the three original settlements, but it has held onto its Early American past with a tenacity that would impress a bulldog. In few places in New England have so many eighteenth and even seventeenth-century dwellings survived in continuous use. More than 116 structures built before 1840 still stand. Wethersfield has its share of museum houses, but far more impressive, we think, is that many of Wethersfield's fine early houses are still private homes. Wethersfield flourished on agricultural trade and the seed business in its heyday, but memory has become its chief occupation now, and the townsfolk pursue their chosen trade very well indeed.

The red brick **Robert Allan Keaney Memorial Cultural Center** at 200 Main Street was built in 1893, making it practically modern by comparison with its surroundings. The Wethersfield Historical Society operates a museum and cultural center within this former school building with an exhibit on the lives of early settlers. There's a $4.00 charge for the museum, but the Visitors Center is free. For a small donation, you can pick up the essential brochure, "A Tour of the Old Village: Wethersfield, Connecticut," which has an excellent map highlighting more historical stops than anyone could make in several days. The center is open Tuesday through Saturday from 10:00 A.M. to 4:00 P.M., Sunday from 1:00 to 4:00 P.M. Telephone: (860) 529–7161.

Cove Park, which marks the old harbor on the Connecticut River, is a short drive out Main Street. As early as 1648 Wethersfield was engaged in trade with the coast and the West Indies from this landing. The Wethersfield Red Onion (ancestor of the Bermuda red onion) was developed here, and along with flax seed, became the heart of the town's trade. A warehouse from 1690 still stands on the river's shore. The town landings moved after a great flood in 1692 washed away six other warehouses and changed the river's course, leaving the cove a shallow estuary rather than a deepwater river bend.

Between the cove and the original town green are many handsomely restored Colonial buildings, including the **Sgt. John Lattimer red clapboard house** from 1690, which stands in front of the Cove Warehouse. Most of the buildings in this section of town are a few years later, dating from 1730 to 1780, although the tiny house at 481 Main Street is a modern restoration of the oldest house in town, built in 1637 for George Hubbard.

No one seems to know if the name is a coincidence, but many of the streets in Old Wethersfield feature early twentieth-century **Hubbard Bungalows,** a distinctive structure of two and one-half stories with a long, sloping roof that covers a front porch running the width of the house. Prominent dormers interrupt the roof on the second story. Many of the bungalows are concentrated on Church and Willard Streets in what is considered one of America's earliest twentieth-century housing developments. Students of domestic architecture tend to go wild in Wethersfield because the small community has examples of almost every house style from the neo-medieval homes of the early seventeenth century to modern ranch houses. We can only surmise that much of New England might look like this had not community-wide fires periodically scoured the village landscapes.

The real showpiece of Americana in Wethersfield is the **Webb-Deane-Stevens Museum** in the heart of the historic district. The cluster of three adjacent historic homes bears the stamp of that dean of the Colonial Revival movement, Wallace Nutting, who once owned the Webb House as part of his "Colonial Chain of Homes." But more modern twists in interpretation and scientific sleuthing have returned the three houses to a look more in keeping with their original periods.

The **Joseph Webb House** is a classic rich merchant's dwelling of the mid-eighteenth century. Built in 1751 and soon enlarged, it was the structure where George Washington and Comte de Rochambeau met for four days in 1781 to plan the final campaign of the Revolution that led to the defeat of Cornwallis at Yorktown. Both the "Council Room," where they met, and the "Washington chamber," where George did indeed sleep, have been restored to their eighteenth-century appearance. The walls of the bedroom, in fact, are still covered with a rare eighteenth-century red flocked wallpaper. Every room is filled with eighteenth-century decorative arts, including fine American and European cabinetry and silver. In 1996, the museum uncovered for the first time in several decades the murals commissioned by Wallace Nutting in 1916 to relate the story of the planning for the Battle of Yorktown.

The **Silas Deane House** was built in 1766 by lawyer Deane, whose political interests soon took him away from Wethersfield. When he left for Paris in 1776 to help negotiate French aid for the Continental Army, he never returned. Accordingly, his home is interpreted to pre-1775, with fine examples of Chinese export porcelain and Queen Anne and Chippendale cabinetry.

The **Isaac Stevens House** represents a slightly later period—it was built in 1788—and a more modest lifestyle. Stevens was a leather tanner and saddle maker, and the house is interpreted to show how his upwardly mobile middle-class family lived in the early Federal period. The house remained in the same family until it was acquired by the Colonial Dames in 1957. In addition to the period family belongings, the Stevens house also displays two fine early Connecticut clocks, a collection of caps, and many examples of early nineteenth-century needlework.

Silas Deane House, Wethersfield, Connecticut

During the summer, admission to the Webb-Deane-Stevens Museum also lets you tour the **Buttolph-Williams House** at 249 Broad Street, reached by a path between the properties. Built in 1720, this house represented a conservative architecture for its time. The exterior is austere and the overhanging stories and tiny casement windows are more medieval than Colonial. The house is open from mid-May to mid-October Tuesday through Sunday from noon to 4:00 P.M.

The Webb-Deane-Stevens Museum is open May through October Tuesday through Sunday from 10:00 A.M. to 5:00 P.M. and November through April Friday through Sunday from 10:00 A.M. to 5:00 P.M. Adults $8.00. Telephone: (860) 529–0612.

Before leaving Wethersfield, you might pay a nostalgic visit to **Comstock, Ferre & Co.,** once one of America's leading seed suppliers. Founded in 1820 to capitalize on the reputation of the excellent seed stocks of the Connecticut River Valley, the company was sold to Franklin Comstock in 1838. His son, William, fairly pioneered mass marketing of packets of garden seeds, and the original border designs for the seed packets are still used on the company's herb packets. Comstock-Ferre is now a retail garden center and seed supplier, but no longer grows its own seed stock. Nonetheless, it is an excellent source for many open-pollinated vegetable and flower seeds as well as some of the early hybrid varieties and tetraploids bred in the early twentieth century. And they always have the Wethersfield Red Onion available as seeds and, in the spring, as sets. The store at 263 Main Street is open daily during the gardening months, and Monday through Saturday during the winter. Telephone: (860) 571–6590.

Before moving up the valley, we suggest a small detour south on Route 99 to the village of **Rocky Hill.** Watch for signs to West Street and **Dinosaur State Park,** where there are more than 2,000 fossil tracks of an early Jurassic carnivorous dinosaur—one of the largest concentrations of dinosaur tracks in a single geological layer in North America. The three-toed impressions, discovered by bulldozer operators in 1966, range from 10 to 16 inches in length and are spaced from 3.5 to 4 feet apart. Although no fossilized bones have been found to positively identify the creatures who left their tracks, scientists believe they were among the first large flesh-eating dinosaurs. Belonging to the Ceratosaur group, they averaged eight feet tall and 18 feet long and lived 200 million years ago. About 500 of the tracks are preserved under a geodesic dome. The park is open daily from 9:00 A.M. to 4:30 P.M.; the exhibition center is open Tuesday through Sunday from 9:00 A.M. to 4:30 P.M. Wheelchair accessible. 400 West Street. Adults $2.00. Telephone: (860) 529–5816.

Closer to the village of Rocky Hill is the modest little **Rocky Hill-Glastonbury ferry,** the nation's oldest continuously operating ferry service. Established in 1655, the ferry was private for the first 260 years but is now run by the state. A small tugboat attached to the side of a floating barge platform putters back and forth across a narrow stretch of the Connecticut River. Vehicles $2.25, walk-on passengers 75 cents. Telephone: (860) 566–7635.

Hartford, Connecticut

From Rocky Hill the easiest way to get to Hartford is to take I–91 north to the Hartford downtown exit. As you exit, the road runs within a few feet of a faded blue onion-shaped dome decorated with golden five-pointed stars. It has an imperial air to it still, though the dome has nothing to do with Russian history and everything to do with Hartford. There was a time when it was a 60-foot-wide icon of Hartford, as recognizable as such latter-day civic symbols as the Golden Gate Bridge in San Francisco or the Gateway Arch in St. Louis.

This was Samuel Colt's dome, and it surmounted his massive brownstone armory where, from the Civil War until 1994, the Colt Manufacturing Company produced weapons that have entered the American psyche, for good or ill. High school history books like to credit Henry Ford and the automotive industry for the assembly line and automated mass production, but Colt and his fellow armorers brought mass production to a fine and deadly art generations earlier. Off these assembly lines came the Single Action Peacemaker (Wyatt Earp's guns, and Billy the

Hartford skyline with Colt Dome, Connecticut

Kid's as well) and a slew of weapons right up through the M–16 that American troops used in the Vietnam War.

Colt opened his first armory on Pearl Street in Hartford in 1846, when his Patent Arms Manufacturing Company (which he had launched in Paterson, New Jersey) received its first major order for revolvers from the Texas Rangers for use in the Mexican War. This armory manufactured approximately 80 percent of the guns solely by machine at a time when industrial mechanization was unusual. In 1855 Colt built the armory that now greets interstate highway drivers, capping it with a dome in deference to Czar Nicholas I, whose Russian imperial army was outfitted with Colt revolvers. After a long period of neglect, the buildings are undergoing rehabilitation by pioneering artists and small businesses. If you want to visit, check in at the Village at Colt's Armory, 106 Wethersfield Avenue. Telephone: (860) 722–6514.

If you do choose to visit Coltsville, stop to marvel at the **Church of the Good Shepherd** at 155 Wyllys Street. Designed by Edward Tuckerman Potter in 1868, it was a commission by Elizabeth Colt in memory of her husband and three children who died as infants. Done in a High Victorian Gothic style, the church was built of Portland red and Ohio yellow sandstones with

granite pillars. Elaborate carvings, stained glass, and wrought iron seem to encrust it with ornamentation—the most striking piece being the "armorer's doors" emblazoned with Colt firearms. Open for Sunday services at 10:00 A.M., otherwise by appointment. Telephone: (860) 525–4289.

Other areas of the city better convey Hartford's Victorian heyday. By the 1870s, Hartford was reputed to be the richest city per capita in the world—a process that began in 1810 with the establishment of the Hartford Fire Insurance Company and the subsequent founding of other insurers. Combined with the skilled manufacturing led by but not exclusive to Colt, Hartford emerged fat and sassy from the Civil War. It was a city aching to reconstruct its self-image the way a newly rich man might build himself a fine mansion.

Probably the best way to see Hartford is to begin at the **Old State House** in the downtown business district. This Charles Bulfinch building hasn't been a capitol for more than a century, but since its 1994 renovation has served as the city's Visitors Center. The Senate chamber on the second floor was the site of the first *Amistad* trial involving fifty-three men taken into slavery in 1839 from Mendae in West Africa. They staged a revolt aboard ship and made landfall not back in Africa, as they attempted, but in New London,

Connecticut. Charged with mutiny, they spent more than a year in jail in New Haven before coming to trial in district court in Hartford. The Hartford judge declared them free, but the case was appealed to the U.S. Supreme Court, where one of their advocates was former President John Quincy Adams. Again, they were set free and the thirty-eight survivors lived in Farmington, Connecticut, until 1841 as they earned their passage back home. The Old State House, located at 800 Main Street, is open Monday through Friday from 10:00 A.M. to 4:00 P.M., Saturday from 11:00 A.M. to 4:00 P.M. Telephone: (860) 522–6766.

Just down the street from the Old State House is the pride of mid-nineteenth-century Hartford, the **Wadsworth Atheneum.** Founded in 1842 and opened to the public in 1844, the Atheneum is America's oldest public art museum and it flourished under the patronage of Hartford's Victorian elite, including the Colt family, Pierpont Morgan, and his son, J.P. Morgan Jr. Among nearly 50,000 artifacts and works of art are one of the best collections in New England of the Hudson River School of landscape painting as well as a few masterpieces of Impressionism. Thanks to outstanding curatorial leadership and a hefty endowment from the Victorians, the Atheneum was one of the first American museums to emphasize modern and contemporary art, mounting the first major U.S. exhibitions of Picasso and of Surrealism. Its holdings include the designs of the Ballets Russe that impresario Sergei Diaghilev had given to his favorite dancer, Lifar, as well as the Wallace Nutting Collection of Pilgrim Century Furniture. Similarly important is the Amistad Foundation's African American collection of more than 6,000 objects documenting three centuries. The museum also has a good cafe and gift shop. The Wadsworth Atheneum is open Tuesday through Sunday from 11:00 A.M. to 5:00 P.M. Admission is $7.00, but is free on Thursdays and before noon on Saturdays. Wheelchair accessible. 600 Main Street. Telephone: (860) 278–2670.

When Hartford was awash with money after the Civil War, it built a showplace state capitol adjacent to its striking public green space, **Bushnell Park.** Bushnell (originally known simply as City Park) was the first public park in the nation to be conceived, built, and paid for by its citizens through popular vote. In 1886, the city dedicated the striking **Soldiers and Sailors Memorial Arch** in memory of the 4,000 Hartford citizens who fought in the Civil War, including the 400 who died for the Union cause. It's a curious piece of memorial sculpture, covered with a terra cotta frieze that represents scenes from the Civil War, telling the story of the war as a triumphant culmination of history that unified the nation.

Near the top of the hill within the park is a white oak tree that is a **scion of the original Charter Oak,** planted on October 19, 1871. The "Charter Oak" is a touchstone in Hartford. In 1660, King Charles II had given Hartford citizens a charter that granted self-rule to Connecticut. When the English governor, Sir Edmund Andros, demanded its return on October 31, 1687, the lights in the room were suddenly extinguished and when the candles were relit, the charter had vanished. Joseph Wadsworth stole away with the parchment and stashed it in the massive oak. The original tree blew down in a storm on August 21, 1856, and according to the plaque at the base of the scion, "At sundown that day bells tolled throughout Hartford." The Charter Oak was estimated to be more than 1,000 years old when it fell.

One of the charming diversions of Bushnell Park is the 1914 Stein & Goldstein **Carousel,** complete with forty-eight painted horses, two chariots, and a 1925 Wurlitzer band organ that pumps out giddy tunes as the ponies go round and round, up and down. The carousel operates from mid-May through August Tuesday through Sunday from 11:00 A.M. to 5:00 P.M. and from mid-April to mid-May and during September on Saturday and Sunday from 11:00 A.M. to 5:00 P.M. It costs 50 cents. Telephone: (860) 246–7739.

The **State Capitol** commands the top of the hill above Bushnell Park. This sumptuous amalgam of palatial styles executed in white Connecticut marble and as adorned as possible with carvings, bas-reliefs, medallions, statues, and inlay work opened in 1878. The building is proof positive that the American version of High Victorian Gothic can match Rococo any day in its extremity of ornament. Polished granite columns, stained-glass windows, and atrium ceilings with hand-stenciled gold leaf accents carry the ornamentation inside. Free tours are given November through March, Monday through Friday from 9:15 A.M. to 1:15 P.M. From April through October, there are also tours on Saturday from 10:15 A.M. to 2:15 P.M. Telephone: (860) 240–0222.

During the same period that all this civic construction was taking place, Hartford became one of the great literary centers of America. Located halfway between the great literary metropolises of the age, Boston and New York, Hartford was home to nine major subscription publishers, who pre-sold books before they were printed. The literary hotbed of Hartford in the 1870s and 1880s was the community of Nook Farm, a development on the west side of the city where Harriet Beecher Stowe, author of *Uncle Tom's Cabin,* lived. Stowe, who was born in Litchfield, was possibly the most famous writer of the immediate post-Civil War era, and her home is now a museum: the **Harriet Beecher Stowe House.** Located at 73 Forest Street, it is open June through Columbus Day and in December Monday through Saturday from 9:30 A.M. to 4:00 P.M. and Sunday from noon to 4:00 P.M. It is closed on Monday the rest of the year. Adults $6.50. Telephone: (860) 525–9317.

Seemingly on the same property, the **Mark Twain House** attracts the larger crowds by far—partly because he remains a more popular author today and partly because his own elaborate Victorian Gothic structure is a wonder to behold. Twain had both his greatest successes and greatest failures in this house, where he lived from 1874 to 1891 and wrote, among other books, *The Adventures of Tom Sawyer* and *The Adventures of Huckleberry Finn.* His well-born wife spared no expense in creating the family home, which was designed by Edward Tuckerman Potter, better known for elaborate neo-Gothic churches. Most of the first-floor interior walls are stenciled with metallic paints in patterns created by the artisans of Louis Comfort Tiffany's firm. To tell the truth, poor boy Samuel Clemens enjoyed the ostentation. The current 90-minute interpretation emphasizes family life, perhaps more than Clemens himself might have but you'll come away with a good understanding of how much a Victorian bourgeois Clemens became. The house

is open Memorial Day through October 15 and the month of December Monday through Saturday from 9:30 A.M. to 5:00 P.M., Sunday from 11:00 A.M. to 5:00 P.M. Open October 16 to Memorial Day (except December) Monday and Wednesday through Saturday from 9:30 A.M. to 5:00 P.M., Sundays from noon to 5:00 P.M. Adults $9.00. 351 Farmington Avenue. Telephone: (860) 493–6411.

Sam Clemens left his house because he went broke on bad investments and had to hit the lecture circuit to recoup. Hartford itself has had a similarly rocky time of it for the last generation but seems to be turning a corner in the effort to resuscitate the city. Perhaps the most promising symbol of recovery is the **New Riverfront,** a project that will take a few more years to completely gel. At this point, Hartford's contribution is the Charter Oak Landing and Riverside Park along the Connecticut River as well as East Hartford's Great River Park across the water. Free concerts and holiday fireworks are luring people back to the water's edge. The **Deep River Navigation Company** also offers a variety of cruises upstream and downstream along the Connecticut River from the Charter Oak Landing. These jaunts are a good way to get a look at the shoreline before you explore the banks farther upstream. Cruises start at $6.00 and depart daily on variable schedule from late May to early September, then week-

Charter Oak, Hartford, Connecticut

ends only through Columbus Day. Telephone: (860) 526–4954.

A Sidetrip to Connecticut's Litchfield Hills

The hill country that rises west of Hartford and Wethersfield has a deep history of its own, starting in the early 1700s as the Connecticut River Valley land was taken and new settlers found the easy rolling hills fertile ground for farming. Today the Litchfield Hills are primarily a summer retreat district, and they make an interesting diversion from the river valley for a short trip of a day or two. The Colonial Revival movement of the early twentieth century took root here with a vengeance, with the result that many a Colonial and early Federal mansion was not only saved but often spruced up in the Williamsburg style to present a visually pleasing vision of country squiredom. The back roads of the Litchfield Hills are lined almost exclusively with deciduous trees, and the crisp autumn frosts that strike the area make it a beautiful area for foliage driving.

The towns of the Litchfield Hills abound with garden centers, antiques shops, and boutiques. If you are an antiques buff in search of early New England furniture—both elegant furniture from Colonial and Federal cabinetmakers and the more casual painted country furniture—look no further. But be prepared to pay auction-level prices. It is not uncommon to find antiques shops where the price tags begin in four figures and climb to six.

To make a driving loop through the Litchfield Hills before continuing upriver, follow Route 6 west from Hartford through Plymouth to Thomaston, where Route 254 leads northwest to Litchfield, shire town of the county. At the end of Route 254, follow Route 202 west. By approaching Litchfield from this direction, you will pass the Chestnut Hill Road entrance for **Haight Vineyard,** the first winery established under Connecticut's 1978 Farm Winery Act. Haight began with ambitious plantings of chardonnay and riesling grapes, and this branch (there's a second winery now in Mystic) still produces a pure riesling, though the chardonnay is blended with other, mostly French-American hybrid grapes in

estate wines. Free tastings and tours are given Monday through Saturday from 10:30 A.M. to 5:30 P.M. and Sunday from noon to 5:00 P.M. Wine is available by the glass at the Fireplace Room Wine Bar and by the bottle. Haight Vineyard is at 29 Chestnut Hill Road. Telephone: (860) 567–4045.

Continue on Route 202 into the center of **Litchfield village,** where parking is free for up to two hours while you shop the boutiques or visit the historic sites. Author Harriet Beecher Stowe was born here, and her father, Lyman Beecher, used to preach at a church on the town green, now gone but marked with a large stone inset with a handsome bronze plaque. We wonder what the church looked like, for Litchfield has three remarkably beautiful churches today—a classic white, high-spired Congregational Church on the east end of the green, a striking multi-colored Methodist church on the west end of the green, and a truly massive, neo-medieval stone Episcopal Church on Route 63 a few hundred yards south from the green. (In case you were wondering, these streets are named for their directions: East Street, West Street, and South Street. Practical folk, those Connecticut Yankees.)

At the corner of East and South Streets stands the Richardsonian stone **Litchfield Historical Society Museum.** The museum owns a number of rather good early American paintings, furniture, and decorative arts and has permanent exhibits on Litchfield-area history. The $4 admission charge also gives you entry to **Tapping Reeve House and Law School** on South Street, where America's first law school was established in 1774. The permanent exhibition, established in 1998, is devoted to the law in the early days of the Republic and the contributions of the school's 1,000 graduates to the new nation. The museum and the Tapping Reeve House and Law School are open from mid-April through mid-November, Tuesday through Saturday from 11:00 A.M. 5:00 P.M. and Sunday from 1:00 to 5:00 P.M.

Three miles south of the town green on Route 63 is **White Flower Farm,** quite possibly the Northeast's finest mail-order nursery for landscape plantings. The nursery's display gardens showcase its flowering perennials, roses, and bulbs in appropriate settings. A self-guided tour is easy

**Tapping Reeve House and Law School,
Litchfield, Connecticut**

if you simply pick up a map at the parking area. Although the company is best known for mail order, all of its offerings are available here as potted plants or bulbs. It also sells a complete line of Shepherd's Garden Seeds, a boutique seed company that White Flower Farm acquired a few years ago from founder Renée Shepherd.

The drive west from Litchfield on Route 202 (West Street) penetrates the scenic heart of the Litchfield Hills. Two miles west of town is the **White Memorial Foundation and Conservation Center,** a 4,000-acre nature preserve with more than 35 miles of trails for hiking, cross-country skiing, birdwatching, camping, and boating. A small nature museum is devoted to local ecology. The grounds are open daily all year. The museum is open Monday through Saturday from 9:00 A.M. to 5:00 P.M. and Sunday from noon to 4:00 P.M.

Route 202 begins to narrow and twist as it approaches the village of Bantam and by the time you approach **New Preston,** you have reached a purely rural world—except for the village center. New Preston is essentially a small clump of buildings at a picturesque waterfall, making it a sterling example of how enclaves formed around important natural resources. The mill buildings have all been converted to antiques and gift shops, a restaurant, and the excellent used bookstore of **Ray Boas,** who specializes in Americana and decorative arts. Boas is open Friday through Monday from 10:30 A.M. to 5:30 P.M. and Tuesday through Thursday by chance. The shop is at 6 Church Street, literally overlooking the falls. Telephone: (860) 868-9596.

Lake Waramaug is often considered one of Connecticut's most scenic lakes, though its shores are dominated by lavish summer homes. But public access is readily available at **Lake Waramaug State Park,** off Route 45. A few hiking trails lace the park, but most people come for the swimming, fishing, and paddle boating. Day use of the park is free Monday through Friday, with a charge of $5.00 per Connecticut car and $8.00 for out-of-state cars on weekends and holidays. Park office telephone: (860) 868-2592.

For a strikingly scenic drive, backtrack a mile from New Preston on Route 202 and turn south on Route 47 to the villages of Washington and Washington Depot. The road drops precipitously over several miles, as these villages lie in a valley between ridges. The road is narrow and turns often, so be careful driving. In the fall, the foliage may prove quite a distraction, as the road is overhung in many places by a canopy of beeches, larches, and various varieties of oak, making this a bronze-and-gold drive.

In Washington, turn right onto Route 199 south and watch for the right-hand turn to Curtis Road, a narrow and rustic roadway through the woods to the **Institute for American Indian Studies.** This little museum in a setting that could have come out of Longfellow's *Hiawatha* is particularly popular with families and day-care operators who parade the children through the replicated Algonquian village and simulated archaeological site. But the Institute is a place of serious study and advocacy for Native Americans in New England. The center has two art galleries with changing exhibits of contemporary Native American work as well as permanent historical exhibits and a very thorough gift shop that runs the gamut from arrowheads and tourist moccasins to beautiful beadwork and jewelry. The shop's selection of serious books and ethnological studies is unusually good, and every title the shop carries has been vetted by the research staff for accuracy. The Institute is open April through December, Monday through Saturday from 10:00 A.M. to 5:00 P.M. and Sunday from noon to 5:00 P.M. From January through March it is closed on Monday and Tuesday. Admission is $5.00. The Institute is located at 38 Curtis Road in Washington. Telephone: (860) 868-0518.

Glebe House and Gerturde Jekyll Garden, Woodbury, Connecticut

Keep following Route 199 south to the junction with Route 317 in Roxbury. The land continues to descend as you reach the lower ridges of the Litchfield Hills and begin to approach the coastal plain. In Roxbury, turn left onto Route 317 toward Woodbury, and enjoy the drive through increasingly open, rolling farm country. Route 317 concludes at a "T" intersection with Route 6 in the village of Woodbury, a handsome and old-timey community in danger of encroachment by strip development on its flanks.

Turn right (south) onto Route 6 and within a mile, watch closely for the sign marking Hollow Road for the **Glebe House.** The house is another fine example of life in late Colonial America. It was built in the 1770s for the Anglican minister of Woodbury on the land the minister was given to support himself. (The land grant is called a glebe, and the minister's house was called a parsonage if in town or a glebe house if on the farm.) The first American bishop of the Episcopal Church was elected here in 1783 when the American worshippers split with the Church of England after the Revolution. Filled with mostly period furnishings from the area, the house is a source of local historical pride. The volunteer tour guides may offer some observations that demonstrate the difficulty of historic interpretation when experts disagree on matters of stylistic authenticity.

Gardeners will want to pay close attention to the grounds, which hold the only garden in the United States designed by the famous British garden expert Gertrude Jekyll. Jekyll never visited but constructed the design from lot drawings at the behest of Standard Oil heiress Annie Burr Jennings, who helped fund the restoration of the Glebe House. Jennings received the plans in 1927 and, for a number of reasons, the garden wasn't planted until 1989. It has now reached full maturity and while not contemporary with the house (colonial gardeners planted mostly herbs and vegetables, not flowers), it has a delightfully old-fashioned feel. The Glebe House Museum & Gertrude Jekyll Garden are open April through November, Tuesday through Sunday from 1:00 to 4:00 P.M. They are located on Hollow Road off Route 6. Adults $4.00. Telephone: (203) 263-2855.

You might want to poke around Woodbury to do some antiques shopping, as the stretch of Route 6 south of the village is lined with a number of outstanding shops, including several that specialize in architectural salvage, others in antique paintings, still others in furniture. Route 6 connects to I–84 about four miles south of the village, allowing for an all-highway return to Hartford where you can connect with I–91 to continue your northward journey.

At Hartford, we recommend connecting with I–91 north to cross the border into Massachusetts, as traffic lights and shopping malls make for slow going on the older river roads between Hartford and Springfield. The landscape near the interstate has a kind of lush and flat quality, as it is a wide flood plain that used to be heavily farmed for broadleaf tobacco. Many of the fields have gone out of cultivation, passing into grasslands where hawks circle overhead watching for rabbits below.

The Mid Valley, Massachusetts

Springfield, Massachusetts

Like Hartford, the sprawling city of Springfield that you see today as you leave I–91 and drive into town is a product of the nineteenth century, when manufacturing made the city wealthy. Ironically, the key to that wealth lies in the early destruction of the first settlement. Founded in 1636 by a dozen farming families from the Massachusetts Bay Colony, Springfield was burned to the ground during King Philip's War (1675–76). Legend has it that Philip himself stood high on a bluff at Forest Hill and commanded his troops to uproot every crop, burn every English building, and kill, scalp, and dismember every English man, woman, and child, leaving their bodies to rot above ground. (The war had reached its most violent phase, and what we might consider atrocities in our own day were common practice.) Philip's troops only achieved part of their mission. Property was entirely destroyed, but about half the settlers escaped with their lives, and when they rebuilt, they focused less on farming and more on sawmills and gristmills. Let the surrounding villages do the heavy lifting—Springfield would process the timber and grain. In the crude frontier world of the Connecticut River Valley, Springfield became the first community of mechanics.

Ultimately this specialization would make Springfield an industrial powerhouse of diversified manufacturing with a specialty in armaments that predated even Hartford's role as an armorer. The Continental Congress established a major arsenal here during the Revolutionary War. When George Washington visited this strategic spot, he was impressed by the town's large number of machinists and chose a site for an armaments factory, which was finally funded by Congress in 1794 as the Springfield Armory. The transition was complete: A river town born of the Puritan plowshare soon thrived by the Federal sword. Boston and Salem suffered through the War of 1812 from lost trade, but Springfield thrived making cannon and guns. During the Civil War the Springfield Armory produced half of the guns used by the Union cause. Hartford made handguns but Springfield issued forth the deadly rifles carried by every enlisted man.

The **Springfield Armory National Historic Site** at 1 Armory Square (the corner of Federal and State Streets) recounts the evolution of guns manufactured here and by private companies of the area as well. Billed as the world's largest collection of firearms, the Main Arsenal occupies a handsome Greek Revival building that was constructed in 1847—the same year that wool merchant John Brown moved here from Akron,

Ohio, and helped establish the Underground Railway stops in the Connecticut River Valley for runaway slaves. The government-operated armory, perhaps best known for the bolt-action .30–06 Springfield Rifle, ceased operations in 1966. The rest of the complex was demilitarized in 1968 and now belongs to Springfield Technical Community College. The Armory is open Tuesday through Sunday from 10:00 A.M. until 5:00 P.M. Admission is free. Telephone: (413) 734–8551.

By the end of the nineteenth century, Springfield was a prosperous community with a broad manufacturing base. The first gasoline powered automobile was made here, along with the first production motorcycle. The **Springfield Indian Motorcycle Museum & Hall of Fame** in an industrial complex at the edge of town displays a number of conveyances from bicycles to toboggans, as well as what appears to be almost every model of the Indian—the first commercial gasoline-powered motorcycle—made until the factory closed in 1953. Many of these legendary American motorcycles are still on the road, showing up for parades and civic events. The museum, open daily from 10:00 A.M. to 5:00 P.M. between March and November and from 1:00 to 5:00 P.M. the rest of the year, is located at 33 Hendee Street. Adults $8.00. Telephone: (413) 781–6500.

Although Springfield has outlived its industrial glory days, much of the wealth generated by manufacturing is still evident. Take a tour through the Forest Park neighborhoods by driving up State Street and following the signs to the right for the zoo. These neighborhoods are filled with one- and two-family Victorian houses built when other cities were constructing tenements—in fact, Springfield once proudly called itself the "city of houses." Readers familiar with the Dr. Seuss book, *Horton Hears a Who,* may recognize some Forest Park landscapes. Dr. Seuss—Theodore Geisel—grew up in Springfield. When Prohibition closed the family brewery, his father ran Forest Park and the Springfield Zoo.

The late nineteenth century was an era of civic-mindedness in Springfield, as elsewhere, and much of the local wealth was funneled into institutions, many of which are found on State Street. Young Henry Hobson Richardson was engaged to design the **Church of the Unity,** his first step toward his trademark monumental medievalism that came to full realization in Boston's Trinity Church. The parishioners paid Louis Comfort Tiffany to make several of the stained-glass windows.

The greatest legacy of Springfield's benefactors is across State Street from the Church of the Unity, where the Quadrangle at the corner of State and Chestnut Streets is surrounded by the Springfield Public Library, two art museums, a gem of a local history museum, and a science museum with a planetarium.

The Quadrangle museums are big enough to be interesting and small enough to sample as a group in a single afternoon. We generally start at the **George Walter Vincent Smith Art Museum** because Smith launched the series of public benefactions that ultimately built the Quadrangle. When he was 35, Smith retired from the carriage-building business with a great fortune. He and his wife, Springfield native Belle Townsley, devoted the rest of their lives to collecting art. In 1896, they built an Italian Renaissance Revival palace (with Tiffany windows) to show their 6,000-item treasure trove.

Smith had the kind of taste you might expect from a man of his class, breeding, and business interests. He purchased a lot of moody, sentimental art and a lot of "guy stuff"—notably armor and weapons, including samurai armor that would rank as national treasures in a Japanese museum. But he also gave some good advice for visiting a museum:

"Make your vision big and view the museum as a whole instead of rushing up to an object and scrutinizing it minutely, and then dashing to another corner and examining something else. . . . At your first visit you should content yourself with getting an impression of the scope of what is there. On your way home you will think over the things you have seen. Certain objects will stand out in your mind—objects which unconsciously have interested you or have piqued your curiosity. You want to know more about them and another day you'll return. . . ."

Smith's counsel is worth remembering as you continue around the Quad.

Next door is the **Springfield Science Museum,** which also contains the Seymour Planetarium, the oldest American-built planetarium in the United States. (Star shows occur at 2:45 P.M. each day.) The African Hall is the centerpiece of the museum, with a trail (actually a ramp) leading past landscapes filled with specimens in appropriate environmental settings. But local natural history proves, in some ways, more evocative. The Connecticut River Valley is full of fossilized footprints from the late Triassic and early Jurassic periods, and one of the treats here is to run your fingers along the indentations made by a thunder lizard stomping across the valley landscape. While many of these dinosaurs were plant-eaters smaller than a human being, some of the tracks belong to large, carnivorous dinosaurs—not Tyrannosaurus rex, but some nasty customers nonetheless.

Many out-of-town visitors skip the **Connecticut Valley Historical Museum,** housed in a Colonial Revival building on the narrow end of the Quadrangle, unless they come to use the extensive genealogy library. Too bad, for this is a local history museum with more than local interest. For example, the miniature portraits by itinerant painter James Sanford Ellsworth present stylized chronicles of the region's farm families in the mid-1800s. The second-floor galleries display antique games produced by Springfield-based Milton Bradley. Among them is the card game, Old Maid, which the company stopped making in the 1960s as an early nod to political sensitivity. We suspect that interactive computer games have already made board and card games seem hopelessly medieval, but those of us who grew up rolling dice and shuffling pasteboard cards on rainy summer afternoons remember the Milton Bradley Company fondly.

From a Springfield resident's point of view, the **Museum of Fine Arts,** built in 1933, is probably the capstone of the Quadrangle. We come away pleased less by the stone-skipping survey of European and American painting than by the museum's strong commitment to collecting and showing post-World War II art—especially Abstract Expressionism. (There's a nice Frank Stella, for example.) Yet the most memorable piece in the entire museum is an immense and bizarre nineteenth-century work by local eccentric painter Erastus Salisbury Field (1805–1900). The central Blacke Court—a two-story skylit space—is dominated by Field's gigantic allegory, "The Historical Monument of the American Republic," a work as compellingly strange as a painting by Hieronymus Bosch. Field made his living by trucking this spectacle of a canvas from town to town and charging admission to see it.

Joint admission to the Springfield Library & Museums at the Quadrangle costs $4.00 for adults, with an extra charge of $1.00 for the planetarium. The museums are open Wednesday through Sunday from noon until 4:00 P.M. They are located at the corner of State and Chestnut Streets. Telephone: (413) 739–3871. Free parking is available in the State Street lot across from the library and in the small Edwards Street lot behind the Connecticut Valley Historical Museum.

At about the same time that George Vincent Smith was accruing his collections of Japanese feudal armor, another Springfield resident, Dr. James Naismith, nailed a couple of peach baskets to the YMCA gymnasium walls and invented the game of basketball in 1891. The **Basketball Hall of Fame** serves as a permanent reminder of Springfield's importance to the sports world. In fact, the Hall of Fame is expanding into new quarters along the river that should be finished around the year 2000. Meantime, the current digs on West Columbus Avenue at Union Street deal in every aspect of the game, from basketball shoe design to trading cards to high school, college, and professional sports. The inductees into the Hall of Fame are found on the third floor, so it's best to begin there and work your way back down. The Hall of Fame has tried very hard to remain up to date and interactive, so you'll find virtual reality simulators as well as a shooting court where baskets are at different heights. The idea is to let a more vertically challenged person get a feel for how low the basket looks to an NBA behemoth. The Hall of Fame is open daily from 9:00 A.M. to 5:00 P.M., until 6:00 P.M. during July and August. Adults $8.00. Telephone: (413) 781–6500.

Entering Pioneer Valley, Massachusetts

Springfield is the southern end of what local boosters have dubbed the Pioneer Valley and modern counter-culture types have called variously "Happy Valley" or "Alternative Valley." (The local entertainment weekly, the *Valley Advocate,* bills itself as the "pioneer in the alternative valley.") In any event, the Connecticut River Valley from Springfield to Brattleboro, Vermont, contains some of the richest agricultural land in the northeastern United States, and arguably some of the most beautiful. Most travelers zip up I–91 to reach a specific destination along the valley, but except where noted we recommend using north-south Route 5 (or, in places, Routes 5 and 10). The old highway has its fitful segments full of stops and starts, but it affords both a better view of the river and an easier pace from which to look at something besides the road.

Before plunging into the human landscape of the Pioneer Valley, spend some time with two remarkable preserves. The first you'll encounter is the **Mount Tom Reservation** on the north side of Holyoke. The mountain is one of a small range of extinct volcanoes flanking the river valley. These cinder cones, which date back more than 300 million years, were among the few in New England not ground flat by erosion and glaciation. During the spring and fall serious and casual birdwatchers from around the world dot the mountain's surface, for Mount Tom appears to serve as a navigational landmark for the annual migrations of hawks, owls, and falcons along the Connecticut River. (The river valley is the principal inland highway of bird migration in New England.) Literally thousands of these birds of prey pass the mountain daily for about two weeks in spring and fall. At the end of September, the Audubon Society sponsors an annual raptor count on Mount Tom. Free. Telephone: (413) 527–4805.

A little farther up Route 5, within the limits of the town of Easthampton, is the **Arcadia Wildlife Sanctuary,** operated by the Massachusetts Audubon Society. This sanctuary protects one of the least common types of forest in the world, the floodplain forest, which is dominated by American sycamores, eastern cottonwoods, and silver maple trees. Many rare aquatic creatures and more than 200 species of birds have been spotted here. A good bird observation tower overlooks a marsh, and there are hiking trails through the 550-acre site. The day-use fee is $3.00. The sanctuary visitor center is located at 127 Combs Road, Easthampton. Telephone: (413) 584–3009. As you head north along Route 5 in Easthampton, just before crossing the Connecticut River, watch for East Street on your left. Turn down East Street and drive for about one mile, turn right on Fort Hill Road, then drive another mile to the sanctuary.

The Five College Area, Massachusetts

The Pioneer Valley is distinguished not only by its natural beauties but also for its concentration of institutions of higher education. The presence of more than 40,000 college students and several thousand faculty and staff creates a culture of learning (with a byproduct of youthful excess) that can be simultaneously refreshing, entertaining, and exasperating.

If you backtrack on Route 5 for five miles to Holyoke, you can detour seven miles on Route 116 to the small village of **South Hadley,** where Mary Lyon founded the Mount Holyoke Female Seminary in 1836. Now **Mount Holyoke College,** it is one of the last holdouts of the Seven Sisters against coeducation. The college's **Art Museum** on Park Street has small but excellent collections that focus on Asian, Egyptian, and Mediterranean art. It is also known for mounting intriguing temporary exhibitions of contemporary work. The museum is open from 11:00 A.M. to 5:00 P.M. Tuesday through Friday, from 1:00 to 5:00 P.M. on Saturday and Sunday. Admission is free. Telephone: (413) 538–2245. The 800-acre campus of Mount Holyoke, with its two lakes, is an especially beautiful example of landscape design by the firm of Frederick Law Olmsted.

From South Hadley, drive along Route 47 through some of the oldest farmland in New England. At the intersection with Route 9 in the venerable village of Hadley, turn left and go two miles to the center of **Northampton,** the economic, social, and entertainment capital of the Five College area.

Although Northampton is only about 21 miles north of Springfield, it is far removed from the quiescent world of that former manufacturing center. "NoHo," as some locals call it, is a college town in spades. Many of the students who attend Smith, Mount Holyoke, Amherst, or Hampshire—or the University of Massachusetts, which dwarfs all of them—fall in love with the counterculture and the natural beauty of the area

and never leave. So Northampton has a substantial overlay of youth cultures from the 1960s, 1970s, 1980s as well as the 1990s. The upshot of this cultural ferment is that there are many good bookstores, cafes, restaurants, and art galleries. Almost every night there is a concert or a poetry reading or a live performance of theater or dance, and the city is considered the jazz and blues capital of western New England. The free local weekly *Valley Advocate* carries excellent listings.

For all its freeswinging present, Northampton has a stern past. In 1740, Puritan divine Jonathan Edwards touched off the "Great Awakening" from his Northampton pulpit. Considered one of the greatest preachers of all time, Edwards launched a revival movement that put the fear of God into people for miles around. (One of his favorite and most rhetorical sermons was "Sinners in the Hands of an Angry God.") Religious hysteria rose to unprecedented heights. People fell down in the streets in trances and reported terrifying visions. Little children were said to pass out with fear of suffering the fires of hell for all eternity. Edwards was so successful that after a decade of hellfire and brimstone, his congregation dismissed him. The Puritan hierarchy summarily packed Edwards off to preach to the heathen in Stockbridge, Massachusetts. Order returned to the Connecticut River Valley, and Edwards grew tired of ministering to the Indians and became president of Princeton College.

The bigger-than-life impulse that Edwards personified carries on in different forms today, including at the celebration of pulp heroics at the **Words & Pictures Museum** on Main Street. During their student days at UMass, Kevin Eastman and his pal Peter Laird started penning a goofy adventure comic strip in a local underground comic book. Stripped of the heaving bosoms and rippling muscles of their early work, their comics eventually evolved into the Teenage Mutant Ninja Turtles. Selling the rights to the characters made Eastman and Laird rich, and Eastman founded this museum of "comic art." (Laird's philanthropy has been quieter.) This museum contains a number of original panels from underground comics, so if you bring young children, you might want to steer them to the G-rated stuff on the second and third floors. Located at 140 Main Street, the museum is open Tuesday through Sunday from noon to 5:00 P.M., until 8:00 P.M. on Thursday. Adults $3.00. Telephone: (413) 586–8545.

The truth is that Northampton's chief attraction is the town itself, and the only admission fee you'll have to pay is the parking meter. Locals are very proud of the in-town shopping center, **Thorne's Marketplace,** at 150 Main Street, because this redeveloped building with more than thirty boutiques drew enough business away from nearby highway malls to cause some of them to close. Just as you can get a glimpse of the local color of an exotic port by walking around its central market, you can get a feel for Northampton by cruising through Thorne's, where household boutiques compete with crystal and astrology shops, a natural foods store, specialty booksellers, several clothiers, and a host of other retailers. The top floor even has a community art gallery and performance space.

Smith College, which occupies a hilltop overlooking the city, rises above it all. Co-ed for several years now, this charter member of the Seven Sisters was founded in 1875 by Sophia Smith of nearby Hatfield to offer non-sectarian Christian-influenced education to "the intelligent gentlewoman." The **Museum of Art** has superb holdings in French impressionist and post-impressionist painters and in the works of Winslow Homer. Admission is free. The museum is open July and August Tuesday through Sunday from noon to 4:00 P.M. During the academic year, it is open Tuesday, Friday, and Saturday from 9:30 A.M. to 4:00 P.M., Wednesday and Sunday from noon to 4:00 P.M. and Thursday from noon until 8:00 P.M. The museum is located at 76 Elm Street at Bedford Terrace. Telephone: (413) 585–2760; TTY: (413) 585–2786. Handicapped parking is available and the museum is wheelchair accessible.

As you will observe, Smith has beautiful grounds. Many of the plants around the campus come from the college's own growing areas. The **Lyman Plant House and Smith College Botanic Gardens** are truly sights worth seeing. The sprawling nineteenth-century conservatory, greenhouses, and outdoor gardens hold more than 3,500 species of plants that range from tropical species to hardy outdoor New England perennials. We particularly enjoy dropping in during the first two weeks of March, when the Lyman House

features a magnificent bulb show that gives us a jump on spring. Admission is free. The Lyman House and adjoining greenhouses and gardens are on College Lane off Elm Street. Telephone: (413) 585–2740.

Heart of the Pioneer Valley, Massachusetts

From Northampton, follow Route 9 east back through Hadley toward **Amherst,** a surprisingly old-fashioned New England village around a pleasant town green. We say "surprisingly" because the presence of 25,000-plus students at the University of Massachusetts does not seem to ruffle at all the long-time townies, many of whom recognize comparatively tiny **Amherst College** as the only significant institution of higher education in town.

In many respects, Amherst is a poet's town. Robert Frost taught at Amherst College for several years and since the early 1970s James Tate has been a mainstay at UMass, where one of the country's leading writing programs attracts young writers in training and many established figures. Poetry and fiction readings are frequent during the academic year at area bookstores and various campus locations.

Arguably, the poet who set the tone for Amherst was Emily Dickinson, who lived most of her life (and wrote all her verse) at 280 Main Street. The **Emily Dickinson Homestead,** which belongs to Amherst College, is open for tours by advance reservation. Tours are given from May through October on Wednesday through Saturday from 1:30 to 3:45 P.M. The same hours apply during March, April, November, and the first half of December but only on Wednesday and Saturday. Telephone: (413) 542–8161. Admission is $3.00. For a particularly good selection of critical writing about Dickinson and for good selections of other local writers, visit the **Jeffrey Amherst Bookshop** at 26 South Pleasant Street. Telephone: (413) 253–3381.

The vast campus of the University of Massachusetts swallows up much of Amherst's landscape, and like rural state university campuses everywhere, it is oriented toward its student population rather than toward outside visitors. Nonetheless, it is worth a visit to tour the

University Gallery in the Fine Arts Center on North Pleasant Street. The largest of the six UMass art galleries, this venue focuses on a superb collection of twentieth-century prints as well as frequently changing temporary exhibits. Telephone: (413) 545–3670.

Route 9 continues east from Amherst toward Worcester via Belchertown (See "Midlands") or by Pelham Road to Pelham, home of insurrectionist Daniel Shays and the western gates of the Quabbin Reservoir. (See "Midlands.") Route 116 from Amherst leads south to South Hadley or north to Sunderland and Deerfield. We suggest ignoring all of them and backtracking on Route 9 west to the village of **Hadley** and the intersection of Route 47.

This crossroads marks what remains of the center of the village of Hadley, a farming community settled in 1659 by religious dissenters from Connecticut. The center of town around the green was once surrounded by a palisade, for Hadley was heavily contested between settlers of European stock and the native tribes they displaced.

It is useful to look at a map to understand why Hadley was worth fighting over: The town is actually a peninsula in the Connecticut River. Virtually every spring the Connecticut overflows its banks and washes over Hadley's fields, leaving behind a deposit of rich silt. The Pocumtuck tribe, who were headquartered a few miles upriver in what became Deerfield, took advantage of this

Tobacco barn

fertile floodplain by farming corn, beans, squash, and tobacco extensively after about A.D. 1400. Friction between the Pocumtucks and the English settlers took a heavy toll along this portion of the river.

To get a picture of what was at stake, you should drive north along Route 47, a road used almost exclusively by locals. **River Road,** as it is known, follows the east bank of the Connecticut past broad fields toward Sunderland. Three centuries of intensive farming have left their mark on the landscape. You will notice in many places an earthen ridge that bars your view of the river. These are the remains of crude levees built by farmers to separate the river bottomland fields—which would flood each spring—from the upland pastures where they grazed their sheep and dairy cattle. Hadley has specialized in various crops over the years. Broom corn was introduced to the area in 1791 and by 1850 Hadley produced most of America's broom straw. That crop was followed by asparagus (Hadley was once America's leading asparagus grower), an industry that succumbed to verticillium wilt around World War II. Hadley then moved into onions, but couldn't compete with California and the Pacific Northwest. The town still grows both asparagus and onions, but the total acreage is relatively small and most of both crops is sold at regional markets in Boston. Sheep and dairy cattle still graze the pastures.

The **Hadley Farm Museum,** housed in a restored 1782 barn, summarizes the town's agricultural past. The building also hints at one of the area's other Colonial occupations—the making of fine furniture. The pediment over the doorway resembles the bonnet tops found on secretaries and highboys made here in the valley, though there is no record of who might have designed it. Inside you'll find a wide collection of household and farm machinery, a broom-making machine from the town's era as a broom capital, and several old vehicles, including a fifteen-passenger stagecoach. Admission is by donation. The museum is open May through Columbus Day Tuesday through Saturday from 10:00 A.M. to 4:30 P.M. and Sunday from 1:30 to 4:30 P.M. It is located at the intersection of Routes 9 and 47. Telephone: (413) 584–8279.

Route 47 is a slow but interesting country

road as it tracks the river, passing farm after farm. About two miles north of the village is your chance to soak in the essence of this riverine agriculture at the **Porter-Phelps-Huntington Historic House Museum** at 130 River Drive. The structure of this 1753 house remains unchanged since 1799 and, even more remarkably, it was owned by the same family until it became a museum in the twentieth century. Seven generations of that family are represented by their personal belongings, and the interpretation takes an interesting approach to focus on three generations of eighteenth-century women—people too often overlooked in "historical" records. The land was rich and generous, but even simple farming had its moments of terror. Toward the end of the French and Indian War the man of the house was away when the building—far removed from Hadley's palisade—was attacked. Miraculously, the woman of the house and her children survived, but a hatchet mark on one of the shutters makes the fragility of life during a frontier war palpably real. The Porter-Phelps-Huntington House presents outdoor concerts, often of period music, from June through August on Sunday afternoons. Guided tours are given from mid-May to mid-October from Saturday to Wednesday between 1:00 and 4:30 P.M. and by appointment during the rest of the year. Adults $4.00, with extra fees for some concerts. Telephone: (413) 584–4699.

As you drive along River Road you will see long, weathered barns in the middle of some fields. These are the surviving tobacco barns. Their sides can be removed to promote air circulation for curing the tobacco or restored to keep rain and wind off the crop. During the nineteenth and twentieth centuries, Connecticut River Valley shade-grown tobacco came to be prized as some of the finest cigar wrapper leaf in the world. Although tobacco growing went into sharp decline in the 1970s and 1980s, it returned in the 1990s with the renewed popularity of fine cigars. Tobacco growing is limited to some extent by the lack of old barns to cure the crop—many were torn down for decorative barn siding in the 1970s.

Many of the farms along River Road exist only because innovative legislation placed them in

Sunderland Bridge over the Connecticut River

agricultural land banks in the 1970s and 1980s. Farmers accepted payment in return for deed clauses that guaranteed that their lands could only be used for agriculture. At the same time, agricultural scientists at the University of Massachusetts and natural foods advocates in the area combined forces to create both the demand for organic produce and the know-how to raise it on fields that had been insulted for decades with pesticides, fungicides, and chemical fertilizers. As a result, truck farming has blossomed along the river in the towns of Hadley, Whatley, Sunderland, and Deerfield. One good reason to drive River Road is to stop at the small vegetable stands or pick-your-own fields at almost every large farm.

In the minuscule center of **Sunderland,** Route 47 crosses Route 116. Turn left toward the looming bluff of Mount Sugarloaf, a "sheepback" or knob of bedrock carved by the glacial action and elongated on its north-south axis. Detour to drive to the top for long views along the river and the fields from the lookout tower, then continue north to the junction of Route 116 and Route 5.

Stay in the Connecticut River Valley by following Routes 5 and 10 northward, you will soon come to **Old Deerfield.** Almost nothing of import has happened in the town since 1704, yet Deerfield's history echoes down the ages. To quote

**The Street in Old Deerfield,
Deerfield, Massachusetts**

the overwrought but accurate observation of a government chronicler of the 1930s, Deerfield "is, and
will probably always remain, the perfect and beautiful statement of the tragic and creative moment
when one civilization is destroyed by another."

The stage for confrontation was set in 1669
when English settlers arrived from Dedham. They
found the Deerfield area already populated by the
Pocumtuck tribe, an Algonquian-speaking people
with a warlike history. This made Deerfield a
peculiar frontier: Civilized people from different
cultures were tending the same crops in the same
ways virtually side by side. Only dress, building
style, and religion differentiated Pocumtuck from
Englishman.

The Pocumtucks had arrived in the valley
about three centuries earlier when they were
pushed eastward out of the Hudson River valley
by some of the Iroquois nations, particularly the
Mohawk. Discovering the fertility of the upper
valley, the Pocumtucks staked out a substantial
portion of the river as their own and fought off
their neighbors to hold it. The land was so rich
that the Pocumtucks accrued agricultural surpluses

that they traded with their hereditary enemies, the
Mohawks, to the west and with the Nipmucks to
the north and east.

The arrival of competing English farmers did
not sit well, and in 1675 the Pocumtucks joined
King Philip's efforts to push the Europeans off the
continent. The Bloody Brook Massacre of 1675
(in what is now South Deerfield) effectively emptied Deerfield of white settlers for seven years. But
it also brought down the wrath of the Colonial
militia, which proceeded to empty the
Connecticut River Valley of all the various tribes.
The Pocumtucks were pushed out again. Those
who survived the Colonists' raids either fled north
to Canada or to northern New England where
they were absorbed into the Abenaki and Sosoki
tribes.

Blood called out to blood on this peculiar
frontier. The white survivors of the Bloody Brook
Massacre returned in 1685 and began to rebuild
their community. A generation later, during the
French-English conflict called Queen Anne's War
in Europe but known simply as the first French
and Indian War here, the Indian allies of the
French wrecked revenge on Deerfield. In 1704
half of the town was burned to the ground, forty-
nine of its inhabitants were slain, and another 110
were spirited off as captives to Montreal. It is conceivable that many of the warriors were descendants of the Pocumtuck survivors who had
already been absorbed into the various tribes in
Quebec. Deerfield's Reverend John Williams kept
a cool head and later wrote an impassioned
account, *The Redeemed Captive,* that remains one
of the primary sources for understanding the
complex relations between Native Americans and
Europeans in the days of the New England frontier.

Once the captives returned during one of
those periodic peace treaties between the English
and French, Deerfield went back to sleep. The
frontier pushed on, and Deerfield was left as a
ghost of itself. Because so little changed, Deerfield
was ripe for rediscovery as a perfect Colonial village when the Colonial Revival enthusiasm flared
after the Civil War. The Pocumtuck Valley
Memorial Association was founded in 1870 to
preserve some of the historic houses along **The
Street,** a perfect measured mile of the original

Deerfield community.

The Street looks a little bare now, as it was long flanked by American elm trees that dated from the town's rebirth in the early 1700s but fell victim to Dutch elm disease in the mid-twentieth century. Many of the Colonial-era structures are private homes, but many others belong to **Historic Deerfield,** successor to the Memorial Association. It costs nothing to walk The Street, but entry to the fourteen Historic Deerfield properties, which range from 1720 to 1850, costs $10. The ticket, however, is good for a week. Real buffs of Colonial decorative arts and furniture will spend a week in the area, returning daily to inspect pewter, silver, textiles, ceramics, and some quite important pieces of antique furniture. Historic Deerfield has developed a strong line of antiques scholarship, and its staff rank among some of the top experts on early American objects. The Information Center is in the Hall Tavern, across from the Deerfield Post Office on The Street. The houses are open daily from 9:30 A.M. to 4:30 P.M., with tours departing about every half hour from April through October and whenever enough visitors have assembled during the rest of the year. Telephone: (413) 774–5581.

Deerfield is redolent of the past even outside the museum houses. Deerfield Academy, a prestigious preparatory school, was founded here in 1797 and while the school has enlarged into more modern quarters, its original building was converted in 1880 into **Memorial Hall Museum.** Here you find more relics, including five period rooms of antique furnishings and fourteen more rooms of thematic exhibits, including some recent ones on Native American culture. The prize exhibit, however, is the "Indian House Door." The 1698 house on which it hung survived the 1704 raid; when it was pulled down in 1848, the tomahawk-scarred front door was preserved. Lest you miss the point, it is proudly displayed with a reproduction hatchet embedded in it. Memorial Hall is located between The Street and Routes 5 and 10. It is open daily from 9:30 A.M. to 4:30 P.M. Admission is $5.00, or is available as part of a $12.00 combination ticket that includes Historic Deerfield.

For all its contemplative, old-fashioned qualities, Deerfield is also the home of the **Yankee Candle Company,** which operates a faux Bavarian village shopping mall on Routes 5 and 10 not far from Historic Deerfield. It's hard to argue with success: Yankee Candle draws close to 2 million visitors per year—not bad for an operation that grew out of 1960s-era hippie candle-making with colored paraffin and milk cartons. You can watch costumed workers create various forms of candles. Telephone: (413) 665–8306.

The Bavarian association of Yankee Candle isn't as far-fetched as it might seem. As far south as Springfield and north into Vermont, the Connecticut River Valley developed in the nineteenth century as America's premier machine tool industrial center, attracting large numbers of skilled machinists from central Europe. Although overshadowed in the ethnic mix by the Poles who came to farm the region at the end of the nineteenth century, the Germans left a legacy in many of the family names and some of the area restaurants.

For many years, the center of that machine tool industry was **Greenfield,** just a few miles north of Deerfield on Routes 5 and 10. The machine tool industry has vanished (Sterritt, the last holdout, hangs on 20 miles toward Boston on Route 2 in Athol) and Greenfield has reverted to a sleepy small town, circa 1955, with a charming overlay of New Age stores next to the Deco-era Garden Theatre, Famous Bill's (good fried fish), and the various offices of county government. The most vibrant industry today in Greenfield and neighboring Turners Falls (east on Route 2) involves soybean products, particularly the manufacture of tofu and tempeh.

Route 2 west of Greenfield is known as the **Mohawk Trail,** a fine highway with long vistas and scenic overlooks. The Mohawk Trail possibly offers the most beautiful fall foliage in Massachusetts, but the glories of its trees are so well-known that looking at the foliage and avoiding hitting another carload of gawkers makes it a test of patience. Better to take almost any of the side roads and drive aimlessly in this countryside dominated by maples, birches, and beeches.

Eight miles west of the Greenfield traffic circle there's a turnoff on the left to **Shelburne Falls.** The center of this village—half in Shelburne, half in Buckland—is the Deerfield River. Park anywhere you find a space here in Foxtown, as the locals call it, and wander down to the river. A small hydroelectric dam continues to generate power at the site of an old machine shop. Below the dam are the village's famous **glacial potholes**—huge rounds gouged out of the rock. The old trolley bridge over the river has been decorated with flowers and decorative plants since the 1920s as a blatant and therefore rather charming tourist attraction. It is called the **Bridge of Flowers,** and if you're lucky, the pharmacy will have some postcards of it. The Deerfield River gorge is steep and dramatic just downriver from Shelburne Falls. Cross the bridge and turn left on Conway Road (which becomes Buckland Road when it crosses into Conway) and within a mile you will reach what even locals concede are the **best fall foliage vistas** anywhere in New England. Having seen landscapes worthy of Alfred Bierstadt, retrace your tracks to Route 2.

The Upper Valley, Vermont and New Hampshire

To continue your journey up the Connecticut River to that self-identified region known as the "Upper Valley"—really the portion of the river that divides New Hampshire and Vermont—return to Greenfield by going east on Route 2 from Shelburne Falls to the Greenfield traffic circle. From this point you can drive on Route 5 north, or, alternatively, on I–91. We generally don't care for interstate highways for anything but convenience, but I–91 between Greenfield and the Vermont border is a truly beautiful, scenic road along the crests of rolling foothills that form the walls of the river valley.

Whether you choose the high road (I–91) or the low road (Route 5), be sure to drive into **Brattleboro, Vermont.** Did you ever wonder what happened to the flower children and communards of Woodstock Nation? Many of them disappeared into conventional lives in the hill towns of the Connecticut River Valley and the Green Mountains. In Brattleboro, they became

entrepreneurs and small businesspeople, fitting in surprisingly well with the native Yankees by sharing the traditional values of hard work and plain speech.

Like Northampton, Brattleboro has to be experienced to be appreciated. Its steep little Main Street is lined with a mixture of post-hippie and old Yankee shops, and the side streets in the central downtown contain clusters of commerce unique in the Connecticut River Valley—candy stores, two brewpubs (the Windham Brewery is the more hospitable), an Art Deco movie theater, guitar shops, neo-hippie clothing boutiques, and several stores devoted to various philosophical, religious, and dietary belief systems. Despite being named fifth best in a survey of "Best Small Towns in America," Brattleboro seems destined to resist the kind of gentrification and gussying-up that tends to overtake such places once they are discovered.

Brattleboro's slogan is "where Vermont begins"—a reference both to being a border town with New Hampshire and Massachusetts and to the fact that Vermont's first permanent settlement, Fort Dummer, was established here in 1724. It is also where Vermont landscape begins. In addition to the river cruises and good paddling available here (see "Staying There"), Brattleboro is the gateway to the mountains.

To continue seeing the Connecticut River Valley, simply keep heading north on Route 5. To connect with the Green Mountains section covered in "Up Country," watch for the intersection of Routes 5 and 9 north of Brattleboro.

The western fork of Route 9 crosses the Green Mountains to Wilmington en route to Bennington on the extremely scenic Molly Stark Highway—another great foliage road that, like the Mohawk Trail, tends toward stall-and-crawl traffic in late September and early October. Route 9 in West Brattleboro passes a pair of handsome covered bridges and offers spectacular scenic views at a turnoff at Hogback Mountain. Much of this territory is covered in the "Up Country" chapter.

A particularly interesting sidetrip may be made by driving east on Route 9 into New Hampshire toward Keene and the Monadnock region, a picturesque countryside dotted with woodsy farms and covered bridges.

Personal Narrative:
Touring Swanzey's Covered Bridges

Covered bridges aren't unique to New England, but we're blessed with nearly 200 that are still standing. Usually painted barn red or allowed to weather to a well-tanned dark brown, they continue to span the little streams and brooks of the back country, providing what Henry Wadsworth Longfellow aptly called "a brief darkness leading from light to light." There used to be about 1,000 New England covered bridges, but increasing traffic and heavier loads rendered many of the old spans obsolete. Fire, flood, and simple neglect also take their toll.

One day when we are visiting Brattleboro, Vermont (which has the Creamery covered bridge over Whetstone Brook on the west side of town near Route 9), we decide to visit nearby Swanzey, New Hampshire, where five standing covered bridges make the little town the unofficial covered bridge capital of New England. Alerted that the Greater Keene Chamber of Commerce hands out a free map of the bridges, we begin by driving 14 miles east from Brattleboro on Route 9 to that handsome shire town of Cheshire County. Routes 9, 10, 12, and 101 all converge in the center of town and the Chamber stands on the north side of Central Square directly behind the Civil War memorial statue. Telephone: (603) 352–1303.

Keene is a pleasant place to tarry. Once known for its glass and pottery (the white pottery made here by the Hampshire Pottery from 1871 to 1926 is highly prized by collectors), Keene has emerged as a college town and shopping center for New Hampshire's Monadnock region, thanks to the civilizing presence of Keene State College. It's a low-key college town, blessed with a number of fine little coffee shops and a downtown that manages to thrive despite the surrounding shopping malls.

In the Chamber they tell us that many people like to bicycle the route, but we are short on time and opt to take our car. Following instructions, we start out in a bridge quest by driving south on Route 12 for 4.1 miles, traveling first on a busy four-lane road, then through a thickly settled area and past a strip mall and the Cheshire County Fairgrounds until we find our right turn onto Flat Roof Mill Road at a large auto dealership.

We follow Flat Roof Mill Road for two miles past ranch houses and farms and a conservation forest until we come to what's been described to us as an "odd" intersection—"odd" because the roads come in at crazy angles. We make a sharp right onto Webber Hill Road and in two-tenths of a mile another right onto Carlton Road, which we follow for one mile to our first bridge.

It is a modest beauty—one of the oldest covered bridges still in use. With a height limit of nine feet four inches, we're glad we're not driving a mobile home. Known as the **Swanzey-Carleton Bridge,** it was constructed around 1789 and rebuilt in 1869 using the Queenpost truss design—a sure sign that it was a farmer's bridge. Most of the early bridges were constructed by farmers and local carpenters to provide safe passage for hay wagons over a stream. They used the construction techniques they knew—the Queenpost and Kingpost truss designs that had developed over the years as supports for barn roofs. The whole point of covering the bridge with a roof and sides was to protect the wooden roadway from excessive weathering. The size of the opening of a bridge, we are told, related to the size of the farmer's hay wagon.

The Ashuelot River and its various branches

Creamery Bridge, Brattleboro, Vermont

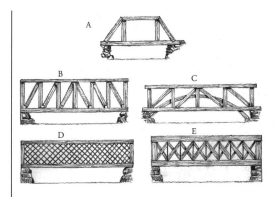

Bridge trusses, including the Queenpost truss (A), multiple Kingpost truss (B), Burr truss (C), Town lattice truss (D), and Howe truss (E)

wind a circuitous path through Swanzey, so those farmers had to construct many bridges. We drive a few hundred yards farther to a "T" intersection, make a right, and drive across the flat country between river branches on Route 32 for a mile and a half. We bear left on Sawyer Crossing Road at the regional high school and stay on the road for seven-tenths of a mile until we encounter the **Cresson Bridge,** also known on area maps as the **Swanzey-Sawyers Crossing Bridge.** This barn-red structure is quite a contrast to the first bridge. Rebuilt from an earlier structure in 1859, it carries two lanes of traffic 159 feet over the Ashuelot. Local records show that it cost $1,735.64 in 1859. The truss system is the most common in these parts—the Town lattice truss, developed by Connecticut engineer Ithiel Town in the early 1830s to exploit the long-fiber strength of wood and carry larger loads over a greater distance. Rather than build bridges, Town licensed his truss for $1.00 per foot—or $2.00 if he caught someone building a lattice bridge without his permission. Because even a rough carpenter could construct the lattice, Town advertised that it could be "built by the mile and cut off by the yard."

After stopping to admire the truss work, which shows signs of recent repair, we stay to our left and follow the twisty, woodsy road for two miles to another T intersection, where we turn left onto busy Route 10 for a half mile, then make a left at the overhead blinking light onto North Winchester Street. ("Watch for

Bob's Auto Service and you'll know you're on the right road," we remember. Apparently the road sign is knocked down every winter by snowplows.) We go straight for a half mile to a T intersection and turn left to pass through the prettiest and most graceful covered bridge yet.

The **Thompson Bridge,** called the **Swanzey-West Swanzey Bridge** on road maps, is another Town lattice truss structure. Built in 1832 by Zodoc Taft for $523.27, it was completely restored and rededicated in 1993. The original two-span bridge also had covered sidewalks on each side, though only one remains. The weathered pinkish color just shows that red barn paint isn't what it used to be.

On the far side of the bridge we make an immediate right onto Homestead Avenue and soon stop at Homestead Cemetery, one of those nice old country burial grounds where the stones calculate generation after generation of people who were born, lived, and died in the same small patch of the world. We keep driving past farms with horses grazing in hilly pastures surrounded by stone walls for 3.1 miles to the junction with Route 10, where we turn left and go 3.1 miles to make a right onto Coombs Bridge Road.

The bridge at this intersection is called the **Winchester-Coombs Bridge,** and it's the first unpainted bridge we encounter. We wonder whether it's cheaper to paint or to replace siding, as half the bridge is clad with shiny, pale new lumber. We decide both approaches must work, since this bridge has stood since 1837, with substantial repairs in 1972. It crosses much higher over the Ashuelot River than the others we have seen, standing on tall stone abutments that have been constructed with fine Yankee stone-wall masonry entirely without mortar—just one stone fitted to another.

After passing through, we turn left and drive one mile through the wooded hills to a four-way intersection. At the crossroads we turn left and stay on the pavement—Verry Brook Road—and drive 3.4 miles along the river, then into classic old New England farmland. This whole area was tilled extensively until the 1840s, when the land played out and settlers left for the richer farmlands of the Ohio Valley. Where the land was left fallow, the New

England forest eventually took over. We can almost mark the era when some of these farms were last worked. Those abandoned first are grown up with hemlocks. Those abandoned at the end of the nineteenth century have grown up in maples, birches, and beeches. And the most recently abandoned—during the Great Depression—are still half open, full of bluestem grass and eastern red cedar trees. But some of the farms are still in business, and we pass rolling pastures grazed by Holsteins. Finally we reach a small grass triangle with traffic merging from the right. We bear left, then stay right at the triangle on Old Spofford Road until we come to our second stop sign in 1.2 miles.

At this second stop sign we bear right onto busy Route 119 and drive 1.4 miles until we pull over to admire the **Winchester-Ashuelot Bridge,** the most impressive and one of the latest of the lot. This two-span bridge with a covered walkway is 160 feet long and clearly gets a lot of traffic. Built in 1864, it's extremely well-maintained, painted red with white trim. Because the sides are unsheathed, the Town lattice truss structure is easy to see—an example, the Chamber's directions say, of "pure American Gothic architecture adapted to bridge building." We couldn't say it better. Satisfied that we have seen the triumphs of country carpentry over natural obstacles, we follow the Ashuelot River west along Route 119 to where it joins the Connecticut, then continue on Route 119 back to Brattleboro, to bring our journey full circle.

Putney, Vermont to Hanover, New Hampshire

From Brattleboro, continue north on Route 5 for nine miles to **Putney, Vermont,** a village known for its apples (about a quarter of the Vermont crop), its makers of fine crafts (more than forty established artisans live here), and its history of progressive thinking. The current incarnation of that thinking is the Putney School, a co-ed prep school where the students help with farm chores, and Landmark College, devoted exclusively to educating students with dyslexia and other learning disabilities. In the 1840s, Putney was home to

a group of Bible-thumping communards who, among other things, found Scriptural support for polygamy. Humphrey Noyes, the group's leader, was charged with adultery in 1847 and subsequently led the whole band through the proverbial wilderness to Oneida, New York, where they went into the silverplate business. Vermonters are very tolerant of eccentricity, but there are certain lines not meant to be crossed.

Not to slight any of the towns along Route 5, but north of Putney we prefer to drive I–91 to exit 11, at which point we cross the river and turn south on New Hampshire Route 12 to **Charlestown, New Hampshire.** Established in 1744, Charlestown was known as **Fort at No. 4,** reflecting the fact that it was the fourth (and northernmost) settlement above the Massachusetts border. It was a harrowing place to live during the French and Indian War, and most of the settlers were carried off to Canada in the 1750s, some never to return, others to remain captive for a decade. Unlike Deerfield, where the original community remained virtually untouched until the revival of interest in Colonial history, the original fort at what became the town of Charlestown fell into complete disrepair. But large sections of it have been rebuilt as both a tourist attraction and a source of civic pride. During the summer, local schoolteachers and some of the older teens act as costumed interpreters. Call before going, as opening hours are sporadic and depend on the availability of interpreters and what else might be going on in town. From Memorial Day to Labor Day you can usually count on the Fort being open on weekends from 10:00 A.M. until 4:00 P.M. Admission is $6.00. Telephone: (603) 826–5700.

From Charlestown, drive north on Route 12 for four miles, then follow Route 12A, which is the old road that follows the Connecticut River so closely that in parts of the spring it may be flooded. You'll drive a lovely seven miles to the 460-foot **Cornish-Windsor Bridge,** the longest two-span wooden covered bridge in the United States, connecting Cornish, New Hampshire, with Windsor, Vermont. The turnout to the **Saint-Gaudens National Historic Site** comes up in another two miles, but before you visit this idyll of artistic sensibility, continue north on Route 12A to the village of Plainfield to gather the fixings for a picnic. Then return to the Saint-Gaudens turnoff for a view of American art at its finest. At the end of the nineteenth century, **Cornish, New Hampshire,** became a retreat for some of New York's leading painters, sculptors, and illustrators.

Most visitors begin their tour at the "Little Studio," where they are startled and perhaps even a little perplexed by the ripe proportions of the statue of a lightly clad goddess Diana, a model for the figure at the top of Madison Square Garden in New York. Beginning in the studio, where an excellent video recounts all the official highlights of the life of Augustus Saint-Gaudens, is the dutiful student approach to the site. But Saint-Gaudens came here to escape programmatic duty, and the spirit of the place is better appreciated by beginning with a picnic lunch beneath the pergola outside the studio. Spread out your repast under the grapevines and let your eyes wander through the hollyhocks to the mountain vistas in the distance. It's as close as you're likely to get to joining the aesthetic aristocrats who frolicked on this hillside a century ago.

Flush with sculptural commissions that stemmed from his masterful statue of Admiral Farragut in Central Park, in 1885 Augustus Saint-Gaudens was looking for a summer place to escape the heat and hubbub of Manhattan. When his childhood friend and lawyer, Charles Beaman, offered to rent (or sell) him a rather ugly former

**Augustus Saint-Gaudens House,
Cornish, New Hampshire**

tavern in Cornish, Saint-Gaudens declined. Fortunately, his wife Augusta (known as "Gussie") had the better eye for landscape, and she prevailed.

"Gus" Saint-Gaudens transformed their home the way he transformed American public sculpture, imbuing a plain vernacular with a heroic classicism. "Aspet," as he named it after his father's birthplace in France, evolved from a rude, chunky farmhouse into an estate with studios, formal gardens, a lawn bowling area, a toboggan run, nature trails, and a pervasive and romantic sense of being well-off. It served as the family summer home from 1885 to 1897, then as their permanent home from 1900 until Saint-Gaudens died in 1907.

As Saint-Gaudens perfected his rural retreat he suffered a fate familiar to those with great summer homes, but his visitors weren't freeloading relatives, but rather the cream of New York social and artistic circles. Many of them ultimately built their own palatial getaways in the Cornish area. A well-heeled bohemia flourished, creating an all-American *belle époque* in the New Hampshire hills.

Despite the company of such bon vivants as Maxwell Parrish, Saint-Gaudens managed to accomplish a lot of work here. After the picnic, enter the Little Studio for a look at some of the sculptor's low-relief portraits and a fine biographical film that certainly made us ashamed of our ignorance about this remarkable sculptor of a century ago. If you wanted a masterful public monument in the Gilded Age, Gus Saint-Gaudens was your man.

You can get a pleasant and speedy art history lesson right on the grounds, because they are covered with copies of his most famous statues, including a new casting of the 1880 Admiral David Farragut statue that made Saint-Gaudens' career. From the Farragut, follow the reflecting pool, lined with several low reliefs, including a copy of the Robert Louis Stevenson memorial, to the Gallery that houses some of Saint-Gaudens' best early and very late work. Here you'll see a selection of exquisite cameos that he cut during his scuffling days in Paris, Rome, and New York, as well as his final masterpieces in miniature: the $10 and $20 gold pieces (known colloquially as the "eagle" and "double eagle") that remain the most beautiful coins ever struck in this country.

Traipse down the lawn to see the graves of the couple if you wish, but by all means take the house tour. The upper levels now serve as National Park Service offices, but the rest of the house gives a feel for Gus's practical turn of mind (his desk on the stairway landing provides a clear view of visitors at the front door) and Gussie's Victorian sensibility (the doilyed and ruffled sitting room).

Once you've passed, however briefly, through the locus of their lives, do what Gus and Gussie almost certainly did: Loll about on the broad porch and watch the day march down the hill in contented rustic splendor. The Saint-Gaudens National Historic Site is open from Memorial Day through October daily 9:00 A.M. to 4:30 P.M. Adults $4.00. Telephone: (603) 675–2175.

From the Saint-Gaudens National Historic Site, continue north on Route 12A to the junction with I–89 on the New Hampshire bank of the Connecticut River. One of the large tributaries of the Connecticut, the White River, flows in just west of this spot at White River Junction, Vermont. Rather than following the river north just yet, we strongly advise taking a little sojourn west along another tributary, the Ottauquechee River. Drive west on I–89 about three miles to exit 2, Route 4 west toward **Woodstock, Vermont.**

Woodstock is easily one of the prettiest resort towns in Vermont, perhaps in all of New England. And if some of its glamour results from rather recent additions and improvements, then it only serves to show what large sums of money can accomplish if dispensed with taste. Scoffers suggest Woodstock might simply be labeled Rockefeller National Park and then sealed off to anyone who doesn't live there. While it is true that the Rockefeller family has been extremely generous to Woodstock (and has profited handsomely from the improvements), such a dismissal misses the point.

There *is* a national park in Woodstock, and it occupies 555 acres donated by the Rockefeller family, but it's called **Marsh-Billings National Historic Park,** and it's dedicated to chronicling the early years of the conservation movement in the United States. Headquarters for the park is the

mansion once occupied by Mary French Rockefeller and her husband, Laurance. Mrs. Rockefeller is the key to the family largesse toward Woodstock, for her grandfather was Frederick Billings.

A little background is in order here. Contrary to popular belief that the American conservation movement sprung fully formed from the head of Theodore Roosevelt and took the immediate form of Yosemite and Yellowstone national parks in the west, it began far earlier in the East, where the destruction of the environment was felt first.

One of the earliest and most influential conservationists was George Perkins Marsh, who was born in Woodstock in 1801. Even as a young man Marsh observed that mud ran through the Woodstock streets after a heavy rain, thanks to the deforestation of Mount Tom, the gentle hill that rises above the town. Later Marsh served in the foreign service in Italy and Turkey and traveled widely in Europe. Making the connection between the ravaged landscape of the Mediterranean and the destruction of his boyhood environment, in 1864 Marsh penned *Man and Nature, or Physical Geography as Modified by Human Action.* It launched the conservation movement.

Frederick Billings retired as president of the Northern Pacific Railroad and came to live in Woodstock in the mid-1860s, where he read Marsh's book and decided to put the ideas into action. In 1869 Billings purchased Marsh's boyhood home on a rise at the base of Mount Tom overlooking the Ottauquechee River. Until his death in 1890, Billings spent his time perfecting an estate that would be a model of progressive farming and forestry. Among his projects was a network of 20 miles of carriage trails and footpaths on the slopes of Mount Tom that lead to the manmade lake at the summit called the Pogue. All the paths are open to the public.

Billings and his descendants maintained the parklands as stewards, all the time summering in the ornate red brick mansion that Billings had built and which now serves as the park's headquarters. Dedicated in June 1998, the park is located just two miles from Woodstock Center. The park is open from June through mid-October daily from 10:00 A.M. to 4:00 P.M. Tours of the mansion or of the grounds cost $5.00. A forest tour is free, as is general admission. All tours last about 75 minutes. Telephone: (802) 457-3368.

The new national park surrounds the grounds of the private, non-profit **Billings Farm & Museum,** created in 1982 by the Rockefellers before they donated the rest of the family property to the Park Service. Billings set up the farm in 1871, stocking it with Jersey cattle that he imported directly from the Isle of Jersey. It remains a working dairy farm, and part of the attraction of the site is watching the various chores. The museum portion is housed in four reconstructed barns to portray the cycle of seasons in Vermont farming. The farm and museum are open from May through late October daily from 10:00 A.M. to 5:00 P.M., November and December on Saturday and Sunday from 10:00 A.M. to 4:00 P.M. Adults $6.50. The museum is located at Route 12 and River Road. Telephone: (802) 457-2355.

The Rockefellers were not simply content to preserve and pass on the conservation visions of Marsh and Billings. They also purchased the decrepit Woodstock Inn, located on the handsome town green, and built an expansive resort on the site that has fooled many a visitor into thinking it's a marvelous relic of the eighteenth century. The 144 rooms are altogether modern in construction, if not in appearance, and the presence of a large hostelry has aided Woodstock in its growth as a resort for winter skiing and summer golfing.

Woodstock is an extremely pleasant place to spend a few days. Its bustling village center is lined with art and craft galleries. It boasts several good and a few outstanding restaurants. The general store, **F.H. Gillingham & Sons,** stocks a superb selection of domestic and imported wines and cheeses alongside Vermont maple products and bins of loose nails. (The proprietors also do a very big mail order business in Vermont country ambience.)

If you continue four miles west on Route 4 from Woodstock, you'll encounter the **Quechee Gorge,** an extremely scenic 161-foot gouge in the rock with the Ottauquechee River running through it, and the almost infinitesimal village of

Quechee, where the Irish glassmaker Simon Pearce has created a small commercial empire on the riverbank.

When you are ready to move on from the genteel tranquility of Woodstock and Quechee, drive east again on Route 4 to I-89 and go a mile to the I-91 junction to go north to **Hanover, New Hampshire.** From I-91, take exit 13 into Hanover.

It is hard to know where Hanover ends and **Dartmouth College** begins. The two have been entwined in a symbiotic embrace since Eleazar Warner established the college in 1769 to educate both English colonists and the local Abenaki tribes. Town and gown grew together, and Dartmouth's vast green functions as the center of the community. But the clock tower and steeple on this green belong not to the Congregational church (as in most New England hamlets) but to the college's chief repository of knowledge, Baker Library.

Like Northampton, Hanover is a college town, but one with far more conservative and low-key traditions. Townspeople see themselves a bit as an outpost of civilization in the wilderness, which may explain why the local newsstands carry more copies of the *New York Times* than of any Vermont or even New Hampshire papers. There's some truth to this point of view. Thanks to the college, Hanover is certainly the center of culture and refinement in the Upper Connecticut River Valley.

Baker Library, anchoring the north side of the Dartmouth Green, is worth visiting to see the extraordinary painted walls of the lower level reading room executed in the mid-1930s by Mexican muralist José Clemente Orozco. The 3,000 square feet of paintings, entitled "Epic of American Civilization," are striking, even garish representations of pre- and post-contact culture in the Americas with fairly strong left-wing themes. Painted in a vigorous Expressionist manner, they rank as some of Orozco's best surviving murals anywhere. A leaflet at the reading room desk deciphers the panels. Upstairs on the first floor, you can visit the special collections room. Among its many treasures are Daniel Webster's copies of the folio volumes of Audubon's *Birds of North*

America. Baker Library is open daily during academic sessions from 8:00 A.M. until midnight. During campus holidays, it closes at 5:00 P.M. Telephone: (603) 646–2560.

On the south side of the Dartmouth Green, across Wheelock Street, are other Dartmouth structures—the Hanover Inn, the Hopkins Center for Performing Arts, and the superb **Hood Museum of Art.** With ten galleries presenting changing exhibitions, the Hood is never the same on successive visits—with the exception of the extraordinary ancient Assyrian bas reliefs that are simply too heavy to move around. The Hood has an excellent collection of Native American basketry, particularly from the Northeast, as well as a smattering of all the major artistic periods of Asian, European, and American art. Its twentieth-century collections, particularly on paper, are one of the museum's real strengths. Admission is free, but a $3.00 donation is suggested. The Hood is open Tuesday to Saturday from 10:00 A.M. to 5:00 P.M. (Wednesday until 9:00 P.M.) and Sunday from noon to 5:00 P.M. Telephone: (603) 646–2808.

Dartmouth students tend to be very involved with outdoors activities—boating, hiking, camping, skiing, and the like. In fact, political conservatism and activist conservationism go hand in hand here. The Outing Club operates a number of facilities in the area that are open to the public. One of the nicest ways to see the Connecticut River from the water is to rent a canoe from the allied **Ledyard Canoe Club.** Located on the river behind the Tuck School (just off the bridge to Norwich, Vermont), the canoe club is open whenever the river water temperature is above 50 degrees. Strong canoeists may want to paddle upriver, where the Connecticut is narrower and the water faster. Downriver from Hanover, the Wilder Dam turns the river into a placid lake. The dam, by the way, has a major fish ladder that is quite active during the spawning seasons. During the summer the canoe club is open from 9:00 A.M. to 8:00 P.M. on weekdays, 10:00 A.M. to 8:00 P.M. on weekends. During the spring and fall, the club is open from 10:00 A.M. to 6:00 P.M. on weekdays, noon to 6:00 P.M. on weekends. Canoes and kayaks can be rented for $5.00 per hour or $15.00

Baker Library, Dartmouth College, Hanover, New Hampshire

for a weekday, $25.00 for a weekend day. Telephone: (603) 643–6709.

The Connecticut River runs far north of Hanover, of course, but once you pass the village of Lyme (see "Staying There") it takes on characteristics of the region of New England we consider to be the North Country—where settlements born of logging concerns have persisted as gateways to the great northern wilderness. You'll find more about that world in the "North Country" chapter.

Staying There

The Lower Valley, Connecticut

Wethersfield, Connecticut

LODGING

Chester Bulkley House. 184 Main Street. Right in the historic village, this circa 1830 Greek Revival home has five guest rooms and period details such as wide pine boards, hard-carved woodwork, and working fireplaces. Three rooms have private baths and two share baths. Telephone: (860) 563–4236. Moderate with breakfast.

FOOD

The Spicy Green Bean Deli. 285 Main Street. Telephone: (860) 563–3100. This popular local spot has good deli style sandwiches and excellent cookies. Breakfast and lunch.

FAIRS, FESTIVALS, AND EVENTS

Wethersfield Weekend Festival. This three-day event on the weekend after Memorial Day weekend pays tribute to Old Wethersfield's Colonial history with costumed performers, concerts, history plays, historic house tours, a Revolutionary encampment, antiques show, and other events. Telephone: (888) 653–9384.

Hartford, Connecticut

For information on the Greater Hartford area, contact the Greater Hartford Tourism District, 234 Murphy Road, Hartford, CT 06114. Telephone: (860) 244–8181 or (800) 793–4480.

LODGING

1895 House. 97 Girard Avenue. Located off Farmington Avenue, close to the Mark Twain House, this 1895 Victorian has a spacious third floor suite with skylight and two comfortable bedrooms with a shared bath on the second floor. Telephone: (860) 232–0014. Inexpensive to moderate with breakfast.

Goodwin Hotel. One Haynes Street. This ornate red-brick hotel is a city landmark. The interior has a late Deco feel. Catering primarily to business travelers during the week, it is a particularly good bargain for weekend visitors. The 124 guest rooms have been recently refurbished with new carpets, drapes, and upholstery. Telephone: (860) 246–7500. Moderate to very expensive.

FOOD

City Steam Brewery Cafe. 942 Main Street. Telephone: (860) 525–1600. Stylish brewpub on the Pacific Northwest model makes light versions of British ales to accompany a contemporary bar menu. Lunch and dinner. Moderate to expensive.

Hot Tomato's. 1 Union Place. Telephone: (860) 249–5100. An outdoor patio and big glass windows give diners a view across the street to Bushnell Park at one of downtown's most popular spots for Italian food with an emphasis on light pastas. Open Monday through Friday for lunch and dinner, Saturday and Sunday for dinner only. Moderate.

Pierpont's. One Haynes Street. Telephone: (860) 246–7500. This restaurant at the Goodwin Hotel is one of the city's power meal venues. The bar is known for its martinis. In keeping with the hotel refurbishment, the restaurant also got a new menu, concentrating on updated classics with creative twists. Breakfast, lunch, and dinner. Moderate to expensive.

36 Lewis Street. Telephone: (860) 278–0436. New owners (as of February 1998) have breathed long-overdue life into the charming dining rooms in this 1826 structure, one of the little historic gems still surviving in downtown. The front room has creamy walls and bronze colored window treatments. The back room has sienna-colored walls and chandeliers. The bar is smart and live jazz fills it with a warm ambience on the weekends. The contemporary grill menu draws on

Connecticut State Capitol building, Hartford

some of the best of classic American and bistro traditions. It's worth dining here just for the wine list, one of the best selected and most reasonably priced in the area. Lunch and dinner. Expensive.

OTHER ATTRACTIONS

The Bushnell. Hartford's major performing arts center presents touring Broadway shows and a travel adventure series and serves as the performance space for the Hartford Ballet, Hartford Symphony, and Connecticut Opera Association. Telephone: (860) 246–6807.

Hartford Stage Company. This ambitious company is known for its productions of American classics and premieres of new plays by some of the finest contemporary playwrights. 50 Church Street. Telephone: (860) 527–5151.

TOURS

Heritage Trails Sightseeing. Two-hour minibus tour departs from local hotels and focuses on Hartford's history. Adults $15. Telephone: (860) 677–8867.

FAIRS, FESTIVALS, AND EVENTS

Canon Greater Hartford Open. This PGA Tour golf tournament takes place in late June through early July at Tournament Players Club at River Highlands in Cromwell. Telephone: (860) 244–8181.

Mark Twain Days. Hartford's favorite son is celebrated in a two-day city-wide festival in mid-July that includes concerts, storytelling, and the Huck Finn/Tom Sawyer Raft Race from Charter Oak Landing. Telephone: (860) 247–0998.

Riverfest. As Hartford shifts its attention back to the riverfront, this early July festival includes fireworks, music, and live entertainment at East Hartford's Great River Park and Charter Oak Landing in Hartford. Telephone: (860) 713–3131.

Rose Weekend. There are more than 900 varieties and 14,000 rose bushes at Elizabeth Park Rose Garden, the first municipally owned rose garden in the country. They are in full bloom during this mid-June celebration that includes concerts, poetry readings, and refreshments. The park is located off Asylum and Prospect Avenues on the border of Hartford and West Hartford. Telephone: (860) 242–0017.

Litchfield, Connecticut

For information on the Litchfield area, contact the Litchfield Hills Travel Council, P.O. Box 968, Litchfield, CT 06759. Telephone: (860) 567–4506.

LODGING

Abel Darling Bed and Breakfast. 102 West Street. There are only two rooms in this stunning 1782 house just west of the town green, but they're all you'd expect in Litchfield: antique furnishings, stenciled walls, wide floorboards, and exposed beams. Telephone: (860) 567–0384. Moderate with breakfast.

FOOD

Village Pub and Restaurant. 25 West Street (on the green). Telephone: (860) 567–8307. This spot has been the local community restaurant since 1890, but it received a major shakeup with new ownership and—more importantly—a new chef in January 1998. There's still a homey warmth about the old booths and the long bar, but the menu now speaks with the eloquence you might expect of a Johnson and Wales graduate. Half the menu features striking New American fish preparations and a number of handmade pastas, but lovers of chicken, pork, and beef will find plenty to suit their palates as well. Lunch and dinner. Moderate to expensive.

FAIRS, FESTIVALS, AND EVENTS

Annual House Tour. This grand event held on the second Saturday of July has been a staple of the Litchfield summer social circuit since 1948. Telephone: (860) 567–9423.

Litchfield Jazz Festival. Three early-August days of jazz and blues performed by some international headliners (Tito Puente, for example) as well as some of Connecticut's journeymen musicians. In 1998 the festival moved to the Goshen Fairgrounds a few miles north of Litchfield. Telephone: (860) 567–4162.

A Taste of the Litchfield Hills. Since 1976, the food and wine producers of the Litchfield Hills have gathered on the last weekend of June for tastings and live entertainment. Telephone: (860) 567–4045.

New Preston, Connecticut

LODGING

Boulders Inn. East Shore Road (Route 45). The rustic 1895 main building of the inn has been joined by some nicer cottages that raise the poshness level a notch or two. The lakeside location is unbeatable, and the inn maintains its own boathouse with canoes and rowboats for guests. Although pricey, the Boulders is one of the more reasonable of the old-time summer getaway inns on Lake Waramaug. Telephone: (860) 868–0541 or (800) 55–BOULDERS. Expensive to very expensive.

The Hopkins Inn. 22 Hopkins Road. With eleven rooms and two apartments, the inn is open from March through December. The inn has its own private beach on Lake Waramaug as well

Hopkins Vineyard, New Preston, Connecticut

as a great view. Telephone: (860) 868–7295. Inexpensive to moderate.

CAMPGROUNDS AND RV PARKS

Lake Waramaug State Park. Off Route 45. Located about 2 miles from village center. The park's seventy-eight campsites do not have utility hookups but there is a dumping station. Sites open mid-May through September. Reservations (at least ten days in advance through the mail) are available, but drive-ups are accepted if space is available. July 4 and Labor weekends are usually fully reserved by April. Telephone: (860) 868–0220.

FOOD

Boulders Inn. East Shore Road (Route 45). Telephone: (860) 868–0541. Creative New American kitchen and extensive wine cellar go a long way toward fine dinners that match the inn's exclusive rooms. Breakfast and dinner daily for guests, open Wednesday through Monday for dinner for non-guests. Very expensive.

The Hopkins Inn. 22 Hopkins Road. Telephone: (860) 868–7295. Traditional New England fare with a little New American flair (duck with all the trimmings instead of turkey, for example). Summer dining available on shaded garden terrace overlooking Lake Waramaug. Breakfast daily, lunch, and dinner Tuesday through Sunday from April through December. Lunch served only on Saturday April, May, November, and December. Expensive.

SHOPPING

Del Mediterraneo. 7 Main Street. Telephone: (860) 868–8070. This shop selects and imports its own line of handmade ceramics and pottery from Spain—nicely suited to the Mediterranean design aesthetic popular in the Litchfield Hills.

Room With a View. Main Street. Telephone: (860) 868–1717. Antiques and decorative objects selected by Marie E. Jainchill, who doubles as as designer and interior decorator.

Woodbury, Connecticut

FOOD

Carole Peck's Good News Café. 694 Main Street (Route 6 south). Telephone: (203) 266–4663. It's worth visiting Woodbury just to eat at Carole Peck's table. Nominally serving "global" cuisine, this splashy, bright restaurant with a surprising sense of fun is for people who like to dine. Peck's repertoire is so deep that it rarely repeats, but she was a pioneer in making "bistro" an all-American word. Lunch and dinner Wednesday through Monday. Expensive.

The Mid Valley, Massachusetts

Springfield, Massachusetts

FOOD

La Florentina Pastry Shop. 883 Main Street. Telephone: (413) 732–3151. "Home of the Rum Cake." The Italian pastries are made from recipes that date back three generations. This was a place to sip cappuccino or espresso at tiny cafe tables long before anyone ever heard of Starbucks.

Student Prince/The Fort. 8 Fort Street. Telephone: (413) 734–7475. Traditional German American fare such as bratwurst and Yaegerschnitzel are served in a decor full of beer steins and German coats of arms. Lunch and dinner. Moderate.

FAIRS, FESTIVALS, AND EVENTS

ACC Fair. This mid-June craft show is juried by the American Crafts Council and features more than 350 of the highest-caliber artisans in the country. Wheelchair accessible. Telephone: (800) 836–3470.

Bright Nights at Forest Park. From late-November to early January, New England's largest lighting display features a two-mile-long, 20-minute drive. One exhibit, "Seussland," pays tribute to Springfield native Theodore Geisel with such familiars as the Cat in the Hat, the Grinch, and Horton and a Who. Telephone: (413) 787–1548.

The Big E, Eastern States Exposition. One of the country's largest agricultural and cultural fairs, features country and popular music, crafts, parades, a circus, horse shows, and an Avenue of the States with replicas of capitol buildings. It takes place for seventeen days from mid-September to early October. Wheelchair accessible. Telephone: (413) 737–2443.

Holyoke, Massachusetts

ACTIVITIES

Mt. Tom. This ski area is only two minutes from I–91, exit 17A. There are eighty-five acres and seventeen trails, with 100 percent snowmaking. So close to population centers, it tends to be a local mountain, with an emphasis on skiing and riding lessons, family outings. All trails are also open at night for the after-work crowd. In the summer there are water sports: wave pool, Alpine Falls water tube ride, water slide. Route 5. Telephone: (413) 532–8736.

Northampton, Massachusetts

For information on the Northampton area contact the Northampton Area Visitors Center, 99 Pleasant Street, Northampton, MA 01060. Telephone: (413) 584–1900.

LODGING

Autumn Inn. 259 Elm Street. Just a short drive from downtown and very convenient to Smith College, this colonial-style motor inn has thirty rooms furnished in a low-key Early American style—Hitchcock furniture, white bedspreads. It also boasts an outdoor pool and barbecue. Telephone: (413) 584–7660. Moderate.

The Hotel Northampton. 36 King Street. This 1927 classic stands on a central downtown site where travelers have stayed since 1786 (at the Wiggins Tavern, now an annex to the hotel). The seventy-five rooms are a little small by today's standards, but the hotel refurbishes them frequently. Telephone: (413) 584–3100. Moderate to expensive.

FOOD

Cha Cha Cha. 134 Main Street. Telephone: (413) 586–7311. This Latin grill specializes in burritos, quesadillas, and salads. The Thai chicken burrito (what can we say? Northampton's a multicultural place) is suprisingly terrific. Free chips and salsa bar. Lunch and dinner. Inexpensive to moderate.

Eastside Grill. 19 Strong Avenue. Telephone: (413) 586–3347. The style here walks a careful line between diner and fancy New American cuisine, with an emphasis on fresh ingredients and intense flavors. Lunch and dinner. Inexpensive to moderate.

Miss Florence Diner. 99 Main Street. Telephone: (413) 584–3137. This classic diner, about three miles west of town on Route 9, opened in 1941 and has changed very little since. The grill is out front so you can watch the action, and the place has become so popular that most of the seating is in an adjoining room. Cream pies (banana, chocolate, coconut) are made daily on the premises. The Miss Florence opens at 4:00 A.M. and serves breakfast all day. Breakfast, lunch, and dinner. Inexpensive.

Paul & Elizabeth's. 150 Main Street at Thorne's Market. Telephone: (413) 584–4832. P&E's pioneered natural foods fine dining in the Pioneer Valley. To appreciate their strengths, enjoy the bread basket, savor the salad, and order one of the fish preparations. (We said "natural foods," not "vegetarian.") Dinner and weekend brunch. Moderate to expensive.

Spoleto. 50 Main Street. Telephone: (413) 586–6313. The spa-inspired light Italian menu is uniformly good, rarely precious and sometimes outstanding. It's *the* place to be seen for local foodies and on weekends the background clamor of conversation makes it seem like a restaurant in a sophisticated urban center. Dinner. Moderate to expensive.

Wiggins Tavern. In The Hotel Northampton, 36 King Street. Telephone: (413) 584–3100. The tavern's been around since 1786 and the hand-hewn exposed beams and massive stone fireplace play up the antiquity. The menu could have been devised by John Adams' chef—it's classic New England fare of roast beef, baked beans, and the like. Breakfast, lunch, and dinner. Moderate to expensive.

OTHER ATTRACTIONS

Iron Horse Music Hall. 20 Center Street. Telephone: (413) 584–0610. This acoustic music venue has developed over the last two decades as one of the top New England stops for blues and jazz musicians, folk singers, and singer-songwriters. Cover prices vary. The Iron Horse also serves dinner (moderate) and a wide selection of beers.

FAIRS, FESTIVALS, AND EVENTS

Paradise City Arts Festival. Juried crafts show is held for three days in mid-October at the Tri-County Fairgrounds and features about 200 exhibitors and a gourmet food fair. Telephone: (413) 586–6324.

SHOPPING

Northampton and the surrounding hilltowns are known for their concentration of fine crafts artists. Much of their work, as well as the work of national artists, finds its way into the galleries on Northampton's Main Street.

Antique Center of Northampton. 9½ Market Street. Telephone: (413) 584–3600. In many ways a typical "group" shop of sixty-plus dealers in antiques and collectibles, this store is particularly strong in Arts & Crafts furniture.

Backyard Birds. 17 Strong Avenue. Telephone: (413) 586–3155. Every imaginable kind of bird feeder—including those designed to keep other critters away from the bird food. If you aren't already convinced of the futility of this attempt, check out the photograph on the wall of a bear chowing down at a feeder.

Webs. Service Center Road. Telephone: (413) 584–2225. This 19,000-square-foot warehouse on the outskirts of town is full of yarn for knitting and weaving. Retail prices reign at the front in the neat showroom, but the bargains are in the back.

Don Muller Gallery. 40 Main Street. Telephone: (413) 586–1119. With a well-selected assortment of fine jewelry, as well as pottery, glass, wood, Muller represents many nationally known crafts artists and handles commissioned works as well as conventional retail sales.

Pinch Pottery. 179 Main Street. Telephone: (413) 586–4509. This small shop has a national reputation for its ceramics and holds small exhibitions in the gallery in the back of the retail shop.

Silverscape Designs. 1 King Street. Telephone: (413) 584–3324. Perhaps befitting the fine jewelry and other crafts items from about 300 artisans, Silverscape occupies a striking Art Deco bank building on the corner of King and Main Streets.

Amherst, Massachusetts

LODGING

Allen House Victorian Inn. 599 Main Street. The owners are restoring this 1886 Victorian to the Aesthetic style with accurate reproduction William Morris, Walter Crane, and Charles Eastlake wallpaper. The bright color and bold designs are a respite from the more common Laura Ashley B&B decor. The Eastlake Room (named for its vintage furniture) along with the parlor and dining room show this vintage house at its best. Telephone: (413) 253–5000. Inexpensive to moderate, with breakfast.

Deerfield/Sunderland/ South Deerfield, Massachusetts

LODGING

Deerfield Inn. 81 The Street. Built in 1884, the inn is smack dab in the middle of The Street in walking distance of all the historic houses. One modern wing was constructed to resemble a tobacco barn, but the property does not carry its attempts at historic evocation too far. Moreover, the comfortable rooms are constantly upgraded. Telephone: (413) 774–5587 or (800) 926–3865. Moderate to expensive with breakfast.

FOOD

Deerfield Inn. 81 The Street. Telephone: (413) 774–5587. In the Colonial outpost of Old Deerfield, the inn's restaurant has made the wise decision that twentieth-century cuisine is far superior to eighteenth-century cuisine. The kitchen draws heavily from local farms for the produce highlighted in the New American menu. Breakfast, lunch, and dinner. Moderate to expensive.

Sienna. 28 Elm Street, South Deerfield. Telephone: (413) 665–0215. With a New York SoHo lineage, Sienna reigns in the Pioneer Valley as the restaurant for foodies. Dining here is something of an occasion for locals, and the fresh-market New American menu can also be a treat for visitors. Dinner. Expensive.

FAIRS, FESTIVALS, AND EVENTS

Old Deerfield Crafts Fairs. Held for two days in late June and in mid-September on the lawn of Memorial Hall Museum. More than 250 exhibitors from seventeen states, often in full costume, demonstrate traditional crafts and sell their wares. Telephone: (413) 774–7476.

Shelburne Falls, Massachusetts

SHOPPING

Crafts. This little village next to the Deerfield River is another crafts mecca. **Salmon Falls Artisans Showroom** (telephone: 413-625-9833)

Bridge of Flowers over Deerfield River, Shelburne Falls, Massachusetts

on Ashfield Street, one block up the hill from the Bridge of Flowers has the work of more than 185 local craftspeople. **Mole Hollow Candles** (telephone: 413–625–6789) has been making smokeless, dripless candles for more than twenty-five years. Their factory store has a good view of the glacial potholes. Next door are glassblowers at **North River Glass** (telephone: 413–625–6422) and across the street is the **Bald Mountain Pottery Studio** (telephone: 413–625–8110).

Greenfield, Massachusetts

FOOD

Basil's. 10 Miles Street. Telephone: (413) 772–6333. Local artwork decorates the walls of this popular spot for pastry, salads, and soups. Lunch. Inexpensive.

FAIRS, FESTIVALS, AND EVENTS

Franklin County Fair. One of the oldest agricultural fairs in the United States is held in mid-September and features horse and oxen draws, sheep and cattle shows, entertainment, and a midway. Telephone: (413) 774–4282.

Green River Music & Balloon Festival. The highlight of this July event is hot-air balloon launches (weather permitting). But there are also music, crafts, and fireworks. Telephone: (413) 773–5463.

The Upper Valley, Vermont and New Hampshire

Brattleboro, Vermont

For information about Brattleboro and the surrounding area, contact the Brattleboro Chamber of Commerce, 182 Main Street, Brattleboro, VT 05301. Telephone: (802) 254–4565.

LODGING

Latchis Hotel. 50 Main Street. The big stucco building is a 1938 Art Deco survivor in the heart of the downtown. The thirty rooms are not far different from what you'd expect at a motel, but the color schemes and furniture design at least evoke the Art Deco era. The ornate old movie house on the premises explains the aroma of popcorn in the hallways. Telephone: (802) 254–6300. Inexpensive to moderate.

FOOD

T.J. Buckley's Uptown Diner. 132 Elliot Street. Telephone: (802) 257–4922. This little red and black diner has become somewhat upscale. With only eight tables and two dinner seatings, reservations are required. The owner-cook apprenticed with a French chef. Entree and salad with wine and coffee is $25. Dessert is extra. Moderate.

Common Ground Collective Restaurant. 25 Elliot Street. Telephone: (802) 257–0855. If R. Crumb's "Mr. Natural" were to visit Brattleboro, he'd eat here. The menu is all vegetarian and mostly organic and the ownership is honest-to-goodness collective. The cashew burgers are actually pretty good and many vegans swear by the seaweed salad. Lunch and dinner. Inexpensive to moderate.

Latchis Grill and Windham Brewery. 6 Flat Street. Telephone: (802) 254–4747. Located in the Latchis Hotel, the restaurant features cozy booths and banquettes and boasts good jazz on the sound system. You can taste the production of the on-site Windham Brewery, including a freshly made root beer. The grilled fish and poultry tend to be overspiced, so keep your order simple and enjoy the beer. The casual pub is upstairs, the classier dining room down below. Lunch and dinner. Inexpensive to moderate.

Marina on the Water. Route 5 (Putney Road). Telephone: (802) 257–7563. This waterside bar and grill overlooks the West River and is a great place for watching the sun go down. It's just what you'd expect at a marina—sandwiches, burgers, pasta, seafood, and steak. Lunch and dinner. Moderate.

Peter Havens. 32 Elliot Street. Telephone: (802) 257–3333. Not everyone in Brattleboro goes out in Birkenstocks. This ten-table, elegant bistro is where you dine when you want to dress suave. The emphasis is on fish with a European accent—shrimp Pernod, for example. Dinner. Expensive.

ACTIVITIES

Connecticut River Safari. Telephone: (802) 257–5008. Located near the riverboat dock on Route 5, Connecticut River Safari rents canoes and kayaks, starting at $10 for two hours. The operators will also arrange to shuttle you upriver or pick you up downriver for additional fees.

TOURS

Belle of Brattleboro Riverboat Cruises. This small (fifty seats) wooden-decked riverboat makes a variety of scenic cruises along the West and Connecticut Rivers that provides a feel for life on the small-town banks. The straight hour-long sightseeing cruises cost $8.00, with additional charges for meals or entertainment. The cruise dock is on Route 5 north of town. Telephone: (802) 254–1263.

FAIRS, FESTIVALS, AND EVENTS

Brattleboro Winter Carnival. This week-long event begins in late February. Along with such standard activities as sleigh rides, snow sculpture competitions, figure skating shows, and dogsled competitions, the festival features a ski-jumping competition on Olympic-size Harris Hill that attracts some of the top international jumpers. Telephone: (802) 258–2511.

Gallery Walk. More than a dozen local galleries hold receptions and offer refreshments and the chance to meet artists on the first Friday of each month. Telephone: (802) 254–4565.

SHOPPING

Musical Instruments. The hills around Brattleboro are alive with the sound of music, all right, and it has nothing to do with the Trapp family. This is a hotbed of New Age sounds, funky jazz, and the whole acoustic music revival (what used to be called "folk music"). Sheet music and jazz instruments are the specialty of **Blue Note Music** (telephone: 802–257–7799) at 61 Main Street, while guitars, mandolins, and other stringed instruments are found at **Maple Leaf Music Company** (telephone: 802–254–5559) at 19 Elliot Street.

Vermont Artisan Designs. 106 Main Street. Telephone: (802) 257–3049. With the work of 300 craftspeople, mainly from Vermont, there is a good selection of well-made items in all price ranges.

Putney, Vermont

FOOD

Curtis' All-American Barbeque. Route 5. Telephone: (802) 387–5474. We don't know what locals do in the winter when this barbeque joint is closed—eat plain and dull food, we guess. Curtis serves hardwood-smoked ribs and chicken with a twenty-five-ingredient sauce and homemade baked beans from the side of an old blue bus parked in a dusty lot. A 370-gallon oil drum serves as his smoker. This is funky and authentic Southern barbecue like you'd never expect in Vermont. Open from April to October, Wednesday through Sunday for lunch and dinner. Inexpensive.

SHOPPING

Green Mountain Spinnery. Across from the Putney Inn. Telephone: (802) 387–4528. The Mill Store sells wool and mohair yarns spun from New England fibers as well as knitting supplies. A guided mill tour is offered on the first and third Tuesdays of each month ($2.00).

Quechee, Vermont

LODGING

Parker House Inn. 16 Main Street. Down in Quechee Village beside the river, this 1857 inn has seven rooms with queen or king beds and a handsome dining room offering a contemporary menu featuring local products. Telephone: (802) 295–6077. Moderate.

FOOD/SHOPPING

Simon Pearce Restaurant. The Mill. Telephone: (802) 295–2711. Irish glass blower Simon Pearce took over this mill site in Quechee Village several years ago for his studio and studio shop. The complex has grown into a mini-destination where the shop carries a range of handmade household goods, including pottery and table dressings that complement Pearce's glass. It's still possible to watch the craftspeople at work blowing glass at the furnace or throwing pots on a wheel. The mill's water chase has been converted into a small hydroelectric plant with explanatory signs. Pearce rightly saw that a shopping complex would fare best with an adjoining restaurant, and this one is very popular for its California-style light pastas and sandwiches. Lunch and dinner. Moderate to expensive.

Woodstock, Vermont

For information about the Woodstock area, contact the Woodstock Area Chamber of Commerce, 18 Central Street, Woodstock, VT 05091. Telephone: (802) 457–3555.

LODGING

Jackson House Inn. 37 Old Route 4 West. This is our idea of a luxurious country inn—a smallish estate with beautiful grounds and the extremely comfortable rooms of a nineteenth-century lumber baron's home as brought stunningly up to date by the Florin family. Telephone: (802) 457–2065 or (800) 448–1890. Moderate to expensive with breakfast.

Shire Motel. 46 Pleasant Street. Set on the banks of the Ottauquechee River on the east end of the village, this nicely kept two-story motel with

thirty-three rooms has views of the river and the Billings Farm. Telephone: (802) 457–2211. Inexpensive to moderate.

Woodstock Inn & Resort. Fourteen The Green. "For two hundred years there's been an Inn on Woodstock's village green," says the literature— but for most of that time, it wasn't this one, which is a faux Colonial inn built by Laurance Rockefeller. The operative word in the name is "resort," for this 144-room hotel is less a country inn than an ocean liner afloat on a sea of grass in a small village. Telephone: (802) 457–1100 or (800) 448–7900. Moderate to very expensive.

FOOD

Bentley's. 3 Elm Street. Telephone: (802) 457–3232. Cheerful, rather eclectic decor with Victorian sofas, potted plants, and coffee shop tables on a couple of levels combines with perky staff to create an eccentric but welcoming air. Avoid the temptation to order anything more complicated than one of the burgers or steaks and enjoy selecting from a wide range of microbrewery beers, including a house-labeled pale ale brewed by Catamount. Lunch and dinner. Moderate.

The Jackson House Inn. 37 Old Route 4 West. Telephone: (802) 457–2065. Chef Brendan Nolan works culinary wonders in this newly expanded dining room—using his seafood connections from Cape Cod to augment the Vermont Fresh network of produce and dairy suppliers. The menu is set up with fixed prices for a three-course choice, or a five-course tasting menu— both between $40 and $50. It's worth every penny for Nolan's classic sense of balance and flavor intensity. Expect delights such as rich slices of duck breast on a bed of leeks, plums, and chard. He does equal wonders with a five-course vegetarian meal. Dinner. Very expensive.

The Prince & the Pauper. 24 Elm Street. Telephone: (802) 457–1818. Small spot with a choice between a very French fixed-price menu of $35 for appetizer, salad, and entree, or an a la carte menu of simple bistro fare (including several grilled pizzas). Reservations are essential for dining room. No reservations are taken for bistro

4

menu, which is served at bar and in lounge. Dinner. Moderate (bistro) to very expensive.

Woodstock Farmers' Market. Route 4, about 1 mile west of town. Telephone: (802) 457–3658. The deli operation at this market emphasizing fresh produce and breads ranks among the region's best. Breakfast items (available until 11:00 A.M.) range from the "New York Minute" of cream cheese and smoked salmon on a bagel to grilled portobello mushrooms, scrambled eggs, and smoked gruyère on a bagel, toast, or English muffin. Excellent sandwiches are available the rest of the time in half and whole sizes. This is also a good spot to pick up entrees to heat up back at the condo, cabin, or campsite. Open daily.

SHOPPING

Gallery on the Green. One The Green. Telephone: (802) 457–4956. This hugely successful gallery primarily represents painters who work in the "nostalgic New England" mode, creating landscapes and farmscapes intended to capture a vanishing rural world. Many artists who lie outside this principal focus are also shown, including some very accomplished color landscape photographers and some carvers of folk art statuary.

F.H. Gillingham & Sons. 16 Elm Street. Telephone: (802) 457–2100 or (800) 344–6668. Established in 1886, this shop has a little bit of almost everything, from food and hardware to homebrew supplies to fine wines. They also offer a mail-order catalog under the name of The Vermont General Store.

Stephen Huneck Gallery. 49 Central Street. Telephone: (802) 457–3206. Stephen Huneck may have begun as a folk artist using dog and cat motifs in his furniture, but he seems to have become a dog industry, with the woodcuts overshadowing the furniture and cast wall sculptures. *Art and Antiques* suggested that he's a fusion of Walt Disney and René Magritte, and they may be right.

Hanover, New Hampshire

For information on the Hanover area, contact the Hanover Chamber of Commerce, P.O. Box 5105, Hanover, NH 03755. Telephone: (603) 643–3512.

LODGING

Chieftain Motor Inn. 84 Lyme Road. Located just north of Dartmouth College, the Chieftain has perfectly clean and comfortable rooms. Although the motel stands near the Connecticut River, the water view is obscured by trees. Telephone: (603) 643–2550, or (800) 845–3557. Inexpensive to moderate.

Hanover Inn. On the Green. Dartmouth owns and operates the inn, which translates into a slightly stuffy Ivy League feel but genuine comfort. Telephone: (603) 643–4300 or (800) 443–7024. Very expensive.

The Trumbull House. 40 Etna Road. Four guest rooms and a suite occupy a 1919 colonial-style home in a luxurious country setting four miles east of Dartmouth. Hiking and cross-country ski trails traverse the sixteen-acre grounds. Telephone: (603) 643–2370 or (800) 651–5141. Moderate with breakfast.

FOOD

Lou's. 30 South Main St. Telephone: (603) 643–3321. Every college town needs a great greasy spoon, and in Hanover it's Lou's. Breakfast is available all day, including Belgian waffles, berry pancakes, cinnamon raisin French toast. And this being a college town, there are also lots of Tex-Mex dishes (quesadilla, tortilla soup, nachos) as well as burgers, gyros, sandwiches. Closes at 3:00 P.M. Monday through Friday and Sunday, closes at 5:00 P.M. on Saturday. Inexpensive.

Daniel Webster Room. At the Hanover Inn, On the Green. Telephone: (603) 643–4300. New American haute cuisine as interpreted by the very talented Michael Gray reigns in this formal and rather elegant room (dark wood chairs, a floral carpet, formal columns) at the Hanover Inn. Gray makes maximum use of produce from Dartmouth's organic farm. Dinner, Sunday brunch. Expensive to very expensive.

Zins. At the Hanover Inn, On the Green.

Telephone: (603) 643–4300. This casual restaurant and wine bar of the Hanover Inn shares an outdoor patio area with the Daniel Webster Room. The Zins tables are the ones with umbrellas. The menu is contemporary Italian-American and there are several wine choices by the glass. Lunch and dinner. Moderate.

OTHER ATTRACTIONS

Hopkins Center. The chief cultural center of the region offers an ambitious program of music, theater, dance, and film. 6041 Lower Level Wilson Hall, Dartmouth College. Telephone: (603) 646–2422.

ACTIVITIES

Dartmouth Outdoor Rentals. Telephone: (603) 646–1747. Rents mountain bikes, climbing shoes, in-line skates, camping gear to the general public as well as to Dartmouth students. Open weekdays 12:30 to 5:00 P.M., weekends from 10:00 A.M. to 5:00 P.M. Robinson Hall, Room 011, Dartmouth College.

Silver Fox Ski-Touring Center. Telephone: (603) 646–2440. Located at Dartmouth Outing Club House, Lower Level Occam Pond. Open Saturday and Sunday from 9:00 A.M. to 4:30 P.M. and Monday through Friday from 11:00 A.M. to 4:30 P.M. Day passes are $5.00. Cross-country ski rentals start at $9.00 per day, snowshoes or ice skates at $10.00 per day.

SHOPPING

The Dartmouth Bookstore. 33 Main Street. Telephone: (603) 643–3616 or (800) 624–8800. Excellent bookstore with a lot of Dartmouth memorabilia and souvenirs.

League of New Hampshire Craftsmen. 13 Lebanon Street. Telephone: (603) 643–5050. The studio craftspeople of the Granite State are some of the best organized in the country. This store is one of seven League shops throughout the state featuring traditional and contemporary crafts.

Norwich, Vermont

LODGING

The Norwich Inn. Main Street. This Victorian-era inn has seen some better days, but it's holding its own. Rooms are reasonable for the area, while the dining is the major attraction. There are fourteen rooms in the inn and seven more in a modest motel on the property. All rooms have private baths and antique furnishings. Telephone: (802) 649–1143. Inexpensive to moderate.

FOOD

The Norwich Inn. Chef Terrence Webb employs his Culinary Institute of America training to prepare a New American menu that emphasizes local produce. The bar enjoys the products of America's smallest brewery, Jasper Murdock's Alehouse. Lunch and dinner. Moderate to expensive.

OTHER ATTRACTIONS

Montshire Museum of Science. Two floors of exhibits explore space, nature, and technology. There are fresh and saltwater aquariums representing different ecosystems around the world. The network of walking trails includes some that pass along the river banks. Open daily from 10:00 A.M. to 5:00 P.M. Adults $5.00. Route 5. Telephone: (802) 649–2200.

Lyme, New Hampshire

ACTIVITIES

Dartmouth Skiway. Telephone: (603) 795–2143. Just fifteen minutes north of Hanover in Lyme Center, this small ski area rarely has lift lines. One quad chair lift services sixteen trails. It's a good place to learn to ski, with excellent instruction and a 400-foot beginner's slope. Dartmouth has a long skiing tradition, having sent eighty-one members to the United States Olympic Ski Team over the years. This modest little ski area lets scholar-athletes hit the books and the slopes every day.

9 · The Great North

Introduction

New England's north country stands in splendid isolation. In a week in July, more people visit tiny Acadia National Park than venture in a year to the Great North, which remains the closest thing to a wilderness redoubt to be found in New England. Because it is so poorly known, the north country serves an essential function in the regional psyche. Those who live there love to regale visitors with tales of how harsh the winters can be (and what sounds like exaggeration often is not). Reports surface every year of some supposedly extinct animal sighted somewhere in the frozen north—a mountain lion, a timber wolf, a devil cat (the wolverine), or a herd of wild caribou. We fully expect some tenderfoot snowmobiler to report a saber-toothed tiger or a mastodon any year now.

Yet parts of the Great North are surprisingly tame. The virgin forest is long gone, and parts of the region in Vermont and New Hampshire are still extensively farmed. The woods are crisscrossed with roads, and while they might be rutted and muddy and virtually impassable in the spring except by logging equipment, they've been there ever since Benedict Arnold and his men carved their way across Maine to attack Quebec in the 1775.

Perhaps even more surprising, some of the most remote parts of the Great North were also some of the first regions of New England to attract tourism. When Henry David Thoreau made his first journey to the Maine woods in the 1840s, he lamented how the presence of tourism had already degraded the wilderness in which he sought a transcendental experience. (The closest he got to transcendence was the animal comfort of having his clothes dry out by the campfire.)

Yet there is still a kind of wildness in these northern boglands and sometimes steep hills. They teem with moose (and black flies), and some remarkably hardy species of flora, including several orchids, survive here and nowhere else in New England. Some of that tourism that Thoreau derided is no more intrusive than well-blazed hiking trails crossing mountain ridges and following river valleys. A new breed of outfitters is as adept at guiding travelers with cameras as an earlier breed was at guiding men with guns.

And while the timber wolves and mountain lions remain the products of overheated imaginations (we think), the Great North is densely populated with other creatures great and small. The widest range of hawks and eagles in New England live here. Moose are so common that they verge on being a nuisance or at least a safety hazard. The Eastern coyote, midway in size between the yippy little Western coyote and the huge timber wolf, has staked its claim all over the region. The ponds and bogs are rich with waterfowl—huge herons, graceful egrets, bitterns, even the snow goose and its dark morph, the blue goose. Its lakes and rivers, which were open to the sea in recent geological times, hold New England's largest specimens of trout and salmon, pickerel and pike.

That said, the Great North really encompasses two rather different regions. One is the tame and sedate farming world of Vermont's Northeast Kingdom, which contains extensive old-growth forest only in its northeast corner. The other is the North Woods, one of America's most enduring and famous forests. Environmentalists and planners alike use this term to describe the twenty-six-million-acre arc of forest from Maine to eastern New York. Although most of it has been logged (some places not more recently than the late eighteenth century), it remains the largest tract of undeveloped land east of the Mississippi River.

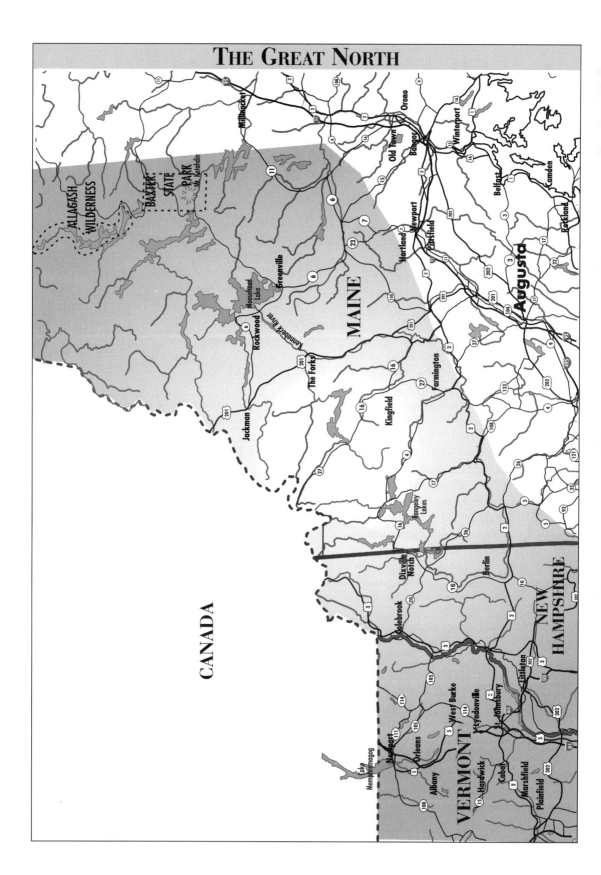

THE GREAT NORTH

Seeing the Great North

The Northeast Kingdom of Vermont

There are those who say that the Northeast Kingdom is a state of mind more than a place, but we're of the opinion that it's a real place that happens to embody a particular mythology about Vermont. Easily the most rural and remote part of the state, it's often defined by what it is not. It certainly is not the Vermont ski country, though it contains two superb alpine skiing mountains, and it is not the Vermont (for the most part) of wealthy rusticators from New York (though examples of the breed can be found playing country squire in many of its towns).

The Northeast Kingdom is a gently rolling land where the mountains play out before they become prairies farther north in Quebec. It is a country of dairy cattle and sugar maples, of birch and beech forests on open hills (a sign that those hills were cut over and farmed as recently as the Civil War), and of spruce-fir bogs in the dark, moist valleys. It is one of the few areas, even in northern New England, where the tamarack tree is found almost everywhere. In the fall, the brushes of green needles on this American larch turn bright gold, adding color and texture to the landscape long after the more showy hardwoods have dropped all their leaves.

The crusty old man of Vermont politics, former Senator George Aiken, is credited with coining the term "Northeast Kingdom" to describe Caledonia, Essex, and Orleans counties. With its distinct culture, physical isolation, and strong traditions, the region seems like a rural New England version of a European principality—Vermont's own Liechtenstein, virtually unpopulated until after the American Revolution, and still barely populated today. Its boosters like to

point to the numbers: 2,053 square miles that include 71,315 acres of public state forest lands and parks, 1,632 acres of federal state forest lands and parks, 37,575 acres of public lakes and ponds, and 3,840 miles of public rivers and streams. Nearly as many snowmobile trails as roads run through the region—some 3,500 miles of groomed snowmobile trails are maintained by local clubs associated with the Vermont Association of Snow Travelers (V.A.S.T.). Telephone: (802) 229–0005 or (888) 884–8001.

St. Johnsbury, Vermont

Located at the strategic highway intersections of Routes 2 and 5 and of I–91 and I–93 as well as at the confluence of Passumpsic, Moose, and Sleeper's Rivers, St. Johnsbury is the cultural and business capital of the Northeast Kingdom. To many travelers' minds "St. Jay" represents the far northern outpost of civilization, as if the rest of the Kingdom were dark and forbidding forest. That's not exactly true, but St. Johnsbury does have the feel of an Athens in the wilds, in large part thanks to the Fairbanks family.

A certain tie-dyed contingent of Northeast Kingdom residents no doubt delights in the irony that the hemp plant was the ultimate source of St. Jay's enlightenment. Back in the 1820s, the town had a factory that cleaned raw hemp fiber and prepared it for market. Experimenting with methods to weigh the massive hemp bundles, young Thaddeus Fairbanks realized that he could connect a weighing device to a platform via a system of levers. In 1830 he received his first patent on the platform scale and went into production. So successful was the business that the town's population tripled in the following four decades and Fairbanks was knighted by the Emperor of Austria for service to humanity. (The Fairbanks Scale

Company remains in business, producing commercial scales both large and small.) Throughout the rest of the nineteenth century, the Fairbanks family transformed St. Johnsbury by founding a private school and establishing two major cultural institutions, the St. Johnsbury Athenaeum and the Fairbanks Museum and Planetarium.

St. Johnsbury exists on two physical levels. The primary business district of **Railroad Street** is on the lower level, following the valley of the Passumpsic River. A rich array of late nineteenth-century buildings attests to the town's flush years immediately following the Civil War. While the storefronts house an odd mixture of "dollar" stores and shops selling high quality crafts, used books, upscale home furnishings, and outdoor gear, the business district has the coherence of a working community. On one hand the Northern Lights Bookstore and Café carries a striking range of contemporary literature (and serves a mean bistro dinner a few nights a week), while just up the street Landry's Drugstore could have sprung fully formed from the Eisenhower era, with its aging neon sign, boxes of Whitman samplers just inside the door, and window full of rubber-stemmed pipes and Zippo-brand lighters.

Roughly parallel to Railroad Street but at the top of a bluff is **Main Street,** which sports a few commercial buildings along with a number of community institutions and several fine homes set far back from the road on shady green lawns. The western end of the street is anchored by St. Johnsbury Academy, founded and endowed by Thaddeus Fairbanks and two of his brothers in 1842. Arrayed along the street are the two other examples of the family's civic generosity.

The **St. Johnsbury Athenaeum** serves as the town's library and public art gallery. A rather handsome red-brick Second Empire building at the head of Eastern Avenue, the library portion opened in 1871, the art gallery two years later. It is one of only fifteen libraries in the country declared a National Historic Landmark. Horace Fairbanks, son of the inventor and briefly governor of Vermont, donated the entire kit and caboodle, including the art collection. Most of the paintings—ranging from charming peasant scenes to a handful of (well-marked) copies of Old Masters—represent the solid, middle-class taste of

well-to-do Americans traveling in Europe in the mid-nineteenth century. The gallery's prize, however, is Alfred Bierstadt's monumental painting, *Domes of the Yosemite.* It occupies an entire wall and is so large that it had to be installed before the gallery could be finished. The opposite wall has narrow steps leading up to a small balcony that provides exactly the right perspective to view this masterpiece of American landscape painting. The library keeps getting new books (relying in part on the generosity of local residents who "adopt an author"), but the gallery is fixed in time—its only change since 1873 was the electrification of the original gaslight system. The Athenaeum is open Monday through Friday 10:00 A.M. to 5:30 P.M., Saturday 9:30 A.M. to 4:00 P.M. Open until 8:00 P.M. Monday and Wednesday. Admission is free, but a $2.00 donation is requested for the art gallery. 30 Main Street. Telephone: (802) 748–8291.

Just a short distance down Main Street is the **Fairbanks Museum & Planetarium,** gift to the town by Franklin Fairbanks, nephew of the scale inventor. Franklin was one of those boys who collected samples of everything around him, and his personal natural history collections actually served as the nucleus of the museum. As an adult, Franklin's private mansion included a "cabinet of curiosities" (a wonderfully old-fashioned term for a room of natural history curios) that he sometimes opened to the public. Eventually his collections grew beyond what even a grand house could hold, so he ordered this natural history museum built for the public in 1891. Constructed of red sandstone in the Richardson Romanesque Revival style, the Fairbanks is a splendid example of an old-fashioned museum.

The initial aim was to construct an exhaustive collection of Vermont flora and fauna, and while the museum didn't quite succeed, there are enough taxidermied specimens here to rival the Smithsonian in Washington. We're usually leery of stuffed animal exhibits, but on our way into town we had spotted a hawk we couldn't identify sitting in a tree by the highway. So we went searching through the collections, and halfway through the bird cases we found it: a red-tailed hawk. (With its wings and feathers folded, it looks like a peregrine falcon on steroids.)

The first floor is devoted to animal specimens, including so many polar bears that the Fairbanks has adopted the beast as its symbol. The museum's first bird taxidermist, William Balch, was among the first museum exhibit designers to create lifelike dioramas. So popular are the specimens that local schoolchildren have mounted a fund-raising campaign to restore them. The balcony area of the museum under the grand, oak, barrel-vaulted ceiling is more of a catchall. Fairbanks encouraged local people to bring back souvenirs when they traveled and items range from South Seas curios to odd "art" from the Caribbean. Like a townwide attic, the Fairbanks is full of the community's quirky history and interests. The museum also houses Vermont's only public planetarium, the Northern New England Weather Center, and a research library for the study of the Northeast Kingdom.

The Fairbanks Museum is open Monday through Saturday 10:00 A.M. to 4:00 P.M., Sunday 1:00 to 5:00 P.M. with extended summer hours. Planetarium shows are given 1:30 P.M. Saturday and Sunday, daily during July and August. Adults $5.00. Corner of Main and Prospect Streets. Telephone: (802) 748–2372.

In the 1880s local entrepreneur George Cary came up with the idea of using maple sugar to flavor plugs of chewing tobacco. At one point his Cary Maple Syrup Company covered five acres on Route 2 on the east side of town, producing several million pounds of maple syrup in addition to the tobacco plugs. Now it is reduced to the more modest and wholesome enterprise named for its one-time subsidiary, Maple Grove, Inc.

If you've ever encountered those tasty little maple leaf candies lined up in a small box, this is where they are made. **Maple Grove Farms of Vermont** began in 1915 when Helen Gray and Ethel McClaren decided to capitalize on their farm's sugar maple trees, herd of Jersey cows that produced sweet butter, and butternut trees to make maple candies that would "sing the song of maple sugar to the ends of the earth." Eventually Helen and Ethel opened a tea room and began shipping candy all over the country. They sold the business to the Cary company in 1929, which rolled it into the operations on Portland Avenue (Route 2). The company makes salad dressing and other food products, too, but the candies and the maple syrup are still the core of the business. The gift shop and welcome center is the first stop, and right next door is a replica sugar shack that shows how maple syrup is made.

Sugaring was Vermont's first industry—the Abenaki people of the region taught settlers how to tap sugar maples by making a gash in the bark and inserting a wooden drip gutter. In March, when the days are warm and the nights are cold, maple sap flows up through the trunk of sugar maples. The colonists soon turned to metal taps and covered buckets to collect the sap. A standard tap hole is $7/16$ inch and the buckets hold sixteen quarts—which is about what a tree produces in twenty-four hours during peak sap flow. Nowadays, most maple farmers collect the harvest by running plastic tubing from the tap holes to a holding tank at sugar shacks located downhill. At the shacks, the sap is heated over a wood fire to concentrate it by evaporation. It takes thirty-five to forty gallons of sap to produce a single gallon of syrup.

Vermont maple syrup is graded on both quality and flavor and the shop has a tasting table so visitors can compare the grades. "Fancy" is pale and has a delicate maple taste. "Grade A light amber" is similar, but slightly darker and more flavorful. "Grade A dark amber" is darker and has an

A farm in Vermont

even deeper taste. "Grade B" is as dark as clover honey and has strong maple flavor. Some maple aficionados claim Grade B is only good for cooking, but we disagree—it makes a robust table syrup even though it is less expensive than the finer grades.

The factory tour shows how the signature maple candies are made. Syrup is heated to 240 degrees, whipped to a creamy consistency and poured into molds. The molds, which date from the 1930s, sit overnight in heated syrup tanks, soaking up more maple flavor. When Maple Grove is in full production, fifty to sixty people work the lines. Tours are offered Monday through Friday 8:00 to 11:45 A.M. and 12:30 to 4:00 P.M. Adults $1.00. 167 Portland Street (Route 2). Telephone: (802) 748–5141.

West of St. Johnsbury, Vermont

People who live in the Northeast Kingdom often do many things to earn a living. In addition to holding down jobs, many of them farm their land to some extent. Half the houses that front on paved roads in the Northeast Kingdom post signs advertising maple syrup for sale. Moreover, many of those houses have cows in a side-yard pasture, some have sheep and a few have llamas standing outside, chewing their cuds. Nor is it surprising to see horses or donkeys grazing in a paddock beside the barn.

With a brief growing season, Northeast Kingdom farmers tend to depend less on crops than on livestock. The average farm in Vermont runs 315 acres and has about seventy cows. In fact, until the 1960s, there were more cows than people in Vermont. That still seems to be the case in the Kingdom. We came across a poem by a Corinth elementary school student in the Bradford *Journal Opinion* that sums up the situation rather well in a brief verse: "Cows, cows everywhere./Herefords, Holsteins, Jerseys, too./Scottish highlanders moo at you."

Every town large enough to have its own zip code also has a general store that sells Vermont cheese, maple syrup, and a variety of teddy bears, potholders, pottery, and "crafts" for tourists in addition to the food and household sundries that the locals buy. Many of these stores also offer homemade cookies and muffins, fresh Green

Mountain Roasters coffee, and hot (or cold) cider in the fall. At this writing, most of them also sell Beanie Babies, but we trust that some other collectible will eventually take their place. (We did encounter a vintage Pet Rock in an antiques and collectibles store at the "bargain" price of $1.25.) Every town big enough to have a general store also has a town green with a bandstand, a Civil War monument, and a white church—usually Congregational. Albany is an exception. The church is Methodist, but even in the Northeast Kingdom people say Albany always has to be different.

The quintessential village of this part of the Kingdom is **Peacham.** Follow Route 2 west from St. Johnsbury to the village of Danville (virtually a suburb of St. Jay) and turn left in the middle of town on Peacham Road. About 3 miles down the road on the left is the **Ewell Pond Wildlife Area**, a good place to watch raccoons and herons fishing in the shallows for small perch and bass. In another 3 miles Peacham appears in the distance as a hilltop punctuated by a white spire. There is not a lot to do or see in Peacham, which is kind of the point of the place. Founded in 1776, it is simply a handsome tree-lined village with a general store, a town library, a post office, a triangular green with Civil War monument, and one of the prettiest village cemeteries in the region. It's no exaggeration that the dead have the town's best view, gazing over a long valley toward the spot where the sun sets behind the Green Mountains in the distance.

Peacham, Vermont

The road perpendicular to the cemetery entrance is the Old Cabot Road, although it's not marked that way, and leads back toward Route 2. It's a scenic drive but not always well-maintained in bad weather. Otherwise, backtrack to Danville and turn west on Route 2 to West Danville, which sits at the head of **Joe's Pond.** Now ringed by summer camps, the substantial pond was named for "Old Joe," an Abenaki who befriended and guided many of the early settlers in these parts. Old Joe was so appreciated that the State of Vermont gave him an annual pension of $70 in his old age. A short distance down Route 2 on the left is Molly's Pond, named for Joe's wife, and at the western end on the right side of Route 2 is Danville Hill Road to Cabot. The turn is hard to miss, as the **Cabot Creamery** has marked it well to encourage visitors.

The Cabot Visitors' Center is easy to spot from a distance by tall storage silos full of milk. The center is dedicated, rather touchingly, we think, to "farm women for their unheralded role in the history of farming." The entrance area is essentially a store of Cabot products and a few other gourmet items that complement them. An astonishing array of samples are laid out—each of the cheeses as well as a selection of dips and other products. This apparent generosity usually has the desired effect: Once people sample, they buy. It's practical to buy dairy products here even in warm weather, as the shop sells inexpensive foam coolers and gives out free ice blocks.

The Cabot Creamery is a farmer-owned cooperative that started in 1919, when each farmer member kicked in $5.00 per cow and a cord of wood. The co-op now includes 1,600 farms throughout New England as members, but the creamery in Cabot only processes milk from Northeast Kingdom farms. The co-op made its first cheddar here in 1930.

It's worth taking the factory tour to see how straightforward it really is to make cheddar cheese. Milk comes in daily by tanker truck from the member farms to keep the silos filled (they hold 130,000 gallons). The vats in which the cheese is made are huge, but they have to be: It takes 33,000 pounds of milk to make 3,500 pounds of cheese. Each vat produces one and one-half tons of cheese over five hours. The vat is filled with milk, to which the workers add the cheese

culture. The mass is stirred continuously and separates into curds and into the watery whey, which is drained off. When the vat is reduced to curds alone, workers walk up and down the sides sprinkling in seasonings for flavored cheeses. The finished curds are pumped into towers and extruded by machine into forty-two-pound blocks that are quickly sealed in heavy plastic, left to age, and later cut into pieces. The creamery also makes three-pound and thirty-eight-pound wheels sealed in wax. Flavor intensity develops with aging, and Cabot ages its cheeses anywhere from a few months to two years at 42 degrees Fahrenheit.

The Cabot Visitors' Center is open June through October daily 9:00 A.M. to 5:00 P.M.; November and December and February through May Monday through Saturday 9:00 A.M. to 4:00 P.M. Factory tour $1.00. Main Street. Telephone: (802) 536–2231.

For a nearby tour of the region's other big agricultural industry return to Route 2 and continue west for about one-quarter mile to **Goodrich's Maple Farm,** the largest sugar house in northern Vermont. Free guided tours of the operation are offered and free samples are available in the gift shop. Route 2 between Marshfield and West Danville (four miles west of the junction of Routes 2 and 15). Telephone: (802) 426–3388 or (800) 639–1854.

The Waldens, the Hardwicks, and Greensboro all lie between Cabot and the next major stop, Craftsbury. Each is a scenic village (or group of villages) with the occasional B&B, antiques shop, farm stand, or other excuse for pulling over to the side of the road and simply walking around. Follow Route 215 north from Cabot to Route 15, then continue north, either turning right onto Route 16 to Greensboro where you'll pick up a back road to Craftsbury, or right onto Route 14 at Hardwick to Craftsbury. Either route is scenic, though we rather favor the somewhat more bucolic Greensboro road because it passes along the shores of **Caspian Lake,** which is noted for the substantial size of its lake trout and landlocked salmon.

The villages of **Craftsbury** and **Craftsbury Common** lie along a turnoff from Route 14 and couldn't be more different. The erstwhile industrial center of the region, Craftsbury, was constructed deep in the valley around a lumber mill. Craftsbury Common, by contrast, is a picturesque residential village planted high on a hill. The white clapboards and picket fences of Craftsbury Common are so perfect that they look more imagined than real, but if you stop and look around, the houses are not the fake fronts of movie sets. It's a real place, albeit one of the few country squire communities in the Northeast Kingdom.

The slightly preppy enthusiasm for the Great Outdoors that dominates Craftsbury may even be a byproduct of the country squires, who, we suspect, all belonged to the Outing Club at their respective Ivy and Little Ivy colleges. The Craftsbury Outdoor Center and Craftsbury Nordic Ski Center (see "Staying There") are the locus for much of this activity, but the entire surrounding countryside is laced with hiking, snowshoe, and cross-country ski trails.

From Craftsbury, Route 14 continues north through Albany to Irasburg, named for Ethan Allen's brother, where it joins Route 5, and on to Coventry, where Routes 14 and 5 part company. Route 14 veers west and undergoes several number changes before arriving at Jay, some 15 miles away. Jay Peak is the Northeast Kingdom's most serious ski area. (See "Staying There.")

From Coventry, Route 5 heads north to Newport, which is the Kingdom's second largest community and only business center to rival St. Johnsbury.

Newport and Lake Memphremagog, Vermont

The 32-mile length of Lake Memphremagog is divided between Vermont and the province of Quebec, with Newport on the south end and our favorite cheese-making monastery, St. Benoit-du-Lac, on the north. In the days before interstate highways in the United States and Crown Highways in Canada, Newport was a major border crossing, and its docks still maintain a small customs and immigration office for traffic coming in from Canada by boat. Some of the first Europeans to come by that route were Roger's Rangers. In 1759 they stopped at the promontory now occupied by Newport as they fled from the surviving warriors of the St. Francis tribe after

slaughtering all the St. Francis women and children. Here the troops split up to forage through the wilderness to safety on the Connecticut River. Divided, they were easy prey for the Indians. (The successful flight through the wilderness of Roger's own small band is described in gripping detail in Kenneth Roberts' 1937 novel *Northwest Passage*.)

Nearly two generations passed before Europeans settled in Newport, which burgeoned in the nineteenth century as a timbering center and then as a rail depot for goods passing between Montreal and Boston. The Canadian influence is particularly evident in St. Mary's Catholic Church, which stands triumphantly on a high promontory above the town. It is a classic Quebec church of the nineteenth century—heavy gray stone, twin bell towers with cupolas like turned spindles, and a shiny metal roof.

The Newport end of Lake Memphremagog is an extremely popular area among fishermen, as its waters contain walleyed pike (troll a plug deep and slow) as well as landlocked salmon. Streams flowing into Memphremagog are particularly good for catching wild trout (brook, brown, and rainbow) on their spawning runs.

Route 5 continues eastward to Derby Center, where it joins Route 5A.

Derby Line, Vermont

At this point it's worth taking a small detour north to the village of Derby Line, which happens to fall exactly at the midway point between the Equator and the North Pole. It also shares a very confusing international border with the village of Stanstead in the town of Rock Island in the province of Quebec. The border is so confusing (it is *not* the little stream) that we managed to cross it while making a U-turn to avoid crossing it. Hence, we had to clear United States Customs before we could continue. Fortunately, the people of this community that straddles the border take it all rather amiably, and the Customs officers are adept at answering questions from befuddled travelers. The locals still make some strong distinctions between citizenships. A Quebec-born woman who has lived in Derby Line most of her life told us that her children, who were born in Derby, are not considered Vermonters. She cited the old Vermont saying, "Just because the cat had her kittens in the oven doesn't make them biscuits."

Follow the road through town as it makes a wide bend to the right to visit the **Haskell Free Library and Opera House.** Depending on your perspective, the building is at 1 Church Street in Stanstead (Rock Island), Quebec, or at International Boundary in Derby Line.

Mary Stewart Haskell, a native of Quebec, had the library built from 1901 to 1904 as a gift to the community at a cost of about $1 million (US). At the time, the international boundary had not been ratified, and many buildings were constructed partly in the United States, partly in Canada. This proved to be the most notable. Inside the library, a black line across the floor divides the countries. Another line crosses the floor in the attached Opera House, which seats 500 at full capacity. Most of the audience is in the United States, most of the stage in Canada. Each room in the library is trimmed in a different local wood and the stained glass in the windows follows a different theme. The library is operated by a private foundation but is free to both Derby Line and Stanstead, Quebec, residents, with books in both French and English.

Open Tuesday through Saturday from 10:00 A.M. to 5:00 P.M., Thursday until 8:00 P.M. Tours of the Opera House (where all the woodwork and the stairs are gorgeous local maple) are available for a suggested donation of $2.00. Telephone: (802) 873–3022 in Vermont, (819) 876–2471 in Quebec.

Lake Willoughby and the Burkes, Vermont

Route 5A south from Derby Center crosses rolling hill country covered with spruce and tamarack until it descends suddenly to Lake Willoughby. The scene is unusually dramatic for this part of Vermont, where landscape tends more toward understatement. But Willoughby is one of the finer flourishes of the last glaciation—a deep furrow carved between granite mountains. Fanciful promoters have hailed it as the "Lucerne of America" for more than a century, but to qualify, the lake would need a city of Lucerne's flair

and sophistication. Instead, it has Westmore—a perfectly fine community, but no Lucerne.

The lake, however, is stunning as it stretches 6 miles and passes between the Scylla and Charybdis of Mount Pisgah (2,731 feet) on the east and Mount Hor (1,592 feet) on the west. While the shores are lined with summer camps and cabins, there are sandy swimming beaches at the north and south extremes of the lake. Fishermen love Willoughby even more than swimmers, as its cold and deep waters make for superb fishing for lake trout and landlocked salmon. Vermont's record lake trout—thirty-four pounds—was pulled from Lake Willoughby. During the summer, the best chances of catching either of these salmonids is to troll deeply with a weighted line and multiple flashers and hope they take the lure for a small school of minnows. The tributary Willoughby River is also famous for its spring run of steelhead trout, a naturalized form of rainbow trout.

The road follows the lake shore and passes along Willoughby State Forest. A parking lot on the left provides access to one of the trailheads leading up Mount Pisgah for some spectacular views. This particular hike of about three hours round trip is considered only moderately difficult.

Landlocked salmon

Route 5A rejoins Route 5 in West Burke, but for a more scenic journey back toward St. Johnsbury, follow the Burke Hollow Road and heed the signs to **East Burke,** site of the Burke Mountain Ski Resort (see "Staying There"). Despite Burke Mountain's efforts to develop as a major resort area, the Burkes stay stubbornly rural and unaffected. Just south of East Burke on Route 114 is Darling Hill Road, where the stunning farm of the **Inn at Mountain View Creamery** (see "Staying There") is worth driving by to appreciate an example of a gentleman's showcase farm.

Route 114 rejoins Route 5 just north of Lyndon Center where the land broadens into wide valleys with small, winding rivers at the bottom. These puny rivers are the modern remains of one-time torrents that flowed off the glaciers. Because they snake back and forth, they posed a problem to early road builders. Lyndon Center, where the Miller's Run and Passumpsic Rivers wind through, has three handsome covered bridges.

The **Miller's Run Bridge** (1878) on Route 122 is painted white. It's a 56-foot queenpost bridge. The other covered bridges in the area are the **Chamberlin Bridge** (1881), a queenpost of 66 feet spanning the South Branch Passumpsic west off Route 5 between York Street and Middle Road, and the **Schoolhouse Bridge** (1879), a 42-foot queenpost spanning the South Branch Passumpsic west off Route 5 by the South Wheelock Branch Road.

The North Woods of New Hampshire and Maine

"This is the forest primeval," intoned Henry Wadsworth Longfellow back in 1847. "The murmuring pines and the hemlocks, bearded with moss, and in garments green, indistinct in the twilight, stand like Druids of old, with voices sad and prophetic, stand like harpers hoar, with beards that rest on their bosoms."

Longfellow was describing the forests of Nova Scotia's Acadia in *Evangeline,* but he could as easily have been writing of his native Maine, where the evergreen forest covers two-thirds of the state. Today, as in Longfellow's time, the area of Maine's "working forest" is about a quarter of the entire area of New England—about the size of Vermont and New Hampshire combined.

The North Woods have never been heavily populated. Abenaki tribes, particularly the Penobscots, sometimes ventured into them on snowshoes in the winter to harvest deer and moose, but permanent ancient settlements have never been uncovered in the region. Both English and French trappers sometimes plied the river systems from the late seventeenth century until the period of the American Revolution, but not until the loggers arrived in the late eighteenth century was there any year-round settlement.

Timbering began in Maine along the coast, of course, and soon proceeded inland following the three great river valleys that drain the North Woods. The first northerly tracts exploited were along the headwaters of the Androscoggin River basin, just east of what is now the White Mountain National Forest. Most early loggers were small landowners who would hire a few men to assist them in the harvest and in running a boom of logs downstream in the spring. But when Maine separated from Massachusetts in 1820, the cash-poor government began to sell off entire townships in the north to raise money. (Even today some of the townships are identified only by number, since they were never settled enough to acquire a name.) Logging switched from an individual to a corporate enterprise, and the scale of operations expanded quickly. The new corporate timber companies abandoned the narrow and twisting Androscoggin for the Kennebec River, which was wider, deeper, and straighter and penetrated many miles farther into the north, with its headwaters at Moosehead Lake. Eager to exploit the timber east of Moosehead, loggers began massive drives on the Penobscot River system, making Bangor the timber capital of the world from the Civil War into the 1880s. By the time that Henry David Thoreau visited the North Woods in the 1840s, a generation of logging had left much of a once-pristine wilderness an ugly bog country of dead stumps, its rivers dammed to facilitate the spring log runs. In 1846, he wrote,

"It is a war against the pines, the only real Aroostook or Penobscot war." By 1890, most of the tall timber that had supplied so many masts to Maine wooden ships was gone.

But forests are a renewable resource, and the invention of pulp paper technology made harvesting non-timber grade trees economical. By the 1920s most of the North Woods was in the hands of international paper and timber companies, which continue to manage the forests. To maneuver their trucks and timbering machinery around, they have cut a network of almost 25,000 miles of timber roads that also provide recreational access to the wilderness. (The roads are almost always unpaved and there is usually a fee to use them.) The timber barons own the land and cut the trees, but they have (so far) left the country open to visitors and, by and large, have preserved the lake waterfronts. Keep in mind that most of this region is private land, and that travelers must yield the right-of-way to logging trucks.

The North Woods may not be the forest primeval, but it is, by and large, a healthy working forest in better shape than it was a century ago. Forest management practices have become more scientific, and the political goodwill of keeping the recreational parts of the forest attractive has meant a successful détente between the paper companies and conservationists. The people who live in and near the North Woods have ambivalent feelings about this system of land management. Clear-cutting followed by use of herbicides to kill unwanted trees sparks protests and concern, but the practices have as many partisans as enemies. (Clear-cutting of small areas can help the forest regenerate and encourages greater diversity of tree ages.) Many people who make their livings from the forest worry more that the woodlands will be carved up into house lots and developed into luxury summer homes. An editorial in the *Maine Times* in the early 1990s encapsulated that fear by proclaiming, "The most dangerous man in the woods is not a man with a chainsaw, but a man with a lawnmower." Vast tracts of the North Woods are owned by multinational conglomerates whose roots lie well outside the region, and while Maine voters have expressed some desire to preserve the forests from development, conservationists have protected less than one percent of the region since 1990.

Even so, it is hard to imagine that the status quo will change quickly in the North Woods—it hasn't changed much since the beginning of the twentieth century, when non-loggers first began to come here in significant numbers to experience the wilds. They were called "sports," and the small industry of hunting and fishing camps to accommodate them came to be called sporting camps.

Many of these camps survive, though their operators today tend to cater as much to travelers with binoculars and cameras as those with shotguns and rifles. The camps are almost invariably found on the shores of the larger ponds and lakes that cover the central part of the North Woods. Often they can be reached only from the air by seaplane or overland by canoe or kayak. The frontier wilderness experience is still very much alive in the North Woods, where the telephones are radio phones and radio broadcasts (to battery-powered radios) are usually shortwave. Most of those who earn their living in the sporting camp industry wouldn't have it any other way. They count themselves rich in starlight and moonglow, and relish the season when the last traveler has gone home and solitude settles over the vast landscape like an evanescent October snow.

Dixville Notch, New Hampshire

The road across New Hampshire from Vermont's Northeast Kingdom to Maine's North Woods

Moose

passes through the northern reaches of the White Mountains. Like northern Maine, this is timber country, but on a smaller scale because it lacks the large rivers that loggers once used to move their harvest to the mills. From St. Johnsbury Route 2 heads east and crosses the Connecticut River to Lancaster, New Hampshire. From Lancaster, the timber towns are strung northward along the river on Route 3, to Colebrook, where Route 26 crosses the high country of northern New Hampshire, passing through Dixville Notch. (A "notch," in Granite State-speak, is a gap between mountain ranges.)

Dixville Notch is a striking piece of alpine scenery, accentuated by **The Balsams,** one of the few surviving back-country resort hotels from the Gilded Age (see "Staying There"). But the tiny community has a reputation that extends beyond its prize location—its polls are the first in the United States to report the vote in the presidential primaries and elections. To maintain their claim to fame, Dixville's thirty or so voters enjoy a late-night party that concludes with casting their ballots at the stroke of midnight.

For those not staying at The Balsams, **Dixville Notch State Park** captures much of the drama of the region, including a scenic gorge and crashing waterfalls on two mountain brooks. The pleasant two-mile round-trip loop hike to Table Rock begins on a gravelly trail that soon gives way to open rock. The view from the top overlooks

**Dixville Notch State Park,
Dixville Notch, New Hampshire**

The Balsams resort, nestled in the valley, and the wild hills that flank it. Other trails lead less directly to nearby peaks. The park has two picnic areas and an historic grave site. Entrance off Route 26. Telephone: (603) 323–2087.

Route 26 begins to descend rapidly as it reaches the river town of Errol, where a left turn onto Route 16 heads northeast into the high spruce bog country leading to the Rangeley Lakes region just over the border in Maine.

Rangeley Lakes, Maine

The town of Rangeley, nestled on the northeast corner of Rangeley Lake, serves as the center of the Rangeley Lakes district, where the buckled peaks of some of Maine's tallest mountains (up to 4,000 feet) surround the remains of an inland sea. The Rangeley Lakes chain comprises not only Rangeley itself, but also Mooselookmeguntic (the largest of the group, at 2 miles wide and 11 miles long) and about ten others, as well as the streams that link them together. In all, the district covers about 450 square miles of little but water and forest where deer and moose abound.

Although the region has been populated—albeit sparsely—since the 1750s, human impact has been surprisingly light. The Rangeley Lakes district can claim some of the most pristine lakes, rivers, and wilderness areas in the world.

The purity of the environment is one reason why Rangeley fishing is world class. In fact, trophy-sized landlocked salmon and native brook trout are caught each season here in the birthplace of contemporary fly fishing. Even by the late 1880s, sporting magazines had identified Rangeley as the home of the largest brook trout in North America—based in large part on the reports of a few New Jersey fly fishers. Trout and salmon fishing are superb in the spring, but fly fishermen know September is the prime season in these cold waters.

We intend no gender bias by the term "fisher*men*," because Rangeley women played a critical role in developing sport fishing in the region. Cornelia Thurza "Flyrod" Crosby was the first registered Maine guide and in the 1880s pioneered the use of the light fly rod and artificial lure. In 1924, local milliner Carrie Stevens created a streamer fly from gray feathers and proceeded to catch a six-pound, thirteen-ounce brook trout, which took second prize in *Field & Stream*'s annual competition. She went on to design other flies, but her original "Grey Ghost" remains one of the classic and most dependable flies used in the Rangeley Lakes.

The 691-acre **Rangeley Lake State Park** is located on the southern shore of the lake, a few miles from Rangeley village. An extraordinarily scenic park, it has wheelchair accessible picnic and camping facilities (see "Staying There") as well as good lake access for swimming and fishing, including a boat launch. The major snowmobile trail through the park joins up with the Interconnected Trail System. The park is a good base for fly fishing enthusiasts, as more than forty trout and salmon ponds and lakes are found within a 10-mile radius. Open May 15 through September 30. Take Route 17 south from Oquossoc at the west end of the lake or Route 4 south from Rangeley. Telephone: (207) 864–3858 or (207) 624–6080 (off-season).

The history of road-building in this part of New England becomes painfully clear at Rangeley. Moosehead Lake lies but 70 miles away by air. By road it is more like 200 miles. "Notches" like those found throughout the White and Green Mountains also penetrate the mountains of northwestern Maine—but in Maine, where the glaciers retreated more recently, they are filled with water. As a result, most major roadways in the north follow the river valleys, which were gouged in a north-south alignment by the ice cover. Only where a tributary river valley cuts between major valley systems do they link up.

Carrabasset Valley, Maine

Fortunately, the Dead River valley stretches between Rangeley Lake and huge Flagstaff Lake to the northeast, and Route 16 follows the valley up to the town of Stratton. Just northwest of Stratton on Route 27 is **Eustis,** the jump-off point to Tim Pond and the rugged canoeing waters of the North Branch Dead River. (See "Staying There.")

Stratton, where Routes 16 and 27 join, is the head of the Carrabasset Valley and contains many rustic but charming lodgings that make good bases for wilderness exploration or for some of the

finest downhill skiing in the eastern United States. About 15 miles south on Routes 16/27 is the access road to **Sugarloaf/USA,** possibly the brightest gem in the American Skiing Company's crown. The 4,237-foot Sugarloaf Mountain is Maine's second tallest mountain, and the resort offers a dizzying variety of ski promotions as well as mountain biking and a championship-quality golf course. (See "Staying There.")

Another 10 miles down the valley is the high country village of **Kingfield,** named for its early proprietor and the first governor of Maine, William King. But the fame of the Kings has been eclipsed by the Stanley family, whose accomplishments are chronicled in the small **Stanley Museum.** Twin brothers Francis Edgar and Freelan Oscar were noteworthy inventors. They developed the dry photographic plate process (a patent that George Eastman swiftly purchased for his nascent Kodak company) and the artists' airbrush. But they are best known for the Stanley Steamer automobile. They built their first steam-powered vehicle in 1896, and in 1899 F.O. Stanley proved the practicality of their technology by driving a Locomobile fitted with their steam engine to the summit of Mount Washington. F.E. Stanley unfortunately died in an automobile accident in 1918 when he crashed into a pile of cordwood to avoid hitting two farm wagons traveling side by side down the road. The Stanley Motor Carriage Company, based in Newton, Massachusetts, closed in 1925, the steamer doomed by the twenty-minute start-up time it required before the driver could go anywhere. Three of the steam powered automobiles are on display in the museum—reminders of what might have been had American automotive habits developed a little differently. The twins' sister, Chansonetta Stanley Emmons, seized on her brothers' invention of dry plate photography and created an impressive body of some of America's earliest documentary photography. The museum has both her photographs and most of her negatives. Open Tuesday through Sunday 1:00 P.M. to 4:00 P.M. Adults $3.00. School Street. Telephone: (207) 265–2769.

From Kingfield, Route 16 follows the Carrabasset Valley southeast to the town of North Anson, where Route 201A heads northward (soon becoming Route 201) along the Kennebec River.

The river views along Route 201 are superb, and it is a rare day in summer when travelers do not spot several packs of whitewater rafters sliding down the river to the relatively placid waters of Wyman Lake (which is really only a wide spot in the Kennebec).

The Forks, Maine

Forty miles north from North Anson, Route 201 reaches The Forks, which takes its name from the confluence of the Dead River from the west and the Kennebec River from the east. This is where the whitewater raft trips generally begin. The season commences with spring run-off trips on both rivers and continues until October on the dam-controlled Kennebec. The 12-mile run through the magnificent **Kennebec Gorge** is nothing short of spectacular, with tall cliffs on either side and a continuous run of whitewater that varies from Class II to Class III. Rafting from The Forks has become so popular that some conservationists have made noises about trying to limit the activity. Presently, about 30,000 people take part in the activity. (See "Staying There.")

Two miles east of The Forks on the road that follows the Kennebec River, a gentle half-mile walk leads to **Moxie Falls,** one of Maine's highest waterfalls. A series of tumbling cataracts over the rocks of Moxie Stream concludes with a rather dramatic 90-foot drop. Hikers can't really get to the falls themselves, but there's a wooden platform well situated for a good view.

Route 201 drills on northward 26 miles through a peculiar landscape typical of this region of New England and no other—the high-elevation spruce bogs. The "lowlands" in this region are about 1,000 feet above sea level, and the surrounding creases of land rise 2,000 to 3,000 feet higher. Some of them form such indistinct peaks that they have never been named as mountains. At the end of this stretch is Jackman, last stop before the province of Quebec.

Jackman, Maine

Jackman, which serves as the de facto capital of the Moose River region, has the feel of a frontier town. It is not uncommon to encounter moose on Main Street, and its little stores did a booming business in American cigarettes when Quebec, only 18 miles away, hiked the tobacco taxes out of sight a few years ago to support its health care system. (We suspect the little towns up the line in Quebec probably did a bang-up business during Prohibition, too.) Jackman is actually one of the oldest communities in the north, as it stands along an eighteenth-century trade route blazed by Indian trappers carrying their furs from the Moosehead Lake region to Quebec City.

Like the Rangeley Lakes area, the Moose River district is legendary among fishermen. More than sixty lakes and ponds dot the region and the beaver-dammed streams provide hundreds of miles of prime habitat for landlocked salmon, big brook trout, huge lake trout, and the small smelt on which the various salmonids love to feed.

The **Bow Trip,** one of the few true wilderness canoe trips available anywhere in New England, begins in Jackman. This 46-mile canoeing trail on the Moose River and its tributaries is equalled only by running the Allagash Wilderness. In some respects, it is purer canoeing, as the Bow Trip passes through much smaller lakes than those of the Allagash. The fishing is, to say the least, unparalleled and it is an excellent way to observe and photograph moose, deer, beaver, fisher, martin, and minks.

The trip begins just south of Jackman at the northeast corner of Attean Pond where a road off Route 201 leads down to a landing. Paddle west along the north shore, keeping the railroad line in sight and taking care for waves raised by westerly winds. At the west end of the lake is a well-marked 1.25-mile portage to Holeb Pond along the railroad right of way. At Holeb, follow the south shore, keeping the rail line in sight on the left. There is a small brook outlet at the west end of the pond that joins the Moose River in about a quarter mile. Paddle east on the Moose River, making a short portage around Holeb Falls as far down as you feel comfortable with the rapids. About 2 miles downriver are more rapids— Spencer Rips—where there are also wilderness camp sites and a good portage for those who would rather be safe than sorry. The Moose River meets up with Attean Pond about two miles south of the landing where the trip began. Ideally the

Canoeing

Bow Trip should be made with an experienced guide, who can also make arrangements for gear. Contact the **Jackman-Moose River Chamber of Commerce** for their list of registered guides. P.O. Box 368, Jackman, ME 04945. Telephone: (207) 668–4171.

The Moose River connects Attean Pond to Wood Pond and then passes eastward through a long series of ponds before it empties into Moosehead Lake. The excellent paved road—Routes 6 and 15—more or less follows this river valley from Jackman for 30 miles eastward to Rockwood, western gateway to Moosehead.

Moosehead Lake, Maine

Moosehead Lake is the largest body of fresh water entirely within the boundaries of any state in the Northeast—an irregularly shaped lake that is 40 miles long and 20 miles wide at its extremities. There are certainly larger lakes in New England (Lake Champlain comes quickly to mind), but Moosehead's 117 square miles qualify it as an inland sea. Moosehead is the low spot in high country, with an elevation of just over 1,000 feet. It drains an almost inconceivable watershed of 1,226 square miles, and the nearby area includes an additional 175,000 acres of water in other lakes, ponds, streams, and rivers.

Lying on or near the headwaters of both the Kennebec and Penobscot river systems, Moosehead played a major role in Maine's massive log drives of the late nineteenth century. Although its 350-mile shoreline was almost completely cut over in the 1830s and 1840s, the lake is ringed in forest again. It is also circled by the 100-mile Moosehead Trail for snowmobiles. Bogs, inlets, and sandy coves characterize its shores and

the lake is dotted with islands and ringed by high mountains. It is almost impossible to gauge the scale of Moosehead from the ground, but from a seaplane its grandeur comes into real focus (see "Staying There"). The outlines of the various bays, irregular as a bull moose's antlers, are clear, and it's a simple matter for the pilot to find a moose swimming across the lake and swoop lower for a better look. (A swimming moose looks like a small motor boat from the air. They are so big and such strong swimmers that they leave a wake behind them.)

Rockwood is on the western shore of Moosehead Lake, 20 miles north of Greenville, which is the other access point by paved highway. Both the hunting and the fly fishing are the best on this end of the lake, and Rockwood is strategically situated at the narrowest and most dramatic point in the lake. The peninsula that looks like an island and looms just a mile offshore from Rockwood's dock is 760-foot **Mount Kineo**. Tangentially attached to the far shore, it is far easier to reach from Rockwood by boat in the summer or by snowmobile over the winter ice.

The **Mount Kineo water shuttle** operates from the state dock in Rockwood from late June through Labor Day. Adults $5.00. Telephone: (207) 534–8812. Kineo once housed resort hotels, but only a few outbuildings remain from its nineteenth-century heyday as a vacation resort. Most travelers go over to hike up the mountain in the footsteps of Henry David Thoreau. Two trail choices are available—the rather steep Indian Trail up the rocky shoulders of the hill or the more gradual Bridle Trail that winds back and forth. The view from the cliffs over the lake is sweeping. Kineo is also suspected to be the source of the earliest stone tools found in New England. Archaeologists from the University of Maine have shown evidence of substantial inhabitation in New England even during the last glaciation. Toolmakers apparently traveled hundreds of miles over the ice sheets to mine the exposed flints of Mount Kineo 8,000 to 12,000 years ago.

Most travelers use **Greenville,** 19 miles down Routes 6 and 15 at the southeastern tip of Moosehead Lake, as a gateway to the North Woods and Moosehead Lake because it lies closer to the interstate highways. As a result, it is home base to many outfitters, guide services, camps, canoe rental operations, and rafting adventure companies. It is also the largest seaplane base in New England. While most of the North Woods adventure outings lie many miles from Greenville in remote locations where the address is only a numbered township, every mode of transportation passes through the little town.

Greenville has a laid-back charm, but it was far livelier a hundred years ago when well-off vacationers came up on the train to spend a few months in some of the monumental stone lodges and fully timbered "camps" they built around the lake. The first steamships set out on the lake in 1836 and until the current road system was built in the 1930s, they carried passengers, livestock, mail, and supplies to large resorts, distant villages, and small hunting camps alike. At the peak of the season circa 1900, about fifty steamships plied the waters of Moosehead, but the **S/S Katahdin** is the only survivor from that era. Built in 1914 at Bath Iron Works, she was downgraded from passenger ship to a towboat that hauled booms of logs until 1975, when she participated in the nation's last log drive and was declared a National Historic Monument. Now the boat offers narrated scenic cruises and serves as the centerpiece of the **Moosehead Marine Museum,** which also has photos and memorabilia related to the lake's steamboat history. Open July through mid-October, Tuesday through Thursday, Saturday, and Sunday. Adults $15. Public Dock. Telephone: (207) 695–2716.

While many canoe rental outfits in the Greenville area will permit you to take their boats out on Moosehead Lake, we reluctantly refuse to endorse the idea. We say "reluctantly" because it's an historic lake for canoeists—Henry David Thoreau made it safely across and wrote glowingly about the experience. But we also lost a good friend on the lake when he and two others apparently swamped and drowned in the cold lake waters even though he was an experienced canoeist and they were all wearing life jackets. Stick to larger craft.

The very name "Moosehead Lake" conjures up images of the huge and ungainly member of the deer family, *Alces alces*. In this case, what might seem tourism hyperbole is true. With a

moose population between 30,000 and 40,000 (and growing rapidly), Maine has more moose than any other state except Alaska. And more of them live in the vicinity of Moosehead Lake than anywhere else in Maine: The rugged mountains and miles of dense forest around the shores of the lake are ideal moose habitat.

Because there are so many moose and they are so big (a mature bull moose can weigh 1,000 to 1,400 pounds and have a rack of antlers 60 inches across, while cows weigh 700 to 900 pounds), few visitors who wish to see moose go home disappointed. They often appear at the side of the road, particularly at dawn and dusk. And although moose are solitary woodland creatures, they tend to feed close to each other. The Chamber of Commerce provides maps marked with areas where moose are likely to be sighted. To keep that information current, visitors are encouraged to register their moose sightings on a giant locator map and in a log book at the regional **Visitor's Center.** Routes 6 and 15. Telephone: (207) 695-2702.

In the spring it can just be a matter of driving down the right road. Moose need salt in their diet and often visit roadsides to lick the residue left from salting the roads in the winter to melt snow and ice. Many moose are even spotted at noon, which with the early morning and late afternoon sightings suggest that their feeding times are not that dissimilar from humans. Moose are herbivores and a mature bull eats forty to fifty pounds of food a day. In the spring to early summer, moose are usually found in or near the water where they can submerge to escape the black flies and voracious deer flies that swarm early in the season. When the fly population declines later in the summer, they will usually be found wading thigh-deep in woodland bogs.

As in all outdoor pursuits, caution and common sense are critical in stalking moose. Keep your distance during rutting season (September to the end of December) when bull moose become aggressive, and during nursing season (calves are born in May and June), when the cows are protective of their young. Although moose have poor eyesight, they have keen senses of smell and hearing and they move very fast for such big creatures. Running moose have been clocked up to 35 miles per hour and a swimming moose can overtake a strong paddler in a canoe. While it is fun to stalk moose on your own, it can be a more satisfying experience to go out with a guide who will teach you about habitat and point out other natural attractions. A range of Moose "hunts" go by van, canoe, even on "bellyboats." (See "Staying There.")

We would be remiss not to point out that moose are also a road hazard. There are more than 600 collisions a year in Maine between moose and motor vehicles. While only a few of these result in human fatalities, almost all of the moose involved fare less well.

Greenville is the usual jump-off point for **West Branch Penobscot River canoe and raft trips.** Canoes can navigate the 42-mile trip on Class I and II waters from Old Roll Dam to the bottom of Chesuncook Lake. The river is fairly narrow and winding for the first half of the trip through historic forest lands, opening into broad Chesuncook for the lower portion of the route. This trip ends above **Ripogenus Dam,** a major landmark in these parts. **Allagash Wilderness Outfitters** will shuttle cars between Roll Dam and Ripogenus Dam. Telephone: (207) 695–2821.

Constructed in 1930, "Rip" controls the flow in the downstream river, which offers some of the most spectacular whitewater in the East and Maine's only Class V waters. Daily **water flow information** is available through Bowater's recorded message: (207) 723–2328.

Beginning at the Ripogenus Dam, the West Branch Penobscot drops more than 70 feet per mile through the steeply walled canyon of Ripogenus Gorge, alternating between sharp drops and calmer waters until it reaches the absolutely impassable Big Eddy. (Some of the pools along this stretch offer outstanding fly fishing for large brook trout and landlocked salmon, known locally as "togue.") Whitewater rafters usually put in at Big Eddy for some spectacular runs over a 23-mile stretch to Spencer Cove on Amajejus Lake. There are several falls and ferocious rapids along the way, which can require either a portage or "lining" a canoe or raft over them. (Lining is the technique of guiding a boat through rough water by controlling it with bow and stern ropes

West Branch Penobscot River, Maine

from shore.) This route, which skirts the southern end of Baxter State Park and Mount Katahdin, is great scenery, but except on the respite of the Nesowadnehunk Deadwater, boaters are usually busier watching where they are going. Rapids like Troublemaker, the Cribworks, and Exterminator welcome thrillseekers with waterfalls, "holes" to surf, and natural waterslides where you can pause and swim. This stretch of river is only for very experienced and skilled boaters in top physical condition and, ideally, should be undertaken in the company of an experienced operator (see "Staying There").

Alllagash Wilderness, Maine

Travelers striking out for the Allagash Wilderness generally drive to Ripogenus Dam—either from Millinocket on Golden Road or from Greenville through Kokadjo on the nameless and rutted dirt

International River Classification System

CLASS I

Very easy canoeing. Waves are small and regular, passages are clear. River may have some sandbanks, manmade obstacles such as bridges or piers, and sections of small waves, usually over a sand or gravel river bed.

CLASS II

Easy canoeing. Rapids of medium difficulty with passages clear and wide. River may contain some ledges.

CLASS III

Medium canoeing. Waves may be numerous and some will be high. Irregular rocks and strong eddies can be expected. Rapids will have clear but narrow passages, requiring some expertise to maneuver. Advance inspection is always a good idea.

CLASS IV

Difficult canoeing. Class IV rivers contain long rapids and often have high and irregular waves. Expect dangerous rocks and boiling eddies. Inspection of river conditions may be difficult, but advance scouting is essential. River requires both strength and finesse to maneuver. Water beyond Class IV is considered uncanoeable except with specialized equipment.

streams that winds through the heart of northern Maine's vast commercial forests. This watery highway was well-known to French and Native trappers at least as far back as the mid-seventeenth century, but not until 1966 did the Maine legislature set it aside as a protected region to "preserve, protect and develop the natural beauty, character and habitat of a unique area." In 1970 it was added to the National Wild and Scenic River System.

There are no permanent human residents in the Allagash and access is limited to a few dirt roads sometimes covered with gravel. As befits a wilderness, the sixty-six campsites along the Allagash are for primitive camping only and rather strict regulations apply to gathering wood for fires and other activities that could degrade the environment. The best way to experience the Allagash Wilderness is from a canoe, and the canoeing is rather straightforward, rising at worst to a Class II river through one 9-mile stretch. The worst hazards are strong winds on the large lakes of the sequence, like Lake Chamberlain. Several companies offer guided trips of seven to ten days through the region (see "Staying There"), and they tend to make the system a rather busy place in July and August. Although there's always a chance of frost at night, September is a more pleasant time to traverse the Allagash. Hunting is permitted in the Allagash (as it is in most of Maine) and there is good fishing for brook trout, landlocked salmon, and lake whitefish. Some hiking trails lead to fire towers that offer panoramic views.

The Allagash Waterway concludes in the village of Allagash in far northern Maine, just before the Allagash River joins the St. John, which becomes the boundary between Maine and New Brunswick just a few miles downriver.

Millinocket, Maine

Great Northern Paper Company more or less built Millinocket in 1901 to house its employees, and despite nationwide increases in the use of recycled paper products, the process of turning virgin wood pulp into paper remains the chief industry of this region. Bowater/Great Northern Paper Company is Maine's largest industrial

track that begins as Lily Bay Road. (Make sure your vehicle has a sound suspension and good tires before trying this road.) Just above the dam is the beginning of Telos Road, which penetrates the heart of the North Woods.

Telos Lake, about 20 slow miles north of Ripogenus Dam, is the southernmost body of water on the **Allagash Wilderness Waterway,** a 92-mile ribbon of lakes, ponds, rivers, and enterprise, producing more than 800,000 tons of paper annually.

Active forestry carried out by a large multinational corporation manages to co-exist with grassroots, conservation-minded recreation in the North Woods. Bowater tries to make its case for modern forest management with the **River Pond Outdoor Classroom and Hiking Trail,** an educational hike along a 5.8-mile loop through areas of harvested and unharvested woods. Bowater claims to harvest less than three percent of their forest holdings each year, although the way they put it—three trees of every hundred—makes it sound like they practice only selective cutting. The trail starts on the Golden Road, just beyond the Debsconeag checkpoint (every entry onto private forest land has a checkpoint). Some of the trail stops are roadside for drivers as well as hikers. For information contact Bowater/Great Northern Paper Company. Telephone: (207) 723–2229.

The presence of the paper industry in the Millinocket region is rivaled only by the access to outdoor sporting activities. To hike along one of the region's most striking natural wonders, drive west on Route 11 to the turnoff for Katahdin Iron Works and continue 13 miles to **Gulf Hagas,** known locally as "The Grand Canyon of the East." This three-mile canyon is accessible only by trail. It was created by the West Branch of the Pleasant River, whose waters run through a 300- to 400-foot deep slate canyon with five major waterfalls, nearly vertical sheer walls, and unusual rock formations. The loop trail around the gorge is about 8.5 miles, with good views of all the features. The Appalachian Trail follows the rim.

Most hikers and mountain climbers heading to Mount Katahdin and Baxter State Park use Millinocket as a jump-off to the southern gate, although Golden Road at Ripogenus Dam also connects with the access road to the southern gate of Baxter State Park.

Baxter State Park, Maine

Former Governor Percival P. Baxter badgered the Maine legislature for years to establish a wilderness park around the flanks of Mount Katahdin, the highest mountain in New England and the first place the sun rises on the United States. His efforts were thwarted every year by frugal (or parsimonious) legislators so Baxter began to acquire the land himself. In 1962, after putting it together parcel by parcel since 1930, he presented the park to the state of Maine as a fait accompli. At least the legislature had the good grace to name the 201,018-acre wilderness after its benefactor.

Most travelers with automobiles enter Baxter State Park's Perimeter Road by Togue Pond Gate off Millinocket Road (an extension of Golden Road). The more northerly Matagmon Gate west of Patten can also be reached by I–95. A daily fee is charged for vehicles entering the park, and vehicles are limited to non-commercial sizes. Pets and other domestic animals are not allowed—perhaps the wardens are afraid someone will smuggle in a flock of sheep.

Baxter chiefly attracts hikers. For one thing, it is the Ultima Thule of the Appalachian Trail—the end of the road that begins down in Georgia. Moreover, the park includes forty-six mountain peaks and ridges—eighteen of them with elevations greater than 3,000 feet—and about 175 miles of trails. Scenic hiking is available for all ability levels. One of the most popular and easiest hikes, for example, is the short, flat loop around **Sandy Stream Pond** near Roaring Brook Campground. It is a great walk for observing both moose and beaver.

At the other extreme are the various trails that lead up to the plateau **summit of Mount Katahdin,** at 5,267 feet. These are strenuous day hikes but well worth the exertion both for the vistas and the alpine environment where nearly a dozen species of wildflowers thrive that otherwise went extinct with the retreat of the glaciers.

 Staying There

The Northeast Kingdom of Vermont

For advance information contact Northeast Kingdom Travel & Tourism Association, The Historic Railroad Station, Main Street, P.O. Box 355, Island Pond, VT 05907. Telephone: (802) 723–9800 or (888) 884–8001. Also Northeast Kingdom Chamber of Commerce, 30 Western Avenue, St. Johnsbury, VT 05819. Telephone: (802) 748–3678 or (800) 639–6379.

NORTHEAST KINGDOM REGIONAL EVENTS

Quad-Lakes Fishing Derby. Adults and children compete for prizes for fish caught in Crystal, Parker, Shadow, and Willoughby lakes, second weekend of September. Telephone: (802) 525–1133.

Vermont's Northeast Kingdom Fall Foliage Festival. Towns of Marshfield, Walden, Cabot, Plainfield, Peacham, Barnet, Groton, and St. Johnsbury band together with variety of events each day in each town for week stretching from the last Sunday of September to the first Sunday of October. Telephone: (802) 536–2472.

St. Johnsbury, Vermont

LODGING

Echo Ledge Farm Inn. Route 2, East St. Johnsbury (exit 1 from I–93, or exit 20 from I–91). With six bedrooms (each with private bath), this 1793 colonial farmhouse offers a country setting and welcomes touring snowmobilers. Telephone: (802) 748–4750. Inexpensive to moderate.

Fairbanks Motor Inn. 32 Western Avenue. Located west of town on Route 2 near the St. Johnsbury Academy, the Fairbanks is the newest of the area motels with forty-five large rooms, each with a private balcony. Telephone: (802) 748–5666. Inexpensive to moderate.

Holiday Motel. 25 Hastings Street. The Holiday offers clean, large, updated rooms just outside the north end of the business district at the junction of Railroad and Hastings Streets. Telephone: (802) 748–8192. Inexpensive to moderate.

CAMPGROUNDS

Moose River Campground. Junction of Routes 2 and 18. With fifty sites, including twenty just for tents, Moose River is conveniently located just three miles east of St. Johnsbury. Although it is nestled in a bend of the Moose River, this is not so much a "resort" campground as a simple and economical base for touring. Bonfire and marshmallow roast held every Saturday night in summer. Telephone: (802) 748–4334 (summer) or (802) 748–8619.

FOOD

Cucina di Gerardo. 213 Railroad Street. Telephone: (802) 748–6772. Wide-ranging Italian menu includes pastas as well as meat and fish entrees. Very popular with locals, especially on the weekends, it also does a bustling business in take-out gourmet pizzas. Lunch and dinner. Moderate.

Northern Lights Book Shop & Café. 79 Railroad Street. Telephone: (802) 748–4457. Excellent bookstore with strong local selections also has a good cafe serving sandwiches, salads, soups, beverages, and snacks. Breakfast and lunch daily, also dinner Thursday through Saturday. Inexpensive.

OTHER ATTRACTIONS

Catamount Arts Center. When New York's SoHo goes country, you get Catamount Arts Center—a surprisingly (and often self-consciously) hip arts venue in rural Vermont. Film series emphasizes independent and art films and a visual arts gallery features local artists. The center also rents artsy videos for film freaks and also produces or sponsors classical music and performance art in larger venues throughout the region. Call for information. 60 Eastern Avenue. Telephone: (802) 748–2600.

ACTIVITIES

All Around Power Equipment. Route 5 North. Telephone: (802) 748–1413. This Polaris dealership sells, services, and, most importantly, rents snowmobiles to take advantage of the V.A.S.T. network, which seems to go almost everywhere in the Northeast Kingdom. Located right off corridor 5F3.

St. Johnsbury Country Club. Telephone: (802) 748–9894 or (800) 748–8899. An interesting mix of nine historic holes designed in the 1920s by two-time British Open winner Willie Park and completed after his death by his brother Mungo with nine modern holes created in 1992. The older holes are extremely scenic and hemmed in at spots by mature trees, requiring significant finesse. The modern holes are designed with the power player in mind. Par 70 for all eighteen holes.

SHOPPING

American Society of Dowsers Bookstore. 99 Railroad Street. Telephone: (802) 748–8565. The Northeast Kingdom is a haven for New Age believers in a number of folk traditions, not the least of which is dowsing for water. This shop not only carries a full range of publications on water witching, but also materials on spiritual applications of crystals and other New Age subjects.

Caplan's Army Store. 110 Railroad Street. Telephone: (802) 748–3236. The Northeast Kingdom has a large number of shops purveying contemporary high-tech clothing and gear to help subscribers to *Outside* magazine enjoy the wilds. They don't shop at Caplan's, but the subscribers to *Field & Stream* do. Head to Caplan's for chamois shirts, wool caps in black and red plaid, big old work boots, hand-warmers, electric socks, and hunter's mittens.

Peter Glenn Ski & Sports. 115 Railroad Street. Telephone: (802) 748–3433. This shop bills itself as "snow ski specialists since 1958," and few other shops have such a wide selection of garb for skiing and snowmobiling. The store also has a good

selection of foot gear and a limited but choice selection of snowshoes.

FAIRS, FESTIVALS, AND EVENTS

Festival of Traditional Crafts. More than forty demonstrators show Early American household and farm skills, fourth weekend in September since 1965 at the Fairbanks Museum. Telephone: (802) 748–2372.

Star Party. Just when the Perseid meteor showers are heating up in mid-August, the Fairbanks Museum & Planetarium hosts a weeklong star party with lectures, planetarium shows, kids' astronomy camp, and organized night sky viewing. Telephone: (802) 748–2372.

Danville, Vermont

CAMPGROUNDS AND RV PARKS

Sugar Ridge RV Village and Campground. 24 Old Stagecoach Road. Brand new campground (1999) with one hundred sites and its own pond is handy to both St. Johnsbury (7 miles) and the charming Joe's Pond (2.5 miles). Telephone: (802) 684–2550.

Groton, Vermont

CAMPGROUNDS AND RV PARKS

Stillwater State Park Campground. Boulder Beach Road. One of four campgrounds in the 25,000-acre Groton State Forest, Stillwater is situated right on Groton Lake. Excellent tent sites (and some RV and trailer sites) and lean-tos are set on lake shore and share a good boat launch. You can paddle or motor right up to some of the campsites. The forest has 22 miles of hiking trails. Telephone: (802) 584–3822 (summer) or (802) 479–4280 (winter).

Peacham, Vermont

ACTIVITIES

Ghosts Walk. Held on July 4 and again in October, the costumed walk through the local cemetery is intended to evoke Peacham's ghosts. Telephone: (802) 594–3432.

East Hardwick, Vermont

LODGING

Brick House Guests. 2 Brick House Road. An 1830s Federal-style house (with Greek Revival porch) has three bedrooms, two of which share a bath. On the grounds is Perennial Pleasures, which sells more than 1,000 antique varieties of flowers to gardeners and to many historic properties. The most popular flower is an heirloom phlox that operator Rachel Kane found growing in an abandoned cellar hole. Telephone: (802) 472–5512. Inexpensive with breakfast.

Greensboro, Vermont

LODGING

Highland Lodge. Route 16 at Caspian Lake. Rambling white farmhouse built as a country inn in the 1860s has several rooms, but there are several cottages on the property as well. The ski touring center has 40 miles of groomed cross-country trails. In the summer, there's a swimming beach. Telephone: (802) 533–2647. Expensive with breakfast and dinner.

Lakeview Inn. Main Street. Lakeview started as a boardinghouse in 1872, but was completely made over in the late 1990s in a simple country style with no Martha Stewart excesses. Twelve bedrooms share three living rooms, and there's also a three-bedroom suite with two double beds and two twins. If you don't feel like going out, you can dine at the Lakeview Inn Cafe on soups, pasta salads, and the like. The cafe is open for breakfast, lunch, and until 7:00 P.M. If you're *really* planning to stay put, you can even shop at Old Forge Scottish Woolens for British sweaters and locally handspun yarns. One wheelchair accessible room. Telephone: (802) 533–2291. Moderate with breakfast.

Craftsbury Common, Vermont

LODGING

Craftsbury Outdoor Center. Lost Nation Road (follow signs from Route 14). This full-service outdoors resort on Lake Hosmer has miles of trails for mountain biking, hiking, cross-country skiing, horseback riding as well as facilities for swimming, canoeing, and sculling. New facilities include 20 kilometers of marked and packed snowshoe trails. The whole orientation is outdoor activity, so while not plush, it's clean and comfortable. Lodging varies from small rooms with shared baths to cottages with private kitchen and bath. Telephone: (802) 586–7767 or (800) 729–7751. Moderate to expensive with breakfast, lunch, and dinner.

The Inn on the Common. For all the local sports activity, Craftsbury need not be entirely Spartan. The Inn on the Common offers genteel country lodgings and elegant dining. The main building dates from late 1700s and fronts on Route 14 and the resort has its own clay tennis courts and swimming pool. Several cross-country skiing packages are offered with trail privileges on Craftsbury Nordic Ski Center trails, which go behind the property. There's even a snow guarantee from January through March: Skiable snow cover or deposit returned in full. Telephone: (802) 586–9619 or (800) 521–2233. Expensive to very expensive with breakfast and dinner.

FAIRS, FESTIVALS, AND EVENTS

Becoming an Outdoors Woman. Annual two-day clinic on first weekend of June at Craftsbury Sports Center is oriented to adult women interested in learning more about traditional outdoors skills. Telephone: (802) 241–3723.

Irasburg, Vermont

FAIRS, FESTIVALS, AND EVENTS

Annual Church Fair. Parade, entertainment, barbecue, hay rides, and live music highlight this mid-July town celebration (since 1953) on the Common. Telephone: (802) 754–6583.

West Glover, Vermont

OTHER ATTRACTIONS

Bread and Puppet Theater Museum. The epic, agitprop productions of Bread and Puppet might be described as Berthold Brecht meets the Muppets. Best known for politically inspired pageants, the members of the company also perform more modest contemporary theater pieces. The company stores its giant puppets, masks, paintings, and graphics in a communal barn here in ultra-conservative West Glover where passersby can marvel at them. The company's annual outdoor performance in August brings hundreds of people to town. Open daily May through October from 10:00 A.M. to 6:00 P.M. Donation requested. Route 122. Telephone: (802) 525–3031.

Jay, Vermont

For advance information on Jay, contact the Jay Peak Area Association, Route 242, Jay, VT 05859. Telephone: (800) 882–7460.

ACTIVITIES

Jay Peak Ski Resort. Route 242. Telephone: (802) 988–9601 or (800) 451–4449. Jay Peak receives the highest annual natural snowfall of all ski areas in the eastern United States. With more than 285 acres of trails (about half expert, a third for intermediate skiers) and more than one hundred acres of glade skiing, Jay Peak is known for a great range of terrain and relatively uncrowded skiing and aerial tram. Snowboarding is allowed on all trails, and groomers leave berms and jumps in place. From the last week of June through Labor Day and during foliage season, aerial tram rides operate daily every half hour from 10:00 A.M. to 4:00 P.M. $8.00. Ski trails are also open for mountain biking with separate trail fees ($5.00) and bike tram charges ($5.00).

Newport, Vermont

ACTIVITIES

Lake Memphremagog Cruises. Tour the scenic lake aboard paddle-wheeler, *Newport's Princess.* Open Memorial Day weekend through October. Many options available, including meal cruises. Basic sightseeing cruises begin at $9.75. Newport City Dock. Telephone: (802) 334–6617.

SHOPPING

Outdoors Gear and Garb. The best stores on Main Street cater to outdoors activities. **Vermont Bike & Ski** (68 Main Street; telephone:

802–334–7560) is a factory outlet store that sells sleek helmets and clingy biking clothing, including the bib-shorts that are an absolute necessity to affect the Tour de France look. Ski gear is oriented to cross-country. For the ultra chic with money to burn, **Bogner Haus** (48 Main Street; telephone: 802–334–0135) has beautiful outdoors clothing to make you look like a movie star on the slopes or trails. With some of the simple jackets going for upwards of $1,000, you might need to star in an extra feature this year. For the rest of us, **The Great Outdoors of Newport** (73 Main Street; telephone: 802–334–2831) carries a really full line of gear, clothing, and footwear for hiking, snowshoeing, cross-country skiing, kayaking, canoeing, and golf. Knowledgeable sales people and a little flexibility on high-ticket items make it a good bet. The shop also rents mountain bikes, canoes, and kayaks in the warm weather, cross-country skis and snowshoes in the winter.

Derby Line, Vermont

LODGING

Derby Village Inn. 46 Main Street. This handsome 1902 Neoclassical building has just five rooms. One is a suite and each has a private bath. During the winter you might curl up with a book by the fireplaces in the living room or sitting room, or settle in with a jigsaw puzzle on the year-round porch. Telephone: (802) 873–3604. Moderate with breakfast.

Westmore, Vermont

LODGING

Willough Vale Inn. Route 5A South. The main inn has seven large rooms with views of the lake as well as one efficiency suite. The four lakefront cottages have living rooms, full kitchens, screened porches, decks, and private docks. The styling is country chic and the setting idyllic. Telephone: (802) 525–4123 or (800) 594–9102. Inexpensive to expensive.

FOOD

Willough Vale Inn. Route 5A South. Telephone: (802) 525–4123 or (800) 594–9102. Restrained tradition (as befits the style of the inn) reigns in the casual Tap Room Bar as well as the more formal main dining room with its white linens and Windsor chairs. Breakfast and dinner. Moderate to expensive.

East Burke, Vermont

LODGING

The Mountain View Creamery. Darling Hill Road. This stunning brick inn is the former creamery of a hilltop dairy farm built in 1883 as a quintessential gentleman's farm. The barn is one of the largest farm structures ever built in Vermont, but Mountain View is far too elegant a place to worry about stepping in cowflaps. The 440-acre farm has groomed cross-country ski trails in the winter, lots of hiking trails the rest of the year, and it's convenient to Burke Mountain. The inn's ten bedrooms are decorated in English country manor style. Telephone: (802) 626–9924 or (800) 572–4509. Moderate with breakfast.

The Village Inn of East Burke. Route 114. Less than 100 yards from the turnoff to Burke Mountain and in the middle of the village, this casual residence has just five guest rooms, each with private bath. Other amenities include a living room fireplace and a fully equipped guest kitchen. Telephone: (802) 626–3161. Inexpensive.

FOOD

Darling's Country Bistro. Darling Hill Road. The dining room at the luxurious Mountain View Creamery was once the center of butter and cheese production at the farm. Now it's the Northeast Kingdom's center of good New American bistro dining. Lunch and dinner Friday through Sunday. Telephone: (802) 626–9924. Moderate to expensive.

OTHER ATTRACTIONS

Burke Mountain. Burke Mountain Road. Telephone: (802) 626–3305; snow reports telephone: (800) 922–BURK. With 2,000 feet of vertical and not a whole lot of horizontal, Burke is a quintessential mountain for snowboarding, though skiers still dominate the slopes. Lifts are limited to quad chairs, but there's rarely a line since most of the skiers are locals. Lacking the extensive lodging infrastructure of the bigger resorts (a situation that could change soon), Burke remains something of a diamond in the rough. Reservations telephone: (800) 541–5480. Thirty-one trails vary from novice to expert. There's also glade skiing in a mostly birch forest. Burke's cross-country area consists of a 95-kilometer network that connects to the four-season Kingdom Trails network. Summer activities include quad chair rides and mountain biking.

Trout River Brewing Co. Main Street. Telephone: (802) 626–3984. Offering four to six styles on tap throughout the year as well as seasonal beers, brewer Laura Gates specializes in unfiltered traditional ales and lagers. The brewery's tasting room opens daily at 11:00 A.M. and sells both retail and wholesale.

FAIRS, FESTIVALS, AND EVENTS

Kingdom Classic Bicycle Race. Annual mountain bike race is held at Burke Mountain Resort second Saturday of September. Telephone: (802) 626–4290 or (802) 626–3305.

Barton, Vermont

FAIRS, FESTIVALS, AND EVENTS

Orleans County Fair. Since 1858 the good folks of Orleans County have celebrated their agricultural lifestyle with this four-day fair in early August at the county fairgrounds. Telephone: (802) 525–6210.

Lyndonville, Vermont

ACTIVITIES

Northeast Farm & Garden Center. East Street. Telephone: (802) 626–8642 or (800) 639–7094. This Ski-Doo and Arctic Cat dealership sells, services, and rents snowmobiles to get onto the V.A.S.T. network at Connector Trail C-552.

FAIRS, FESTIVALS, AND EVENTS

Annual Dowsing School & Convention. Weeklong gathering of dowsers and those interested in the subject gathers during early August. Telephone: (802) 684–3417.

Caledonia County Fair. The good folks of Caledonia County have celebrated their agricultural lifestyle since 1846 with this five-day fair in early August at the county fairgrounds. Telephone: (802) 626–5538 or (802) 626–5917.

The North Woods of New Hampshire and Maine

Dixville Notch, New Hampshire

For advance information, contact the North Country Chamber of Commerce, Colebrook, NH 03576. Telephone: (603) 237–8939 or (800) 698–8939.

LODGING

The Balsams. Few grand hotels from the Gilded Age are left in New England, but the core of the Balsams has been around since 1866 and its present grand sprawl dates from the turn of the century. From a distance, the resort resembles a clump of red-roofed white mushrooms sitting at the edge of a tiny mountain lake between 800-foot cliffs. The rooms are country comfortable, as if designed not by Martha Stewart but by her great-grandmother. The pace at the Balsams reflects an earlier era of mountain rusticating, when travelers came on the train and spent weeks or even months staying put, enjoying the natural setting and letting someone else do the heavy lifting. The room rate includes all meals, evening entertainment, and unlimited use of the facilities: golf, tennis, swimming, boating, fishing, mountain bike trails, alpine and cross-country skiing (67 kilometers of groomed trails), snowboarding and showshoeing (32 kilometers of dedicated trails). For the 1998 winter season, the Balsams completed a snowmobile trail to link the hotel to the New Hampshire snowmobile trail system. The Dixville Peak Snowmobile Trail ascends 3,940 feet for a magnificent view of the Great North Woods. Telephone: (603) 255–3400 or (800) 255–0600. Expensive to very expensive with breakfast, lunch, and dinner. Many packages and promotions are available.

Rangeley Lakes, Maine

For advance information contact Rangeley Lakes Chamber of Commerce, P.O. Box 317, Rangeley, ME 04970. Telephone: (800) MT–LAKES.

LODGING

Grant's Kennebago Camps. Kennebago Lake Road West. One of the original sporting camps from the turn of the century, Kennebago Camps still delivers the wilderness experience that drew "sports" in the first place but has upgraded the facilities to offer modern amenities in lakeside cabins. Activities include superb lake and stream fishing, swimming, and guided or unguided nature hikes. Pets welcome. Telephone: (207) 282–5264 (winter), (207) 864–3608 (summer) or (800) 633–4815. Moderate to expensive with breakfast, lunch, and dinner.

Rangeley Inn. Main Street. The core of this venerable hostelry is the three-story main inn, built in 1877 and expanded over the years. While the

The Balsams, Dixville Notch, New Hampshire

rooms in the motel behind the inn on Haley Pond do not have such a nostalgic atmosphere, some of them do feature wood stove fireplaces or whirlpool baths. Telephone: (207) 864–3341 or (800) MOMENTS. Moderate.

Town & Lake Motel. Main Street. Located right on Rangeley Lake, this property offers a choice of accommodations that range from two-bedroom shorefront cottages with fireplace and kitchen to motel units, some with kitchenettes. The motel has its own dock, should you prefer to arrive by canoe. Telephone: (207) 864–3755. Moderate.

Campgrounds and RV Parks

Rangeley Lake State Park. South Shore Drive. One of the most easily reached campgrounds in the area has fifty campsites among fragrant spruce and fir trees on a mile of shoreline on the south shore of the lake. It also has a concrete boat launching ramp. Sites and facilities are wheelchair accessible. Telephone: (207) 864–3858 mid-May through September, (207) 624–6080 October through mid-May.

Food

Rangeley Inn. Main Street. Telephone: (207) 864–3341. Rangeley does not lie in a section of Maine noted for its haute cuisine, but the Rangeley Inn's dining room offers solid traditional New England fare that is a welcome relief from the rubber pizza that has become the national food of rural northern New England. Lunch and dinner. Moderate.

Activities

Dockside Sports Center. The center not only rents canoes, powerboats, and jet skis during the summer, but is one of the few dealers in Maine that also rents snowmobiles in the winter. Rangeley has become something of a snowmobiling mecca, connecting to 140 miles of trails. Town Cove. Telephone: (207) 864–2424.

Rangeley Mountain Bike Touring Company. Catering to all seasons, this shop rents cross-country ski gear in the winter and bikes and kayaks in summer. The shop also provides good route maps for cyclists who hope to see wildlife such as bear and moose but also want to stay clear of log trucks. 53 Main Street. Telephone: (207) 864–5799.

Rangeley Region Sport Shop. This shop will give up the ghost—the Grey Ghost, that is—as well as hundreds of other varieties of dry and wet flies, many of them tied locally. It also rents canoes and kayaks and the staff makes recommendations of fishing guides. 85 Main Street. Telephone: (207) 864–5615.

Saddleback Ski Resort. Saddleback is a small mountain with a big feel. Only two chairlifts service the summit, but the 1,830-foot vertical drop and rugged setting make it a favorite with skiers who enjoy an unhomogenized experience. Saddleback offered glade skiing and narrow, winding trails before the bigger ski areas sought to re-create these retro slopes. Forty downhill trails overlook the town and Rangeley Lake. There are also 50 kilometers of groomed cross-country trails, which double as hiking trails in the summer, with hikes that range from easy 1.5-mile saunters to 17-mile rugged expeditions. Saddleback Road. Telephone: (207) 864–5671.

Fairs, Festivals, and Events

Logging Museum Festival Days. In the best woodsman's tradition, this two-day event in late July includes a logging competition and bean-hole dinner. It's also a good chance to visit the Rangeley Lakes Region Logging Museum, which displays work by local woodcarvers, as well as covering the history of the logging industry. Open July and August, Saturday and Sunday 11:00 A.M. to 2:00 P.M. Telephone: (207) 864–5595

Old Time Fiddler's Contest. This mid-July event, held since 1980, is open to all levels of competition. Telephone: (207) 864–2117.

Rangeley/Budweiser Snodeo. This three-day event in late January includes snowmobile displays, games, parade, and fireworks. Telephone: (207) 864–5364.

Rangeley Lakes Sled Dog Races. Racers compete for best overall time in junior through unlimited divisions during this two-day event in early March. Telephone: (207) 864–5362.

Carrabasset Valley, Maine

LODGING

Herbert Inn. Main Street, Kingfield. The Herbert is probably where Grandpa and his dad stayed on their big adventure to northern Maine. A bit frayed around the edges, this huge old hotel exudes a country charm entirely unaffected by metropolitan country chic. Sit out on the front porch and count the cars en route to Sugarloaf. Telephone: (207) 265–2000 or (800) THE–HERB. Inexpensive to moderate.

The Inn on Winter's Hill. Winter Hill Road, Kingfield. When it was built in 1890, this residence was the town's grandest. Among its distinctions was the first domestic central heating system. Just in case, there are also three fireplaces. The mansion itself has four posh bedrooms and the attached barn contains sixteen additional, less expensive rooms. There's access to great cross-country skiing trails from the back door. Telephone: (207) 265–5421 or (800) 233–WNTR. Moderate to expensive with breakfast.

Tim Pond Camps. Tim Pond, Eustis. Started in the 1850s, Tim Pond may be the oldest sporting camp in the country, but its pleasures never go out of style—trout fishing, wildlife watching (deer, moose, occasional bear, loon, songbirds). Telephone: (207) 243–2947. Expensive with breakfast, lunch, and dinner.

White Wolf Inn & Restaurant. Route 27, Stratton. There's a lot to be said for staying north of Sugarloaf rather than south, especially if you're looking for value. The White Wolf Inn has ten rooms done in woodsy Maine country decor. Each has a private bath and most can accommodate four people or more. Catering to an outdoorsy clientele, White Wolf has become a frequent stopover for European travelers sojourning in the woods as they make their way from Boston to Quebec and Montreal. The inn's mascot, Lima, is a white wolf hybrid. Telephone: (207) 246–2922. Inexpensive.

FOOD

Julia's. The Inn on Winter's Hill, Main Street, Kingfield. Telephone: (207) 265–5426. In a classy room fit for a Victorian country squire, Julia's serves elegant French-influenced contemporary cuisine—duck breast, chicken with Calvados sauce, and the like. Dinner. Moderate to expensive.

White Wolf Inn & Restaurant. Route 27, Stratton. Telephone: (207) 246–2922. The menu at White Wolf is eclectic, ranging from burgers and pizza to venison and buffalo steaks. In this region of vegetable-challenged cooking, the salad bar is a welcome relief. Dinner. Inexpensive to moderate.

OTHER ATTRACTIONS

Grand Falls. King and Bartlett Township. Arguably New England's most striking horseshoe falls, Grand Falls can be reached only by dirt road, preferably in dry weather unless your vehicle is equipped with four-wheel drive. From Route 27 north of Eustis about 1 mile, make a right onto the King and Bartlett Road. Cross the bridge and bear right and continue for several miles to mile marker #9. Bear left and continue to the falls—about 17 miles in all. Remote as the location is, the state maintains a picnic site next to the falls.

ACTIVITIES

Sugarloaf Ski Touring Center. Fifty-seven miles of groomed trails weave through the area with occasional views of Sugarloaf Mountain and the Bigelow Range. The center is located about a mile south of the Sugarloaf access road on Route 27, Kingfield. Telephone: (207) 237–6830.

Sugarloaf/USA. At 4,237 feet, the legendary ski mountain of Sugarloaf is the second highest mountain in Maine. (Mount Katahdin is taller, but has no ski trails.) With dependable natural snowfall augmented by aggressive snowmaking, Sugarloaf has one of the longest ski seasons in New England and a tremendous variety of trails. Its 2,820-foot vertical drop is second in New England only to Killington. The American Skiing Company has pumped major investments in the area over the last five years to boost snowmaking capacity, open new trails, and to add quad chairlifts, including the longest and fastest chairlift in North America. During the summer, duffers flock to the mountain- and forest-view, 18-hole golf course, designed by Robert Trent Jones, Jr. It's generally considered one of the most challenging and scenic in the country and hosts a number of pro tournament events. The resort also has 50 miles of hiking and mountain biking trails and a stocked twelve-acre trout pond. It also rents rowboats and canoes. Lift rates range $60–$92 for two-day passes. For information on lodging packages, call (800) 843–5623.

FAIRS, FESTIVALS, AND EVENTS

White White World Week. This winter carnival held at Sugarloaf for five days in late January includes fireworks, a torchlight parade, live music, and other events. As one of New England's premiere ski mountains, Sugarloaf also hosts a number of ski and snowboard competitions throughout the season. Call for details. Telephone: (207) 237–2000.

The Forks, Maine

ACTIVITIES

Whitewater Rafting. About a dozen professional rafting operators work from this region. They include **Magic Falls Rafting,** which offers inflatable kayak trips on the lower Kennebec and the Dead rivers; telephone: (800) 207–RAFT; **Moxie Outdoor Adventures,** which is based at a classic Maine sporting camp on Lake Moxie; telephone: (207) 663–2231 or (800) 866–6943; the longest-operating outfitter, **Northern Outdoors,** which also offers ropes courses, rock-climbing, mountain biking, fishing, snowmobiling, as well as lodging; telephone: (207) 663–4466 or (800) 765–7238; and **Professional River Runners** in West Forks, which offers overnight camping trips along the rivers; telephone: (207) 663–2229 or (800) 325–3911.

Jackman, Maine

LODGING

Sally Mountain Cabins. These cabins with cooking facilities make a good base for a fishing vacation. The proprietors will handle all arrangements (including non-resident licenses) for fishing expe-

ditions and guided canoe trips in the region. Telephone: (207) 668–5621. Inexpensive.

Moosehead Lake, Maine

For advance information, contact the Moosehead Lake Region Chamber of Commerce, P.O. Box 581, Greenville, ME 04441. Telephone: (207) 695–2702.

LODGING

Beaver Cove Camps. Beaver Cove, Greenville. Close to Greenville center, these fully equipped housekeeping cabins on Moosehead Lake are open year-round to take advantage of seasonal outdoor activities. Telephone: (207) 695–3717 or (800) 577–3717. Moderate.

The Birches. Many veterans of Moosehead Lake expeditions swear by this sixty-year-old, 11,000-acre wilderness resort. Lodging options include rooms in a log lodge, lakeside log housekeeping cottages, cabin tents, or yurts. The Birches is also a full-service outfitter for expeditions into the woods north of Moosehead and operates **Wilderness Expeditions,** one of the first whitewater rafting companies in the area, with trips on the Kennebec, Penobscot, Dead, Rapid, Allagash, and St. John Rivers. Telephone: (207) 534–2242 or (800) 825–WILD. Moderate.

Gray Ghost Camps. On the Moose River, Route 15, Rockwood. Named after the most popular artificial wet fly in the area, Gray Ghost caters to fly fishermen with modern, fully equipped housekeeping cottages. Telephone: (207) 534–7362. Inexpensive.

Greenville Inn. Norris Street, Greenville. Set up on a hill above the lake in the center of town, the Greenville Inn has a definite country grace without a shred of fussiness—unless you count the linen doilies in the parlor. Most of the guest rooms in the main building share baths, but private cottages are also available on the grounds. Telephone: (207) 695–2206 or (888) 695–6000. Moderate to expensive with breakfast.

Greenwood Motel. Rockwood Road, Greenville Junction. Located on the side of Little Squaw

Mountain in a rural setting, this motel is directly on Maine's Interconnected Trail System for snowmobiles and offers snowmobiling, hunting, and fishing packages. The motel also rents snowmobiles and ice houses. Telephone: (207) 695–3321 or (800) 477–4386. Inexpensive with breakfast.

Indian Hill Motel. West Cove, Routes 6 and 15, Greenville. Because it sits atop a hill as you enter Greenville, all the rooms in this motel have views of the lake and mountains. There are also cottages and efficiency motel units, as well as canoes, a paddleboat, and barbecue grills for guest use. Free docking for guests with their own boats. Telephone: (207) 695–2623 or (800) 771–4620. Inexpensive.

Kineo View Motor Lodge. Route 15, Greenville. A half-mile driveway leads to this motor lodge set on fifty-five acres. Each room has a private balcony with a 180-degree view of Moosehead Lake and the surrounding mountains. Telephone: (207) 695–4470 or (800) 659–VIEW. Inexpensive to moderate with breakfast.

Lodge at Moosehead. Lily Bay Road, Greenville. *Architectural Digest* meets *Field & Stream* at the Lodge at Moosehead, where exceptional hand-carved furniture sets the tone for elegant rusticity in both guest rooms and public areas. The long view of Lily Bay on Moosehead is impressive, especially at sunset. All rooms have whirlpool baths and fireplaces and the newest rooms in a separate building feature beds hung from the ceilings with old log chains. Telephone: (207) 695–4400. Expensive to very expensive with breakfast.

CAMPGROUNDS AND RV PARKS

Lily Bay State Park. About nine miles north of Greenville on the east shore of Moosehead Lake, the park has fishing, boating, hiking, and swimming as well as ninety-one campsites, many along the shore. Telephone: (207) 287–3834.

Old Mill Campground. Route 24, Rockwood. With fifty nicely landscaped sites and great views of the lake, Old Mill offers direct access to swimming, boating, and fishing. Telephone: (207) 534–7333.

FOOD

Greenville Inn. Norris Street, Greenville. Telephone: (207) 695–2206. Greenville may be a woodsy kind of town, but its visitors clearly appreciate some of the finer things in life—which happens to include the New American grill-oriented menu at the Greenville Inn, with a range from contemporary light pastas to grilled salmon and the ubiquitous "smashed" potatoes. Dinner. Moderate to expensive.

ACTIVITIES

Backwoods Adventure. Main Street, Greenville. The Greenville area may contain more water than dry land, making a canoe a mode of transportation sometimes more convenient than a motor vehicle. This shop rents both canoes and kayaks. Telephone: (207) 695–0977.

Folsom's Air Service. The largest seaplane operator in the Northeast, Folsom's ferries folks into remote camps and fishing lakes and also offers sightseeing flights. Ask about the fly-in day on Chamberlain Lake—round-trip air transport, box lunch, and use of canoes and camp. Sightseeing flights begin at $20 per person. Greenville. Telephone: (207) 695–2821.

Maine Guide Fly Shop & Guide Service. Main Street, Greenville. In addition to providing equipment, this shop rents canoes and offers guided drift boat fly fishing trips on the Penobscot and Kennebec Rivers for landlocked salmon and brook trout. One of the more unique services, they will fit moose-watchers with camouflage belly boats (floating platforms) to paddle eye-to-eye with moose. Telephone: (207) 695–2266.

Moose Safaris. Moose can be easily spotted at roadside bogs near dusk and dawn, but for those who want to be sure to spot the big creatures, several operators arrange moose sighting safaris and cruises. Two good choices are **Main Street Station,** Main Street, Greenville; telephone: (207) 695–2375; and **Moose River Store,** Route 15, Rockwood; telephone: (207) 534–7352.

Whitewater Rafting. **Eastern River Expeditions** in Greenville offers trips on the Penobscot, Dead, and Kennebec Rivers; telephone: (800) 634–

7238; **North Country Outfitters on Moosehead Lake** in Rockwood offers trips on the Allagash, St. John, and Moose Rivers as well as the West Branch of the Penobscot; telephone: (207) 534–7333. Other outfitters with trips on the West Branch include **Moxie Outdoor Adventures**; telephone: (207) 663–2231 or (800) 866–6943; and **Northern Outdoors;** telephone: (207) 663–4466 or (800) 765–7238;

FAIRS, FESTIVALS, AND EVENTS

Down East Sled Dog Races. This two-day event is held in Greenville in late January. Telephone: (207) 695–3440.

Ice Fishing Tournament. Moosehead Lake is known for its ice fishing, which begins on January 1 and ends March 30. This week-long event is held in early March. Telephone: (207) 534–2261.

International Seaplane Fly-in Weekend. Events include a craft fair, a supper, and a breakfast, but the real attraction of this four-day, mid-September event in Greenville is the congregation of planes, including some real old-timers, and the tales their pilots have to tell. Telephone: (207) 695–2821.

Hiking

MooseMainea. More moose live at Moosehead Lake than anywhere else in Maine—a fact celebrated with nearly a month of promotional activities from mid-May through mid-June, including a canoe race, rowing regatta, antique auto parade, and Tour De Moose mountain biking events. Telephone: (207) 695–2702.

Winter Festival. This nine-day event in mid-February includes snowmobile races, cross-country ski races, a parade, fireworks, and other activities. Telephone: (207) 695–2702.

SHOPPING

Indian Hill Trading Post. Route 15, Greenville. Telephone: (207) 695–2014. The largest sporting goods store in the area also provides non-resident hunting and fishing licenses.

Allagash Wilderness, Maine

Wilderness is not necessarily free of bureaucracy. For advance information on rules, regulations, permits, fees, and licenses regarding the Allagash Wilderness Waterway, contact the Bureau of Parks and Recreation, State House Station 22, Augusta, ME 04333. Telephone: (207) 287–3821. Or, contact Northern Region, Bureau of Parks and Lands, 106 Hogan Road, Bangor, ME 04401. Telephone: (207) 941–4014 (May through October), (207) 723–8518 (November through April).

For information about the private road system in the North Woods, contact the organization of private land owners, North Maine Woods, Inc., P.O. Box 421, Ashland, Maine 04732. Telephone: (207) 435–6213.

LODGING

Chesuncook Lake House. Chesuncook Village (Township T5 R13, at the northwest end of Chesuncook Lake). Sports have been *really* getting away from it all here since 1864. This inn and cottages 40 miles north of Moosehead Lake is accessible by water or air only. In addition to fishing, swimming, and hiking, the proprietors offer canoe trips on the Upper West Branch of the Penobscot River. Radio phone: (207) 745–5330. Moderate to expensive with breakfast, lunch, and dinner.

Nugent's Chamberlain Lake Camps. Located within the boundary of the Allagash Wilderness Waterway, about 60 miles from Millinocket, Nugent's is reached on logging roads. Founded in 1936, the camp on 17-mile-long Chamberlain Lake has been saved from any traces of modernization by the strict regulations governing the Allagash Wilderness Waterway. There is no running water, but you can scrub up at the excellent community bathhouse. Telephone: (207) 944–5991. Moderate with breakfast, lunch, and dinner.

ACTIVITIES

Allagash Canoe Trips. Since 1953 this company has organized wilderness expeditions on the Allagash, St. John, Penobscot, Kennebec, and Moose River watersheds. P.O. Box 713, Greenville, ME 04441. Telephone: (207) 695–3668.

Millinocket, Maine

For advance information contact the Katahdin Area Chamber of Commerce, 1029 Central Street, Millinocket, ME 04462. Telephone: (207) 723–4443.

LODGING

Big Moose Inn, Cabins & Campground. Millinocket Lake. Located near Baxter State Park on the lower flanks of Mount Katahdin and surrounded by lakes, this property offers cabins, B&B rooms in the inn, and campsites as well as a "home cooking" restaurant and direct access to international snowmobile trails. Like so many operators of lodging in these parts, the proprietors can also arrange whitewater raft trips and seaplane tours to augment such activities as fishing, hiking, swimming, and boating. Telephone: (207) 723–8391. Moderate.

ACTIVITIES

Snowmobiling. Snowfall in the Millinocket region and farther north is as sure as death and taxes, so snowmobiling is a popular activity. More than 350 miles of groomed trails surround Millinocket. The **New England Outdoor Center** arranges guided day trips and guided lodge-to-lodge overnight trips and also rents Ski-doos for independent exploring. Trailside lodging is also available. Located in Millinocket near Baxter State Park. Telephone: (800) 766–7238.

FAIRS, FESTIVALS, AND EVENTS.

Paperfest. This Labor Day weekend event celebrates the region's main industry with a carnival, craft and book sales, food, dance, and other events. Telephone: (207) 723–4443.

Baxter State Park, Maine

For advance information on Baxter State Park, contact Baxter State Park Headquarters, 64 Balsam Drive, Millinocket, ME 04462. Telephone: (207) 723–5140.

CAMPGROUNDS AND RV PARKS

Baxter State Park. Accommodations in ten separate camping areas within the park include lean-tos, cabins, bunkhouses, and tent pitches, but they fill up quickly. Reservations are accepted after January 1 and must be made in advance. Contact the Reservations Clerk at the address above.

Bibliography

New England-wide

GENERAL DESCRIPTION AND TRAVEL

Howells, Bob. *Backroads of New England.* Houston: Gulf Publishing Company, 1995.

Levine, Miriam. *A Guide to Writer's Homes in New England.* Bedford, Mass.: Applewood Books, 1997.

Magley, Beverly. *National Forest Scenic Byways.* Billings, Mont.: Falcon Press Publishing Company, Inc., 1990.

HISTORICAL/CULTURAL

Allen, Richard Sanders. *Covered Bridges of the Northeast.* Brattleboro, Vt.: The Stephen Greene Press, 1957.

Blumenson, John J.G. *Identifying American Architecture.* New York: W.W. Norton & Company, 1977.

Braun, Esther K. and David P. *The First Peoples of the Northeast.* Lincoln, Mass.: Moccasin Hill Press, 1994.

Brown, Dona. *Inventing New England: Regional Tourism in the Nineteenth Century.* Washington, D.C.: Smithsonian Institution Press, 1995.

Faison, S. Lane, Jr. *The Art Museums of New England.* Boston: David R. Godine Publisher, 1982.

Johnson, Steven F. *Ninnuock (The People): The Algonkian People of New England.* Marlborough, Mass.: Bliss Publishing Company, Inc., 1995.

Laing, Alexander. *American Ships.* New York: American Heritage Press, 1971.

Lepore, Jill. *The Name of War: King Philip's War and the Origins of American Identity.* New York: Alfred A. Knopf, Inc., 1998.

Wilmerding, John. *A History of American Maritime Painting.* Boston: Little Brown & Co., 1968.

Workers of the Federal Writers' Project of the Works Progress Administration. *Connecticut: A Guide to its Roads, Lore, and People.* 1938. *Maine: A Guide 'Down East.'* 1937. *Massachusetts: A Guide to its Places and People.* 1937. *New Hampshire: A Guide to the Granite State.* 1938. *Rhode Island: A Guide to the Smallest State.* 1937. *Vermont: A Guide to the Green Mountain State.* 1937. Boston: Houghton Mifflin Company.

NATURAL HISTORY AND GEOLOGY

Alden, Peter and Cassie, Brian. *National Audubon Society Field Guide to New England.* New York: Alfred A. Knopf, Inc., 1998.

Raymo, Chet and Maureen E. *Written in Stone: A Geological History of the Northeastern United States.* Old Saybrook, Conn.: Globe Pequot Press, 1989. Out of print.

Roberts, David C. *Geology: Eastern North America.* Boston: Peterson Field Guides, Houghton Mifflin Company, 1996.

Wessels, Tom. *Reading the Forested Landscape: A Natural History of New England.* Woodstock, Vt.: The Countryman Press, 1998.

Round stone barn, Hancock Shaker Village, Pittsfield, Massachusetts

RECREATION AND NAVIGATION

Gabler, Ray. *New England White Water River Guide, Second Edition.* Boston: Appalachian Mountain Club Books, 1981.

Jermanok, Stephen. *Outside Magazine's Adventure Guide to New England.* New York: Macmillan Travel/Simon & Schuster, Inc., 1996.

Perry, John and Jane Greverus. *Sierra Club Guide to the Natural Areas of New England.* San Francisco: Sierra Club, 1990.

The Mid Coast

HISTORICAL/CULTURAL

Cape Ann Historical Association. *Gloucester at Mid-Century: The World of Fitz Hugh Lane 1840-1865.* Gloucester, Mass.: Cape Ann Historical Association, 1989.

Morison, Samuel Eliot. *Maritime History of Massachusetts.* Boston: Houghton Mifflin Company, 1921.

Seelye, John. *Memory's Nation: The Place of Plymouth Rock.* Chapel Hill: University of North Carolina Press, 1998.

State Street Trust Company. *Whale Fishery of New England.* Boston: State Street Trust Company, 1915.

RECREATION AND NAVIGATION

Cape Cod (& the Islands) & North Shore Bicycle and Road Map. Cambridge: Rubel BikeMaps, 1997.

LITERATURE

Beston, Henry. *The Outermost House.* New York: Viking Press, 1962. Classic naturalist musing on dune life on Cape Cod.

Junger, Sebastian. *The Perfect Storm.* New York: Norton, 1997.

Kipling, Rudyard. *Captains Courageous.* New York: Doubleday, 1897. Swashbuckling adventure among the fishing captains of Gloucester.

Melville, Herman. *Moby-Dick.* Berkeley: University of California Press, 1981.

Mulloney, Stephen. *Traces of Thoreau.* Boston: Northeastern University Press, 1998. Author retraces Thoreau's journey by foot and public transportation through Cape Cod.

Thoreau, Henry David. *Prose Works: Selections.* New York: Literary Classics of the United States, 1985. Includes *Walden, Cape Cod, Maine Woods,* and selected essays.

The Hub

GENERAL DESCRIPTION AND TRAVEL

Carlock, Marty. *A Guide to Public Art in Greater Boston: From Newburyport to Plymouth.* Cambridge and Boston: Harvard Common Press, 1993.

Kales, Emily and David. *All About the Boston Harbor Islands.* Hingham, Mass.: Hewitts Cove Publishing Co., Inc., 1983.

Morris, Jerry. *Boston Globe Guide to Boston.* Old Saybrook, Conn.: Globe Pequot Press, 1998.

Southworth, Michael and Susan. *AIA Guide to Boston.* Old Saybrook, Conn.: Globe Pequot Press, 1992.

Wilson, Susan. *Boston Sites and Insights.* Boston: Beacon Press, 1994.

HISTORICAL/CULTURAL

Fischer, David Hackett. *Paul Revere's Ride.* New York: Oxford University Press, 1994.

O'Connor, Thomas H. *Bibles, Brahmins and Bosses: A Short History of Boston.* Boston: Trustees of the Boston Public Library, 1991.

Shand-Tucci, Douglass. *The Art of Scandal: The Life and Times of Isabella Stewart Gardner.* New York: Harper-Collins Publishers, Inc., 1997.

Whitehill, Walter Muir. *Boston: A Topographical History.* Cambridge: Belknap Press, 1959, 1975.

RECREATION AND NAVIGATION

Sinai, Lee. *Exploring In and Around Boston on Bike and Foot.* Boston: Appalachian Mountain Club Books, 1996.

LITERATURE

Carroll, James. *Mortal Friends.* Boston: Little Brown & Company, 1978. *The City Below.* Boston: Houghton Mifflin, 1994. Sweeping family sagas set in Boston.

Lowell, Robert. *Life Studies and For the Union Dead.* New York: Noonday Press, 1964.

McCloskey, Robert. *Make Way for Ducklings.* New York: Viking Press, 1941.

Parker, Robert B. *The Godwulf Manuscript.* New York: Delacorte Press, 1974. First of the series of mystery novels featuring Boston-based detective Spenser.

Thoreau, Henry David. *Walden; or, Life in the Woods.* New York: Dover Thrift Editions, 1995.

West Quoddy Head Light, Maine

Porter, Eliot. *Summer Island.* San Francisco: Sierra Club, 1966. Eliot Porter's paean in prose and photographs to Penobscot Bay's Great Spruce Head Island, owned by the Porter family since 1910.

Rothe, Robert. *Acadia: The Story Behind the Scenery.* Las Vegas: K.C. Publications, 1995.

Ralston, Peter. *Sightings: A Maine Coast Odyssey.* Camden: Down East Books, 1998. Combines photography of islands and their inhabitants with the story of the founding of the Island Foundation dedicated to their preservation.

RECREATION AND NAVIGATION

AMC Guide to Mount Desert and Acadia National Park. Boston: Appalachian Mountain Club Books, 1993.

Gibson, John. *Fifty Hikes in Southern Maine: Day Hikes & Backpacking Trips from the Coast to Katahdin.* Castine, Maine: Backcountry Publications, 1983.

St. Germain, Tom. *A Walk in the Park: Acadia's Hiking Guide.* Bar Harbor, Maine: Parkman Publications, 1996.

The North Coast

HISTORICAL/CULTURAL

Duncan, Roger F. *Coastal Maine: A Maritime History.* New York: W.W. Norton, 1992.

LITERATURE

Jewett, Sarah Orne. *The Country of the Pointed Firs and Other Stories.* New York: W.W. Norton,

1981. Classic local color stories of life in and around Tenants Harbor, Maine.

McCloskey, Robert. *Blueberries for Sal.* New York: Viking, 1948. *One Morning in Maine.* New York: Viking, 1952. Classic children's books.

Moore, Ruth. *The Weir.* New York: William Morrow and Co., 1943. Story of fishing family on Gott's Island.

Shreve, Anita. *The Weight of Water.* Boston: Little, Brown and Company, 1997. Fictional retelling of the 1873 murders of two women on the Isles of Shoals.

Small, Connie. *The Lighthouse Keeper's Wife.* Orono: University of Maine Press, 1986. Memoirs of her twenty-eight years as a lighthouse keeper's wife along the Maine and New Hampshire coasts.

White, E.B. *Charlotte's Web.* New York: Harper & Brothers, 1952. This classic tale was inspired by the Blue Hill Fair, which White visited from his summer home in Brooklin, Maine.

Up Country

GENERAL DESCRIPTION AND TRAVEL

Sternfield, Jonathan and Stevens, Lauren. *The Berkshire Book.* Lee, Mass.: Berkshire House Publishers, Inc, 1998.

HISTORICAL/CULTURAL

Burns, Deborah E. and Stevens, Lauren R. *Most Excellent Majesty: A History of Mount Greylock.* Pittsfield, Mass.: Berkshire Natural Resources Council, Inc., 1988.

Craig, Theresa. *Edith Wharton A House Full of Rooms: Architecture, Interiors, and Gardens.* New York: The Monacelli Press, 1996.

Owens, Carole. *The Berkshire Cottages: A Vanishing Era.* Englewood Cliffs, N.J: Cottage Press, Inc., 1984.

Randall, Peter E. *Mount Washington: A Guide and Short History.* Woodstock, Vt.: Countryman Press, 1992.

Wharton, Edith and Codman, Ogden, Jr. *The Decoration of Houses.* New York: W.W. Norton & Company, 1978, 1997. The revised and expanded version of the authors' 1902 book.

NATURAL HISTORY AND GEOLOGY

Laubach, Rene E. *A Guide to Natural Places in the Berkshire Hills.* Lee, Mass.: Berkshire House Publishers, 1997.

**Conway Scenic Railroad,
North Conway, New Hampshire**

Slack, Nancy G. and Bell, Allison W. *AMC Field Guide to New England Alpine Summits*. Boston: Appalachian Mountain Club Books, 1996.

RECREATION AND NAVIGATION

Appalachian Mountain Club. *Appalachian Trail Guide to Maine*. Boston: Appalachian Mountain Club Books, 1993.

Appalachian Mountain Club. *Appalachian Trail Guide to Massachusetts and Rhode Island*. Boston: Appalachian Mountain Club Books, 1998.

Appalachian Mountain Club. *Appalachian Trail Guide to New Hampshire and Vermont*. Boston: Appalachian Mountain Club Books, 1992.

Cuyler, Lewis. *Bike Rides in the Berkshire Hills*. Lee, Mass.: Berkshire House Publishers, 1997.

Daniell, Gene and Burroughs, Jon. *AMC White Mountain Guide, 26th edition*. Boston: Appalachian Mountain Club, 1998.

Green Mountain Club. *Guide Book of the Long Trail*. Montpelier, Vt.: Green Mountain Club, 1990.

Stevens, Lauren, R. *Hikes & Walks in the Berkshire Hills*. Lee, Mass.: Berkshire House Publishers, 1998.

LITERATURE

Fracher, Judy. *Hey, Lady! How Did You Get Way Up Here?* Etna, N.H.: Durand Press, 1996. Account of reaching a personal goal of climbing all the "4,000 footers" in the White Mountains.

Mayor, Archer. *Borderlines* (1994), *Disposable Man* (1999), *Fruits of the Poisonous Tree* (1995), *The Ragman's Memory* (1997). New York: Warner Books. Mystery novels feature Brattleboro, Vermont, police detective Joe Gunther.

Melville, Herman. *Pierre*. Short novel set in backdrop of the Berkshires. Available in various collections of Melville fiction.

Rockwell, Norman. *My Adventures as an Illustrator*. New York: Abrams, 1995.

Wharton, Edith. *Edith Wharton's New England*. Lenox, Mass.: The Mount, 1995. This edition includes *Ethan Frome*, perhaps the most famous of Wharton's novellas, and seven of her most interesting New England tales.

The Lakes Region
HISTORICAL/CULTURAL

Skees, Suzanne. *God Among the Shakers: A Search for Stillness and Faith at Sabbathday Lake*. New York: Hyperion, 1998. A profile of life and belief among the last eight remaining members of the Shaker sect in Maine.

Sprigg, June. *Simple Gifts: A Memoir of a Shaker Village*. New York: Alfred Knopf, 1998. Story of Canterbury Shaker Village and the last seven sisters living there.

The Midlands
HISTORICAL/CULTURAL

Macaulay, David. *Mill*. Boston: Houghton Mifflin Company, 1983. Details construction, planning, and operation of mills typical to those developed in New England during the nineteenth century. This heavily illustrated children's book is equally interesting to adults.

Dublin, Thomas. *Lowell: The Story of an Industrial City*. Washington, D.C.: National Park Service Division of Publications, 1992.

Dunwell, Steve. *The Run of the Mill*. Boston: Godine, 1978. Excellent account of the New England textile industry.

LITERATURE

Kerouac, Jack. *Maggie Cassidy*. New York: Viking Penguin, 1993.

Kerouac, Jack. *The Town and the City.* Toronto: Ameron, Ltd, 1976.

Larcom, Lucy. *A New England Girlhood: Outlined from Memory.* Hanover, N.H.: New England University Press, 1985. This 1889 memoir by one of the Lowell mill girls remains the key account of the early days of Lowell manufacturing.

The Connecticut River Valley

HISTORICAL/CULTURAL

Delaney, Edmund. *The Connecticut River, New England's Historic Waterway.* Old Saybrook, Conn.: Globe Pequot Press, 1983.

Hard, Walter. *Rivers of America: The Connecticut.* New York: Rinehart & Company, Inc. 1947.

The Great North

NATURAL HISTORY AND GEOLOGY

Heinrich, Bernd. *The Trees in My Forest.* New York: HarperCollins, 1998.

RECREATION AND NAVIGATION

AMC River Guide: Maine, Second Edition. Boston, Appalachian Mountain Club Books, 1991.

Appalachian Trail Guide to Maine. Boston: Appalachian Mountain Club Books, 1993.

Caputo, Chloe. *Fifty Hikes in Northern Maine.* Castine, Maine: Backcountry Publications, 1983.

Clark, Stephen. *Katahdin: A Guide to Baxter State Park & Katahdin.* Unity, Maine: North Country Press, 1985.

DeLorme Map & Guide to Baxter State Park & Mount Katahdin. Freeport, Maine: DeLorme Publishing Company, 1998.

Kellogg, Zip. *Maine Geographic: Canoeing, Volume 3: Northern Rivers.* Freeport, Maine: DeLorme Publishing Company, 1986.

LITERATURE

McPhee, John. *The Survival of the Bark Canoe.* New York: Farrar Straus, 1982. Modern classic of traveling North Woods in a canoe.

Mosher, Howard Frank. Novels set in what he calls "Kingdom County" include: *A Stranger in the Kingdom,* New York: Doubleday/Dell, 1989; *Where the Rivers Flow North,* New York: Viking/Penguin, 1978; and *Northern Borders,* New York: Doubleday, 1994.

Pelletier, Cathie. *The Bubble Reputation.* 1993. *The Funeral Makers.* 1987. *The Weight of Winter.* 1991. New York: Crown Publishers. Chronicler of Maine's far north, where a manic sense of humor helps ensure winter survival.

Rich, Louise Dickinson. *We Took to the Woods.* New York: J.B. Lippincott Co., 1942. *My Neck of the Woods.* Camden, Maine: Down East Books, 1998. Long before the "back to the land" movement, the author's family plunged into the forests of northwestern Maine.

Roberts, Kenneth. *Northwest Passage.* New York: Doubleday, 1946.

Thoreau, Henry David. *The Maine Woods.* Boston: Houghton Mifflin, 1906.

Index

C

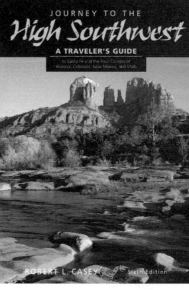

About the Authors

Patricia Harris and David Lyon grew up in the Connecticut River Valley near Hartford and on the west coast of Maine's Penobscot Bay, respectively. They have been a writing team based in Cambridge, Massachusetts, since 1982, specializing in art, popular culture, food and travel. Their articles have appeared in a wide variety of art, travel, and general-interest magazines and in major newspapers across North America. Among their several books is *Romantic Days and Nights*® *in Boston* (Globe Pequot Press). They are restaurant reviewers for the Microsoft city web site Boston Sidewalk.